HOW MUCH PAIN CAN OUR HEARTS ENDURE

By David Mahon

Woodbridge Publishers
1200 Century away, Thorpe Park,
Leeds, LS158ZA

Copyright © 2023 by David Mahon
All Rights Reserved

First Edition

ISBN (Paperback): 978-1-916849-27-3

WOODBRIDGE
PUBLISHERS

ACKNOWLEDGEMENT

I would like to thank my beautiful wife Audrey for putting up with me for all that we have been through and supporting me with this autobiography. I would not be alive without her.

Also, my father Michael has been my rock, he's a diamond of the highest class and I would be nothing without him.

All my family and friends that have had my back in the dark times.

The Doctors and Nurses at St Luke's Hospital Rathgar and the Eye & Ear Hospital.

My Legal team, especially Tony Collier.

All the people that should be still with us but unfortunately are not.

And finally, I would like to acknowledge the support and love I have received from my late brother Owen, who passed away in 2023 from Cancer, he was the best brother ever. Owen always had a joke or two. R.I.P Owen.

Thanks to everyone who reads my autobiography and a percentage will go to Cancer Research in honour of Owen Mahon.

DEDICATION

This book is dedicated to my wife Audrey and my father Michael:

The most beautiful things in the world cannot be seen or touched; they must be felt in the heart. Mick and Audrey will never fully know how much I love them.

Table of Contents

Acknowledgement ii

Dedication iii

Prologue vi

Dave's Early Years 1

Rory 24

Mick's Cancer 77

A Different World 81

Welcome To Spain/Bienvenido A Espana 91

Commitments 98

Through The Storm 108

Engagement 118

Happier Times 124

Cancer (K) 148

Early Warnings 154

Amy's Disappearance 165

Wow Factor 307

Amy's Disappearance – Early Days 310

Moving Back From Spain 337

Amy's Dublin Garden 364

Nostalgia 365

Dean's Last Night 370

Hammer To Fall 403

West Life 429

The Wedding 442

Trial By Fire 451

Prisoner # 84976 512

Infamous 515

Cancer - Dave 538

Epilogue 644

PROLOGUE

Today is the fourth day of my twenty-four-hour lock–up. I'm up on the west two landing in Wheatfield prison. This is what is known as a 'punishment wing' and inmates are sent here for breaking the rules. My neighbours, such as they are, have been sent up here for all kinds of misdemeanours—fighting; selling drugs, passing drugs on a visit etc… No recreation time (time out of cell) isn't the only punishment. They'll face further losses of "privileges" such as the loss of visits, phone calls, and 'grat' (your prison wages called a gratuity). Loss is very much on my mind today.

My indignities don't end there though, because I'm being punished for doing nothing wrong. I've been moved here, very much against my will, because there has been a threat to my life. That's what I was told anyway, when the screws came into my cell back on the east one landing, an "enhanced" landing for inmates that obey the rules, and told me to "get some things like bedclothes and toiletries" before my unceremonious march to the place.

Logic, of course, would suggest that the person who made the threat against me—a breach of prison rules if ever there was one—would be the one to be moved here, but the I.P.S. (Irish prison service) doesn't do logic. You get to learn that fast. Chiefs and governors come and go since I've moved here, assuring me that I'll be "moved back tomorrow," but as the song goes, 'tomorrow never comes.'

Loss of privileges, loss of friends, and the loss of the few tiny comforts I've learned to enjoy, but even greater losses consumed me. My brother Rory never bothered anybody and was the life and soul wherever he went. Today is the seventh of August 2017, exactly twenty years since Rory's passing, and my world is an even-darker place... this is my story.

DAVE'S EARLY YEARS

Of all the biographies and auto-biographies I've ever read, the part that I almost always glaze over out of sheer boredom is this part; the compulsory trip through the good old days, the "look how cute as a baby I was" section that I call the 'early years' or 'mandatory fluff filling.' It is for this reason that I shall keep this as brief as possible!

I was born in a period of time known to some as the long-sixties or, to most normal folk, 1971. If there was anything 'special or unusual' about my birth, it was that I was born in the very house I grew up in (as opposed to a maternity hospital), our family home in Santry, a suburb in north Dublin.

For the sake of completeness, I was an April baby (13th), which makes me a 'Ram' for all you astrologers out there.

Ireland was a very different palace back in the 1970's. Television came in a massive wooden box that you had to walk up to and press buttons in order to change a channel, of which, there weren't that many! You knew you were doing well if you could watch it in colour, as most of them were black and white.

A telephone was something that lived in a tall, sheltered box at the end of a road or in every few homes with people lucky enough to afford one. They had to remain permanently affixed to a plug in the wall if you wanted them to work. Texts was a fancy name for books, a 'tweet' was something birds did, and you had to use a contraption known as cameras in order to take photographs.

If you needed a 'flash' for your photo, you could buy them separately—usually at a chemist—where you'd also bring your roll of film to see how your photos turned out. Facebook would be a book or magazine with people's faces in it, and as for the 'web,' well, that's where the spiders lived. In short, not at all like today.

There were many cultural differences, too. For example, the cinema was dominated by Star Wars, superheroes, and a giant shark, nothing like the summer block busters of 2018... Oh... maybe not so different after all! We had a show called 'Opportunity Knocks', which was the X-Factor and Britain's Got Talent of its day, and 'Come Dancing' was the Strictly of my childhood... only without all the fun and glamour.

I was the baby of the family, which means I was born last. It's a Dublin thing because everyone is a baby at some point, I guess. I had two older sisters and three brothers, older too, obviously!

I was truly blessed by having two wonderful, loving parents. I mean, they were 'normal' in the sense that they were not cruel, barbaric psychopaths with weird Dickensian learnings. They instilled values like hard work, respect for your neighbours (especially the elderly), and to always say 'please' and 'thank you', but more than anything else, they worked bloody hard at providing a clean, warm home where we always felt safe and loved.

In order to pay for the nappies that I was filling with a wondrous orange-goo with annoying regularity, and lots of other family-related essentials, my father, Mick, managed a few fish and chips shops in Dublin. They were owned by the Beshoff family, and their crowning glory was Roscoes in Marlborough Street, Dublin 1. The other shops were located on either side of the Liffey, one in Kimmage on the South and the other on the Malahide road.

It wouldn't be an exaggeration to say that people literally came from miles around just to have a 'one and one' from Roscoes. Honestly, I still hear about it to this day. What I also hear, far more than how the fish and chips were, is "what a lovely man" the manager was. My father. He has—and always has had—one of those infectious personalities.

He worked every hour God sent and every day of the week that filled them just to keep a roof over the heads of his ever-growing brood. It must've been physically and emotionally exhausting for him, and no matter how long he'd last, he'd eventually have to stop. Thank God it did, and not in a tragic way, as it probably would've.

Instead, salvation came in an automotive shape, in that a friend of his drove a Taxi and recommended that Mick do the same. It wasn't an easy decision, as my father loved the fish and chips shops and is incredibly loyal, but family loyalty trumps all in the Mahon household.

From his first day behind the wheel of a car with a taxi-plate on the roof, he loved it and never looked back... well, apart from his rear-view mirrors and other rules of the road, but you get what I mean!

Yes, the hours were still long and not always sociable, but he could choose his own, so the money was good, and we all benefitted from some more daddy-time. My eldest brother—Owen—followed my father into the taxi business (almost said "Ranks" but you know!), and just like the old-man, he's a very hard worker and excellent provider for his four children and grandchildren. Owen is a great guy and has always been supportive of his siblings and extended family.

My other brother, Terry, is a musician of all things. He not only plays a range of musical instruments, but he teaches people how to play as well. If that wasn't already annoyingly talented enough, he also writes and composes too. He is probably my closest brother, and apart from being extremely creative, he's also a real character, the sort of guy who'd be the heart and soul of any night out. Unfortunately, he separated from his wife, but they've somehow managed to maintain a fantastic relationship, and they continue to get along famously. Their pride and joy is their daughter, Emma, who is now in her twenties and has grown into a lovely young lady.

Speaking of ladies, that allows me to segway nicely in the direction of my female siblings. My eldest sister, Olivia, married her childhood sweetheart and their picture-book romance is still as strong as ever. He's a terrific guy and they have raised four young boys into four great men, each of them a perfect culmination of the best their parents possess. Anytime I'm ever asked to describe Olivia, I can unfailingly sum her up in three words, 'A real lady.'

That sounds like a lot for my other sister, Dorry, to live up to, and thankfully, she does! Dorry was a smart, strong, and independent woman long before Beyoncé started writing songs about it. Through many hardships—financial, ex-husbands, etc.—she raised five children single-handedly and away from home, as she's been living in England for over thirty years now. It's funny, her children are in their thirties at this stage, yet I still think of them as "Dorry's kids," maybe it's just an Irish thing?

Okay, for those of you good at maths out there and noticed missing siblings… congratulations, well spotted. He was my older brother Rory, and he was such a unique character that he's got an entire chapter all to himself. You could write books just about him… in fact, my father did just that, but I'll introduce you to him later. As for now, we'll whistle–stop through the rest of my obligatory childhood fluffy!

Having two taxi-drivers in the family to look up to, it's not such a stretch to know that my childhood memories are mostly related to transportation of some kind. My earliest memory, in fact, is of bombing all over the place on my little tri-cycle, mostly bumping into things and falling off, generally being an annoying little pain in everyone's ass, but c'mon, I must've been adorable too, right?

Nah, didn't think so either. When I wasn't carrying out the world's worst Evil Knievel impersonation, I remember having to go to school. That's right, I used the word "having" when it came to school because I hated it. All of it. Everything about it. For those of you out there who turned up to Larkhill Primary School in Whitehall at the ripe old age of four and enjoyed filling the intervening years into your teens with nostalgic reverence, then I doff my virtual cap to you because I didn't.

Someone once said that you only ever do two days in prison—your first day and last day—but it doesn't apply to Dave Mahon's schooldays. Day one felt like having pins stuck in my eyes, and every day that came after that added an extra pin.

Finishing national school felt exactly the way having several thousand pins removed from your body would or probably should feel. My sense of all-over body-pain relief lasted only as long as the school holidays, as then I was shipped over to St. Aidan's Secondary School, a Christian Brothers establishment. The Christian Brothers haven't exactly been basking in the balmy sun of good news lately, but as far as my experience with them went, I found them alright, and no, nothing 'funny' happened. I stayed there until I'd sit both my intermediate certificate (or 'the inter' as the junior cert was less formally known) and leaving certificate exams. It killed me having to stay that long in school, and whilst all my friends were stuck indoors studying, I couldn't have cared less. It showed, too, as I failed my leaving cert and, again, couldn't care less. All I wanted to do was work.

I got my first job when I was twelve years old. My first paying job that is, as I'd worked as an altar-boy before that. I'd heard from one of my friends (what a little liar he bloody turned out to be!) that you'd get "loads" of money for regular mass and as for weddings and funerals, you could probably retire to Hawaii. After a few of those, I was going to be Magnum—once I could grow his moustache— and drive that big red Ferrari all over the island and play with those big Doberman Pinschers he had.

Naturally, I'd have to get a few weddings under my belt first, to bring Ma over too, but that was fine. I could wait a couple of weeks. I got home, told Ma the good news, and wow, she was overjoyed! You see, I wasn't just an altar boy in her eyes, I was something far holier than that. I was somewhere just north of a pope and south of an angel. She, and I kid you not actually, beamed with pride at seeing me in my junior saint costume upstaging the priest on the altar in Whitehall Church that first time. To her, I was saying mass. Funny that, as years later, Audrey would accuse me of the very same thing. But that's a different story!

Back to the late seventies though, and with my first mass under my belt, I went straight to the priest for my money.

"Bless you child, but you don't get paid for altar service!"

I thought he was joking. He wasn't. It took a long time before I got my mitts on a wedding gig, and well, Tom Selleck and I still haven't crossed paths. Even worse though, was that I was stuck with the bloody things. No way could I just jack-it-in, it would've broken Kay's heart. Things you do for your mammy, eh?!

So paid employment didn't properly happen for me until I was twelve. We were now into the 1980s, a decade of electro-pop music, weird haircuts, and something about 'A Flock of Seagulls!'

While U.2. filled stadiums and made their millions, I was pushing drugs… up a hill… on my bike! I was the official delivery boy for Conway's pharmacy on Swords Road, hitting the big time fifteen big ones every week! Literally, fifteen ones! It was a king's ransom for me, though. I was a working-man with my own transport, just like my dad and big brother. They had it easy, though, as they never got soaked in the rain or attacked by German shepherds.

True story that, I got bitten to bits by four Alsatians one day, and only for some quick thinking on my part—I used my bike as a bike shield and weapon—or I could have been killed. Nowadays, your parents would be straight into a solicitor's office on the way to the hospital to sign off on the lawsuits, but they were simpler times. Nope, junior Mahon didn't inherit his millions for such a serious breach of health and safety, all I got was a mammy-patch–up-job, and that was followed by:

"Did you get paid?"

"I did."

"Well???

Ah yes, the taxman… Well, tax-Ma, really. Eight pounds (yes, pre-euro things called punts) for her and seven of those bad boys for me. I loved that little job and stuck with it for seven or eight years, even when I was doing other jobs. I guess my dad's 'loyalty' apple didn't fall far from the tree. It also gave me the perfect excuse to hang up my ceremonial altar robes, handing them down to the next generation. In ex-altar boy tradition, I passed them off with the promise of big money, my replacement no doubt having dreams of flying out to Los Angeles to join the A-team with all his promised loot. Well, it was the 80's what would he know about Magnum?

When I turned 15, I was expected to do 'the inter,' and that would've involved studying. I had been doing my delivery job for three years at that stage, so work wasn't going to be a good enough excuse as I was used to the school work juggling. I needed something else, and quick.

I got lucky again. Another job involving deliveries, this time, coal. This was hard, tough, dirty, physical work, but I loved it. No need for a gym membership when you are lifting 50kg bags of coal and anthracite when you aren't even 50 kg yourself!

Coal, obviously, is a combustible fossil fuel, so it is in greater demand the colder the weather. That's all well and good until you have to deliver it during the snow. I've always been reluctant to tell the 'coal' story because there's just no earthly way of telling it without sounding like an 'oul grand-da'—you think you have it tough? You don't know you're born... back in my day, I had to deliver sacks of coal in the snow! But I did. I'll move on!

A good psychologist would analyse my life patterns and notice that I started working at a young age and always worked 'transport' type jobs (deliveries) and took quantum leaps every three years. At twelve years old, it was prescribed (prescription); at fifteen years old, it was coal... then at eighteen years old, I delivered... People!

No I didn't become a mid-wife. I became a taxi-driver, a real job for me, a perfect job. Heck, it was a family business! I've always loved meeting people and having a laugh, and I certainly wasn't afraid of hard work, so it was a nice fit for me.

Driving my father's taxi was, for me, the greatest job in the world. I did the day shift, and he did the night. It was obvious from my leaving cert results that I wasn't going to be troubling the world of academics, so my father helped to fight my corner with Ma, and so at the tender age of eighteen, I became Ireland's youngest taxi-driver ever. Life was good and I even kept the chemist job as it only took half an hour by car. Mainly though, it was because I became quite close to the owners. In fairness to them, they gave me a pay raise for my loyalty—twenty-five pounds a week, back in the big time! No way would I tell my Ma that though... although she probably guessed knowing her!

I guess I should mention here, too, that I wasn't 'money-mad' as a young man. I was just A.B.S. Anything But School! I did (still do) possess an altruistic side, and year after year, I'd volunteer at sales-of-work for St. Michaels House on the

Ballymun road and would bake little cakes, e.t.c., to try and raise more money for them.

One year I got my photograph in the paper for doing just that, and between that and my altar duties, my mother developed a repetitive strain injury from polishing my halo!

Years later, I'd go on to do a parachute jump to raise money for the National Council for the Blind, so it's something that never left me. In the twelve or so years that I drove taxis, I'd always be heavily involved in what was known as 'The Annual Handicap Outing,' but that title wouldn't be "P.C." enough today. No matter, we brought a lot of happiness and respite to many deserving families, and that can only ever be a good thing.

Ask any Dublin taxi-driver from my era what question they are most asked, and to a man (or woman), you'll get the same answer:

"Who's the most famous person you met?"

Fame, as we know, is a subjective thing. Who was more famous? Elvis or the Beatles, for example. So for that reason, here is a list of people you might have heard of, in no particular order. You can argue among yourselves as to who the most famous was!

Bob Geldof, Coronation Street stars, Keith Duffy, Tony Bennett, Paul Costelloe, Martin Sheen, the Corrs, cast and crew from Glenroe, Gay Byrne, Freddie Starr, Yazz (from the Plastic Population), Cliff Richard, to name just a few. By far, the most interesting celebrity/personality to talk to me through my rearview mirror was John Gotti's daughter. I hadn't a clue who 'The Teflon Don, boss of bosses, Dapper Don' was when she hailed me. She was just a very glamorous beauty who spoke with a strong 'Nooow Yorik' accent.

But do you know what? For all her obvious wealth and celebrity status (to everyone, bar me!), she was the most normal and down-to-earth person you'd ever hope to meet. She was just great craic and, to my mind, a million miles away from the kind of world with which her name will forever be synonymous. Of course, when I found out—a day or two later—exactly who she was, I replayed that entire journey slowly through my mind, you know, just in case!

Hey, I loved The Sopranos as much as the next guy, but I didn't want them coming after me! A question I'm seldom asked, however, is "Who is the most interesting person you've ever had in your taxi?" which is a real shame as that's a much better question. There's no singular answer to that question, but I'll share a few of my favourites with you.

I remember a particularly busy Christmas Eve one year, and I was lining up at the Gresham taxi rank on Dublin's O'Connell Street. The shops were all closed or closing, and it was around 4 pm when I noticed this guy getting into the first taxi in line, getting out after a minute, and then jumping into the next... then the next... and the next until he finally got into the back of my taxi...

"Will ya' take me to Finglas?"

"Yeah, no problem."

"Nice one."

"Why did the other lads not take you?"

"Cause I'm drunk."

"Ah, no harm in that bud, sure it's Christmas, after all.

So we started off on our journey, the usual chit-chart, then:

"Will you go through Smithfield?"

"Smithfield? Why there?"

"I want to buy a Christmas tree."

"A real one?"

"Yeah!"

"How are you going to get it home?"

"In the back of your car."

"Are you mad? With all those pine- needles going everywhere?"

-No reply-

"Do you have kids?"

"Yes."

"Are you married?"

"Yes."

"And you're buying your Christmas tree now?"

To be honest with you, I felt sorry for the guy, so I took him to Smithfield and he bought his tree. It was just as well I was driving a hatch–back! We had a great laugh, though, all the way out to Finglas, there was just something that clicked between us and I was sorry when the journey had to end. As I pulled up outside his house, a woman came storming out of it and burst through his garden gates with nothing but bad intentions etched all over her face. I looked from her back to my passenger via the rearview mirror. The look on his face confirmed it before he said it;

"OH. MY. Jesus… That'll be the wife!"

If I was writing a collection of books, then I might have had room to include all the colourful metaphors and eerily imaginative threats to his life and genitalia that composed the better part of her tirade, but I don't, so let's just say that she effed and blinded him to an inch of his life. I'm sure she was a lovely person, but I was glad I wasn't married to her, phew! Discretion, I'm always told, is the better course of value, but let's be honest, I'd rather be a live dog than a dead warhorse, so I left them at it and busied myself with the task of Christmas tree removal from the boot. No good deed goes unpunished, so when she saw me sneaking around to the boot, she diverted her angst at me! She assumed that we were friends and that I was at fault for having him out "on the bather." I tried explaining to her that I was only the taxi driver – an honest to God victim of circumstances-but she was having none of it:

"Ah, so you're only a taxi driver. Did I get that right?"

"Well yeah!"

"Well" (mocking me), that's where your session must've started because so's he! Hope you're proud of yourself, Christmas eve… And so I took my medicine; no way was I going to get anywhere with her. I didn't do the best of jobs getting the tree out either, leaving more needles in the boot than on the branches, which she noticed (looks could kill? I was nuked!) Snatching it

out of my quivering paw with one hand and skull–hauling him back into the house with the other. I don't know who fitted their front door for them or what hinges he used doing it, but with the slam that door got. I can only applaud him as it didn't fall down! Then it dawned on me. I hadn't been paid! "Happy Christmas," I said to myself as my poor passenger was only hearing one thing for the rest of the holidays, and drove home, laughing all the way.

Another time I was waiting in line up in the ranks at Dublin airport when an unusually well-dressed man approached us. It was obvious that he was a bit worse for wear and after a couple of brief consultations with the drivers ahead of me, he jumped into my car.

"Hi, can you take me to Belfast please?"

"Sure. No problem."

"Thank you."

"Why did the other lads not want to take you?"

I was expecting the usual "because I am drunk" or "it's too far," I'll be clocking off soon or something, but this was much better:

"Oh! Because I have no money!"

I just started to laugh; what else could I do? I took an instant liking to him.

"But don't worry, I'll pay you when I get there, I promise."

By way of context, this was still during the troubles and to put it mildly, taxis wearing southern tags and reg–plates weren't always welcome. It wasn't my first trip over the border either, as I once had the privilege of driving Barry Mc Guigan back in the day. It wasn't long after his father had died and again, we got on like a house on fire. Then again, there would be something wrong with you if you couldn't get along with an absolute gentleman like him. Anyway, back to my Belfast buddy….

"Do you have your passport with you?"
I knew he'd have to, so if he said 'no', that would be the end of the trip-

"Yes"

"Give it to me. If you don't pay me when we get there, I'll have to keep it."

"Okay, sure."

Yes, it was a gamble – and my peers would later comment about me being mad-but I like a challenge. Off we went on our unusual journey, with neither one of us having a penny to our name on us in cash. I had to use my visa card to fill up on petrol, but it was one of the best trips, I'd had, we literally laughed all the way and the guy was churning our stories to beat the band. If even half of them were true, then the guy was clinically insane and not just "a bit mad." More than once, my little inner voice wondered what on earth I thought I was doing, but I stuck with it.

When we got to Dundalk he asked me if we could pull in for pint!

"A pint? Sure, you've no money!"

"You can buy me a few drinks and I'll fix you up when we get to Belfast."

"Yeah, but I've no money either!"

"Then use your visa card."

Okay, full disclosure? I thought the guy was a bit of a con man; there was just something about him so I thought, 'In for a penny, in for a pound,' and I bought us a few pints. I only had a shandy, of course. Ahem! Moving swiftly on....

The border was never a pleasant crossing back then. It was manned by British army paratroopers in full combat fatigues and armed to the hilt. They were constantly on full-alert –mode and treated every car as a possible terror attack or enemy of the state. You had to have your wits about you and be prepared to answer plenty of inane questions. We got lucky and only had 15 minutes of grilling at gunpoint before moving on.

My passenger proceeded to tell me that he was home to see his mother, whom he hadn't seen in over six years, and was going to give her a lovely surprise. He was a famous jockey and had been living in Germany. I knew that jockeys weren't usually very big, so I took a good look at him. He was small alright, so short he even made me feel like Wilt 'The Stilt' chamberlain!

"What's your mother's house like?"

"Oh, it's beautiful, fantastic, located in one of our leafier boroughs."

Yeah, he kinda talked like that! As we got closer to his family home, he directed me via a series of "left here" or "right here" and so on. Before long, I hadn't a clue where we were. In my southern taxi in Belfast. During the troubles with no money and a fairly mad passenger… How do I always manage to get into these situations?

Before I knew it, we'd pulled into what I'll generously coin as a "fairly rough-looking housing estate." Surely broken bottles, burnt out cars and sectarian spray paint couldn't be this guy's idea of a "leafy borough", could it? Well, yes it could and he pointed me in the direction of a large house on the corner. Did you ever get so scared that you could barely hear anything because of the noise of your own heart pounding through your chest and ears? That was me.

I drove past his house-ever so casually so I could park the car facing out of the estate, you know, just in case. He got out.

"I'll be back to you in a minute."

"No problem."

You can bet the farm on the fact that I left my engine running. A few minutes passed-each one elongated into my mini-lifetimes where I saw a different version of my own death-before he came back out of the house and walked back towards me. Something felt wrong. There was. He was crying, oh God. The movie theatre in my mind was replaying Norman Bates scenes on a loop. This guy had probably walked into the wrong house, couldn't find his mother and murdered everybody. I was sure to be next. A million frantic thoughts flashed across my mind. I had his passport. I had his luggage in the boot (oh God, what if it's full of body parts??). No use to me, but well, it was something. Wasn't it? So I got out of my car, locked it and walked toward him. The little voice in my head was screaming his lungs out-, "What are you doing?" Have you never seen a bloody horror movie?? This is the part where you always get killed! Run! Run!

"Are you alright, bud? What's wrong?"

"(Sniff)" Come on inside the house."

"Okay."

[inner voice- "Okay? O-bloody-k?? Run! Run! Get out of here"]

So, I sauntered into the house like the world's biggest fool and met with his sister… whom he also hadn't seen in six years. She was the reason for his tears. She'd just dropped the most awful bombshell on him. His mother had died three years ago.

I regret to tell you that I didn't know at that point if this was all part of the scam, a bit of stage-craft if you like but it wasn't. He asked his sister to pay me and she did, in sterling too, so I was very well paid for his unusual gig. It relaxed me a great deal because now I didn't feel like I was going to be "just another victim", but it was bittersweet. I'd doubted this guy and there he was, still absolutely inconsolable, having "just" lost his mother. His poor sister was also in a very vulnerable state, no doubt re-living the tragedy through the shocking rawness of her brother's tears. Nature hates a vacuum and I hate awkward silences, so stuck between two grieving siblings, I just had to say sometimes to bring everything back to earth. I could see that his sister was desperate for someone to say something, so I directed my question to her:

"Why didn't somebody contact him to let him know about his mother?"

"We did, I mean, we tried, but nobody knew his exact whereabouts" suddenly all of his stories on our journey north started to make sense. My goodness, this guy has certainly lived the life, shall we say, the high life! Spoiler alert, I checked him out on Google years later, he was everything he claimed to be… and more! But as with everything else in my life, no name-no pack drill, a taxi man's confidentiality goes deeper than any confession box. He started trying to compose himself:

"Right, so Dave, can you bring me back to the airport?"

"Okay."

"I'll pay you, naturally."

"No, no, not at all, sure I'm going that way."

His sister couldn't believe her ears. She was desperate to have a bit more time with her brother (why wouldn't she?) and begged him to stay. He looked at me;

"Would you stay in a kip like this?"

I laughed.

"What are you laughing at?"

"Jesus, only a short while ago you were telling me how beautiful it was here!"

Now it was his turn to laugh (thank God).

"Anyway, look, maybe it'd be for the best if you stayed a few nights."
He didn't comment, but her eyes expressed fathoms of gratitude. They gave each other a big hug and I went back to my taxi to get his luggage and gave him back his passport.

"Hey Dave?"

"Yeah?"

"Hang on, I've got a present for you before you go."

He handed me a fancy little box.

"You're not to open it until you get home, right?"

"Okay, thank you very much."

"Can you give me your number though? I'll give you a call when I'm going back to the airport and I'll get you to drive me."
"Yeah, here (handed it to him)."

We said our goodbyes after that, I began my long journey home. I got a few queer looks from the paratroopers as I crossed the border, trying to figure out where "All" those Dublin taxis were coming from, sensing an invasion or something, I supposed! That mysterious box didn't half give me a scare at the border though my inner paranoid voice screaming and ranting about, "They played you! It's a bloody bomb! How could you be so stupid??" I waited until I was about 20 miles south of the border before finally giving in to my curiosity and pulling into opening it. I lifted it up to my ear to give it a little listen first in case it was ticking. It was. Oh God. I waited until all the traffic cleared-both sides of the road and then opened it. Hey if I was going to be blown up, no point in taking anyone else out. My paranoid voice was well and truly humiliated when I looked inside to see two beautiful gold watches, ladies and gents. What a lovely gesture; I was delighted I took a chance on him. He called me a few days later looking for a lift as a promised-but I said no, told him to get another taxi, as it would've cost him a fortune. By the way, I do

20

know a few taxi drivers who would love to have exploited that situation, but that was never me.

"Ah, c'mon Dave, I'd love to have a few more pints with you!"

"Sure, I can't drink and drive. Are you mad?!"

"Ah, go on, take a chance!"

"I'll tell you what, I'll meet you at the Coachman's Inn, it's a pub beside the airport, how's that?"

"Good man! I'll meet you there!"

Do you know what he did! We had a nice few pints and a great laugh. What a lovely guy.

Sadly though, not all my experiences have a happy ending like that. There's one other story I'll share with you (otherwise, I'd never stop!) and it concerns a young lady. I was still only a 'pup' myself at the time and when she hailed my taxis, I was struck by how beautiful and elegant she was. She looked like an actress or pop star.

"How is it going?"

"Good, thanks."

"Where can I take you?"

"Fitzwilliam Square."

To anyone reading this that is not familiar with Dublin, Fitzwilliam Square during the day is a highly sought–after piece of office real estate. Old Georgian houses, resplendent in their immaculate refurbishment, overlook the small "square", a grassy, wooded area in an otherwise concrete jungle. The 'park', I guess you could describe it, is home to the ultra-exclusive Fitzwilliam lawn tennis club and regularly hosts major tournaments. After dark, however, it's a different story. It's an area better known for prostitution. This fare was after office hours.

"Fitzwilliam Square? Em… are you sure?"

"Yes."

"Okay. Do you know why I asked?"

"I do."

"Right okay."

"What's the matter?"

"I'm sorry, it's just… well, you don't look like… ya' know?"

"I don't. Thanks, very kind of you."

"Do you mind if I asked you why… You know?"

"For my daughter."

"Sorry??"

"My daughter. Her communion is coming up. I need the money. I've no other way to pay for everything."

"Have you ever… like… before?"

"No. Tonight is my first time."

I couldn't believe what I was hearing. This woman was not only stunning, she also came across as delicate-not street-smart - and worse, a young mother. Young and 'Green' as I was, even I know that there were a lot of violent scumbags out there, only ready to beat the living hell out of women they paid for sex, cutting and slashing their faces out of badness, and worse. I tried to tell her just how mad I thought she was and did everything I could to talk her out of it, try to find another way. As the saying goes, the lady was not for turning and so, with a heavy heart, I dropped her off at Fitzwilliam. I drove off in a bit of a daze. I couldn't believe what was happening, I was perplexed. I didn't know what to do, but I knew I had to do something. I turned the car around and drove back to Fitzwilliam, a slightly circuitous route given the Dublin city directional system, but at least I had a plan. I was going to find out exactly how much she needed and give her whatever I could. It wouldn't have been enough for a Communion dress, but I could always arrange to drop out to her again some other day to give her some more money, but only on the condition that she wouldn't enter "the business."

I had only left her minutes earlier-literally-but she was gone. Someone must have picked her up. I never found out if that was the case or if she made her little girl's Communion day as special as she had planned. I never saw her again but I often think about her and hope that she is okay. I also hope that her daughter never had to find out the cost of her Communion, the real cost.

I supposed I should end my taxi-story section of this book with something that almost ended every chapter of my story. It happened back in 1994, a time when Brit-pop was exploding onto the scene. I exploded onto the scene a bit myself through my front window. It was a car crash that should've killed me. I was over tired, it was the middle of the night and it was pelting it down with rain. I reacted too late to an aqua-plane skid and drove straight into a brick wall. Thank God it wasn't another car. I actually walked away from the accident, blood streaming down my face, pumping out of the glass shards from my windscreen in complete shock. Some kind motorist saw me and picked me up. That's how I got home, I don't remember it, I was told about it. I don't even know if I said 'thank you' to the person who drove me home, so if that was you, dear reader, then I'm sorry for not doing it sooner, but thank you. A friend of mine dropped me around to the crash site the following day to help me get my taxi collected and dropped off at the repair shop. When I saw the state of the car, my legs turned to jelly. I've heard that expression dozens of times and supposed that as a writer (of sorts), I should really use something more original but anything else would be a lie. My legs turned to-jelly. We got the car onto a tow truck and when we got it to the garage, the manager did the mechanic thing of sucking his breath through his teeth:

"Well, the poor bastard is brown bread (dead) anyway. Did you know him?"

"Yeah, it was me?"

He couldn't believe it. I didn't blame him and I still couldn't believe it. I showed him the cuts on my face and head, like Jesus showing Thomas the wounds on his hands, only then could he believe. It was indeed, a lucky escape and the significance of it never left me. Years later, when the taxi–business (as I knew it) came to an inglorious end, this again replayed in my mind. I had to take stock.

Everything was turning to crap. It seemed like there was a strike every other day and the transport minister of the day decided to tear up the rule book and de-regulate taxis. It was a monumental farce and life–changing for everyone I'd worked and grown up with. Overnight the price of a taxi–license plummeted from £80,000 (or thereabouts) down to £5,000. In real terms, 1,834 taxi-drivers lost £75,000 overnight. Nobody can just absorb a hit like that. This was a pension for most of those drivers and for the unfortunate ones only starting out, they had to mortgage their homes as when you were buying the goodwill of a license, you couldn't obtain a loan. It hit me harder than most because I had two licenses at the time, but I was also lucky because I had bowed out of taxi-ing for good. I had already taken my first step in the property business, as there were a lot of important things going on in my life apart from driving.

When I was 17, I was in a fairly serious relationship with a girl I'd been going out with for a few years. She was my first love and we had a great time together. Looking back, it was inevitable and we got pregnant towards the pagan autumn of 1988 and on April 10th 1989, just days before I turned 18 (she was only 21 herself), she gave birth to a beautiful baby boy, Graham. He changed everything!

Before he came into the world and made it a better place, his mother and I socialized all over Dublin's city centre. At such a young age, we favoured the 19th O'Connell and Fairview cinema as locations we'd term 'our usual haunts.' We were about the most unprepared parents you could ever hope to imagine, but you learn fast. We were only kids ourselves and one of the hardest things we had to do was tell our parents, which we decided to do individually. I don't know where I managed to get the courage to tell my folks, but I did. Graham's mother was extremely private, so I won't use her name out of respect for her privacy: (She has died since writing this book).

"Ma. Da… "X" is pregnant."

Subtle as a sledgehammer, eh? I can remember it like it was yesterday. I didn't want to just blurt it out like that, in my mind, I had a wonderfully well worded discourse composed, all about 'love' and 'maturity' and about being "ready for this responsibility", but I bottled it! That's how "mature" I was. I was expecting a bit of war but it didn't happen, thank God. My mother was delighted and my father - typical Mick- "Do her parents know yet?"

"They will tonight!"

I think he was trying to see if I wanted him to come with me, but he didn't need to. Graham's mum was a far stronger person than I was! It all went very well, all things considered. If you ask any of my friends to describe me back then, it would've been something along these lines- "a quiet young man bordering on shy unless he knew you." It's always the quiet one, isn't it?!

Graham was born in the Rotunda Maternity Hospital in Dublin 1, the city centre. A northsider like me! It's not only a famous Dublin landmark - the world's oldest working maternity hospital- but also one of the best, certainly the staff are anyway. I fell in love with him the second I saw him, head over heels fully, completely and unconditionally. I was crying with excitement – "It's a boy! It's a little boy!" And the next thing I remember is Mick bringing me across the road to a pub to wet the baby's 'head' as we say around these parts. I ordered two pints.

"I am sorry son, can't serve you."

"What? Why?"

"You're too young for alcohol."

My father almost fell off the stool laughing!

"Do you know what, you're dead right, he is too young! But, seeing as he has just fathered a child, maybe you could give him a pint on this occasion?!"

He did, so fair play to him. Ironically, three days later I would reach the legal age, a warning sign, in hindsight, of our youth and immaturity. His mother and I tried our best, especially for Graham, but we broke up a couple of years later. Graham's mother, to her eternal credit, did a fabulous job raising him, flawless, in my opinion. Unfortunately, I was only a Saturday father, a visiting dad, but I loved every precious second, I had with him. We have some great memories-off playing in the park, both in Fairview and Santry-of taking him to the play zone in Santry and Kinsealy, bringing him off swimming and like most other dads, I'm still sick of McDonald's food to this day! My most important memories of his early years revolve around him being with my mother. She completely doted upon him. She had plenty of grandchildren, even great grandchildren, but she always paid special attention to Graham. I know I really shouldn't say it, but I really do think that he was her favourite! Graham is now a strapping, really handsome man of 29 yrs. He visited me regularly in Spain and we still have a great relationship to this day. He is extremely well read; he has travelled extensively and you couldn't wish to meet a more courteous, well-mannered young man. He is settled down with his own partner now and I couldn't possibly love him or be more proud of him than I already am. I can take no credit for his up-bringing or how well he turned out, that's entirely on his mother and the amazing job she did.

As Graham grew from a child into a man, you might as well say that I was going through a mourning phase myself. In my early twenties, I was earning lots of money but putting in the hours to do it. Still, life was pretty good and only getting better. I ended up meeting another beautiful girl and after some time, we got very serious. We ended up moving in together into a very opulent apartment complex called Venetian Hall, just off Howth Road in north Dublin. This was my first time living with someone and it was also my first time living away from home. I was really slumming it-a posh pad in upmarket Clontarf, complete with its own swimming pool – nice work if you can get it. I really was living with the dream; I had a beautiful partner, a good job, a great place to live and made the time to enjoy golf, go to the gym, go for a swim and even rack up the odd frame of snooker. I wasn't half-bad at snooker as a kid, I got proper lessons and everything, wanting someday to be the next Steve Davis, but I loved cars even more, so once I got behind a wheel… well, the rest is history, I suppose.

My girlfriend and I made the most of our good fortune, we had some great laughs, socialized out at bars and discos and I even "let" her beat me at tennis from time to time (like I ever had a chance). Unfortunately, my father had his battle with cancer at this time, and well everything changed. I ended up having to work every hour God sent and my girlfriend and I tried and failed to get pregnant, which only added to our growing frustrations. We tried everything and visited St James's Hospital regularly, but for all the world, it was never going to happen. This was a crippling blow for her and with me not around as much, the stress finally told on us and our relationship sadly ended. Like with Graham's mother, we ended on good terms and I eventually left the apartment when my father battled cancer. He retired and after a while, I found that I too wanted a break. Wanted? I needed one. I was still in my early twenties and looked and felt like I was carrying the world and its problems on my shoulders. Life was too short, so I decided to rent out my taxi and went over to England to be with my sister Dorry.

Although I didn't fully acknowledge it at the time, travelling over to England was the start of scratching a nagging itch I'd had since birth. Going overseas spared off some latent 'adventure' gene that had embedded itself into my D.N.A. It seems really obvious-looking back-as I wanted to travel from the start–crawl, walk, run, swim, trike, bike, car and now I was airborne, although only a puddle–jump compared to what lay ahead. I was also stationed at the airport for most of my taxi life, so again easy to spot in hindsight. For me, travel equalled freedom, but also a test. Could I make it away from home?

Growing up, the product of a working-class North Dublin household. I had a strong appreciation for family. It was clear to me that stretching my legs into the "foreign" workforce would be much more achievable with family support. Dorry is my big sister and a real "mammy" in the sense that she was the matriarch of her family, doing it alone. I, of course, wanted to spend time with my sister and her children, she was delighted to have a rare helping hand around the house and I had a secure base of operations. Everyone was happy, a rare thing! I had no bills and didn't "have" to work, but I didn't come all this way to be a lounge lizard. I had to stay occupied and I needed to work, but at what?

Most people of my generation who travelled to England back then would have done one or two things–building or bar work. Both paid well and didn't not appeal to me, but they were my fall back-position, I wanted to test myself. Try something new, be creative. I love cars, always have and I loved tinkering around with cars ever since I could look under the bonnet of dad's car as a kid and hand him his tools as he fixed it, but absorbing it all as I did. I saw an old Volkswagen camper van lying in a neglected state of disrepair and gathering dust. Now you didn't see an awful lot of these back in Dublin but they were dotted around the U.K. Not everywhere, not a very common site, but you'd see them around. I checked out his particular V.W., looked under the hood, kicked the tires etc, and made a very modest offer to a very grateful owner who couldn't wait to get rid of it. I got it up to Dorry's place and she allowed me to work on it at the side of her house. Fair play to her, as I don't know if I would've been so accommodating if my brother brought a bunch of scrap to my home!

Then a strange thing happened. I got stuck into it and not only did I fix it, but I also gave it a bit of a polish/make-over and sold it for a profit. It was easy, too easy, it must've been a fluke with my still-warm profits burning through my pocket. I bought another one. Another fixer-upper. I did it again, more profit! I hadn't found a 'new–job'; rather, I'd identified a niche market. British owners didn't want the hassle of repairing V.W. camper vans, Australians loved V.W. camper vans with "character" (my interpretation of a just fixed V.W. with more miles on the clock than the orient express) and I loved bringing them back to life. What I loved even more, was the interaction of the meet-greet –feet on the street of it all. I was a salesman, and I loved it.

I was making a lot of money, meeting new people, cutting deals and not exactly killing myself. I took my time, an arrangement of one a week for the twenty weeks I did it. Dorry was delighted she had extra help around the house and another

27

income helping out; with a single mother raising five children, she could finally save a few pounds. I was able to save up a few bob as well but knew I couldn't stay at Dorry's forever. It was only a short stay and I'd been there long enough. I've always preferred to be the guy to leave the party and not be 'asked' to, so I decided to move on before wearing out my welcome. My adventurous spirit yearned to boldly go where I'd never gone before… Backpacking!

I was young, single, footloose and fancy free, so I pointed blindly at the map and hit Belgium. So, I made it to Bruges before Colin Farrell and went to Brussels to see where the sprouts lived! From there, I crossed the border into the flat but very beautiful Netherlands, visited Amsterdam. From there, I headed south and saw quite a lot of France before crossing the 'Pyrenees' into Spain. From the moment I stepped foot on the Spanish soil, I loved its hot, fragrant air, I knew I'd found my home. Over the years, I have travelled the world, all over Africa, South and North America, Asia and most European countries, but nothing ever came close to my first impression of Spain. I loved everything about it, especially the people, as they were just like the Irish-warm, friendly, loved life and were family oriented. I had a whale of a time but after a month or so, I found myself back in Ireland driving a taxi-again, but not aimlessly. I had a dream now, something to work towards and by God, was I ever determined to get it.

Don't get me wrong, it was great to be able to travel, to work and then fall back into your taxi when you get back, but reality bites. I was back living with my parents. That was all good before, but now. I'd gotten used to living on my own, so I decided to try and get my toes on the property ladder. Everywhere I'd bring a fare, I'd have a look at what was for sale; Swords and the newly built Clare Hall development looked very appealing, but I stumbled upon a beautiful house in Dunshaughlin and my head was turned I had some money saved and this was where it was going. It was a massive, four bedroomed detached property that had a deposit within my range. It was a dream home for me and my first, but dreams don't always come cheap. It was going for £70,000 a kings-ransom back then, as Clare Hall was going for just under £50,000 on average. I went in and met with the taxi federation, as I needed a mortgage, and they recommended a broker for me. His name was Martin Kelly and he got me a mortgage straight away. I was off and running my first step into a whole new world.

Dunshaughlin wasn't Santry though and Co Meath wasn't Dublin. At first, I found it to be a very clannish and cliquey town, but then all the Dublin commuters started moving in and that suited me just fine. Martin and I stayed in touch and had plenty of property-related meetings, all of which fascinated me. Still, I now had a mortgage that needed to be paid, so not only was I driving taxis, but I was also starting to hone my newly discovered sales skills, buying and selling a few second-hand cars and vans. This was at the time when mobile phones were only at the cusp of their brick-like market entry and could only be used for making and receiving calls, the dinosaur times that they were! It was a fortuitous time for me, though, as I didn't require an office or a secretary, I could sit and wait for callers, and they came. I was still only twenty-three years old and as free as a bird.

I was starting to make new friends in Dunshaughlin and having great times there. My family would regularly pop out to visit but when they'd leave, Santry would suddenly feel far away. That would soon bleed into my psyche when I was driving "all the way" to work and then "all the way" home. Nowadays, with a much improved road infrastructure, it's "only up the road" or a "short-spin" as we used to say, but subconsciously, I was talking my way out of it. Before long, I rented out my house and upped sticks back to Dublin.

I found a convenient room that was available to rent in the nearby suburb of Glasnevin, humorously referred to as "The Dead-Centre of Dublin" because of its massive cemetery, home and final resting place to many Irish Revolutionary Heroes. It was a strange experience for me, though, living so close to my family but with a different family, so I threw myself headfirst into my work rather than go back to my rented room. I couldn't settle there, feeling like some kind of a weird Cuckoo before realizing at some point that the bird analogy was on the money. I missed my family and like all Irish sons, I missed my mammy and all the home comforts. I moved back to Santry with the intention of buying another house whilst maintaining a heavy work schedule. That little plan took longer than expected, but that's getting ahead of ourselves. First of all, there's somebody I'd like you to meet. Ladies and gentlemen, allow me to introduce my older brother his name is Rory.

Rory

My brother was a product of the real sixties, unlike his baby brother. Rory came into the world when the decade nurtured flower power, making peace not war and was backed by a soundtrack containing Elvis, the Beatles Woodstock and the Doors. In so many ways, Rory was the embodiment of the decade that bore him; a peacemaker, a lover of great music and, as we'll see later, the real power behind flowers when it came to getting his way! Like the rest of us, he was a home birth in Santry and his too, was a healthy delivery. All was good in the world of Rory, until his fourth birthday.

I'm sure that one of the very last items on my parents list of 'what to expect on my son's 4th birthday' would be for him to slip into a coma, yet that mysterious occurrence happened to him. Completely out of the blue, the last thing my parents expected. He was rushed to Temple Street Children's Hospital, where he stayed for three days. Despite the best efforts of the excellent hospital staff, they drew a blank, completely flummoxed as to what was wrong with him. They arranged for his transfer to St. Vincent's hospital, over on the south side, where a more specialist team were assigned to him. rounds of tests there, it became apparent that there was a blockage to his brain caused by excess fluid and serious surgical intervention was required. Don't forget that was pre-decimal Ireland. A time where any such surgery was touch and go at best, but for a small child like Rory? Not a favourable prognosis. My parents had no choices left, if they wanted him to live.

Thank God the operation was an amazing success but also not perfect. The little boy who fell asleep before his 4th birthday woke up after it a changed person, requiring medication for the rest of his natural life, but at least he was alive to take it. Some things never changed though, and Rory, the pre-coma rogue emerged from the briefly enforced hibernation as Rory the rascal! He was absolutely fearless and spent his every waking hour terrorizing the poor staff at St. Vincent's! There are some spectacular views from the top floor of that super tall hospital and Rory loved them so much he tried several times to climb over the balcony for a close inspection! This resulted in several changes to hospital policy – (A) board up access to the balconies, (B) keep everyone with a bad heart away from Rory Mahon and (C) if something looks dangerous. Then Rory Mahon will find it, nail it down! The era of Mahon-mischief had arrived!

The wonderful staff at St. Vincent's were always delighted to see people so seriously ill on arrival, depart from their cane in better shape. Still, you can be sure they also breathed a collective sigh of relief when Rory was well enough to go home…. especially their worn-out maintenance crew!

Rory still looked like pre-coma Rory, but… he was not quite the same and never would be. He started to suffer from severe epileptic seizures and sadly, I have no memories of my brother where these "fits", as they were then known, weren't a part of his D.N.A. Let's be clear, I don't mean the odd seizure now and then; this was every day and not just once a day either. Even when I was a toddler and he'd be "looking after me" (the way that most second youngest siblings lay claim to the youngest as being "theirs"), teaching me how to play with building blocks and such, then –wham–Rory's on the floor, all the toys are up-ended and slowly sprayed in his blood. It was terrifying for both of us but it also became 'normal' and created a close bond between us. Closer than closer, my toddler's brain stretched to its limit trying to understand why life was so unfair to "Ror" and I must've made an early–age promise to myself that I'd never be cruel or impatient with him because I never was… sometimes I could've bloody swung for him though!

Over the years, I've come to meet a lot of people who grew up with siblings who would today be described as having learning difficulties or special needs. Back in 1970s Ireland, our brothers and sisters were known as being 'handicapped,' which is viewed as a derogatory term these days. Back then though, you had a handicapped brother/sister and sometimes they'd be lovingly described as being 'special.' Well, Rory was very special, very special and unlike my other older brothers, I'd end up looking after him, but so what? That's what families are supposed to do, isn't it? Not every household was blessed with characters as large as Rory and as you'll see, they didn't come much bigger!

Rory's coma came at a very bad time for him-age-wise as he ended up becoming problematic in terms of getting him a place at school. However, Kay-our-mother-wasn't the type of woman to sit meekly and accept the word "no" when it came to her children, so after a brief meeting with the local school, Rory was on the books! He started Larkhill Boys school like the rest of the family (boys) and even though he only lasted a few days there. I'd still hear stories of his time there over twenty years later! I'm unsure how to feel about that, as nobody remembers me even being there and I went through all these phases! Anyway, a few days into what was to become his short-lived Larkhill academic experience, my father received a phone call. He'd been summoned to the principal's office for what was probably the first time in his life, nice one Rory!

"I'm sorry, Mr. Mahon, but we don't feel that young Rory is ideally suited for this school…."

To be fair, my parents knew this was coming as they had totally blagged Rory's way into school, but nothing ventured…! My father collected Rory from his classroom immediately and proudly held his little hand as they walked out of those gates forever.

"Daddy?"

"Yes, Rory."

"Why am I leaving this school?"

My father looked down into Rory's little face, his son's eyes starting to well up and a slight quiver in his lower lip. He thought that he'd done something wrong. My dad smiled at him and then nodded his head back in the direction of his classroom.

"You see that school, Rory?"

"Yes."

"Well, Rory, you are too good for that school."

Rory's entire demeanour changed instantly and he suddenly beamed with pride:

"Yes, Daddy, I'm too good for that school."

But where to next for Rory, as he had to go to school somewhere? The answer to our prayers. Actually, wasn't too far from our doorstep. Just off the Ballymun road, a literal stones-throw from our housing estate sat the large campus of St. Michael's House, a school for children with mental and /or physical handicaps. Rory loved it, they adored him and he came on leaps and bounds.

Every so often the careers (as the 'teachers' were called) would take the children (clients nowadays) away on little trips and stayover's known as 'breakaways.' These are excellent ideas for all concerned, including the parents who get some much-needed respite. One of Rory's favourite breakaway destinations was down in Brittas Bay, Co-Wicklow. It's a beautiful spot, sitting on the cusp of the sunny-south-east coastline. Rory-who was extremely athletic, winning track and field trophies-was also an extremely gifted swimmer, so wherever there was water, Rory would be in his element.

One time, a really nice priest took them off fishing down in Brittas. He carefully lined up all the children in a secure row, helped bait their rods and cast off for them, and then began telling them lovely little fishing stories to help pass the time.

"….and of course, our lord himself was a fisherman; did you know that? Yes, yes he was, as were some of his apostles…."

Whether Rory was bored or had heard it all before, nobody knows, but he got bored and snuck away…

"….and of course, Jesus was an excellent fisherman, so he was, oh dear, an excellent fisherman. Do you know why? Well, because he was a fisher-of-man, do you see? So…"

Rory re-emerged, hands behind his back……wearing "the look."

"….and after Jesus had filled the nets with fish …."

-Rory strikes-
"….do you know what he said? He said…

-splash!

"…. he said…. OH! Fuck!! Oh fuck, oh Jesus, that's, that's cold!"

Rory had taken off one of his wellies and filled it up with cold seawater, then snuck around behind the priest and let him have it!

"Who…who…oh that's cold, who did that?"

One of the many reasons why Rory was never a master criminal? He couldn't keep a straight face! He was doubled over with laughter, and his latest prank had gone much better than he had expected. The more he laughed, the more the other children laughed too. Brittas Bay basked in a chorus of children's laughter:

"Father?"

"(shivering) Y…Yes, Rory?

"Did Jesus really say that?"

"Em… did, he… eh... I think so…."

"Where was I exactly?? When Jesus filled the nets and said –oh fuck, oh fuck, its cold!!"

The whole gang exploded into laughter all over again; even the priest managed to laugh it off eventually, but he'd always keep a close eye on Rory after that. I don't know how many Hail Marys Rory got in confession for that stunt, but I'm sure it was well worth it!

Not all of Rory's fishing adventures ended as happily. Fishing was a big part of our childhood, and our father would regularly take us up to Clogher Head to cast-off a few lines and try our luck. Sometimes we'd only have the one rod to share between us and on those occasions, we'd always let Rory have the first cast. He was an explosive ball of pent-up energy at the best of times, so patience wouldn't have been one of his strong points, especially when our father would affix feathers to the line to help attract Mackerel. It took time and patience, so more often than not, Rory would run up and down the pier looking for mischief until the rod was finally ready. One of us would always go with him to make sure he didn't get into too much trouble. It was just as well. My dad, having gotten the rod loaded and ready, waited for ages for Rory to return, but- assuming he'd found something else to do in the meantime-in his absence Mick cast off anyway. It would've been an otherwise great fishing story for him, as no sooner had the float settled on the water than he got a bite. Two, to be more precise, two mackerel on a single cast, an amateur's dream start, and just as he reeled them in, he heard a distant shout:

"Da! Da! Help! Rory's in the harbour, he's drowning!"

The fish, the rod and the feathers were lost to the sea as Mick threw them and double-timed them down the pier and dove straight into the water. My older brother was only barely keeping Rory afloat by holding onto his hair for dear life. Between them, they managed to pull Rory out to safely and dry him off. My father didn't even need to ask what happened; it wasn't the first near miss–or the last. Rory had been charging up and down the pier, then-just as quick and unexpected as a hic-cup-took a seizure and fell into the harbour. If my brother hadn't been so alert or my dad so quick to act, then that would've been that for Rory, game over. Just. Like. That. When Rory came out of his seizure, he was sore all over and confused:

"Why am I all wet?"

"You fell in."

"I did?"

"You did. Do you not remember falling in?"

"No."

That's just how it went with Rory back then, he could take a seizure and when he'd recovered, he'd have no idea of what happened, no memory of the incident what – so - ever.

My poor father needed eyes in the back of his head sometimes. One time my dad was about to reverse his car out of the drive to give me a lift to school. Rory used to get collected from our garden gate by St. Michael's special bus, but when Mick noticed that Rory wasn't waiting in his usual spot, he asked me to get out to see where he was.

"Da! Da! Stop the car, stop the car!"

Rory was under the car, mid-seizure. He was less than four-inches from a certain tragedy.

My mother wasn't exempt from frequent Rory – induced heart-attacks either. She went shopping with her sister one time whilst my father was recovering in hospital. Next thing she knows, there's a request over the shop's P.A. system.

"Could a Mrs-Kay Mahon please come to the reception desk? Kay Mahon to the reception desk, please, thank you."

Naturally, my mother feared the worst. Mick had undergone a very serious operation; clearly, something terrible had happened. Why else would someone go to the trouble of tracking her down and getting her paged? She made her way to reception with her heart bursting out of her chest in frightened panic.

"Howaya's ma!"

"Rory?!"

"I knew you were here!"

"Is… everything alright?"

"Ah, not really."

"[oh god, please, no, no] what's…. what's wrong Rory?"

"Can I have a fiver? I want to buy something!"

She was too relieved to even give out to him and just gave him the money! No matter what he'd do, you couldn't stay mad at him for long.

It wasn't just because he was family, either. One of his favourite pastimes was kicking a football on the street with some of the local lads. If they weren't about (for whatever reason), he'd just kick the ball by himself, but he wasn't always the most accurate with his shots. Now back then, every street in Dublin had a neighbour who'd confiscate your ball if it happened to land in their garden. So, let's set the scene: a beautiful hot summer day, Mick pottering about in his praised garden, Rory kicking the ball all over the place waiting for the other lads to appear, and a neighbour in her garden watering her plants. It doesn't take a rocket scientist this one, does it?! Bang-Rory hoofs the ball into the sky, splat-the ball lands in the neighbour's garden. She gathers up the ball and gives poor oul Rory a right, rollicking about kicking the ball into her garden and saying that he wouldn't be getting it back. That was that. At some point, the other footballers come out to play, and there's Rory sitting on the curb, sulking with his head in his hands.

"Are we playing ball, Rory?"

"Nah"

"Why not?"

"No ball."

"How come?"

"(pointing) Ah, she took it."

All the other boys knew the score. If your ball lands in Mrs. X's garden, it was a goner, still, boys will be boys, and Rory was an easy target:

"Ah, Rory, you're not gonna let her away with that, are ya?"

"What do u mean?"

"Knock on her door and tell her she better give it back."

And so Rory boldly went where no other boy had gone before.

"What do YOU want??"

"Give me the ball back, will ya?"

You know that old saying about 'the straw that broke the camel's back'? This was the equivalent of a hay bale on the back of dear old Mrs X:

"(Roaring) Your Ball Back??"

"y…. y…yes…please"

"(Louder) Never! It's Gone-Gone - Do you hear me??"

She really went off on one, going into a full rant, easily eclipsing five or so minutes. Finally, she stopped to take a breath. Rory took this as his cue to respond:

"Ah, would you ever cool down…"

"Cool Down?!! Did You Just Tell Me To "Cool Down?"

"Well…"

"How-Dare-You 'Cool Down,' is it? Well, I'll…"

She never fully realised the rest of that particular sermonette because-out of the corner of his eye - Rory spotted her garden hose and (Rory being Rory) turned it on her until she was drenched.

"Now, that's better, isn't it?! You're much cooler now!"

All of these fair-weather football friends thought that he was the cat's meow for doing that, and he therefore thought that it was okay too, so he headed on home. It wasn't the end of the matter, though.

When she eventually dried herself off and calmed down half a notch, she stormed down to see my parents, ready to upload a rain of retribution. My mother saw her coming and went to meet her at the front gate; the sooner this was going to be over, the better, so I went with her too. Heck, if Rory was in the dog house. I might as well keep him company. Rory stood just behind us. The anger of the tirade being unloaded at our poor mother clearly had something to do with him. Then just like that, her face contorted into a 'what's happing' expression and the void created by the audio vacuum of her sudden silence started to fill with little moans and a choking sound. As one, we all looked at the patch of ground behind my mother. It was Rory. He'd taken another seizure, and this was an especially bad one. He'd also managed to wallop his head off the corner of the pillar at the end of our gate and busted his head wide open. He'd lost a lot of blood by the time we managed to get him off to the hospital.

It wasn't the poor lady's fault, but she blamed herself and felt truly awful about the whole thing. Rory got home a few days later and she called around to the house to see him, full of apologies and to be fair, she turned out to be a lovely neighbour in the end, especially when the chips were down like all good neighbours do. That day though, she was just relieved to see Rory looking back at himself again.

"See you later, Rory. Get well soon."

"Thank you, bye, bye."

"Bye, Rory."

"Missus?"

"Yes, Rory."

"Don't forget to bring me my ball back!"

That was just Rory, though, he wasn't trying to be a smart-ass. It was just how he was wired.

To be fair to our neighbour, it wasn't as if she was some kind of heartless monster either because to look at Rory, you'd never think that there was anything wrong with him. In all honesty, he was an incredibly handsome young man and he was not exactly short of admired either. This could be a blessing and a curse for him because unfortunately, the world is full of insensitive idiots. You'd always get the jack-the-lad types who'd know about his condition and dare him to go up to girls in front of their boyfriends and say the most inappropriate things to them, hoping to get him into trouble. He had lots of very near-misses with angry, jealous boyfriends, but thankfully common sense managed to prevail. Well, that and the fact that he had a lot of very protective brothers who wouldn't have thought twice about getting involved or coming to his aid. The seizures, continued to come thick and fast and we were living with a ticking time bomb.

They say that a close shave rubs some of the luck off, and if that were true, then Rory was on borrowed time. One day my sister took him to the shops-he was only around six or seven years of age-when he took a seizure right in the middle of crossing a very busy road. Somehow my sister (who wasn't much older than him) managed to stop a car from running over him. I'll never forget what the driver said to her:

"You're lucky you stopped me. I thought that he was an old sack left in the middle of the road."

My poor parents were at the end of their tether. The above example; the Mackerel fishing, the seizure under the car and many-many-more. I could honestly fill the rest of this book with stories about "The Day Rory Nearly Died", but as my brother, what can you do?

The doctors, the hospitals and all the healthcare experts told us that he was on the correct medication, correct dosages etc, so there was nothing they could really do for him except to patch him up every so often. A lot of other parents at St. Michael's house started bringing their children off to Lourdes in the hope that the divine one could fix what science couldn't. What would there be to lose? With that, my father brought him over when he was twelve; my mother hated flying, so it was a boys-only trip for them!

Just to clarify, the Mahon family are not now, nor have ever been a bunch 'holy - Joe's,' so for the atmosphere over there to have the effect it did on my father speaks volumes about faith and hopelessness. The absolute certainty of some of 'the faithful' over there about miracle cures for their sick and dying loved ones was both tragic and inspirational, an oxymoron for all the right reasons. It moved my father to tears more than once and he isn't exactly what you'd call a 'Crier.' On their last day over there, Rory was very confused:

"Dad?"

"Yes, Rory."

"Why are you crying?"

"Because I love you, Rory!"

This was and is a beautiful sentiment, a loving bond between father and son, but Rory saw things differently. Dad is crying. Therefore, Dad is sad. So, make him happy. It was time for "The Joke."

Rory loved a good joke and knew a few good ones. Some of them weren't even that dirty! But when he decided that the moment required a "break glass in case of emergency" type joke, he'd bring out "the joke" as we all came to know it. For anyone who ever met him, this will forever be Rory's:

"Dad?"

"Do you want to hear a funny joke? It'll make you happy!"

My father was too choked up to answer him. They were over there to try and make Rory better and now here he was, trying to make his daddy better. This, more than anything else, was the real Rory, all heart, no malice.

"C'mon, Dad Dad, do you want to hear it??!"

"(struggling) Phew Phew....eh...yes Rory, thanks."

"Okay, are you ready Dad Dad?!"

"(putting the brave face together) ready!"

"Okay! So, do you know the way you have an umpire in cricket?"

"I do."

"And you have a referee in football?"

"Yep."

"Then, what would you have in bowls?"

At this point, you insert guess after guess after guess. The more wrong you are, the funnier he finds his joke to be. He'd be in fits of giggles with each and every "No!" he'd shut down with until eventually, you'd surrender, just like my father:

"Okay, Rory, I give up! What do you put in bowls?"

"(fits of giggles) Do you really give up?!"

"Yes!!"

"Are you sure!? (Almost wetting himself!)"

"Yes! Will you ever bloody tell me!!?"

"Goldfish!!!"

Nobody-seriously, nobody! –found his punch line funnier than Rory. He would be in absolute hysterics at the end, tears running down his face, actually sweating from laughter! Do you know what, the first couple of times, you couldn't help but join in with him, but by the ten thousand times, it wasn't quite so, but he never lost any enjoyment from it. Literally, a gift that kept on giving to him. That, dear reader, was Rory's joke! Trust me, it's much funnier when he tells it!

When he got back from Lourdes, life continued as normal for him, seizure after seizure with cruel idiots sometimes 'getting off' on the fact that he could so easily be exploited. The scariest time of the year for my parents - without a doubt – was Halloween, for those very reasons. Rory was always happy to make friends and eager to help. Sometimes too eager. He'd be bigger and older than the other kids he'd hung around with from the area, so there was no better man to get stuck in and collect wood and fuel for the bonfire (known colloquially back then as "The Bomber"). Then Rory, naturally enough he'd wanted to taste the fruits of his labour when it came to Halloween night, but it was far too dangerous for him. Year after year, the 'unfairness' of it all got harder on him, so my parents had to come up with creative distractions for him. For such reasons, they regularly attended Halloween Balls with him or basically, went anywhere where it was safe and "so much better than that dirty old bonfire." But even that had a shelf-life. So, how do you keep him indoors? Luckily my mother had the answer.

Two words- 'Super' and 'Mario' hid a multitude of dangerous situations and kept him home. Happily, so. My mother would sit for hours with him, patiently playing Mario. Before long, the Kay/Rory absences started getting longer, then longer and still, you wouldn't know that they were even home sometimes until you'd hear a laugh, a scream or a torrent of abuse about the little plumber from the Nintendo room! My mother was just as bad if not worse than Rory for it; she was hooked! Still, that's not to say that Rory's day of mischief was over.

Boys will be boys and teenagers will always push the boundaries. As a helpful soul, Rory was blind to the manipulation of others. He was a very convenient resource for the local teenagers to tap into, to go into an off-licence and buy alcohol for them. More often than not, we'd only find out that he was doing this after we'd ask him to go to the shops for a few massages and he'd tell us that he couldn't because he'd been barred from the shopping centre. But still, the seizure continued and there seemed like no hope was ever going to come. Then he turned nineteen and this changed again.

My parents had never given up hope of finding a solution to his seizure issues. No, they would never get them cured completely, but surely there had to be a way to at least deal with their frequency? The answer, it appeared, could be found in the Richmond Hospital (now defunct and turned into a court) in Dublin city–centre. The usual battery of extensive tests was conducted and then a proposal was put forward to my parents: "We can operate on him and we're confident that it will alleviate the frequency of his seizures.... however, the survival rate is 50/50 at best..."

Jesus, what a choice to make kill your son via surgery or just let one of his many near misses "Hit" someday and let him die that way. When the only thing you got left in your life is a pocketful of change, you've got to be really careful about how you spend it, so to say that my parents agonized over this decision from every angle-front and back, inside and out. It would be an understatement and do them a grave disservice. When logic failed them, they turned to God and prayed on it long into the night. When time ran out and they were forced into making a decision, they trusted in the rule of Occam's Razor–all things being equal, the simplest explanation is usually the right one.

I can't even begin to contemplate how they felt going into meet that team of surgeons and put their signatures at the bottom of a document that gave the medics permission to put Rory into a sleep he might never wake up from. I hope I never have to endure those emotions. But thank God they did because Rory's surgery was a great success. He'd still be prone to seizures and have to rely on medication, but they'd never come with such horrific regularity again. No free lunch though, as a result of the surgery, he'd been fitted with two wires through his brain and inside his nose, keeping the top of his skull in place. One of the more obvious side-effects of this surgery was that it resulted in him having in 'sniff.' All the time, because of the location of the wires. It caused a reflexive suffering to 'clear' the blockage, so it wasn't something he could control and you could see people's reaction to it on planes or public transport wasn't favourable, but they weren't to know. It taught all of us in the Mahon family to be a lot more tolerant of others, though, as there-but for the grace of God could be another Rory.

I don't know if it was because we were the youngest sibling or if it was down to some other reason, but we both grew up with a love for vehicles and all things transportation related. Bikes were Rory's transport of choice from a very early age, but he wasn't allowed to have one for the longest time due to his obvious medical issues. How did he eventually get one? In a word, persistence!

"Can I have a bike?"

"No."

"Ah, please."

"No."

"C'mon."

"No."

"Why not?"

"Can I have a bike?"

"Will you get me a bike?"

"I want a bloody bike!!"

Day after day, week in, week out and on, and on, and on. Eventually, my mother broke and sent my father out to get him a bicycle. Mick bought a second-hand one for him because, knowing Rory, a new one would be lost or stolen or just given away to someone he felt sorry for; his heart truly was like that. To Rory, though, this bike was all his dreams realised into one fantastical metal machine on two–wheels. Once he sorted out his balance, promised to be careful and wear his helmet at all times (discarded as soon as he was out of sight, naturally), he was off. Every street corner was an adventure and every other cyclist he met in the neighbourhood was a fellow explorer and brother of the handle-bar! He was completely happy and then his natural inquisitive took over. Why should he need mud-grounds? Why doesn't he have a bell? Before long, Rory started tinkering around with Dad's tools and would dismantle his bike to make be–spoke modifications (no pun intended!) and then try to put it back together again. Let's say that his dismantling skills far outweighed his assembly skills and Mick became quite adept at reconstructing bicycles! I'll never forget his first puncture because it gave me a rare opportunity to flex my 'mechanical muscles' and help him to fix it. Wow, was that ever a mistake! He correctly surmised that if and if an absolute go been and like I surely was, could fix a puncture, then he could. He was right, he could and just to prove it, he'd go out of his way to find nails on the road or broken glass so that he could puncture-then repair his tyres. It cost my parents a small fortune on puncture repair kits, pumps (usually lost or else given away to someone who 'needed one' more), repair patches etc. Then he worked out how to change the bulbs and batteries on his lamp, so there was another almost mortgage in repair and maintenance outlay! When he wasn't upgrading his bike, he was being heart–in-the-mouth dangerous on it.

There was a very busy –and dangerous road close to where we grew up called the Swords Road. All day –every day-cars, vans, buses and trucks would zoom up and down it and it was a famous accident black spot. Rory was cycling home on it and spotted a car laden with several canoes on its roof rack, so he decided to swerve in front of it. The poor driver had to slam hard down on his brakes to avoid hitting him, casually causing the canoes to come loose and then bounce all over the road into other traffic. The furious driver jumped out his car and grabbed Rory by the scruff and started to berate him at the top of his voice. Luckily for Rory, a lady called Joan Duffy from his club happened to be there and very kindly explained the situation to the driver, who then let him go. When Joan quizzed Rory about what he did, he just laughed and told her that he wanted to test the brakes on the man's car, then hopped back on his bike and cycled home.

Another time he was taking a short cut home. Where the port tunnel now is and he must have been cycling in a very creative manner because the Garda pulled him over. After giving them his name and address they told him that he couldn't cycle like that on a public road:

"Can't I?"

"No."

"Well, you know where I live. You bring it home for me!"

With that, he trusted his bike at the guards and ran home. The Garda beat him to the door through, and after my father had to explain Rory's condition to them, they took it well and left the bike with him and friendly terms-no sooner had they gone when Rory got back into the house, having climbed over the wall to the rear

44

of our house. It wasn't the first or the last brush with the law he'd have. Again, I could fill another book with those tales, but one really stands out.

It was about half past five or so on a winter's evening when he was cycling home and got pulled over by a Garda. I won't mention the name of the officer, but suffice it to say that every driver on the roads of Dublin's north side during the mid-eighties to mid-nineties would've had a bit of a brush with him at some point. The nicest thing I've ever heard said about him was that he was "A Total Bastard." Anyway, he squares up to Rory:

"Where the fuck do you think you're going?"

"Emm.... home?"

"Fuckin' smart arse, are ya?"

"No .... I'm going home. "

"This your bike?"

"Yeah."

"Where's your Fuckin lights, huh? No lamp, no lights. Do you want to get killed?"

"No."

"You're a danger to yourself and others. I am giving you a summons?"

Rory was very troubled when he got home and this was so unusual that it really stood out. My father had a little chat with him to see what was wrong.

"Dad, what's a summons?"

"Why do you want to know about that, Rory?"

He told Mick what happened and about how his lamp had been stolen and how scary the whole experience had been for him. My Da eased his mind, promised to buy him (yet another!) a new lamp and then that was that. Well almost.

Several weeks later, Rory gets served with a summons and he is absolutely clueless about why. Mick explained to him about the night he got stopped for not having a lamp on his bike and that he was told he'd receive a summons:

"So, you'll have to go to court."

"What's court?

"Well.... let's see.... it's a place people have to go to when they do something wrong."

A look of absolute horror and disbelief shot across Rory's face:

"Really, Dad Dad, really??"

"I'm afraid so."

"Why did you do something wrong Dad Dad?"

"It's not for me Rory. It's for you!"

And so, the dreaded court date arrived. My poor father had gone through what Rory was supposed to say so many times that he repeated it in his sleep! Then the moment of truth arrived and the judge called Rory:

"You are Mr. Mahon?"

"I am."

"Do you have anything to say for yourself?"

"Huh?"

"Mr. Mahon, what have you got to say on the matter?"

"Huh?"

"Mr. Mahon, what have you got to say on the matter?"

"Huh? What are you talking about?"

"(Big, Long, Sigh) Well, Mr. Mahon, you were summoned before me to court today to answer the charge against you, namely that you, on the evening of January

10[th,] did only cycle your bicycle without adequate lighting. Now, I ask you again, have you anything to say for yourself?"

That was a bit of a mouthful for me, let alone Rory, so all of Mick's careful preparation went out the window. Rory was scared and kept looking at my father and back to the judge in panicked agitation. My father calmly mouthed his instruction slowly to Rory, who then composed himself and looked to the judge:

"Sergeant, I told the policeman my lamp was stolen!"
Mick just buried his head in his hands and gave me his best "oh my God." look. To be fair, the judge was no fool. It was clear and obvious that Rory didn't exactly fit the usual profile of an accused man in the dock. He then cast his gaze over to my father and saw a family resemblance:

"Excuse me, sir, but are you the father?"

"Yes, your honour, I am."

He then looked at Rory, then back to my father in an almost avuncular way:

"Am I correct in thinking, Mr. Mahon–senior–that-your son would have..." He just let the sentence hang there like that; his look and his tone afforded Rory the silent, knowing dignity of what didn't need to be said out loud for all to hear.

"Yes, your honour, you would.''

"Thank you."

"Garda 'X' do you still wish to proceed?"

"Yes, I do judge, yes."

"Do you not see something very wrong with that decision?"

"No judge. No, I don't. This is a very serious....."

"I'll stop you right their guard. You are correct about one thing. This is a very serious issue."

"Judge?"

"Garda X, have you been trained to observe at all?"

"Yes, judge."

"Yes?"

"Yes, judge."

"Have you, with all of your experience and training, observed anything at all about Mr. Mahon, eh- Rory Mahon, here before me?"

"Judge, on the 10th of January I..."

"Don't try to fence with me, guard.''

"Judge?

"Simply put, guard, do you observe anything, shall we say – 'different' about the man before me?

"As I said previously judge on January 10th!... I…"

"And as I said previously guard, don't fence with me, Garda 'X' I put it to you like this, there is something demonstrably wrong with the situation we find ourselves in today and your obstinacy isn't helping matters. This young man shouldn't be here. Simple. I also think that you know this and further, that on the night in question, you knew it then but still proceeded to push the matter now, Garda 'X,' you are what I would colloquially describe as a 'frequent flyer' before my court and if I was to check my records, I'm sure I'd find that most if not all – of your "visit" here are for minor traffic-related incidents, would I be correct?"

"Judge?"

"Garda 'X' if you ever – EVER waste my courts time with this. ... NONSENSE, again, and I refer explicitly to young Mr Mahon's case, and I KNOW you know to what I refer, then I'll be taking this up with your superiors. Am I clear?"

"Yes, judge."

"Case dismissed. Young Mr Mahon, please get a lamp for your bike. Next!"

I was never so glad to be in a courtroom! On the way out of the court building, another guard, a young one called me aside and whispered something I won't repeat, but he was almost as happy as we were!

Just thinking about Rory speaking, or rather – 'performing' in a public place, brings me nicely around to another of his tales-singing! He first started showing more than a passing interest in music when he started going to St. Michael's house and before long, he'd be inviting a few school friends home and they'd listen to records and sing along to them. Initially, they wouldn't exactly be 'in tune,' but pretty quickly, Rory started to shine and he'd start belting out Elvis tunes and all manner of folks ballads. His attempts at Shaken Stevens and the gravelly tunes of Rod Stewart, well, not everything met with success; we'll leave it at that! He definitely took after our older brother and our mother in the musical gene pool. As for me, I honestly couldn't carry a tune in a bucket! It was a massive relief for my parents to have him enjoy and love something that they could all share in and so it was that Sunday night at Clontarf Castle became a regular feature in all of our lives.

The setting was perfect for Rory as the crowd consisted of mostly working–class people like ourselves. He could enjoy a few pints under Kay and Mick's watchful eyes and the music felt as though it was specifically tailored to his exact taste. As for the headline acts, by and large, you couldn't hope for a better, more down-to-earth group of people. Sonny Knowles would be one of the better known and respected singers around the Irish circuit, and with his beautiful voice and hard–working ethics, his success is well deserved. What maybe isn't so well-known about him is his humanity and consideration for others. Especially people like Rory. You see, when Rory was at home and listening to a song he liked, or if we were all out somewhere together and our mother (an incredible singer in her own right) was finally hassled into singing a song, he'd just dive right in and sing along. He couldn't care less if you were Elvis on the radio, Kay at a wedding or Sonny Knowles on a stage; he'd join in if he liked the tune, with no fear of social conventions or worrying what people might think. So anyway, one of our first 'Sonny-Night' the 'bold' Mr Knowles, is up on–stage belting out a song when all of a sudden, a familiar face joins him.

Maybe "joins him" is a bit generous. Poor Sonny was left in the shade in that "impromptu" duet and happily relinquished control of his microphone as his band led into their next number. Everyone sitting at our table was in convulsions laughing at the confidence and brass-neck of him... well, not quite 'everyone!' Kay and Mick didn't know where to look! Were we going to be thrown out and barred? Would the audience kick up a fuss, demand a refund or generally just turn ugly on us? What was Sonny bloody Knowles going to make out of this? They had nothing to worry about. As soon as the next song was over, Rory handed the microphone back:

"What's your name then?"

"(fuss and mumbled) Rory Mahon."

"I'm sorry, Rory-man, is that what you said?!"

"No! Rory. Mahon!"

"Well, Rory Mahon, you're a great singer!"

"Thank you. Sonny. You're good too, you know!"

"Well, thanks very much, Rory!"

"No, you are! Isn't he Ma? Tell him!"

"Oh, you're here with your mother?"

"Yeah! And my da and me brother, and our friends... "

"And where are they sitting Rory?"

"There! (pointing)"

With that, the spotlight moved from the stage onto our table, where a very uncomfortable Mick and Kay gave a little wave and looked for a hole in the ground to swallow them up!

"That lady couldn't be your mother, Rory, she is far too young!"

My mother wasn't the blushing kind, but she flushed bright enough right then to sit on a rocky shore and direct ships safely into port!

"She is, silly! She's old! She's very glamorous though. That's why they all call her 'glamorous Kay!"

You wouldn't have thought it possible for my Ma's face to have burned brighter, but it did! She must've wanted to strangle him-anything-to shut him up!

"Oh, glamorous Kay? Hello, glamorous Kay (waving!)!"

Rory was enjoying this, but Kay wasn't! She wouldn't kill me for that, but not Rory! She gave a little wave back and then beckoned Rory back over. It was a great night and fair play to Sonny Knowles for the way he handled it; a great professional! As for Rory, he had tasted the limelight and from that night on, he became a regular on Sonny's stage.

And it was never a problem. Sadly, not everyone was as generous as him. In fact, one or two other headline acts got very prissy and precious over their status. There was one in particular who looked at the castle as a stepping stone to a Vegas residency. Aka Elvis or Sinatra, but at his age, that ship had well and truly sailed, but he had a terrible attitude. Don't get me wrong, Rory didn't have any divine right to invade a stage and try to take over, I'd never say or assert that he did, but the sign of a god performance (or person) is how they read their room. The good people in attendance were used to Rory and encouraged him up onto the stage at times. They didn't take kindly to him being treated with scorn or disrespect and they made their feelings known. This particular singer would keep snatching his mic back out of Rory's confused hands, only to a chorus of:

"Rore - Ree! Rore - Ree! Roar - Ree!"

He'd moodily hand the microphone back:

"Okay, okay, but just one song."

Rory would duly oblige and then hand the mic back.....psyches! It would be a dummy move-and he'd launch into another song, sometimes even a third there was a price to pay if you didn't trust Rory properly, it seemed!

That was his Sunday night "gig," Saturdays would usually be at the Red Parrot, but Mondays were father and son events at The Wexford Inn. There was a fabulous folk band that played there regularly called 'The Vagabonds' and their set list would've included all the great ballads from The Dubliners. The Wolfe Tones, The Furies and songs like those. It was nectar from the Gods for him and wouldn't you know it, he'd soon worked his way into their show! I cannot speak highly enough of those guys because, in their kind and unselfish way of doing things, they made my brother feel like the star of their show. They even put together and special intro for him.

"And now, ladies and gentlemen, please show your appreciation for our special guest joining us on stage-all the way from Dublin's Northside – THE ONE. The only Rory!" He'd milk all the applause like some old theatre tart and join the boys in a few songs. In his mind, he was Elvis; Jagger, Bowie and Bono rolled into one and do you know what? He wasn't half bad! I'd love to think that somehow someday a member of that band reads this book and if they do, please know that however and whenever this book finds you. You made my brother's dreams come true and the Mahon family will never forget that. That, in somewhat of a nutshell, was Rory's music career, of which, a little more later, but before that, a few words on his 'actual' career.

Hand on heart-how many employers do you know of today that go out of their way to hire employees with special needs or a learning disability of some kind? I'm erring on the side of caution here by saying that your answer is probably in the single digit percentile and a low single digit at that. Back in the 1980s'and 1990's, it would've only been a tiny fraction of that, tiny fraction but this was the world Rory faced when he left school. It wasn't like he needed to work; my parents cared for his needs more than adequately, but he looked at his brothers and sisters; they were working, why wouldn't he? My brother had the get-up-and–go of many an able-bodied person that wouldn't even look for a job and then some. His up-and-at-cm attitude inspires me to this day. It was one thing for him to get a job. It was quite another for him to keep it.

St. Michael's house ran a work experience programme for their older students-like-Rory-and they'd find jobs that suited a student's skills and/or personality. Rory loved all animals, especially horses (John Wayne and cowboy movies had a lot to do with that!) and so when a job opened up over at the R.D.S. (Royal Dublin Society) in Ballsbridge, South Dublin, -to help with horses at the prestigious horse show-Rory was the obvious choice. As ever, he loved getting stuck in and helping out where he could. When he got home after his first day, it was all he could talk about at the dinner table. I think he knew the name of every horse and what colour they were by the end of the meal! All good, so one day turns into two into three and so on, with Rory becoming more confident and independent as he went on. Then he reached a week, and my father received a phone call.

"Da?"

"Hiya, Rory."

"I'm finished early. Can you pick me up?"

My father collected him and then–on the drive home-more out of making conversation than anything else: "How come you had an early finish?"

"Ah, I got sacked."

"Sacked? Why did they sack you?"

"I got caught smoking."

"You got sacked for smoking?"

"Yeah!"

"That seems a little bit strict. Where were you smoking?"

"In the hay shed."

He was lucky again. The danger was always there, though. He just seemed glued to it. Mick had to explain to him the dangers of smoking (not the first time) and how easily hay could catch fire and how–no matter what job he'd have–he'd get sacked if he didn't do what he was told.

He eventually moved on to another job; this time, it was working out of Cathal Brugha Barracks over in Rathmines. As before, he starts off with all guns blazing (maybe not the smartest thing to say about somebody working at a military location, but still!), loved the job and the job suited him. All good. Ah, but this is Rory, so a few days pass and then Mick receives another phone call:

"Mick?"

"Hello, yes?"

"Rory's father?"

"(now what?) Yes, what's the problem?"

"We need you to come and collect Rory."

"No problem, is he eh... is he okay?"

"I'd say he's doing better than that, and you'll see when you get here!"

Mick could've sworn that he heard a slight giggle in the sergeant's voice before he hung up, but no matter, on to Rathmines.

"Hello, I'm here to collect Rory please."

"You the father?"

"I am ..."

"Sarge! Rory 's dad is here. Will I send him to the mess?"

"Go on ahead, sir, you'll find Rory in the mess."

My father parked his car and walked into the mess, where he was greeted by a familiar sight, Rory holding court at the bar, taking song requests!"

"Hiya da! Are you having a pint?!"

"Rory, have you been drinking?"

"Have I what!! It's only 50p a pint!"

"Rory, you're supposed to be working."

"Da, (tutting) 50p. A pint!!"

"Time to go home, Rory."

"Ahh, da!"

"Now!"

Another awkward drive home with da for Rory, when he was once again told what he should and shouldn't be doing at work. Kay wasn't one bit impressed with him when he got home either and she was fresh out of sympathy for his sore head the following morning too! That's what brothers are for, though, so I looked after him on the sly:

"Jesus, Rory, sacked again."

"Yeah, I know."

"For drinking!"

"Yeah!"

"How come you were drinking?"

"50p a pint, Dave!"

"No way, 50 pence?!"

"Yeah, great, isn't it?!"

"Don't blame you, Rory!"

Just my luck; Kay was listening. She'd felt bad about letting Rory suffer and was quietly coming up the stairs with a glass of water and a Panadol for him so as not to disturb him.

"David Mahon!"

"My full name, never good. Not Dave, David and anything else; it was full name time, I was "in for it", as we used to say:

"Hiya ma, everything alri..."

"I don't know who bloody worse, you or him!"

"Ma, I was only..."

"Don't even go there with me – "Don't blame you, Rory, only 50 pence–how is that supposed to help him, huh? Well?"

I wasn't going to get a word in edgewise, so I sat on Rory's bed getting medicine of the ear-bashing variety while Rory got his much-needed pain relief. No sooner had he swallowed his last drop of water than:

"(groggy) ma?"

"Yes, love?"

"Love?! How did that just happen?!!

"Can you give out to Dave downstairs?! Need to sleep this off!"

"Course I will Rory. You get plenty of rest."

Then she tucked him in and kissed him on the head before turning to me:

"You downstairs! I'm not furnished with you yet!"

She wasn't either, and I was persona–non-grata for the rest of the day! That's the story of my life, though, no good deed went unpunished. So, with Kay on the warpath and Rory needing (wanting) a job, Mick decided to bring him off to work with him, where he could keep an eye on him.

A great idea with just one teeny-tiny flaw. He was a taxi driver so he couldn't take him on a fare! The solution was to let him wait with the other taxi drivers in the holding rank area of Dublin airport when Mick was on the job. Remember that 'get-up-and–go' I mentioned earlier? Rory knew that if a job wouldn't come to him, then he'd come to it, and so he decided to try something out:

"Anyone wants to get their cash washed?"

They did! A lot of the hours spent at a taxi rank are idle-no fares/waiting for a call, etc.-so the lads would read the paper, play cards or whatever. But their cars still had to get washed and you couldn't risk doing it yourself if a fare came. Rory had spotted a viable business opportunity and basically became his own boss! With the few bobs he had on him, he went off and bought a bucket, a 'shammy' (chamois) and a bottle of washing up liquid. When Mick returned to the airport, he couldn't believe his eyes:

"Hiya da!"

"Rory? What are you doing?!"

"Washing cars! The lads are letting me. It's my new job!"

"That's great! Well done!"

"Da, do you want me to wash your taxi?"

"That'd be great, Rory, thank you!"

"No problem da, just give me the two quid first!"

He wasn't joking either, and it was two pounds a head, family or not! No room for sentimentality when it comes to business eh?! That little business opportunity developed into the making of the man that Rory was to become. It wasn't just a job for him. It provided him with a sense of identity and provided my family with a massive peace-of–mind that money couldn't buy. He was earning, independent and surrounded by workers/customers who were like an extended family of close friends; it was a truly perfect fit for Rory!

As popular as he was with all the drivers up there, he could test their patience. As well! One of the busiest and usually–more-patient of them was none other than a man named John Usher. At the time, he was the president of the Irish taxi-drivers Federation and on one occasion, he swung by the airport rank to have a chat with the lads in the canteen:

"Howya John."

"Ah, Hiya Rory, are you working hard?!"

"Not right now. Whose taxi is that you're driving?"

"Well, Rory, that's mine and (beaming smile) she's brand new!"

"Wow.... very nice... needs a clean, though!"

"(laughing)All right, Rory–fair enough! Do a good job now, won't you?!"

With that, he went into the canteen to take care of some business, allowing Rory to get fresh water into his bucket and take care of his own business. Now I don't know about you, but I've never had to wash a brand-new car before, and I can't imagine that I'd need to go anywhere near the windows, as they'd be as clear as ice water as it was. John's windows were no exception   maybe even the one he'd left rolled down at the driver's door! Yep, Rory didn't notice that there wasn't a window there until the bucket full of muddy water he threw at it   went straight through and all over the front seats. With that, John walked out of the canteen......

"Finished already, Rory? That was quick!"

"Ah yeah, John! I couldn't leave you waiting around, could I?"

"(laughing) good man Rory."

"You owe me a pound."

"No bother, here you are."

Rory snatched it out of his hand and suddenly "remembered" he was late for dinner…

"Bye bye, John."

"See ya' Rory, safe home on that bike, d'ya hear me?"

But Rory was already out of earshot and pedalling like it was the Tour de France. John opened the driver's door, carefully climbed into the driving seat so as not to crease his lovely new suit- and 'Squelch.' why was it so wet?

"What the f... Rorrrry!!"

I was glad not to be working anywhere near John that day, I can tell you! To his eternal credit, he (eventually!) saw the funny side of it and uttered what was to become the mantra of the airport taxi drivers- "Ah sure, that's Rory, what can you do?!"

John had an office based in Summerhill on Dublin's north inner city where the federation was located and Rory–realising the internal role he occupied in the taxi-business-would often drop in to say 'hello' to everyone. There was a lovely lady who worked there called Doreen and she was especially fond of him. Well, usually, that is! Rory happened to pop in there one morning full of beans; for some reason-and, poor Doreen was suffering the effects of the 'session' from the previous night. Not a great combination. Now, even at home, Rory couldn't enter a room without a slamming door and a big story by way of an intro:

"The lads in the airport are driving me mad!" -or-

"I got another bloody puncture." -or-

"Guards stopped me for not having my lamp–light on."

There was always something, never a dull moment! I'm sure, as far as Doreen was concerned anyway-Rory's 'Herd-of-Elephants' entrance that morning must've reverberated around her pounding head like a million ball-bearing bouncing off a sheet of mental.

"Rory.... I'm not well.... I..."

"What?? What's the wrong door?"

"Sssh! I've got an awful headache..."

"Ah, you were on the drink, weren't you?!"

"Please, Rory-sssh!"

"Weren't you?! Weren't you?!"

"Rory, you're driving me mad."

"Weren't you?! Weren't you?!"

"Yes - yes!! Now go, get out!"

"ha-ha – you have a hangover!"

"Rory - go!!"

He left pretty sharpish as Doreen wasn't the sort of person you could expect to poke with a stick and get away with it, not even Rory! Still, it was "Rory", so she felt terrible about shouting at him, and no doubt promised herself she'd make it up to him. A couple of hours later, she got her chance as Rory bounded back into the office with the soft-padded tip-toe of an angry rhino with a toothache:

"Hello, Doreen, are you better?!"

"Look, Rory, about earlier, I'm really sorry... "

"You don't look better??"

"Eh.... what? Oh, okay, yeah... no, I'm not any better, but look ..."

"Doreen- look!!"

"Huh? Rory.... is that . "

"I gotcha a large Brandy; the man said it helps hangovers!"

"(choked) Ah Jesus Rory, Ah, aren't you very good?! Ah, bless your heart!"

"Do you feel better?!"

"I will after this, Rory, Ah, you're just the best, do you know that?!"

"I hope it makes you feel well."

". and after me shouting at you and all, I feel terrible, Rory. I don't deserve you!"

"Okay, Doreen, you get better now, bye, bye!"

And he was gone. Doreen enjoyed her brandy and it did in fact, help with her hangover. Between the brandy and Rory's kindness, her mood lifted considerably and she managed to get through the rest of the day. With her shift over, she put on her coat, locked the office and decided to treat herself to another little brandy on the way home; sure why not? The Sunset House in Ballybough was the 'local' for the federation workers and she was on the way home, so she settled into her usual seat and ordered her drink when the barman brought her drink over to her, he also handed her a fairly hefty looking receipt:

"Sorry love, I think you've given me the wrong receipt."

59

"No."

"Sorry? I only got here. This drink (pointing) is all I've ordered."

"Okay...?"

"Yeah, so why am I being changed for two large brandy and a couple of pints of Guinness?"

"Ah, come on now, Doreen, you're forgetting about the drinks earlier!"

"Earlier? I was at work all day."

"Yeah, a fella' came in here earlier, said he would drop the brandy over to you and that you'd be in later to settle up, so...."

"(to herself) The little bastard, I'll bleeding kill him!"

"Excuse me?!"

"Not you-Rory!"

You see, that little episode tells you a lot about him, he had an absolute heart of gold, so genuinely considerate, loving and caring for others, but didn't always quite grasp the entire concept! There was no badness in him, none at all. But if you fell victim to one of "his" pranks, you mightn't think so.

Back in the airport, Rory was still making money and winning new customers, but not everyone would return for repeat business. A case in point would be when he was cleaning a certain taxi and another driver-for a laugh-decided to involve Rory in a prank:

"Be sure to give that taxi a really good scrub, Rory."

"Always do. "

"Yeah, but this fella is really fussy if he finds so much as a speck of dirt ... "

"He won't."

"He will."

"He won't!"

"Ah, Rory, what about back here-look at the dirt of his exhaust pipe?"

"What do you mean?"

"You'll have to stick a few hose pipes right up there, to get all that dirt out."

"Are you sure?"

"Absolutely."

And so, Rory did what he was led to believe his customer wanted, much to the amusement of all the other drivers looking. Suffice it to say that he lost another customer that day and couldn't for the life of him work out why. On the up-side, it at least gave him a different opening–salvo when he got home from work that evening, slammed the garage door (as usual!) and began his pre-dinner rituals:

"Bleeding lads are driving me mad, ma! You won't believe what happened today!"

Of course, he wasn't always so forthcoming about his day! By far, the most infamous example of this was the day a transporter van crossed his path.

Rory, like the rest of the Mahon males, had a passion for all things with wheels and an engine, so something the size, shape and dimension of a vehicle transporter was a sight to behold. As luck would have it, Rory was having a quiet period in his carwash, so he ambled over to have a nosey. Another stroke of luck for–Rory, the truck driver, was up to his tonsils and needed to off-load his truck pronto, as the airport police were on his case about blocking up a busy area. It was an impressive sight to see the truck driver fly up and down the transporter reversing cars off the ramp and into tight parking spaces like they were on magnets.

"You look busy there."

"Busy's not the word pal, I'm up to me bollix!"

"I'd love to drive a car off that top ramp..."

As I said before, to look at Rory, you'd never think that there was anything wrong with him. I'm sure that the poor truck driver made a very quick calculation in his head and assumed that Rory-clearly an adult obviously worked at the taxi rank, so therefore, he must've been an experienced taxi driver. Well, you know what they say about assumptions, don't you? Unfortunately, due to his many afflictions, but particularly because of his seizures, Rory could never be allowed to drive, legally or otherwise. If ever proof of this were needed, all one would have to do would be to talk to the Garda, who, noticing his erratic cycling one night, was about to pull him (thinking he was drunk) when BANG-he hit the deck in a full-on epileptic fit, smashing his head off the road repeatedly as he seized. The

61

poor guard thought Rory was a goner for sure because of all the blood alone. Now imagine, if you can, the same scenario, only behind the wheel of a half-town mental box travelling at 30mph. It's a no-brainer. Rory didn't think so; in fact, he really fancied himself as a driver.

"Would you?"

"Yeah!"

"You'd be doing me a big favour pal, and all the keys are in them. Cheers!"

"Nice one!!"

Naturally, Rory ran up to the top deck, started a car and started to reverse it... All the way over to the edge until a car wheel went over it. Do you know that scene at the end of the Michael Cain movie 'The Italian Job'? Not unlike that! Thankfully it only took Rory one wheel over the edge to recognise that he was out of his depth, so out he got, quickly dismounted the transporter, jumped on to his bike and then cycled home like the very hounds of hell were chasing him. Yet another lucky escape from a near-death experience. Not so lucky for the poor trunk driver. By the time he noticed the overhanging car and the missing Rory, he knew he was in a world of brown smelly stuff. A special crane had to be hired out in order to get the car safely back onto the trunk. Everyone was furious, from the rental company to the airport police and as for the poor driver, he was apoplectic with rage-who could blame him? Rory took a few days off after that incident, but it wasn't his last driving officer. There are too many stories to go into about him crashing my father's car or just taking the first car he'd noticed at the taxi rank with the keys left in the ignition, but I'll finish his auto–misdemeanours with a little something he did for the Irish tourist board.

Quite often, tourists returning rental cars on their way back home would confuse the taxi rank as a drop-off point for Hertz or whoever. The law of averages being what it is, Rory was bound to be thrown a set of rental keys at some point and on that fateful day, Rory decided to be helpful:

"Sorry, mister, this is the taxi rank, not the car-hire place."

"Oh, where I go then?"

"Is that an American accent?"

"Why, yes, it is!"

"What part?"

"New York City."

"Ah, move into the passenger side so I'll take you."

New York was meant to be a dangerous place to drive, but this poor devil hadn't reckoned on the Rory-factored. My brother had what I'll generously call a "heavy" foot when it came to driving, so our American friend was treated to a helter-skelter pedal-to-the-metal thrill ride up and down the footpaths, down the wrong side of the road at high-speed detour to the car hire office.

"Jesus Christ.... Jesus Christ .... jee-sus-H-Christ! Did you not even realize that you were on the wrong side of the god-damn road??!"

"Of course, I did! I just wanted to make you feel at home!"

The poor man was still in shock when Rory held out his hand to shake it (as was his way) and wish him all the best. The New Yorker took this to be another nod to his homeland and struck a fiver in his hand.

"What's that a fiver?"

"Yeah, is that not enough?"

"Huh?"

"Em.... your tip, that's about right, isn't it?"

"(Realisation hitting him) Ah yeah, that's grand, bye-bye!"

All I'll add to that story is that a whole new world opened up to my brother that day and on many occasions after that, his hand-shake hand didn't return to his pocket empty!

As much as he loved his job, loved cars and "helping" people, music was always his first love. Elvis was his absolute favourite singer-ever-and nothing could come close to him. My father decided to take him over to Graceland once and as soon as he dropped the surprise bomb shed, my phone started to ring. I was working at the time, so it could only have been one person:

63

"Hiya Rory, what's up?"

"Dave?!"

"Yeah, yeah, I'm here!"

"(singing) don't... Be-cruel.... to a heart ..."

"That's true! Bleeding Elvis again, Rory!"

"Guess what?!"

"What?"

"No, guess what!"

"(sigh) I don't know, eh. ...you got a new record?"

"No. guess!"

"I did guess!"

"Another guess!"

"Rory, I'm working! Just tell me!"

"Me and da are going to Graceland!"

"What?!"

"You'd better come!!"

"What? Where did you say??"

"Da's bringing me to Elvis's Gaff for my 30th birthday. You're coming, Dave. Aren't ya? Say you'll come too, Dave, you HAVE to! Say it! Say it!"

There would only ever be one answer he'd accept. Once he'd decided I was going with him, it was a done deal:

"Okay, I'll go. Did da get my ticket as well?"

"Are you 30?"

"Well, no. "

"So, get it yourself. Bye bye, Dave!"

As soon as I got home, I made a bee line for my father. He saw me coming and just buried his head in his hands.

"I know, I know I heard."

"Graceland da? You don't even like Elvis!"

"(sigh) I know ..."

"I don't even like Elvis!!"

"I know ... I know."

"How did he do it?!"

Rory spent enough time around my father to know that he spent every spare minute he had on his back garden. It was (and still is) his pride and joy, a spectacular monument of horticultural excellence developed lovingly over decades. My brother, a cute–whore and Elvis fanatic, gave Mick two options for his 30th birthday party-1 Graceland or 2 big party bashes for (literally) hundreds of people out in the back garden. Mick's nightmare-dozens of clumsy people he doesn't know trampling his flowers underfoot, vomiting into his pond and using his delicate nursery as a latrine:

"I'll book the tickets for Graceland right now, Rory!!"

When Rory saw that I was home, he didn't give me a second's peace:

"Did you book your ticket yet?"

"Did you?"

"Did you??"

"Did you???"

I picked up the phone, booked my ticket and then before I knew it, we were up-up-and away and enroute to the U.S. of A. The travel time from Dublin Airport to O' Hare International in Chicago is approximately six hours. How would I know that? Did I mention that Rory brought a camcorder on the trip and recorded EVERYTHING?! Packing our cases, all on camera. Booking in, all on cameras.

Boarding the aircraft, all on camera. You get the idea! So yeah, I can prove that it's a six-hour flight!!

To be honest, my father and I were delighted to have rare distracted by his video–dairy because it meant that he wouldn't try to sneak down a few extra drinks, something we always had to watch out for. It would have been a nightmare scenario. Rory fell into a full-Blown seizure (from too much alcohol) in a self-contained pressurized tube tense-of-thousands-of-feet above the freezing Atlantic Ocean. What we got instead was merry-Rory, the ultimate showman!

Not being a stranger to singing in public, he noticed a lot of bored and restless people all around a captive (literally!) audience. More specifically-his, audience. He handed me his camera and told me to record him, then gave Mick "the look." This is a family thing. My brother, the musician and my mother have the same exact expression when about to burst into songs we just know it as "The Look", and it's pointless to try stopping what follows:

"I met my luuur…. by de gas-yard-wallll."

"Suddenly, a small chorus just joins in."

"D-Ree-amed a "D-ree-im, by–de-ol-ed KA-NAL..."

Out of nowhere, the in-flight entertainment went from whatever dull movie was on to an all-out sing-song. A good ol Dublin pub ballad-fest was guiding us sonically into Chi-Town. Irish rebel- songs were proving the soundtrack of entry into one of Americans largest Irish emigrant populations, inspired by my brother! Not too many peoples can say that, I suppose!

We finally arrived-all on camera. Collected our luggage and move through customs-all on camera. Walking through the beautifully lit airport complex, we all turned into wide eyed tourists, marvelling at how different everything was from "back home." My eyes were like saucers at the taxi rank:

"Wow, da, look at all the huge American cars!"

"Dave?"

"Yeah?"

"They are just called "cars" over here!"

Rory went into convulsions laughing - "Good one, da!" It was a typical example of the high spirits we were in, and even the taxi journey to our hotel was a laugh. With Rory sticking his camera into whatever caught his eyes. The U.S style taxi meter was something he'd have to show the lads in the canteen when he got her home. Our taxi driver didn't know that and it was obvious from his nervous looks from Rory to the meter-back to Rory that he thought we were recording him for possible fraud. I don't know Chicago half as well as I know Dublin, but I'd bet dollars to doughnuts that we weren't taken the "long way round" on that journey! As for the hotel, lovely and everything that you'd expect from the numerous American TV shows we've been fed over the years, with one surprise addition, the in-house entertainment. On our first night there, we got lucky to witness the U.S. debut of a now up–and-coming Irish singer. Like U-2, he too was from the north side of Dublin and treated us to unique renditions of everything from The Dubliners to Elvis and blasted out a few Tom Jones tracks, but that's "Not unusual," and yes, I went there, sorry! As for the name of his mystery superstar. I think it was Rory…. something!

Rory was quite grounded as superstars went, as not long after his impromptu concert, my father tipped me on the shoulder and whispered:

"David, you're not going to believe what he is doing now!"

He was right, I couldn't! He had set up his camera in the main reception area and was conducting an interview with the Chinese receptionist! My father and I hid behind a row of desks listing in to make sure he was safe and figured on staying hidden for the few minutes of the interview. Well over half an hour later, there was still no end in sight, so Mick, ever the gentleman, attempted to put the young girl out of her misery:

"Are you alright there, miss? I hope my son isn't taking up too much of your time?"

"Oh, he's your son?"

"Yes."

"You must be very proud of him."

"Absolutely."

"I mean, he's so charming, and as for that voice, well!!!"

"Oookaaay?''

"And he's so generous too! I still can't believe this video will be shown all over Ireland when he gets home!"

"Neither can I miss. Say goodnight Rory!"

We gave him plenty of stick about that back in the hotel room and we laughed long into the very small hours, local time. The next morning Rory got up with the birds, Mick and I were like a couple of jet–lagged zombies. After ordering our breakfast, we headed out to see and record all the sites. As great as Chicago was though, and as spectacular as some of the sights were, my father and I felt like we kept hearing a broken record;

"Hey Rory, we are on a boat in one of the great lakes!"

"Yeah, when are we going to Elvis's Gaff?"

"Hey Rory, this is where Al Capone used to run his business from!"

"Yeah, when are you going to Elvis's Gaff?"

"Wow, Rory, we are over 1300 feet in the air. This is the tallest building in the world (As it was at the time), beats our liberty hall, doesn't it?!"

"Yeah. Can we go to Graceland now?"

When we got back to the hotel, worn out from a great day of sightseeing, we met with a most unusual sight-all the hotel guests lined up on each side of a red carpet. I caught Mick's eye and called him over for a quiet word out of Rory's ear short:

"Jesus da, what's this about? Please tell me Rory didn't do anything….?"

"I was just thinking the exact same thing son, I mean, remember the interview?"

"With the receptionist last night?"

"Yeah."

"Oh god…."

Our fears were interrupted by Rory's big, hearty laughter!

"Da, Dave, look!"

It was a duck run. Apparently, our hotel had the unusual custom of letting like ducks travel down its elevators from the upper floors, then parade down the red carpet to a water fountain in the lobby. Naturally, Rory made sure that they all made it safely:

"Good man, Rory, you're like a marine for these birds!"

"Huh?"

"You never leave a duck behind!"

"Yeah, now can we go to Graceland?"

And so, it was that we enjoyed our last night in Chicago, with a few beers, a lovely meal and Rory clutching our special tour bus tickets to Graceland:

"Dave, we can't be late; the bus leaves at 9 am."

"I know, Rory."

"Da, we can't be late; the bus leaves at 9 am."

"I know, Rory."

"Hey, Rory."

"Dave?"

"What time does the bus leave at?"

"Smack!"

 A slap into the back of my head from Mick!

"You're bleedin' worse! He won't stop now!"

"Dave?"

"(rubbing my head) what Rory?"

"We can't be late. The bus leaves at 9 am."

My father shot me a look that withered me to the grounds;

"What did I tell you? Huh? Eijit!"

He was right…. of course, he was!

I had the alarm set for half seven the following morning. Apparently, we couldn't be late because the bus was…. well, you know. Imagine my delight a full hour earlier-when I woke to Rory's camera struck in my face and all the light on;

"Come on, Dave! Wake up! We can't be late!"

Guess what? We weren't late. We were the very first people in line. Like, ages before anyone else. The bus arrived, we took our seats and it left at 9:40 am! We had to wait for a few late strangers. Rory was not impressed, so most of the journey involved our quieter than usual cameraman. Next thing we know, Graceland sat in front of us. The Holy Grail. The Promised Land. The queues went on forever. Rory's face dropped. Then our bus driver uttered words Rory could've done without:

"Wow, guys, I've never seen it so crowded. Hope you guys can still get in!" Our late-comers sat three rows behind us and when we collectively looked back and glared at them, they suddenly wanted to be anywhere else but Graceland. Our hotel was on Beal Street and Rory had us in and out of there quicker than greased lighting, we had a long line to wait in. Suppose there is one thing that the Yanks can do better than anyone else, its razz–mataze. As long as the queue was, we still made it into "Elvis Gaff" in short order. Then we had to face another little drama, at the entrance were a series of safe deposit boxes with big signs declaring "No Photographs. No unauthorized filming. By order." All cameras etc., had to be left in the safe deposit boxes. Rory was decidedly unimpressed. To soften the blow, I pointed him toward the numerous merchandise stands. These exist in my mind, to this very day, an image of the world's biggest kid having stumbled into the biggest toy shop on earth; that's the closest thing I can describe to how Rory reacted!

"Dave! Dave! Quick-quick-look!"

I'm going to level with you here, dear reader, I am no Elvis fan. If I hear him on the radio or whatever, I'll listen to him but only because of family memories and such. But even I have to admit that there was something almost contagious about seeing/wanting/coveting all of that Elvis memorabilia when I was there. Everything looks and feels like a work of art–probably because I was surrounded by avid fans who commented about everything from key chains to T-shirts as being "awesome!" - when in the cold light of day, you see it for what it really is, useless old Tat. As I contemplated purchasing a horrid "Merry Christmas Elvis" snow globe, I spotted Rory's green T-shirt (penny's best!) flying over my head…. sans Rory.

"Sir-sir, please! You can't do that here, sir-please…."

A topless, smiling, pasty-white Irishman loomed ahead of me, squeezing into a white T-shirt with the face of "The King" printed on the front…

"Hey, c'mon now sir, you must first purchase the item…."

My brothers grinning mug popped through the neck of the shirt;

"Relax –The- kax-There will ya?!"

In a single-fluid motion, he dumped nine more T-shirts in the assistant's outstretched arms and a wad of cash. He ended up leaving of "concessions area" (as the tatty memorabilia stand so grandly announced itself) with Elvis merchandise of every size and shape. I left with an abandoned pen's T-shirts and an ugly snow globe I still can't believe I paid actual currency for!

As we walked past the front gates, I found myself laboured with carrying all of Rory's purchases so that he could sign his name on the gates. A tradition of sorts, I believe. Don't ask me how he knew that or where the maker came from as it appeared and then disappeared with a magician's flourish. There's something just weird about walking into another man's house without him actually inviting you, at least, that's how I felt. The whole building is, well, so Elvis, which probably sounds silly as it's his house-but everything just looks kind of abandoned, like the lord of the manor might soon return. Don't get me wrong, there's something cool and exciting about walking in the actual footsteps of the most famous person who ever lived too, and Rory's little smile said so, almost, 'Now you understand, don't you?' I honestly did.

One of the oddest things about the living room (apart from the trapped in 1960's Americans snapshot of it all) was that everything was covered in plastic, except for his T.V.…which was in bits. Actually, the T.V. was the weirdest thing I ever saw and it confused Rory as well. As soon as the tour guide entered his line of sight, he sought answers:

"Here, 'scuse me… yeah–you!"

"Ahm, may I help you, sir?"

"(pointing)What's the story with the telly?"

"Oh, you mean the bullet hole through the screen?"

"De what?"

"The round Elvis shot, sir."

(Really, really confused) He what?"

"Oh, he was receiving negative comments, so he shot the T.V. sir."

"Did he not have a remote control?!"

Now it was time for the guide to be confused. Why would anyone have a TV remote when you could just use a legal weapon to blow it up? Unfortunately, it was a bit of a damning indictment about the state of Elvis's life back then, surrounding yourself with sycophantic 'yes-men' who wouldn't call you out on crap like that. It was a curse the tour guides also suffered, as they thought it was just another slab of 'Elvis cool' to brag about. Mick saw the wheels moving in my brother's mind:

"Rory"

"Yes, da?"

"Forget it. You're not getting a gun to change channels!"

Rory thought this was the second funniest thing ever…. after "The joke," of course!

"Okay y'all, can ya' Fall-o me Ta' Da' Bac-o-Da prop–r-Tee."

Which we did and quickly came face to long-face with a really old looking horse. Well, I say "old," I should qualify that he survived a flood on Noah's boat.

"Mister-what's the story with the horse?"

"Oh, he's just old, sir. You know, he belonged to Elvis himself!"

I wasn't sure if this guy was trying to yank Rory's chain or not, so I piped up!

"Really? How is he still alive, then?

He approached me in a conspiratory whisper:

"Plenty of steroids, sir, plenty of steroids!"

Rory felt a bit left out, the check of me knowing something about Elvis he didn't:

"Were you asking about going upstairs, Dave?"

"Oh no sir, no-no-no, no one is allowed upstairs."

"Why?"

"Orders from Priscilla, sir."

Then it was Rory's turn to whisper conspiratorially in my ear:

"That was his wife, Dave!"

I was glad he could clear that mystery for me! We had a look around at a few bits and pieces after that then Mr Tour guide put on his serious voice:

"Okay folks... (sigh) this here, well (nodding solemnly)... this is the tough part..."

This guy was good, he let the words just 'hang' there.... second after agonizing second. He had commanded silence and rapt attention through so few words... and was loving it.

"This.... (pause) is the final resting place of.... Elvis. Aaron. Presley. The king!"

There was aside from the odd gasp-a universal silence. It was like we had all just only heard Elvis died. It was quite moving and unexpectedly mournful. Just a few feet in front of where we stood, a rather large American lady sobbed into her 'Elvis lives!' handkerchief (you couldn't make up that level of irony, could you?!)

"I can't believe he is gone..."

Guess who's unselfish, loving nature just had to make it right?

"Are you alright, missus?''

"(Sniff) Y… yes, thank you…. oh, and its 'miss!'

"Why are you crying?"

"(blowing into her handkerchief, tears freely flowing) I…. I can't believe he left us…."

"What are you crying about? He's been dead for 20 years!!"

Suddenly the whole scene changed, mournful silence shattered by infectious laughter, even 'Miss' mourner saw the funny side. My father and I looked hopefully around for another large hole…. to disappear into! That was Rory's thought, no filter. At some point, I can't remember if it was before or after the 'Funeral,' we had a look at the Elvis fleet. This was a collection of his truly humungous cars and motorbikes, or, as Mr. Tour guide put it, "Mr. Presley's Automobile collection. Its near priceless valuation makes it almost uninsurable, so please, folks don't go past the security ropes. "Cos if you break it, you bought it!" Cars. Big, old, classic cars. Not just my kryptonite but Mick's as well. It's no wonder we got distracted and didn't notice Rory slip away.

"Pssst-Dave, Dave!"

"Rory?"

"Sssh! Not so loud, I'll be caught."

"Caught? (Looking around) where are you?"

"Behind you! Quick! Take a photo!"

I turned, eyes half-closed, hoping against hope that what I feared was not happening was all in my mind. It wasn't. Lying stretched on the hood of a priceless car was Rory. Oh. Holy. Divine. Jesus.

"(Loud Whisper) Rory. What. The F..."

"Quick! C'mon (Throws a camera at me)."

74

"Where did you get a camera from? They're not allowed past..."

"(Mick) Quick David, we've got bigger problems than the camera!"

-click-

"Now get back over this side of that bleedin' rope-NOW!"

Sounds too good to be true? I still have the picture! The 'king' was definitely a petrolhead, though and it came as no surprise to me (given his vast wealth) to discover that his love for burning fuel extended to the aviation type too.

We were shown his two private jets, one of which was "His" and the other he gave to Lisa Marie. Rory kindly explained to everyone that she "was his daughter" before the tour guide, which ruffled his feathers a bit! We all expected a bit more from them, to be honest. The king had a super-sized bed in his one–very Rock 'N' Roll-and a fully fitted out bar. This was stocked with only one beverage. Water. How much of a let-down was that?! Lisa Marie's jet was a case study in opulence. No corners were cut in fitting out her aircraft with the best of everything-the thick piled carpet covering every inch, even the ceiling. We eventually left Graceland with a treasure –trove of Rory's memorabilia and no insurance claims, so it was a great day! Back at our hotel –dubbed "Heartbreak Hotel" by…. you know-we enjoyed a well-stocked bar more in line with the tastes of three discerning Irish men! As Rory finished his second beer, he started laughing away to himself. Mick and I assumed that he was happy and exhausted after Graceland and that his alcohol allowance was making him giddy. Boy, were we wrong!

"Are you alright there, Rory? Are you a bit drunk?"

"Ha-ha-ha, I know something you don't know!"

"Ah, time for bed Rory, you're a bit tipsy there."

"I'm not, look!!"

With that, he turned his camcorder toward us, so we could see whatever it was he wanted to show us better:

"Rory, why does this look like Graceland?"

"Because it is!"

Somehow-and to this day, I still don't know exactly how he did it-he perfectly pirated every pixel of our Graceland tour. I was with him about 95% of the time and I didn't see his commander once, not even a glimpse. Rory defying the odds and scraping through once again, it was uncanny! The rest of our trip went incident free-as much as any day with Rory could be truly free of incident-and then we packed up our stuff and headed home. Rory insisted on keeping all of his Elvis memorabilia under the big American flag he purchased "to keep it safe," was his persistent reasoning. When we arrived home, everyone had to watch his video journal, and I do mean everyone!

As he was busy re–living his holiday with the next person (and then the next….!) I had to get back to work to start paying for it! Rory managed to grace us with his presence out in the airport ranks eventually and started listing off who had and hadn't seen Graceland with him yet. I'm sure he cleaned a car or two as well on our first Saturday back; it killed me that I had to work. It was one of those days where all I wanted to do was go out for a few pints and relax, but it was my busiest time, worse luck. As I headed back out to the airport with yet another fare, I noticed Rory's slightly uncoordinated rambling gait as he cycled home. He'd recognize my taxi a mile off as well, so over the years, we'd managed to develop a very subtle sign language/shorthand for such occasions:

"Going for a pint, Dave?"

"Can't, working!"

"Alright. Bye bye!"

And so, he headed off to the Red Parrot in Dorset Street and I continued on with my taxing. I was cursing him through, as he'd really put the "Goo" on me for a few pints–nothing worse is there?! As I got absolutely slammed that night, I didn't get a minute for myself, but it made the time go faster and eventually, at stupid–o'clock' in the morning, I managed to crawl into my bed for some much-needed sleep.

As so often seems the case when you get that tired, it seems like your head only hits the pillow before it's time to get up again. This was slightly different in that my head only did touch the pillow before Mick came into me:

"Are you home long?"

"Just in Da, busy one."

"You didn't see Rory on your travels, did you?"

"Not since last light, on his way home from work."

"Do you know if he was going out?"

"Red parrot, I assume, Saturday night, sing song, isn't it?"

"Yeah."

"Asked me for a few pints too, wouldn't have minded!"

"Dave, he didn't come home."

Okay, this was different, but then again, this was Rory. He was a devil for losing track of time or forgetting things, so it wasn't a red alert situation. Mick called around to the usual suspects, but no joy, no Rory. I placed a phone call to the Red Parrot. No answer, probably too early. My father and I jumped into my taxi and we drove out. Getting there quickly and it dawned on me-Sunday morning. No traffic! I parked at the Royal canal bridge and knocked on the doors of the Red Parrot. . There was no answer again, no red alert just yet, as we still had to call around the hospitals. Rory, like other epileptics, suffered the usual chronic disease of his central nervous system. In real language, his convulsions (Seizures or "Fits") led to impairment, a loss of consciousness, or both. Rory sat at the serious end of the scale and suffered grand mal convulsions (severe seizures accompanied by unconsciousness) rather than petit mals' (of much briefer duration), so calling the hospital for him was nothing new. I can't remember if it was our first call or not, but it was the Matter Hospital who told us about a man matching Rory's description being taken to the city morgue. It was a shock to hear that-obviously-but Rory's was a fairly general description around Dublin, so yes, we did hit the panic button but we also knew how many times he'd defied death and turned up on the doorstep laughing historically in the past. As I drove there, Mick related what he was told:

"...body found in the Royal Canal... near Red Parrot..."

I surmised from those bites of information that it wouldn't be Rory, as he knew the area far too well and he was a great swimmer, drunk or sober. Anyway, we'd arrived at the morgue. Time to mark it off the list and continue our search.

My father met the man in charge and told him who we were and why we were there. He confirmed that the body did indeed match that of Rory and asked if we'd

77

identify the body. It's hard to write this. Mentally and emotionally, I don't want to move past this point, but I have to. It's just like being there. At the morgue. I didn't want to go into that cold room. If I didn't go in, he wouldn't be dead. If I go in and he's dead, then... Then what? I looked at my father, our eyes met and our expressions didn't require words. Whatever comes next, life will never be the same again. A near miss rubs the good luck off? Please, God, just one more near miss, that's all I ask....

The first thing that hits you is the cold. It's unreal. It's too cold. It's why we store meat in refrigerated units, but it doesn't seem right when it's humans. Especially when it's your family 'sleeping' soundly on a cold and impersonal slab of concrete was a lifeless facsimile of my brother. 'Ror Ror', my baby name of him; the demon tormentor go my patience, my drinking buddy, my workmate, my big brother, my reason for believing the world wasn't such a big bad place after all.... Gone? I moved in for a closer look and to this day I wish I hadn't. I can never un-see the pool of his precious blood, now so dark and cold, at the back of his head.

I don't recall the next series of events but at some stage. We were taken from him and ushered into another room. I know I didn't want to leave him. But I can't remember if I put up a fight. I remember screaming a dark, empty howl that took every ounce of strength out of my body, but no sound came out. I remember looking out a window and seeing my brother Terry outside. He saw my face and just knew. I nodded at the unasked question. Yes, it's true. He was with his wife Barbara, who was pregnant. Her bump would one day grow into my beautiful Goddaughter Emma, now in her 20's. I didn't want my last memory of Rory to be what I saw in the other room. There's a poem I heard once- 'Stop the Clocks' or something. I wanted to stop and then reverse the clock. I wanted to go back 24 hrs–less-and meet him on the old airport road again, only this time say 'YES' to the few pints. Go out with him, listen to him singing his heart out and get him home safely. Do you know what, not just that night, but all the nights and God knows we went out plenty as it was. I supposed it's my conscience, but I'll always feel I should've done more. I'm forever haunted by frequent aftershocks of what might've been. Especially once we heard everything.

He went to the Red Parrot, sang, had a great time and waited outside for his taxi home. I was driving a taxi at the exact time, mere miles away and I would've collected him had I passed. He got cold waiting around, so he brought a bag of chips to keep warm while he waited. The irony of my father's two occupations being the last thing Rory would think about, chips and taxi. A feed of drink and a cold night waiting around, nature decided to call, but nowhere was open. All he could do was sidle down the embankment beside the bridge to relieve himself. His good manners and need for privacy conspiring against him in the end. Unknown to Rory-and to me weeks later when I checked in the cold light of day, was a wire stretched across where he stood, at ankle level. It almost tripped me too. It caused my brother to lose his balance and fall to his death. I remember meeting Bertie, Ahern-local TD- about it. His response? Not fit for print, but Rory wasn't the first or last to die at that spot and there was lots of empty talk about budgets. I went back and removed it myself. Permanently. Fuck him. My brother should still be alive.

Jesus, was his funeral tough. I remember saying goodbye to him before the lid was sealed on the little wooden box that would be his final home. I protested like a child, not wanting them to close the door on him. My brother-in-law eventually forced me out of the room where he was lying in wake. It was at Massey's funeral home on Beaumont Road. He kept on telling me to "let him go," but I couldn't. I kept fighting my way back in to say "Goodbye" one more time, then one last time and so on. For what I knew would be the absolute last time I'd see his face, I did something I've never told anybody until now. My mother bought me a beautiful gold-chain Celtic Cross for my 21st birthday. I took it off and made Rory a promise; "I'm only lending you this, I'm not giving it to you. Next time you see me, you have to give it back." I've never let another piece of jewellery around my neck since. Rory's still minding my chain. I'll get it back. I made him a promise.

The people of Massey's said that Rory's funeral was the most expensive they'd ever staged. What a strange thing to say. Such was Rory's popularity, it was always going to be huge. We just never imagined how huge. Some of the roughest, toughest taxi-man in Dublin put a charity–do-together for Rory in the Royal Oak in Finglas to help pay towards the funeral costs. Totally off their own backs and completely unsolicited. Their reasons? "Hey, it's Rory!"

As the funeral cars passed our home in Santry, a guard of honour stretched out on both sides of the road leading the way. All day, people kept telling me how "Time Was a Great Healer," but for me, the counter-argument always speaks louder when it's come to Rory. Time doesn't so much "heal" but simply provides time for you to grow callous to help you cope with the pain. We entered that big church in Whitehall, Rory and meme, to the sound of a choir singing Bette Milers 'The wind beneath my wings,' and I would've given anything to hear him grab the mic and take over one last time. It would've been its biggest gig too, no room inside, standing room only in the car park we played two Elvis songs for him in the church-'You were always on my mind' and 'I saw you crying in the Chapel Chapel!' Every note, every lyric, every beat drove nails into my heart. Still do. Before Rory was finally laid to rest at his last stop, with no crazier car rides or falling off his bike, my father took out the American flag Rory bought on our holiday. He looked at me and no words were needed. I remembered Rory's words too. Mick draped it over Rory's coffin and patted it fondly, finally. And with a tiny wink, quietly spoke:

"To keep you safe now."

I visited Rory's grave every day. Mostly during the night, when it was just us. The lads up at the airport erected a plaque shortly afterwards:

"In honour of Rory Mahon, from his taxi driver friends."

He wouldn't love that, right there at his taxi wash too. I went straight out to his grave to tell him all about it, but was not overcome with grief I fell on my knees crying. A man came over to see if I was okay, assuming it was my wife, at first.

"Must've been somebody very special."

"He was. It's my brother Rory."

"Rory? Jesus, I knew him! Wait till I tell you a story about him…"

That was Rory!

Rory

Rory with Elvis's car

Mick's Cancer

The year was 1994, Ireland was a thriving economic tiger about to roar onto the world stage and we still had an international football team capable of going to the big events. In short, it was a great time to be a chatty Dublin taxi driver; that is exactly what Mick and I were doing. These were halcyon days of having money and very little responsibilities. I was still living in the family home in Santry, but I was looking out for a place of my own too, but not overly so, I knew I had it handy. One could very easily be forgiven for thinking that there wasn't a cloud in the endless blue skies of my life back then... until of course, one did. A big black angry cloud that soon plunged our little family into darkness.

The first sign of its presence happened as I was chilling out in my room-and from the bathroom- I heard what could only have been grooms of pain. That in itself was strange, but then when I saw Mick coming out of the bathroom, that was stranger still. My father is old school in the quintessential way that only men of his generation can be-you chopped your finger off when it got caught in the car door? Ah, I'll be grand, sure I've lots of fingers, you wouldn't miss one-that sort of thing. Believe it or not, I have no memory of my father being sick before this... ever!

He came into my room, white as a sheet and looked at me with sad, tortured eyes. 'I'm passing blood,' What? Is Mick passing blood? Can't be. 'Show me da, we'll see how bad it is.' He brought me over to the toilet and you can't un-see what I saw. He had passed a blood clot as big and thick as an egg... it was enormous. My reaction was an absolute no-brainer- "Da, we're off to the hospital NOW!" He gave me one of those "it's-not-that-serious" looks but in fairness to him, he didn't argue. He just shrugged his weary shoulders and followed me out to the car.

Just as I turned the key in the ignition, Mick went into what I thought was taxi-driver mode- "where are you going, Beaumont?" I was expecting a quick lesson from the old maestro on going down to such and such, swing a left, avoid this place and so on, but instead, I got something completely out of the blue- "head down by the top of Collins Ave, I want to pop into the E.B.S. I didn't react too well to that, if I'm honest. I had a right go at him about putting stupid things like money or bills etc., ahead of his health but as stubborn as I am, I learned it at his feet- so we made the pit-stop he requested. Of course, we did!

Sometimes your parents do things that shock or embarrass (or both!) you when you're growing up. This one we'll put in the 'shock' section. Picture the scene- there's me sitting outside in the taxi, waiting impatiently for my never-sick-father to do whatever unnecessary business he insisted on, only for him to walk out of the E.B.S. ashen-faced carrying a bag of money. As I write this, it's hard not to smile at the thought of my father, easily one of the most inoffensive men who ever lived, robbing a bank in broad daylight, but that is how it looked! The reality, however was far from funny.

"Jesus da, what's in the bag?"

"It's my life saving son. It's all I have."

"You're not thinking of checking out on me?"

"I think I am."

That's my father. Right there. He's convinced that he's about to die and is clearly in unbearable pain, but he insists on cashing out his life's savings to make sure that his family will be looked after, not a single thought about himself.

Mick was seen to fairly quickly by the always excellent staff at Beaumont Hospital and thank God he was because he was diagnosed with kidney cancer after a few hours. He was immediately booked in for surgery the following morning, such was their concern. I often think about those few hours waiting around in Beaumont. Mick was waiting for his 'death sentence,' cold sweat beading on his forehead from what had to be unmerciful pain, yet not so much of a whisper of complaint out of him. Like I said old-school. They don't make them like that anymore. I also can't forget what was going through my own thoughts, my world, so blissfully happy and uncomplicated only hours earlier, was in ruins. My father, only fifty-five years of age, a father of six, was passing egg-sized blood clots in his urine as a result of kidney cancer which required as close to emergency surgery as it gets. At the time, it was the worst possible news I could've imagined.

Everything moved so fast–too fast-but the next thing I remember is Mick having a pre-surgery conference with his team. Although I can't be sure of every detail, it ended exactly like this.

"Well, Mr Mahon, you are in God's hands now."

"I won't be in God's hands doc, I'll be in yours."

"You're putting me under a lot of pressure!"

He was smiling as he said that and then walked away with his team. He was a lovely guy and fair play to him; he handled the surgical pressure perfectly. Then again, as a former Irish international rugby player, he was probably used to pressure.

The weeks following Mick's surgery brought a different kind of pressure. Ask any taxi driver and they'll tell you the same thing, if you don't work, you don't get paid. It's that simple. He'd already cashed out his life savings and to be honest, it wasn't nearly enough to get my parents through the rest of their days, but it would help him get through some of the time he'd need to recuperate. We are a close-knit family, so for me, the writing on the wall I was going to work as much as I could for as long as I could. It fell upon my shoulders to help support my mum, dad, Rory and myself, and I was grateful to be in a position to do that. The downside was that I'd have no time for relationships etc., but that was a small price to pay.

That was the way of things for a few months until Mick decided to drop another bombshell- "I'm retiring." Two seemingly innocent little words that make up a tiny innocuous sentence that I'm sure is used hundreds of times a day throughout the world. Well, not in the Mahon household, as poor Mick was soon to discover.

"What??" It wasn't a question. It was an explosion! Kay had lost her bickie!

"You are too young to retire!! You're. " Well, let's just say that Kay had quite a bit more to say, and not too much of it is fit for publication.

Due to the massive hours I had been working, I had managed to squirrel away a nice little nest egg, so unbeknown to Mick, I went out and brought him a beautiful new maroon coloured Toyota Carina. I threw him the keys, "All yours da, taxed-insured, full of fuel, off you go!" I had made it as easy as possible for him to tread water back into the world of work, but not for the money. This was an effort to get him back out to familiarity, to what he loved doing. My father was not just a popular taxi driver but also a very popular person. I thought it would do him good to see how much he was missed and how much he means to people. I was blue in the face hearing, "How's Mick? Tell him we were asking for him..." From every corner of the city, but especially up in the Dublin airport when myself and Rory worked most of the time. Ever the gentleman, he gave it a try for me, for Ma-but as much as we all thought we knew him, he knew himself better. He had always known that he wouldn't be able to maintain his pre-surgical lifestyle, and he was right. His first instinct had been the best possible decision all along.

My father retired from the full-time workplace at the tender age of fifty-six. It was a day of momentous decision in our house, as Kay wasn't to be outdone or outshone by anybody:

"Well, so am I."

"So am I what?"

"Retiring."

"What? What do you mean "Retiring!? Sure, you don't even work!"

Oh yeah, Mick went there. I did mention him being old school. It was a bad choice of words. Game–set and match for Kay followed:

"I'll never cook or clean again, that's your job now."

In fairness, he stuck to that arrangement from that day forward and it was a benefit to us all, as he was a far better cook than my Ma! So that's how Mick got through the first of his major health scares and how round one of the cancer fight was won. Cancer, as we all know, isn't a very gracious loser.

A Different World

Rory's death hit my family harder than we could ever have imagined. My mother never got over it and my father still grieves to this day, I guess we all do. It was strange, but in a way, our fractured little family was never quite as close again, the Rory, shaped hole in our lives weakened by the glue that held us all together was gone forever. My other brother–Terry, was lost for quite a while afterwards, the special music bond between them ripped apart far too soon. I was no different.

When I went back to work, it wasn't the same. All my life as a taxi driver up 'till that point involved Rory. When driving to or from the airport, I'd catch myself looking out for him, and the crushing pain of his loss would hit my raw emotions every single time. Whereas once I loved parking up in the airport ranks, chewing the fat with the lads and hearing whatever new adventures Rory got into, now I hated it. All it was for me now was an empty shell, a place of darkness and despair. I found myself turning down fare after fare if I thought they might want to go anywhere near the Red Parrot. I just couldn't handle it.

When you can't face going to work, you stay at home. Even that was a problem. I loved my house out in Dunshaughlin, I had it pretty much the way I wanted it, but even there, I faced too many little reminders. My phone would ring. "That's Rory," I'd instinctively think. I pass the bus on my way home and that would remind me of the times Rory would pop out to see me, "I'm on the bus, Dave!" Like it was the best thing in the world. Well, initially, then he cycled all the way out to see me once he knew the way. Thank God I was in that day, as he wouldn't have made the journey back. My friends and family would visit me often, and we'd plenty of shenanigans and some good times out there, but inside, I was miserable. I took a fare out past Kinsealy one day and saw a house on the market. It was a no-brainer.

Kinsealy is based out in North Country Dublin and if you've ever heard of it, that's probably because C.J Haughy had a huge house out there. In fact, he passed away in it too, but that wasn't the house I bought, worse luck! Kinsealy was a much better location for me-work wise- and for my friends and family to visit. It also gave me a fresh start of sorts, emotionally. My social life actually developed into something I could now properly call 'social' and a 'life.' my proximity to Tamango's, Gibneys, Swords and Malahide gave me a new lease for and renewed taste for human company outside of work. I was starting to broaden my horizons culturally, emotionally and professionally.

I needed to exercise the travel demon out of my mind. Airport equalled Rory. Airport travel equalled Memphis; equalled Rory. I decided to travel to new pastures, places where I wouldn't 'see' Rory around every corner. Two places became popular choices for me back then, Liverpool in the U.K. and Spain, mostly Gran Canaries at the time. Eventually, my friend Martin suggested that we take a look at the property market on Merseyside. We were spending enough time over there. Why not? What sounded like a 'mad idea' over a pint turned into a 'nice little earner' to quote Del Boy Trotter! In fact, for a calendar year, we made forty separate journeys over there, flew out on a Wednesday morning and caught the red-eye home. We'd eventually progress to the stage where we'd bring clients over to view and then purchase apartments from us. We dealt primarily with high-end apartments around the Albert Dock and South Ferry Quay, so good quality products were an easy sell. Martin was already a big-time property magnate and I was only learning my craft and hovering up the crumbs off his table, but I was a quick study with a passion for the business.

Thankfully Martin liked what he saw in me and when he phoned me one evening about an 'opportunity' out in Spain, I caught the first flight out. It was an apartment in a part of Spain called Marbella, a well-known tourist destination. The building itself hadn't yet been completed, so I spoke to the developer over the phone and struck a deal" off the plans," as it's known in the trade. I had dipped my toes into Spain and still had plenty of time to conduct market research before the last brick was laid. Risky? Maybe, but my time with Martin had given me a bit of a sixth sense for these things, so we killed two birds with one stone. We'd take a few days 'R' and 'R' and check out what else Marbella had to offer.

Sometimes in business, appearances speak louder than words and can be better than any references on a C.V. résumé. We stayed at the best hotel in the area, the five-star Gualdimina, and arranged to meet the sales team dedicated to showing us some property-right there, on "Our Turf." I only had one stipulation with Martin.

"Whatever happens here, don't let them know that I have another place here in Spain."

I had my reasons and he assured me that he'd play ball.

Our main point of contact from their sales team was Irish born (I know, us Paddy's turn up everywhere, don't we?!) but brought up in South Africa. He had the coolest accent I'd ever heard and with his relaxed personality combined with an encyclopaedia knowledge of Costa del Sol properties, I knew right away that I was on a winner. His name was Tommy and even though I didn't know it at the time, he'd go on to be one of the best friends I'd ever have. He showed us all over the Costa del Sol, strange and exotic places such as Estepona, San Pedro, La Cala de Mijas Calahonda and Fuengirola - that would one day sounds as familiar and every day to me as Moore Street and Ballymun. I wasn't much of a "poker player" back then as I viewed each new property wide eyes as wide as saucers in my innocent wonderment, but I didn't care. I loved it all-the weather, the people, the country and all the freedom it brought me. Disappointingly my friend had told Tommy behind my back about the property I had already purchased. Tommy decided to use that to get a rise out of me:

"So Dave, what do you think of this spot?"

"Ah, it's spectacular, I love it!"

"Hmm…"

"What? What are you "humming" about??"

"Ah… nothing, don't worry about it…"

"No! (of course, I was worried!!) Go on, say what's on your mind."

"It's just… well… it's never going to increase in value."

(gulp) wh… why?"

"Oh, you know, with all the mafiosa living here and…"

"The what?? The bleeding mafia?!"

"Well, not all of them…. but enough of them….."

I noticed a crooked smile-not on his mouth-but in his eyes.

"Dream on, Tommy! This is like Beverly Hills and you know it!!"

He cracked up laughing and then I did too, possibly for the first real time since Rory. Right there, right then, a friendship was born. I also bought another apartment off the plans, in the same area-only the golf course this time. That was the beginning of Mahon Estates, but at that moment in time, I was just a guy trying his luck and putting a bit of a portfolio together.

My trip over to Spain and back were beginning to force my hand a little in terms of making me evaluate my options. The taxi business wasn't really doing it for me anymore. I was living in a different world from the 17yr old me. My father was retired and Rory was gone, so my heart just wasn't in it. At this time, the taxi business was going through a major change as well and now wheelchair accessible taxis and licenses were being normalized. I ended up getting one and then rented both of my taxi plates out. This was money my father could use as his pension, so my parents were happy and more importantly looked after.

I took stock. My taxi career was over, essentially, at least until such time as I could cope with my grief, if ever. The rent from my plates went to Kay and Mick, my savings together with income from Spanish and Liverpudlian properties, was more than enough to tide me over. I'd no girlfriend, no Rory and nothing to anchor me to Ireland. I had a good friend over in Spain and Tommy had all the contacts I'd need. Rainy, miserable Ireland with heartache on every corner or sunny Spain, a fresh start and a new friend who was madder than I was, an honest-to-God laugh-a-minute lunatic. Decision? Come on, what would you have done? I told all my friends and family. They'd miss me but couldn't and wouldn't fault my logic. I packed my bags and had a going away party!

When I got off the plane at Malaga airport, Tommy was waiting and drove me straight to my hotel.

"Welcome home, Dave! You don't speak the lingo; you don't know an awful lot about the country, but you have a passion for the business and more importantly, you're got me! Now first things first, we're going on the piss. This will take a few days!"

True to this word, it did! I can't remember even sleeping in that hotel before I checked out-as Tommy's insistence:

''You can stay at my place. Plenty of rooms, just me and Dylan.''

Dylan was his son, by the way. He was born in South Africa and was a lovely young man. Tommy's place was located in a picturesque fishing village called La Cala de Mijas and looking out over it from his balcony that first morning I knew I'd made the best decision for me. Then Tommy dropped another bombshell:

"By the way, I've just been promoted at work."

"Yeah? Fair play to you. So, what are you now?"

"Well, David, you are now looking at management!"

"You?!!"

"Don't sound so shocked! I'm the new manager at Inter-reality……"

"Well, congratulations, Mr Manager… sir!"

"…..and in my first act, you have been granted an interview!"

He knew I was hungry to learn the business, so it was yet another lovely gesture on his part, my fairy Godfather! There was just one small snag… I'd never had a job interview before!

The process, I soon discovered, is quite nuanced in that you need to know to say "yes," for example– "are you a team player?" I wanted to tell the guy that my 'team' consisted of me, Tommy and as much money and fun as we could generate! But I had to pull in my horns with an 'enthusiastic' "yes!" and leave it there. As Tommy explained to me later:

"You got the job, but you didn't exactly "ace" the interview, did you?!"

And he was right! No matter, the Tommy and Dave show was soon on the road and at the end of my first month, we sold five properties between us, with the 'Rookie' here wiping Tommy's eye there to two! I was so green that I failed to realize how rare this volume of sales was until the owner of the company came to our little office to heap praise on us in front of the entire sales team. It was embarrassing but also motivational. I'd arrived. Oh, and in the great cosmic rule of coincidence, the owner of Spain's largest realtor was….. Irish! A man by the name of Darragh Mc Anthony, Paddy's running the world!

Nothing in this world is ever perfect, though, and the big-black-fly-in-the-ointment of my new job was getting paid! The work, people, etc.-couldn't ask for better, but you had to wait a very long time for the commission's cheques to arrive. This was a very different adjustment for a cash-business taxi driver to make, but I never starved.

I sold a few more properties under Tommy's guidance. I also learned to make friends with a lot of the right people too. It's a lucrative business, so getting to know the lawyers, mortgage brokers and interior designers within the industry was priceless. Business was going so well for me that I could soon book myself a holiday back to Ireland. It was great to catch up with all my family and friends, all of whom were eager and delighted to hear all about my new life in the sun, my best friend, Darrin, couldn't wait to get me out of the house in Santry and out to the pub for a long overdue catch-up.

Funny how life works out sometimes. Our plan for that night was simple-go out for a few quiet pints and chew the fat, no hassle, no fuss. It was probably for that reason that we ended up going to a pub we weren't very well known at Kiely's bar in Coolock village so as not to bump into a load of familiar faces and end up on a bender. So, in we walked, Darrin ordered our first round of drinks and then I looked around to find a seat for us. Everywhere to the right-hand side looked packed and noisy and when I looked left, well, I only saw one thing.

I was never a believer in 'Love at first sight' or 'Instant attraction,' all of that was the stuff of nonsense, the pulp-romantic-fiction novels of Mills and Boon and such…. until then. Luckily, I was never exactly the shy type, so I made an immediate bee-line for her and introduced myself. We hit it off straight away and laughed all night. Darrin got on well with her friend, so it worked out well, but our friends were only playing the roles of 'wingmen' for us, which was fine. The last thing on my mind, as I entered the pub that night was to fall in love, but that's exactly what happened. I left the pub later that same night with two of the most beautiful words I had ever heard reverberating around my mind, 'Audrey Fitzpatrick.' She was all I could think about and all I ever wanted to think about again.

We dated for a while afterwards and I'd be like a kid waiting for Christmas between each date, eagerly awaiting the next, then the next. I used to work out in the gym at total fitness in Clare Hall and purely by chance, Audrey did too. The first time I bumped into her there, I accused her of stalking me! She still denies it to this day, but I'm not convinced! Audrey knew that I lived over in Spain and that I was only ever in Ireland for holidays, but she also had more than an inkling that I was very serious about her because I was back and forth with an increased regularly and when I was back home, I called her every day. Audrey was always upfront and honest with me, so right from the word 'go,' she told me she was divorced after a very traumatic marriage and had two children. I explained that I wouldn't mess her around or fill her full of empty promises and thankfully, she believed in me and trusted me enough to meet her children.

From the second I saw their beautiful little faces, I fell in love with them too. Dean, her eldest, was twelve years old, already tall and full of mischief and corny jokes, he was adorable. Amy, the youngest of eight years, was a happy bouncing ball of energy that would've put the Duracell bunny to shame! It was obvious that Audrey wasn't just the girl of my dreams. She was better than that, she was a world-class mother with a bond of love with her children you'd have to see to believe. Audrey was the real deal and she deserved the best of everything. I was determined to make sure that she got it and when I say 'Audrey,' that included Amy and Dean too.

If you were to ask any Irish son what the acid–test was for wives and girlfriends, they'd more often than not agree with mine. If the mammy likes her, she's passed! Well, Kay didn't like Audrey, she loved the very bones of her and when she saw how she was with Dean and Amy, it was a done deal, they were family and it was up to me to make that 'official,' I simply couldn't ask for any better. All I had to do was convince Andrey…. easy, right?!

Well, not really, no! First of all, I had to work out the logistics, I lived in Spain, but Audrey, Amy and Dean didn't. That meant me having to make absolutely sure that my business could support a family and not just for a while, but for good. Tommy as always was a great sounding board and I hit him for advice. He knew me, knew how I felt about Audrey and witnessed firsthand how I set up a property business for myself after his boss kept messing around playing God with my commissions. Spain worked a lot on back-handers back then so to set up a legitimate business in the face of such corruption, with the language barrier, the cultural dynamic and what was essentially a computer-based illiteracy, "Took balls," as he put it.

"Dave, you're a determined, stubborn son of a bitch. You'll make it work, don't worry!"

It was hard to argue with Tommy, but he was also as cute as they came.

"How do you know she's "The one," Dave?"

"Trust me, I know."

"First date –where?"

"The bloody stream, in Howth."

"Interesting, no hesitation, okay, kid's names?"

"Dean and Amy."

"Okay, describe the little girl… go!"

"A chatty little ball of energy, long-lovely brown hair all the way down to her back-side and a smile that lights the whole room up, from her eyes."

"And the boy?"

"Dean, he's tall now and is definitely going to be a six-footer, love's football is a typical mischievous kid with an endless supply of corny jokes and a man after my own heart at how he tries to get out of school."

"Audrey body wise?"

"Smoking ho….. here, hang on a bleeding minute!"

"(laughing) ah, you've got it, bad kid! What are you waiting for?!

As it happened, waiting for Audrey to up-sticks and moreover would be worth it as we had a lot of balls to juggle. As I look back on it now, I wonder how we ever did it–her house in Clare hall… her job at applied magnetics, the children's schools, my own living arrangements and not to mention the inconsiderable emotional upheaval. Audrey and I had been together for three years before I asked her to move over and that included me moving back to Ireland for good–if that suited me better.

One of the many lies and misconceptions about our relationship and eventual move over to Spain was that it was an ill thought out, spur of the moment, selfish decision. This, dear reader, couldn't be further from the truth. Yes, we were madly in love and dying to give it a go, but Audrey was and is the brains of the family. She thought through every possible scenario, inside out, backwards and forwards and then some. She came out to the Costa for a week's holiday on her own to get a feel for the place. We stayed at Estepona in a penthouse overlooking the port. As my culinary skills wouldn't come near something Gordon Ramsay flushed down the toilet, we ate out every night but this also proved to Audrey how inexpensive it could be. We'd take long, leisurely walks on the famed white sands of Marbella. Audrey drank in the feel of the place whilst I drank in her responses. No amount of talking about or writing about how it feels to live in such a place can ever truly do it justice. It must be felt and experienced.

For me, there was only one place on earth better than living on the Costa and that was living there with Audrey. That entire week, we felt alive every day. Back in Ireland, you merely 'exist' in comparison. Blue-clear-skies, endless blue water on the horizon, mountains, the heat, the wildlife, the aroma, the sounds, it's just endlessly invigorating. When you've come from a cold, dark, wet little island in the North Atlantic, you just cannot beat the feeling of slipping into shorts, T-shirts and a pair of flip-flops with the sun on your back. Every conversation we had that week boiled down to the same common denominator:

"Dave, I've made a decision."

"Whatever you decide, I'm with you all the way."

"Amy, will be 12 in February."

"Okay?"

"So, she'll be finished in primary school in May…."

"Yes!"

"Let's bring the kids over for a holiday and see what they think."

"Sounds great. Let's do it."

I booked a little holiday for us in Torremolinos and that entailed, in essence, myself, Amy and Dean turning into fish as the only time we left the pool was to eat, sleep and do all the other activities the hotel laid on for us. Dean turned out to be a crack shot at archery and Amy as well, she was a force of nature. She loved being able to eat out every day and on one of the days, she sat across from a "large" English couple. Between them, everything on the menu was ordered and Amy, a shy, stick-thin 12 year old, ate all around her. This was nothing new to us, but as we left the dining area, the English couple beckoned Andrey over:

"s'cuse me, but is she your daughter?"

"Yes, is there a problem?"

"Are we on candid camera or "summink'?"

"I'm sorry?"

"Well, we've just watched her eat her own body-weight in food, but there isn't so much as a pick on 'er…

'ow's that?"

Before Audrey could formulate a cohesive response, Amy ambled over:

"What's for tea ma? I'm starving,'"

Poor Audrey, what could she say?! But that's just Amy for you. The holiday was a great success and so, in June 2004, Audrey decided to move over to Spain. Oh, in case you were wondering, Amy had her favourite Chinese-for tea that night. Decision made, it was a new life for all of us, a different world for Dean and Amy to live in, but leaving Ireland wasn't going to be as simple as that...

Welcome To Spain/Bienvenido a Espana

Audrey and her ex-husband were not getting on at all, well to put it mildly and this was making everything difficult, awkward and Audrey was deeply unhappy. Being so close to her children, they immediately picked up on this and this only added to Audrey's woes. The last thing she wanted was for her children to be stuck in the middle of all that hassle, yet through no fault of her making, that's exactly the predicament she found herself in.

As that was going on in Ireland, I was juggling my properties and rentals in order to find somewhere we could all call home. This was by far the cosier of our two problems to solve, so as I waited for Audrey to dot all the 'I's' and cross all the T's in Dublin, I furnished our new home with some nice individual flourishes for each of the children.

Finally, on the 19th of June 2004, Audrey packed all of the belongings she needed into five suitcases and headed to the airport with Amy and Dean for "another holiday." Audrey's family knew the truth but also the reason for the pretence. The kids have been through enough emotional distress, a 'holiday' was something they could all look forward to at long last. In fairness to Audrey, it was one hell of a convincing pretence, as she quite literally upped sticks and left. She left her house in a Clare Hall with every piece of furniture still in situ, even their dog! Obviously, arrangements were made for the dogs to be looked after, but in fairness to her family, they played their parts to perfection, "Enjoy your holidays" with cheerful waves and smiling faces as Audrey and the kids left in the Taxi. Audrey's niece Beverley couldn't quite hold it together, she was the sister Amy never had. This added to the children's suspicions, but they kept their own counsel on that at the time. I don't mean that in a bad way because God only knew how they were processing what was happening. Audrey and I both come from families with sets of parents who stayed together happily for 50 years or more. What did we know about parents breaking up?

Even though the arrivals board at Malaga Airport stated quite clearly that their flights had yet to take off, I was pacing up and down the arrival hall with nervous impatience. By chance, Tommy happened to be passing through, albeit briefly-

"Are you alright there, Dave?! You look like a mad dog with a hammer stuck up its arse!!"

Then he burst into laughter and left me there looking like an even bigger idiot! With friends like that... well, you know the rest! Back in Dublin, Audrey thought she'd never get on the plane, terrified that something bad would happen any second. She didn't feel so much like she was migrating, it felt like more of an escape. She did what all mothers do and kept the brave face on so far as she could tell Dean was grand, just dying to take off, the flight still being a novelty. She couldn't tell if anything was up with Amy or not:

"Are you alright, love?"

"Grand, ma, why?"

"Just asking!"

"Actually... ma'?"

"(Heart Thumping) Yeah?"

"I'm starving! Can we get some food?"

No, Amy was grand as well! And so, after yet another pit stop to refuel Amy-Dean was too excited to eat-their flight was called and soon they were thousands of feet above Irish soil. Back in Malaga, the flight from Dublin changed on the arrivals board from "Boarding" to "Landing at..." So, yours truly, the 'Mad Dog' with a most unusual method of storing tools, well, according to Tommy, started pacing quicker than ever.

When they walked through the arrivals gate, 600 years after taking off – so it felt anyway! I was greeted by a sight, a 'vision' I'll never forget. Dean, being the tallest, was the first one I saw and his beaming, excited, boyish smile made my wait melt into nothing. Running literally at his heel was Amy, a big stupid grin all over her face, her eyes radiating a joyous heat not even the Spanish sun could ever equal, and we smothered each other in hugs. It still rates highly in my most treasured, happy memories. When I looked back at the arrivals gate, my heart thumped out of my chest. Audrey-my Audrey-looking tired, relieved, happy and more beautiful than any woman ever had a right to, beaming at the welcome I just received. I made fun of her (always our go-to ice breaker) by putting my sunglasses on and slagging her about all the matching pink suitcases, she was also dressed in pink with bleached-blonde hair and sun-bed-darkened skin, Beyoncé would have envied! It was the perfect start to our new lives together and so with our car loaded, we headed off to our hotel. Yep-hotel-don't forget we still had to break the news to the kids.

It wasn't just any hotel either. I had to set the wheels in motion, even at a subconscious level, so I booked us a suite at the First Flatotel, which is an aparthotel, so there were enough bedrooms for all of us. I could tell who picked what room by the clothes left immediately on the floors of each one as a blur shaped Amy and Dean raced past us, yelping, "Beat you to the post!" as they went. Audrey was only half a step behind them, warning, "Factor 20 first, you'll burn…. wait!" I just laughed and followed them out! That set the tone for our first three weeks.

Despite Audrey's best Irish Mammy generous application of sun cream, Amy still managed to burn a bit at first but then tanned beautifully. We were no more than 60 feet from the beach (Las Yuccas) at any given time. So, Dean quickly discovered the joys all teenage boys remember from such close encounters with bikini-clad girls his own age and a bit beyond. Amy spent a bit of time drooling at the sights on the beach too-the ice cream stand, hot dogs and burger bars and so on. I asked Audrey if all the swimming was giving her an appetite;

"No."

"What then?"

"Dave, she's a bottomless pit. There's no filling her!"

She wasn't wrong! Still, time flies when you're having fun and we were, all of us. But there is only so much 'touristy' stuff you can do before the novelty starts to wear off. So, I began introducing them to all of the friends I'd managed to make since moving there. A lot of the socializing included Bar-B-Q's and swimming in their private pools, so it was right up their street! More importantly, they were starting to get a taste for the real Spain and its people and that was something I had hoped would soften the blow. No matter howhow we were going to do it, Audrey and I continually had our hearts in our mouths, second guessing ourselves, hoping we were doing the right things. Time elapsed and it was the end of the 'Holiday,' so it was crunch time for everyone.

The kids weren't happy. That is an understatement, unfortunately. What about home? What about our friends? Do our feelings not matter? Hey, I never said we were the Waltons, did I?! Of course, it was a shock, of course, they felt cheated by the 'Holiday' façade. But love conquers all-, thank God. It took more than a few days, to be really honest. But they came around slowly but surely. What they didn't know was what the alternatives were. There was a reason why Audrey was granted a legal separation after only a few months-virtually, unheard of from a monster who psychologically abused his wife and kids so badly she was granted a lifetime barring order from him. It was time for phase two.

Remember that 'new home' which I mentioned earlier, the one I furnished? It was an apartment I had rented, roughly six miles from where I worked, in a resort called Riviera Del Sol. It was essentially a gated community with all its own amenities, including a golf course. I didn't use my own home because I wanted something fresh and new-no baggage-a journey we could all start together. Do you know what? It worked!

I claim no credit for it. All the credit belongs to Dean and Amy, and them alone. They were such lovely kids that they quickly made friends and once you've got good friends-no matter how old you get-then you start blending in. Friends make life bearable. Friends plus family equals happiness and once more, Audrey and I had the two happy-smiling-hugging kids we met at the airport again. The pool, situated just outside our window, would soon be known as "Amy's pool" because she lived in the bloody thing! Dean and I would put in a major shift in the swimming stakes too, but Amy was a bloody mermaid! A stranger from another planet would be forgiven for thinking that Amy could only speak the following words;

"Ma, I'm going to the pool," and

"Ma, is there anything to eat?"

For a little slip of a thing, who could out-eat a professional wrestler, she would mostly insist on the following items to be included in every meal-Brussel sprouts, Roast potatoes and Ketchup- while waiting for dinner to be served, she usually scoffs a ketchup sandwich or three. To Amy, anything goes on a "Ketchup Combo"- ice cream, crisps, sugar, fruit, anything. Interestingly, cannibalism wasn't her thing, this mermaid doesn't eat fish! Dean was more like me-if it's on my plate, then it's fair game, I'll give it a go! With Audrey and the kids starting to settle, I went back to work, not just for the money but for the normality. I was used to working, Audrey and the kids were used to each other. It gave us all a bit of breathing room and time to miss one another.

One of the great misconceptions about the property game is that you've loads of money and are cash rich. The reality is somewhat different; you are 'book-value' rich but cash poor and as anybody worth their salt in business will tell you, cash is king. That was why I found myself doing a few odd jobs here and there-painting, decorating, tiling-that kind of thing to keep us ticking over. Sometimes I'd just go out and do a few building nixers, as I was never one just just to sit around. The kids were back to being grand again, Audrey was happy, I was busy, the Sun was shining, all good. Audrey's family came over to us for a visit and stayed with us for a while. This was a great time for all concerned, especially the kids, who loved having more family around and proudly showed off all the local sites of interest. Dean, in particular, was in his element explaining how such and such a road led to this place or that and how the little lizards "were actually called Geckos," stuff you just didn't get back in Ireland.

I was tiling a bathroom in a Villa a couple of miles south of home. One morning and got chatting with the client, as you do;

"And where are you living yourself, Dave?"

"Ah, just north of here, Eagle Golf Park in Riviera."

"Well, you'd better watch yourself up there, Dave, I heard a few mad Irish women are up there on holidays".

"I know, they're Audrey's sisters!"

My sister Dorrie also joined us from England for a bit. She loves nothing more than swimming in the Mediterranean Sea and catching a few rays, so with such low maintenance as that, she enjoyed her stay too. It was important for me to have her there, not for me per se, but for Audrey and the kids to meet my side of the family and see that we were just as normal as they were-Audrey's parents were in their 80s and had never been on a plane before, so they didn't make it over, nor did my Ma, as she was terrified of flying. Before we knew it, the summer season had ended and it was time for me to utter my three most hated words when I was a kid- 'Back to School.' The 'Child Dave' that still resides in my mind stared me down something fierce – "You bleedin' big hypocrite"- and he was right! What I didn't appreciate until those words escaped from my lips was that 'Child Dave' was only in the ha'penny place.

My heart went out to Audrey. She was damned if she did, damned if she didn't. Jesus, I wouldn't be an Irish Mammy for all the tea in China, I don't know how they do it. When we'd be alone, she'd express the emotional wrestling she was going through; the kids didn't want to go to school, they hated her and she was stupid. They wanted to go home. Ireland was stupid, the teachers are stupid, nobody understands them and pretty much every guilt trip you wanted to throw on the list. This is where Irish Mammy's really earn their corn, there's a tough, decisive edge to them that Daddy's can't replicate.

"Well, they're 12 and 14, I'm their mother, and I'll make the decision."

Riviera was close to an area called Calahonda, the only English-speaking school around. We wanted the best for Dean and Amy, so private schooling was a gift. They wouldn't appreciate it until graduation, or that was the plan anyway. Every parent wants a life for their children better than the one they had. It was our intention for the children to rub shoulders with motivated go-setters, the kids who–like them–would one day progress into leaders of the industry. The flip side to that coin was public schooling where every subject was taught in Spanish and they'd fall behind (not being native speakers) and get lost in the system. Okay, So Calahonda International College was expensive-over €20,000 per year- but that wasn't Amy or Dean's fault that was on us. But so, what? This was about their futures and we could afford it.

When we brought them to school for a look around, even 'Child Dave' would've been impressed; the facilities were that good. They had a swimming pool, a gym, packed lunches weren't allowed! Because; "Chef cooks for them three times a day."

There were summer and winter uniforms, the same with P.E gear and each class was restricted to 15 pupils only. They knew some of the pupils there already, as luckily, they'd made friends during the summer break. Looking back, it still looks like we did the right thing, at least on paper anyway.

Then the reality of starting school kicked in and Dean wasn't best pleased. Not one bit. I used to think that I hated school (Well, I did!), but Dean left me in the shade. Compared to him, I was 'Swotty Mc 'swot-face, perfect and Head boy,' I think it's fair to say that he hated School! I know he hated it back in Ireland too, but I wasn't prepared for it to follow him to Spain as well. Audrey saw the look of shock on my face and just laughed.

"You can get that look off your face. I told you this would happen!"

As is the case with siblings, across the globe, what one hates, the other loves. Amy is one smart cookie. She loved school and was good at it too. She is painfully shy until she gets to know you (Then you can't shut her up) but still loves meeting new people and seeing new things. Yet, as nervous as the kids were about starting school, we were worse and tried our best not to let it show. They'd already been through so much in their young lives, they deserved happiness and that's all we thought about.

It was time to take stock again. Move Audrey and the kids over- check. Have a few holiday breaks- check. Get some family over to make the transition easier for the kids-check. Move into rented accommodation to see how we work as a family unit-check. Find a decent school-check. Find a more permanent home-pending.

Commitments

There comes in every relationship a time to make it work or make a break. Ever since I laid eyes on Audrey, I was determined to make it work just when I thought I couldn't possibly love her anymore, she allowed Dean and Amy into my life and I knew-KNEW- that I'd never need or want anything or anybody else in my life ever again. I'd hit the jackpot, won the lottery, whatever else you want to call it. I'd found my purpose, my one true love and two perfect extensions – living, breathing – extensions of her massive heart. But.

There's always that. The "But" in my case was, to be honest, a little bit of insecurity. What if I mess this up? Audrey had given me everything, open, honest, transparent, brave and unselfish. How could I make her see that I was for Real? That I wasn't like a ghost from her past who looked too good to be true and wasn't? That's not me. She'd moved lock, stock and two smoking barrels of love and energy over to Spain to me and I couldn't match that. She'd proved her side of the deal. The insecure 'me' felt I had to do the same. But how? Write a poem? Jump out of a plane? Skinny dip on Las Yuccas beach? Then the penny dropped.

Nothing quite says 'let's plant roots together' like, well – planting Roots together! Buying a house together not for business, not for profit – for us that's pretty permanent. When Audrey agreed to do it, it was all my Christmas coming at once. It was to be the very first "US" thing of serious meaning and magnitude. Audrey had given up her house in Clare Hall and now she'd own her own home, our home. But!!

Always a bloody 'but'! This time it was made of paper and beautifully encapsulated in Red-Tape. It's known as a Cedula de Habitabilidad, that's a Habitation certificate for you and me. It needed a whacking great pair of scissors to cut through all of that Red-Tape too, a year's worth of cutting, but we got there eventually and it wasn't like we were homeless as we stayed at my old apartment in Gualdimina, but it was worth it. Our home. Brand squeaky – shiny new. Never a living soul in it before us, all ours to make our own mark, our own memories, and boy did we!

We used to decamp to one of our favourite social haunts – Tricky Ricky's - where I'd let the family down appallingly with my terrible singing voice!! Nothing was safe from my howls – U.2; Tom Jones, Elvis, all the hits my brother could knock out of the park, I slowly strangled! Back in Ireland, I'd never do it, I'd be barred from every sing-song on the island, but in Spain the worse you got, the better the craic was, so it was all good! Just as well, I never had a problem laughing at myself or others doing so!

Another local joke at my expense was that I was the only "Baldy" in the whole of Spain who got a bill for £600.00 every time I went to the hairdresser seriously! Okay, it wasn't for any artistry on my barren head, but for the work, Audrey would get done-the usual 'service' with added hair extensions, blond, of course. They only added to her beauty, so I would've paid double that, happily.

Come to think of it, Audrey has a habit of giving me G.B.H of the credit card variety, especially at Christmas! One year in particular, she must've bought everyone in Spain a present, at least that's how it looked to me and as always, she'd start ticking names off her own Christmas checklist from the start of November. I'm much more 'Average– bloke' in how I do the festive shopping and so it was on Christmas Eve that she dragged me around the shops to help me. That whole day my ears were chewed off about how stupid it was to leave everything to the last minute and how I should take a leaf out of her book, yadda – yadda - yadda. Guys - are you feelin' me on this?! Lo and behold, I'm pulling out of the car-park of Dunnes stores in Fuengirola, my checklist ticked and sitting in the boot when Audrey says the strangest thing…

"Oh-oh…"

"What's up?"

"Dave… I'm after forgetting to buy something…"

"(My best, I swear I'm not gloating voice!!) Surely not…"

"(mortified) No. I have. Something big…"

"(only 'slightly' smug!) On your checklist was it… hmm?!"

"Oh, shut up and turn the car around."

"Something 'big,' you say?!"

"The turkey?"

"The bleeding Turkey?!!"

I screeched the car into a space ass close to the entrance as I could. Audrey sprang out of her chair like a jack-in-the-box and disappeared back into the shops,

A woman on a mission. As is her want, she was gone for ages and eventually returned with a big smile on her face… A lot more presents and a Turkey.

"What else did you buy?"

"Ah, just a few bits and pieces."

Then the receipt fell out of her purse, so I picked it up for her, but not before taking a sly glance!

"£200.00?!!"

Of course. I had a little moan about it-not because of the amount, but because I'd been getting it in the neck all day! To this day, we laugh about it, the £200.00 turkey, happy memories. Oh, and no, I still haven't learned to start shopping in November. I'm still a bloke!

It was a car that seemed to attract funny stories because another time, back in the early days, we were all driving from Torremolinos to Marbella when, for the lack of anything better to say, I committed on a wall we were passing, Yes that's right, a wall. It just seemed to go on and on forever and it had lovely, intricate stonework. I told Audrey that I thought it was a nice wall, nothing more:

"(mumbled) oh yeah, lovely."

"What was that, Dean?"

"Just saying, you know, it's a bloody wall!"

"Is that the Great Wall of China, Dave?"

Amy, just like her mother, having yet another 'blonde' moment. Some achievement for a brunette, I think you'll agree?! Okay, now I appreciate that this probably doesn't read as particularly funny, but we laughed so much, I actually had to pull the car over. You see, you had to know Dean and in particular, his frequent fits of giggles. Even those little words fail to capture it, because he had one of 'Those' laughs, you know, the ones I mean. Dean was the guy who you'd hear laughing in a dark cinema that gets everyone else laughing. He was that guy, the spark that lit the flame that made you laugh. Now, if you can multiply that with the strength of a baby-Gurgle-Giggle and you're somewhere in the ballpark! Sometimes I was the owner of the dumb comment to set him off. Other times it was Audrey, but the lion's share belonged to Amy. Don't think for a second that

Amy is an airhead, far from it, trust me on that. Except when it comes to maths, but hey, even Achilles had his heel, didn't he?

Dean was a Fecker to her because he knew she'd cock up even the easier sums! He'd go out of his way to bring the conversation around to something maths related and straight away, Audrey and I could see it coming! As siblings do, Amy knew Deans weak spots too and teased him mercilessly about them, typical kids. One of the Deans areas of improvement would concern motor mechanics. In his mind, he was the next stig and Mc Giver rolled into one… only he wasn't! I'll never forget the look on his face the year we bought him a scrambler motorbike for Christmas. We hid it in a friend's house up until the day, as he was a devil for rummaging around, and when he was presented with it, he had to make several urgent trips to the toilet, bless him. He'd always have to do that when he got really excited. Another little foible Amy was also able to exploit! Anyway, he loved his scrambler and if he wasn't riding it to Hell and back, he'd tinker around with it to "improve" it. After one of Deans many improper math tests on Amy, she waited until he was mid-Giggle before delivering a stunning retort way out of left field?

"Hey, Dean, how's the scrambler? Did you manage to put it back together?!"

"Wow, I'd never seen an about-turn like that before!"

"What are you saying, Amy?"

"Dave, look under his bed!"

Sure enough, under his bed was the carcass of his paired bike and half-yes, HALF of my tool collection!

"Dean?"

"Dave?"

"A saw??"

"Emmm…"

"An axe??"

"Well… eh…"

"A wood plane?!!"

I'm no mechanic, but even I knew certain things! To be fair, Dean was a bit of a man after my own heart in lots of ways, and our shared love of all things motor-connected bonded us in a way I'll always treasure. So, what was Amy doing when Dean was demolishing his bike and getting us into fits of Giggles? Well, she was not studying for a math degree, but she was shining in other academic areas. Something we never knew, though, was that she was a natural born thespian.

School plays. Two words that automatically trigger a snooze fest for most people-me included. I'd some neck to be so flippant about them because I'd never been in or attended one before, but hey, perceptions do influence outcomes. Amy was to appear in her Christmas play in the English school and Audrey asked me along. Funnily enough, I didn't mind because (And only because) it was Amy, so there we were, sitting front and centre, the manifestation of moral support. Then Amy came on stage. Wow. Seriously, I mean it – Wow! Talk about owning a stage! To be clear-no, showboating or over-acting. She was natural, fluid and my-God-was she brave. She's one of the shyest people I know, but on stage, confidence personified. It was only a school play-dime a dozen- but I sat utterly transfixed. Audrey noticed that I went uncharacteristically quiet, so she stole a quick glance in my direction. She slagged me off about this-to this day-but I sat there in tears!

"(Whispering) Are you okay?"

I couldn't take my eyes off Amy, so I just nodded in the affirmative.

"(very low whispered) Dave, you're saying!"

I was just so proud of her and I couldn't believe what I was seeing. It's about the proudest of anyone I've ever been.

Seeing as it was Christmas and we were all so proud of our Amy, A slap-up meal was in order, not a Chinese or a pizza affair but a proper slap-up Christmas dinner with all the trimmings. I booked it for Christmas Eve, so this obviously wasn't the year of the world's most expensive Turkey! You should've seen Dean and Amy, dressed to the nines and acting all so suave and grown up, being waited on hand and foot, just perfect! Of course, Dean disappeared off with his mates as soon as he was full, but Amy, even more than food, loved all the attention and talking to different people, once she knew them, of course! We knew the owner – Sam and he saw to everything and made Amy feel like a princess. There's a photo of myself and Audrey (looking great) from that night and it's one of my all-time favourites. Amy took it.

Going out for family meals was something I loved to do until the kids got all 'Grown-up' and wanted to go out with their mates instead. The tragedy all parents face at some point when we realise we're 'old' and 'not cool,' but that's life. Anyway back when Audrey was still cool (I was never cool, so I've been told… by everyone… Always!), we decided to head inland on a drive. Why? Because it was lashing rain. Yeah, in Spain. Dean made the journey extra Long with endless renditions of!

"The rain in Spain falls mainly on the… Brain! Psyche!"

I could use that brilliant excuse as a perfectly valid reason for me getting… well… (whisper it) L.O.S.T but let's not dwell on that, okay?! Good. Moving swiftly on… Not only were we-you know the "L" word- but I couldn't even remember the name of the bloody place we were supposed to be going to complete brain freeze. I eventually stumbled upon a small Spanish village (Spain being the perfect place to stumble upon such things!) and sitting there, minding its own business, was an Indian restaurant of all things. Happy Days! So making it all look like I knew exactly what I was doing the whole time (Hey, I'm a man, it's what we do!) I parked up and we swiftly decamped inside, out of the downpour.

I'd been driving for hours and as we say in old Santry, "Needed the Jax," so I set about my business but not before making a mental note about the spaghetti western /one horse town look we got upon arrival. It wasn't the sudden silence or the rubber-necked gawks we got either, it was the single tooth I counted amongst the locals. Anyway, I did my necessary and when I walked back toward our table, Dean was off on a Giggle spasm. Then Amy. Then Audrey.

"Dave! You look as though you just saw a Ghost!"

"Audrey… (whispering) Not. Here. Okay?"

But the kids were out of control now, struggling to breath from laughing every time they looked at me.

"Ah, just bleedin' tell us and stop being such a drama queen!"

I swear to God, Amy was laughing so hard when Audrey said that, she actually made a 'Honk!' noise and that just put Dean over the top-not tears-but snots from laughing. Every local yokel in the place was also double up, not that they could understand our thick Dublin brand of Hibreno - English, but down to the contagion that was Dean's giggles – remember that 'SPARK' I spoke about earlier? This is a perfect example of it.

"Dave, tell us – please!"

"Okay. Look, I had to, you know, sit down in there?"

"(Laughing) Go on!!"

"And, well, there's a urinal in front of me, right!??"

"(Tears flowing) Y… yes!!!"

"So this guy comes and well guess the rest-but there was no door or dividing wall between us."

 -At this stag,e Audrey can't even talk, just a nod 'go-on.'

"So, Ugh, I Saw… You know… everything!"

I don't ever remember hearing Audrey roar-yes, ROAR-with laughter until that point! Actual minutes-literal, not figurative- passed before she could even try to speak! Amy and Dean? Forget about it! With that, the urinal-man walked out of the toilet. Audrey exploded laughing when she saw him and (Thank God for her Dub-accent) howled:

"The dirty bastard!!"

That did it, I think the entire town went into hysterics, even urinal-man who, like everyone but us- hadn't a Scooby-doo about what we found so funny! Dean and Amy didn't even realise until the journey home that Audrey had used "the B-word" in front of them so hard that they laughed. I was scarred for life-poor me!

When we sorta'-kinda' calmed down, a woman brought food over:

"Audrey, did you all order?"

"Yep."

"Did you order for me?"

"Nope."

Why not? Right? Well, you see (and the kids loved this!) I'd always order the same dish at Indian restaurants, but it's never on the menu. Audrey rolls her eyes up at this "indulgence," but it's a simple enough dish. Anyway, it's not on the menu, so she refuses to order it-point blank-fair enough, I suppose.

-Broken English, sure, but better than my 'smashed' Spanish!

"Yes, I'll have Butter Chicken, please."

"Sorry."

"Butter Chicken."

"Ce?"

"BUT.TER. CHICK.EN."

-Cue the Dean Giggles, Amy's snorts and Audrey 'trying not to laugh.' Don't forget I have a strong Dublin Accent at the best of times, so she's hearing a close. Approximation of "Buddha-Chicken." I know this because of her bewildered look as she pointed at the little Buddha statuette by the cash register. Okay, time to break out my best 'ES-PAN-E-OYlE':

"ME. GIUSTA. POLLA. LA. MANTEQUILLA (chicken with butter-sort of!)."

This was worse! No food is being consumed at our table for fear of choking! Then the manager, I- assume-comes down to me with perfect English. Dave's - Dublino English equals…? He points at the bloody statue again. I don't need to explain to you how my loving, 'supportive' family reacted to that, do I? Didn't think so. Sometimes you just gotta admit defeat:

"Sweet and Sour Chicken, please."

"Thank you, sir!"

Problem is well and truly solved.

It was a wet miserable Spanish day, but only on the outside. We spent the guts of it in that little restaurant, laughing, joking and enjoying each other's company. You couldn't plan out a day like that. It would never work. Do you know what? The food wasn't half bad either! We always enjoyed going out for meals together, but for me, anyway-maybe as a result of my upbringing, nothing would-or will- ever top a home-cooked meal. On that front, I also hit the jackpot.

Audrey has many outstanding traits and up there amongst the top of them are her cooking skills. Honesty, hand her A Turnip and a bag of Tayto and she'll make something delicious out of it. I've always enjoyed my food and have never taken a cooked meal for granted. During the long, cold winters when we'd be apart (in those terrible but Temporary times still ahead of us at this stage), I'd have given anything for her famous chicken and roast potato dish, it doesn't sound all that memorable, but take it from me, you wouldn't forget it if you tasted it. Of all the many meals she cooked by herself for Amy and Dean, I'd be lying if I said I didn't enjoy and appreciate each and every one of them. Breakfast, dinner or tea. Not a bad one out of them all. Until, that is, I tried my own hand at it! I couldn't cook to save my life, so I'd have been a fool not to have tried to learn from someone who could. Just as well for me, that 'patience' was another one of her many attributes because even the rats down at the local dump were rumoured to have turned their noses up at my earlier abandoned efforts! I stuck at it, though and then, like a young chick being kicked out of the nest as an encouragement to spread its wings and fly, I was given the Christmas dinner to do. Thank God Audrey hung around to supervise as it went well. One of Amy's favourite foods is Brussels sprouts and she ate the ones I cooked, so that's more than enough for me. Incidentally, Amy's are second only to Audrey's when she cooks them, and I'm not usually a fan of the wee green beastie.

That dinner fulfilled the trick that Audrey had hoped for, I'd been bitten by the cooking bug and then - after a lot of trial and error - I discovered my niche, my signature dish' as Gordon Ramsay would put it (and when I was cooking it, actually thought I was him, but that a different story!) were chicken fajitas. I thought I was great! I'd fly out to the local shops, pick up all the Mexican sauces, guacamole, Jalapenos, hot spicy sauces, chicken, mince-meat and of course, the wraps. I'd insist upon a clear, clean and empty cooking space and then let the magic happen! When everything was cooked up "(To perfection -naturally!!)" I'd wrap 'em all up into tidy pockets, garnish with thick slices of hard cheese (usually cheddar) and then lace (artistically of course!) with three precisely placed cocktail sticks. When the cheese had melted-just so-I'd serve. How do you know when your dish is successful? For me, it was when Dean, Amy and especially Audrey wolfed it down without any hint of a wisecrack. Amy and Dean grew to love it so much I'd find myself cooking it at least once a week. This didn't give Audrey any real kitchen respite thought as I'd end up using every pot/pan and dish in the kitchen and leave a huge mess! It was the only meal to have its own soundtrack:

"Is it nice? What do you think? Be honest. Are you sure? Would you like a bit more?

It was just the kid in me, looking for (and getting!!) approval for my culinary masterpiece. Hey, I never claimed to be 'mature' in my life and I'm not starting now!

I remember chatting to a few lads at a bar on the Costa and they were giving it 'the large one' about being footloose and commitment free and just assumed that I was too because of my relaxed, satisfied and chilled out demeanour. The truth though, was that I had never had so many commitments and responsible in my life: Businesses, mortgages, loans, rents and then, the cherry on the cream on the top of the cake that was my life, a family I loved more than life itself. Audrey was settled, working hard and enjoying her new life. The kids were settled, attending the best school money could buy and living in a perfect climate of endless sunshine. On the surface, we wanted for nothing. When I'd gone home after those few pints, I sat out on my sun-kissed balcony, cuddled my beautiful Audrey, sipped on an ice-cool Jack Daniels and closed my eyes in a state of bliss. Life wasn't just good, it was perfect. I should've kept my eyes open a little longer as off in the distance, storm clouds were gathering.

Through the storm

Business was booming and Audrey had developed a specialization for interior design and home-planning. She was using the experience she'd had in moving over to Spain to help other people trying to do the same. It was a unique service that only Mahon Estates (our company) was providing and it worked like a dream. When you're so busy, sometimes you only see what you want to see. What we saw was two children living a healthy lifestyle. Swimming before and after school, socializing with a bunch of well-mannered, 'ivy-league' type kids and only the occasional subtle changes, one of which was Amy's accent. If anything, we expected it to be more Spanish if anything, but it became something - closer to the south of England. If I were to guess, I'd say London or one of its many environs. How so? Well, the usual stuff, I suppose, instead of:

"Alright, Dave, wats - De-Story?"

We'd get a closer approximation of,

"Aw – Ri - Mate, 'ow's it goin' then, eh?"

I'd understand if we'd moved to Essex or something, but this was the Costa del Sol, so I didn't get it. But Audrey did. Amy was trying to fit in with the other girls at school. Well, that was only half the story.

The question we should've asked ourselves (in hindsight, that smug, always 20-20 version of our guilty feelings) was – why? Once you start figuring out that bit, the rest of the pieces fit into place. To fit in with her friends, they all had those accents. What was wrong with how Amy spoke? Nothing, but it was different to the rest and with kids – especially teenagers – 'different' isn't good; different is a bulls-eye. Like all bullying, it started off small - little comments about her accent; then taking her belongings and throwing them in the bin, excluding her from parties and events.

Amy is too much like Audrey in that, it's my problem, I'll solve it by myself and leave me alone: that kind of thing. She didn't "ask" us for help, but the signs were there, albeit subtle. For example, when some of her books went missing, she mentioned it in passing, no big deal. Only it was after a while, Audrey started noticing blood on Amy's clothes. This was from her scratching on her psoriasis, a condition that worsens under stress. We still kick ourselves for not noticing sooner than we did. When it did come out, Audrey did what I believed at the time to be the right thing – by reporting it to the teachers. Ever heard of a school management team who were aware of a bullying problem before the parents paid a visit? No? Me either, so of course, they were "shocked" and said all the right things. Did it work? No, of course, it didn't, it never does. To cut an extremely long and even more annoying story short, Audrey took her out of the school in April 2005, with nothing – whatsoever – being done about the bullying. She was absolutely correct. Anything less than that decisive action would've been cruel and irresponsible, so good on her I didn't find out about how bad it was until much later, and after my initial anger and feelings of hurt for the poor Amy, I made a mental note to keep a closer eye out. I thought-and who would blame me really – that paying top dollar for "the best" school around would negate certain things, such as concerns for bullying, but hands up, I got that wrong. It wouldn't happen again.

We enrolled Dean and Amy in the local state school La Cala de Mijas in September 2005 and despite the best intentions, it developed into a bit of a fool's errand. Amy tried her best for the first few months – as she'll never shy from a challenge (like her mum) – but unless you are a native Spanish speaker, you've no chance. Amy does have a better-than-average grasp of the Spanish language, but that was never going to be enough. She tried though. Dean was too much like me when it came to school – he just didn't want to be there. If you told him that Pamela Anderson was his teacher and once a month, he'd get to have lunch with her, he still wouldn't have gone, at his age, I would've at least "thought" about it! Despite our best efforts, Dean left school (officially, as he was never bloody there!) at 16, and Amy at 14.

Sibling rivalry went into overdrive at that point. Dean got a job working on the sites, so Amy piped up:

"Dean is working, I want to work."

"You can't. You're too young."

"It's not fair. I will work."

And so, it went on and on and on. Audrey was starting to lose her patience. Whilst our business was flying, I was the busier of the two of us as I was always off wheeling and dealing, therefore, Audrey was at home more and feeling the burn of all the tantrums. Amy had been going on about heading back to Ireland to finish her education, so Audrey relented and brought her back. It lasted a day. Sometimes the grass looks greener, and Ireland is as green as it gets... until she realised the reality of what she was walking into. It was a quick study for her; no matter how beautiful the promise made to you is, you can't fill it if it's empty.

While all of this was going on, Audrey and I had chatted about finding her something else to get her teeth into, as the Interior Design wasn't giving her enough to do. A lot of her free time was also down to Dean, as he was a working man. Loving it – and not giving her G.B.H of the ear-hole like Amy! Out of nowhere, I spotted a bar in Calahonda called 'Elvis on the Rocks' and it was the name that grabbed my attention more than anything. When you spend your life looking for Elvis stuff to tell your brother about, it stings your heart when you see one, he would've loved instantly. I looked it over, checked out the location and had a Baldrick moment, he of Blackadder fame:

"Audrey, I have a cunning plan!"

We popped out to it. For a drink later that week. It was a small enough bar located under a high-rise building on the beachfront. The locals were mostly working class and of Spanish and Moroccan descent. I'll never forget Audrey's reaction when we walked into it for the first time:

"Dave, this is a kip!"

"Well… fair enough, it's a bit untidy alright, but…"

"Untidy? Dave, even the mice are wearing overalls. It's filthy!"

"Ah, now, it's not that bad…"

"Really?! See that guy selling food at the bar?"

"Eh, yeah??"

"Ask him if that nest of cockroaches beside the serving area is this bar's idea of a Happy-meal Toy or if they're extra. We're leaving, I'm starting to scratch and itch just being here… it's crawling!"

I was trying to gather up the courage to explain why I'd brought her there when the cat let itself out of the bag:

"Dave! This must be Audrey, yes?!"

"Hiya Steve! Yeah… eh…"

116

I was given "the look," Every guy, everywhere, knows that 'look', it's the one you get when you say or do something to displease your better half and not only does it articulate their apparent displeasure, it also serves as a warning – "Wait. Just. You. Wait 'till I get you home!" I was hurtling down that infamous creek once again and losing control of the paddle.

Introductions made; it was down to business. Steve had fallen on hard times, a mixture of gambling and alcohol but none of us are immune to life's difficulties. God knows we haven't been either. II had planned to see if we could find something in a similar location, use the stuff that worked – location, music, etc. – and run it properly. But the more we spoke, the more obvious the glint in Audrey's eye became. As far as I know, I was still in the dog house, so I tried smoothing things over on the drive home:

"Well, it's not – like – 'Terrible,' is it?"

"Make the deal, Dave."

"Huh?"

"Take it."

"Yeah, but as you said, it's a kip!"

"Today, that's true. Tomorrow… that's different. I'll smarten it up."

"Are you sure?"

"I put manners on you, didn't I? It'll work!"

The deal took a few weeks to finalize as Spain doesn't just have red in its flag. It's their favourite colour of tape to tie you up in too. Also, you can only purchase the lease as most deals like this were leasehold. When we did get the keys, the first thing we did was called in an Irish Building crew. There was only ever one man from this job, my friend Mick. He was 65 years and at the time, but even then, he was running the London, Dublin and New York marathons every year when my own business was slow, he's the guy to throw me a bit of cash-Flow-work (as I called it), but there was no slacking with him, friend or no friend. Mick had a few Argentinian lads in his crew then as well, nice guys and solid workers – of course, they were – Mick doesn't suffer fools.

After a week, we had completely gutted the premises and Audrey was in her element, directing the traffic and ensuring everything was 'just so.' Both inside and

117

out – despite still being a work in progress – it already had an Irish-bare look about it. I decided to pop back to Ireland to buy some Irish memorabilia for the bar and had my sister (Olivia) take some photographs of famous Irish landmarks and popular Dublin pubs.

I was flying back and forth from Spain to Ireland regularly and life just couldn't get any better. Business in Spain was well, we have bought a bar and it's almost renovated. We are going to call it the Beachcomber, or the name was Audrey's choice, because I drank in the Beachcomber and in Kilister many years ago and so did Audrey. We frequented a lot of waterholes over the years, I always wondered how we had never bumped into each other before.

I was back in Ireland for a weekend to visit my folks and as usual, I had a great weekend. My flight was at 10 o'clock or thereabouts, so I had to be in the airport at 8 A.M. Mick would always insist on driving me to the airport no matter what time my flight was at.

On this particular trip to Dublin Airport, my father was a bit quiet, I asked him if he was okay, and he said he was fine and it was just a bit early. I thought I was just 'waffling on as usual,' when we arrived at the airport, Mick suggested that he comes in for a cup of tea. I thought this very unusual as he has never done this before. He would always just drop me there. I knew something was up; maybe he had some bad news for me, who knows. We went into Dublin Airport, had our tea. I asked again, if he was alright and that you seemed very quiet. He said that he was fine, of he went. I thought this was a bit strange. I told him I love him and that I would ring him when I land in Malaga.

I landed in Malaga.

I had a normal flight and proceeded to well, just get on with it.

I called him when I landed in Malaga, but there was no answer, so I called my mother and she answered. The usual question she asked.

"Did you have a good flight and what is the weather like?"

"I said great, and it's lovely and sunny. How is Da? He seemed very quiet on the way to the airport."

"He's great."

The next day I was in the bar with the builders doing the renovators and just getting on with life, but there was something niggling at me, my father is never that quiet, so I decided to call him, but no answer. I got my mother again, I asked to speak to Da. She said he was not here and sure he'd call you back. I knew there was something up.

The day after that, my friend Bubbles from Dublin called me.

"How is your father?"

"why."

"He's in hospital, I think."

He realized I didn't know anything.

"I'll call you back."

I called my mother and asked why is Mick in the hospital, how did you find out. It doesn't matter, what's wrong.

"Your father had a heart attack."

"FUCK."

"We didn't want you to know,"

"Why?"

"cause you would only fly back and you are in the middle of opening up a bar."

Typical Mick. He is the most selfless man I know. My mother insisted I not come home, but of course I did.

The flight landed, I got a taxi straight to the matter hospital. It was quite late, I walked into intensive care and saw my father all wired up; this is a sight I will never forget till my dying day.

The man, my father, a super hero, lying there so helpless and nothing I can do, only look. I went quietly into the room and leaned on him, gave him a kiss, he woke up, his eyes opened up wide, he frightened the shit out of me. I said are you alright, he just stared at me and pulled the covers off himself. He was naked apart from the tubes everywhere. Am I alright he said to me. I'm cut from here to here, pointing to his lower stomach, and you just leaned on top of me, of course, I'm not alright, and back into his sleep. I felt like a complete fool.

His nurses told me that the drugs he was on were making him hallucinate and they had a great time with him. Mick recovered very well and after a few months or so he told me exactly what had happened when he drove me to the airport, he got an unmerciful bang in the chest. Still, he didn't want to say anything and he knew something was wrong; that's why he suggested we went into the airport for a cup of tea, he said that his heart just didn't feel Wright. When he said good bye to me, he drove straight to his doctor in Mountjoy square, Dr Killen. He passed his house in Santry, all the time holding his heart.

When he got to the Doctor, the Doctor said you are having a serious heart attack, I will call an ambulance for you, and you have to go straight to hospital.

My father said no, I will drive, it's only around the corner, the Dr. insisted, but so did Mick. He drove from the Dr. in Mountjoy Square around to the front of the matter, packed his Micra, Mick walked up to the matter, "Bang," Mick grabbed the railings outside the matter hospital, and he fell to the ground. A passer-by called for help and the doctor in the matter done the rest.

Talk about old school.

"He had a quadruple bypass."

He managed to weather that particular storm, thank God, but it made me even more grateful than ever to still have him in my life. Back over in Spain, Mick (the builder) had his own ideas about how the bar should look and Audrey had hers. Mick is a force of nature, a very strong-willed and determined man. He's been barking orders since birth and always gets his own way. Audrey crushed him! When the bar was finished and we hung up 'The Beachcomber' sign, it looked great, it was a wonderful sense of accomplishment and even Mick had to admit that Audrey was right! I loved seeing Audrey's face when the barrels of beer, cooling systems, pumps, fridges and even the beer mats arrived in. It was all in her eyes. "I've achieved something. Little old me," She'd come a long way from being a worried mum at Dublin airport, nervously counting the seconds until they could board the plane.

The rest of the bar was fitted out in wood, glass bricks and black and white photos of Dublin watering holes, plus a large open hatch, where passer-by could stop for a beer. It wasn't exactly the Wembley Arena in terms of capacity, though as we'd only hold between 15 to 20 people safely, but remember, this was Spain, so it was all about the terraces and that's where no stone was left unturned. Audrey made sure that we'd brand new benches, a bar-B-Q area and fitted Awnings; tarp's and sun shades bring our capacity up to 100 plus, not too shabby, eh? There was a lot of interest from the locals as to who these 'crazy foreigners' were, but it was all good;

"You must chain down all the furniture, or else it will be stolen!"

-OR-

"bring it inside at night-time, and you won't have to chain it."

Their hearts were in the right place. It was a beautiful spot in its own way though, especially as the nearest bar to our one was over 300 meters for us (part of a large restaurant) and that-in the Costa – is almost unheard of. Before we knew it, the day we thought would never come upon us had arrived. Our grand opening!

We saw to it that our bar was fully stocked with alcohol (Sorry, Elvis) in every brand, type and label you could think of. I spent most of the day on my own in the bar (our "opening" time was set for 6 pm), going through everything in painstaking detail. Were the cooling systems working and set to the right temperature? Check. Was the floor swept, mopped and buffed? Check. Had all the glasses been washed and stacked properly? Check. Had all the bulbs, switches, sockets and fuses been checked? Check. I sat in every seat and thought – As a punter, would I like it 'here' and when all were laid out to your satisfaction, I made sure that all Olivia's pictures were hung straight and positioned to maximum effect. I checked my watch every few minutes to do my own little 'count-down' until 6 pm. At every stroke of the hour, I knew, for example, that Audrey would be getting her hair done etc., so I was primed and ready, so was The Beachcomber. I called my father to see if he was ok, and he said he was doing great.

He asked about the bar.

I said I'm standing in the bar waiting till 6 for the big opening. I have everything done, I have every drink under the sun at my disposal and guess what? I'm drinking brandy, no, no, no water, we had a good laugh.

I took a bottle of mineral water from the fridge, dropped two chunks of ice into a tall glass and poured the first drink of the night. I decided upon something non-alcoholic as it was going to be a very long and important night. I sashayed around to the other side of the bar to sit on a stool and pursue my handwork at a leisurely pace until six-bells. That's when it dawned on me, I'd forgotten to get the bloody bar stools! We'd been meticulous over every tiny detail and somehow, barstools – the cornerstone of every drinking establishment – had slipped through the net. I shouted something that would've sounded like "clucking Bell" to the untrained ear as I checked my watch - only two hours to go – what was I going to do? I jumped into my jeep on autopilot and drove up to a bar owned by a friend of mine called Bernard. The difference between his place and ours was in a word, size! His was huge and as luck would have it, 'The Joshua Tree' didn't have its owner present when I got there, so I liberated ten of his finest barstools and set them up in 'The Beachcomber.' If the bar didn't live up to its name, then I certainly did, combing the beachfront properties for salvageable timber and finding a new home for it!

Just before six, Audrey and the kids arrived, all manned – dressed to the nines – And looking like they'd just dropped in from the catwalk. Audrey had also rustled together. An impressive cornucopia of finger food (there's just something about her egg and onion sandwiches with a hint of pepper that makes my mouth water), so everything was set. As soon as we opened the doors, the place filled up with more than a hundred happy customers outside too. It was a very cosmopolitan crowd – Irish (of course), English, Spanish, Moroccan. You never name them all – and quite a few friends came out of the woodwork as well. Mick, if you're reading this, don't get angry, it's only a figure of speech, and of course, there was nothing wrong with your actual woodwork!

My business brain quickly grasped a few important essentials and in particular, the local drinking preferences. The Irish and English, well, what you'd expect to be fair, but the Mediterranean's couldn't get enough Jameson or Remy Martin, not something I'd noticed before. Our beer barrels were changing over nicely and bottles of wine got 'inhaled' as it normally is; good food never hangs around too long, does it? Toward the end of the night, I noticed a friendly face:

"Congratulations Audrey, Dave. The bar is beautiful, a real credit to you both." It was Bernard, his wife and kids, came to wish as well.

"Thanks, Bernard, you got enough to drink? Need anything?"

"I've got a drink here, thanks, but can I ask you something?"

"Absolutely."

"Where did you get the bar stools from?"

"Oh, those, I robbed them off you!"

"(laughing) Cheeky bastard!"

"Well, Bernard, it was 'The Joshua Tree', so it was all "In the name of love!" wasn't it?!" We had a good laugh about it. Bernard is cool like that and trust me, he more than got his own back! I can't remember the exact time we closed that night, but It was well into the wee small hours and then some. Audrey and I were utterly spent, beyond exhausted, but delighted. It had been a roaring success and the kids enjoyed themselves (except for being sent home early but hey, teenagers!) And we'd announced 'The Beachcomber' onto the Costa in the best way possible. Its success was already guaranteed and after only a few short days, holiday makers who'd frequented our little bar were booking their next holidays with a view to our bar still being open, such was the craic they'd had. The locals really took to us, "open arms" doesn't even come close to the welcome we received and we befriended some great local characters along the way. Remember, though, this was Spain, so we inevitably had the Guardia Civil Sniff around at least once a week for a few "sips," but that was a good thing, as it knitted us into the fabric of Spanish society.

The bar was a godsend in so many ways, nor was the least of which the boon to Audrey's Sanity. Finally, she could escape the tantrums at home. Now she could have them at The Beachcomber! Amy was still pushing for parity with Dean's 'employed' status, but no matter how many times she was told, "You're too young," she just refused to listen. There was another bar that Audrey and I frequented called "Paddy's," but everyone knew it as 'Evo's. Amy had used her own initiative and secured a little job for herself there, collecting glasses. She's her mother's daughter through and through, strong, determined and creative. So when we found ourselves having our own bar, Amy figured on a few hours of paid employment. A reasonable request… kind of!

Audrey, also a reasonable assumption, figured on Amy doing what she in Evo's and also a few more bits and pieces considering it was a family business. Amy was not of the same opinion. You see, now that she'd gained "experience" at Evo's, then her rates would be higher! Not only that but if she was going to be shown how to – pull a point – for example, then that also equated to more money! You can't help but admire her guile sometimes! Still, anything for a quiet life, so we gained an expensive but experienced bar worker and Audrey has one less moan to contend with! All in all, we had weathered a number of storms, sorted them out and now that everything was settled again, I decided to make another important statement on our future. I was going to propose…

Engagement

I knew from the moment I saw her that Audrey was the woman. For me, there was no one else; there couldn't be anyone else. For me, the sun rose and set with her. She'd given me everything I'd ever dreamed of and just continued to give, day after day. We'd lived together at that stage for a good while, we were a perfect fit. We looked like a family. We acted like a family. So, why not make it official?

I booked a table for four at a lovely place called Chris De Bell's with two of our friends, Avril and Dawn. I didn't even have an engagement ring with me, but I just couldn't wait another second, I'm impulsive like that. I got down on one knee and asked Audrey to marry me. You never know how these things are going to work out, I mean, you 'think' you do and you 'hope' that it'll all go to plan, but when you're down on that knee, you're vulnerable and expecting the sum of your fears to bite you on the ass. She said, "Yes!" oh, thanks be to God, phew! Never in doubt…!! We were both on cloud nine, but me a bit more, I think! Okay, so now the not-so-small matter of getting a ring. Well, after letting our families know first, of course! Oh, and our friends… look, you get the idea, we were excited!

My mother was ecstatic about our engagement and hardly had the phone back in its cradle before popping out to buy a wedding outfit. Sadly, she didn't survive the cancer that had already injected its poison into her and didn't get to see us married. We buried her in that same wedding outfit.

We went around every jewellery shop in Spain looking for the ring, so it was just as well I didn't have a ring for the proposal when I think of it! Of course, my Del-Boy Spanish (Bon-Jour!) didn't exactly help, but I did know the name of a good jeweller in LA CALA, so we ended up there. This wasn't the next day, by the way; this was weeks later. The ring that Audrey settled on came on a random trip through a shopping Centre in LA, Canada, in a shop called Roger M. As we were looking at it, the owner Roger – came over to assist us and he was so posh, he was po – sssh. He was good for a laugh and I pretended to know all about diamonds, bragging as usual.

"How do you know so much about diamonds, sir?"

"Oh, from my many travels, South Africa in particular."

"Oh, do tell."

"Yes. Cape Town, to be precise. I was examining this un-cut diamond."

"Hmm, so you know a thing or two about diamonds then?"

"Oh yes, I know all about the 5 C's."

"(little chortle) Oh no, no, no sir, I'm afraid it's the 4 C's."

"You sure about that?"

"Yes, sir. Positive."

"Well, In Ireland, we call it the 5 C's."

"(Getting a bit shirty) Explain yourself then."

"Okay, the 5 C's, here goes – one, clarity."

"Yes."

"Two, class."

"Yes."

"Three, karat."

"Yes, yes…"

"Four, cut."

"Yes sir. And now, the eh… fifth??"

"You really don't know, do you?!"

"Sir. I can assure you, there is no fifth. There are only four."

"Well, I don't know how it is over here, but back in Ireland, you need to have cash!"

The whole place erupted with laughter, except for Roger. His English – Butler Act didn't go down too well with me, so I wasn't exactly quiet! We bought the ring though, so that brought a bit of a reluctant smile to his otherwise slapped–looking puss. The ring was a little large for my dearest's petit – digits, so we had to come back to get it re-sized. Audrey was delighted, though as she commented about the fact that it was the first major purchase, she'd seen me make where I didn't hassle or bargain over the price. My response: my heartfelt and sincere:

"Audrey, in years to come, I don't want you saying that I even bargained down your engagement ring."

She laughed. She knew me too well. She still does! A few days later, we both took a day off to go to the bank and make a large cash withdrawal. Not only for the ring but also for a new-ish car. I was buying a Mercedes that day, but that wasn't the big money item; our major spend was probably going to be the dinner and drinks we'd planned later! A great day lay ahead but this was us, so expect a few bumps in the road.

Not having a car until later that day, we decided to walk to the bank. Along the way, a taxi driver recognized Audrey from all the school runs. She'd used him for. I had no cash on me but the driver agreed to drive us for free, a good start. When we got to the bank, they had the money ready for us, but it was all in €500.00 notes denominations. We hailed another taxi outside the bank and got him to take us to the garage in Marbella. A modest enough distance, no more than a few minutes' drive. At most. As we pulled into the garage, the manager was giving my car a bit of a rub, recognized me and we nodded a 'Hello' at each other. All good.

"How much do I owe you, pal?"

I'd a five euro note and a couple of euro coins set by for his tip, it's nice to be nice.

"Twenty euros."

"Sorry, did you say twenty... euros??"

"Twenty euros."

"Look pal, we're not a couple of tourists, don't try ripping us off, alright?"

"Twenty euros."

"I'm not giving you twenty, pal, no way."

With that, he whipped out his phone and called the Guardia. It took them less than a minute to arrive. That's an impressive response time. You might want to remember that little factoid for later. Anyway, they wanted to know what the problem was so I explained the rip-off to them. They agreed, but here's the kicker, in Spain, you have to do something where you "denounce" the driver and all that stuff or else forget about your complaint. I have been getting ripped off – on principle – but I agreed to pay the driver and just move on. But I hadn't enough cash, so I asked Audrey to dip into the withdrawal funds.

"Dave, all I have are €500.00 notes."

She didn't need to say anymore, the remainder didn't need saying. If we pulled out tens of thousands of Euros in €500.00 notes, well, it was the Costa (Del Crime), so it would've opened more cans of worms than we had plates for. The safer course was what I did next.

"I'm sorry, officer, but we have no more cash."

"Si."

"So, eh… can you get me to the nearest bank machine?"

"Si."

Fair play. They drove me there and back and the taxi – driver had to wait for us. In fact, because the Guardia responded to the call in the Spanish version of a Paddy – wagon, Audrey and I had to climb into the back of it like common criminals. Thank God for Audrey's sense of humour because she thought this whole caper was absolutely hilarious! Unfortunately for me, she also found one of the Guardia to be very easy on the eye. That only made me grumpier! Once back at the garage, I paid the corrupt taxi – driver in the requisite amount of cash and a generous tip of every Spanish expletive I'd ever heard. My panting words totally confused him:

"Good enough for ya', you pox-bottle!"

He was too. The only thing is, when all of this was happening, the garage manager witnessed every act of it unfold before his very eyes. I can't imagine what he thought about the well-dressed and respectable couple getting into a row with a local Taxi-man and then getting carts off in the back of a Paddy Wagon only to return again to pay off their fare and then their Mercedes in large cash denominations! You can bet your bottom dollar that he checked each and every Bank-note we gave him with greater than average care. Once again, my life had descended into a bad episode of Mr. Bean. It's a gift I have… or a curse, you decide!

Mercifully all our Euros were legit, the deal got done and we drove away from that garage absolutely wetting ourselves! We drove straight to the La Canada Shopping Centre in Marbella to pick up the polished and ready engagement ring. It was a short journey, €100.00 in a corrupt cab, short. There's a lot to be said about having your own wheels! Roger, 'the butler', was delighted to see us (and our money), and Audrey was delighted with the finished product. Just for laughs, I decided to bargain down Roger in front of Audrey and it worked!

I managed to get a couple of hundred Euros off it, and everyone was happy. What a topsy-turvy day that was. Our next stop was at Estepona, where Audrey and I had our first holiday together. It was a spur-of-the-moment thing, spontaneity being my middle name and all!!

Obviously, that meant that we'd have nothing booked, nobody knew where we were going, so we'd be guaranteed not to bump into anyone we knew. In the spirit of our impossible to predict "us" days, we selected a Spanish restaurant completely at random and ordered a local delicacy and a bottle of celebratory champagne. This was a place we'd never stepped a foot inside or never even heard of it before. Yet, as we sat there chewing our food and sipping our bubbles, I just happened to notice an old acquaintance of mine. This guy had been avoiding me for weeks because he owned me a few hundred quid from a bar tab, so carpe-diem, I went straight over to his table. He almost died of shock and clearly thought that I'd pursued him to this exact spot because he paid me straight away and apologized profusely! That was an unexpected but most welcome bonus.

Having spent a wonderfully romantic afternoon together, we stopped in at a place on our way home called Orange Square. We were regulars at this spot, a picturesque Rectangular Affair with lovely orange trees sprinkled roundabout. The aromatic waft of soothing, fresh citrus is a sensation that never wanes. We met our good friend Tony there (always a possibility as he owns it!) and shared our wonderful news with him. He was completely overjoyed for us and presented us with the gift of a wooden sculpture. You may know of it as it's a replica of the famous 'Thinking Man' and we treasure it to this day. It was a great way to end our day and then we went home.

I always worry about how the kids react to big news, so it was a joy and a relief to see Dean's happy reaction; he was delighted for us. Amy and Audrey got all girlie and giddy, which is every bit as gorgeous as it sounds. Amy then tried it on and turned it around her finger three times before making a wish. Once complete, a look of realization flashed across her face:

"Hey ma, when you die, can I have your ring?!"

Only Amy! We all laughed. How could you not?! A family dinner was decided as the best way to celebrate and where better than Dean and Amy's favourite restaurant, the slow boat in Calahonda, Chinese obviously. The food was top-notch, the atmosphere was untouchable and the company was perfect. Even down to the staff, who were excellent, knew the kids and loved them, we couldn't have asked for better.

Now that we were engaged, we talked about having a baby. We'd actually discussed it quite a few times before our engagement but nothing too serious. However, now that we had a ring on Audrey's finger, the goalposts had changed. Now it was a reality and we wanted the kids on board.

Dean, as was his wait, couldn't have been any more blasé about it – Ah yeah, whatever! – whereas Amy got very excited!

"Yes! I'd love a little sister… or a brother!"

That was that. It was definitely on the cards now. Then life got in the way again…

Happier Times

I suppose at some point in your life, you experience a real once-off moment, something that means the world to you but not necessarily a hill of beans to anyone else. A trip to a Garden centre did that for me; I know, it sounds reverting already, doesn't it?! It was back in Spain and the horticultural establishment in question was a good, solid drive inland. So, I rounded up a posse! Riding shotgun with me was one of my all-time best friends, Gavin. Everyone loves Gavin and if you don't - you're the problem - he was (and is) just that good. To everyone he meets. Our kids only knew him for 5 minutes before everything was "Uncle Gavin" this and "Uncle Gavin" that, a truly unique gentleman who, conversely, could also be very outspoken, so he was great company. Bringing up the rear in my little gardening wagon trail was a van containing some of the staff I had working for me at the time.

Having given some thought as to best describe what I was like once I got to the Garden centre, I'd have to make a comparison with that housewife's farewell 90's game show – 'Supermarket Sweep - the one where people ran around a supermarket stuffing their trolley with anything and everything as quickly and possible. That was me, only with plants, trees and water - features, instead of beans, beer and cornflakes! Yet another way of describing it would've been to compare it to Audrey running through a clothing boutique and "filling her boots," but not - even Bill Gates could've paid that bill!! Still, my little excursion wasn't cheap either because I kind of lost the run of myself in a retail frenzy, adding white shine, slate and all kinds of everything. Really. There was way too much stuff to bring back ourselves, so I ended up having to get it all delivered, which duly arrived to Amy's house - a few days later.

What a sight that was! The Argentinian lads I had working for us at the time couldn't hide their shock. At the onerous tasks that the truck delivered for them to do, but fair play to them, when everything was built, fitted and planted, we had an award-winning garden surrounding us. I didn't do it for that purpose; I did it for our family. A haven to relax in, an Eden without serpents. It was damn – near perfect. The kids had a safe place to play in or to chill out in the sun, listening to a bit of music. Audrey loved lying out in it, bathing in the scorching Spanish heat and typical man that I am; I went and installed one of those B.B.Q's with all the bells and whistles—an N.A.S.A scientist would take years to figure out. No problem to the worst chef in the world who claimed its dominion in true cave-man fashion. Let's just say if you enjoy your burgers on the very-well-done side of 'well-done,' then you wouldn't have starved! I can never think about that garden without a smile. Some priceless times were had there.

'Uncle Gavin' would regularly visit 'Eden' and suffer cremated meat A-la Dave but thankfully, he'd reciprocate at his place, complete with a private pool. He's a dab-hand at the 'oul Bar-B-Q too,' so good food plus water plus 'Un Gavin' equalled two deliriously happy kids every time. He was exceptionally good with them. Sadly, 'Uncle Gavin' has to live in a nursing home in the U.K. these days, but his love and friendship will outlive us both.

I can remember another time when I was doing my home-improvement thing and wanted to do a bit of tiling on the top floor of our three-storey house. It was a workout in itself lugging those heavy tiles up our cold marble stairs, so it didn't come as too much of a surprise when I lost my footing. It was a surprise when I was falling up the stairs, yes you read that right, I fell up the stairs. There's no point asking me how I managed that act of Anti-Newtonian physics, but I did it... somehow! As the famous star trek character famously espoused – "Ye, Canne change da laws of physics," –I guess he left an important part out – because you pay the price if you do! My price? A busted knee, a real humdinger of an injury and believe me, it hurt like a bastard. It was off to the hospital for 'physics-boy' here.

We went to the hospital in Marbella and thank god we had private insurance at the time because it got me seen straight away. I managed to end up with a doctor who spoke better English than I did:

"Mr. Mahon, you have indented your knee."

"Okay. Eh, what's that?!"

"You see this swelling (points) here?"

(Did I see it?! It looked like my knee swallowed a beach ball!)

"Yeah, I see the swelling. Alright!"

"That's because all the blood has pooled in this area. That's why it's so painful."

"Right, eh, do I take something for the swelling or something?"

"No, no, no, I'll drain it."

"How are you going to do that? Wave your Harry Potter wand over it or something?!

"(Laughing) No! Of course not… with a needle."

"(still laughing) A needle?! Ah, no problem, work away."

"You're… not afraid of needles then?"

"Me? Nah, not at all – work away… What in the name of Jesus is that??"

"Oh, this? That's my needle…"

Dear reader, I am not squeamish and I have no issues about needles or getting stitches, any of that stuff. However, when your knee is awaiting sponsorship from the N.B.A and your doctor produces a syringe that once belonged in a giant's sewing basket, even I get nervous. If you brought this thing to a harbour, you'd have Greenpeace lecturing you on the evils of whaling. I wasn't laughing then. He had a nurse clean and swab – Gentle as a fairy's cough – around the top of my knee (Good thing she was tall) and then rested the tip of his harpoon against it:

"Okay, Mr. Mahon, you may feel a slight pinch…"

"AAAAAAAAAAAAGGGGHHHHHHH!!!"

"… or maybe, a lot of pain! I bet you miss Harry Potter now, don't you?!" Smug git. The pain – intense as it was – was fleeing and as soon as the draining process began, the relief was palpable. Thank god that was over, a few hours rest and I'd be back at home and finish off the tiling;

"Mr. Mahon, I'd like you to look at your drainage fluid with me."

"Okay, but it just looks like a lot of blood to me, doc."

"Yes, but you see here (points) and here (again)."

"Em… okay, what's that?"

"That's some of your bone and gristle. This is not a good sign, I'm afraid."

"Balls. So, another harpooning job then, is it?"

"Oh, no."

"Good."

"We need to operate."

"Oh."

"Immediately."

This came as a shock to me as I'd never needed to have an operation before. I guess you never do forget your first time, do you?! Anyway, it went well and I emerged with the 'Gift' of two self-tapping 60-millimetre screws in my knee. I didn't know it at the time, but that was a foreshadowing of my future body parts.

Where (like Darth Vader!) I'd become more machine than man... well, not quite! I got on famously with that doctor and he had a terrific sense of humour. As I found out later on, over a few brandies! Turns out that he had spent many years in Ireland, so that explained how clued-in he was, we were having great banter. What a lovely guy.

It did mean, though, that I was restricted to crutches for the first couple of weeks; rehabilitation is what I was told it was. Anyway, it's no fun being in "dry dock" when you're so used to doing your own thing, but at least I had Amy to keep me company and look after me;

"I'm making a sandwich; would you like one?"

"Yes, thanks, that'd be great."

Happy days – A thoughtful, considerate teenager – what were the chances, eh?!

"Amy, I can't reach the remote control, you wouldn't mind getting it for me?"

"Sure, no problem."

Cool. I asked her that once or twice and in fairness, she obliged. Then I felt a bit thirsty, so she made me a cup of tea. When the day grew too hot, I got her to open the sliding patio doors and then it got too cold, so I got her to close them again. I thought – "this is great" and never once considered what a complete pain in the arse I was being – typical sick man pity – and Amy was an Angel about everything.

"Davey, I'm heading out to see Ma. Will you be okay?"

"Ah, I'll be great, no problem, see you later."

And off she went. All was good on planet Earth and everyone was happy. Then Audrey came home wearing one of her secret smiles.

"I eh, met up with Amy earlier."

"Yeah? Ah, I'll tell you, she's an Angel that one, made me tea, sandwiches, she's great."

"(Laughing now) really?!"

"Yeah. What are you laughing at?"

"(Laughing Hard) When I met her, Ma, please don't leave me with Davey again. He had me doing everything for him – tea/food/Remote Control/Doors open – Doors closed!!"

"I didn't think I was that bad…"

As I said, typical bloke! But I had a plan and I needed Audrey to play her part in it, which of course, she did so; we just waited for Amy to come home and;

"Hiya Amy… have a good day?"

"Yeah, was alright. I'm starving…"

"Are you making sandwiches?"

"(Cautious) Yeah…?"

"Ah, good. Make me one as well."

Yes, "please," Yes, "Thank You." I knew what I was doing alright!

"Amy?"

"Yeah?"

"How's that sambo coming on??"

"(Biting her tongue) N…e…a…r…l…y…… done"

"As you're there, throw the kettle on as well, I'm gasping for a cup of tea." (Stomp-stomp-stomp- 'click'-stomp-stomp-st…)

"Amy?"

"(inaudible comment under her breath) What?"

"Remote control."

I couldn't see it as she was standing behind me, but I felt that 1,000-yard stare burning through the back of my head! Then Audrey – bang on cue – came into the room, complete poker-face;

"You alright there, Amy?"

Amy was about to blow a gasket, then the realization hit her;

"MA? You… you told him, didn't you?"

"That you were moaning about him? Yes, I did."

Amy was about to go straight into the red, a sub-atomic strap, then Audrey's poker face cracked, then mine, then Amy's. We ended up having a great laugh that night, and many others at my expense, the worst man-baby patient in the world! Amy has many strings to her bow, a whole quiver full of talents, you might say.

For example, when our property business really started to catch fire, I found myself running from pillar to post – a meeting here, a phone call there – not to mention the amount of queries when I was sitting down for a quiet pint, I was having a bit of a moan about it to Audrey one night (feeling sorry for myself with some first world problems, poor little me!) and she landed on a fantastic and brilliantly simple solution get our own website, as I had the whole evening of moaning planned out! But, dear reader, I'm nothing if not creative when it comes to a good moan, so I improvise. I'd show 'em!

"A website? Sure, what do we know about bloody websites?"

(Told you I was creative; see how seamless that moan-transition was? Genius!)

"Now I'll probably have to trawl through all the papers (sigh) and find someone to, I don't know – build? One, then, well, how much that is going to cost…"

(I had my soap-box, I was in full flow, and nothing was going to spoil my moan, happy day!)

"… then you have to worry about security, getting hacked…"

"I'll build a website for you, Davey."

(A voice too small and nonchalant to be Audrey's, it had to be Amy, the spoil-sport!!)

"You?"

"Yes!"

"Do you know how to do something like that?"

"Of course, I do, sure, that's easy."

(Admittedly, she did spend a lot of time on that computer. Never thought that might've helped!)

"Okay, good. Go ahead, so."

Right enough, she hopped onto the computer and started tapping away like a whirling Dervish – where once there were fingers, there was now a flesh coloured blur. I've heard slower machine guns, there was no-way she was building a website. This had to be another of her jokes at this old dinosaur's expense;

"What do you want to call your company?"

(Yep, it had to be wind-up. She'd caught me flat, though. Think of a name… think… think…)

"Oh, eh Mahon Estates."

"(Snort) Yeah, okay!"

"What??!"

"Nothing. What colours do you want?"

"Eh (She did it – again! I hadn't thought this through). I suppose, well, blue is my favourite colour."

"Blue? Alright. What font and font size do you want?"

"What???"

And on the little construction project went, Amy putting flesh, bones and personality onto our new website quicker than it took me to figure out that "Font" is to do with lettering and writing style and not something you found in a church to hold Holy-Water. Even at such a tender age, women can multitask as Amy

136

introduced me to a whole new language – web design, HTML, bits, bytes, R.A.M, R.O.M, MCAFFEE, Acrobat, Rip, Zip, etc. – whilst explaining to Davey – O - Saurus how many "bits" made up a "Byte" and that zips weren't just for trousers. In less than two hours, she'd created a fully functioning, very professional, commercial website. It was the quickest couple of hours I could remember as we laughed all the way through it. I didn't have to pretend to be computer illiterate because I was!! But I did play up on it a bit too. Amy knew this but didn't show me any mercy in her sledging of my failure to grasp the basics. I guess all kids like a bit of light-hearted revenge! Looking back at it now, Amy – you created Mahon Estates that night, and all the fonts, colours and eh… "Stuff!! Are down to you, too.

Our little office also gets conceived that night. Amy did such an outstanding job on the website; I wanted a proper computer desk for the house to show it off properly. So, we turned part of the sitting room into our original office. I like to view myself as 'Dave-Mahon/Handy-Man,' so I bought one of those pre-packed jobs from IKEA. I mean, how hard could that be, right? Well, as my fellow handyman the world over would vouch – not the easiest task to set yourself! So, what did I do? Recruited Amy, of course and just to rub it in further regarding the whole website business, she wasn't just better than me at the IKEA jigsaw puzzle from hell. She was way better. It left me wondering what use – if any I had left in the world. Even this "simple, boys' stuff," as she put it, was out of my wheelhouse. Even on my best day with those things, I'd end up with a stray nut, belt or screw, but nothing ever fell asunder. This kid had everything matching on her side.

"My" side, well, it took me a lot longer (entirely down to the torrent of abuse I was receiving from any younger, faster – smarter help), and yet, it didn't quite fit. All it took by way of corrective action was the insertion of an unorthodox and 'not– included' component. No, not batteries. A phonebook. Kids these days have no idea what such things are. Anyway, using one as a centre balance to support my side of the desk is as plausible as my other explanation! We set the computer on top of the desk, everything stayed solid and safe, so job done. If you didn't notice the phone book and one or two extra bits and bobs, then it looked as advertised on the box… Almost! It stayed that way for years – unbreakable – and we always had a giggle when we looked at it, though always at my expense! But every party has a pooper, and Audrey, 'little miss House-proud' herself, always fussing over this and that in keeping the house perfectly clean, considered it a bit of an eye-sore, well my – side of it anyway! Even from such an early age, Amy had talents and skills beyond her years [that's why I know there's hope].

Having said that, I don't want to be accused of having rose-coloured glasses or that she was "perfect." But she was. I mean, she'd clean my car for a few extra quid, even though it would be worse 'after' than 'before,' but I never let on.

"I suppose you want me to pay you now?"

"Ah, c'mon Davey, a nice clean car, it's only fair!"

"Oh, alright (Handing over), here's a few "Pounds" for you."

"(Laughing) Pound?? Come back from the 1980's will ya'? It's euros!!"

"What are you going to spend your few "pounds" on? Records? Tapes?"

"Oh my god!! Davey, don't you exist anymore, except in museums!!"

I used to say the same goofy stuff to Dean as well, with similar results! To them, I must've gone to school with Moses and lived in a world of black and white before they were born and suddenly everything came into full colour!

Speaking of black and white, that reminds me of the time we all went to a Spanish zoo for the first time. We eventually reached the Penguin enclosure and as it's an 'Arctic' enclosure, the temperature was turned way down:

"Ah ma, aren't those little penguins so cute!"

"Yeah, they're lovely little things."

"But Ma, look, they must be freezing in here. It's so cold!"

"Eh Amy, it's meant to be cold, it's their natural habitat!"

"But Ma, that one's shivering!!"

She just didn't get it, the blondest of blond moments from a brunette! On the drive home, we used to have little sing–a–longs on the radio, especially to a song called "Key-Yeah," I think, you know the one – "Take it, take it, take it like a Polaroid picture?" Well, my version was… like a Polaroid pizza and it cracked them up every time.' Even today, that song contains so many memories.

Dean Fitzpatrick

Amy is not camera-shy

Amy Fitzpatrick Posing

Dave, Audrey, and Dean in Audrey's holiday home, Wexford, Ireland

Audrey and Deano in Wexford

Audrey Living the Life in Spain

Dave and Audrey enjoying the sun

Audrey, with her beautiful blue eyes, enjoying a glass of wine in the Costa del Sol

Audrey soaking up the sun in her garden

Audrey relaxing, with not a care in the world

Dave soaking up the sun in his garden

Dave having a large cocktail in Spain, life couldn't be better.

Dave in his Bar, in the Costa Del Sol. (The Beachcomber)

Audrey Doing all the work in her Bar. (The Beachcomber)

Audrey and her father-in-law Mick.

Amy's Home in The Costa del Sol Spain

Amy loving Spain

Dean in his grandparents home

Amy loving life

Dean, Audrey and Amy in Spain

Mahon Estates was a thriving business in Spain

Amy's Home

Amy after her swim

Amy, Dave and Dean's last Christmas dinner in Spain

Dave and Amy at the wildlife park Spain

Amy learning the guitar

Cancer (K)

When I was very young, cancer was the bogeyman. It was the sort of thing you'd see the housewives silently mouthing to each other at the shops or over-hearing that such and such "has the BIG C," like even mentioning the word was a bad enough omen in itself. Almost as though if you said it, it'll find you. It was a terrible, God-awful thing that luckily only ever happened to other people. Nowadays, at least, we all know someone who has or has had it and unfortunately, it's still as God–awful as it always was.

Cancer has haunted my family for years. I guess almost every family in Ireland, if not beyond, could say the same thing. It's an indiscriminate killer, it shows no remorse and gives no warning. The last thing I ever expected to hear from my dad – when I received a call from him as I drove down the road from my Spanish home on a perfect sunny day- was that my mother had cancer. He started filling up as the words left his mouth and somehow, I managed to pull safely over onto the path. It's a life-changing event to hear that your mother has been diagnosed with a killer disease, but for the life of me, I can't remember anything else he said after that. I know that I called him back, but no other details are there. Cancer, in all its black, rapport – equals - gloom, just echoed around my mind. Shock, denial, heartache and everything else you can think of, were all there. Audrey knew as soon as she saw me that something terrible had happened and after I shared the horrible news with her, I was on the first flight home.

Walking into the family home in Santry, my mother - K- seemed ok physically, but I could tell she was deeply upset just by looking at her. My sister Dorry arrived home from England too and together, we went to Ks' hospital appointment in Beaumont the very next day with my dad, - Mick.

Mick sat in on K's consultation with the doctor. I noticed how the nurse kept looking at me and my gut feeling was that something was seriously wrong. Ten agonizing minutes later and my parents shuffled out of the office. My mum was in a state of shock, dazed and confused. Mick was bravely fighting back tears. I'll never be able to shake the sight of my parents, my protectors, the people I've loved and admired the most in the world, looking so fragile and broken. Dorry and I went in to see the doctor and explained who we were. Our wonderful, glamorous mother, only sixty-eight years old, had small cell lung cancer, a result of years of smoking." I'm sorry, but your mother has only five months to live."

I asked the doctor if there was anything we could do. "No, just chemo (chemotherapy)." I asked, "What about America? I mean, you hear about people going over there all the time and getting cured. They're always developing new cures, new medications and so on over there?"

"No. Look, you're entitled to a second opinion, but to be honest, she's too far gone. The cancer is in the lungs and will spread rapidly."

There it was cold and honest. There was nothing more to say. All four of us walked out of the hospital as quiet as Church mice. The first thing my mother does? Typical K, she lights up a smoke! When we got home, Mick got K settled and then asked as if we had told her that she had only five minutes left to live. We told him that we hadn't. "Well, don't." And we never did.

My wonderful mother, a woman who lived selflessly and tirelessly for her children, grandchildren and great grandchildren, "glamorous Kathleen," started on the chemotherapy treatment and went downhill fast. I remember one occasion, for instance, when we were in the kitchen and out of nowhere, she noticed her hair falling out for the first time. Only something as purely evil as cancer could ever inflict a treatment as cruel as chemo on its victims. Staring, dumbfounded into handfuls of her hair, I could almost hear her heart breaking. She buried herself into one of my father's big hugs and went into floods of tears... we all did. But such was her strength of character, a primal instinct to protect her family, surging against what must've been a tidal wave of emotions. She looked absolutely deadpan at myself and Mick and said, "At least you two will never have to worry about losing your hair... you're both bald!"

At some point, she recognized that she was probably dying and it was then the conversations started about not wanting to die in a hospital. Due to work commitments, I had to travel back and forth from Spain every couple of weeks and her rapid decline each time was painfully obvious. Mick did more than any husband ever could, nursing her tirelessly throughout everything twenty-four-seven, never a word of complaint or thought of self-pity. A perfect caregiver and as role models go, a son couldn't ask for more. Now, having said that, it didn't stop me from getting into his bad books!

In happier times, my mother enjoyed the odd social drink at The Coachman's Inn, so just for a treat, I took her and Mick there for something small to eat- loss of appetite, yet another side effect of the dreaded chemo. But all things considered, it was a wonderful, memorable day. K started having a few glasses of Guinness and was thoroughly enjoying them, thank God but Mick, understandably, had a bit of a moan at me because he knew that K would be really sick afterwards. But she was my mother and when (if ever) would I get to do something like that again? I do admit to feeling bad about having to bring the little session at the Coachman's to an end, as K was really enjoying herself, but I didn't want to push it, so into the car we went.

As I drove past Kealys, I spotted my mother in my rear-view mirror... or more specifically, the famous twinkle in her eye, so what else could I do.... It was into Kealys! I didn't look at Mick as I drove into the car park... I didn't have to; his stare had already burned two holes into the back of my head! In hindsight, Kealys was a no-barrier; we had absolutely great craic slagging and joking like we did in the good old days when we hadn't a care in the world. We eventually got back on the road, but another glance at K in the rear-view mirror confirmed our fare - another twinkle of devilment- "Fancy a spin out to Howth Ma?" The Summit was our next stop!

I don't know how well you know Howth – if at all? – But the Summit is a beautiful spot with unspoiled picturesque views over Dublin Bay. Fate is not without a sense of irony, though as this was the low point of our day. Cancer drains your energy like air gushing out of a balloon and K just got flat-out tired. It was completely understandable, of course, but it burst the happy little bubble we were living in that day. That's how quickly everything changes- not a care in the world one minute, the next, you have the weight of the world on your shoulders. Cancer doesn't let you forget that it's around, back into the car and straight home to Santry.

Mick, being Ks' perfect caregiver, was one hundred percent correct about the toll the day out would take on her. God love her, she was up all that night getting sick and of course, Mick was with her every step of the way. It kills me to know that, as that was never my intention and I hate that it made her so unwell. Having said that, it was the last proper day out we all had together and I'll never regret seeing the joy, mischief and happiness of the old-K that one final time.

Unfortunately, the rest of my memories after that involve my mother lying in bed in a weakened condition. The pain she went through in those final months was inhuman, but she never lost her sense of humour or spirit of rebelliousness. To put it delicately, K was a bit "safe" with her money, despite knowing full- well that I wasn't short "of a few bobs" at that time, but I was still her little boy. One time, during a visit to her, she directed me to the side of her sick bed to where she had a sum of money and offered it to me. Naturally, I politely declined and then after a few minutes, left her to see if Mick needed a hand with anything. When he saw me, he noticed that I had a bit of a wry smile and was chuckling away to myself. He asked me, "What was so funny," I replied, "Jesus Mick, you'd know K wasn't well. She just offered me a good few quid!" He asked me "how much," and when I told him, he said, "What?! Sure, she's only after taking that off me for the housekeeping!" My poor Da, always getting it from all sides! With K being so unwell, we never stopped to think about the toll that this was taking on him too.

As much as I wanted to stay and lend a hand, I was still back and forth to Spain quite a bit. Inevitably, it was in Spain that the call I dreaded the most came through. It was Mick, "You'd better come home .... your mother is close to dying," the pain in his voice was matched only by his infinite bravery. I was deeply shocked but couldn't understand why at the time. I mean, I knew that she had cancer; I knew that she was given only 5 months to live. I had seen her deteriorate bit by bit then rapidly before my very eyes... but I still wasn't prepared for it. I don't think you ever could be.

One thing was for sure, I wasn't hanging about. As the call ended, I was already on the way to the airport. The rest of my life could wait, my mother couldn't. What happened next was like something out of a bad movie. Turns out that there were no more flights available out of Malaga. Audrey was online looking for any other flights or cancellations, anything, nothing not that day or the next. In my head, K's clock was ticking down to zero, her life ebbing away with every painful second that passed and there's me stuck in Spain like a bloody idiot. I'm a useless failure of a good-for-nothing son, I can't even make it home in time to say "goodbye" to my mother, pathetic. In the movies, they'd cut to a clock up on the wall and then pan down to the hero manufacturing a last-minute rescue out of the blue. All the issues and story threads are tied together into a nice little bow as the credits roll to a happy and satisfying conclusion. Trouble was this was the real world and happy endings are as rare as hen's teeth.

And yet... the one remaining aircraft on the runway was going to Dublin. It was fully booked (in fact, "overbooked"), so I had no chance of getting on board, or had I? Being a frequent flying customer, I was well-known to a lot of the staff there, so I approached a woman I recognized at the ticket desk and detailed my predicament. "Sorry," no, I begged; I pleaded, I bribed, I caused a huge fuss (security was called at one point). "Look, we can't help, sorry" I offered to make a huge donation to the charity of their choice. "No" The clock in my head was counting down, images of K dying and asking where I was, dying without me there, thinking I didn't care...

If you were to ask anybody that knows me about my stance on religion, they'll all agree in unison that I am not a religious man. But what happened next was so wonderfully unexpected that I'd say it borders on the miraculous in my dejected, crest-fallen state. I never noticed that there was a lady standing quite near to me who heard everything. Her next words to me, "Come down to me, I'll get you on that flight," may as well have come on the wings of angels as far as I'm concerned. This beautiful human being, both complete stranger and Good Samaritan all in one, with the kindest act of unselfish charity I'd ever known. I still think of her often, wherever she is and if by some cosmic coincidence, you are that person and are reading this, then please know that you will always and forever be in my heart. I can never thank you enough.

That flight didn't arrive in Dublin until well into the night, after eleven / just before midnight... my bloody countdown clock hammering into overdrive. Out of the arrivals area (tick) into a taxi rank (tock), the memory of Rory always washing the cars there (you can't have her yet Rory, I haven't said "goodbye" yet) and then straight to Santry.

I didn't know what to expect (am I too late??), but I was rushed upstairs. I was rushed upstairs as soon as I got in the door, there we were middle of the night and Kwas in her bed, eyes closed. Sure, where else and what else would she be doing at this hour of the night? Normal, right? Snap out of it, Dave.

As soon as I walked into her room, K became very excited, so much so that I thought that she might have taken a fit or something. I remember talking to her, but what would be the last thing you'd say to your dying mother? Again, nothing prepares you for this. Her reaction told me all I'll ever need to know for a fact that she knew I was there and that she knew what I was saying. Knowing K, I'd say that somewhere in there was a good ticking off for leaving it so late. I wouldn't put it past her!

I lay down beside my mother for our last few hours together. As I listened to her breathing, I noticed it slowly at first grow ever fainter until, eventually, she exhaled her last. No more pain Ma. You went out your own way in your own bed in your own house (like you said MA, not in a hospital) surrounded by my father, Dorry, Terry, myself and someone who gave her the last rights. I love you, Ma. REST IN PEACE.

It's funny, the stuff that stays with you. I can't remember too much else after that, maybe shock, or exhaustion from Spain or a combination of the two, but what I'll never forget is my mother's remains being taken from the house. I just remember them placing her into what looked like a cheap coffin box and then struggling down the stairs. I don't know, maybe that's the norm? Either way, it wasn't K, not nearly glamorous enough.

My mother died two days shy of her birthday on November 7th. As I buried my mother, my thought turned to the man breaking his heart at the side of her grave. Mick, how was he going to get through this? Whatever was going through his mind, I hoped that survivor guilt hadn't anything to do with it. You see, cancer had visited Mick as well, only he got lucky and got the better of it.

Kathleen and Michael Mahon

Early Warnings

It was the end of another busy day for all of us property was busy, the bar was flying and Christmas was coming. I wasn't long back from Ireland after burying my dear mother and I was emotionally and spent. As I thought a good night's sleep was all the tonic, I needed on that cold December night. Murphy's Law at something – silly- o'clock' in the morning, my mobile phone buzzed and vibrated like a wasp on steroids until I finally answered. It's irritating, squawk!

"Yeah."

"Hello, is this Mr. David Mahon?"

"Yes."

"This is Marbella Hospital…"

"(Wide awake now) Yes, yes, what… what is it?"

"I'm afraid your son, Dean Fitzpatrick, has been rushed into us. Can you make your way here as soon as possible, please?"

"I'm on my way."

Audrey and I got out of that bed like it was on fire and got dressed in such a frenzy that I couldn't remember where I'd left my car key. I found the house keys alright and as Audrey checked on Amy, left her a note in case she woke up and in all that time, I still couldn't find my accursed bloody keys. Audrey threw me her spare set and we ran out of the door. No car, Bollix. That's all I bloody need. I scrolled through the contacts in my phone.

"Dave, where is the bleeding car?"

"(still scrolling) don't know, probably stolen."

"Stolen?!"

"Yeah, hang on Audrey, I'm calling Richie."

Richie was a friend who lived nearby-

"Richie? Dave, sorry about the late hour. How soon can you get here? Thanks. We need a lift to the hospital, it's Dean."

160

I hung up and looked over at Audrey. "Ten minutes." He was dead on, exactly ten.

"What happened to Dean?"

"I don't know. We'll have to see what the situation is when we get there."

"Where's your car, Dave?"

"No idea, I think someone nicked it, but I'll worry about that later."

"Jesus. Took your car of all the nights, bastards."

"Do us a favour Ritchie, drop us off at the front entrance before you park, will you?"

"No brother, I'll follow you in."

The front entrance was- literally- like a war zone. To my tired eyes, it looked like a military checkpoint, armed soldiers with gun holsters, armoured trucks, M-16 assault guns, the works. Serious dudes. Audrey and I speculated on what could've been going down; maybe a politician was shot or something. Whatever it was, somebody was in a world of trouble. Thank God, it didn't affect us, we'd enough of our own. We overheard some of the hospital staff gossiping outside on their smoke break?

"I can't remember seeing four national Policia trucks here before. You only see them for serious crimes…. I wouldn't want to be him "

That was a bit frightening, to be honest. Not only is it unsettling to be around guns and ammunition, but what if there was a shoot-out and Dean got caught in a cross-fire or something? Audrey and I assumed the worst and feared everything. Where was Dean? What the hell was going on? We stood at the main reception desk and impatiently waited our turn;

"We were called in, our son, Dean Fitzpatrick, can you tell me…."

"Are you the parents?"

"Yes, can you…."

"This way please."

It happened quickly. The administrator gave a subtle signal to somebody behind us and the next thing, the three of us were being rushed, under heavily armed escort, into a side room, under armed guard. I make no apology for the tone of the only question my mind could process;

"What the fuck is all this shit? Where's Dean?"

Audrey realized what was going on about a millisecond before I did. Dean was the patient under armed guard. She collapsed into my arms with shock and my knees actually went weak with the shock of what I was seeing in front of my eyes. Dean was lying unconscious in the hospital bed, hands and feet chained and shackled to the iron bars of the bed. His face- his whole body in fact had been battened black, blue, yellow, purple and every colour in-between. I actually thought he was dead or in a coma at best. There were only a couple of ways this could've happened. I thought he either fell (or was pushed) off a tall building or else had been near the epicentre of a bomb blast. I'd never seen poor Audrey so upset, she couldn't even speak and the floor around us both was drenched by her tears. I didn't even know where to start; I could only look around at all the faces until the doctor strode in. Thank God, at least he spoke English.

"You're the parents, I presume, yes?"

"Yes. What happened? Is he, you know, going to live?"

"Yes, Dean was in a car."

"Crash? Accident? What?"

"No."

"No? What? What happened?"

"He was in a car. He went through a police checkpoint. He didn't stop."

That was it. He just stopped talking. Huh? Did I miss something there?

"So how is he like this (pointing) then, huh? Is he going to be alright?"

This was excruciating, it was already stressful enough and now we were being forced into pulling hen's-teeth.

"That is a question for the National Police."

"No, it's not. I'm asking you. You're the bloody doctor."

162

"Ask then."

"Is he going to be okay?"

"We will see when he wakes up."

"Which will be when exactly?"

"In a few hours or so."

"So, he's definitely going to wake up then?"

"He should. We'll see."

He should? Why was he still all chained up? Audrey and I were completely in pieces, it was shattering our hearts to have to see poor Dean like that. We didn't get a minute to ourselves though, as no sooner had the doctor left us than a senior member of the Nacional Police came to speak to us.

"Your boy was driving a wine-coloured Mercedes motor car, yes?"

"Yes, that's my car (at least I knew what happened to it now)."

"He approached a roadblock at Riviera and refused to stop."

"Okay. So, did he have an accident? Is everyone else alright?"

"No, he didn't have an accident. But he did hit one of our officers."

"Is your officer okay?"

"He was standing at the roadblock. We don't know about his condition."

"Sorry to hear that. So how did Dean end up like this?"

"There was a struggle."

"A struggle?"

"When he got out of the car."

With that, he gave us a smarmy grin, turned on his heel and walked away. It took a couple of minutes for the penny to drop. Poor Dean didn't get hit by a truck; he got hammered to bits by a police force seeking vengeance. Now we had bigger problems. The most urgent and by far the most important was Dean. Was he going to be okay? Would there be any lasting damage? Secondly, should Dean pull out of this unscathed, would he have a prison sentence hanging over him? We could worry about prison later. In fairness to Richie, he came into the hospital and tried to find out as much as he possibly could, but like the rest of us, he was faced with a silent blue wall.

It was hours later when Dean's eye finally opened and it appeared to me that he thought he'd woken up on Mars or Neptune or something. He didn't have a clue where he was. Initially, I put this down to blunt force trauma he'd been inflicted with around his neck and head that would discombobulate anybody. Then I figured that it was a combination of his wounds and the medication the doctors must have administered him, so I decided to ask them.

"No, we don't think so."

"What do you mean – No?"

"We know from our tests that he had taken some narcotics."

Oh, for God's sake, will this night of disasters ever bloody end? This was an even bigger, more serious problem than we dared to believe – Drugs? On top of everything else?

We sat at his side the entire night and into the morning until he finally started coming to his senses. Audrey's eyes were almost bloodshot from tears and lack of sleep. They were the first sight Dean's eyes could focus on around, if possible, he felt even worse. Then he told us what happened.

He told us that he didn't stop at the checkpoint at the Riviera, fair enough, that much we knew from the cops. Then he added some colour to the picture that the officer smugly omitted;

"So, they chased after me, I panicked and then they dragged me out of the car……"

I knew what was coming; I'd lived in Spain long enough and knew how their cops operated. It broke both of our hearts to hear how the beating began and then, when it was obvious that he wasn't even trying to fight back (not that he could've anyway, they were like a pack of wild dogs ripping a lamb apart), how the real beating went down. He couldn't remember at what stage he lost consciousness, but he remembered that they worked over all his more sensitive areas first to maximize the pain and suffering they were so adept at docking out. When the doctors told the cops that Dean was awake and "talking to his parents," they immediately discharged him, but not home to us. He was placed under arrest and taken to Fuengirola police station.

"He's not well. Can we take him home first?"

"No."

"Please, he's been beaten half to death."

"No."

"We want to see him."

"Come tomorrow when he sleeps off whatever he's taken."

"You mean what the doctors gave him for his pain?"

"No, the narcotics."

That was a long and difficult night. Audrey and I didn't sleep, we chatted the night away- me trying to provide reassurances- Audrey telling me a lot more about young Dean. The boy I met for the first time had already been through the mill. I never knew that the young lad who – like me -loved cars, hated school and was always up for a laugh had endured horrific times and turned to drugs at the tender age of eleven. Eleven. Jesus Christ! Audrey knows my stance when it comes to drugs- I'm a zero-tolerance type of guy, always have been, but that night I learned a hard lesson not everything with horns is a demon.

That afternoon (we didn't sleep, so we are into the next day), we went to Fuengirola police station to see Dean. Clearly, he was still black and blue, but the handcuffs were still on. The poor kid was terrified, confused and now that he'd seen Audrey, he just wanted his MA. None of us had the Spanish skills or peace of mind to communicate effectively, so we were given a translator by the name of Franco Rey, who was actually a nice enough guy.

"How old is Dean?"

"17."

"Then he will need to be interviewed with an adult present."

"I'm his mother. I'll do it. What are we looking at?"

"Charges, I'm afraid."

"What charges?"

We expected one or two, but what came next was a list of charges that would've made Saddam Hussein blush. It was fiction hour at the O.K corral, as far as I'm concerned. Franco managed to get to the crux of the matter.

"The officer that Dean hit with the car is badly injured."

That explained it. It was vengeance, pure and simple. Let me qualify that Dean did wrong – he was completely in the wrong – but this was a farce. Audrey and I were mad as hell with him, but family first, the cops were trying to make him look like a young Ted Bundy, so no, we weren't having it. No way. The pressure being applied on poor Dean was intense and the poor kid couldn't stop crying. I had to buy him some time, so I asked for a conference without Dean present. That was facilitated readily and then- through Franco – I insisted on answers to three questions;

"What are you charging Dean with? What will happen to him and How's the Officer?"

Their answers made interesting reading;

"Dean hasn't been charged. They went to see what the officer wants to do."

"What if he's charged?"

"Then he'll more than likely to prison time."

"But he's only 17 years old."

"Doesn't matter."

Audrey was in a state of complete shock. I can't blame her. Who wouldn't be?

However, I noticed something. While all the talk and accusations were being thrown around the room, one very important detail was getting buried;

"Excuse me, Franco?"

"Dave?"

"Explain to the police that my step-son, Dean Fitzpatrick, was battered by them."

"...And that his beating was such that he was hospitalized..."

"...that physically he's still black and blue."

"...and that he is a minor."

"Dave, they say that this is old news, so what?"

"Now tell them that I'm demanding the name- or the names- of the Officer- or Officers- that did this to him."

"Dave.... I, look......Dave ......"

"Now."

Annoyed as I still was with Dean, he wasn't going to prison for this. I was sticking up for him the only way I knew how, and this was an avenue worth exploring. What followed was a lot of huddled and hushed discussions in little groups with big green/blue uniforms. Every time a break in conflab happened, I was given evil eyes. It wouldn't have taken Darren Browne to read their thoughts and the atmosphere grew quietly hostile. A case study – in passive aggressiveness-stalemate. Okay, time to push my luck;

"Franco, ask the cops to let Dean go."

"Okay."

"...so that we can all get some much-needed rest, let the hair sit, and we'll revisit the situation over the next few days."

"Okay."

"How do they feel about that?"

"They still don't know what to do, their officer is seriously injured..."

"So is. Dean, tell them to show a bit of compassion. He's in bits, a kid."

"They don't like their officers being attacked."

"Do I need to call in my solicitors?"

That brought them back into another blue hurdle before deciding on letting Dean go home for a few days; he was too exhausted and battered to go far anyway. I was brought out to the back of the station, past the cells (nothing fancy there, I can tell you) and out back to the car pool. I was taken to my car, nicely parked but woefully out of place. No car of mine belongs in a police station, so I made it my business to give it a slow and deliberate once-over. Guess what, dear reader? Not – a bloody- scratch. I double, then triple checked it. Nothing, nada, no damage at all, interesting. Just how badly injured could this cop be? I drove us home and we all had some much-needed sleep.

When I woke up, I went to Dean to pay a visit. It wasn't an argument; my rest had brought me clarity. Specifically, it jogged my memory. To be even more specific, I felt guilty about something… this might've been my fault;

"Morning Dean. How're you doing?"

"Sore. Tired."

"Listen, I need to talk to you about something…"

"Ah, Dave, leave it out, will ya? I'm not in the…."

"Please, just hear me out, okay?"

"(tutting) Okay."

"Thanks. Do you remember when I brought you to the bar a few weeks ago?"

"(sighs) Yeah."

"And I bought you a couple of pints…"

"Yeah."

"Well, I sort of knew it wasn't your thing, you know?"

"Go on."

"Look Dean, you're a young man now and… well, when I was your age, pints were the thing, you know what I mean?"

"No."

"I know you smoked a bit of grass."

"What?! Eh, look…. Dave…., eh..."

"I'm not condoning it, Dean, I hate all drugs -you know that- but I guess what I'm saying is, to each their own and all of that, but drugs Dean, c'mon…."

"Dave, I, look, I'm not into…."

"Dean, your mother and I saw the toxicology report. We know you were on something. You broke through a checkpoint and hit a cop. A cop, Dean! Look, what we're not talking about here, is the fact that you did all of this in a car you stole. From me!"

"Dave…. I…."

"I'm not finished. I'm not mad about the car."

"What?"

"Don't think for one second that I'm happy about it. I'm not. But when I was your age, I used to take my father's taxi without him knowing about it."

"Jesus - you?"

"Yeah… the difference between us though, Dean, is that I used it to earn money and I gave half to my mother. I also never – never - did drugs."

"Okay…."

"But then, I embarrassed you that night too."

"Huh?"

"That woman chatting you up, I didn't help you, I know she was too old for you- but I went a bit far on the slagging. I'm sorry about that, truly. I also noticed that you hardly touched a drop of alcohol all night, so I let you drive me home…"

"I know… you said I was a natural!"

"You are. You're actually a very good driver. In fact, when you turn 18, I'll see about getting you your own wheels..."

"Yeah?!!"

"Yeah, but this other nonsense... the drugs... the stealing… it's got to stop."

"I could be in prison, Dave."

"Yeah, but look, trust. Trust is the thing, Dean. Trust me to deal with this. I'll trust you to turn things around, alright?"

"All right."

"Right. Let me make a few phone calls."

I got onto Franco, he got onto the cops and we all met up again. Without Dean, he was still recovering. Turned out, the cops hadn't realized that we lived in Spain and that Dean- apart from this incident was a good kid, a nice young man with a family that loved him and wanted to make amends. The cop that he hit, somehow made it off "life-support" (moryah) and decided not to press charges. No free lunch though, there were conditions. The deal was when Dean turned 18, it would be better if he left Spain. Otherwise, as an adult, then adult charges may appear. Franco arranged for Dean to come back to the station the next day—another condition. The cops wanted to put the fear of God into him. They really gave it to him and laid it on thick, when they started telling him that he would be ''raped in prison.'' Audrey and I called a halt and we walked him out. Enough's enough. Maybe that was bad or weak parenting on our part, you decide, but it's what we did. As we walked out of the Municipal building in Fuengirola, we noticed a young and Spanish secretary making a bee-line for Dean. She was friendly. Very friendly. It was all in Spanish. So, Audrey and I couldn't follow along properly, but Franco could;

"She's telling him that he's cute... too good looking for prison…"

Audrey was not impressed, then in her best Dublin accent:

"Oi! That's my son you're talking to!"

So thus, ended that possible romance! Dean didn't attempt to complain, he was in enough trouble!

Amy's Disappearance

This story never gets any easier to write. Difficult isn't a big enough word to describe it, but it's the best I can do. Before writing this book, I'd already written about 70,000 words on this subject, not including the book Audrey and I wrote when we lived in Spain (with the help of Mick o' Toole) called "Please Find My Amy." One of the hardest parts about my writing on Amy's disappearance is the fact that it still feels as raw as yesterday yet as distant as several lifetimes ago. Yes, I know that sounds oxymoronic, but that's all a part of the mindset that consumes you when a child goes missing. Down is up, backwards is forwards and they're only the bits you can make sense of.

I guess we should start from Christmas 2007. Dean, Amy, Audrey and I had been living in Spain for over four years. We were a normal "modern" family. We were nothing out of the ordinary. All of us wanted were some things everyone else wanted, peace, security, happiness and a better future for the children. I wasn't in a very festive frame of mind as I'd only buried my loving mother, Kay, a month previously in November at Christmas. So heavily embedded with the word "family" that you only truly appreciate its significance when you lose a loved one just before it. It was my first Christmas without Kay and every song on the radio, every advert on TV, everything made me distraught with pain, a time for family, mother hugs, mother's cooking, Christmas dinners, everyone around to Ma's house and so it was ripping my heart out, to be honest, and remember thinking that this was as bad as it gets. I wanted 2008 to just happen and vanquish 2007 to the bin forever. Now, all I want is to relive Christmas of '07 again and not only appreciate just how very special it would prove to be but also not let Amy out of my sight. Again. Ever. Anyway, back to December again.

I was moody heartbroken and generally moping around, moaning about everything. I didn't want Audrey to even put up a Christmas tree out of respect for Kay, but maybe this was just an Irish tradition. As usual, Audrey snapped me out of it and made me see sense. There are four of us in this relationship and we have to be Irish about the kids. She was right, of course and Kay would've told me the same thing, too. Funny though, isn't it how we still call them "kids" even if they're teenagers? Maybe this is an Irish thing, too?

So, I did the only thing I could do. I just soldiered on and tried to make the best of it.

Audrey, like the rest of the Irish mammies around the world, has Christmas day down to a fine art, only with one little difference. She's the biggest kid in the world on Christmas morning! She woke up before the kids and got everyone under the tree so that we could all open our presents together. That done, she set to work with Amy on putting the Christmas dinner on. Due to the sunny climate, most people in Spain go outside to have their meals or more often than not, go out to a restaurant, but Audrey is a traditionalist when it comes to these things. So is Amy, and her job was to prepare all the veggies, especially her favourite (and her forte) Brussels sprouts. Dean again was much more useful as a chocolate poker in the kitchen, so we retired to the living room like the country gents we thought we were. So, when the food was on, Audrey's next step was the customary phone calls home to Ireland to wish our families a "happy Christmas." That was Audrey's parents, her siblings and her niece. For me, it was my father, brother, sister and Graham, my son.

Audrey and I enjoyed a little aperitif (or two!). Before dinner, I gave Amy and Dean a glass of, as Audrey calls it, "fake wine" (non-alcoholic) to make them feel "all grown up" and to include them as much as possible. When I sat down for dinner, it was presented as beautifully as ever. Audrey – a brilliant cook at the best of times really outdid herself that year and created a truly excellent meal. To be honest, I'm not really one for sprouts, but I tried one to keep Amy happy. I'm glad I did, as she did a great job on them and that's the truth talking, not nostalgia. I was so stuffed after my meal that I waddled into the living room like a heavily pregnant duck and flopped onto the couch, eventually dozing off in front of the telly. Audrey changed into her new PJ's and joined me. Dean and Amy did what every other teenager does after the Christmas dinner, shot out the door and met up with their friends, like I said, normal people doing normal stuff.

The only exception (at this juncture) was that I'd kept a good bit of work on over the festive period as Audrey had initially planned on bringing Amy back to Ireland on the boring day of St. Stephen's Day but had to cancel due to Dean's behaviour. They had rescheduled the flight for Amy's 16th birthday the following February. So having thought that the girls would be away, on top of the usual business associated with Christmas (still a lot of Irish and English ex-pats down to visit, rent and buy in the Costa), I didn't feel the time pass and before we knew New Year's Eve was upon us. Be careful what you wish for. I wished in 2007 over so many times and I couldn't wait to ring 2008 in. Amy would turn 16, Dean 18 and Audrey would hit the big four-o, but my young bride will never look a day older than 29 to me! We were planning a big family cruise to mark the year of so many special milestones and not to leave my little self out, I wanted to buy a Toyota Landcruiser jeep. In situ, Audrey wanted it in black. That was the topic of conversation as we got ourselves ready to go out on New Year's Eve. Audrey asked the kids if they wanted to come out with us (typical mammy thing to do - don't let the kids feel left out!) But the look of abject horror on their faces belled their sweet and how-eyed refusals to do so. Of course, they had their own plans; we were the old fogies, the dinosaurs and do you know what? Dean right too! Dean had a night out planned with his mates and Amy wanted to babysit with her friend, Ashley. This was a simple task as it was only looking after Ashley's little brother, but Amy was really excited because it meant having a sleepover.

That little snap-shot right there, that's Amy. A couple of weeks shy of her sweet 16th and she's full of jumping beans having a babysitting sleepover on New Year's Eve. Even at that, teenagers being what they are, Amy could've come home an hour later over some silly falling out, that's the unpredictability of teenage girls. At least my very limited one anyway. Amy was due to meet at her friend's house at 6 pm. So, we said our goodbyes at a quarter to 6, the short distance taking less than the 15 minutes she'd allowed herself. The deal was that she could stay the night, and the next, if everything was going well, Audrey knew the family. So, all was good.

The funny thing is that neither Audrey nor I were particularly pushed about going out that night, but we decided to go to an Irish bar where we knew the owners and most of the patrons. Audrey had a solid-gold cast in iron rule with the kids. No matter what, they had to call at around midnight to wish each other a "happy new year." Sure enough, at 11:53 pm. Audrey's phone started ringing.

Why do I know such an exact detail? Because we've been through this literally tens of thousands of times. Anyway, New Year's Eve in a noisy Irish ex-pat bar and fireworks exploding outside like it was the D-day landings. Audrey missed that call... and the next because, on top of all that noise, her phone was in her bag. We only noticed this when the bells started ringing and Audrey took out her phone… which, right on cue, started to ring again. It was Amy, dependable as ever, Audrey walked out to the little courtyard so that she could hear her in peace. To this day, I'll never forget the happy jolly conversation they were having and just before the call ended, Amy laughed because of her cheeky comment:

"Ma, don't get too drunk!"

Amy and Audrey both love to have the last word, so that round went to Amy, I asked Audrey to let me have a look at her phone to see what number Amy was calling from. It was a landline. I asked Audrey if she recognized the number.

"Yes, that's Debbie's number, Ashley's mother."

"Where do they live?"

"Calle los olivos."

This was about 1 km from our house, so the number area code and all that matched, so that proves that she was exactly where she said she'd be. Even I was a teenager once (and was far from an angel), so you have to check; it's also very important to notice too that I also spoke to Amy on that call. We wished each other a happy new year and shared a couple of laughs. I distinctly recall slagging her about her maths "skills" because Audrey tried to explain to her that she couldn't call Ireland for another hour due to the time-zone difference and Amy struggled to understand it. All good natured, normal stuff. I wish to god that I could remember every word, every inflection, every nuance in perfect clarity, but I can't, god for the life of me. Why do I wish that? Because that was the last time we spoke to Amy. For now, we stayed at the party a little bit longer and got home at about 1 am. 2008 was finally here and I could put my horror of 2007 behind me once and for all, boy was I ever wrong about that. I've always been an early to bed, early to rise kinda guy, so that night was no exception. I had no reason to think otherwise. I can't even remember if Audrey stayed up or not. The next morning, we got up, had a nice leisurely breakfast and just took it easy.

Apart from the fact that it was New Year's Day, it was just business as usual, a very ordinary day. Dean had arranged to stay over at his friend's house for New Year's night as well, so we weren't expecting to see him around. He was going to a café, an ear-full from Audrey when he did call or arrive home though as he hadn't called to wish her a "happy new year." All Audrey and I can remember doing that morning is having breakfast, chilling out and making a few phone calls. There was no point trying to call Amy, as she was not known for an early morning when she stayed over with Ashley. They'd messed about on the computer until the waste of the small hours, perhaps as far as 4 a.m. and then crawl into bed and snore away until late afternoon. In a word, teenagers. Given how it was still the holiday season, there was every possibility she'd stay over for another night, possibly two, so we weren't worried. In fact, no warning signs or red flags whatsoever. I really cannot stress this enough. Everything was as normal as could be.

At some point, possibly lunchtime, possibly later, we received a phone call inviting us to a private party in La Casa de Mijas, at a Dutch bar where Steve Nelson was playing. This was an opportunity not to be missed. As he was a hugely – popular entertainer up and down the Costa for many years and we felt honoured to be invited to such an event. We were asked to be there at 7 pm. So we were, tardiness is a pet hate both of us share. We enjoyed the lovely buffet style food that was laid on and just for a laugh. I stuck a sandwich in Steve's mouth as he was halfway through a song. He took it all in great spirits and somehow managed to sing and eat while playing the song. Not a bother to him; it was a great party and perhaps the most memorable part for Audrey and me was his unique take a Lynyrd Skynyrd's "sweet home Alabama." It's a little play on words replacing "Alabama with Calahonda." I'm sure you're probably thinking, "so what" and on the face of it, I tend to see your point. However, after a conversation, Audrey would go on to have with him. One of Amy's friends, we found out that this was one of her favourite songs and they'd sing it at the top of their voices. I love it, too. But I can't listen to it anymore. Even thinking about those opening chords fills me with tears. But that was still to come.

Audrey and I were dead on our feet by 8 pm and even though we were having a ball, we left at 9 pm, the old fart lightweights that we were. Going out two nights in a row didn't use to be a big deal, but the settled life gives you a bit of sense! I hit the hay as soon as my feet crossed the threshold of our home and Audrey sat up for a while watching T.V. in case Amy came home. We'd normally leave the back patio door unlocked in case the kids were going to be late home. As it made a very distinctive "squeak" when you opened it, so even if we were asleep, we'd hear it opening. We didn't hear it 'squeak' that night, not even Audrey, who conked out in front of the television and slept on the sofa. It didn't squeak because Amy didn't come home.

Audrey woke up just after 6 am, made some tea and thus checked Amy's and Dean's rooms to see if she came home. By the way, Dean's room would be cleaner than Amy's, so it wouldn't be that unusual for her to sleep in his bed if it was free rather than navigate her own untidy little minefield. I got up somewhere between 8 and 9 am, a bit late for me but then I'd been "out" for two nights running, so well within the rules still; it was now the 2nd of January and work wasn't going to do itself so we popped out after a light breakfast.

At this stage, we had rented the Beachcomber out to a local man as its initial novelty –newness had worn off and it became "just another bar" business wise on the Costa. It still generated a bit of income for us and allowed us to plough more of ourselves into the property business, and that's exactly what we were doing up until post-lunchtime on January 2nd, pressing flesh and cutting a few deals with the ex-pats we were meeting at the usual watering holes. Business as usual, nothing to see here, no worries if I was to be pedantic, then I'd say that the only thing slightly out of the ordinary was that Audrey still hadn't heard from Amy, but that's being overly picky because of hindsight. Audrey had spoken to Amy (and Dean) many times about keeping in touch and getting permission... "ask first" type of conversation, so it wasn't a signal of trouble ahead or anything like it. Ask yourself honestly with teenage kids staying over with friends over the New-year period with people known to you or your wife. Would you have been concerned yet? Add to that premise the fact that both of the kids had hinted and or mentioned that one night would probably run into two and that the clock was yet to strike three, so that was the middle of the night for them therefore, not calling you was hardly a surprise. When we walked back into our house, it was as empty as we left it. Then the clock struck three times and Audrey reached for her phone.

She hit the speed dial and her face was like thunder. Whoever she was about to call Dean or Amy-she was going to get a severe tongue lashing. I caught her eye and she mouthed

"I'm going to bleeding kill her."

So, she called Debbie's house.

"Hiya Debbie, is Amy there? This is Audrey."

"No"

"Oh! Is she on her way home? Has she just left or something?"

I wasn't really listening. I'd heard this song too many times before. It was a bit boring, to be honest, she'd say "yeah," and then Audrey would spit feathers unti Amy walked in and world war III would kick off. But Audrey's reaction wasn't what I'd been expecting, obviously, I couldn't have heard what was said to Audrey, but I knew by her face; her breathing from some other primal instinct that a bombshell had just landed. Audrey put the handset into the cradle and turned to me, looking as scared as I'd never seen her.

"Debbie said she left her house last night."

"What?"

"She said she walked home."

"Last night? What time?"

"Half nine."

That was it, the moment that would change our lives forever. Only it hadn't announced its importance yet. We did what anyone else probably would've done. We called all of her friends, starting with Kim, her best pal, nothing. Then Rebecca, another friend Nothing. Every friend we called had the same response!

176

"No, we haven't seen her, but you know what she's like, she's probably gone to see "such -and –such and lost track of time…"

We called every single "such and such" that was mentioned. Nothing, nothing and yet more nothing. Audrey and I had a massive circle of friends and acquaintances all over Costa. Everyone knew us and knew the kids. Still nothing. Every time we dialled another number, we'd steal a glance back to the squeaky more and more realistic, I could see she was in turmoil, thinking the unthinkable but afraid to vocalise it because then it's true. So it fell to me to say it.

"Audrey, this is getting serious, I think we should call the police."

Jesus, just writing these words again puts shivers down my spine. So she hadn't been seen by anybody we knew in what was then only 18 hours… "only" 18 hours. How long does it take for a trail to go cold? Stupid thoughts and reasoning shoot through your mind like the rule of three. A human being cannot live for 3 minutes without air, 3 days without water or 3 weeks without food. So, she was grand; we were worrying too much. The lightweight dinosaurs that leave parties at 9pmp worrying like a pair of old – farts over nothing. So now I'll ask you the question what do you do when your teenager goes missing?

You don't want to even think about it, do you? There is no instruction manual you can turn to or a download a checklist. You can get off Google, for instance, because missing kids is something that happens to other people, not you. Until it does, sometimes you'll get lucky and your son or daughter will walk back in the front door as soon as you start talking to the police. Sometimes the police will say "thank god" and leave it at that and sometimes they won't and come down on you like a ton of bricks for "wasting police resources," hey, who wants that? But sometimes, you don't get lucky. Your child doesn't walk back in the door and the police that you're on the phone to don't speak your language and because you were panicking to begin with, the whole thing snowballs into an ugly, unintelligible mess and your daughter is still missing. Another call, another dead-end and your child is still missing. Believe me, those thoughts don't even scratch the surface of what went through our minds. The number to call was 002, that's the number of the Guardia Civil, that's how it works in Spain. It was the number we had on our fridge, which was just as well because we were in such a state; we would've dialled 999 or something. What happens then-wrong number? Your child is still missing, tick-tock. Audrey picked up the phone, dialled 002 then hung up. I knew why we were being stupid. Then again, Amy wasn't home... tick tock. So she picked up and dialled again. Then hung up again. Same reason, the same primal reflex intuitive. You only call the cops when you're nowhere left to turn. Third time, lucky third times, a charm, the human rule of three, Audrey dialled again and this time she waited until they answered. I couldn't do it, my Spanish wasn't good enough, Audrey's was conversational so that was our best shot.

"How can we help you?"

"My daughter is missing."

Holy shit, now it's real; it's an actual event. This is happening. This is serious.

"What is her name?"

"How tall is she?"

"What is the colour of her eyes?"

"What is the colour of her hair?"

"What was she wearing?"

"Where did she stay?"

"Tell us the address."

"When did you last speak to her?"

Every question and every answer drove coffin nails into Audrey's soul; I could see it on her face. I'm her rock, the breadwinner the man. I'm supposed to give her hope and reassurances. I was petrified, I couldn't believe what I was hearing.

"Had we other kids?"

"Did she stay overnight often?

Did they know something we didn't? Didn't this sort of thing happen all the time? Why weren't they telling us that they get thousands of these calls and they never amount to anything serious? Why did we feel like a black hole had opened up in our living room and sucked out? All the hope in the world? The Guardia ended the call by telling Audrey that they'd send Amy's details on to the Guardia Civil, who would start looking around immediately, but that we were to go the police station first thing the next day. Audrey and I could only look at each other in muted shock. There are only so many times you can say, think or feel- "This can't be happening," before you snap yourself back into action. We started calling around every number in our phones, on our phone lists, then re-calling around every number in our phones, on our phone lists, then re-calling people. Then the door opened and squeaked before closing again with a thud.

"Amy! Is that you?"

It was Dean… of course, it was Dean, what were we thinking? We updated him on everything we knew, which wasn't a whole lot.

"Ma, I think something serious has happened to her?"

He was only articulating what we were too afraid to say right from the start, that was his opinion. He went out to a few of his friend's houses to shake a few trees and we returned to the phones. I checked the time; it was coming up at ten o'clock p.m. The first 24 hours had elapsed. Where are you, Amy? Please just walk back in the door, I swear to God, we won't give out, please we couldn't rest, couldn't settle. So we went for a drive around the area, stopping here and there, asking questions looking in doorways, side streets, you name it. You do all you can and still feel like the world's most useless prick because nothing is working. Nobody had seen her… nobody saw anything. What more can we possibly do?

It's a night I'll never forget but don't want to remember. I've often tried to piece together my thoughts from that night put them into some semblance of order and apply some cold-hard logic to them. Forget about it, there is none. There's a nagging itch at the back of your mind, just out of reach like an answer. You just can't remember, but it's "on the tip of your tongue" and you want desperately to scratch it. That itch is telling you that you're missing something huge and obvious that will locate Amy in two seconds flat, but you are too old, too tired or too dumb to see it, hidden in plain sight. That's what it's like. It's also like being given a ten thousand piece jigsaw puzzle where all the pieces look the same and you don't have a picture to guide you along to how it should look. What do you do? Start with the edges, right? We'd done that, we'd called everyone, informed the police and gone out looking for ourselves. Now what? Slowly try each and every piece until one of them "kinda" fits? Oh, sorry, I should've mentioned this earlier… you're against the clock and if you don't solve it before the buzzer goes, then I'm sorry, but one of your children has to die. The puzzle just got a lot harder, didn't it? This was no jigsaw puzzle. This is Amy…. tick… tock… where is she; tick…. tock…. is she Alive? … tick…. tock   every second counts.

Dean came back. He was worn out, visibly upset and panic made him mad with nervous energy.

"I'm telling ya," something bad happened; I can feel it in my gut."

Audrey smothered him in a hug. And did her best to reassure him;

"Ah, you know what your sister's like, Dean. She'll be back tomorrow full of apologies before raiding the fridge!"

It settles him   a bit. I kept thinking about my brother, Rory. He was missing, too. I stood right over the bridge where he died under and never even knew. Was he still there at that stage? I don't know, was he still alive there? I don't know, what if we found and had gotten him to the hospital in time?

Then Audrey decided to call her best friend Paula and shared her worse fears. She also asked Paula to stick some credit on Amy's Irish phone because we did not think we could do it from Spain. Maybe that was the missing puzzle piece; it was all going to be as simple as that "Sorry, I'd no credit, now wouldn't be something." Or she arrived back in the door. We could not rule that out. We'll never rule that out.

I called my best friend, Darren, the absolute go – to – guy where the chips are down and he did not disappoint.

"Ah, come on out of that, Dave. Do you not remember that I went missing for a few days when I was a teenager? Remember? I ran away!

"Oh, yes."

"She'll be back Dave, don't worry too much…"

It was so good to hear from our friends. It helped… it really did, but we still didn't sleep. Not a wink, I paced up and down the whole night, wearing a channel into the carpet. C'mon Dave, think and watching every hour of the clock tick past. It's funny. Back then, we were measuring her absence in hours and minutes.

At 6 am, we thought about just going in, but with shift changes, the hustle and bustle of hand-overs plus people leaving late or finishing early etc. We waited until 8 am. Best to have all the right people in situ, wide awake and fully focused on finding our Amy. That's exactly what we did. I had another little panic attack (of sorts) on the drive over to the station – will they have an interpreter present or will we have to get one? I cursed myself. All those years living in Spain and I hadn't bothered learning the lingo, gobshite. I'd have to rely on Audrey's conversational Spanish again, piling the pressure on her even more.

We popped up to the station and knocked on the glass door of the little public office. Dean stayed at home, just in case. A Guardia civil officer opened the hatch.

"Si?"

"Hello-eh, Hola. We are here about Amy. Fitz. Pat. Rick?"

"Oh, yes, Amy Fitzpatrick! Come in..."

Wow. That was unexpected, we'd been dreading the whole let's go through all of the same questions all over again because we're as dumb as the Irish police and never bother passing on time-sensitive information etc., but they weren't. They were the opposite, professionally organized and courteous. They had done their homework and were ready to go, it was bitter–sweet. Great that they were so on top of everything, but also terrifying that they were so on top of the situation. Surely a teenager missing for more than 36 hours wasn't such a big deal, right??

We needed to officially begin the search and this entailed singing a written statement known as a no-brainer. Job done. We were then given an official translator lady and were shown into a small office with two uniformed officers. Then the questions began. Seven hours of questions, every big thing, every small thing, every minute painstaking detail.

Everything personally, I welcomed it all because it was a measure of how seriously they were treating this. A situation we had felt stupid for initially reporting. Once again, my thoughts drifted back to Rory and the little red clock in my brain. Angrily counted down the seconds, screaming. We're wasting time. Dave, she could be lying in a ditch and you're sitting here answering questions about what shade of blue her eyes are? I tried hiding those kinds of thoughts from Audrey, but she can see into my soul at will, so she knew anyway. Then the officers gave us the first official set of instructions for Amy's case:

"Can you make some phone calls?"

"Absolutely."

"Start with her friends."

"Done it, but we'll do it again, whatever it takes."

"Good, her school friends? Everyone, she knows?"

"Same answer. Anything else?"

"No, just keep trying, looking at the most likely scenario? She ran away. We see this all the time and she'll be back in a few days."

That tickled our ears for sure from the get go, that's all we wanted to hear right then and there. A snap-shot of that frozen moment in time looked something like this. She's gone less than 48 hrs, a very professional and organized police force is all over this and their experts and experience, their "sixth sense," if you will, was telling them that she'd run away. She'd run away for a couple of days and would come back with her tail between her legs.

I'm not going to say that Audrey and I breathed a collective sigh of relief and thought, "Thanks be to god for that," because honestly, we didn't but uncertainly felt a lot closer to realizing that dream than we would see her again. How mad is that? As we thanked the police and turned to leave, we had a Colombo moment from them:

"Excuse me – sorry-just – one-more thing?"

"Yes?"

"Did either of you have an argument with her?"

"No, absolutely not (looking at each other to confirm), no, definitely not."

"Good. How was she? What was her demeanour?"

"As in?"

"Did she sound upset about anything? Any tantrums?"

"No."

"How would you describe her mood, as far as you could tell?"

"To be honest, she was in great form, slagging Audrey off, telling her not to get drunk and I was having a bit of banter with her about time-zone and doing sums, so very happy. Genuinely sincere, yeah, no problem."

When you enjoy a relationship as close and intimate as love, Audrey and I have a quizzical look at each other and can say a multitude of things. That last line of questioning now had us more worried than ever. Another festival for the surreal because we also still expected to get home and find Amy with her bum sticking out of the fridge as usual.

"Hiya Ma, did you forget I was coming back today? Where's my dinner?" We zombie-walked back to the car then I asked Audrey if she remembered the details (names, numbers etc.) of the police officers or translators. She didn't, nor did I. How bloody thick were we? Okay, back to your jigsaw puzzle-what now? Tick-tock come on, think, what do you do next? Go home in case she shows up, or somebody calls the landline? Dean was covering all of those bags, so come on, what? Thank you! You can't just do nothing tick-tock make a decision; your child's life depends on this.....

That dear reader, is what the inside of my mind (Audrey's too) looked like, twenty-four-seven. So, what did we do? The only thing we thought we could do, we drove around anywhere and everywhere with our phones glued to the sides of our heads. All the while making good on our commitment to re-call everyone. All over again, just as the Guardia asked us to, every time our phones would ring. We'd go from naught to sixty on the hope-meter – "Amy?!" Only for it to die again instantly when it wasn't her. Then, darkness replaced it. Was it news about her lying in a hospital bed? A ransom demand? Or God forgive us, someone to tell us she was dead. Less than forty hours since her last confirmed sighting and we're already living on tenterhooks, our nerves stretched beyond their actual limits. We tried not to spend too much time on any one call to any one person tick-tock remember? Forty one hours in, still nothing, no one knows. More calls, more driving. Forty two hours.... forty three.... forty four.... nothing, "haven't seen her" "no" … "She might be with such and such…" nothing. The only time the engine of my car wasn't turned on was when I had to re-fuel after covering every inch of Calahonda twice over. We once again tried Riviera Park. Where the kids sometimes hang out. Nothing, we went to El Zoco and Almirantie, a large commercial area. Where we had our bar and our friends had their bars, like the Joshua tree, owned by our friend, Bernard. Again, nothing. It is now approaching forty eight hours and I'm sick to my teeth hearing "no" Audrey and I haven't had a blink, let alone sleep, the entire time and still we push on. A smart person, smarter than us anyway, would insist on one or both of us getting some rest at this point, probably have something to say about being "counter-productive" and "greater chance of mistakes" being made and so on. Audrey used the keys she had from working in the Joshua tree to look around inside. Again nothing. Joshua, the guy the tree is named after, was overcome but was hobbled in the process. Well, we were wrestling too against a formless, heartless invisible enemy called "time" and the unknown and like old Joshua, we too felt honked but not yet overcome, not ever.

On and on and on we "no"….. "not seen here" "missing? Really?"….. "ah, she'll turn up," and on and on and on. We drop into a bar called Tricky Ricky's, a meeting place for all of our friends and tons of people known to Amy. If she had run away or was mad at us for whatever reason, then this was the place and these were the people who'd know or would have an inkling of a thought, an idea, a whisper, something… nothing. Fuck, why on earth can we not catch a break?

There's a small wooded area near "the beachcomber," and in it resided a few tramps. Nice enough fellows in their own way and I used to throw them the odd pint or sandwich or whatever, it's nice to be nice, they were eager to help but once again, not a trace. Not a clue, derelict buildings, internet cafes, shops, banks, and supermarkets not so much as a near miss. Beaches, bus stations, taxi ranks, cinemas, nada. I even read graffiti under bridges, random walls and street corners, looking for clues. The only half-clue. I found it was Dean's name on a wall and I'm pretty sure that was our Dean. At this stage, I'd dropped Audrey home to be with Dean and help him to deal with this awful situation. I was conscious of not calling them, as I knew only too well the disappointment of it not being Amy or news of her whereabouts. It killed me to eventually go home because –ironically- it would've literally killed me not to. I was worn out, dead on my feet, actually shaking with exhaustion. Something I would never have thought possible, I couldn't even look Dean and Audrey in the eyes when I dragged my feet into the house. I'd let them down, I'd come here without her, I'd let Amy down. I didn't find her. I hadn't just failed… I'd failed utterly, completely, the most failed fail in the history of failure, snap out of it Dave, your family needs you. Stay strong.

"Come on, Dean, Audrey, we'll get there."

This was more for Dean than Audrey and she was grateful for that but Dean?

"We won't. She's gone. I'm telling you this bad."

"Come on, Dean, don't give up on her. The police are looking. We're looking, all of her friends, everyone from school, bank managers, bar and restaurant staff, public transport people, foremen, local maddens, all of our friends, everyone we knew, even down to the tramps out in the woods, not hundreds, but thousands of eyes searching every inch of the Costa, keep- strong-believe!"

Nice words, sure, but in my heart, I was more on Dean's wavelength than I liked to admit. If she wasn't hurt somewhere off the grid or taken by some opportunistic piece of shit (being so close to Morocco and knowing their local reputations changes where it was a Moroccan opportunist), then we'd be lucky, very lucky. So far, we weren't feeling too blessed by lady luck, so my heart continued to plumb the depths.

"Dave, it's time we called home to our families."

Audrey was right but this was another milestone moment I never wanted to happen. With every milestone come another nail hammered into the lid of Amy's coffin and I couldn't face that. It's almost as though she's hanging off a cliff and I'm gripping her hand. Going to the police meant she was hanging on by only four fingers by telling all of our friends and covering every inch of the coast she knew about down etc. Their fingers calling our families was firing out the last distress signal into the sky and loosening Amy's trip to just two fingers. How long could she last with such a poor and weakened grip? How long could anyone? Fuck me, what a nightmare.

If you're reading any part of this book, you'll know that my father, Mick, is a rock. Unshakeable. I wanted my dad to make all this just go away, I called him first. Never in doubt.

"Hello, da?"

"Is that you, Dave?"

"Ya, I.. it's…. it's Amy… Da, she's gone missing.."

"What do you mean, she's gone missing…..?"

I started bringing him up to date fighting back tears and lost. So I hung up. I never hang – up on Mick, so that made me worse I called him again. He was full of love and understanding, melting my heart and I broke down again. So it hung up again. Jesus… what's happening with me? I called him-again-and damn the tears, I made it through to where we were at.

"Cheer up, son, she's as bright as a button, that girl. She'll turn up any minute, try not to worry."

I was consumed with negativity though, too tired to make sense or listen to it.

"Try and get some rest son. Maybe she ran away, you know what kids are like. Oh, how I wanted to hear that, to believe it for it to be true. Maybe it was? Maybe it is? Mick and Audrey gave me the strength to call the rest of my family and friends. Then, Audrey did the same. Seeing Audrey upset kills me. I can't bear it not for a second, it's not a good place to be in, the thing is, Audrey can be emotionally soft and emotionally strong all at the same time and seeing her negotiate thus impossible feelings of hurt, despair and hopelessness. As she went through call after call home to tell parents, siblings, friends and other relatives the news, we still tried to proceed, was remarkable. She's a truly amazing woman and I love her so much.

You soon realize who your real friends and when a crisis comes calling. Over the next two days, the oasis hotel, a regular haunt of Amy's, had 30 extra guests on their book. Our friends and families, sixty more eyes, thirty more brains and thirty more hearts full of love and determination to find our Amy and get her home. Thirty souls who had only a singular motive put us to work to show us the way. We'll look until our eyes bleed. It's a powerful thing. It's humbling, Amy please, God, if you're reading this somewhere, know this – this is all for you, people who never even had a passport got emergency ones Just for you. All these people put their lives on hold for you. People love you Amy, not because you went missing, they love you for the beautiful amazing woman you are and the girl you were, know that. Please… Okay?

Technology is a thing and it's everywhere. All kids love it and Amy was no exception. If you're now thinking – just trace her cell phone!-well, we didn't. We didn't have to because we found it the day we learned of her disappearance. It was in her bedroom together with all her make-up and money. Not the action of a girl about to run away or planning to voluntarily disappear… Don't you think?

These days every second story in the news about footprints, carbon or electronic. Early 2008 was no different and like every other teenager, Amy lived a lot of her life in cyberspace. Whether that be on the phone, msn or bsbo. We checked her emails, her phone and her electronic accounts, but there had been zero activity across any of those platforms since New Year's Eve. Audrey and I would be the first to admit that we're no scholars when it comes to computers, so we drafted with the help of a friend of mine, Richard O'Shea. Everyone just knew him as Richie. A self-confessed technophile who had lived for twenty years or so in Spain and even though he didn't like to admit it, he was a fluent Spanish speaker.

He was also a bit of a wide-boy in that he'd be the go-to-guy if you wanted a dodgy old car or shall we say, a "convenient" supply of licenses or insurance certificates. In hindsight not 100% trustworthy, but at the time, we could still all ensure Amy's disappearance in hours and we were desperately fighting against the clock. We'd asked the cops to help us with the electronic stuff and they were dragging their feet about it, but I'm not worried that way, so we arranged to meet Richie at the Hotel Oceania. This was a maturely agreeable location because his girlfriend works there and it was also a spot, we'd taken to have our meetings with pretty much everyone involved. Audrey and I brought our computer tower down with us for him to have a look at because we quickly appreciated how important it could be to unlock a much-needed clue to her whereabouts.

It's the footprint analogy that did it for me. Like playing hide-and-seek deep snow, no matter where you go, you can't help but leave a trail of footprints behind you, betraying even the best hideouts. A computer works the same way, little electronic footprints that can't be snowed over a history of learned behaviours, personal performances and individual choices. Computers, for all their scary and mysterious powers, area dumb animal at the end of the day …you tell it what to do, it does it and then endlessly waits for your next command. We didn't know that at the time. We also didn't know how easy it would be to command the dumb animal to delete its records or carry out all manner of convert commands. It was a task the cops should've taken ownership of from the start because now we'll never know if riches was economical with a lot of facts, I'd only find out much later. Things like the not-so-important fact that he was giving Amy driving lessons or that the months he'd spend around at our house working on the Mahon estates website, Amy had put something easily as good together in under an hour when your little girl goes missing then the whole world is a suspect until they're not. Richie chose to search through the possible treasure trove of secrets contained in that tower beyond prying eyes in the reception area of the Oceania whilst Audrey and I split ourselves to meet as many people there as we could. The course of our investigations took us from hotel to hotel, to pubs, to homes and of course, the never ending barrage of calls and texts to our phones. We were all over the place physically and emotionally. Is Richie a suspect? Does he continue to remain a suspect? Dear reader, you have the facts. I'll let you decide.

We were in constant touch with the Guardia Civil- "Civil Any news?"… "updates?"…. "What next?" And the next time we dropped into them, they had a different translator on hand. He was a very distinguished gentleman in his 60's, spruced up constantly and very good looking. You could say "movie-star" looks and you wouldn't be too far off, as he was once an actor on the short-lived BBC drama-El Dorado, back in 1992-1993. Apparently, he played the doctor on it and was also a reporter once upon a time-but I couldn't care less about all that, he was a darn good translator and a connected guy with all the local authorities, in a word, useful.

He was an absolute godsend as far as we were concerned and not just when it came to Amy when Dean fell afoul of the layover there, he proved to be every bit as useful as having an "insider" with the cops he was a good guy and saw clearly that Dean's misdemeanours were influenced by the frustrations he felt over his sister's continued absence. A rare oasis of common sense, something I'll never again take for granted.

We would've been lost without him and to give him all the credit he richly earned. He put his heart and soul into Amy's case, maybe even left a bit of his own soul in it. He had all the top-brass on his speed dial and didn't have any frustrating language barriers to contend with, his name is Franco Ray and everyone seems to know him, not only that, people liked him too, we couldn't have built a better middleman if we had been given the parts to do so. Yet, for all contacts hard work and goodwill he brought no Amy, no news, no clues… nothing.

At some point, we stopped counting the hours and minutes. We started going by "day four" or "day ten" or whatever. This snowballed first into "week two" and "week six," and then unbelievably, we were counting in terms of months. Dean, Audrey and I had literally poured ourselves into the un-fillable void Amy had left and achieved nothing. I can't tell you when exactly we started drowning in darkness or started to consider the twenty-four-seven worry –a thorn existence we'd fallen into to be nothing more than an exercise in daily idleness and object futility but I can promise you we pushed through it and pushed on ever and always onwards, always hope. Well wishes were an unexpected source of strength we badly needed, but I'd waste some of that energy on biting my tongue. For every "nothing is insurmountable, Dave!" I'd say "thanks" instead of "Go fuck yourself, what would you know about it?" That sat caged in the back of my mind. No matter how hard we worked, no matter how many favours we asked, markers called in or how many hours we worked every day ended the same-Audrey crying herself to sleep, which wouldn't come and no sign of Amy. I felt that we were motionless but direct the results don't lie, no Amy.

For all the good you feel you're doing, you're overwhelmed by the irredeemable awfulness that your little girl isn't at home where she should be. You've failed. You're miserable because your breath cannot respond to that which it cannot rationalize or intuit and sympathy for all the kindness it holds cannot alter the facts. Amy is still missing. Nobody seems to know anything and bless their hearts, they're all putting in an honest shift and looking hard. Asking difficult questions, not taking "no" for an answer, but it can't last. They've got their own lives to go back to.

At some point, probably the first Friday but it's all a horrible blur at this stage –the media got involved. Nothing leads the news like a tragedy, so it didn't take too long for sky news. Some English channels and the print-media from Spain and Ireland to dip their dirty little toes into the river of hopelessness we'd found ourselves in. Myself, Dean and Audrey felt like we were holding our breath, afraid to breathe lest we miss some vital tidbit about Amy and now the circus had come to town. Did they help? The cynic in me would point at the scoreboard and highlight the fact that we were no closer to getting Amy back, so-no however, the realize in me would counter that argument with the strongest of rebuttals-Amy's face was everywhere, her disappearance was no longer a local "secret", or just another case and none of that hurt our search or detracted from our efforts. The world certainly as we knew it was aware of Amy Fitzpatrick, her check pout, her baby–blue eyes, a study of bottomless beauty staring out at the world, our most recent photo of her. An image that would go on to generate over half–million "missing posters" was everywhere it didn't hurt.

We were back and forth to the Guardia Civil more often than most of their employees. It had escalated up the chair. "Amy" was now an operation at the high table. In Spain, there are different types and different types and different levels of police in these forces. You'd have the local police who would look after minor issues such as parking tickets, driving offences and such up a level, you have the Guardia civil who'd also look after central traffic issues, but up the chain then to anti-drugs, terrorism and the like then, sitting at the top of the food-chain you've got the national the most serious crimes and now also Amy's case. She was common to all levels of Spanish policing, or so we were told. Pretty early on, we could see roadblock all around Riviera, Calahonda and La Cala. At one stage I got a call to meet the Guardia at my house. We didn't know what to expect (obviously, we were hoping for a long overdue family reunion), so I drove as fast as I could. Every second could count once again. Did I break the speed limit? Yes, did I slow down when I saw a checkpoint almost outside my house? No, of course, I didn't because I was in such a hurry to find out what the Guardia wanted… Good or bad. Then, the two officers had a rapid exchange of words before the one on my left reached for his side-arm. I stopped then alright. The officer to my right took a quick look in my window and then said something in Spanish to his colleague, but I made out "parents" and "Amy Fitzpatrick" in there somewhere. It all happened in a matter of seconds, but without trying to dramatize a bad gangster movie out of it, they were creating a visible presence like that up and down the Costa.

We were back inside our house (although to this very day, we still call it "Amy's house") in a matter of minutes after that and some other officers were waiting for us:

"What's up? What's the story? Have you found something??"

"Yes. Prepare yourselves (opening a bag), clothes….. of a young girl……."

"They're not Amy's."

Audrey's words, true but no less devastating. Fuck, I really thought they'd found a clue, some kind of a lead to crack the case. Another blank, yet another dead end. Infuriatingly, this was only the first of several such occasions and trust me, you never learn from each new experience rather than almost every other response in human nature; for example – don't touch something hot, but you do, you burn yourself and never do anything that dumb again because it hurts counter intuitively, the pain of another red-hearing in Amy's disappearance hurts way more than any mere something here…. "you open up your heart and expose it's native nakedness to the world, then bam! Slammed shut another coffin nail. It's not the death by a thousand cuts, it's the time of a thousand heartbreaks and one's heart can only endure much. Some of those experiences were worse than others, especially the calls where you'd be told to drive to a remote location, arrive at it and be faced with all manner of police tape and officers in forensic uniforms. Sheepishly approaching you with an evidence bag packed full of something, that's when you actually pray for no news, because until you actually get a look inside the evidence bag. Your mind fills in all the gruesome possibilities – body parts? Blood-stained clothing? And then you'll see an old shoe or something else equally impossible to be Amy's. Do you give the cops a good lash for getting you all worked up? Do you fucking take every piece of help you can get. So, what if they got it wrong, at least they were trying; not everyone was.

I had a few life-long friends, guys I would happily have taken a bullet for, guys I would've given my last penny to if they needed it, you know, stuff really good friends do for each other? When I first told these people about Amy, I broke down in tears and not for effect. These guys had cried with me and for me many times in the past. Not all of them came over to help me, but Amy. It's hurting me then and it hurts more now. I know Audrey feels the same way about some actual blood – relatives who left with the first exodus of press cameras. Richie was a really good friend but someone I only met in Spain. Then he got arrested, he was later released without charge but jokingly boasted to me about Amy. Getting all of his outstanding charges dropped (car and driving/packing charges), but he never let any of the details of his arrest and/or questioning out. He also never answered the simplest question in the world to any degree of satisfaction.

"Where were you on the night Amy disappeared?"

Again, you have the facts, make of them what you will. Before Richie's story started to jar with inconsistencies, there was somebody else who pinged off my radar with worrying regularity. Her name is Debbie Rose.

In case you've gone, "How do I know that name?" Then that's because you read it earlier. She is the mother of the friend Amy stayed over with on New Year's Eve. She's the woman Audrey telephoned to find out where Amy was and told us that she'd left the previous night. Now, if you don't object, please just pause for a second and let that sink in.

Ready? Okay, so here is where the disconnection in my brain begins – I put myself in Debbie Rose's shoes. Her daughter has stayed over at my house, and now she's missing. Please do the same thing with me so far. Right, maybe this is an Irish thing (and I doubt that), but suddenly, I'm wrecked with guilt. I'd consumed with:

"Fuck, I hope she's okay."

"Jesus, she was last seen at my house?"

"I'd better do something to help."

"If she doesn't turn up soon…. I'm in the frame…"

"I'd better do something to help." And quick!

General thoughts and words to that or similar, I would imagine most people would be thinking? Please, just a bit further, I promise, here's what Debbie Rose did…. "Nothing" is it me or is that not at best…. "Odd"…. or at worst – "suspicious"? I've always found it to be suspicious, but the "good-boy-Dave" of me fobbed it off as "odd" at the start because Amy was going to walk in the door any second.

I've written comprehensively about the volume of calls-texts-etc. Audrey and I made at the very beginning and that never let up until much, much later when we weren't making the calls, we were receiving them. Everybody we called would call us back over the hours – days-weeks and months that followed, everybody that is except Debbie Rose, mother of a daughter the same age (-ish) as Amy. The last adult to have a confirmed sighting of a teenage minor who was left in her care. The woman who broke the news to us. Then, when Audrey called her back, she added colour to the initial report, telling us that Amy took a shortcut down a dark and dangerous path of all the "little" details to omit, that I'm sure you agree a bit of a whopper. And now, here's a simple question that's never been answered to my satisfaction.

"How do you know she took it?"

If I were back in her shoes, I'd also feel a responsibility to account for my allowing a teenage girl to take such a route alone, but maybe that is just me because of the landline number that showed up on Audrey's phone when Amy called on new year's, we know that she was definitely in the Rose household. That is a fact. It is undeniably 100% proof. So, a puzzle is placed on the board, the picture looks like Amy is 100% where she said she was and Debbie Rose 100% is the last confirmed person to admit to having seen Amy.

When the media started really running the "Amy story" on all formats, Audrey and I had to decamp ourselves at the hotel Oceania as an ad-hoc but functional H.Q or base of operations. When the T.V. cameras were rolling, Debbie Rose would turn up, dressed and made-up to the nines, as a professional hair-dresser, she had that boxed off too. She'd appear as the camera lights came on, easily the most glamorous person in the room, hog the attention and then disappear when the lights blinked out and the cameras stopped rolling. Once, I could almost forgive out of a sense of "well maybe she is just nervous" or something twice is bordering on narcissism three times is totally taking the piss, four and beyond is no longer forgivable. It's ghoulish. It's the type of behaviour that the lizard parts of our brains click into red alert. About the exact same six balls – pack where murderers turn up to gloat at their victim's funeral. It's wrong, nothing right about it, totally out of sine. When the weeks dragged on, I couldn't let that particular itch go unscratched. I decided to have a word about it with the Guardia Civil.

At the initial meetings, we were two very grateful little Irish people, so thankful for any help the cops could give when we met over Debbie Rose, the glories weren't so much off; they were a distant memory. The little Irish mice were now starving hungry lions and weren't in the mood to eat any more shit.

"We want you to examine Debbie Rose's phone records."

Once again, Audrey and I were ahead of the curve because seriously, how many famous cases had been on the news around that time, relying on phone records as a means of prosecution? A complete slam-dunks of a request a no-brainer.

"Why do you want her phone records?"

We couldn't believe what we were hearing but ever onward:

"Because we've already proved Amy used that phone to call us on New Year's Eve, but who else did they call? Surely, they called other people, two teenage girls alone with a phone at New Year's, of course they did. Amy might've called a girlfriend who's yet to come forward or a boyfriend we didn't know about."

"So, why else do you want them?"

"There could be an Irish number on it we might recognize?"

"And if you can't?"

"Then there's an Irish number on it that we don't recognize, which is even better for us because we've exhausted the numbers we know."

"Hmmm... leave it to us."

That wasn't the first, second or last time we'd asked for those records and to this day, I don't know if the Guardia actually bothered putting them together. You're probably thinking that they must have, or of course they did, but they have different laws in Spain than in Ireland. Probably another hangover from the Franco era, as "a man's private home is his castle." What this distils down to was that Debbie Rose would have to have given her consent to release them, which I don't think she did. Why did I say that? Because months later, I asked again (and again and again) before we were finally told.

"It's gone too late to retrieve those records now."

It is "definitive" – per-se-but to me, it's as good as because of the choice and order of the words they used: not-

"Too late to examine them, "but –

"Too late to retrieve those….."

That, in turn, raises more unanswered questions- Did she refuse to grant them? If so, why? If not - Why didn't the cops get them? In fact, we go back to square one- Did they ever ask for them? It can actually drive you insane, and that's only one of the many threads we were pulling on to unravel this god-forsaken – mystery and all of them were just as ambiguous. Audrey and I, to a fault, are straight talkers. Yes is yes. No is no. We grew increasingly despondent and frustrated by the cat-and-mouse nature of what became every little thing. Our thought rhythms were already all over the place; we didn't need the additional assistance. We made a judgement call, stuff the cops and their red tape. We'll try using the back door, so to speak.

We made contact with a Spanish guy who was high raking employee at Teleonica. We knew him from our experiences of getting all the houses and business phones set up, we offered him a 'fee' to do the research for us and he agreed. I'll never forget his response, the same rare positivity, a lone pearl in a heap of pebbles:

"No problem, I'll get records for you!"

A few days later, he got back in touch as agreed.

"Cannot get them... strange!"

Cannot catch a break. Everything we touched turned into shit. Those simple phone records could've made all the difference in getting our Amy back to us. What next? Well, we still had money, so why not get a private detective? Being Irish, we decided to look into one of our own, but the top of the food chain on our Emerald Isle turned out to be nothing more than an oul gobshite who'd help you with catching an unfaithful spouse but was an otherwise white bread low level bottom feeder we asked around and discovered a guy recommended by Clarence Mitchell. He came highly recommended and seemed to be the best around. They were world-renowned as it happened. We made a few calls and had a series of meetings at Puerto Banus with this crew of P.I's it was quite a cloak and dagger;

"Then they insist on certain rules, for example, tell nobody you are using private detectives."

"Why?"

"We cannot work privately with discretion if anyone knows."

Hence, "private detectives, I guess," naturally a few of the parasitic red-top Irish hacks decided to stay on the Costa to "follow the story" (works on their tan) and had to write something, so among their many fictions, they almost got something right "with all their money why don't the Mahon's just hire a private investigator?" We had, but that was none of their business. It also justified our choice of P.I firm because it doesn't take an awful lot of joining up the dots from us not using an Irish firm to the arrival of that story, does it?

Looking back at the scoreboard, the P.I firm didn't help us find Amy and cost us a lot of money in the process, but they produced reams of priceless reports. Information of a gold standard a lot of our suspicious about Debbie Rose and the reluctance of the Guardia civil to engage with her, confirmed we weren't going mad, it was "a thing"… It truly was. It transpired that she had been in a relationship with a member of the Guardia Civil but had split up prior to Amy's disappearance. The house Amy had spent her last known night in had witnessed a fair amount of domestic violence. It had been reported contemporaneously to Fuengirola Guardia station and was, therefore a matter of record.

We had printouts of Debbies schooling in England, her employment history, her marriage break-up, her hair dressing salons etc. All in a neat file. Not just Debbie Rose either, by the way, we had other persons of interest looked into, but Debbie was the last person to see Amy and had displayed a complete lack of concern ever since we brought our case to the police:

"We need to go up and ask her a lot of questions."

"No. You cannot go near Ms. Rose."

"What?? Did you even read the report?"

"You cannot go near Ms. Rose."

"Amy could be there."

"Unlikely."

"But you're not sure?"

"Well… no."

"She could be hidden up there!"

"Where?"

"I don't know…. maybe under the floorboards for all we know."

"What makes you say that?"

"Fuck off, would you? We've all seen movies and TV and all that. Anything is possible these days."

"I don't think so."

"Really? So, it's more likely that she vanished into thin air, like magic?"

"I didn't say that."

"No, you don't seem to be saying anything, do you?"

"Here, a man's home is his castle, same for women."

"Have you even searched that house yet?"

"We're doing all we can."

Bollox, I don't know how I didn't just storm up to that house and tear it down. Brick by brick. I'd still love to do it even if nothing came out of it. It's another thing crossed off the list, allowing us to focus our attention somewhere else.

We went back to the detective agency and brought them up to speed.

"What should we do with all this info on Debbie Rose?"

"Show it to the senior members of the Guardia Civil, but we must warn you, they won't like that you employed us."

We agreed and called an emergency meeting with some of the top brass. First thing we did was to hand over copies of our reports.

"Where did you get this??"

Not happy that whole Latino, macho-pride thing was well and truly out of joint, the P.I s were spot on.

"We are in charge of this investigation! Understand?"

"We don't care. What are you going to do with this information?"

"Humph…we'll look into it."

"So, you didn't know that stuff?"

"This is our investigation. "

"Yeah? This is our daughter and you should've known this already."

"Anything else?"

"Yeah, you should've known about the domestic violence. It was reported to you before Amy went missing."

"What are you trying to say?"

"Are you deliberately hiding stuff from us?"

"No"

"So you're doing it by accident then?"

"No, what else have you got?"

"Rumours."

"Not always reliable."

"We know that's why they're called rumours."

"Tell us."

"We've heard that she arranges parties for rich clients in Puerto Bauns. Private ones, on yachts…. Dodgy... stuff…"

"We'll look into it."

Did they? I'm not sure they did. Rumours of other, convert, "unusual" things followed Debbie Rose like a bad smell. I was warned in no uncertain terms not to go anywhere near Debbie's house, so I didn't. I became a bad smell in that I too followed her around secretly. Let me clarify that I'm not some kind of a stalker. I followed anyone who I thought may have had anything to do with Amy's disappearance, but Debbie Rose was like "too easy." She went to work, she went home, she went to work, she went home-rinse, and repeat. No social life? (She owned two hairdressing salons) and never socialized? Audrey and I have known a lot of hair-dressers over the years and without exception, they work hard and socialized, not Debbie Rose, though well dear reader, these are the facts I'll let you decide.

If you read our other book – "please find my Amy" then you'll probably be shocked by what you've just read about Richie and Debbie Rose. Not a surprise really because we had, shall we say, "creative /editorial difference," but I don't this time, I don't have a filter I say it like it is. I also promise if you didn't read the "Amy" book, then you won't know about our next suspect, Dougie.

Desperate times call for desperate measures. At this stage of things, Audrey, Dean and I had started to lose faith and respect for the police. Some of them were going above and beyond for Amy, but for the most part, she'd become yesterday's news and we (me and Audrey in particular) were becoming a bit of irritation for them look, no better man than me to be aware – very much so of my shortcomings and imperfections, but I was doing the best I could we all were. However, I'm also a bit of a sponge for new ideas and after a consultation with Audrey, I turned to the other side of the coin. The dark side had its seedy underbelly where demands roamed and angels feared to tread. If the beings of daylight couldn't help us, maybe the creatures of the night could? We'd go on to make serious strides with these people and I'll go into that a bit later, but Dougie was on my radar.

Sometimes in life, you get a lucky break and god-knows we were overdue in that little department. I was approached by a lady with an English accent at a supermarket in La Cala. Amy's face was everywhere because, unlike the boys in Spanish blue, we were doing our jobs properly. Anyway, Audrey and I were plastered on a few walls and T.V. screens as well, so it wasn't uncommon to be approached and wished well by kindly strangers. Long story short, that's what I assumed to be happening on this particular day, only the conversation turned different and this lady told me about Dougie. He too, was English, but even amongst the British villains, he was considered a low-life piece of shit whose name kept coming up in connection to Amy. He was also known to at least one of Amy's friends.

Many people who gossip never bother to check the facts, so if this lady were a gossip or just trying to settle a score with Dougie, I'd be a worse fool. Thankfully, I wasn't. I did my homework via the underworld, established a ring of truth to the story and a meeting was arranged with him, albeit under false –pretences. The first thing I noticed about the guy was that he was "pure poison," if you didn't know anything else about him, you'd tell that he'd been inside more times than he'd been to school. The second thing I noticed was that he carried a firearm. It was in one of those shoulder holsters you'd seen on a T.V. detective show. Not a smart move. Too difficult to reach in a hurry, too much room for a clumsy manoeuvre to happen. My "father protector" sense was working in high gear because I'd soused this guy out in seconds.

If he'd dropped so much of a shift of a hint of a clue about knowing where Amy was, I'd already decided to drop him and pistol-whip him into the Bollox with his own "piece" until I got her back, in my defence I hadn't slept properly in months, we'd no leads and the police had gone to sleep I was that desperate. Let me also add I don't usually have such thoughts on first meeting a person, but again, something felt immediately "off" about this guy. I didn't like him, so we didn't get into any small talk:

"Do you know Amy Fitzpatrick?"

"Eh… n…. no."

"Are you sure? Amy? The young Irish girl who's missing?"

"Oh-eh."

"Heard of her now. Have you?"

"Yeah, yeah sure, yeah I mean, I don't know her, but I heard all about her, sure."

There was something about the look on his face when he said he didn't know her that I couldn't quite put my finger on. I quickly looked at his gun, his groin – and back to his gun again. Two seconds maximum, he was in his 50's seemed like he'd taken something, it wouldn't be difficult, but worse I wanted to hurt him. Instinctual couldn't be helped. The thing is, I had to see this through, Amy is just too important. It wasn't easy, believe me, I swallowed all my pride and every piece of morality I had and started "buddying up" to him like we were plasma head was a war zone of doubt and anger, but one thought won out "This is for Amy, This is for Amy…" he fell for it and then the problem wasn't to get him talking but to stop him.

It was all the usual bullish bravado you'd get from a macho 13 year old with a few girls nearby.

"I battered this guy, special forces "e wuz…"

"Yeah gave it to this bird good "n" and yeah!"

Then he showed me his gun by opening his jacket and pointing:

"That's why I carry a "tool" see, fuckin mad, me."

Deep breaths and then rinse and repeat this Dougie character was a loud mouth and a liability. Unless he came out with something soon. I was leaving –no- "goodbye" or "kiss me arse" I'd just leave. I felt dirty just being near him, three showers and a Turkish bath dirty, that's a minimum finally, he hit a chord.

"Yeah (such and such) a friend of yours Amy, I believe?"

Amy, who he didn't "know" but "heard all about?? (balls-gun-belt-groin)

"Yeah? Go on"

"Yeah, mate, feisty! Took 'er on a road trip to Belgium, didn't I ?!!"

(I had no idea what this meant at the time)

"Really! Wow (actually wanting to vomit seriously)! Why's that?"

"Well, apart from the obvious (winked), it smooths out optics wiff the ol bill, doesn't it?"

"So, c'mon Dougie, did you have sex with her?"

"Did I ever mate! Fuck yeah!!

This pathetic boastful piece of shit had not just told me but loudly bragged about having sexual intercourse with a 15 year old girl legally that made it rape, she being under the age of consent, was unable to give her consent. It wasn't hers to give. That makes him a paedophile. The lowest of the low, I swear to god and I've been nothing but honest all the way through this book, so I'm not going to change now. If I had been there for any reason other than Amy, I'd have killed him stone dead. Think of me what you will, whether I should've just killed him anyway or whatever, but I needed to find out if this reptile was also capable of abducting a girl too. My love for Amy, for Audrey and Dean was all that held me back and even at that once, he'd out-lived his usefulness to me. I was dropping a dime on him to the underworld, then the cops; his exit from his world would come alright. Even villains have rules and paedos aren't welcome anywhere.

I left that meeting shortly afterwards none the wiser, but he was going to ask around (his paedo-network probably) to see if Amy might've gone off with an older man his parting words?

"Mate, don't tell anyone we wuz talking "bout this don't wanna" have a name for being associated with a missing girl, now do I?"

When I got back to Audrey and Dean, I was visibly wound-up but to be honest didn't think he had anything to do with Amy's disappearance. He was still alive and in possession of his genitals, but maybe not too much longer. A couple of days later, I ran into Amy's friend, the one Dougie bragged about raping:

"I met a friend of yours the other day."

"Who?"

"Dougie."

"Ah yeah, how is he?"

Oh god, she actually knew him. My heart broke; every horrible thought rushed into my mind. Please god, don't let it be this, not Amy.

"Did you go on a road trip with him to Belgium?"

"I did, yeah"

"I'm sorry to ask, but he said he had sex with you. Did he?"

"Eh…. no, but he tried to."

Ugh, shitty bastard, I choked back on my own sick. Then asked if he knew Amy.

"Oh yeah, of course she does."

"(fuck) Really?"

"Sure, Amy was in his apartment lots of times"

I looked at Audrey. We didn't know whether to laugh, cry, shout, scream, vomit or jump off the nearest bridge. What had Amy gotten herself into? Who were these people she'd been spending time with? If this girl was telling us the truth, then Dougie probably wasn't a paedo after all, but he was definitely of child rape. What else on top of that? At the time, we had no reason to doubt this girl, as why would we? Later on, we were told by the Guardia that she had a bit of a reputation for being "easy" (their word, not ours), but I don't know if there's any truth to that. The truth is not a matter of personal opinion and as we'd later discover for ourselves, cops love nothing better than a salacious rumour. We looked at the address we'd been given for him. I couldn't believe what I was seeing.

It was only a couple of miles from Debbie Rose. Did they know each other? Chances are they did; then I was struck by an ugly connection they shared her seedy private parties and his proclivity rings and abduction clubs seemed frighteningly real and terrifyingly close to homey called Dougie.

I got no answer. He'd disappeared seemed to be too much of that happening for my taste, so we looked once more at his address by complete fluke, we were able to get access to his keys, the first time either of us had been near an estate agency since Amy's disappearance for good reason. I'll never understand or forgive myself, for we stopped off at the Guardia civil station to update them. We that is, Audrey and I, had finally managed to piece more conclusive evidence together. We had three viable suspects and a potential link into the chain of other similar, local disappearances. Not only that, but also keys to an apartment that we were sure was ripe for a rice harvest of crucial D.N.A. evidence for a spruce of criminality got to be had to be to the honest we were excited, confident that we might actually click a few puzzle pieces into place. We handed everything over and waited and waited and waited. Tick tock…

"Okay, Dave, Audrey…. Do not go near this apartment."

"What??! Why not????"

"You might contaminate the scene with your own D.N.A. or spoil the pre-existing forensic signature."

"So, what are you going to do then? Amy could be there! Still!!"

"We are sending in our scientific team, forensics, D.N.A. ballistics etc. You'd only be in the way or accidentally destroy key evidence. It's a very specialized task, no offence."

No offence taken. We'd done our bit and found the suspect's motive, opportunity, suspicion and a location for them, so what did we know? For all the work we'd put in and dangerous situations we'd willingly walk into, we'd been rewarded not with Amy or news of Amy but with a polite fobbing off. Audrey and I, to this very day-don't believe that they so much as looked in the window of that apartment. We'd handed them a gilt-edged opportunity to do something constructive, but a tree without roots is only a piece of wood. There's no polite way of putting it. They'd fucked us over again. Why? That's an answer I'd love to give you another classic example of the Monty Hall problem.

That, by the way, is based on the game show competition where you have an opportunity to win a car. It's just behind one of three doors, so one has a car and two are empty. Your odds are one in three. So, you culminate door number "1." It's empty. You select door number "2", so far so good. The host then offers you the chance to change your mind. What do you do? Most people will stick with door number "2", the original choice. Why? Because it's worked so far and your odds are now better, it's a 50-50 shootout. That's why most people don't win. The solution to the Monty Hall problem is to change to door number "3" because statistically, your odds jump from 50 – 50 to 2/3. That's why I mention it, if you ever find yourself in the position Audrey and I did, then change your mind. Go to the apartment first, maybe Audrey would spot an item of clothing or a piece of her daughter's jewellery from the off. Don't rely on the cops in fact, don't rely on anyone but yourselves.

It also helps if you befriend the shadow community as early as possible. It's one of our many regrets as the cops sat around on the apartment keys and smoked their brains out. Our other friends established the following facts: Dougie had left in a hurry, not the Costa, but Spain. He'd left a lot of expensive, personal items behind, including a big plasma T.V. The only thing missing from his apartment? I remember having a few guesses laptop? P.C? Stereo system? Not even close. I would still be guessing because I can't honestly say I would ever have thought to say "mattress" send a shiver up your spine? It did for us. Now, I beg your indulgence once again, dear reader, but please – ask yourself, why get rid of your mattress?

Creepy, isn't it? Where do those answers bring you? Disgusting, horrific, painful. Our minds went straight into the darkness of that poor girl, Milly Dowler. The similarities frighten and haunt me still. Doggie's drug dealer friend lived in the apartment above him and spun some tale to the landlord about a leak dripping down on it, but that was absolute horse shit. There is nothing quite so terrible as a child rapist, but a child rapist/abductor enabler runs it close; you see, right there sits the problem. Somebody somewhere knows something. They just won't tell us. Please just pick up the phone, send that email, post that letter, send a pigeon. I don't care. Mark it any way you want; we'll guarantee you confidentiality if that's what you want. Happiness is contingent on making the right choices, please make the right choice. That's all we can ask.

Meanwhile, back at the ranch, we had a missing Englishman to locate and answer some questions. We went to the Guardia. Yeah, why bother, right? Well, to be fair (not that I think they deserve it), some of them barred up and made preparations to go to England. They were stopped by some arsehole of a magistrate who wouldn't sanction it. The dark side answered our request again within 24 hours of my cry for help. Some "friends" of ours knocked on his door in England; he wasn't there, but his wife was with their two kids. I wonder if they'll ever know what a disgusting blight on the world he truly is. Anyway, my phone number was left with her and he called me not so long afterwards!

"Dave?"

"Dougie?"

"Mate, what's going on? Fucking 'ell I already ad a chat wif you, told ya', I know fuck all "bout your Amy."

"Don't lie to me because I know that's all you are. You're a fucking liar, you lied to my face, you said you didn't know Amy…"

"Dave, mate, I.. "

"Get your arse back over here now, pronto."

"Don't know about that mate."

"Have it your way. I'll go over to you so."

"Mate, I've made a lot of calls to Spain too much talk "bout me, I don't."

"Fine, I'll be "eddin back over there."

"Fine, I'll see you over there so."

Then he hung up the weasel. I didn't get to speak to him again, but almost did. We traced his moments until he, true to form, ended back up in prison. An English prison.

Thankfully my nefarious of spies were not only able to locate the prison he was in, but also provided the contact details right down to his cell number. He was back in "the system" and was afforded all the legal protections that came with it, so after chatting to the prison governor myself (as the interpreter for my Spanish lawyer, honestly you couldn't make this stuff up, could you?!). We were denied access to him/had no other choice but to present all the facts to the Spanish authorities. Neither the police nor magistrates gave it so much as a second glance. I'm sure I'll be accused of being disingenuous for saying this, but in their eyes, this was "only some lost Irish girl" in a case that had now (potentially) crossed into U.K. waters, so she wasn't worth the effort or expense. To them, not us. There are many things that now, years later, through the introspective lens of hindsight annoy me to my core and keep me awake at night. This is one such thing we have that amounts to nothing more than a caged pervert. Now, hence to slither away to, no more rocks to hide under with at least a 50/50 chance of throwing a clue over direction, so what do you do? Nothing, we weren't allowed blah-blah-blah "jurisdictional" this or "chain of evidence" that and on and on. Meanwhile, our little girl still hasn't come home. Talk about frustrating unless you've walked in our unwanted shoes, you've no idea. OH, by the way, the police were also investigating a line of enquiry where Amy had supposedly struck up a friendship with an older man, so it wasn't like our information about Dougie went against the grain or would've depleted their resources in any way. We couldn't have dove-tailed any better with their investigation if we'd planned it. Yet we'd still managed to hit a brick wall. We still can't make any sense out of it, but maybe you can see something we couldn't. There was another suspect who came to light much later, but we'll come back to him, as I guess I'd better take this opportunity to first tell you what the Guardia civil. Actually, did you see, at first, they inspired confidence in us.

Nothing quite says "major" operation like the sight of high-ranking police officers, spruced up in more badges and rosettes than a church for first communion - barking orders to their underlings, pointing hither and together in that furiously direct way that only those with "command" bona-fides can pull off properly. We were treated to all that pomp and circumstance, gawping in wide-eyed amazement at how lucky we were, us little "oul Dave 'n' Audrey" from Dublin, to have help

205

of this magnitude to bring our Amy home. Just as we were thinking, "Wow, it doesn't get bigger than this!" We heard its low at first and then building to a deafening crescendo, the 'whuppa-whuppa whuppa' of helicopters overhead as in directly overhead.

When you see a helicopter in the movie, it's like, "meh," so what? However, when you see and hear one directly over your head so close you could almost shake hands with the two officers sitting in the cockpit, their green and white uniforms sticking out against the pale – blue sky like a stairway in a scrap yard a colourful homage to Amy's eyes and nationality in one foul cosmic coincidence it's a different matter. The eleven-year-old-boy inside of you wants to jump up and down and point in biddy excitement at what is undoubtedly a spectacular occurrence. Well, we felt none of it.

You see?? Nothing else says, "Oh my god," this is real. Our daughter is missing and could be hurt, injured, dead or dying, like seeing an army of police officers with air support. It is not only sight but a sound that evokes terror, heartache and desperation into our very blood cells to this day, probably forever although it would be impossible to locate the exact day/hour/minute/second when Audrey and I first felt that Amy wouldn't be home anytime soon, this is close to it, helicopters have that Pavlovian effect on us each time we hear them every spin of the propellers saying "she's gone" this is how it feels, remember this in the dark leaded knot in your stomachs".

Yet for all of that, we must also give deserved credit to the Guardia civil for throwing the kitchen sink in those early days of investigation. Fine-tooth combs couldn't have sifted through the dirt track Amy used to go home on (according to Debbie Rose) any better. They were beyond thorough and extensive, so fair play to them. Then again, that was easy for them. Here's a thing, though; they didn't find anything untoward along that dirt track, nothing. Hmmm….

Remember when I related how good a swimmer Amy was, how she swam every day, sometimes for hours each day? (Please, God she still does.) it follows, therefore, that she'd have a lot of strength in her legs. Think about that-kicking water several thousand times every day over and over. That's muscle memory right there. Think of the other benefits like increased lung capacity, a solid core and upper body strength that is not too farfetched obviously really a fact literally. Now re-examine Debbie Rose's dirt track story. Have you gotten there yet? Well, here's where I am in scenarios: 1. Amy is abducted there. Do you seriously expect me to believe that she wouldn't have kicked out (fast and very hard) and made a run for it? Or scenario 2. Amy is abducted and completely overpowered; therefore no chance to run. Not only does Amy have certainly enhanced lung capacity, but believe me, she had a set of pipes too. She would've screamed at full volume for help and drawn (for them) unwanted attention bottom-line? It is an effort to common sense to believe that Amy would've gone anywhere without a struggle and for no sign, no prints, not so much as a hair to be there or near there is pure fiction that's the realm of little green men and alien abductions as far as I'm concerned. To put another nail in that balloon, Audrey doesn't believe and never did I, that Amy would've walked home that way. I've always been a big believer in a mother's instinct for their children and Audrey's especially.

Still, helicopters can bring you to places you can't get to on foot or in a car and they get there fast. Really fast. They also allow a much broader search area than Audrey, Dean and I could have seen on our own, quite literally, a helicopter view. Still nothing. They flew over every park, cliff and ravine in hells creations and once again, the song remained the same - "sorry, no sign of Amy." There were officers combining every back alley and crack house and still, that song repeated its chorus, over and over and over. Nature hates a vacuum and in the absence of hope and logic, Audrey and I started to think that maybe we shouldn't have made such a fuss because maybe Amy was too afraid to come home. She would be too embarrassed to just walk back in the door now after causing all that commotion and ridiculous thoughts to be having, but that is where your mind goes. The whole Irish thing of "ah sure it'll be grand," sure she is not gone that long really-be weary of letting that get a hold on you. It's poisonous, elusive and pervasive. It softened our resolve briefly, no more than a few seconds at a time, but it kept coming back like a bad headline. The only positive thing I can say about it is that it strengthened our bond. When I was in the "ah-sure's," Audrey would snap me back into affirmative action and vice-versa. These are situations where complete honesty and trust with your partner are essential.

We had too much work to do and negative time to do it. Every passing minute – too late and it was killing us in lots of ways; we'd started to take our attention away from Dean. It wasn't anybody's fault, and he was searching at full-on pedal to the metal frantic pace too - his only sister was missing, he'd rather be damned than sit around not finding her. But we were seeing less and less of each other and at times, that was a blessing. Why? To put it bluntly, a lot of our own investigation led down dark alleys where we'd be faced with questions such as:

"Are you sure she wasn't taken for prostitution?"

"How do you know she wasn't sold off for body parts?"

"Have you tried the on-line kiddie porn sites?"

Fuck me, it got even worse than that and every time I had to hear some shit like that, a little part of me died, but I thank God that Dean wasn't there to hear it. The situation was already too much and if I was struggling to keep a lid on my emotions, then what chance did he have? No way, something you should never have to hear and I hope he never did. The whole sick-to-the-pit of your soul reality though, was that anything was possible, nothing including that grotesque bit was off the table. If you have a sick enough mind, then who knows what evil shit people get up to? Finding your missing child invokes all primal sensibilities and gives you a second/third/fourth wind when mane-mortals doing a job had long since collapsed into oblivion, but when you hear some of the sick alternatives out there. You go into overdrive. You don't even remember to sleep, let alone eat. But you arc a mere mortal, you are not super-human even though you're operating at superhuman capacity. A crash will happen sooner or later and you're only fooling yourself if you think that somehow you'll be immune. Thoughts and ideas that would never have crossed your mind in the early stages were now consuming you. No idea was too stupid. No stone would be left unturned and no avenue would go unexplored.

I can't think of any parent I've ever known who wanted to hear the following words:

"A lot of young girls disappear and go on the game to re-invert themselves…. maybe your daughter is now a prostitute?"

Dear reader, I must ask… Are you a parent? Have you got a daughter(s)? If you answered "yes" to either or both, then your reaction in any other circumstances would surely be to at least punch the person asking you that question. God, how I wanted to, but then again, maybe their lack of tact was counterbalanced by a genuine desire to help? Regardless of the motive, you swallow your anger and knuckle on down to work; then I asked a question I never thought I would:

"Where can I find a prostitute?"

The answer came to me in the form of a Chinese massage parlour in a place called El Zoco. As soon as I entered the building, it just screamed, knocking shop. This wasn't the place to come to for my orthodox physical being, approached by a fairly slight oriental lady.

"Can I help you, sir?"

"Yes, please I'm eh…. looking for a girl."

"Yes, sir. We have lots of girls."

"(realising how it sounded) No, sorry you didn't understand. I'm actually looking for a young girl."

"Oh, (considers me) well, okay sir, we got young girl, very nice."

"What? You have a young girl? Here?"

"Yes sir, whatever you desire, young girl… old girl… all here."

"Ah, for fuck's sake, you don't understand."

"Sir?"

"I'm looking for my daughter, Amy Fitzpatrick?"

"Oh no, sir, she's not here."

"How do you know?"

"Oh, we know of Amy Fitzpatrick, she disappeared. There are posters everywhere."

"Okay, have you seen her around? Heard anything?"

"No sir, so sorry. We hope you find Amy."

Thank you so much. Can you please keep your eyes and ears open for her."

It was a typical response, people know about Amy. It was also a good way to gauge the temperature. No leads, nothing. I went over again to every knocking shop and street corner in town, nothing. Everyone sincerely wanted to help with the posters, but well, you know the rest. We printed off "Tricky Ricky's" thousands of posters; the first ones of Amy where she was dressed in a school uniform. We were slated for using this photo, but can't please all the people all of the time, as the posters were not of political correctness the media had a bit of a moan about them;

"Not very appropriate her being dressed up like a school girl… tut, tut, tut." Audrey and I didn't quite know how to react to that. Do they think we had a portfolio of photos? And we weren't in the right frame of mind to source an appropriate one!

"Really? Go fuck yourself; find our Amy."

Is it a bit too politically correct as a response? No, Audrey and I don't really do the whole "P.C thing. We just want Amy home sorry about that, anyway, it was the most recent photo that we had of her and that is exactly what the Guardia civil told us to do. Yet, for all the kindness and positivity we were getting from the majority, there was always the crass and negative minority. You might not believe that anyone could be so stupid or so insensitive, but the following question was actually put to us, and not just once.

"Could Amy not have left a better photo of herself?"

Yep, that happened. What do these people think? Do they honestly believe that there is a professional photo gallery somewhere that people must go to before getting abducted? As I said, thank god for the majority of logical and reasonably minded people, lots of which were our friends who were absolutely terrific in getting feet on the street and putting up Amy's posters on every spare patch of wall/bus shelter/bridge and window. If they weren't bill-posting, they were handing out flyers with Amy's photograph front and centre. Everyone, it seemed, was very helpful, but then:

"Dave, do you have a minute?"

"What's up?"

"Your woman here won't let us put Amy's poster up in her shop."

"(pointing to the shop owner) Are you serious??"

"Yes, very…"

"Why don't you let us put her poster up?"

"Eggs."

"I'm sorry – eggs?? What does that even mean??"

"At Halloween… Amy threw eggs at my window."

"Okay???"

"So, no poster."

"Look, I don't know if she did or not…"

"….she did."

"….but look, she's missing. This is not a prank, this is very serious."

"Not in my shop. You have plenty of posters up everywhere else."

She wouldn't budge and never even had the good grace to wish us luck in our search. We didn't argue with her; it was her shop. It was a poor decision on her part because everyone knew about it within minutes and her business suffered as a result… Ah, well.

Amy had been reported missing on Wednesday, January 2nd. By Friday the 4th, the media had sniffed out the story and were all over it. It was our first encounter with the behemoth that is the news cycle and we were completely out of our depth. Amy was now the "missing Irish teenager, Amy Fitzpatrick," and it all felt like she was no longer just missing, but her identity her individually had been taken from us too. This, dear reader, is something I hope you never have to experience. I wouldn't wish it on anyone.

The first time we saw her image on the television, it didn't feel real… it's another of those out… of... body this-has-to-be-happing-to-someone-else moments. Amy isn't a T.V. star or a pop star or my kind of public personality to be on TV all the time she's
……you know "Amy," our little Amy, Amy Fitzpatrick, the little mermaid of the Costa del Sol. Missing kids on the TV? Nah, that doesn't happen to us, that's something some other poor family has to deal with; then you change the channel:

"Irish teenager Amy Fitzpatrick is missing …"

No, it can't be. We change over to another channel.

"A massive manhunt is underway in Spain for the missing teenager Amy Fitzpatrick, originally from Ireland."

How many different ways can they say it? The answer would shock you, but the problem stayed the same, no Amy. There are certain things you can write, for example. The Guardia Civil organised a search party that just didn't' get near to describing the meaning of the actual words. The magnitude behind it all. Those seven words don't even rate enough to construct a sentence, yet this is what they don't tell you – your daughter is missing. You can't find her, so you are a failure. You are such a total and complete fuck-up you can't locate another human being, a living, breathing thing-not a set of car keys. How could you be so careless? You obviously don't love her enough otherwise, she wouldn't be missing. You have to go to another group of fully grown adult people who have enough to be doing and aren't nearly as stupid as to misplace one of their kids to try and find yours. They're too nice to come out and say it to you, but they can't believe how dumb you are and your child for getting lost. Hang on, this is real now, isn't it? She's really gone like gone-gone what if we can't find her? What happens then? What if she doesn't come home by herself… there's so much more those words say without saying, but you get the point. Now, try to imagine that torrent of internal abuse coming at you every minute of every day, but multiply that by a factor of ten whenever you hear it on the radio or read it in a newspaper. By a factor of twenty, if it's on the T.V. and yet the irony, you need to continually fan those flames until you get her home, as having her image and details on a permanent public loop is not just your best shot, it's the only one left. Anyone who ever thought letting a child vanish and handing all the responsibility over to the police to sort out was the end of the matter read on.

Search parties are a great idea, covering multiple locations simultaneously, hundreds of eager-fresh eyes scanning for the minutest details. So how do you get one? In Spain, the Guardia did it for us; starting from La Cala de Mijas, who would you recruit into a search party? To be fair, we were given the pick of the crop, we had groups taken from the Red Cross, rescue teams, hill walkers, etc., people with first-hand experience and know what to do. It was a controlled grouping because when an Irish G.A.A team based in the Costa del Sol called to offer their assistance for the search party, the Guardia wouldn't hear of it. Maybe they know what they were doing maybe we can trust cops to get these things right after years of collection experience. Maybe we shouldn't.

All of us turned up and were told to wait inside a tent. There were plenty of tents actually, which was just as well because there were plenty of us, a small army of friends. Thank God for all of their support because we would've been totally lost without them. There are very horrible memories from that time, but one of the worst – by far-was seeing what all of this was doing to Dean. Look, we had all cried – even wailed-but there was just something about the sight of the tents and the organisation of the search teams that registered with him; it broke him. He was a strong, tough and proud kid, he hated appearing "weak or vulnerable" in front of anyone, so to collapse emotionally in such a public area should give you some idea as to his fragile state. It was horrible, the closest thing I've ever seen to a kid holding his heart in his hands, crying uncontrollably and in a low – defeated voice. Repeating, "Ma looks, it's broken, my heart is broken, make it better." Worse, neither I or Audrey could do anything, we were being pulled from pillar to post by what felt like everyone to answer "this question about Amy" or that "question about her" that we (and I hate even saying this) neglected his needs. I wish that weren't the case, but once again, this isn't a book of excuses or written through rose – coloured glasses; you deserve the truth. Truth doesn't contradict itself, so you should have no problem spotting a lie should you come across a monumental discrepancy between what I write and something you may read in a newspaper or else online. I mention this now because we're coming up to some media-stuff shortly and as you'll see, our version of events won't always tally.

Back at the search site, Dean was as low as I'd ever seen him. Thank God for Audrey's sisters because they played a blinder with him and not just the day either to be fair, they really looked after him and spoiled him as rotten as anybody could to try and take his mind off the horror story unfolding around him. Funny little images come to mind like the time. Audrey caught him smoking a cigarette (who could blame him?). I'd known for a while that he smoked but promised not to "rat" on him to Audrey that first time she'd seen him pulling on a ciggie, it killed her but she let him off the hook. How we both wished that- that –could be the biggest problem to deal with. The soundtrack from that day wasn't Audrey giving out to her son. It was the sound of his heartbroken screams of pain. It was the constant:

"Dave! Over here…"

"Audrey! Can I ask if…."

But sometimes, we couldn't even hear ourselves think:

"Whuppa-whuppa-whuppa-whuppa."

More helicopters, some flying off in the distance, others hovering low overhead, a couple more landed and powered down. I know they were there for Amy, I know they performed an otherwise impossible function, but my God, did they stir-up a horrible sensation in the pits of our stomachs. As that difficult, productive, exhaustive, but ultimately fruitless day drew to an end, we heard the first of what would become a constant intrusion:

"Dave, Audrey –give us a story!"

213

There were lots of requests like that, everyone shouting and scrambling over each other to get to us first, but Franco Rey signalled to us to say nothing and beckoned us to come over to him. Along that short walk over to him, a man's (whom I later discovered to be a journalist) shoulder charged me – hard and deliberate in my chest. It was clearly a tactic of provocation. Perhaps he wanted me to attack him, get involved in a brawl of some kind? I don't know, but had I taken the bait, it would've undone all the good that had been done that day for Amy, so I didn't however, it has been another hard and exhausting day and my patience was hanging by a thread and I wanted him to know that he was out of order, so I gave him a "look" that was all his waiting opportunist friend a photographer –needed –click. That was the photo the media uses of me for months. Not helpful. Franco copped it.

"Dave, Audrey, don't engage with the media."

"What? We need them for Amy! Why not use them?"

"I can tell you from my own personal experience that they are a scum sucking bunch of lying bastard parasitic leeches; they couldn't give a fuck about you: Audrey, Dean, any of it they smell blood, Amy's blood. They actually want for Amy to be dead."

"What??"

"And not just dead but death by the most horrific methods. If it was slow, painful or the cream on top of the cake-sexual with sexual residence discovered on her corpse, then it's party-time for them; if they could link that to you Dave, they'd fill their pants with happy-joy-shit because you'd be the Spanish Hannibal Lecter if Amy isn't found. They'll go through yours and Audrey's private lives with a fine tooth comb and let me tell you, none of us are angels."

"France, you're talking a load of Bollox."

"Oh?"

"Think what you like, we've nothing to hide and Amy won't be found, dead know why?"

"Do tell."

"Because we're going to find her, that's why and the media will help us."

"I think it's a mistake."

"Noted, we're getting Amy home."

So, Amy was big news. We had never seen a media circus like it. Scores of TV cameras, myriads of journalists from everywhere and from among the crowed we could just about make out some Irish accents. We later discovered that a group of Irish reporters had made the trip down. That was good we recognized one of them, it was Paul Reynolds from R.T.E and he gave Audrey and me a little nod. We reciprocated and then Audrey agreed to say a few words.

"I just want to say thank you to everybody, all the press, all the police and I'd just appealed to everybody especially down in Spain. All the Irish and the British communities, anybody that knows anything if they can remember anything – even if it stupid: something small, something they think they might have seen, just ring up anytime, day or night.

There, it was short – sweet and to the point. That's Audrey encapsulated right there. It stands as accurate and as vital today as it did then. To be honest, we welcomed all the media attention, scary as hell but necessary. We started pumping out interviews left, right and centre. Anything to keep Amy's photo on the T.V. screens on the front of newspapers and in the public conciseness. We did our jobs, on that score, nobody can ever say we didn't. Then all of a sudden, the big empty pond of hopelessness that had remained still and life less for so long had a ripple; we got a phone call from a friend of ours:

"Dave, I've heard something you need to know."

"Go on, I'm listening."

"It's about Amy."

"Go on."

"The Guardia have a suspect."

"Who?"

"Richard O' Shea."

"Fuck off, Richie??"

215

We spoke to Richie and he confirmed that he was called into the station because "they had a few questions" for him. We were too shocked to ask him how it went, why he was a suspect or anything else. Like I said, when you're not sleeping and living in a constant state of stress, you'll make mistakes. Not pushing him on those questions was a mistake, but we'd never thought for a minute that he would've had anything to do with Amy's disappearance even though you need to be suspicious of everyone well, we think it now, he has outstanding answers we need to hear.

The media had set up camp on the Costa and even though we hardly got a moment of peace, they were a great help, ten out of ten, I won't blame them. As much as we managed to saturate all the local haunts and hot-spots with posters and pamphlets, we were only in the ha' penny place in comparison to the global reach possessed by the associated news media and for that, we'll never be able to thank them. But still no Amy. Here we go once again, dear reader. What would you do next? For us, the answer sat with the tool in our "disappearance" tool box produced the biggest "bang" for the buck… a press conference.

Have you ever given a press – conference before? No? We hadn't either and the thought of it was overwhelming. Naturally, Franco was dead against it:

"You can't do this. They will look into your private lives every little aspect will be fair game."

"We've nothing to hide."

"You're missing the point. Audrey – you've had a messy divorce, your son Dean has been in trouble with the law, and you – Dave, you've said it yourself, you are "no angel" and everybody has a past. Your lives will never be the same again, please – I implore you-don't do this."

"Franco, we hear you, but Amy needs this."

"You're still not listening to me. I was a reporter; even now, I could still tear you to shreds.

"Fine…. Look, give us a few minutes to think about it."

Actually, that was rhetorical; we took time out. Regardless, I went off by myself to have a drink and consider the pros and cons. The glass had barely touched my lips when I had a very brutal epiphany.

"Fuck Franco, fuck the media and fuck me for even contemplating the thought of not doing it. Amy's out there, still we don't know where or how much time she might have left, Dave, stop being such a prick and get your shit together."

That's what we did; Franco was upset.

"Haven't you listened to a fucking word I've said??"

"Franco, take that attitude and shove it up your arse."

"What?"

If your daughter ever went missing, you'd do exactly the same thing."

"Well…"

"So here's how it is: I'll pray to god and pray to the devil in order to find Amy. Nothing or no-one will ever get in the way of that."

Choose your battles carefully, or so they say, so Franco dusted off his pride and set about doing something we wouldn't have been capable of doing, organising a press conference. We picked the venue, a happy and familiar place utilising home-field advantage, if you will, the Oceania in La Cala de Mijas, the nicest hotel in the whole of Spain. It didn't hurt knowing the owners, who happened to be good friends of ours and they gladly gave us the use of their facilities to stage the conference.

For such a huge event, you'd be surprised how quickly it got arranged and as we drove into the Oceania, we were blown away by the sight before us, scores of reporters swarming over every inch of the hotel. We'd never seen anything like it before. I remember parking the car and looking into Audrey's face, mirroring my wide-eyed look of dumfounded. In my own dulcet tones, I managed to eloquently capture the moment in just two little words – "Fuck me." I still couldn't be more succinct. Thank God for the army of supportive friends and family with us, as only for them I might've bottled the whole thing. Even getting out of the car and into the hotel was a terrifying ordeal. Audrey and I gripped each other's hands and thought of Amy. As we walked into the hotel and got swallowed up by the media masses; every step we took had another question thrown at us and the "click-white" of thousands of cameras dulled our senses, already blinded by the fit inducing photo-flashes flickering like a thousand splendid suns through our closed eyelids. They were like carrion feeders at a carcass, stripping all the flesh off the bone, then bone feeders, further reducing the remains to a cloud of dissipating dust. We

217

weren't and never will be used to that kind of behaviour. Whatever new world we'd just gotten ourselves into, one thing was for sure, we weren't and never will be used to that kind of behaviour. Whatever new world we'd just gotten ourselves into, one thing was for sure we weren't in Kansas anymore, Dorothy.

Franco barged his way over to us and started trying to tell us the itinerary, but we couldn't hear a word of what he said over the noise of the reporters. I, however, have never had much of a problem being heard, so I told him to talk to the media:

"Try to calm them down, get them to behave themselves a bit and we'll do the conference in a while, 15 minutes maybe." We genuinely needed at least that to let our heads catch up with the rest of us before we went "in" the room. We had to have a moment to try to compose ourselves. Franco agreed and then told us that he'd prepared something for Audrey to read.

"Read what, like now or something??"

"No, to read out to the press."

"Oh, okay, give it to me so."

"No."

"What?"

"No."

"Why not?"

"I don't want to read it first or rehearse it, just read it out straight, more natural."

Now we truly were in the merry –old-land-of Oz, better Audrey than me in that particular situation. I have no problem speaking in public, but don't ever ask me to read something out in public. I've never been comfortable doing that (probably the latest hang-over from school! Suppose.) We noticed a Guardia standing off to the side in his civvies, then finding a seat and sitting alone. We'd copped him straight away because he used to drink at our bar and for reasons I won't go into, we know that he was more crooked than a shepherd's staff, but so what he came there to help us. We went over to say "hello" to him (the least we should do), but he knew no English, so Audrey took care of the Spanish greetings! He wished us luck before we headed back over to a very worried looking Franco Rey:

"How do you know him?!"

"Ah, he used to drink in our bar."

"(gasps) He is a bandit."

"We know!"

"Okay, quick, let's get going."

We were ushered over to a massive table longer than a shipping container and loaded down with more microphones and recording devices than you'd find at a level 42 concert. Everything was powered on God-knows what those million tiny red lights had picked up already. In the centre of that electronic spiders-web sat a few empty chairs facing into the micro phones like a dress rehearsal for a firing squad.

"You sit… here!"

"(to-Franco) Where's the Guardia civil?"

"Oh, they wouldn't come to something like this!"

Wrong choice of words, Franco. I was absolutely furious, but I'd learned a lesson after my brush with that asshole cameraman /journalist, so I kept schtum, took Audrey's hand, got up and we walked away, stormed away would be closer to the truth and as we walked, the cameras exploded into action. Franco shit his parts in an effect to catch up with us:

"(gritted teeth) What the fuck are you doing there??"

"The press conference is off Franco, unless you get us a decorated officer with all his bells and whistles. on, and one actually assigned to Amy's case too, no day-trippers."

"What for??"

To answer questions and be held accountable for his answers; otherwise, he could just fob us off, but those days are over. Besides, what would we know about an investigation? Let the media grill them, hopefully, they'll be able to ask all the questions we don't know or can't think of. Audrey took a breath and then agreed. Just between us, reader, we were never going to cancel. Are you crazy?! But we couldn't take the chance of giving Amy's first press conference any veneer of amateur hour. It was vital, in our opinion, to set off on the right foot. In our heart of hearts, we prayed that Amy would get to see this. See how much she is loved, see how hollow our lives were without her and that, no matter what. She'll be welcomed back with arms wide open. We also hoped that whoever was responsible for her absence was watching us too. We wanted them to know that we weren't going anywhere without our daughter. Subconsciously too, I suppose it was a show of strength to the coward responsible – "hey you, you gutless piece of shit, loot at us. Really, look at us. Do you see any quitters in front of you? That's right, you don't, sitting in front of you loud and clear are loving parents who want what you stole brought back home safe and sound. By the way, we're also hunters supported by an army of other hunters. Some are in uniform, most without and if we all gotta hurt you, we will. We'll find you too. eventually and when that happens, well there'll be a reckoning, "let's leave it at that." Let's be honest, it's harder to send that message without police presence, right?

We had held-up in the ladies' toilets while we waited to get away from everyone but also to stay out of sight. It's more worrying when people can't see you to read your body language or whatever it is these armchair psychologists profess to know; it also afforded Audrey the opportunity to "tear me a new one" for that stunt if she wanted to. She didn't thank god, all she said was:

"Dave, what are you doing??"

I got off lightly; Audrey and I would walk through the gates of hell for each other (some would argue that we've already done that), confident that whatever reason we had for doing so, the other one would support it 100%, don't think that a day goes by where I don't realise how lucky we are to have that, because it doesn't. Anyway, after I explained my reasons to Audrey, she rowed right in with me. A united front, thank God. I'd be dishonest to say that I know down to the minute how long we waited it out, but I'd be confident in saying that it was no more than 20 minutes. Franco led us out and as we crossed the foyer, we got another little nod of encouragement from our bandit friend. A few undercover officers noticed this (missed nothing, it seemed) and approached us:

"You know – him??"

"Yeah, why?"

"A fucking ban-dido, that's why!"

220

We didn't observe a single differ sit near or speak or even acknowledge their ban-dido colleagues. Interesting, sitting at our table, however, was an officer in close enough approximation to what we wanted, another horde-won battle for Amy. We took our seats and then I went deaf or at least I thought I did because the low murmur of white noise that had constantly been there just died flick of a switch type silence. Holy shit, we better not fuck this up. I'm not sure what stage – fright is exactly, but my mouth went as dry as a baggers arse and I gave Audrey a sheepish look and held her hand. Then, this amazing wife of mine, this "lioness," held up. The page Franco gave her and started to read it out.

"I just want to appeal to anyone out there who may have seen Amy to get in touch with the Guardia civil. Somebody must know something. She is a popular girl with lots of friends from school and from around the area. A girl doesn't just disappear, doesn't just vanish from the face of the earth.

I was blown away by the strength, composure and courage of my Audrey. You hear stories about mothers over-turning crashed cars to get their kids out to safety and think, "Hmm," I don't know about that. Well, this was the oral equivalent, she continued:

"So, I'm asking if people can just look back on the night and if they do remember seeing a teenage girl waiting alone in the area where she was last seen. Even the slightest bit of information may be important and lead us to finding her..."

Right then, right there, she finally broke down. I can't even begin to explain to you how hard that was for her to do. I still can't believe it myself, but she did better than I would have, that's for damn sure. Her emotions were raw and honest, but Franco's little "plan" had worked. He was playing this little chess game at least ten-moves ahead of us, the advantage of not being personally invested in the outcome, I suppose. Fair play to him. We needed that level of detachment if we were even going to be effective. Because Audrey couldn't see through the oceans of tears that finally broke through, she couldn't finish reading out the rest of the statement. Her niece-Nicola. A beautiful person who loved the ground Amy walked on took up the reins:

"I'm just terrified that someone has got Amy and is holding her against her will. If that is the case, then please just let her go. We just want Amy back. We are devastated. Every day that goes by, we are more and more worried that something has happened to her. I also want to send a message to Amy- if you decided to run away, then please come back your brother, Dean misses you and we all love you so very much, please come home. You are not in any trouble, we just want you back. Don't be frightened; we just want Amy home.

In the absence of any better way of saying it, the press conference was a great success. Now, at last, the Irish, English and Spanish press had more than just a few tired old sound bites to run with. Now they had something big, something "juicy" (an industry word, not mine) that personified "Amy Fitzpatrick" no longer a name or just a jumble of words like "missing Irish teenager," now she was "somebody human." A huge advantage, why? Well, studies show that in situations where (and I'll refer to them properly) those sick -weirdo – fucks who take children against their will start seeing them less as "objects" and more like "people," they are less likely to hurt or, god forbid, kill them. It appears easier to destroy an object, whereas destroying a "person" has psychological conflicts for them. Let's not plough that field any more than it has to, eh?

The media, as expected, had no end to their question, but guess what? We loved them for it because they were doing their jobs and that was a level of power and influence that fed starving nations and put wars to an end. We had secured a global weapon to fight a "local" problem and we were going to give them as much ammunition to load their weapons whenever and however they wanted it. That's the deal and it's a fair one of their first questions was exactly what was needed!

"Audrey, is there something you hold with you or would like to hold with you to remember Amy by?"

"Yeah. ...the fridge!!"

It was easy to see where all the Irish journalists were sitting because that was where all the laughter came from! Unfortunately, the silence from the Spanish media was defeating. Audrey's little joke was lost in translation shit that was awkward.

"Fridge? What is fridge?"

We then had to explain that Amy's favourite place was at the fridge, her nose sticking in and her arse poking out. Even though she was as slim as a cat-walk model, she ate like a junk-yard dog (Amy, if you're reading this, I'm sorry, but it's true!!) Look, we all know that this is not a laughing matter none of this nightmare is even remotely funny; it's as far from funny as east is to west, but we're Irish and making light of adversity is what we do better than anyone, in Spain, it translates

222

as "black humour," and it's what we'd call "gallows humour" and fuck it, Audrey had just begged the world to give her baby back and broke down after inhuman pressure, her moment of levity was a survival tool if anything, hardly an indictable offence so give her a break, happily the rest of that conference and the subsequent ones, all of them went smoothly. We got to know and understand the rules of these encounters and to be fair, they got to know us and our strange little Irish quirks. Press conferences were one thing our domestic discussions were heartbreakingly brutal; they had to be:

"Do you think she ran away?"

"No"

"Maybe she met a fella – an older man? English may be?"

"Why English?"

"There is a lot more of them around than the Irish."

"Fair point. What else? Prostitution?"

"God forbid. Drugged? Then held against her will?"

"Jesus, what if she's just lying there in a river like Rory was?"

"Fuck's sake, hope not Jesus."

"Human trafficking?"

It went on – and-on-and like that. We didn't have a bull nation as to what had happened, so we filled that annoying little void with as much horror and negative as we could. This is a phenomenon common to a lot of parents of missing children around the world. How fucked up is that? The best-case scenario is always that the child just upped and ran away-always. We knew that in our scenario, that wasn't true because she would've been home long-ago, or at the very least, someone would've seen her.

After we got home from the press conference, we had a multitude of calls and correspondence to address and reply to and it was in the throes of such productivity that Franco called our home. He wanted to see how we were after that monumental event and if we were holding up okay.

"We're exhausted but buzzing if that makes any sense?"

"It does. You're going at 200mph it's tiring, but 100 hyped-up to stop."

"Something like that, Audrey did unbelievably well. I'm so proud of her."

"As you should be. Did we cover all of the bases?"

"To be honest, no."

"No?"

"No, when Audrey was speaking, my thoughts were all about her, what she must be going through-emotionally how both of our hearts weren't broken; they are smashed beyond any hope of repair. Even if Amy came home-now-we'll never get all those lost days back, how will she cope? Will she be the same person-how could she be??"

"But?"

"I would have loved to have spoken my mind... "

"Why didn't you?"

"Because I wanted to say that if I get my hands on the person or persons responsible for this, or if they have harmed her in any way I will kill them, you know, something along those lines..."

"Oh, Dave, Dave, Dave, you can't, you cannot ... "

"Why not? Why does everybody always say the same sort of things over and over? Why can't they say something real? Raw? From the heart? Tell me I'm wrong! Show me one parent –just one anywhere in the world. He isn't thinking those thoughts or thoughts like them? Amy's parent who is looking down the barrel of abduction, kidnap. or worse?"

"Because the media might not like it, it gives the wrong sequence of sound bites."

"Fuck the media and fuck their sound-bites."

"Unfortunately, Dave, this is the world we live in. "

"Yeah, but until one of their children - your children – disappears and goes missing, nobody will understand."

"Yes, Dave, I hear you, I do. But you've left something out."

"What??"

224

"Say you did say that. Say the media ran with it. Now, he says that someone did take Amy. They watch Audrey breaking her heart and then see you beside her and issuing verbal threats."

"Right?"

"Dave, people like that would probably "get off on it.""

"What???"

"That's what we're dealing with. That's why you never hear such raw and brutal honesty."

You could've knocked me down with a feather. We were definitely through the looking glass. Now a whole new darker territory; as if to punctuate that fact, we received a call from the police. They'd found something and wanted us to confirm that it was Amy's! That was it, nothing more, was it clothes? Hair? God forbid – a body part? Or the absolute worst case-her body? The horror of not knowing what could come next lines with you like a relentless, satanic shadow you stumble around in an ever-present darkness where no light gets in. Audrey and I had to meet the police "immediately" over in front of Debbie Rose's house. We met the police car, or rather its full-on high beams, between Debbie Rose's house and the darkened dirt track where Amy supposedly made her way home. We didn't see an ambulance or a coroner's van; that was a good "sigh," I knew then, that it wasn't the worst-case-scenario. I was handed a guard's evidence bag. No parent of a missing child ever wants that. No talk, just an evidence bag. No talk, just a solemn handover. I couldn't breathe, I tried to swallow, but my mouth had evaporated all of its moisture. I had a very simple task look in the bag and speak "Yay" or "Nay" as to whatever it was Amy's, I cracked it open a pad and then slowly looked down. Clothing fuck. This is it   trousers or pants of some type (I'd later be told that they are called "leggings"), black in colour, they looked like ladies' trousers, alright   ! I didn't know part of me wanted to have something, a lead of some description to get us to Amy. But I didn't know I wasn't the man for this particular job, what do I know about women's clothing? I looked over to Audrey, then showed them to her;

"What do you think, Audrey?"

"No"

"No?"

"Sure, they're huge for too big to be Amy's."

225

Of course, they were. What the fuck was I even thinking? You could've put Amy's into them. Gobshite, the Guardia then showed Audrey a shoe. Even I could've gotten that one right, it looked like a yeti owned it, not a teenager, another brick wall. The endless labyrinth search continued as fruitless as always something that's a blessing. I don't think I could handle identifying Amy like I did Rory, but then. Well then, you've got that complex old problem that parents of the disappeared refer to as "closure." Negative thoughts are always negative thoughts. This, dear reader, is what hopelessness likes. How many times can you push your body beyond its limit of psychological and emotional boundaries only to go to bed, hope for sleep that might "come and think over and that you've achieved.... Nothing. All your efforts count for shit. You'd have been better off doing nothing from day one, fuck it, sure, the result is just the same, only that is something you could never do, and love doesn't allow that. Love gives you a strength you never thought you had. Love is persistent; it doesn't keep a count of the failures and whispers in your ear, "c'mon, just one last push, this could be the one! You can do it!!" When the relentless failures dull your senses, your partner (your "Audrey") kicks in and takes over, then you're for her brings you back sounds easy. It leaves a scar and sometimes you can't see the wound until it's pointed out to you. Then you have to sit up and take notice because you're dying.

Whilst our health was definitely taking a hammering, our business was, too. Why give a shit? "Because we had a life," and also, we have to pay for all of the search materials and costs, etc. "Just" because your child is missing doesn't cut any slack with the banks, especially in Spain. We were falling behind on our mortgages and credit card payments. All the usual fun stuff it took for me to stand in an office of a friend of mine in Fuengirola to notice how much I'd taken my eye off the ball.

It transpired that this "friend" of mine owed me a little bit of money. You know, just shy of $70,000, how I had let it get that far was obvious. How he had wasn't, it was opportunist at best. Almost all of my friends and family had been badgering me to go back to work.

"C'mon, Dave, sure Amy only ran away, you need to stay on top of things...."

Stuff like that, I'd put it on the never-never; next week, then next month and the next and the next. You don't see the time go. But next-month never came and a goal without a deadline is only a dream. That day was my deedless day. I guess you could say that our discussions had reached the halfway point,, which, in hindsight is disgraceful as he should've just paid out what he owed because (a) he owed it and (b) it was obvious where every cent was going to go but be that as it may, it had to go into "discussions" we never got finish that transaction because my phone started ringing:

"David Mahon?"

"Yes?"

"This is the Guardia Civil, at Fuengirola station."

"Okay?"

"We need you to come and see us."

"Sure, no problem. Have you got something??"

"Well, we need you to have a look at some forensics..."

All the strength left my body like snapping your fingers, quick as that you know when you hear people say things like "Oh, I went weak at the knees" or some such? I actually really went weak in the knees, not a figure of speech. I reached out, grabbed a chair that luckily was nearby and collapsed into it. My hands were shaking uncontrollably; all my muscles went on strike or got "shacked" or something because I had no say in what they were doing. I felt like I was going to faint-why? Because I'd forgotten to breathe, that satanic shadow loomed right over me, smiled its terrible –awful-grin at me and filled my head with an unspeakable evil. "Forensics" could only mean one thing, even a "thick" like me knew that it was over. We'd lost Amy forever. I started trying to reason away my fears:

"Please, God, was it quick."

"Hopefully, it was an accidental death. No "funny-business," please."

Then, I snapped myself out of my mental fog. Where was I? How would I get to the police station from here? You start off with easy questions like that and build yourself back up. I was ten minutes away from my date with destiny; no further than that, I had to focus, something was missing... of course, Audrey! That's what the shock of the word "forensics" did to me. It pulled the plug in my head and drained all sense out of it. I took out my phone, called Audrey and told her the news. Another very difficult call. I asked her to come up to Fuengirola and then she asked a very simple question:

"Can you give me a lift?"

Questions don't come much easier than that, but I didn't know how to answer her! I couldn't tell her that I was shaking like a wet dog because I couldn't control the muscles in my own body, that I couldn't walk, let alone drive.

"Eh..... no... no, eh, I'll meet you there. Just jump into a taxi..."

Audrey booked her taxi and ended up giving me a lift to the police station.

"How come you're not driving?"

"I can't."

"What? What do you mean?"

"Look.... Audrey ... this isn't going to be good."

"(heart sinking) oh god. ...what is it? Dave? What haven't you told me?"

"They want us to look at some forensics. They don't call you unless they have news."

"Oh, Jesus ....."

The taxi stopped outside the Guardia civil station, a building that had seen more of us than Dean had in recent weeks and it was the last place in the entire universe I wanted to be. I have to tell you, that short walk through the door was one of the longest of our lives. Think about that. Every step forward feels like acceleration into your daughter's death. You are rushing into the nuts and bolts of how she died everything in "glorious Technicolor." As they used to say, forensic details..... literally. Anyway, we pushed through the doors and announced ourselves.... quietly, we were ushered over to a group of uniforms and with them was Franco.

"What is it?? Do you have bad news for us?"

In these moments, everything slows down. You read into every look, every nuance, every sigh or shoulder shrug; life hangs in the little details. Are they making eye contact or avoiding it? What does either one mean anyway? Their choice of language – words are important-always-but so too is the parlance with which they are delivered. You aren't living on your nerves. You are living on the tiny precipice at the external of where your endings taper into nothingness. The

228

slightest drop in the temperature, the softest breeze and you're over the edge, lost forever-

"Please come into this room with us."

Hmm- "please," a request of kindness. A soft word, a don't strictly the grieving parent's word? Why do they want us to go into a room? Are they expecting us to have a bad reaction? A hysterical, terrible reaction, maybe? We follow them into the room, operation entirely on autopilot. This is going to be "the" room we'll have nightmares about once its terrible secrets reveal themselves sight you can't unseen words, you'll never unhear that will echo into eternity. This will be the room to end all rooms. This will kill us both we'll never come back from this; enough is enough, this is too much.

"Please sit down; have a seat."

Another "please," another kindness, followed by another one- "sit-down" -the passive position. It's much easier to control hysteria when the subjects are seated. You don't want to deliver bad news to standing people. Too many variables in play to control, will they faint? Run? Get violent? Hug you? No better to deliver bad news, the worst news, to seated, passive participants. They opened a bag, took out a magazine and handed it over to us. It was one of those glossy publications with pictures of models on every page. One of the pages had a tag, a marker for us to go to.

"You see the model on this page, this girl?"

"Yes."

"Is.... this... Amy?"

"No."

"No???"

"No, that's not Amy."

"Oh."

"What do you mean – "oh?" Is this why you brought us here??"

"Well... yes."

"You thought this (pointing) looked like Amy??"

"Yes."

"That's it? That's your forensic???"

"Yes."

"Oh, my god.... c'mon Audrey, we're out of here."

I was glad we hadn't driven there because we were both fit to be tied. A magazine with a picture of a girl that sorta/kinda had a passing similarity to Amy? Fuckin eejits, splashy/flashy/glossy Spanish magazine, with their office, they could have sent the page to us, "contact us" they had our address details, emails/websites – the whole nine yards, a monkey sitting in a pool of his own piss could've picked up a phone.

"Hello, that model on page 22. ..is her name Amy? No? Okay, thank you."

Job done, Q.E.D., simple as that. Not for the first time, we stormed out of that police station – biting our tongues – trying desperately not to let them feel the full verbal slaughter their incompetence deserved. We still needed them; they were the only game in town with the resources necessary to find Amy fuck me-rock? Meet hard place. We needed a drink. It took several large brandys. I feel like a few more now just thinking about it.

Our consolations that day were two-fold first, Amy is still alive. We have hope (we still do) that second lightning couldn't strike twice. We'd never have to go through that again rant at our insistence – would let them know how wrong that had all been handled, so just keep looking onwards and upwards tick-tock. Time passes, new leads and new disappointments. Nobody is telling the "back soon just ran away for attention" story any more. Now, each time we enter a large group, hushed whispers of Amy's demise grow louder. We hear words like "tragic" and "awful" but don't pursue the conversation. We can't. We don't blame them; it's nothing we haven't already thought about and cried about every other day. Our morals are low, our funds are dwindling and our health, well we don't even recognize ourselves anymore. The mirror in our home reflects a different couple back at us, an older couple haggard, broken and exhausted. They look like a version of Dave and Audrey walking out of Auschwitz. There is no spark of life in their eyes. They look beaten. Time relentlessly goes on, no news, no leads and no Amy. Hope and terror see-saw with every knock on the door, every new email and every text or call. Then, out of the blue, I get together "might be something" call from the police,

"Did Amy ever go to a dentist?"

A smart question. A different approach, perhaps?

"Yes, she did."

"Where did she go?"

Encouraging, why didn't we think of this before? Very specific questions, these:

"To the one in Calahonda."

"Dave, go there and get her dental records. Bring them to us."

Shit. Dental records. We all watch TV. We all know what this means.

"Do you have news for us?"

"We can't discuss this."

Short, punchy responses. No chit-chat. No bullshit. This was different. I called Audrey, yet another call I wish I'd never had to make. Even she sensed something different this time. I wasn't imagining things, but that's where the good news ended. For the first time, she couldn't go with me not to the dentist, the shock just too much for straws-camels backs bridges too far. Choose your own analogy; a mother's heart can only shatter into so many pieces and hers had no more "break" left to give, not that day. I made another journey into the valley of death alone and I feared all evil.

I knew the girl working at the dentist's reception desk and explained the situation to her. The look on her face said it all, she'd been asked for dental records. For the police before, it was always the same reason. It never deviated, it was a scientific coffin nail. She got me what I asked for-no fuss and as she handed them over to me, her rapidly watering eyes betrayed her strong, hopefully, "good luck," she meant it too; we needed it. Amy needed it more. In my hands lay the answer we'd been waiting for. But not this way, I drove to the station in Fuengirola. Another excruciating drive. The number of times I thought about those records, "losing" them or just not handing them over as I made the short journey would probably surprise you. I parked my car and just sat there, staring at the brown envelope, A4 size, quite light in weight, not even close to an extra postage charge and yet its contents hung heavily on whatever future myself, Audrey, Dean and Amy were about to have. Imminent doom has strange effects on a man;

"C'mon Dave, open the door.... just open the door..."

You start all these little mantras inside your head, baby-stepping your path into your oblivion:

"Good job, now, take the keys out of the ignition....."

"Okay, just pick the envelope up, don't think – do- it's only an envelope."

That was the hardest part. I didn't want to touch it-see it-acknowledge it, it was an agent of evil, it was killing Amy and I knew – knew- that when I handed it over, I was delivering the death stroke. That envelope contained Amy's wedding day, the birth of all the children she was ever going to have once it sealed. To break the seal, for the Guardia civil to peek inside it and use its contents to reveal what they surely suspected was to let the genie out and seal Amy's tomb. To not hand it over was to live forever in ignorance but with a distant spark of hope. Dear reader, pray you never have to walk in those shoes. I walked in through the double doors of my gates of hell and announced my business to the desk sergeant – the anti-St. Peter's guide into the realm of eternal tournament:

"Oh yes, we were told to expect you. You have the records?"

"Yes, Amy's dental records are in this envelope as requested."

"I'll take them from you. Thank you."

"Huh?"

"I said thank you. I'll pass them on."

"Is that it?"

"Huh??"

"I thought I was coming here to identify a body or something?

"No, we just need her dental records."

"Yeah, but ...why?"

"Oh, just for files, you know."

"I'm sorry, could you just..."

"Our files. It's much easier if you get them for us."

"You're eh.... serious, right??"

"Of course."

Smug, unprofessional prick, oh, I was beyond angry now. If anybody's face was crying out for a slap, it was his, but I couldn't - Guardia civil and all of that crap. So I did the only thing I could do. I put both my hands on his counter and stretched my neck over it until I could see his feet;

"Everything okay, Mr. Mahon?"

"Grand yeah"

"Eh. ... what are you doing?"

"Looking"

"Looking? For what?"

"Well, I can see your phone on the desk."

Yes, why are you looking at my shoes?"

"I'm not, I'm looking for a puddle of piss."

"Excuse me?"

"Do you like bananas?"

"Eh. ... yes??"

"(Whispered under my breath) I bet you do, fuckin ape."

"What was that?"

"Hmm?"

"Did you say something?"

"No, anyway, if you want anything else, let me know, okay?"

"Eh. ... yes, thank you."

Arsehole, I practically took those double doors off their hinges on my way out. This was not how I thought I was going to feel leaving the Guardia Civil that day. That is not under my circumstances. My relief at not having to identify her body or news of that kind, no way. Thank God for that blessing, but I was utterly stupefied by how crass and unprofessional they were being. A mad dog with a hammer up its arse could see that requesting dental records wasn't a big goal, it was a game changer; such things conjure a miasma of pain, fear, hopes, dreams, and memories that suck the last vestiges of strength from you. I sat stewing in my car for a couple of minutes before calling Audrey. I know she was balancing on tenterhooks waiting for the hammer to fall, but I needed every ounce of composure to not smash my phone off the ground, so I was waiting; waited until I could hold not crush to pieces-the handset, then dialled. I told her everything and waited for her reaction. I won't labour the point, but if I thought that I had been angry, then Audrey's was on another level entirely. Who could blame her? Up until that day, we had, so far, managed to wear our proverbial "brave faces" to keep the sunny side out. For lots of reasons, none more important than Dean. If he (in our estimation) had noticed that behind our dodgy plasterwork lay a bunch of free-floating cracks ready to expose the decay forming behind them, he might fall into an abyss he'd never leave. But that day hit us so hard it was impossible to recover. Audrey-showing resolve nobody out of a comic book would possess- we got up off the floor as we balanced on the ropes all of us had been left with mental scars that cut so deep the fight was almost stopped, but Audrey and I had made it to the bell and readied ourselves for Amy's next round. We were so far behind on points that only a knockout was going to save us. In the blue corner, Dean's trainer had seen enough and thrown in the towel. Sadly, we had to almost slip and break our necks on that towel. Sadly, we had to almost slip and break our necks on that towel before we saw it, but that comes later.

The bell that we heard to announce the next round was that of a ring-tone:
"Hello"

"Dave, it's not Amy, okay?"

"Who's that? Franco?"

"It's not Amy Dave it's not Amy – right?"

"Franco? What's not Amy? What are you on about???"

"Look, Dave, I got a call from the Guardia Civil. They found a body ..."

"A body?? Where? Where Franco? Tell me... "

La Cala.... around your area... look..."

"Oh god, no, no, no, no."

"Dave, it's not Amy"

"Are you sure?"

"Yes."

Are you 100% sure?"

"Yes. Dave, this is what they tell me, okay?"

"Okay, I'll tell Audrey. Franco, keep me posted on regular updates."

I clicked off, held Audrey and told her word for word what I heard. The earlier boring analogy isn't a bad one because we went into the emotional equivalent of a punch-drunk wobble. Shock intervened and gave us a standing count.

"How can he be sure-100% sure it's not Amy?"

"He told me it was a male body."

"Is he sure about that, Dave?"

"Yes, he's been told that, honestly."

In a movie, the phones would start ringing, and all hell would break loose? Sometimes, life is movie-shaped. Our phones-both, mobiles and land line screamed into action and as we answered them-no mean feat, there phones/two people we couldn't hear what was being said, why?

-Whuppa-whuppa-whuppa-whuppa

News reporters outside our house in a helicopter, low enough to clean out the gutters if they felt so inclined, friends and family on the phones, backed up on long "call holding" lines as we answered whatever we could;

"Is it Amy?"

"Have they found Amy? Is she dead?"

"Hey, did you hear they found a body?"

235

It was already all over the news back home in Ireland that the body of a person had been found "in the area where Amy Fitzpatrick went missing." Everything happens like that as fast as that. Fuck me. We'd been told, no, assured by Franco that it was male remains –not Amy's-that had been discovered, but suddenly we'd been inundated by calls, reporters, helicopters and Irish news outlets linking (Albert tenuously) the remains to Amy. How would you have reacted? What happens next? The only thing I could do.

"Franco, don't fucking lie to me. Is it Amy??"

"No, Dave, i told you, it's a man 100%, not Amy."

"Then why are the Irish news linking her to it?"

"Because that's what they do. Dave, it's a man, he was murdered."

"Murdered???"

"Yes, murdered."

"Who is it? Do you know his name?"

"No"

God love that poor man and his family. I mean that with all my heart, I really do. I never found out his name and it wasn't from a lack of effort either. Whoever this poor unfortunate soul was, his death barely received a column inch in the papers-no name –a "forgotten" statistic under an advert for marmalade or something. As for us, we were getting our first taste of the insidious propaganda machine that Franco had warned us about. We weren't in Ireland at the time for obvious reasons, but we received a lot of feedback about certain publications heralding Amy's death in huge headlines, only for the article to state that it wasn't her, but someone else enough said.

All that nonsense from the print media got me back to thinking about that magazine the Guardia Civil showed us. Okay, they show an absence of any class, but maybe their idea held merit? Who knew? But it was an avenue we hadn't explored. So why not? So, working on the premise that Amy had run away to become a model (we know existed in the realm where logic had gift town anyway), then we'd run with that. I made a ton of calls to all the modelling agencies I could find and also a call to Peter O' Brien. Peter – Irish, so one of our own, a Finglas lad has done well, he is one of the top fashion designers around, he has to be. He designed clothes for the likes of Princess Diana to Diana Ross. Was it a long shot? Admittedly, it was, but you've got to try and in fairness to Peter, he said that he'd send Amy's picture around to all of his colleagues. We dove-tailed our blanket email campaign to all the modelling agencies with this, but we never heard a single word back in response from anyone.

We started picking up little signals from the Guardia civil. Nothing obvious but detectable-that they were getting a wee bit annoyed at us. We hadn't gone away, we weren't ever going to give up and we had dumped an absolute tornado of media attention onto their home soil. We were extremely demanding of ourselves and we enforced our high standards on every part of Amy's campaign, especially theirs. We were fully transparent, with nothing to hide and were loud and upfront about everything; even when we'd drop the ball, that happened more often. Then we'd like, but they were based on long shorts. For example, we received so many prank calls it beggared belief:

"Amy is in a house in Mijas."

"Ma, this is Amy, I put a fiver on my phone; I needed to call you."

All of the likes of the above (I could fill at least a chapter reciting them all, but why bother?) We were/absolute bunkum, but we had to try. We also had to report these "leads" to the Guardia Civil, who'd "waste resources" on yet another wild goose chase. So, long story short, we felt a little show of strength was forthcoming. We were right; we were summoned to a cafe /restaurant called Los Olivious. It was a new place to the ever involving fabric of the Costa, but yet again, we found ourselves on the doorsteps of Debbie Rose's house. Funny how we continue to boomerang back there, don't you think? It was an interesting location, too, in the sense that it was very clean, very Spanish and the kids had been to it several times. To be honest, it was all very perplexing.

We weren't too far away when we received the call, so we arrived there within minutes. The reception that awaited us was shaking an army of Guardia civil. The place was completely surrounded, crawling with uniforms and Franco, they'd given this a lot of thought right down the friendly neighbourhood translator. It was a full military press in terms of police services. They all had a representative in this little consortium. First thoughts? This is too bit of a spectacle for there not to be news of major significance; you'd think the same thing, too, wouldn't you? Well all aboard the logic express as it's about to leave town:

"Audrey, Dave –welcome! Please, be seated!"

"O... hey? What's up?"

"Please, let us first make an introduction ...."

This was a long enough process made twice as long because of Spanish/English translation delays. Multi-lingual boredom of the arse-numbing variety:

"Now, we'll explain to you what Interpol is and its function, nothing Google couldn't have told us in a paragraph in English."

"Now, we'll tell you what Europol is.... "

Straight out of the Wikipedia blurb.....but longer. Again, we sat there and just listened. Then, listened again in English; maybe this was some archaise Spanish protocol. The appetizer before the main course. ... we hoped.

"So, as you can see-we are doing everything in the search for Amy."

"Is that it? (I couldn't help myself)"

"Yes!!"

"Do you want to explain the North Pole (northpol) to us next?"

"Excuse me?"

"Or maybe, the south –pole (southpol)?

"Em..."

"Do you think we're stupid or something?"

I can't remember what useless nonsense they replied with, but whatever it was, it wasn't worth another second of your life or mine. We'd go on to have many useless, unproductive meetings with the Guardia civil here, there and in Malaga. Franco attended as many as he could but eventually gave up the ghost and moved on to other things, he needed to earn a living, I supposed, so good luck to him. We'd been in a lot of talks with the Irish government –one of our citizens is missing, please help, and they pulled a useless, untidy, unkempt, unprofessional scarecrow out of a broom-closet slapped an "Irish ambassador" name tag on his chest and shipped his un-interested ass down for a few press conferences and

238

meetings with the Guardia civil. His name is Peter Gunning and he now resides in a book of the most useless things ever invented wedged between motor–bike ashtrays and the solid sieve. You know him. You've met him. He's the guy you can't wait to leave the pub early so that you can look at your mates and hear the collective.

"Fuckin eejits!!"

That's him. That's Peter, that's the guy who attended the meeting with his P.A, took a few minutes that was discussed and reported them back to mopping out the toilets; if he is repetitive of what passes for ambassadors from this country, then whatever you do don't lose your passport. He won't help you find that because he's incapable of finding his way to a dry-cleaners. Thank you, Irish government. For sending Peter Gunning to help us find Amy. What the fuck where you thinking?? Look, you've read enough about me now to know that I can't shut my mouth. I have to speak my mind and I spoke my mind to this guy more than once. At one point, I remember storming out of a meeting, getting into my car and driving home- convinced that nobody gave a fuck about finding Amy. I opened the front door, walked into the hallway and fell to my knees. The weight, the pressure of all the relentless negativity and on top, apathy had finally broken me. I did something I'd never done before, or since, I howled. It's a sound I didn't even think I could make; it wasn't even a thing I'd even thought about doing. I didn't even think it was me, I didn't know what that strange noise was or where it was coming from until I took a breath and it stopped. What the hell is all that about? Somewhere in the back of my mind, I thought that I'd died, that the noise was the sound of death or something equally stupid. Do you know what? It was a comforting thought. I'd died doing my best. I'd nothing more to give and my little heart just gave up. Kaput. I went down fighting. That's all you can do.

The next thing I knew was a soft, warm feeling on my arm. I remember thinking that it must be a good sign. Maybe I'd gone to heaven and some kind angel was welcoming me? I opened my eyes; Heaven looked a lot like the floor of Amy's house. I looked at my arm and located the source of the soft, warm heat. Audrey's hand. Words aren't always necessary. She sat on the floor beside me, put her arms around me and cradled my crying head into her bosom. I grew up and can't remember crying. I'm not or was not a crying man. Now I was broken. Rory's death had changed me forever. I was no longer immune to tragedy. Then, only months before, I'd lain down beside my mother as she died, ending forever the world I once knew. Then Amy didn't come home and nobody can tell us why. The situation decayed daily; where once we had all the help in the world and everybody cared about getting her back, now we had nothing. No Amy, no help. Nothing. The world stopped caring about returning the most beautiful whip-smart princess back to her castle, which crumbled around us. Headlines replaced deadlines; finding a new story replaced finding the story of our missing Amy. Not a crying man? I cried that night for Ma, for Rory, for Amy the future. Audrey saved my life that night; she saved my heart, my mind, my everything. She picked me up, found me again and made me realise what real strength was. She had it; I needed to catch up. Fuck that, I was going to catch up then we were going to find Amy even if it killed us.

That event had a massive impact on both of us. I was so angry at myself that I felt that I'd let Audrey down more than anything else; how dare I get so upset in front of her like that? Did I not think that she already had enough to be dealing with?? Stupid I know but then you're not thinking straight, you're just not a great example. This would happen just after my collapse; we were out on a drive, chasing up another dead-end when a car passed us on the other side of the road. So far, normal. Only there was a teenage girl sitting in the passenger seat.

"Audrey! Audrey! That was Amy!!"

I slammed the brakes through the floor and spun the steering wheel, gravity and rubber against concrete combined with mass plus motion, protecting us on to the other side of the road facing the right way. I hit the accelerator with everything I had and gave chase. They were 600 metres ahead... 500... 400... I used every trick I'd learned over the years of driving to propel us forward ever faster when to shift gears up then down. When to steer/oversteer, we caught them, then overtook them and forced them into a controlled stoppage. I was up and out of the car as Audrey began un-clicking her seatbelt. I pulled the passenger door open and pulled Amy out to freedom!

Only it wasn't Amy. It was a very confused and agonized girl looking desperately at her equally terrified and frozen mother. I'd traumatised an innocent mother and daughter and almost killed us all through reckless driving for nothing. Fuck, I couldn't apologise to those lovely people enough and I've nothing but the height of respect for them in how they responded. They quickly realised who I was and what I thought I was doing and were beyond sympathetic and kind. We were in a very bad emotional state and they could've behaved like assholes, but they didn't. They showed a spirit of forgiveness and generosity so sadly absent from the world these days, look I'll upset any applecart when it comes to finding Amy and apologise later if I have to, but their reaction gave us a little bit more hope. Not everybody was a total prick who couldn't care about Amy; good people still existed and we'd just found some. Still, no Amy, though she was now being spotted everywhere. A feast had replaced a famine. The poor young girl I pulled out of the car had a passing resemblance to Amy. A girl was brought from Coin (a neighbouring town) to Fuengirola Guardia station amid a bustle of high expectations and celebratory fanfare. Same age as Amy? Check same height? Check same very slim build? Put a check in that box, too. What was she wearing? Clothes so similar to Amy's that they might as well have been hers. We were met by one of the senior officers assigned to search when we got to the station:

"It's her! It's Amy!"

"Are you sure?"

"Yes!"

"How sure?"

"110%, it's her!"

"Is she okay? Is she healthy?"

"Yes-yes-yes!"

Our nightmare was over at last! Amy was home! Unharmed! Oh, thank god we got a little glimpse at her through the crowd of officers – her beautiful dark hair... her face was in a half-profile range same Amy make-up and eye-liner our hearts were fit to burst, oh Amy, you're home... you'll never be let out of our sight ever again! She noticed a gaggle of commotion heading towards her and turned to face us full-on. She looked a little different? Maybe she hadn't eaten enough or something, that was probably it. Then, our hearts sank. It was the "almost Amy." A good enough replica to double for her in a movie long shot but not Amy, not even Irish. Bollix... so close.

Audrey's family owned a holiday home in Co Wexford faced on Ireland's sunny south eastern coastline. Amy was spotted there next. Again feasible, she might've upped sticks and skipped back over to Ireland and where better to lay low than at a holiday home in the depths of an Irish winter? The "missing" posters and photographs were all over Ireland at that stage too, so a reliable eye-witness sighting gave us the licence plate of the car she got into and everything had to be her; it had to be our missing Amy. The Garda tracked the car down. It belonged to a local man; the girl in question looked a bit like Amy. But of course, we'd gone down another blank; there are only two ways you can deal with those particular

241

situations. Hang your head and bemoan your bad luck, or take the positives We chose the latter, why? Because it shows us that people were looking for her and cared enough to call the authorities with information that might lead to her return. As her parents, we couldn't hope for anything more. We were (and continue to be) truly humbled by the love that was shown for her near – misses, such as they gave us some renewed vigour, the hopelessness I felt at my collapse was eddying away, bit by tiny bit, but another kick in the Bollox was just around the corner.

I'd taken my eyes off the ball health-wise, I wasn't sleeping. I wasn't eating properly and I wasn't exercising. I was also knocking back a bottle of Jack Daniels (at least) every day. That was one of my coping mechanisms for dealing with the pain of trying to find Amy. I wouldn't recommend it. My health had taken a bit of a nose-drive, to put it mildly. I only went to the doctor because, to be honest, Audrey moaned me into it. She was right, of course, but I'm typical of my gender and generation. I don't need a doctor, "Yeah, right," I had undergone a series of tests and the doctors wanted me to come back a week later. So, like a good little boy, I popped back to them in Calahonda a week or so later.

"Dave, you need to sit down."

"(worst bugs-bunny impression ever) what's up doc?!"

"You need to stop drinking. Now… right now."

"I'll be grand."

"I disagree. So do your test results.'

"Look, I need a drink at the end of the day to relax… "

"Fine, you'll be dead in two years."

"What?!"

"You're right. Don't listen, have your drink. But you'll die in under 2 years."

"Oh, okay eh.... thanks doc. "

Audrey was in the car waiting for me and knew from my face that whatever news I'd been given was a long way from a clean bill of health. I never lie to Audrey and vice-versa, and I told her my news:

"Well, what are you going to do?"

"I'm going to go on the lash today and then..."

"Then what?"

"Then I'm hitting the booze on the head."

That is precisely what happened. Audrey and I even managed to laugh about it. But that's how we got through the horrific minefield of shit that our lives had become. So, no more beers and Captain Jack was on shore leave for the foreseeable, but that didn't mean that the stress just upped and left. Did it fuck, but the campaign wasn't going to run itself, so we muddled through like that for the next four months.

I'd started eating better and had gone back to training, too; it's funny how a death – sentence of 2 years can focus the mind. I was a member of a gym in Dona Lola, an urbanisation in Spain, right on the midterm part of the Costa del Sol, with tennis courts and pools outside and a gym, saunas and Jacuzzi. All the usual stuff inside. Audrey was also a member and our times there during the campaign were little heavens of relaxation. I had a workout, picked up Audrey and we drove home refreshed and ready to pick up the reins of Amy's search again. When I pulled up outside of our home, I saw a sight that made me feel sick to my very stomach.

Some horrible bastards had popped our side window and broken into our home. Amy's home, Amy's house, felt akin to a violation of our family itself, for fuck's sake; now what? We walked carefully through the house, not just in case we disturbed any evidence but, more importantly, in case our home invaders were still there. They weren't lucky for them our home was completely ransacked.

"Call the police, Dave."

"What for? What'll they do?"

I noticed a gun on our sofa. It was an old antique Spanish pistol that I had up on the wall, completely ornamental. The burglars must've left it there for quick access, a convenient weapon to beat us with had we returned mid-robbery.

"Audrey, don't touch that."

"Why not?"

"There could be useful fingerprints on it. Fuck it, I'll call the Guardia."

"I'll do it; they might know who we are at this stage!"

There's our gallows humour again, so Audrey put a call in;

"We need you to come to the station to fill out a report (Denounce)."

"No, I'm not leaving this house with the window off its hinges."

"Why not?"

"They might come back. Can you not come to us instead?"

"Okay."

Jesus, talk about amateur hour. What did they expect us to do, dust our own place off for prints and bring them the results of that too? Think about that too? Think about that for a second, please. The home of one of the most high-profile missing teens in the history of the Costa, if not Spain itself, has just been burgled. Isn't that just the teeniest bit, I don't know, suspicious?? Let us take this opportunity to address the whispering campaigns that are shady but inevitably follow every tragedy. I'm the "wicked" step-dad (whereas step-mothers have a benign /fairy persona), and Audrey is a "poor" mother. Great, so now the Guardia civil have a Willy Wonka golden ticket to enter our home under the guise of a "forensic robbery investigation" should've dragged his sorry ass over to what was now an actual crime scene and see what was stolen and who the likely culprit(s) were. Why such a senior investigation? Think about it, what else had been stolen? Amy, of course, could this be related? It's too close to home for it not to be, isn't it? You and I, the general Joe-soaps and "uneducated masses," might put it down to an unfortunate coincidence (maybe it is?) But detectives are trained to climate coincidences from any serious crimes with immediate effect, the very first thing to go out the window in the realm of possibility, ergo, not a coincidence, it must be connected. Therefore, it's a lead (or possible lead) to be explored in finding Amy, right? Has to be because I wouldn't know what signs to look out for or notice any tell-tale patterns to determine what to do next, would you? I guess what I'm trying to say is that for instance, the evil step-dad story is true and Amy ran away because I'm such a total bastard. She then waits for Audrey and I to leave the house, breaks back in and slices up all of my clothes, etc., but Dean's and Audrey's belongings remain untouched. That would be important for Intel to have, wouldn't it? To me, it is anyway.

So, in the absence of a speedy response from the boys in green/blue, Audrey and I had a good look around to assess the damage and to see what was taken. Do you know something? That was a much tougher ask than seems obvious because we had really put housekeeping chores on the back-burner. If I could just qualify that comment further; all three of us had made finding Amy the number one, two, three and four priority in our lives. Quite literally nothing else mattered, like migrating birds; we ate on the wing so our car and home were full of take–away and who gives a damn about watering plants or making beds when every second is another second close to finding Amy or another bit further from ever seeing her again? Our home was a mess, but a mess you can always clean, Amy is irreplaceable.

Unfortunately, other things are too. Our lap-top had been taken and let me plant this flag straight away. I couldn't give a flying fuck about that, it's a bit of technology, insufficient. However, on it was stored all of our personal details, including all of Amy's photographs and photos we had of her, another part of Amy we'll never see again? There was all the usual business type stuff on it too, but also Bertie Ahern's (P.M of Ireland at home) mobile phone number, so that might have caused a security issue, but that's not our problem. He had an entire defence force to protect him. We were still waiting for the Guardia Civil to arrive. My mother had only died a couple of months prior to Amy's disappearance and her jewellery (most of which my father had passed on to me) was still at our house because I didn't want to start processing that still hurt until the New Year, and then Amy disappeared. It had just sat there out in the open. Thank God I'd already bequeathed her engagement ring and watch to my sisters but the rest was probably going to go to Audrey and Amy, if I'm honest. A little way of making our own history as a family and having heirlooms to pass down, but sadly that little pipe dream ended that day, fuckers.

Audrey and I had the wonderful experience of walking into our bedroom and seeing first-hand exactly how savage those assholes could be. Drawers were ripped out of cabinets and dressers, with the contests flung everywhere and anywhere. The place looked like a tiger had a nervous breakdown in it. That's the only way I can describe that frenzied mess we had obviously been hit by a team of highly experienced, cracks – commandos of a high rank because they missed nothing. I'm sure that as they threw our clothes, etc., around like confetti, they would've noticed a big brown envelope thick with cash, it even had pink writing on it because it contained the proceeds of the walk that Audrey and I had done for a breast cancer charity. I think the event was called "pink-a-mar-a-thon" or something like that. Anyway, the gobshite completely misses it! Audrey couldn't believe she was actually holding it in her hands:

"Well, Dave, the thieves weren't Irish anyway."

"Why do you stay that?"

"Cos, they didn't take the brown envelope!"

A silly but true joke about our morally corrupt leaders and that little moment of dark humour still had us mid-boggled when the Guardia civil finally arrived. Of course, we knew each other at that stage, so introductions weren't necessary. We showed them everything we'd noticed ourselves up until that point, so they started looking around and doing their thing-fingerprints and asking inane questions until they thought they'd done enough, well, they hadn't.

"Did you take any fingerprints off this gun yet?"

"Gun?! What gun??"

"Eh, (pointing) this one!"

"Is that.... loaded?"

"No... It's only an ornament."

"Hmm... (Looking at it from a distance)... No."

"No? Why not? They definitely moved it, so contact points or something?"

"Well... em... well because we... em ...can't take prints off a gun. Impossible"

Time passed and we would much later meet up with a couple of serious hombres who, let's just say, "know a thing or two about fingerprints and their jaws hit the floor when we related this story to them. They not only knew that it was an obvious lie from the Guardia civil but, further from personal experience, no less knew that fingerprints could be obtained from guns thrown into rivers and lakes if not wiped properly. But back to the burglary...

"Well, you haven't even looked upstairs yet?"

"Did they go upstairs?"

"Jesus. .. of course they bleeding did, why else would I say it?"

So, reluctantly, they traipsed up the stairs and got as far as our bedroom door,

"De Puta Madre!"

This is "sons of bitches" in Spanish or a close enough approximation anyway.

"What? Because of the bedroom? Nah, they didn't touch it."

"Que? (What??)"

"Yeah. The bedroom always looks like that!"

They just started laughing; we all did more gallows humour, but once again, that was the Irish coming out of us, reverting back to what we know when the chips are down. It's a bit like putting on an old favourite coat when it gets cold, I suppose.

"Lads, before you leave, can I ask you a question?"

"Si"

"Do you think that this might have anything to do with what happened to Amy?"

"Porque/Why?"

"Well, I don't know, but it should at least be looked into and discussed, no??"

"We don't believe it was anything to do with Amy, but who knows?"

And on that bombshell, they left Audrey and I. We could only gape at each other in speechlessness. What the fuck was that???

How much pain can one heart endure? That's a little quote or saying that I've sprinkled throughout this book because not only is it pertinence with regards to human breaking points, but it also relates to the fusing together of two hearts into one. Mine and Audrey's. In stupefied silence, we put the house back together as best we could, if only we could put our lives back together as easily with Amy its crowning glory, our princess back home and in residence you have to dream. You have to send positive thoughts and energies out into the universe every so often. Who's to say it isn't picked up and acted upon? Where's the harm in keeping hope fed and watered? We sat back, exhausted and shocked equally, in our then cleaned house. That's the word I'd started using for the place I'd once called "home" looking back, that's when I wanted out of there, I just didn't cop it quickly enough;

"What was here before this house, Dave?"

"Dunno-why?"

"Was it built on a graveyard or something?"

I knew where she was going with this, there are at least two famous houses in horror movies that were built on a graveyard-poltergeist and Amy was born in each case, some freaky shit happened to the occupants and it was down to the "evil house" or, more to the point, the graveyard they were built upon. It's all fiction, of course, although some people would argue that they are based on these events. Why argue, who knows? Here's what I knew, though in poltergeist, a little girl goes missing and as for Amityville, look at the word, it's Amy Biville. Did I point that out to Audrey at the time? Did I? Fuck.

"Don't go there, Audrey, it's not the house,"

"Are you sure about that?"

"Honestly? No, I'm not. C'mon, let's go out for a drive, get a bite to eat?"

Some questions don't need to be answered –Tricky-Rickie's. It's a weird thing, you go at 90mph all day, every day, burning energy and calories at the rate of an Olympian, but you never think to eat. Your brain can't process hopelessness, desperation and then hope (again) whilst checking every face – twice - to see if it's Amy and think about food or register hunger. You then get so hungry that the thought of cooking becomes vomit, so you get take-out. Then you get your food, pick at it and discard most of it. We actually ate that day, though and better still, Audrey even managed a few glasses of wine, too. I didn't, I was on the wagon for four months at that stage. Four long months. Over sixteen weeks without the sharp, sweet treacle of Mr. John Daniels lovingly sliding its way down my throat, tickling my taste buds and depositing itself comfortably into the warm embrace of my stomach. I didn't miss it much, didn't miss it much, did I?!!

"Audrey, I'm nipping out for a quick walk. I need to clear my head."

"Okay."

"I'll be back in a few minutes."

Walking in one of life's simple pleasures, fresh air, going at your own pace under your own steam, just going where your feet take you. It's also a Mahon family trait, and we walk our troubles away, at least, we try to anyway. When I walk, the inside of my head is like a movie screen, snapshots of memories: thoughts, images and voices of those gone and those still with us get cobbled together into a cohesive little bite-sized package. I like to call an "idea," there's no hard or fast rule on how long it takes to collect an idea; you just wait until the arrival. It didn't take too long that day. Thank god. It was more of a plan than an idea. I went back into Audrey.

"Sorry, I couldn't stop thinking about my mother..."

"No problem, everything okay?"

"Ah yeah, you know me."

"Exactly – I know you! What's on your mind?"

"I kept thinking about what I'd say to her... you know... all this going on."

"Or what she'd say to you ..."

"Exactly! So, what I kept "hearing" in "her" voice was for me to go ahead and book A holiday for us - just us - and that we were to just go and enjoy ourselves. "She wouldn't have been too far off, would she?"

"So that's exactly what I did. I walked up to our travel agent (I'd been using this guy for years) and booked our flights and a hotel (I gave her the package)"

"Dave (big smile), these are dated for tomorrow!"

"So you okay with that?"

"Yeah, but only because your mammy told you to do it!"

She was thrilled and Audrey also knew Kay well enough to know that is probably what she would've advised us to do. We both just needed to hear it, if that makes any sense to you.

The very next day, we landed in Tenerife feeling a mixture of guilt for "abandoning our posts" but a massive wave of relief too, from getting away from that bloody house. We travelled to the north of the island, away from the rambunctious play de Los America, where all the tourists went. We needed downtime, plenty of peace and quiet. After dropping our stuff off at the hotel, we went out for a walk and came across a bar we liked the look of called "Bogart's." I did my dopey-nerdy thing and delivered the worst Bogart impersonation of "here's looking at you kid" ever, and even as Audrey giggled at my stupidity, my brain was hardwiring itself around another of his quotes "of all the bars in all the world you decided to walk into this one" god what I would've given to have said that right then to Amy. No way was I going to say that out loud to Audrey. Her eyes were smiling for the first time since New Year's Eve; I'd spare her as much "reality" as I could.

I left Audrey at a quiet little table and went up to the bar. I ordered her a glass or vino blanco e auga con gas and then just looked at the barman and said nothing. As he prepared Audrey's drink, I did the sums in my head... 4 months of the booze... dead in 2 years if I don't stop drinking... Amy... Kay...

"And for you, sir?"

"Fuck it. Give me a cocktail."

"We do thousands of cocktails sir. Anything in particular?"

It's a cocktail bar called Bogart's and I just asked a stupid question. If they had bloody cocktails, what bleeding planet was I on? The planet "sober" wasn't doing me any favours.

"Give me the biggest baddest cocktail you've got."

"That, I can do sir!"

"Sir?"

"Not telling you your job, but if it helps, I'm partial to a Jack Daniel!"

"Well, in that case, I'll make sure that Mr. Daniels makes an appearance!"

When he stopped throwing different bottles over his shoulder and under his legs and put down the metal – mixer-shaker things, he handed me a monstrous glass of liquid memory loss. Well, to call it a glass is disrespectful, a bit like calling the Eiffel Tower a lump of metal; this was closer to a transparent bucket. I needed two hands to lift it and if I couldn't drink it, I could bob for apples in it as it was longer than my head! Audrey's reaction to seeing it was priceless; she laughed so much that I swear I could almost smell pee at one point. Ever the entertainer (in my own head anyway), I decided to sidle on over to one of the many board statues and basically talk a load of absolute drunken bollox to it, but myself and Audrey had a much needed laugh and that's all that mattered. We got absolutely hammered and despite my doctor's orders to the contrary, it was the best tonic we could've had.

Yeah, there's always one of them, isn't there? Audrey and I had been "on stage" in the public eye even since Amy's disappearance became "news." Even in our newly inebriated condition, we had a nagging little voice at the back of our minds;

"Tut-tut-tut, whatever would people think out drinking and having a laugh when your daughter is missing – or worse? Fine parents, you are alright, a couple of no-good drunks..."

I caught Audrey that thought (or its first cousin) and immediately saw the spark leave her Eyes shit. Just one day, please?

"Don't do that Audrey."

"(Sheepishly) do what?"

"Feel guilty, that's what."

"Yeah, but what would people thi..."

"Think? Fuck them and fuck the begrudges."

I was right. I'm still right no matter what you do, you'll never satisfy the agenda of the morality police anyway, so don't even try. Walk in our shoes for 5 minutes and then try judging us, until then, fuck you. If nothing else, Tenerife had given this old dog a bit of fighting his bite again and boy, were we even going to need that soon. We'd been on the island less than 24 hours, had a good laugh and a bit of a walk and already Audrey was reluctant to stay any longer. "Just in case Amy comes back and there's nobody to let her in or welcome her." I went over to my suitcase and opened it:

"Dave, what are you doing??"

"I knew we'd end up having this conversation."

"Ah, Dave, look, I'm sorry, look-we'll stay."

Poor Audrey thought that I'd gotten into a huff and started packing our cases. What I was actually doing was unpacking Amy's posters! Audrey had put some in her case too, of course, she bloody did! We just looked at each and laughed – "Leaving me bollox!!" We slept that night. That was something. It almost felt normal. The next morning, we trekked out after a light breakfast (and I was hungover; (have to be honest!) Armed to the hilt with Amy's posters, we were like the "Costa-on-tour" as we handed out posters. Anywhere and everywhere to shopkeepers, doctors, passers-by, it didn't matter to us. Everyone was so kind and supportive; it was another humbling experience we got a resounding "yes" from everyone we asked, bar one of all people, who was an officer behind the desk at the local Guardia civil station;

"No?? Why not??"

He just smiled at us and then pointed over at a noticeboard on the wall. I wasn't in any humour for smugness or smart arsed theatres, not that day. I looked over at the notice board anyway. I was pleasantly surprised it was a poster of Amy, already in situ. Somewhere, somebody had been doing their job properly and I was glad of it. But it was bitter-sweet. It was sad, I was sad. More than any other time. I just really missed her at that point. I can't explain it; it's just one of those things. We finished our blanket coverage of the island, jumped on a plane and headed back to the house. Neither of us would refer to it as "home" anymore. It is and forever will be "Amy's house" to us and whenever she returns, that will be our home, wherever that may be.

As much as we needed that breakaway, it made us miss Amy all the more. To the best of our knowledge, she was nowhere near our house, yet being away from it felt like we were further away from her than ever. For all we knew, she could've been within spitting distance from us in Tenerife but were just not programmed that way. Go figure, I literally dragged myself back into Amy's house and as I started unpacking my clothes and other bits and pieces, I noticed a few more missing items from the house. Stuff we hadn't reported to the police because we simply hadn't noticed due to a desperate cocktail of shock, exhaustion and apathy towards anything that didn't help to solve the Amy puzzle. If nothing else, our break had burned away some of the scales from my eyes. What else hadn't I noticed before? Some vital clue to finding Amy, perhaps? I was filled with new motivation. I dared to think positive thoughts. Then, I noticed that my watch had been stolen. It was Rory's Graceland watch, one of the many trinkets and souvenirs from our best-ever holiday together. It wasn't much to look at, hardly a rare gem or collectable work of art, but to me, it's priceless and irreplaceable like Rory, like Amy. Curse my bloody stupidity for thinking anything could be any different. In a dictionary, you'd find a fancy word like "disbanding" or "crestfallen" to describe how that little revelation made me feel, though they lack the sickening hopelessness that comes with it. Sometimes your childhood vernacular, your hometown lexicon, says it better and easier. My spirit sat on a hard cold rock in a bitterly cold rainstorm and said, "fuck this. All of it. Enough." Then I slapped myself out of my little pity party and got back into the serious business of finding Amy. I can feel sorry for myself when she comes home; otherwise, it's a waste of valuable productive energy.

We were only back on the road no more than a minute before Franco called us. He was at the Guardia civil station waiting for us. Immediately, I assumed that it was in relation to Amy's news? Updates? Something positive, please God? Nope, not even close. All it was some standard report we had to fill out for the burglary. Ah well, at least I could put Rory's watch and the other bits on it now. It was good to have Franco there to translate for us; it meant that we could just tell him the whole ugly truth and he'd translate it all in an instant. Saves time, that precious commodity we never seem to have enough of. I then started to get that annoying little voice in the back of my head again. This time, it warned me about the Guardia officer; something seemed "off" about him. All of the communication – oral-was in Spanish, but his body language was all wrong.

"Franco, is there a problem here?"

"No, no, no problem. Why?"

His body language and attitude seem way off. I'm not wrong, am I?"

"Well... no, maybe not."

"So, what's his problem?"

"How do I put this, your total value of stolen assets?"

"No idea?"

"Yeah, thought Dave, it's between $30,000-$40,000."

"So?"

"Well, this officer wrote something in this comment section (pointing at it)."

"Franco, I don't know what that says. It's bleeding Spanish!"

"Okay, it doesn't matter. Don't worry about it."

"No, I will worry about it. What does it say?"

"Its most accurate translation would be – insurance job "or something like that".

"Well, that's good to know. Say this, eh, "officer," that we don't have any insurance, so he can cross that off his list, right?"

Like so many of our dealings with the Guardia Civil, nothing ever came of this and we never saw any of those items again. As far as the Guardia Civil were concerned, "it was probably the work of Spanish gypsies," so that was that... Case closed. However, if they had looked further than the end of their noses, they would've seen something – we believe to have been of major significance—Amy's phone, the very handset that we had on The Late Late Show. Audrey had wanted to carry it around with her everywhere (who would blame her), another spiritual link to her little baby bunting, her Amylou. In our wisdom, we decided to leave it at home, lest it get lost or stolen out of her handbag. It would be "safer" there. Another great decision. Fuck me, we couldn't do anything right, could we? Still, we found ourselves stuck in Fuengirola Guardia civil station, our home from home and with Franco, so we decided (now the burglary report was done) to have a "progress report" of such with the investigation team. It's only when stuff is read back to you that you realise how much you've dove:

"When you first met with us..."

"Your family history..."

"The run-away theory..."

"The abduction theory .. "

"Press coverage and media conferences. "

"Search terms, house to house campaign... "

"Similar circumstance, list of suspects. "

And on and on and on, wow, we'd done a lot. More than enough, you'd have thought, way more. I mean, an aircraft crashed into the Andes and the survivors started eating each other – they were found, without a fraction of the time, resources and manpower we'd already put into this and that was up in the Andes, I mean the fucking Andes!! A vast mountain range hundreds and hundreds of miles from civilization, we were in the Costa del Sol, surrounded by people, cameras, technology, police coast guards, sniffer dogs and between us, we couldn't find a

254

missing teenage girl, whose face was plastered across every T.V, newspaper and website across several European countries?? Riddle me that one, Batman.

Don't get me wrong, as we referred to the lengthy progress report, we (at times) felt good about ourselves and how much we'd achieved, but do you know what? It's all for nothing. Where's Amy?? We may as well have banged our heads off a brick wall for all the good it was doing. Even calling that meeting had been made into a big deal. Why? Because their communications with us were becoming much less frequent, that's why. And that really pissed us off. What was wrong with them? Did they think that we were going to just roll over and go away? Did they think that we were going to let them forget about our Amy? The simple answer to those questions was a responding "no way!" That would never happen. It was yet another meeting where we'd felt isolated again and the language barrier was shutting us out of information about our own daughter. The search for Amy had made us look at our problem - all problems in a different way than we had before. This was another such example – we felt shut out, isolated and starved of communication. Fine, the simple answer was to get back in, to be made more inclusive and to drive the communication process, so how do you do that? Well, dear reader, how?

We played to our strengths. Amy was (and I still loathe to even use this expression) still "big news" both at home and abroad. We're Irish, we know the lingo and had an "in" with the media. They were the tools we had, so we went back to Ireland and looked for support from the Irish government. Sounds easy? Trust me, it's not. Bertie Ahern was the Irish prime minister at the time and we'd been warned all over town to be careful in our dealings with him. One of the nice recommendations we'd received concerning him was that he was "sloppy and similar to two eels fucking in a bucket of warm snot," as I said, that was one of the better ones. I'd already had dealings with him concerning the circumstances leading to the death of my brother, Rory, so my expectations weren't very high. But one other universal point of agreement concerning "about Bertie" was that he was an opportunistic media whore. So far, once the stack was tipped a little in Amy's favour, we had no trouble getting his attention, thanks in no small part to the media. Audrey and I didn't care much for media or political games. We just wanted one simple thing, Amy home, so we gave Bertie this man-of-steel/man-of-the people moment and he, in turn arranged a meeting in Malaga for us with the heads of all the local police forces and Interpol.

We left Ireland, flew to Malaga and had our meeting with the above mention people. Bertie had come through for Amy, so we'll give him due credit for that. It was certainly a "top-table" level meeting and it was great to sit with such great investigative minds. Their collective skills and experiences were priceless. A "think-tank" of information that money couldn't buy. That's what made it so depressing of all the notes and "leads" we gleaned from that experience, nothing quite jumped off the page like the best criminal investigative minds. Agreeing that finding a missing person was a zero-sum-equation. They are – by-far-the most difficult cases to solve and the low-percentage levels of successful investigations are morbidly depressing. Better minds than mine and Audrey's should take a good look into that someday because whatever the current best practice is, it isn't working. How many more children have to disappear before it reaches the door of some influential celebrity or politician before those methods are revised? Normal people like you and I? Our families don't stand a snowball enhance in hell. Yet another bundle of joy we got from our meeting was the pervasive evil of the internet. In itself a wonderful intention, but the websites we'd been hearing about were the worst things in the world.

"Here, look at this link..."

"You see, how it gains access to this site..."

"Now you see how easy it is to groom girls like Amy.."

"Then, this is how the meetings are arranged.... abductions."

"Which leads to sexual torture sites, such as these. ?"

"Or even these ones.... 'Snuff' sites –where people pay to see young girls killed live online"

Something's you should never see and those sites top my list. Something you can never unsee and those horrific – demonic images haunt me to this day. We also left our esteemed experts with some food for thought of our own:

"We always felt that the Guardia civil have done a fabulous job."

We saw little flashes of pride all around the table, unspoken, barely perceptible, but there. They liked praise.

"I mean, wow-helicopters!"

More little "tells" from the poker table;

"Sniffer dogs, amazing!"

Clearly, these guys never played serious poker games;

"Organizing the search and rescue personnel, the Red Cross folks all the houses of meetings such as these..."

This was it; the moment I'd been building up to their guard was down;

"But still no Amy- what's that about?"

Silence. I'd popped their little ego balloons, good. We were met with a stony silence – temporally, but it happened. We looked around the table, looking each person in the eye. They just sat there, as conservative as cats, not knowing how to break the uncomfortable silence we'd created. I had no more intention of disrupting the power of this moment than they had of appearing our gnawing anxieties. Never underestimate the power of silence. Sometimes, it says more than an hour of oration. The rebellious voice at the back of my head was practically singing.

"Tick-tock mother-fuckers, how do u like it?!!"

"Mr. Mahon (at last, they blinked first!) Might we suggest counselling for you, for Audrey and for Dean?"

You know my rebellious internal voice well enough by now, so you'd be correct what you think he's telling me to respond with, but reality bites and sometimes you've got to hold your tongue and remember the bigger picture. Their door had been wide open for us, quite generous when you consider we had only lived there for three years, only "tourists" in the great scheme of things. This was their country and not ours; it was good to remember that. They had agreed to this and other meetings and in fairness, they had all of their angles covered. They were on the ball.

"Why, thank you, that's really considerate, we are most grateful for everything."

My mother always told me that manners don't cost anything, but having to suck that up was maybe an exception to that rule. Four little words got me through. Four little words gave me the sense to shut up and to get through so many more dark nights of the search still ahead. Do this for Amy.

Audrey and Dean went to these sessions once or twice, but there was a problem. The lady-lovely, though she was, was Spanish. That is in no way, shape or form a racist or nationalistic slur far from it. Rather, it's another observation on how being in a strange land only deepens your despair again. She had excellent English but not a command of our Hibreno English and the little subseries of our expressions or humour that tend to get lost in translation. For example, you'll hear out and around any Irish pub something like, "I was out with such and such the other nights for a few pints. We'd great craic, he's a bleeding mad bastard!" Now, to your ears and mine, that is a synopsis of a great night out with someone known to both parties as being a bit of a wit "quick with a joke, or to light up your smoke. As the song goes, however to the ear of our Spanish counsellor friend, the words "mad" plus "bastard" equals a character of dangerous habits and an altogether unsavoury person. That type of thing. For that reason or similar reasons, Audrey and Dean found it more frustrating than helpful, but at least they tried. I didn't. I was too much of "a man" and found such practices to be a sign of weakness. Did you ever see John Wayne go to a shrink? Or Steve Mc 'Queen.' No. Nor did I. I was too strong mentally for all of that new-age touchy feeling nonsense. I'm very happy to report that I've grown up an awful lot since then and now I really appreciate the precarious nature of mental health. Seeing somebody who can help you is the true test of strength that there is, but men of my generation, like me, had to be brought to their knees (literally in my case) before realising that they don't have a grasp of things after all.

Our big meetings, arranged by the Irish government and the Spanish authorities, seemed to morph into monthly affairs, which was great because any mention of Amy at the inter-governmental level could only keep her search alive. No matter how hard any set of parents can work and push, you cannot compete with the system. If you can work with them, you've some chance, but without them, the losing battle you've been fighting is all but lost. We gripped hold of those monthly meetings with everything we had; we knew the cost of keeping them. The Spanish provided a lovely lady called Ana Marie Perkins to translate. She was very knowledgeable and had worked her way up to become the official translator for the Guardia Civil, no mean feat. However, it also - sadly – made her use to us partially effective to qualify. Audrey or I would push for certain answers quite strongly, passionately we were living with loss and a ticking clock pounding around in our heads, but Mrs. Perkin's translations were passive. Too passive, to be honest. In her defence, she didn't want to bite the hands feeding her, but to her determent – fuck that shit – Amy's life is on the line; get another job. We can't get another Amy, we also knew that she was only replaying fractions of our points across- what took us 5 minutes to say, she'd replay in a couple of short sentences. We couldn't sustain that level of apathy, so after two such meetings, we went out and hired our own translator. He was also a Spanish lawyer, which couldn't hurt.

We took him along to the next couple of meetings thinking that it would make a difference. It didn't… bollox, I guess when the police have nothing new to say or have no new leads or evidence, then it doesn't matter who translates it. Audrey and I had our own chats about the lack of progress and decided to go out on a bit of a limb and once again change translators. Heck – "out on a limb" – we weren't even within shouting distance of a bloody limb. Desperate times need a different focus, so we threw in with a solicitor the Guardia civil had no time for;

"Stay away from him. He is, as you say – "dodgy," be careful."

"Be careful"? Bollox to that, we'd been nothing but careful and gotten nowhere. This was a guy who'd push their buttons, or so we hoped. Oh boy, did he! He was the only translator we ever met who truly spoke our language. I didn't mean Hiberno-English or Gaelic either. This guy loved to roll up his sleeves and fight them effing and blinding like a trooper. He brought the passion, ruthlessness and balls – to-the-door, bravery that had been so obviously lacking. We like him straight away. I was right to get this guy. Sadly, I was also right about the Guardia Civil and their half-assed incompetence. Audrey had feared it but refused to believe it at first. This is not a criticism or an "I told you so," she needed to believe that these guys were the mutts nuts and would find Amy because what was the alternative? Think about it. After spending a few hours with these new guys, our worst fears were realised… they'd been staring us in the face all along.

We made some calls to the Irish government. I don't recall exactly what it was we said, but the meaning was clear;

"Our daughter is missing. The Spanish branch of the Keystone cops are on the case and we need you to put some muscle behind us quickly."

Their response was predictably disappointing.

"It's a Spanish investigation and we cannot intervene."

"But Amy is an Irish citizen!!"

Same response, we started to compile a dossier of sorts, in the hope that if we could prove professional misconduct or incompetence, then somebody somewhere would come to our aid. We also had to be discreet because we couldn't afford to lose our monthly meetings and kept high tale was better than none. This is all the information that the media were too afraid or complicit to report. I'm not, instead of them fanning the flames of numerous baseless whispering campaigns, they should have broken out their best sparkly crayons and written about some of the following. In fact, it needed to have been screamed from the roof-tops, for example, a week or thereabouts after Amy was first reported missing. Dean (Together with myself and Audrey) visited the first track near Debbie Rose's house, where she claimed Amy had gone missing. Dean was not only able to tell the Guardia civil that there were C.C.T.V cameras on top of the lamppost there, he went as far as to point them out. Dean, a kid these "experienced" officer "specialists" assigned to our case, seemed genuinely surprised by that little fact and worse, did nothing about them. Yet, rather than admit that, they lied, telling us that they were examined, but nothing was found. We asked some other officers:

"Oh, those cameras weren't working."

So, who do you believe? We asked to look at the footage anyway...

"Why?"

"Because we might recognise someone on the camera that you didn't."

"No, there's nothing or them."

"What, on all of them??"

"Nothing."

"Well, then it shouldn't cause any difficulties for us to view footage of nothing then, should it?"

"You're not authorized."

There was a brick wall just begging for my head to bang off. Unbelievable. How many man-hours would that simple little task have saved? How many red herrings could've been avoided by one stroke of the pen, crossing the dirt track off the endless list of possibilities? Alternatively, how close might we have gotten to finding the person responsible for taking Amy? We'll never know because they didn't try to do their jobs properly. Whether it was by accident or design, that would be something for an impartial tribunal to decide, wouldn't it? Once again, dear reader, I ask you to enter into darkness and put yourself in our shoes, knowing the importance of what you now know, of how easy it is to sit down and watch a couple of videos and the enormity of the finding (or not) therein on a scale of one to ten, how angry and frustrated would you be. Audrey and I don't have the luxury of imagining what we know and taking it from us. It's worse than you can possibly believe.

Having a fearless translator gave us insights into information we didn't want to know but had to hear. On more than one occasion through "unofficial" channels, we learned that the Guardia civil thought that we'd give up quickly and piss off back to Ireland or wherever they're from. When we inquired why such a horrible attitude existed, we were told, "to free men up for proper police work, ease off on the search for Amy and stick her file up on the top shelf," but you get the idea. We now had proof of what I'd long suspected the Guardia civil couldn't find their arse with both hands and it was time to delve deeper into the dark side.

I've already alluded to the use of the underworld in fits and starts, - but I haven't gone into just how far up the totem we went or how far into the mire, depending on your own sensibilities. When most Irish people hear about the underworld in Spain, their thoughts are usually drawn to alternatives and Marbella. We had already been up there delivering leaflets, putting up posters and meeting with the massive ex-pat population up there. It was an easy "sell" for want of a better world because we'd been on both Ireland's Late Late show and the BBC's documentary programme about missing people, so the huge Irish and even larger British populations up there were already well-versed on Amy's disappearance. We met with no resistance, only support, and especially from the Spanish lads who consistently proved themselves to be every bit as family oriented as the Irish, if not more. So Gangsters? Criminal element? We were too busy to notice who was a gangster and who wasn't. In fact, the only criminal' element we knew about was a lot closer to home.

It was never anything more than a storm in a teacup best, but you can never legislate for people's stupidity. Without making a gangster movie out of it, I'll ask you a question? Your next door neighbour has suffered a recent tragedy? Something concerning their youngest child? Suddenly, a song comes on the radio that reminds the heartbroken mother of happier times with her child, it's not a ghetto-blaster or a surround–sound system out of a movie theatre. It's one of those little radios you'd see in kitchens, say so anyway this song comes on the mother raises the volume up a notch and goes into that safe little cocoon of the soul, trying to process the sad enduring of everything. One song, three minutes? Five at the extreme end? One song, it's over life and volume goes back to normal. What would you do? Let it go on or make a big fuss about it? I know you can see what happened already. I wasn't even at home at the time because Audrey needed her own space that day. It always seems to happen like that, doesn't it? Also, bear in mind this is the middle of the afternoon, not four in the morning. Audrey hears the door banging off its hinges. Context: Is this another robbery? Audrey is home alone. Terrifyingly bad enough to be rudely awoken out of her little Amy memory, but to the 'thum-thum-thum-thum' of fist against timber? Context: Is this the Guardia civil banging the door down with news of Amy's disappearance? Audrey opens the door, what now? And what then happens will announce itself into her life? Standing on our door-step, fist posed for another thump on our door, is the outrageously ugly woman who happened to live next door;

"Turn the music down; it's unacceptable. Too noisy."

"No."

"Excuse me?"

"Do you not realise what I'm going through? What's been happening here?"

"Yes, of course I know, but that doesn't change the facts; your music is still too high."

"Do you know what?"

"What?"

"The best thing you can do is go and fuck off with yourself."

And with that, Audrey slammed the door in her face; proper order for Audrey. We didn't even have a TV or a radio to lower down anymore because it had been done before Miss Piggy started hopping her chubby little hooves off the door. All she was short of screeching was, "I'll huff, and I'll puff and I'll turn your radio down." I was blissfully unaware of all this. Then my phone buzzed in my pocket. Audrey was in an awful state, thinking and vocalising stuff no husband or partner ever wants to hear. She wasn't going to survive the rest of the day on her own, so I got back to the house within minutes after the call ended. I'm not being overly dramatic when I say that I was relieved to find Audrey still in one piece when I came through the door. As I sit here writing about this years later, I'm still stumped at how selfish and cruel Cynthia was. That's not her real name, by the way, it's what I call her, though Mrs c.Unt, because she is unbelievable, as I sat out on the back porch, Audrey sobbing into my arms, "Cynthia" popped her head over the fence and started abusing me?!! A child could see that Audrey was in a very delicate state, 'heartbroken.' Cynthia was a 100 miles an hour (Alcohol can be a terrible thing), and still this harpies spat bile and venom. I still can't believe that happened and I was there! Worse was to come, of course it was. This is Dave and Audrey, misery doesn't skimp on the portions when it comes to us. There was a dividing gate between the two properties. Her husband, a man so fucking dull he pissed dust, burst through and struggled to think of something tough to say. I did it for him.

"Get the fuck off my property, I'm not asking."

He blinked once, twice, thrice, that's how you know he was thinking. I stood up and away from Audrey. This wasn't going to be his day. He didn't need a foolish blink to process the inevitable outcome. He turned to walk away and then a blur moved between us. Do you remember that mad bitch of a nanny in the "Omen?" The one who viscously attacks Gregory Peck at the end of the movie, in a frenzy of satanic blood-lust. That blur was 'Cynthia' in her devil nanny attack on Audrey. Not verbal this time, but physical, a punch; holy fuck, I was now scared for Audrey. How the hell was I supposed to save her from this bleedin wildcat? I needn't have worried. Bang!! Audrey let go a right hand that would've sent McGregor off looking for marbles. Cynthia's eyes rolled into the back of her head and she stumbled back a good few step. I quickly turned to see if Audrey was okay and it was lucky that I did because she was steamed up, a follow-through left that would've taken 'Cynthia's' head off her shoulder because she shed no neck as it was just a fat deposit her head sat on. I stood between them and 'Mr Unt' took his horpie back to his house. That wasn't the end of it.

The next morning our neighbour, the pair of 'cunts,' went to the Guardia Civil and made a formal complaint. We ended up in court in Fuengirola. They were changing Audrey with assault; honestly, you couldn't make this up. The aggressor, who trespassed, was the one pressing changes. Thank God Audrey didn't connect with that left hook or the helicopters would've been out again. Franco arrives out with some Guardia officers. We didn't have the time or mental capacity to process the pile of shit. It took the Guardia less than a minute to piece together what happened and they had a chat with 'Mr Unt' he, in tune, asked:

(On the steps of the court)

Have a quiet word with me;

"Look Dave, in hindsight, let's not be too hasty."

"Hasty? Us??"

"Look, we'll drop the changes."

"No."

"What… what?? We're neighbours, for god's sake!"

"You guys aren't neighbours in the sense that's what I grew up to believe."

"Meaning??"

"Our daughter goes missing. You do fuck – all. No "hello or goodbye" or "kiss – me-arse" nothing.

"Well, if you're implying…"

"But as soon as the radio volume goes up, you're all over Audrey?"

"Now look, see here…"

"Do you know what, I'm glad we're here at court…"

"You are? Why?

"Well, first of all, your wife assaulted Audrey first and she was trespassing."

"What do you mean "first" as if you've any other cause for complaint? I don't think so!"

"Until your lunatic of a wife assaulted Audrey! Would you agree, but unfortunately for you, in Audrey's distressed state, a lot of other things came to light…"

"Well, she's obviously fore…"

"Shut your face! She told me about all your passive–aggressive bullshit. Turning the electricity off in the house when I wasn't there? Giving Amy a hard time??"

I really wanted to hit him over that and given the small squelchy noise emanating from him. I guess he knew it too; he slithered away, his lawyer threw themselves at our mercy, accepting all blame (as they should), and we were advised

264

to accept, so we did the settlement fully in our favour. We never spoke to them again, no loss there. But that massing voice in my head wouldn't quit. I couldn't relax. Something didn't fit… then it hit me like a bulldozer. When the Guardia Civil came to our house about the assault, they didn't have a clue who our neighbours were. Not even one. They were total strangers. So what do you say? So, I put my nagging voice on? Here's what we missed: Amy goes missing, check, search is put together, check friends and family provide statements, check Guardia civil canvas the area doing house to house enquires, as usually neighbours and locals notice things no "check" in that box as it hadn't been done. Audrey and I thought we'd gotten the wrong end of the stick, but we hadn't. We checked, asked and then checked again;

"Ah, come on lads, what the fuck??"

"No, it isn't necessary."

"What? What's that supposed to mean???"

"Everybody knows about Amy, they would've come forward if they saw anything."

Well, fuck me sideways if that wasn't the dumbest thing I'd ever heard. Let's just say, for argument's sake, that one of our neighbours abducted her, using the logic and reasoning of the Guardia Civil, then the kidnapper would just hand himself in? I've never claimed to be a Sherlock Holmes, but seriously, there are more than one or two little flaws in that strategy, aren't there? The large snapping noise you just heard was the camel's back. Fuck that, we'd had more than enough revelation of the "oh-my-fucking-Jesus-what?? Variety no more… we'd keep them on the periphery from then on when angles drop the ball, the demons control the game. We just needed to go directly to the prince of darkness; we'd had enough dealing with all the minions.

It was an easy decision to make and our only regrets are that we didn't do it sooner. We were born and raised into law-abiding families and we therefore knew that the police are the good guys. They'll search relentlessly until they find her or else die trying. Also, they're super-smart, much brighter than your average "fools" like us…. I cannot stress this enough, dear reader – that's complete nonsense. If your child goes missing, meet with local crime bosses; you've some chance there at least. We gave the cops everything from day one and hid nothing – ultimately – superficial searches and headline – hogging-helicopter fly-byes, they basically did fuck. All the posters, all the media, all the interviews, all the expenses that was us, not them. We were very lucky to be in a position to do that because otherwise, you wouldn't be reading this. You'd be going, "Amy, who?" As we all do about, so many other poor children vanished without a trace. Our businesses were turning to shit like everything else in our little orbit, but we didn't care; we'll find her today. Then tomorrow, then next week. Meanwhile, the banks continue draining your accounts and they get paid regardless. When Audrey and I started our move away from the Guardia Civil we decided to offer a reward. How much is Amy worth? She's priceless. How much did we have? That was a finite amount, sadly. How much do we offer? How much would you offer, long story short, we started off high and ended up with a zenith figure of one million euros, but let me qualify that right now. We didn't have a million euros, not even close to half that much, but a lot of friends and wealthy business people chipper in and committed to "X" amount if it came to it. Sadly, it didn't. It led to an awful lot of crazy calls from vultures in human form, jackals sniffing around the bones of what they hoped were Amy's remains. However, one blessing came out of it and some big-time members of the underworld took note; getting an all-important "sit down" with people of considerable influence was no longer a pipe dream.

Again, a bit of context; a million euros is less than chump change for these people. Their interest and then involvement in Amy's disappearance was not financial. One person in particular lost a lot of his own money helping out. Even mob bosses have mammies and daddies, little girls are universal. Whatever people do in their profession shows in their own business and not a world I agree with or pass comment about. When a person approaches you as a genuinely sincere person, a family man who's sharing your pain, you treat him as such. Who are you or I to judge another human being anyway, right? In any event, the million euro reward was neither the first nor the last, but it made different elements sit up and take notice.

Audrey is far from conservative and is generally quite open-minded. Yet even at that, it took a while for me to get her fully on board the underworld bus. I had help in the end from the Guardia Civil. No, it's not that they sat us both down and said, "Hey, you know the guy that buys and sells fake Rolex, well he might know something!" Far from it, it took months of consistent incompetence we'd them with volumes of notes we'd gleaned from our feel-on-the-street interaction with the public. Nothing would happen. We'd go to them with different rumours. We'd heard about Amy - "Sorry, we cannot and will not act on any rumour," even a junior infant knows that a stopped clock tells the time correct twice a day. All we needed was for one rumour to bear fruit, but no dice, baby. As for the non-events, the phone records, house-to-house enquiries and lack of search at Debbie Rose's house, well, I needn't go on. Once I started hanging out at street corners, it was a no-brainer. Audrey became happy, more than happy and even better at English local criminals in the search for her baby girl than I was. At least one pair of nervous all-seeing criminal eyes on every street and junction in the Costa del Sol? You bet your life we tapped into those resources. Karma can be a bitch, but it can also be your friend. My decent upbringing had installed a help-if-you-can – help mentality that I've managed to hang onto before Amy's disappearance. I'd been quite generous to the locals, even the criminals – if they were in need, nothing to put Bob Geldof out of business, but a cup of coffee here, a sandwich, these little gestures, small kindness they'd been remembered and appreciated, thank God to a person they all wanted to help and promised to keep eyes out no matter how small we'd hear every whisper about Amy, priceless, useless too at times but boy, what an infrastructure to have. You have to take the rough with the smooth, especially with criminals. So we had to park our prejudices and cosy-up to the shit as well, the low-level junkie sellers purveyors of cocaine-hashish and God-knows what pills they pedalled along with it, but hey, we prayed to God and the Devil when it comes to getting Amy.

We know one little Moroccan man very well and he was on relatively good terms with us and the kids. We saw him as a bit of a small time crook, a diet – version of Arthur Daly but he really came through for us in the early days. He told us that Amy had been in a nightclub in El Zoco on the night that she had disappeared with an older man. This, if true, wasn't big news, it was massive news. We pushed him really hard on its truth. It was massive news assured (by his source) that it was 100% true; we went straight to the Guardia Civil with this information, but they were completely underwhelmed. Their few appeared to be more about who gave us the information than what it meant. Then, as in now, all these years later, we kept stum about our sources. We gave a commitment from day one that we'd give nothing less than absolute confidentiality and it's something we'll always honour. What did the boys in blue (technically green in Spain, but it's what we refer to them as anyway) do about it? Your guess is as good as mine as they never committed anything to us except to tell us that the source of our information was Yusuf, he's one of our informers, but we'll neither confirm nor deny that allegation. What I can say is that Yusuf was known to us, but then so was everybody on the Costa back then. He has sadly passed on since it is my opinion that the Guardia Civil never acted on his information, but I don't have a monopoly on being correct, so they may have done so behind our backs. Nothing could stop Audrey and me from investigating it further, so we went up to the nightclub owner and put our information to him. He claimed not to have known Amy and wouldn't have known if she was there or not on the night in question.

"Fair enough, but we want to ask you something. Do you have CCTV in operation?"

"Of course I do."

"Can we have a look at your tapes from New Year's Eve?"

"They're long gone. We only keep records for 48 hours and then record over them. Standard practice for us. "Okay, did the Guardia Civil come in looking for them?"

"From time to time but not for New Year's, no."

"Did they come here to ask any questions about Amy?"

"No, never."

Fuckers, still we gave them the benefit of the doubt. Maybe in all the frantic confusion of the search, a single night club slipped through the net. It wasn't impossible; it was human. In order to ease the pressure off our ever worried mind we did a circuit of all the other nightclubs. None of them had been interviewed and none had CCTV on file for more than 24 hours; it just wasn't the way things worked at the time. Some didn't even have recording facilities, just dummy cameras that were employed for preventative methods. Shit.

Audrey and I left and we made a bee-live back to Fuengirola police station. They got both barrels off us in surround sound. Our response? An irritated shrug of the shoulders.

"Why aren't you taking this seriously?"

"I can assure you, as professionals of law enforcement, that i.e. ?."

"Bollox, you did nothing with the information we sweated to get you."

"What do you want for us to do, to go to a nightclub?"

"Yeah, why not?"

We called their stupid bluff. Of course, we did and they agreed and dragged their pre-pubescent stroppy asses along after us. But only to one of the nightclubs as they were "really quite busy." I'll be generous and say that they asked all of the relevant questions. It was far too little, much too late. I'm no fool and easily recognized the painting by numbers, matter of fact, tick-box exercise it meant to them. In short, they didn't care a shite one way or another. Grumpy, demanding, Irish asshole parents? Check, now onto something important, el classico is on the box later or whatever it is they did between the so-called investigative works.

Amy and Rory kept coming into my mind in ample–style fashion, panicking me into the belief that she was lying under a bridge or something, drawing her last breath. I'd missed Rory; I'd die before missing Amy. No fucking way, do your jobs, you shower of wankers, ugh it was soul destroying. At the very least, they should've been over those night – clubs like a rash, no more "iron-first-in-a-velvet-glove" bullshit, we were deep into overtime, this was "break-glass-in-case-of-emergency" time, gloves off and hands fitted with razor wire to hell with the consequence. Squeeze hard enough and anyone will talk. Then reality hit me. What would they do if they got news? Proof? Anything? There was a way of finding out.

Let me preface this by saying that were any other circumstances, a deliberate attempt at wasting police time is dangerous, illegal and utterly stupid. Let me also add some context, Amy was as gone as gone could get, I'd slept less than 3 hours a week on average existing on a cocktail of coffee, wits, anger, terror, love and desperation. But I still stand by my actions. You, however, have your own mind and set of moral values, so don't be afraid to think it was completely wrong. Maybe it's still raw as scald reality blinds me still? Like a plug, the Guardia will not act unless all three prongs are in union. There is evidence you must have some (but not always corruption is far from unheard of) hear, say, or rumour isn't considered (unless again it fits one of their many narratives, in which case a rumour is enough of a smoking gun for the judge to sign off on a warrant) and lastly the pre-Franco assumption that a Spanish man's home is his castle and never shall his moat be breached. That extends to vehicles and such as well, not that it ever stopped me from kicking in the odd door or two in their view in order to qualify (or not) certain leads we'd been given. Anyway, I was sitting strewing over a coffee in an area called Elvira and decided to call the Guardia civil anonymously from there:

"Hello, is that the Spanish police? (I couldn't be too knowledgeable)."

"Si, this is the Guardia Civil how can we assist you?"

"Is that Irish girl still missing?"

"Si."

"Amy Fitzmaurice?"

"Fitzpatrick sir, Amy. Fitz Patrick."

"But it's "Amy" anyway, right?"

"Si."

"Well, I'm sitting now in a bar called "X" and there are 4 men here and to be honest, they are quite loud and they've mentioned 'Amy' a few times now and that they know where she is!"

"Are you certain of that, sir?"

"Yes! Do you want me to hold them her for you?"

"No! We'll take it from here. Those men might be dangerous.

"Yeah but there's a reward. What about that?"

"Please sir, sit tight; we'll handle everything…"

The call ended shortly after that. I wasn't to "approach the men" or do anything; I set the stopwatch "Let's see what the response time is like. I was across the streets, safely hidden from view, a minute passed. Then another ten, then half an hour! Not so much as a traffic warden. An hour, two, three, four hours. Nothing. Fuck that, I'd gotten my answer loud and clear. I met Audrey and told her how I'd spent the best part of the day, time we could've put to better use. We went through the usual back and forth:

"Are you sure you didn't miss them?

"What if they were in undercover. How would you have known?"

"Do you know how much trouble you would've gotten into??"

Don't think, for one, that we don't scrutinize. With every move we make when it comes to Amy, it was obvious we only had our card left to pay. We'd stay in the same game as the underworld, but we'd go to the high-stakes table. We'd meet with the top people, the pinnacle of that pyramid, the apex, as with all things Amy; No names. We might need these people again and they were good enough more than good enough to help us, so we owe them. But you've got to swim through a world of shit to get out of the sewage. We met them all along the way. The wannabes, the plastic gangsters and the spoofers. You come across them in every country, but there's a special element in the Costa that attracts them, like wasps to a picnic. Let's start at the bottom, the English ones. Some were "okay-ish" and gave an approximation of helpfulness at some level. For the mass part, though, they were name dropping nobody's:

"Fuck-in-ell make me and the twins, you know, the krays?"

"Me and our Ron, we were as thick as thieves' mate back in da day..."

Balh-balh – bollox. If it wasn't the Adams, it was the Richardson's or the great train robbery, utter rubbish, but finally we got a mid-level somebody,

"Alwigh mate," erd you was looking for me yeah?"

(Typically cockney, finished every sentence with a question)

"Yes, we believe you might be able to help us find our daughter, Amy."

"Okay."

"Great, can you put the word out amongst your contacts and maybe advise us to how best to proceed? We'd be most appreciative."

"You probably" heard about all my mass–au–ge parlors, eh?

(You've got to constantly massage their ego sometimes).

"Yep, I heard you've got them in a few different countries, that you also sell a few-high-end cars and that you run your own business... drugs too."

He looked taken aback. Shit had I said too much? It wouldn't be the first or last time I'd done that; I'd blown it. These next words are same combinations of colourful metaphors telling us where we should go. He'd probably pound me into little pieces for "taking liberties…"

"Fuckin' 'ell, you have done your "own work, haven't you? I'm impressed, aren't I?"

Some egos can be so large they can blind you. This guy had an ego so large that it had another – smarter ego orbit around it. I got lucky; I'd needed to take that as a test for when I'd meet the very top guys. Still, as long as I played to this particular ego, Amy had a chance. He listened to us and agreed with what we put to him. He felt a bit conscious, I suppose, around Audrey when talking about his scenography and massage parlours.

"You know, Dave me, 'oul china all those girls working for me, they want to do it, know was I mean? Like, nobody fors' em, they is willing participants, yeah?"

He tried to make it sound "cool," like it was the greatest career option for any young woman trying to make her way in the world. He was a hell of a salesman; it was easy to see how his casual patter could ensure and recruit the young and native. He was a huge, powerful guy and was seriously connected. Yes, there was something genuine I liked about him, in spite of everything. He had an easy charm and lots of charisma. I guess in Dublin, we'd call him a 'character.' Yet if I thought for a naive – second that he'd have coarse Amy and work any of that bullshit, I'd have driven over him until his bones turned into powder, sealing my own fate into the bargain and to be honest, I think he knew that, he certainly allowed my direct comments once or twice, which in a weird way earned me a bit of "cred" with him hey-whatever it takes.

"You are more than welcome to visit any of my "brof-ils" in Spain anywhere. I'll even cover the 'ol expenses, won't I?"

I declined his eh, 'tempting offer,' but at least he was willing to leave none of his own stones unturned for us and that was commendable. I've always thought that this guy should've been in the movies. I mean, he had that whole 'look' the fashion sense, all the 'bling' a model girlfriend and his arm (an actual porn star) and a big flashy muscle sports car and as for his house, phew-straight off MTVs' cribs programme! It was too spotless to have ever been lived in; that's the sort of guy he is, but at least he was true to his word. He told us that he'd look and that he'd help and did exactly that—a rare diamond in the very rough.

We then moved up another notch on the pyramid to another English gangster. Again, no names/no park drill for his sake as well as our own. This is seriously well known in fact, he'd be infamous along the Costa. No play boy antics here, just all business, the real deal. Our meeting would either go well, or else we'd end up as shark bait out in the med. That's not fancy poetic license either; that's a fact. Were we nervous about meeting this guy? More terrified than nervous, but when it's for Amy, you grow a bigger set of balls, you just do. We'd been advised not to take this guy's time with flattery or ego just tell him what we had to say and hope for the best. I have just read that last sentence back and it still chills me. We really did stick our lives on the line and talk about being in the moment; anyway, we gave him a brief back story and asked for help;

"I've seen the posters, I've read the papers, I've seen all the extra filth (cops) about too, like flies around shit. Sorry for your troubles."

"So… can you help us then?"

"Course I will. I'll get my cadaver dogs down from England get "em to search a few places of interest."

"Sorry, eh…. Cadaver dogs? What eh…"

"We use these dogs to sniff out all sorts – clothing, blood… even death."

"Oh… fuck..."

"Yeah, don't worry about it, I'll cover the costs. I've ever got a few best cops on the Pay Role. I'll do my own investigation. Understand??"

We understand! Did we ever! It felt as though all of our Christmases came at once. An unlimited budget, a lead investigator who was feared by those in the uniforms as well as the rest of us, specially trained dogs and a guy everyone wanted to keep happy. People in fact, went miles out of their way to keep this particular homage happy, so now we'd have people bending backwards, selling their own granny to get into his good books. We couldn't have asked for better. When we started to get invited to his house for meetings, we not only realised how "poor" we were in comparison but what was more impressive were the brain storming session we'd have a birthing ground for some amazing ideas, at last, we felt that we were getting somewhere.

We took a breath, then took stock as a gangster was doing his things so Amy would be found sooner, not later; that's the unsubtle impression he conveyed. So, we looked at ourselves, our house needed another professional cleaning. We're not pigs, just busier than the busiest thing that was ever busy, then we looked at Dean. For the first time since Amy didn't come home, we took a long hard look at him. He was 18, no longer a kid technically, but he was only a big lost boy... no sister, no hope, shame on us we neglected him. Thus, no other word for it, I wish there was we'd neglected him; he knew it too and had started acting out more and more. He was on the threshold of getting back onto the Guardia Civil and we'd more than ridden our luck with them as it was. We had a full and frank discussion with him and it was agreed by all of us that it was better for him – for all of us – to go back to Ireland; it was what he wanted. He knew the Guardia were still snarling at this traffic accident and his heart wasn't in Spain anymore, not since Amy... for Audrey and I could now provide Amy with our total focus and besides, we were getting into bed with some proper dangerous gangsters; we didn't want Dean anywhere near them that wouldn't have helped anyone; it was heartbreaking to have the house devoid of children. Now, it was truly only a shell. Then I took a serious look at Audrey... oh God...

I'm not a doctor. I'm not medically craned. I'm also not blind, nor am I an idiot. The woman that was standing beside me wasn't Audrey. I hardly recognized her; she looked like she was ready to fall down dead any minute. You hear about people "letting themselves go" or what not, but this was too much. We went to the doctor and we both received a server talking to, but Audrey was in a lot of terrible pain. She was told straight that she needed to step back away from everything or she'd die. In fact, it was going to take a lot for her to just live; that's how far she'd fallen to any other person at any other time. The reaction to such news would've been earth–shattering a long holiday followed by constant medical care and a vegan fat-free diet for life, not Audrey. We discussed it. She wasn't having any of it- "I'll take a break or to hospital-whatever you want once my baby gets home." It wasn't always as polite as that. Then we made our way up to Mr. Gangster's house for a status update, sure we could both be dead the next day anyway, so what was the difference? We got more of the same promises and shows of strength. He had an impressive collection of weapons in his domestic arsenal, anything shy of a Russian invasion and he was covered.

I'm not the sort of person to go out of my way and many people, especially when they're helping Amy, but so far, all Mr. Gangster land done was talk-the-talk. We'd yet to see evidence of anything he'd promised. I left a few more empty days pass and then got him on the phone.

"What's the story with these dogs of yours?"

"Oh yeah, I must organise that they're still over in England."

"England? You told us weeks ago that you'd have them over!"

"I did? Oh well."

"Oh well? What about your investigation news that's, how's coming on?"

"Oh, yeah… I'll start that when I get the dogs here…"

"What? You haven't even started it yet?"

"Calm down, calm down…."

"Calm down?

"Do you know what you are?"

"No. Tell me"

"(Shouting) You're a no-good Count!"

Then I slammed the phone down, seething with rage. Audrey was staring at me with her mouth and eyes making massive "O" shapes:

"Dave… that wasn't… who I think it was … was it?

"It was. Fuck him anyway."

"Dave. Maybe you shouldn't have said that to him. These aren't guys you mess with…"

"Audrey, when it comes to Amy, this is what we have to do. Anyway, this guy is full of shit; let him go and fuck himself."

"You know nobody seems willing to do anything?"

275

"No, because we are the two people in the world who care about Amy. This is why we are sitting here alone.

Fuck me, it had degraded way past the point of depression. We would've welcomed death into our house that night, greeted him like an old friend and sank into his eternal sweet arms, happy to be finished with life. We didn't wake up the following morning…. because we didn't sleep, we just lay there depressed and without any hope. When the darkness outside began to fade, I told Audrey to get ready and we went to a local café for breakfast and some caffeine.

Capture the scene; we go up to the counter, order our meal and then proceed to our table, just and I do mean just, as our bums sink into our seats. A couple of cars screech to a halt outside. The otherwise empty café bearing myself, Audrey and the staff immediately filled up with an army of tattoocd muscle men, weird? The very tall, very muscular and very well-dressed man enters the doorway. This isn't a movie or a work of fiction; this shit happened and it happened like that. Who do you think this particular gentleman was? Why none other than me gangster and a squadron of some of his entourage of personal soldiers. Holy shit. Now, I'm not the biggest man in the world, but even I couldn't find a rock large enough to hide under. So anyway, this silverback lopes this way over to our table and flashes his most sincere wolf grin."

"Do you remember what you said to me last night?"

(I'm dead anyway, so what's the difference?)

"Yeah, I do; I called you a non-good-cunt. Now I'm saying it to your face, you're a non-good-cunt."

"How – fucking – dare you tell us that you were going to do this, that and the other for Amy. Then you do fuck all! Who do you think you are?"

(slow, bad – guy laugh), you're either mad, or else you've got some set of bollocks. Then he turned on his heel and walked outside to a table set up with good friends, his cronies. I'll be honest with you, my heart nearly battered its way out of my chest as I sat watching King Kong and his troupe of ninja warriors tear chunks of meat off the bone in the name of "breakfast," a sudden and shocking realisation hit me, I was a gobshite. Anyone of these hunter–killer types could probably have ripped my flesh off my bones with their bare teeth and yet, I had given their alpha a dog stick and put it up to him? Foolish if not suicidal. No matter what, he'd left me alive and hey. Who knew maybe he'd make good at some point on his earlier promises? I waited until Kong and company finished their feasts, then called the waiter over, who was actually a friend of ours.

"Do me a favour. Give me their bill."

"Are you sure Dave?"

"Yeah, just give it here."

I paid the most insignificant bill and Mr. Gangster's shadow left over the table.

"Thanks for picking up the Tab. Nice of you."

"No problem, least we can do."

"He (put out his paw, I shook it), I wish you two the best of luck in your search for Amy."

That was that. It could've been a lot worse; it could've been a miraculous piece of good fortune had he lived up to his own hype but that's life when you're facing ever insurmountable odds in darkest times. You'll literally try anything. It reminds me of a nature show I once watched when a tiger attacked a deer of some kind but failed and the deer had a lucky escape. The mournful narrator conveyed to us the idiot view – something along the lines of how over 999 of these attacks and in failure, the tiger has to keep trying or else, its cubs will die. So far, Audrey and I were close to 100% failure, but we'd keep trying anyway. Amy wasn't going to starve, not on our watch. We'll fight for the life of our "cubs" against any odds. Time wasn't helping us; our silverback friend loved to hear himself talk like so many "gangsters" even when there's nothing in it for them other than their own self aggrading. I just hope that Mr. Gangster doesn't rear this or need real help himself someday.

We then looked a little closer to home (so to speak and met with a person whom we were told was in the I.R.A) one of the many difficulties you face in dealing with this particular group in their famed level of secrecy... Is it the "actual" I.R.A or the "real" I.R.A or, the "continuity "or the" I can't believe it's not the better version? Then you throw in the whole "needy gangster element of whether or not this person is an actual somebody or just a hopeless Ulsterman with delusions of

277

meritocracy. I'd spent my whole life avoiding people like that, but you do what you have to do for your little girl. And then we eventually managed to get a face to face meeting with a person "in command," but it wasn't in Spain and it wasn't in Ireland. I prefer not to say anything more about where we met for two reasons – our commitment to confidentially and their insistence upon it. The people who we met were, to me, the real deal, they talked the talk and walked the walk. They know a lot about missing people in general, but not Amy specifically.

One of the new ideas we heard at that meeting concerned not where Amy was taken but where she was taken to. It is their considered opinion that Amy was definitely taken and they suggested that we look to Africa. Specifically, North Africa, as it is so easy to just disappear from there, we really didn't want to hear that or what else they said. On a map of North Africa, you are immediately drawn to a big bright patch of yellow. A desert and not just any old desert either – the Sahara. That doesn't come much deadlier than that, do they?

"Deserts go on for miles and miles in every direction, so it's almost impossible to track in them. Also, if someone needs to die, it'll look like heat exhaustion or any number of plausible alternatives if the body is found at all."

We really didn't need to hear that either. Deserts? Death? A tiny needle in the world's biggest deadliest haystack? All of our work, efforts, and blood, sweat and tears had suddenly evaporated into a bunch of nothing, especially if that were true. Fuck!

"Look, we have a good bit of activity around that part of the world, so we'll get the word out on the street about Amy. We'll get back to you."

"Thanks, when do you think that will be?"

"We contact you, you don't contact us."

Fair enough, I'd heard that particular line before, but never with that cold level of menace. It took a few months, but we did get to have another meeting with them.

"We've heard nothing back; no one's seen her. Nobody's talking."

Fuck. That was another sickening but-punch, another flicker of hope trampled underfoot. I was utterly deflated and Audrey tried consoling me, but I was past that.

"Audrey, if the I.R.A. can't find Amy, then we are in big trouble. Even bigger trouble than we think."

And here we are, years later, with nothing. No sightings, no, nothing, but she's not forgotten, never will be and we will find her. Looking back through the lens of hindsight. I continue to question myself, looking for an impossible answer. Were those guys the real deal? Were they even involved? Could we have climbed further up that ladder and spoken to the "generals," or whatever it is they are called? Would we have done so only to sit in front of the same people anyway? It's a never–ending series of questions. Leading to more questions pulling you around in ever-expansive circles. It's counterintuitive and counterproductive and draining all at the same time. It's so tiring. No, it's late and I want to go to bed; tired but tired of life, tired of failure, tired of looking for reasons not to jump off a bridge or walk out into the sea with rocks in my pockets. Will the next time I hear about deserts – human trafficking –prostitution – drugs - or serial killers be the last one I can take? I know that my nerves were shot; Audrey was in ever-greater danger because suddenly she was starting to get little pains here and there that weren't going away, they were growing into bigger, more violent attacks. She was dying facts.

We went into another scheduled meeting with the Guardia Civil and listened to the usual "no update" diatribe, but we also got something else this time, something different:

"We know that you are both meeting with the underworld."

"That's hardly a secret, so what?"

"No, it's good. Go ahead and talk to them because they definitely won't talk to us."

We'd never disclosed where exactly we were getting our information from, but it didn't matter because law enforcement didn't want to know. They did nothing with it anyway, not since the very early days. Most people who read the papers or listen to the news about Amy or any missing person never fully appreciate the power that they possess. Yes, dear reader, that includes you. Politicians only give a damn when the general public – voters-want something done en-mass politicians tell the police what to do in no uncertain terms in what amounts – more or less - to "get this fucking done quickly!" No better organisation on the planet than the "ol police" to read off a list of excuses as to why they can't do their jobs and so begins the next set of bullshit. Power tends to see who gets stuck with the scorn and opinion of the public. When the papers go into a tie-break they point the finger of blame at the judiciary this is when your daily mail (or insert whatever right-wing pulp that suits) will scream headlines of the low-hanging – fruit variety along the trend of "useless laws are killing children!" or "hero cops frustrated by arcane judges that type of things. All the while, nothing gets done. Next time you see those headlines look for what is missing… in this instance-who the fuck is looking for Amy? Governments, judiciary, police and media, four little fingers in the same glove where public interests are represented by horribly deformed thumbs. Smiling gobshites shaking hands and making empty promises they never hope to fulfil, that's the recipe for what constitutes concerning media optics when you need all the fingers in that glove squeezing into a tight helpful first. I wish you luck with that. In those media dispatches, you'll often come across this tired old (but for them – effective) "line;" ... The family are receiving consular assistance at this time…" This is the get-out-of- jail-free card that the aforementioned unholy alliance relies upon to show that they are doing something or in the news – media speak. "We are doing all we can to assist the family. Be rest assured that no stone will be left unturned…." It sickens me every time that I see it because I know from experience what it really means. At best, it is a paper – trail for wannabe do-gooders because, on paper you do get assistance at the consular level, but you have to beg like a dog for that. What help does it provide? The best way I can describe it is if you imagine being in a car accident, the injured party is bleeding to death in front of you. You have a phone, so you could call for help. You have a belt around your waist that you could use as a tourniquet to stem the flow of blood. You could do any number of things, but here's what you actually do;

"There, that must really hurt. I wish you every success."

Helpful, isn't it? Ah, well, at least their "hearts" are in the right place, eh?

Yet again, our best hope lay with the underworld.

Audrey and I continued to make strides up the pyramid, but we weren't there yet. At one of our meetings, we were asked if we had considered using a "mouse-trap." I didn't have a clue what the guys were talking about, but it was one of those occasions when it was better to just shut up and listen. It was good that I did because my head was full of thoughts about famous west-end plays of the long running variety and useless quotes about ruling the world with the design of better working mousetraps. I was one – hundred-percent positive that I didn't want to hear the answer, but…

"So, what's a mousetrap then?"

"Have you never heard of it before?"

"No."

"Alright, it's easy enough. All you have to do is set up an account on the internet and pretend that you are looking for a child fitting Amy's description.

"Well, we are looking for that exactly that! How does that help?"

"Because of this bit, you're looking to buy one."

"I'm sorry, did you just say…"

"Buy. Yeah, you heard that right."

"Are you for f…."

"Real? Yeah. Hence, the best bit, you're buying for sex."

"Bollox off, no fucking way, I'm no pervert forget about…"

"I thought you said you'd do anything to find her?"

"We will, but…"

"Then you can't ignore the idea."

"Fine, we'll give it some thought."

Holy shit. What wasn't discussed was that only a couple of days before that meeting, I'd made the front pages of some of the local rags for…. drinking coffee and reading a paper in a local café. Big news, huh? Audrey and I were just grateful that I wasn't having a pint at the time because then the whole Irish –alcoholic– abusive stepfather cliché would've been dusted off. Now I was considering the idea of going on-live and looking to buy a pubescent teenage girl matching Amy's description for sex. What could possibly go wrong? Well, everything actually, but that smart arse of a gangster had really put it up to me. Was I willing to do anything to get Amy back or was I full of shit like the silverback? Every fibre of my very being screamed caution and yet, what if?

Audrey and I went through the possibilities at some length, believe me, and finally, we decided to bite the bullet and go to the Guardia Civil. What myself and Audrey didn't discuss and really should've was our health. I've already said that Audrey was dying; well, she couldn't hide it anymore, even her eyes betrayed her, custard–yellow where the whites used to be. I was sneaking off to get sick and on the good days, there wasn't too much blood. It's different to explain how your mind works, but it's a powerful thing. Laser focus blocks out pain, which can tell you as a fact, but your body is a machine and if you don't give it periodic maintenance well, you know the rest. I would imagine that the two officers we meet with in Fuengirola thought that we'd come straight off the set of "The Walking Dead" or something, but laser focus and all that. This meeting and what we discussed would change Audrey forever had I known that beforehand it should never have taken place. I'd have gone alone. The only reason I didn't was because it all felt too perverted to discuss it without her there. It seems silly now, but at the time, I feared that the Guardia civil might've thought- "Oh yeah, brings the misses all the time except when he wants to "pretend" buying young girls for sex? Fucking paedo…." Even writing that makes me want to dry heave, it's fucking disgusting, no matter what way you look at it. Anyway… I did have Audrey with me and we discussed the demon deed:

"Do you know what a mousetrap is?"

"Yes, sure we know of them. Why?"

"Well, you see, we met someone and…"

"Who?''

"You know better than to ask us that by now, right?"

"Si, but we have to try, no?! Please…"

"Anyway, neither myself or Audrey are particularly good on computers…."

"Go on…"

"Well, it was suggested that we advertise for a young girl-Amy's description to buy her…. for sex."

"Si anything else?"

"Isn't that enough?"

"Well, don't limit yourselves to just sex, you know?"

"No."

"Well, we see all kinds, you know-hunting games, live sex shows…."

The list of the grotesque seemed infinite. We honestly live in a sick and fucked – up world. Not much scared me then, even less now, but those "dark web" internet sites are beyond terrifying. Human beings have degraded as a species to something far below the level of a mere commodity. I wouldn't put a bag of sugar through the indignities out there, what's being done to people every day. I won't ever consider those sites and Amy…. I just can't. That must've been the moment when Audrey's strength finally went. She's a trooper, too strong for her own good. Nobody knew; we could see that she wasn't well and far from her best, but we couldn't have anticipated this before we left the Guardia Civil. They advised us against such a course of action and had we had the expertise ourselves to log on to the dark web and set up the mousetrap (Also known as a honey trap in some circles), then we would have done it, of that, I have no doubt. However, without the support of law enforcement or government backing, then we would've been rightly screwed had we caught someone. We asked the Guardia civil that if we couldn't do it, then could they. They had the infrastructure, the expertise and the full power and might of the Spanish government behind them. Would they have somebody to set this up and check it intermittently? The honest answer is I don't know; they've yet to get back to us about it.

Audrey was unusually quiet on the journey back to the house. She seemed out of it. When we walked back inside, I went to put the kettle on and turned to tell Audrey something. She wasn't there? I came out of the kitchen and saw her on the hallway floor. I rushed over to her and put my hand on her head, moving it gently from side to side.

"Audrey! Audrey, can you hear me? Are you alright?"

Nothing: She was cold to the touch and unresponsive. I felt around for her pulse and had trouble finding it, but it was there, faint and weak. It hadn't been too long ago that we'd been in this exact spot when I'd broken down and she raised me back up. I'd wanted to die that night (and honestly, part of me did) and now here we were again. Roles reversed; the easy option would've been to just curl up beside her and hold her until she passed peacefully from this world. Just like I did with my mother not too long before, with Audrey gone, my health already in the toilet, I'd have just laid down beside her, holding her remains until I, too, was gone. It wouldn't have taken long; she was and is my reason to live. I don't know how long it would've taken until we were discovered, as nobody gave a shit about us anymore. It was just us and the dwindling hope of seeing Amy again; we were truly alone. For all of our friends, family supporters and well-wishers, we'd never been so isolated. Well, fuck all of that. I wasn't quitting on Audrey or Amy and never will. I could've called an ambulance and sat there holding her and talking to her until it arrived.

In a TV show, all the paramedics would burst through the doors, laden with bags full of all kinds of life-saving apparatus, stretchers, and oxygen the whole nine yards. On the TV, everything happens in one, slick movement. In reality, it's chaos, but organised chaos, as these people knew their stuff. Life-saving gizmos attached and are up and away in the back of a wailing ambulance driving at the frantic pace of Lewis Hamilton on crack cocaine. I know this because I've seen it plenty of times in Ireland. Had I called the ambulance for Audrey in Spain, her dust-covered – skeleton would still be waiting. Why? Because they're shit.

Thank God, I always make it a practice to leave a good drop of petrol in my car because if I had stopped for petrol or anything that night, then Audrey would be dead. I had her in my car and on the road to the hospital before I even realised what I was doing, talking to her the whole time, begging her to just "hang in there." I had been in a hospital in Marbella before getting a serious operation on my knee, so I instinctively drove there. Like a homing pigeon with a medical degree, a hospital is a hospital…. except when it isn't. This was Spain, not Ireland, when I'd been there with my knee. I had insurance and all the usual bells and whistles that go with such things. Since then, since Amy, I'd barely remembered to shave, let alone review insurance policies for private medical care, so I drove us in a "hornets" nest without knowing it. Lucky Dave strikes again.

I grabbed a doctor as soon as I entered the hospital and pretty much imposed Audrey on him. He was a decent man, to be fair and went into "gotta – save-my-patient" mode straight away. How bad was Audrey? Really bad. A lot more dead than alive, deader than any live person has a right to be.

"How is she, doc? Is she okay? Is she going to make it?"

"Prepare yourself for the worst. She's touch and go. It's not looking good."

"What is it?"

"I can't tell she's losing a lot of blood..."

"What can I do? What do you need?"

"Out of the way!"

With that, she was stretchered off into a treatment room surrounded by nervous people in white coats. If it had been in English, I still wouldn't have known what they said, it was all "si, si" this and long-Latin-sounding-medical-term-that. I was frozen in shock. Now what? How the fuck did it come to this? Losing blood? How the hell did it come to this? It could've been a minute; it could've been an hour. I was too shocked to have any real concept of time. But the next thing I remember is the doctor walking towards me, his hands dripping with blood, my Audrey's blood. In these situations, you read facial expressions other tells with a keen awareness of the world's best poker players. We all have this gift only the most of us; it takes extreme stress, nervous shock-whatever-to bring it to life. He was covered in Audrey's blood, his expression was grim-apologetic. He was flanked by two suited administration people. Stony faced business like, whatever it was I was about to hear, I knew it was bad.

"Your wife? She needs a blood transfusion now."

"Well, do it then!"

"She needs hysterectomy – now too, or she dies, yes?

"For fuck's sake, do it, whatever it takes, don't let her die!"

Enter the weasel-necked tight ass fuck bureaucrats."

"You have no insurance cover."

"I don't?"

"No, no insurance, no blood, si?"

"Did you not hear (pointing) to him?? She's dying, for fuck's sake, how much is it?"

"Sir, this is a private hospital. You can't just…"

"Don't fucking give it all "that" shite, how much? Cash?"

It was like talking to pencil-pushing – knob-ends. All over the world, hiding behind the fussy little clipboards, the most powerful tool in the known universe. Time – killing reams of paperwork. We went to and from a bit, no give-in with them at all, so then they dropped the shiny cherry of this cake of shit.

"You must take your wife and go now, or we'll call the Guardia Civil and you must make arrangements to pay us. What you owe us."

I stood slack-jawed and open–mouthed at the doctor, Audrey's blood still dropping off the ends of his-finger-tips, its little crimson cascade forming tiny puddles of the precious life-giving liquid that its owner could ill – afford to lose. Yet there it was Audrey's life was not important enough for this. American owned /accountant managed Spanish hospital to break paperwork protocols, the blood they needed to transfer dripping off a doctor, shrugging his shoulders in a polite "Well, what can I do about it?" Way, the client type (doesn't get more specific when you think about it) pooling and concealing its desperate rosacea shapes, destined to end up in a filthy mop-bucket with the rest of the detritus soiling their pristine corridors. Well, I've said it before and I'll say it again "Fuck that for a game of soldiers;"

"Call the Guardia civil?? Go ahead, sees if I give a fuck, what are they going to do? Charge me for bringing my sick and dying partner to the hospital? Good luck with that, you pencil-necked prick."

"Well, I…. I…, how dare…."

"Whatever fuck off.? You (to the doctor) are you going to treat her or let her die?"

"I agree – yes-she should have blood and needs immediate treatments.

"But…."

"But nothing. Is there somewhere else?"

Don't forget all this time Audrey is bleeding out. Heart rate, pulse and all other vital signs plummeting into the abyss. Yet again, the language barrier wasn't helping, so I called our solicitor/translator/friend, Juan Delfante, to interfere:

"Yes-of-course, where are you Dave, exactly?"

"The private hospital in Marbella"

"Okay, I'm in Malaga, I'm in a taxi, I'm on the way... put the account cunt back on."

I did and Audrey was immediately put into an ambulance and rushed to the public hospital. I know you can't get an ambulance in Spain, not if you even tried buying one and yet there we were in an ambulance rushing from a hospital to…. a hospital. Who ever said that life wasn't without its ironies? Upon arrival at the public hospital, it was déjà-vu only in analogue as opposed to digital, but the care and treatment were of the gold standard. You get who you pay for. There are exceptions to every rule. Audrey was saved, there's no other way of expressing it to you, the solid medical professionals who saw to that. Accept our perpetual thanks and gratitude to Juan Delfante, wherever you may be (you crazy bastard!), ditto and for too many other reasons to recount about the private hospital? We agreed to pay 50% upfront in cash worth every penny to keep Audrey alive and pennies are all they care about health doesn't get a seat at the church of the immaculate currency and never will oh, and for all of their cash-clinical expertise and fancy expensive tests-Audrey didn't need a hysterectomy. It was one of the first things the "poor" relations in the public emergency room told us. Now and I swear to God, I'm not being bitchy-if they said that to Audrey and me, then two questions arise: why and who else? The "why" of it seems (to me anyway) to be born out of financial gain-the more procedures they do, the greater the revenue; their attitude and evidence speak for themselves. The other question, the "who else of it all," well, that's deeply troubling. It is only in very recent times that this little emerald isle of ours was embroiled in the Dr. Neary scandal, something very similar, I'm sure you will agree. I am not for a second trying to make light of the horrors that those poor women have and continue to live with. But maybe there is a scandal of even more epic proportions waiting to explode in Spain. This, God forbid, could be a global problem, so doesn't that at least warrant a look? It's improbable that such identical issues should arise thousands of miles apart for the same generation of women, isn't it?

Anyway, Audrey was making a good recovery (thank God) and I got to have a quick update with Juan, so what better time than to fill in his back story? As you already know, he wasn't our first multi-purpose solicitor and to be honest he came with an extremely bad reputation. Franco Ray – the all-singing/all-dancing God amongst lesser men- was never really our guy. He was the Guardia's and always will be; that's not sour grapes, but he did a lot of good for us. It wasn't until we met Juan that we realised what could really be done. Look at this current example – a drop of a hat and the guy is in a taxi from Malaga to Marbella for those of you unaccustomed to Spain. That's on par with being in Wexford and needing a taxi to the far side of Dublin. How many people do you know would do that for you? That's Juan, though. He's that kind of guy, young in his 30s, Spanish with perfect English language skills and a textbook "loveable rogue" if you ever met one. Audrey and I took to him immediately and him to us, he did things for us that we could never have achieved ourselves.... I mean, I know little or nothing about football, but for those of you in the know, I'm sure you've heard of F.C. Barcelona. Not only did he have Amy's name mentioned at one of their games against Madrid, but he got her name, her photograph and details of who-how-and where to make contact finished up and across the giant screen and scoreboard during the match. That was huge and nobody else –including us could've organised that. Imagine you were in our shoes and somebody did that for your child, how grateful would you be?

"Or he might not. We won't know unless we try?"

We were then given a crash course in armchair psychology. It was like something ripped off the pages of a Thomas Harris novel - do not approach the glass, don't let Dr. Lecter inside your head-nonsense. Did we go and visit Wilson anyway? No, but not for their reasons, it was all logistical. You see, it takes months to get the clearance we would've needed to see Wilson in prison (A) by the time we get that, he'd have been moved to prison (B) In Spain, they use that tactic as a punishment tool for people like Wilson because he had once sliced up a Spanish Prison Guard. He also received an additional 5 years to his 18-year stretch for doing that, giving him the grand total of 23 years.

Around the same time as Amy's disappearance in January 2008, a Romanian girl was abducted from Pearse Street in Dublin's south inner city. She, or rather her remains, were recovered in 2008 and her name was Mariora Rosta. Wilson's Cousin was subsequently arrested and charged with her horrific death. She was raped and violently tortured before her murder. He was acquitted. The Irish Garda doesn't see any connection. I guess Black kitten/Black cat only applies when it suits them. We must be the mad ones, eh? We had many more meetings with both the Garda and the Guardia Civil about trying to get the area in Coin searched again, but (you guessed) it never happened. We even had discussions with the underworld about having the house - the land - the whole mess searched again and even they were flabbergasted at the failure of the policing authorities to get this done. Their methodology in doing it would've been far more thorough, but given how Wilson was a gun for hire and had killed people (we'll never know how many) in the past, he was a 'somebody' and therefore knew only too well how to cover his tracks;

"Dave, he'd know how the police think."

"What do you mean?"

"Well, for a start, he'd know that they'd have to obtain a search warrant."

"Right."

"And only the courts can grant them, especially a rented property."

"Okay?"

"Dave, well you probably don't want to hear this next bit…"

"Go on."

"Sure?"

"Yes and no, but yeah, I'll need to know it, unfortunately."

"He could just dig a hole past the perimeter of his boundary walls or fences."

"Yeah, so what does that mean?"

"Simply put, the Guardia execute a warrant for his premises. The search begins and ends there. That's it."

"Right?"

"So, therefore, they can't touch any of the neighbouring properties without evidence or probable cause of some kind."

"Why is that a problem?"

"You've dealt with the Guardia; you know what they're like!"

"True that."

"Besides, everything in this country comes down to currency; even their bleedin' uniforms are money-coloured! An extended search would be very expensive; therefore, they'd never be given a warrant, simple as that, really."

I can put my hand on my heart and tell you that I would never have put those pieces together like that. These people think differently; it's an intelligence of a different kind and when you play chess on their board, they're so many moves ahead that the game is over before it even begins. They tap into that primordial murk in the back of the lizard part of the brain that you don't like to even acknowledge. It makes you think differently too, and criminal, paranoid thoughts breed like cockroaches. I couldn't help but think that maybe they weren't telling me something?

"Are you trying to tell me that Amy is up there? In that General area?"

"No, Dave, no way. If we knew something, we'd tell you."

I believe that 100%. They weren't gossip or rumour mongers; they knew to talk and not to talk. Amy's info was something they'd definitely share with us. There's a lot to be said about the criminal code. Audrey and I were back and forth to Spain like yo-yos. Attending meeting after useless meeting with both sets of law enforcement of Government officials. I don't know where the money came from to pay for all that travel, but our friends and families never saw us go too short. The easy solution would've been to sell a story to the media, but it's something we'd never do; that's blood money. Unfortunately, the same thing can't be said about our Garda and Government. They could learn a lot of morality from the criminal code, how messed-up is that?

Out of nowhere, the newspapers "stumbled" upon the Wilson story. On the TV, radio and internet - all media platforms - Eric 'Lucky' Wilson was being named as the 'Main suspect in the Disappearance of Irish Teenager, Amy Fitzpatrick.' The only people - on media-friendly terms - we'd shared that extremely confidential information with were... the Police and Governments. This was an uncontrollable media circus born out of our knowledge and control but mainly out of greed. Pure and Simple. The eye-catching irony about all the coverage wasn't "Convicted killer" or "Gun for hire" but his photograph. He was just 23 years old and – pains me to say it - a very good-looking bloke, so it's entirely possible that a guy like that (and being Irish into the bargain) might well have met up with Amy that night. Alternatively, he might have absolutely nothing to do with Amy's disappearance. What do we know? Audrey and I are just two - exhausted, exasperated, heartbroken and desperate- parents trying to find our missing daughter. We don't have the training or the skills that the police have (or should have), and thankfully, we don't possess their shameless greed either. If it wasn't him, wouldn't it be great (for all concerned) to strike him off our list of suspects?

Eventually, the penny dropped and the Garda decided to bless us with a "liaison officer." We immediately felt that it was another in a long line of fob-offs. It's not like we were strangers to them at this stage. Audrey and I decided to travel the short journey from my father's house in Santry to Coolock Village, where Coolock Garda Station is based;

"Can we speak to Det. Sgt. Eddie Carroll, please?"

"What about?"

"We've got to meet with him."

So, off the desk, the sergeant stormed, huffing and puffing under his breath like an anti-Christ because he wasn't on a need-to-know basis. He returned with an equally ecstatic - to-see us, Carroll;

"Looking for me?"

"That depends. Are you Eddie Carroll?"

"Detective. Sergeant. Carroll, yes."

"Then, yes."

"What's all this about?"

291

"You're our liaison officer."

"Well, this is news to me."

"Have you ever been to Spain?"

"No, never."

To paraphrase white snake, here we went again, on our own. Think about it. We were told by the Top Brass at An Garda Siochana that we were to travel to Coolock to meet our liaison officer. We complied, as always. You'd think that an e-mail or maybe even a phone call to let him know his new duty wouldn't have been too difficult a chore to organise, wouldn't you? Welcome to Garda Land. To top it off, this shining example of intellect knew nothing about Amy's disappearance and didn't know (or care, seemingly) about being our liaison officer, oh, and never so much as stood in Spain for five seconds. We'd spent years pushing Amy's appeal on every media platform for years, up to saturation point, and this guy had never even heard of her? A local girl? Wow, we could just see him finding her, couldn't we? We were totally screwed, but what can you do? So, we gave him as much information as he could handle and let him at it. I'm not blaming him, he's just a local guard (or 'Bobby' if you were in England) trying to do his job. He looked busy enough before we got to him, so I guess we were the last thing he needed. I'd like to say that we had now reached the lowest link on the chain, but even that locked too grand and unassailable for us. We'd have been better off driving out to Howth Harbour, walking to the end of the pier and screaming into the wind. That way, at least, you'd have some hope of the wind carrying your voice off to someone who might help. If you think that's an attempt at humour, it's not. Neither is this next part; after months upon months of nothing, we met again with Eddie Carroll. He told us that he'd looked exhaustively into Wilson and that we'd been misinformed; he hadn't been in Spain during the time of Amy's disappearance. Rather, he'd been up in Northern Ireland. This was progress - of sorts - because at least now we could tick Wilson off the lists of suspects - narrow the search and your odds increase accordingly. So, we arranged another meeting with Fergus Healy up in the Garda Headquarters;

"Are you aware that Wilson was up the North when Amy went missing?"

"Oh yeah."

"Well, we need to remove him from our list of suspects, so are you 100% sure about this?"

"Ah yeah, we're pretty sure."

"Pretty sure?"

"Yeah, pretty sure."

"So, not definitive then?"

"Em... What?"

"As in, not 100% sure. 'Pretty sure' doesn't inspire me with confidence, you know?"

"Well.... no.... not 100%"

"Then he's back on the list, sorry."

"What? Why?"

"Well, you know he also had several allies, right?"

"Oh... we only know of two..."

"Oh, sweet Jesus, there's THREE that we know about!!"

"T... th... Three, you say?"

"So, you'd agree then, you've got a lot of loose ends to tie up there, haven't you?"

"Em... let me think."

"No need - that question was rhetorical; he's a loose end and I don't like loose ends."

"Why?"

"They make me nervous, as they should you."

"Well, we're still pretty sure that he was up N..."

"What - North?? Maybe his allies - or one of them was, he's definitely smart enough to do that."

"How do you know that?"

"Well, he's kept one ally hidden from you, and look at the size of your office and all those medals and awards you have, eh?"

"I, eh…. I see your point."

"I mean, he must be even smarter than you!"

"Well, I, eh, I don't know about that (sarcasm was lost on this guy) …"

"Well, I don't care. Do you have any CCTV of him up North at that time?"

"No."

"Eye-witnesses?"

"No."

"Mobile phone tracking or triangulation?"

"No."

"What route did he travel?"

"We don't know."

"When did he leave the North?"

"We can't answer that."

That's the Garda Siochana for you, good, aren't they? Inspire confidence in you yet? We'd go on to discover that they'd convicted people - for life - on less than that, but that's another story. What's important here is what you are starting to see unfolding before you. They said and did a whole lot of nothing. We had given them everything every step of the way. The Guardia Civil too, had both sets of high-ranking, high powerful sets of government officials and this is the typical response. Not good enough, not nearly good enough and yet they stay in their jobs and positions of power, safely ensconced up in their Ivory towers, places where their children aren't taken and tragedy doesn't darken their doorways. Not like us, not like the plebs, we've raised our voices, shouted - screamed – and once even overturned a table full of drinks out of frustration at their apathetic attitudes. But we always stayed to the end, always endured because it's what you do, you stick it out. Only that particular day, at that particular meeting with Fergus Healy and his high-ranking security detail, did the rules change. There was a breach in our collective protocol; Audrey -like me- couldn't, just COULD NOT believe what she was hearing. So, she stood up, glared at the table of dumb inefficiency and stormed out. Nobody saw that, least of all me. By right, I really should've jumped up out of my chair and gone out after her because her health is paramount to me. Always will be, but I didn't. I stayed and continued to listen in disbelief at the lies, apathy and management speaking nonsense (i.e., at the end of the day/ in the fullness of time/ all things considered, etc.) that said the square root of nothing in flowery phrases. Just think, that was what they were saying to our faces. Just imagine what they were saying amongst their own members, or worse - what they relayed back to the Guardia Civil. If it was anything like that, then the 'Thick Irish' shame we've heard about for so long will continue gaining traction.

You couldn't leave them in charge of a cup of coffee, so there was no way we were not going to continue doing our own investigations. I continued my research on Wilson and there can be no two - ways about it, he's a bad pill. Let me expand on that, do not under any circumstances take what you read in the newspapers or online as being true. Sometimes, the only truth in them is the date on the top of each page and I kid you not. The online stuff is just as bad, sometimes; even worse, it depends on how good the cat-coaxing skills are of those keyboard cowards on any given day. We were very fortunate (some days) to have trusted access to the reliable underworld, if that doesn't sound too oxymoronic. They continued to have fingers on the criminal pulse at all times, so I believe what I heard. For example, when Eric (not so) 'Lucky' Wilson got pinched and then charged for the murder of 'Tall' Dan, it was said that he was a gun for hire, a hitman. My sources informed me that he had "ten notches under his belt"- that he was responsible for ten killings in two different countries. One of his victims (it is alleged) was a Dublin man by the name of Patrick (Paddy) Doyle, who was shot dead in a neighbouring town, Estepona. That is quite literally the next town down from Marbella and this happened in February 2008. That's right, only a month after Amy disappeared, less than thirty miles away, no distance really, especially in Spain. Then again, maybe he was in Northern Ireland at that time? To be honest with you, I don't know because I can't know, Audrey and I don't have the resources to ever be sure. It is also very important to state - right here and now - that this book is not an attempt (veiled or otherwise) to pin Amy's disappearance on Wilson. He's a bad'un for sure, but we cannot claim anything more than that. I'll go further, that is not by way of some sort of legal disclaimer. It's purely and simply nothing more than a matter of fact. Here we are, all these years and all we – can tell you for absolute certainty is that we don't know. I've given you every shred of every lead we ever got, so it's up to you to decide. There are several suspects and it could be any one of them; it probably - more than likely - is. Then again, it could just as easily have been a complete opportunist. What we do know, though, is how great things could've been had the Police done their jobs properly from day one. What we thought was good, in reality, should've been so much better.

We only hope that someday we'll be able to cross person "X" off our list and then reconsolidate and refocus our efforts. Maybe even move on with our own lives someday. Who knows? I've been told on many occasions about killers attending the scene of their crimes after the fact, gloating in a sense at not having been caught, a morbid sense of accomplishment perhaps? It is with that same Ghoulish longing that I expect the low-down piece of shit who took Amy to have bought this book (or Trophy?) and salivate over his or her own "brilliance" on every page. If that person is you, then know this, I'll see you in Hell. We're not going to give up the search. Our meetings with the Guardia Civil have essentially run their course and our contact with the Garda Siochana was pointless. So once again, it is and will remain me and Audrey against the world. The world is a big place, but smaller than you'd think. We'll find you eventually, and Amy.

A massive part of our 'Taken' Rulebook didn't involve Liam Nelson croaking down a telephone line about a 'unique set of skills or nonsense' like that; rather, it involved good old-fashioned leg were??

Audrey looking very frail after Amy's disappearance.

Guardia Civil searching for Amy, in fairness the Guardia did a lot in the early days.

Dave and Audrey's first book "Please Find My Amy."

Dave, Audrey and the Mayor of the canary island.

The three mothers of missing children,
Yeremi Vargas, Sara Morales and Amy Fitzpatrick

Dave and Audrey have a meeting back in Ireland with the minister for foreign affairs Michael Martin

BUCKINGHAM PALACE

The Private Secretary has been

asked by The Queen to thank you for your

correspondence which has been received

by Buckingham Palace, and to say that the

enclosed reply is sent to you on her

behalf.

Letter from the Queen and 10 Downing St, even though Amy is not English.

1O DOWNING STREET
LONDON SW1A 2AA
www.pm.gov.uk

From the Direct Communications Unit   4 August 2008

Dear Ms Fitzpatrick

   I am writing on behalf of the Prime Minister to thank you for your letter of 21 July.

   This is receiving attention and a reply will be sent to you as soon as possible.

Yours sincerely

E. Adams

MRS E ADAMS

Ms Audrey Fitzpatrick

PH.: 0034 617561319
Email: missingamy@live.co.uk

9, Los Lomas de Riviera Club,
Riviera del Sol,
Mijas Costa,
29649
Malaga.
Spain

To Whom it May Concern,
Could this letter please be passed on to Her Majesty?

My name is Audrey Fitzpatrick, my daughter Amy has been missing for 6½ months now. She was 15 went she went missing 01/01/08 walking home from her friends house. She has since turned 16, has missed her brothers 18th, my 40th and so many other things.

The reason I'm writing to you is, we live on the Costa del Sol in a mainly British community, full of British tourists any yet the British media have failed to follow Amy's story even after being asked repeatadly.

Is there anyway you can use your influence to get them to publise Amy's story? My phone number and email address are at the top. Please help, Amys photo needs to be out there all the time.

Kind Regards

Audrey Fitzpatrick

3rd September 2008

Our reference: 62124

Mrs A Fitzpatrick
Las Lomas de Riviera club
Riviera del Sol
Mifas Costa
29649 Malaga
Spain

Foreign &
Commonwealth
Office

London SW1A 2AH

Minister for Europe

Dear Mrs Fitzpatrick

Thank you for your letter to the Prime Minister about the disappearance of your daughter, Amy Fitzpatrick, in Spain. I am replying as Minister for Europe at the Foreign and Commonwealth Office (FCO).

This must be a very distressing time for you and your family.

The Irish Embassy in Madrid and the Irish Department of Foreign Affairs in Dublin are the correct points of contact, as the FCO can only provide consular assistance to British nationals.

I understand that the Irish Embassy in Madrid is providing you with assistance. You could approach them for advice on the best way to get coverage of Amy's disappearance into the press, both locally in the Malaga region and more widely. I have also enclosed contact details for several organisations, which I hope will be helpful in tracing Amy.

Yours

Jim Murphy MP
Minister for Europe

303

Dave And Audrey met another Taoiseach (Prime Minister) Brian Cowen.

Audrey has another meeting with the Taoiseach (Prime Minister) Enda Kenny

Audrey and Dave having a meeting with yet another Taoiseach (Prime Minister)
Berti Ahearn

Dave and Audrey at the WOW factor in Spain

Guardia Civil searching for Amy

Beautiful blue eyes.

Audrey is at death's door

Two large billboards posters in Spain, one in English and the other in Spanish. We were told to take them down, as it was bad for tourism. (Now what do you think?)

For a very long time I didn't touch anything in Amy's bedroom

THE AMY FITZPATRICK STORY

PLEASE FIND MY

AMY

by her mother
Audrey Fitzpatrick

This is the Las Lomas de Riviera Club, where we lived, and below is the stretch of road it's thought Amy may have walked along to get home

Wow Factor

Audrey's relentless efforts in the Amy campaign continue to this day. She is online constantly with all the many contacts we've built up over the years, but before we had that priceless database, we really did lean heavily upon the kindness of strangers in the early days. Two such people come to mind, two lovely girls originally from England and had moved to Gibraltar. They wrote a song for Amy.

They were of Amy's vintage, maybe a year younger, so no more than 14 years old or so. To help with their writing process, they asked to meet up with us, so of course, we agreed it was an honour to meet up with two obese ,kind-hearted young ladies and their mother. It really humbled us that such children, especially, would even think of doing than let alone do it. They decided upon what was, in my opinion – the perfect song title- "Somebody's Lost Princess," for all the mean-spirited and apathetic people we come across, it did the heart good as seeing that such lovely people still existed.

It was also the time of year for the reality T.V. shows to start remounting, even in Spain, and like the X-factor in Britain, the 'wow factor' was the flavour of the month in Spain. It worked to essentially the same format as its more famous snail-mote, even down to the judging panel, Simon Cowell's brother and one of the judges from Strictly Comes Dancing. There was even a wealthy, Alan sugar/apprentice type judge called Bassim Haidar to tick the local businessman made good box.

As for us, in the long list of contacts we'd built up over the years, we'd managed to count at least one in the recording business, so we were only too delighted to secure several hours at a recording studio again, the kindness of friends we weren't changed for the studio time, a lovely gesture because it's far from cheap. It made those two girls very happy too, so it was one of those rare, win-win situations. Finally, the night of the wow factor arrived, held at the Torrequebrada Hotel in Benalmadena. As the girls were still too young to compete as entrees, they were allowed to set up on the stage and kick off the pre-show. I guess you'd call it. They were introduced by a well-known radio personality from the Costa called Maurice Boland.

He made a point of going through a lengthy dissertation about Amy's disappearance before allowing the girls to sing. It was strange, as much as we love Amy's case to be vocalised to the masses and you could never have enough 'air-time,' he was effectively singing to the choir because everybody in that room knew all about Amy and it couldn't have helped the already nervous girls on the biggest stage of their lives. Finally, he spoke very well about what the girls had done and why they were there and then it was down to them.

For a fact, I was more nervous than they were – I was thinking about how young they were and the delay coupled with the huge crowd – but I shouldn't have worried. They weren't good, they were spectacular! When they say the words "somebody lost princess," my face morphed into a leaky sponge. Then, when I saw video footage of Amy and her best friend Kim on the giant screen behind them, all those beautiful happy times, our beautiful happy daughter – laughing, joking and pouting – blissfully unaware of the horrors in front of her, I had the emotional equivalent of a heart attack. I couldn't breathe for the heaving of my tear-laden-gulps for air. I'm not a big crier; there was no earthly exploration for that amount of tears to come out of my face and so, the coward that I am, disappeared off to the toilets. You couldn't stay there another moment. It's not desperation or anger; it's a horrific hybrid entity that I hope you never experience.

When the performance was over, Audrey's manifested eyes never left the stage as she stood to applaud two young girls, she couldn't have been more proud of them as if they were her own. She instinctively reached across for my hand, obviously for comfort and support. That's when she realised that the coward writing this wasn't there. Nor my prouder moment, but Audrey knows me better than I know myself, so no explorations were necessary. I exited the bathroom at about that second anyway. Hearing the thunderous applause confirmed that it was safe to do so. It was a standing ovation, every eye in the house blinking our tears like smarties at a kid's party. I started to crumble again, so we held each other and cried our hearts out. Who won? I couldn't tell you if my life deepened on it. All I could do was concentrate on not crying until we got home.

At the end of the evening, we met one of the judges – Bassim - the local Billionaire businessman. He seemed like a good guy – married to an Irish girl from Cork and was very well informed on Amy's campaign. He insisted on donating a few thousand euros for it and as usual, I felt really awkward about accepting it, but what do you do, slap everyone down when they only want to help? I asked him to make the cheque out to the private investigations company we were using and he duly obliged. That was another bill paid anyway.

Audrey and I will never forget that night and we've never really discussed my sharpish existence during the performance; we don't have to. Audrey sees the same reaction from me wherever she plays the YouTube videos of Amy and Kim singing.

I love them too much to watch, if you can figure that one out. Not Audrey, though, she feels closer to Amy every time she watches them and from what I've learned about a mother's infusion over the years. I want to rule that out. There is one YouTube video on my bucket list that I'll never tire of watching on shy away from the one where all three of us are reunited. What a day that's going to be.

Amy's Disappearance – Early Days

Our legs took us far and wide but not too far from the reasonable bounds of probability. I guess the 6-hour drive up to Alicante, to the much larger population of Irish ex-pats, is as good a place to start as any. You must always consider what could be possible (a wide and difficult option) against what seems most likely (narrower-faster), and that is based on known behaviours. So, what did we know about Amy at that age? First, the obvious- young, very good-looking, firm, strong vocal and above average intelligence. Was she a "typical" teenage girl, in so far as there is such a thing? Yes, most definitely – she loved music, dancing, boys and was technologically proficient. Did she live on her phone? Sometimes, but not always, case in point, there is no activity on it or the social media sites for days. Was it possible that she might have met for want of a better phrase - a "cute boy" and went off with him somewhere? Of course, it was. Hence, Alicante wasn't a bad place to begin our road-trip. In fact, it was a smart choice. Was it a long shot? At first, we thought so, but it was better than sitting around the places we'd searched already, hoping for a miracle. That was mental torture.

It's a long, exhausting drive from Amy's house up to Alicante at the best of times, but even more so when you are leading a convoy of media vehicles. We were followed everywhere we went by the T.V. and newspapers. It was relentless, but it was all for Amy, so we endured it. One of the things Audrey and I discussed on that journey was where – exactly we should start our search when we got there. It was only then that it dawned on me that I didn't know just one or two people up there. Then of course, the Irish, being who we are would network all the other ex-pats over a pint or at a sporting event or something, so we had a fantastic set of resources to tap into, and we did, however, despite having been there a couple of times in the past, I still couldn't find the bloody hotel that I'd booked us into which led to no end of grief from Audrey- "some bleeding taxi-driver you must've been!" But it gave us some much needed levity. I ended up driving into a random hotel to ask for directions and so eventually, I got us to our hotel. We went to a place called "Torrevieja." Because that was the main Irish area – Irish bars and all the best of it and it seemed as though everyone knew who we were and what we were doing there. It was a little disconnecting at first, but then you've got to step back and acknowledge the great job that the media were doing for us, haven't you? Credit where credit due, ten out of ten on that one:

"Alright, Dave, Audrey, what's the story?"

"Any news on Amy?"

"Do you think you'll find her up here?"

"Have you tried...?"

But by far and away, the most frequent question we were asked was:

"What can I help you with? What do you need?"

The Spanish-Irish, as they are becoming known as a beautiful bunch of people who offered all and asked for nothing in return. Many sincere thanks guys, we were eventually directed to the local radio station up there, where we made another appeal for Amy.

This is actually a good time to mention a word or two about appeals and interviews. If you were a child of my generation or older, then you'll probably equate the word "interview" with the likes of Michael Parkinson, Terry Wogan or Jonathan Ross. You'd then probably remember all those famous celebrities on those various talk shows over the years. I know I did up until Amy's case. That's what interviews meant to me, famous people asking other famous people questions in front of T.V. cameras and an adoring audience. It was the realm of the rich and famous and not for the likes of Audrey and me. Then everything changed when Bob Geldof appeared on our screens in the early 80s, scruffy and snarling, appealing for aid for starving African children, that wasn't only an appeal, but it was something for normal people, not superstars. I guess what I'm trying to say is that it was accessible. It also worked, it is with those weighty, terrifying expectations that Audrey and I walked into the glare of T.V. camera's-normal people with no formal training – reaching out to an audience of people we'll never know, probably never meet and we just bared our souls for all to see. No matter what way you want to try and dress that up, it boils down to two simple words- not normal! It also isn't as easy as "Parky" makes it look; then again, they weren't looking for a young girl, lost, stolen or murdered… Each of those words weighs heavy upon your heart and adds to your interview difficulties. It isn't even like Audrey or I have a problem speaking; we don't. Each of us could talk for Ireland at an international level, but when you're given "X" amount of time to reach as many people as you can, to keep them interested long enough to not switch channels and by the way, if you're dull, inaudible or otherwise "not easy T.V" then nobody else will touch you. That's pressing; it's also exhausting. The same applies across the board, whether that be on the radio, in a newspaper or even in a bar (or in our situation, all of the above on the same day). It drains you physically, psychologically and spiritually. You run on autopilot.

After our interviews and appeals, we walked around Torrevieja, handing out flyers and leaving them by the thousands in places where we knew they would get distributed for us. Some days, you got a few minutes to sit down to a meal, but you didn't take them, you'd eat "on-the-wing" in case you missed that person, that opportunity, that would make all the difference. Alone, we'd covered a lot, but every single Irish person out there gave us such generosity of their time, resources and energy. To even say "thank you" to them is too small and twice a gesture, but it's all we've got. You guys made a difference – a real difference, and I hope you can take that on board. It was only ever going to be a flying visit and so inevitably, we had to leave. Our hearts were heavy though not "just'' because we didn't find Amy or because we were leaving a 'cocoon' of love and support for Amy that had to be experienced to believe, rather it was that thought of going back to Amy's house and her not being there. That house was no longer a home; it was an illness. It made us feel sick; it frightened us, depressed us and we couldn't stand it anymore. But where else was she going to go if she came home? What if we weren't there??? No idea.

So, it's time for a bit more role reversal. You live in a large country, the second biggest by area in Western Europe. To put it into Irish terms, it's well over twice the size of the U.K., so pretty big for such a large place. It's only got around 41 million inhabitants, so it's quite sparse but that's 41 million people to cross off your list of suspects, 41 million people to put Amy's appeal in front of in the dream of generating 80 million eyes looking for her across 504, 800 km. Within this massive land mass, you reside in a region known as Andalusia, which just so happens to be the main tourist destination. Tourism inevitably accounts for a further 52 million people added to the land mass annually. Now you have a potential list of 93 million suspects who dream of having 180/186 million eyes searching for her. There lies a problem, more tourists than inhabitants, most of which are British, German and Spanish; therefore, it is the second most popular tourist destination. Only France beats it and guess what? France is on the other side, hence one massive black hole to fill and you have to put your faith in border controls to prevent her leaving the country. To the west sits Portugal, a massive border that may or may not be plugged with more holes and escape routes than a teabag. To the west, the Mediterranean Sea, the largest sea in the world, a gateway to Europe, Africa, Asia and the Arab nations. To the south, within spitting distance on a map, sits Morocco, only a tiny straight separate you. Come to think of it, can you think of a worse place to have her child taken from? No, neither can I.

Without wishing to upset the Moroccan nation, it is a country held in bitter disdain by most of the inhabitants along the Costa. It seems to send over more than its quota of "bandits" and Audrey and I were told more than once that "the Moroccans" probably took her; they have form. "I checked, they did have 'form' alright," so I decided to go there and see what I could see. I didn't want Audrey to travel, from what I'd heard, it wasn't going to be safe for me, let alone her, and I'll never put Audrey in harm's way. So I travelled over and brought a thick, fresh supply of Amy's posters with me. A new territory, a new hope? I'm sure there are places of rich and exquisite beauty in Morocco, but I didn't see any. In fact, what I saw only filled me with dread, despair and hope? Not here.

Of the many reports I'd received about Morocco, the most plausible were amongst those concerning its proximity to Spain and the ease by which one could be smuggled there from Spain. As I said, on a map, it's only spitting distance. My natural curiosity can be my greatest ally at times, but mostly, it leads me into areas I could happily have lived the rest of my life never knowing:

"Why are so many people smuggled over to North Africa?"

"Ah, Dave, you'd be better off not knowing."

"No, go on, tell me."

"Well, you, you know prostitution and eh…. Stuff."

"Stuff??"

"Dave, I don't want to say it…"

"Stuff??"

"Dave, I really don't want to say it..."

"Bleeding, tell me. Will ya?"

"Body parts"

"What??"

"Body parts. Yeah, you heard it right."

See what I mean? Stuff you could live your life happily, never knowing about. This is the world we live in! Everybody and any part of your body is seemingly available for purchase. God help any of the Guardia civil - or any other agencies- that have to deal with these cases. Please, God, Audrey and I will never have to be the poor, unfortunate parent who has to answer the door someday to such news. Please, God, none of us are. When you are confronted by the harsh reality of these facts, your heart races, "doing ninety," as we used to say as kids, you read books about little throw-away facts and one I've always remembered (although I cannot vouch for its accuracy) is that the human heart beats a million times in a lifetime. Apparently, it's why all these old yogi masters live for as long as they can slow their hearts down so much; they "buy" out extra years to their lives. As I faced that particular voyage, I lost a couple of years, my heart pumped like the Tasmanian devil after swallowing a bucket of sugar.

Something else happens too, that you need to guard yourself again should you ever end up in our shoes - you start doubting yourself. About everything like - who were we kidding, thinking that by going to Morocco, we were somehow going to find Amy just like that? You still go, you'll still do anything -whatever it takes to find her, but your self-doubt defeats you every time. Don't let it. Also, there was that bloody language barrier again. I took a friend of mine along with me, Chris, he speaks a few languages, at six-foot-two and well able to handle himself, he had many optional extras if it came to that. We drove to the southernmost tip of Spain and boarded the boat to Morocco, the Tarifa-to-Tangiers express, as it's sometimes called for purely sarcastic reasons. I've always hated boats as I'm prone to sea sickness, so it was the worst start to an already horrible journey. I spent the time sussing everybody out. Who looked like a smuggler? Who looked like they were being brought against their will? What was the security like? Were there any places to hide people, etc.? I'm not exactly Columbo, so I arrived at our destination suspecting everything and doing nothing, well, how could I? One thing is for sure though, it could easily be done and I'm sure it's not a good prognosis for Amy's search.

Arriving in Tangiers was a bit of an eye-opener. Chris and I were - by far -the two best dressed men in the town. It's not like we arrived in full evening -dress, top "n" tails en-route to the opera, we were normal enough smart casual, I think it's called? Pretty much everybody else there looked as though their clothes had been taken off the bodies on a battle-field, the place was like a war-zone you didn't just see poverty all around you, you could smell it. It was the same on the boat, it's not a judgement, it's a fact, a basic observation. I don't recall seeing even the most rudimental suitcases or travel language, it was all patched together plastic bags, not even newish ones. It was a different plant for me. I was light-headed and green from sea sickness and throwing up, but I wasn't experiencing hallucinations. I wasn't imagining it; sometimes reality is just weird enough by itself.

Spain, especially where we live, was all-year hot, so I was used to warm climates, but Moroccan heat was different, "rougher." I supposed the smells too were different, a blend of spices sweet and heat rolled into one aromatic sandwich. The air definitely gave off a dirty, polluted texture; from experience, I've learned that one of the first stops to make (wherever you are) in any information- gathering exercise is to the local taxi drivers. I used to be one myself, there is not much they don't notice. Sure enough, there was a taxi rank nearby, so we sauntered on over. We asked if they wouldn't mind distributing some of Amy's posters among their colleagues and once again, that dreaded language barrier. I did manage to get through to a few of them and Chris looked after the ones I couldn't. They agreed to do so and got us off on the right foot. Well, so we thought. When I looked back over my shoulder at them, I noticed that they were all laughing -big joke? So I gave them a filthy look, the miserable bastards; you can only imagine what it was they said or thought and that certainly soured my mood.

We walked around the town randomly handing out flyers, trying to make our intentions clear, through a lot of broken English combined with hand signals and nods of the head, on our little sojourn, I kept a keen eye out for somewhere to stay. The little cheap hotels were a non-runner. I refused to pay and stay anywhere a cockroach turns its nose up, so we were extremely limited in terms of choice. Most of the inns were nothing more than a hotchpotch of loose timber, rusted metal and a concrete-type subsistence that stank of piss. Please, God, don't let Amy be anywhere near this kip. Every street corner had its local gang of tugs, hard eyes, betraying cruel and vicious inert. Never have I been so glad to travel without Audrey; I would've been sliced to pieces trying to protect a woman with the blondest hair and bluest eyes in that particular Islamic nation. Nope, our boys trip was the safest option. This wasn't Alicante; this was a horse of a different colour entirely. Gone were the Irish bars and the Cead Mile Failte gone to be the instant recognition and the united goal of helping Amy. As a Muslim country, bars and pubs weren't allowed, so there was no collective meeting spot to head to. It was all random, ad-hoc. I wasn't so much a fish out of water, more a fish out of whiskey! As one of my good Spanish friends would say to me in such situations:

"Dave, you must change the brain, yes? Change the brain!"

This basically equates to "think differently," but it's so much more fun when he says it, and always accompanied by his little mime where he unscrews his head and puts the other one on! Either way, he'd have been right, I had to change my approach, so we headed to the nearest police station. That turned out to be another entry into our book of the bizarre. Two police officers were posted outside of it, and as we approached, they blocked our way. I tried to commerce a line of communication with him, but I might as well have tried reciting Macbeth to a duck for all the good it did, so I turned it over to Chris. He, at least, quacked in the correct manner, but still, we were refused entry. Then he showed them some of Amy's posters, but they still wouldn't let us cross their threshold, pricks. I was furious but couldn't let them see that. As I'd imagine, I'd have joined entry then, alright! The problem is I'd still be there if they are that difficult to get into... well, you know the rest. I still don't know why they wouldn't let us in, maybe they were hiding something... or someone? I've had a bad omen about that place ever since.

"Change-deee-brain, change-deee-brain!"

We then moved on to a few not so nice places. How do I even begin to describe them... okay remember that scene in the movie "train spotting" where Ewan Mc Gregor's character has to grope around "the dirtiest toilet in Scotland" to fish out his drugs? I wish that had been where we went, as that was Buckingham Palace by comparison. It was home to the lowest of the low, no redeeming qualities whatsoever, when the humans went home, darkness followed and with the night came the rats. Not rats as we know them, not our "posh" Irish rodents; these brazen motherfuckers were huge and didn't scurry off at the first sign of people. Oh no, these things would force you off their footpath and onto the street! I'm not joking, sirs and I couldn't believe what we were witnessing. They had long mutated snouts full of inter-looking teeth that weren't designed for a warning nip. If they got a hold of you, then parts of you were coming off. You know you're in a bad area when even the local rats can beat the crap out of you. Just as I was trying to imagine how big and mean the cats would have to be, I felt a large, heavy thud on my back. I remember this like it happened yesterday and as I turned to see what it was, I prayed it wasn't the paw of the local alley-cat. It wasn't; it was Chris's hand;

"Dave, please don't leave me here."

"Leave you here?! The bleeding size of you, I'm the one that should be worried!

322

"Ah, Dave, don't mess. Did you see that rat?

"See it?! I could've put a saddle on the bloody thing!"

"C'mon, let's go. I don't like it here."

So much for my big protector! We stayed for a couple of days more, sticking Amy's posters up everywhere we could and trying as best we could to see if anyone knew or saw something. We got nowhere fast, really, but at least we'd covered another territory. If Amy was there, it might have strengthened her to know that she wasn't forgotten, she was loved and we were looking. Sometimes, that's all you can do. Sometimes that's enough. On the positive side of the equation, even more people knew about Amy's disappearance. Oh and with no other full-moons that week, we avoided the wee-rodents long enough to get safely to our boat.

Talk about déjà-vu?! Same boat, same smells, same everything. How can I know for sure that it wasn't similar from the same fleet? Easy, Amy's posters I'd put up were still there, another result because they weren't torn down and they had a captive audience; at least twice a day, every day for the duration, happy days. Once again, Chris and I were the best dressed passengers and only ones with actual luggage, again That's not bragging or me trying to be fictitious, but it's relevant why? Well, as soon as we disembarked the vessel, we, like everyone else headed over to the customs checkpoint. It was little more than a sign with 'customs' on it in a different language and people just crowded through it unhindered until myself and Chris got there,

"Excuse me, please, passports?"

"Here."

"Why travel to Morocco?"

We showed them Amy's posters and then the Guardia Civil came over. Lots of parasitic discussion in Spanish, future glances at us - to them-to us whilst every drug struggler at the terminal sauntered on by thinking that Christmas had come early. Meanwhile, Chris and I, "white boys on tour," -are burning up (no shade) and perspiring like Brian Cowen jogging around a sauna in a duffle coat. Naturally, our sweat was nothing more than a sign of weakness at being "caught," and worse now, I desperately needed that toilet, so I did the human equivalent of the pre-poo doggy dance. Lest my accident should befall me, of course, I couldn't just ask for the toilet as rule one in the drug smugglers handbook, when you are caught, the first thing to do is to flush the evidence. I don't think we could have looked any more guilty if we'd have worn masks matching jumpers in black and white stripes and carried large black sacks with "swag" emblazoned across them. All the while, this bloody chuckle brother's sketch continued looking from me -to you-to me to you, etc. So, in my very best Spanish (not very good, hardly even Spanish), I asked to speak to whoever was in charge. A commanding officer was summoned and a few painful butt-clenching moments later, he arrived. A captain of some description. I showed him all of the Amy memorabilia and kept talking until I saw the little light bulb come to life in his head. Then I asked to use the toilet and when he said that I could, I high-tailed it out of there, leaving Chris behind. When I got back, Chris and I were free to go. As we journeyed back to Amy's house."

"Jesus, Dave, you missed it!"

"Missed what?"

"The captain! He ate the bollox out of those customs lads!"

"Yeah?!"

"Oh, yeah! He said that you were the stepfather of missing Amy Fitzpatrick, that they should've known who you were and that they were to put Amy's posters up everywhere!"

Fair play to him for that and given how huge Amy's campaign was at that time, the shame on those officers for not recognizing her (not me) because when we think about it, isn't that their job? To find missing people to stop drugs and people being imported and exported illegally, in essence, to notice stuff? It doesn't inspire confidence. All other captors would've needed to do was dress her down and the eagle-eyed customs officers wouldn't have given her a second glance. Muppets, looking back maybe Chris and I did stick out and looked out of place but that's not an excuse for shoddy police work.

Back on the Costa, I met up with a few Moroccans here and there and told them about my experience in their country. Their responses?

"Why do you think we left it!!?"

Like anywhere else on our little planet, there is good and bad everywhere. That is all about balance, but I didn't see a lot of nice people when I was over there and I can only comment on what I see and experience myself. We got more people speaking about Amy, so it wasn't a total failure. When we were away from home just in case the Guardia Civil actually had news for us, unlikely as that sounds.

Till this day, you can upload Amy's poster off the internet. Please feel free to do so and put them up in your car, office, place of business, shop window, anywhere and everywhere. Audrey wanted us to hit Puerto Rico (the one in Grand Canaries) because of its heavy tourism throughout. It was a place I was already very familiar with from my younger years when my friend Darrin and I used to paint the town red there and Playa des Ingles. Audrey and I were so deeply involved and immersed in the Amy campaign that we never noticed what else was happening in the news, both from Grand Canaries.

Their names are Yermi Vargas and Sara Morales, a little boy and a little girl. The people of Grand Canaries were aware of these two beautiful little angels, but it was never reported in the Irish news. Mainland Spain was also oblivious to their disappearances. Two more working-class families left distraught and devastated. This was in 2009, so not too long after Amy, we decided to combine our respective efforts and do a joint campaign for all three missing children. Little Yermi was only 7 years old, Sara was 12, how heart breaking was that? For the Spanish mainland, we had Amy's face at the top of the poster with Sara and Yermi at the bottom, in the Grand Canaries that was reversed. These two beautiful children are from an area called Vecindario Canaries Island. Dear reader, I really cannot over-emphasise how lovely the people of these islands are when you spend your holiday there. All the blue-collar workers, like bar staff, cleaners or sanitation professionals, all have their own lives to lead; when they go home like the rest of us, this particular area Vecindario is one unfamiliar to most Irish. It's a bit out of the way, but it is a beautiful, spotless area and the people there are as warm and compassionate as you're likely to find anywhere on Earth.

Whilst en route there, Audrey and I called a few T.V. and radio stations in the Canaries to let them know we'd be around for a week or two and asked if they'd be interested in doing a few interviews with us to highlight Amy's disappearance. Every one of them was interested, but we didn't book any appointment with them or anything. We simply provided the name and address of the hotel we were staying at, as well as our obligatory mobile phone and email details. When we landed at the airport, the next thing we did was jump in a taxi and head directly to our hotel. I can't remember the exact time, but it was late enough and all I could think about doing was dropping in our bags and grabbing a glass of wine before bedtime. Well, you know what they say about the best laid plans of mice and men, don't you?

When we walked into the hotel reception, I thought I was having a seizure, flashing lights, 'clicklty-clicklty-clack' spotlights, microphones-it was like a cattle market. The first thing that comes into your mind is that all "this" has to be for someone else, it was all too much. A part of you wants to turn around and see J-lo or Lady Gaga being ushered through the throng by bodyguards the size of supervillains out of an Avengers movie. But it doesn't happen because that would be normal?!! Nope, that whole media circus was waiting for us and not patiently either. It was question-after question, in Spanish English and god knows how many other dialects. I suppose if you are Brad Pitt or Madonna, you get used to it, but it's little owl Dave "n" Audrey from nowheresville North Dublin, it is the quintessential double-edged sword on one side. You just want everywhere to piss off and leave you alone on the other too much media attention isn't half enough. Your little girl is out there somewhere and this is your best shot at getting her home.

Audrey and I are no different to anyone else, we get tongue-tied, nervous, embarrassed and every other emotion you'd expect to encounter at such times and we're also not immune to making mistakes. We were beyond tired, as it was if we were courted every interview and answered all questions right there and then we'd have made a ball of it, so we agreed to one interview there and then and rescheduled the rest for the following day as we never refuse interview for Amy. It was still well after stupid-o-clock in the morning when we finished up, I'd love to say "the next morning,'' but a couple of hours later (literally), Audrey and I gave up and showered. Audrey also put in a call to the mother of little Yermi.

We arranged to meet at our hotel later that day. I won't even attempt to guess what day or even month that was because by then, they had all blended into one long beige carpet of fug. One day, Amy was with us; the next she wasn't and that was how my calendar worked with my forward planner stuck on a permanent "tomorrow we bring Amy home." Phone calls were made; Audrey and I crept out of the room on husband mouse feet and padded our silent way down to the breakfast bar only to be aware of how the other guests felt about the boisterous hullabaloo "we'd'' caused all through the night, if they were sleeping on we weren't going to disturb them. Yep, you guessed it! The breakfast suite was wall-to-ceiling full of reporters. Here we go again.

We decided to have a few interviews, just sound bites really here and there, until Yermi's mother arrived. It was only fair we waited for her up in our room, away from the media so as to present a united front. When she arrived at our hotel, we got a call from our reception desk and we headed on down to meet her. She was obviously fluent in Spanish (her native language) and hardly looked old enough to have a kid, let alone have one 7 year old, but like us, she too was in her 30s. She was another lightning bolt of nervous energy, top marks for her efforts in trying to find Yermi up till that point, too. We all hit it off immediately and just clicked at every level, joined in a shared but unwelcome brotherhood, parents of a missing child.

She was an incredible boost to Amy's cause. She very quickly brought us up to speed on what T.V. shows to do and just as importantly – which ones to avoid. Between us, we carved up the media scrum, maximising our collective messages across every available format in record time. Yes, we were all up to our eyes (and then some), but it felt fulfilling, like we were actually making a difference, A few days later, Sara's mother joined up with us, too. At first sight, I thought that she was Sara's grandmother, but such are the ravages one endures during such tribulation the pressure takes a toll. She looked so old and so tired it broke my heart. I tried to make her feel a bit better about herself in my usual self-deprecating way by poking fun at myself;

"Nah, you don't look that bad. Look at me, I used to be six-foot-seven. Before all this!"

As ever, the language barrier, my "hilarious" joke got lost in the translation; nothing kills a joke quicker than having to have it all explained in detail in "This is why it's funny." Another promising career comes crashing down in flames! She was another lovely, hard-working lady who lived in a heart-aching stupor of desperation, another unwilling member of our tragic brotherhood. She fitted in perfectly; Audrey and I were blessed in other ways too, in that we had great friends in the Canaries. Steve York is a prime example, a real friend. He put up Amy's poster all over the island; there wasn't a wall, window, or available space he didn't utilise. He also had that rare gift of knowing all the right people in all the right places and never once gave us a bum steer.

Our little brotherhood was pumping out on overdrive and I know that Audrey and I were conducting T.V., radio and newspaper interviews four times a day on average. That doesn't sound like much as you sit there and read it, but trust me, it's exhausting when we weren't bill posting, doing interviews, we'd all sit around together to do a brain-storming session. Something was born out of one of those sessions; it was the idea of having a demonstration in Vecindario, one of our better ones, to be sure.

The whole of the grand canaries was now aware that there were missing children. The Irish community would've known about Amy, the Spanish islanders about the two Spanish kids. Yermi and Sara's mothers had a lot of friends and family travel over for the event. Together with the support groups that they already had in-situ we had hoped to get a few hundred people to turn up, maybe as many as a thousand if we were being particularly bullish so we made sure to bring enough posters and flyers with us. Five hundred was going to be more than enough, or so we thought! As a conservation estimate, I'd say that ten thousand people turned up at least. Yes, you read that correctly, ten thousand. It was incredibly moving and not one of our little brotherhood was aware (until it happened) of the level of support we had with such a large gathering. The politicians, of course, were watching and taking notice. Therefore, it was no great shock-on a day of great shocks-to see the mayor of the Canaries arrive. He was most welcome and just like everyone else, he made us feel at ease.

"A great turn-out, yes?!"

"Unbelievable, we're blown away, we never expected this."

"Everything going okay today for you?"

"Brilliant, yeah, thanks for coming, by the way, means a lot to us."

"Is there anything I can do for you?"

"Well, yeah, actually there is!"

"Name it, whatever you need."

"Can you print off more posters for us? You see these ones (with the 3 kids)?"

"Yes, of course! Straight away."

He immediately called over one of his aides and sent them off on a print run right there and then. Then, he gave me an awkward, troubled look and discreetly called me to one side.

"It's great to see so many people supporting you and the other parents, yes?"

Absolutely, something on your mind, though, have you?"

"Yes, I have to be straight with you, okay?"

"Of course, yeah, go on, what's up?"

"Well, I called the Irish consulate to see if they would send a representative today."

"Okay?"

"Yes, you're Irish. Amy's Irish, far from home, okay?"

"Go on."

"They say no."

"I thought as much."

"You do? Why?"

"They said no to us too. No excuse, no reason, just a flat 'no' and hung up."

"This is true, Dave, same for me!"

I was never in my life more ashamed of being Irish than right then in that moment. How dare they, how dare the Irish government let us down. Let Amy, one of their young citizens, down like that. They should be ashamed and embarrassed reading this, arseholes! I wish they had been there to see how the folks from the Canaries did things; they do it right. It's from the heart, it's sincere and it's professional, something the Irish government will never attain without a root and branch make-over. How long do we need to anaesthetic ourselves against their ineptitude? They are driven, invariably, by one of three motives: money, political need or stupidity. Sometimes all three at once, our prime minister of the day Bertie Ahern was so corrupt it sweated into the very folds of his skin.

"Eh... eh... a.... anything I can d-d-do for ya Dave, y'know just ask."

We did ask, so did the mayor of a foreign town and we all know the result, as a friend of mine used to put it."

"Piss in one hand, hope in the other, see which one fails up first."

Crude, but he's not wrong. Hope is a very expensive commodity, but what use is life without it? You can't allow these fools to get in your way so we didn't, we pushed on and on through the mine. It was a blessing to receive boxes, actual boxes of posters not half an hour later from the mayor's office, we are still waiting for an email from our own government. That was our Amy cannon loaded again, so off we went, pressing the flesh, getting her image out there. The media's appetite was as insatiable as ever:

"Dave, any chance of an interview?"

"No problem."

Question asked and answered not once, twice or twenty times either. We finished so late that night; we got back to our hotel after the milkman, went up to the room for a quick nap and then went into the shower, dressed out the door and did it all again day after day. To date, Audrey and I have never failed to do a TV interview together, but one exception was that day (the day after the demonstration) when, as usual, we both travelled to the TV station/studio for yet another appeal for Amy, but also this time for the other two children as well as the other mother's also travelled there, the producer decided that it would be better for just three mothers to do the appeal. To be honest, I thought it was a fabulous idea, the power of three mothers united in a tragically common cause- absolute gold-dust, a massive point of internet and topic of conversation that would be throughout the land. Audrey, however, wasn't too happy.

To be fair to her, it was going to be a massive undertaking to do the show. It was an hour long show, that's not easy no matter how experienced you are; also it was a Spanish programme, don't forget. So, it was all going to be in Spanish. Audrey's Spanish is on a level I'll never achieve, but it's still only "conversational" in comparison to native speakers, which the other guests and presenters all were. I know she needed and wanted my support-just as much as I do hers-but she had to do a solo run on this one. It was too good an opportunity, too big of a conversation not to be a part of:

"C'mon Audrey, you'll be great!"

"I won't Dave, we always do these together!"

"Audrey."

"What?"

"It's for Amy."

That was all I had to say, it's all I'd ever have to say. She was gone straight over to her seat, then – lights, camera, action. I don't know what your experiences are with watching Spanish T.V. shows, but to my untrained Irish ear, they sound like they're going at a hundred miles an hour; it's such a 'quick' language, if that makes sense. Anyway, in fairness to Audrey, she understood everything that was being discussed in real time but had to wait a second or two to hear the translator in her earpiece. To speed things along (as television is such an important media), she'd give all of her answers in English and the interviewer would go through the same process. Audrey had to go through an hour of live television like that and as I watched backstage, I was never more proud of her. She will never stop looking for Amy Fitzpatrick, her little girl-her baby Amylou. After a while, you do so many interviews that you wonder (and you really do) if they actually accomplish anything or is it all just "vanity" for want for a better way of putting it? Well, the following morning, we heard a soft (I guess you could almost say "polite") knocking at our door in the hotel. When we opened up, we were met by a queue of cleaning staff. All were looking for posters of Amy, Yermi and Sara. It was a rare moment of such naked beauty, kindness and humanity in our lives since Amy's disappearance that we will never forget it. Nor will I ever be able to forget oh looks of love and desire to just help in their faces; it re-energises you, makes you take that extra step and silences that naggings naysayer in the back of your mind. There are still good people in the world and your message is getting through. You will find Amy and they are some of the reasons why.

It wasn't just the hotel cleaning staff either; we started receiving poster requests from all sides. The local taxi-drivers pulled up beside you and asked for posters, the ones who didn't already have them up. We'd walk into bars, pubs and clubs; if Amy's poster wasn't already there, it would be on our way out. Never a problem, those wonderful souls were only too happy to help. For all of my troubles and tribulations with Spanish banks, to their credit, they never had a problem with Amy's posters in their windows. It was thrilling to see so many posters everywhere we looked, but it was also heart-breaking. I love looking at her face but hate the reasons why the posters have to exit. I'd get lost in those beautiful blue eyes, so full of love, devilment and a whole wonderful future in front of them. I'd look at her eye-lashes and makeup and smile, remembering her applying it so many times and the craic we'd have slagging each other off stupid little nothing things that seemed so funny at the time, laughing at the giddy-nonsense of it all. Her cheeky little pout on every poster whenever you look and those silly clothes she has on, part of a costume for Halloween. How many people have looked at that picture on that poster by now? How many of them would look at it and think something negative about her because of that pout or those clothes, not knowing that it is but a snap-shot in time, a careless throw-away second in a life that was anything but how she looks in that image? How many people would see that poster and know how Amy would've just "died" of embarrassment at us using "that" photo of her when there are literally hundreds of better ones? I'd been lost in those thoughts, apologizing to her;

"The bleeding state of me, that picture!"

"We know, but it's the most recent one we had. It's what you do Amy."

"No way Dave, I wouldn't even show that to my friends. Now it's who I am?"

"Amy, please, we had to get your face out there quickly. We did our best…."

Sometimes, the conversation would end with us laughing about it. Other times, she had taken the bedroom door off its hinges, slamming it with temper about how stupid I was and how she'd "never live it (photo) down and how I wouldn't understand. I'd happily have that conversation end with her poking my eyes out once we had her home. That's only ever going to happen if Audrey and I make it, so that's heart-breaking really; it's not dangerous to the hundreds and hundreds of people who have and continue to support us. It's just that at some point, you've all got your own lives and families to look after. Ours will never be able to settle without those bluest of blue doe-eyes and cheeky pout at the other side of the dinner table. Quite often, I'd drift away, get lost in thought, staring at her poster and then eventually it dawned on me. That was my rest break I'd say "sleep," but c'mon, who am I kidding? Sleep? That was a luxury neither of us could afford. So if I was that tired, then how much worse must Audrey have been?

"Audrey?"

"Yeah…"

"We need a morning off, we, n…."

"What??? No! We can't we…"

"Audrey, stop – listen! We're burnt out! Look at us, really look."

"I'll stop when Amy's home."

"We just need a couple of hours to rest."

"Why?"

"It'll do us good. You'll see let the brain re-set."

Audrey wasn't easily convinced, but I got her there in the end; I talked her into a trip down to the beach for a couple of hours. Just sit in the sand, have a bite to eat, maybe a glass of wine and get a bit of sun like normal people. It was always going to be impossible, but I had to try. We shuffled on down to a little half-moon shaped beach in Puerto Rico like a couple of O.A.P.'s, not the thirty something we were at the time. We ate a small breakfast and lay in the sun for a bit. I had a little swim and Audrey fought against her self-imposed guilt and tried to relax and rest. She doesn't swim. We must've been there for a whole twenty minutes before I saw him. Ask anybody who has any experience of being followed around by the media and they'll tell you the same thing- you develop a sixth sense when they are around. I almost "sensed" this guy before I saw him. It was one of those "under-cover" photographers, the sniper in the tables arsenal who has a rule that is lower than a snake's belly, but this wasn't the time or place for me to throw his cameras into the depths of the med and to bounce him in after that vile intrusive instrument of his. It was on my mind, though I won't lie to you. He couldn't see me, so I was able to see the line of sight his lens was focused on. It was on Audrey, of course and like almost every other woman on that beach, she was lying down topless. It's not a big deal over there, still I could just imagine the seedy headlines those pictures would've generated for the local low-class Sunday world and Olive Press equivalent rag, so I felt that an intervention was called for;

"How are ya? You alright there, bud?"

"(white as a ghost) Eh, em…"

"Is that my wife you're taking pictures of?"

"Oh… eh… yes"

"Why?"

"Well… em… I'm a journalist… and… eh…"

"So, you want a story, is that it?"

"Eh."

"Look pal, we're just an ordinary couple alright?"

"Yes, but…"

"No, no buts we are normal people in an extraordinary situation, a tragedy, okay?"

"Y… yes."

"And if you want to consult with your colleagues, you'll find that we're quite amenable to giving interviews. We never say "no" because we believe they'll help us find our daughter."

"O… Kay."

"So, if you want an interview, just ask."

"Okay."

"Or if you want to take some photographs, all you have to do is ask, yes?"

"Okay, sure."

That was it; no aggression, no attitude, just a bit of honesty and some basic respect, nothing untoward. It was enough to make him pack up his stuff and make a sheepish exit, though. I'll say this much for him, he never did anything with those photographs, so fair play to him. We managed another hour or so of sun and then we were back out on the trail again. Audrey and I returned to that island countless times to keep the campaign going and even though we still had an Amy-shaped gap at our dinner table, our collective "successes" could be measured by the fact that everyone in Spain – mainland and island was known aware of Yermi Vargas and Sara Morales. It goes without saying that Amy Fitzpatrick was also known, but at that stage, she was ingrained into the Spanish psyche.

As puzzling as Amy's disappearance is, Yermi and Sara's is even more so when you think about it. As soon as each of those children went missing, the entire island went into a virtual shutdown. No planes and ships on to the island and not so much as a kite or paddle boat off it. So where the bloody hell did they go? It's difficult not to speculate on the existence of a highly organised team of kidnappers/abduction specialists operating within the Spanish borders at that time, isn't it? Surely, coincidence only stretches probability so far, right? The truth is, we just don't know and your guess is every bit as valid as mine. You are also encouraged not to dabble in speculative theories-which I agree with for the most part, but sometimes you just have to indulge your creative juice and see where they take you. Who knows, you may just stumble upon the solution. It's not as if stranger things haven't happened is it?

At one point, Audrey and I received an invitation from Yermi's mother to come and meet the rest of her family. Not even the ever-annoying language barrier could confess the unconditional love and acceptance showcased upon us by those beautiful, amazing people. Yermi's uncle, the younger brother of his mother, was there to translate for us and god love him; he couldn't contain his excitement at having us there, he was hyper! Whereas our house had evolved into a debilitating illness, theirs had blossomed into a soft bubble of love. Every time we entered it, it felt like receiving a hug, that's the only way to describe how it felt. As for how it looked aesthetically, well, it was a normal enough, semi-detached property with neighbours on one side. An empty parcel of wasteland on the other, perhaps car-marked once upon a time for future development. It wasn't vast by any stretch of the imagination, but it was an area where little Yermi used to play in. I looked at it, close to home safe (no hazards, etc.) and about as close to being a "side garden" as it gets. One minute, Yermi was playing there, happy as Lary and the next, he was gone. The only trace left of him was his teddy bear. One of his favourite toys and definitely something he wouldn't have left behind, just those two little words – teddy bear conjures up a heartbroken little boy, small hands desperately reaching out trying to grasp it as he's snatched away. He would call for it, mourned for it and then the cruellest blow of all, when he realised that he'd never see it or his mammy, family or friends ever again. He'd want to bury his distraught little face into something familiar, something he'd have shared, maybe cried with. It's a safe, fun and familiar smell providing a refuge of warmth and safety than a teddy bear. Nothing in the world would make sense to him; he'd want his mammy. Who among us at that age would've been any different?

It takes a particular brand of sick-evil-bastard to do such a thing; I'll never understand their capacity for such wanton cruelty. To see and hear his mother and his grandparents talk about him and how much he is missed… Jesus, it rips your heart out. When his mother brought myself and Audrey up to show us his bedroom, I knew it was going to be tough, there was nothing that was going to be there that was going to stop my heartbreaking, but I never once showed my discomfort she's a proud mother who loves her son so much that being around his things and chatting about him, keeps him "with" her. What we didn't expect to see when she opened the door to his room was an Aladdin's cave of gift-wrapped presents;

"Why are all these presents here?"

"They are for Yermi, they are his."

"Oh, okay."

"Yes, for all his birthdays, Christmas and other special occasions, we still buy presents for Yermi, wrap them up and leave them here for him. Can you imagine his happy face when he comes home to open them?!"

That did it. Audrey and I just choked on our tears; they wouldn't stop. Even as I write this, I'm choking up all over again. It was such a sweet, lovely thing to do and the joy, the belief in this poor woman's face as she told us, was inspiring but tragically so. We sometimes think about how many presents there are today for Yermi to come home to. His mother and siblings, grandparents and other family members will still buy them, wrap them and keep them safe. Someday, our phone will ring and it will be Yermi's mother, calling – joyfully to describe how happy Yermi is with all his presents, how handsome he now is and how delighted he is to be home and wasn't forgotten. I pray for that call, I pray for that day, please God, it comes soon.

So far, the three children on those posters haven't been found yet to make it home, but they will. Audrey continues to stay in touch with Sara's and Yermi's families to this day, and not just theirs but many more. Sadly, the most exclusive club in the world has a growing membership. Mostly, Audrey would communicate with them over the internet and one such person advised us back in the day to leave Spain and just start a new life. Somewhere - anywhere else. I thought it was mad and insensitive advice to give anyone in our situation, but now, all these years later, I think she may have been right. Something else people kept saying to us was that it would be great for us to attain some "closure" I wanted to throttle each and every one of them because your closure equals "death." Again, looking back, maybe they were right. Hope is all you have and eventually, all you're left with, your constant companion, your curse, the curse of "hope." It repulses me on every level to think that some sick bastard may be out there somewhere, living in their dog-shit apartment reading this book or the "Please find my Amy" book and getting their sick thrills out of it. I'd love to say that it's probably only me being paranoid, but sadly, I've seen enough of the real world to know better than that the organisation "missing abroad" was set up after Amy's disappearance and this is down to one person, Audrey, who has also been responsible for helping return bodies back home to the U.K. for "closure," ironic, isn't it? Audrey is simply a force of nature who just doesn't quit. She regularly speaks to membership families across the globe for Torquay to Tokyo, Alabama, to Alice Springs and Dublin to Durban. It doesn't matter; we're all suffering the same. We all bleed, don't we?

Finally, something fell our way that wasn't another bill or news of yet family tragedies, it was an invitation. Specifically, it was from England, the B.B.C to be exact. They had compiled a list of missing people's cases and wanted to include Amy in their program. This was brilliant news in the context of trying to find her, not in any other way, naturally, at that time, the U.K. had a population estimated at over 65 million people, that's almost 30 times that of the Irish republican, it was May 2008. That's another 120 million plus eyes, potentially looking for her and that's on top of the Spanish figures. Of course, we accepted their invitation; it was a complete no-brainer. It was also yet another platform by which to keep Amy "fresh" over in Spain. How? Well, most English speaking ex-pats over in Spain watch all the English channels and read the British newspapers, including the Irish people. Potentially, we'd be able to have Amy's appeal in sound and vision in each of those homes as well as out in the streets and wherever else our posting efforts led us. At no point since the days following her disappearance were we so 'sure' of success.

When we arrived in England, the first thing I did was to call my sister, Dory, and tell her which hotel we were staying at. She's a rock and one of the most positive people on the planet her energy was an essential ingredient to our BBC debut, as believe me the very thought of appearing on "BBC Missing" terrified us both, she's also brilliant company and when she turned up the day before we were to record the BBC show she brought her wonderful children with her. Uncle Dave and Aunty Audrey were more excited to see them than they were us, so that's saying something! It was the perfect cocoon of fun and happy times from the cold hard world we endured the rest of the time. I'm sure it was a measure of nervous tension there, but it was definitely a highlight.

One of the first things to hit us when we turned up to the show was how old and haggard the rest of the people were. Obviously, we weren't the only parents of a missing child there, but we were totally taken aback by the 'wear-and-tear' on those around us. Stupid thoughts entered the stupid zone in my head, stuff like maybe they were asked to distress themselves or something in order to 'beef up' the show's impact or something? In hindsight, I forgive myself for thinking it because they still look 'wrong' to qualify. Audrey and I are the least snobbish, pretentious people you'll ever meet, so it's not a 'clothing' or fashion issue. We were there to represent Amy, so I'd be damned if we were going to turn up looking anything less than respectable. Even today, when we have nothing, hardly two pennies to rub together, we'd still "splash out" in pennies and try to look our best for her. Maybe it's an Irish thing, a generation of Irish mammies tucking your shirt in and wet-licking back your hair before you leave the house for fear you might "make a show of us?" But it wasn't just the clothes; it was like when we met Sara's mother in Spain, these people had aged decades, not years. In my mirror, we hadn't, but then maybe we had as well? What you couldn't see, at least on the super filed level, was the decaying process internally, but we'll come back to that.

When we started chatting to the other parents, we were hearing horror-stories, tales of how this woman's son was missing for six years, that woman's daughter for seven and so on. The reality started hitting Audrey and me like a ton of bricks, but that wouldn't happen to us. We were 'Dave 'n' Audrey', and nobody was more invested and highly motivated than us to find our child. We had the drive, we had the money and we were surely sorely mistaken. It was a glimpse into a future we were never going to let happen. Fate, not for the first time, had other ideas; it happens that way sometimes. As for the show itself, it went as well as could be expected, really nothing new or earth-shattering questions such as:

"Did she run away?"

"How can you be so sure?"

"Was she really happy at home?"

"Did she have a boyfriend?"

They were old-hat to us at that stage, but they were along the lines of enquiry we'd peppered the Guardia civil with and them us. Therefore, things being equal, they were good questions. More importantly, our answers to those questions took Amy off the dull studio floor and into the hearts and minds of those watching on. You've got to make your child a living, breathing, vibrant person; don't be content to leave them as impersonal statistics on a spreadsheet of despair. That's the easy option you may as well never turn up. Fight for your child, fight their corner for them, don't give up and never-ever let them think out there in the universe somewhere that you've had enough. Your fight and your spirit might be the only thing keeping them alive; don't let them down. I know we won't, no rest for the wicked (or the good!). So the next day, we were back on a plane, back to Ireland.

The purpose of our trip was strictly business. Amy business this time, we were to appear on The Late Late Show. For those of you out there with only a passing interest or conversational knowledge of Ireland, then that name probably won't jump off the page. However, if you've even spent time on the Emerald Isle, then you already know the point I'm about to make. From an Irish perspective, The Late Late Show is our letterman, our Parkinson; it's the only talk show in town. If you want to grab the attention of a million Irish people in one go, it's what you do. Not that any of that means anything to myself or Audrey other than it's useful to Amy. The day after the show was going to be Audrey's birthday, so I pushed the boat out a bit and booked us in at the Westbury Hotel. That's Dublin's Savoy or Waldorf, depending on which side of the pond you inhabit. I had all of our friends and family meet us on the day of the show (at the hotel), and we had a pleasant day, none of us were really in the humour of celebrating. Still, we were never short when it comes to support and love; we are truly blessed in that sense. A call came to our room early enough that evening to let us know that our "car had arrived." This was a bit of a bone of contention for me, to be honest. The producers of the show insist on sending a car for their guests. It's a nice touch, "very showbiz," I supposed, but it's also very clever. Why? Because that way, they maintain a measure of control over you. It's easy to know if you will-or-won't turn up or if you'll be late, etc. So they can plan around problems if they happen. It was never going to be an issue with us, when we make an Amy commitment it's as good as done, so I'd say it's a tactic they found successful back when they'd have the likes of an Oliver Reed on the show, rest in peace. So why did I have an issue with it? Simple, really, Audrey and I always pay our own way and stand on our own two feet. Amy is our daughter, our responsibility and she cannot be bought by complimentary flights, hotels, or "contributions" for stories or interviews. Amy is not a commodity and cannot be bought, unlike so many other parents of missing or murdered children we've come across. Grief isn't a business plan, certainly not to us. To me, "our car" was an attempt at trying to buy us, so I made a point of letting the producers know this until that phone call to our room. I still considered getting a taxi.

Maybe that was a contributing factor to our nervousness that night, maybe not. I don't know, but we were nervous and we aren't usually. Parked outside the hotel was one of those large black stretch limousines, which had the obligatory tinted window and the whole nine yards. I thought it then and I think it now. It was a bit much. Anyway, in we got and as the car slowly "moored" its way out of the Westbury's collection port. A typical Dublin couple walked by us, pressing their faces up against the tainted glass, trying – unsuccessfully to peer inside.

"Jesus, what? How the "under-half" bleeding lives!"

If only they knew in that car at that time, it wasn't Bono or Sting, but an ordinary couple. Much like themselves – who would've given anything to just walk through the city as carefree as they were. How the other half lived?

For five agonisingly heart-breaking months, we wondered that, too. The half where you don't have a care in the world and all your family sit down for dinner... together.

When we got to the R.T.E studios at Montrose in Donnybrook, an affluent suburb on Dublin's south side, we had a quick meet and greet with the show's host, Pat Kenny. Pat endured a lot of stick (pardon the pun) over the years for his "wooden" interview technique, earning him the nickname of "pat-the-plank," but I found him okay. In fact, I'll go further than that, he was one of the nicest interviewers I've ever met. He seemed extremely down to earth and empathetic to our predicament. I think that he has a daughter Amy's age, so maybe that was why. To be fair, all of the staff we meet at R.T.E were very nice to us and everyone seemed to know about Amy.

Backstage in what is called "the green room" (no, it's not green!), we met with some of the other guests who were on that night. To be honest, I don't know who they were- someone from the Corrs and an actress from Coronation Street, but I can't remember her name. What I do remember about her though, was how choked up she was after our segment was over and she hugged us and gave us her best wishes and support. She didn't have to and we appreciate that, Audrey went to get her makeup done before the show, so I went to join her and got mine done as well! I sat beside a guy called Paul Costello (a very famous designer I later discovered!), and he asked me why I was appearing on the show; I wasn't in the humour for small talk:

"Ah, we just are."

"Are you in one of those boy bands?!"

Well, that just cracked everybody up! Fair play to him because I was a bit uptight and that did help. Before we knew it, the runners collected us and we were back on live TV again.

The show itself went as well as could be. Pat was sympathetic and asked a lot of the right questions, which allowed us to keep humanizing Amy, leaving her off the statistics pages. It went well, a typical enough interview as far as I was concerned, the only difference being that it was on Irish television, so there was a bit more pressure-home crowd and all of that. What I didn't know was that Audrey had a little something hidden up her sleeve.

She had sent The Late Late Show photographs of Amy, totally unknown to yours, because Audrey knows how difficult it is for me to look upon them emotionally. Next thing I know (and don't forget this is on live TV), all of those photos start scrolling across a big screen in video format. The pictures were difficult enough, but the accompanying soundtrack was provided by her friend Kim's singing voice. It took every ounce of strength I had and then to tap into my hidden reserves to not curl up into a weeping ball of pain. It still does. It's such a beautiful montage of Amy – being Amy-singing her little heart out, not a care in the world. What I see is the moments between those moments, the time when she'd surface anywhere between the hours of 1 am-2 am (as parents of teenagers the world over know only too well), creeping down the stairs wrapped up in her duvet her raccoon like eyes peeping out behind smudged mascara;

"How much do you charge?"

"Huh?"

"For haunting houses!"

"(Tut)"

It was one of our "things." Surprisingly, it never got old, we both enjoyed it. Not that the slagging was all one-sided either she used to dig out my cowboy boots, slip them on and clamp after us in a pimp-Frankenstein-mock walk (which was how she perceived my "walk" to be!) shouting.

"Rr..Dee..ree, Rr..Dee..ree!"

In what I can only generously describe as the worst Dave Mahon impersonation ever attempted! But do you know what? It absolutely cracked her up, that same contagious laugh I see on that video montage, that same happy full of beans Amy that I love and miss so much I'd happily sell my dying breath to see her do that "Dave walk" one more time or even the slightest hint of an echo of her modern take on my voice, I'd die a happy complete and relieved man. Somehow, I didn't collapse into an emotional heap and I managed to ride out the rest of the show on a cautious fragile auto-pilot. That was that, another show done, another appeal out into the wide-blue-yonder and on to the next one. Be it on the radio, newspaper or carrier – pigeon, we never said no. Never a minute's peace, but those three magic words moved you on- "it's about Amy" for me, it was also about another word too-

"Rr-der-ee!" I will hear it again.

As we packed up our bags back at the Westbury, I remember pausing for a minute, looking around and breathing it all in, the room, the furnishing, the ambience and then catching Audrey's eyes:

"In happier times, we'll come back here and stay for a few nights,"

"Yeah?"

"We'll do a bit of shopping on Grafton Street and stop off for a pint in Brussels just like normal people do."

"That'd be nice."

As we went back and forth from pillar to post-Spain/Ireland/UK/whenever to keep breathing life into Amy's campaign, I thought back to that room. My happy place, a sanctuary from the storm. When Amy's home, we'll all stay: me, Amy, Dean and of course – "Rr-der-ee."

Moving Back from Spain

I stood on the balcony of our apartment and looked out over the calm darkness of the midnight on the Med. It was still warm, even to my body, so many years living there and it was as quick and calm as a sleeping baby. My mind, however, was a tempest, a perfect contrast to the surrounding, outer calm. I glanced over my shoulder and looked into our dark living room. Audrey was sleeping. Good. Thank God. But she was also sleeping more and more these days. When Amy had first disappeared, an elephant gun wouldn't have knocked her out. Now, she spent more time asleep than awake. I turned back to take in one last view of what was once my little slice of heaven. I had made my decision.

I was ill; I didn't know quite how bad, but I knew I was a long way from a bill of good health, clean or otherwise. Audrey was even worse, way worse. Our fridge and presses were empty and so were our pockets and bank accounts. No money for food, for petrol, or medication, let alone to see a doctor. No leads for Amy either. Still, so, I made the dreaded phone call to Mick;

"Da?"

"Hiya Dave, any news on Amy?"

"No, no. unfortunately, Da."

"Yeah?"

"Can I borrow some money off you?"

Seven little words I hadn't uttered since I wore short trousers and ran about with a snotty nose. That's exactly where I was again - psychologically- a little boy running home to his daddy. Fuck!

"Of course, you can son. Can I ask what it's for?"

"Plane tickets Da. Two of them. One way. Back to Dublin."

"Would you not buy return tickets Dave? Cheaper doing a round-trip?"

"We won't be coming back Da. We're done!"

I let Audrey sleep on and wake up in her own good time. This was not a conversation to be had by rousing your partner from their slumbers. As usual, she read my face and knew. I had news. I came straight out with it, just blurted it right out, some things you can't sugar coat. We both knew it was coming and then there it was, inevitability staring us in the face. We held each other and cried for I don't know how long. No words were necessary. Everything had already been said before, anyway. From an outside looking in, it looks like a complete no-brainer, but for us, it was torture. It was Dante meets Milton, a lost paradise in the seventh circle of hell. We weren't just leaving the sun, sea, sand - the "Life," we were leaving Amy. The decision was made and the tickets were bought, but it still took us a couple of days to process what we were doing. It took Audrey a long time to make the move over to Spain, an excited Dean and Amy in tow, now.... well, "Now" we were a lifetime away from that.

We were all borrowed out and too ill to work. What was the cost of Amy's search up until the point? Well, its toll was legion, if I'm to be completely honest. Emotionally, I'd never experienced it like this before. It was an all-consuming world-killer of an enemy, Marvel Bad-Guy in scope. The 'Terminator,' I guess, you'd call it, because just when you'd reach the point where you'd foolishly think, "That's it, I just can't hurt any more, it's not possible" then Wham! Another fresh cut through the soggy, bleeding mess that was once called your heart. Mentally, you exist on an outer-limit screenplay, somewhere between anger and despair, where all is dark and everything tries to kill you. Your thought process is sharpened to a needlepoint where the only thing that exists is finding Amy, finding Amy, finding Amy. Your dad has the flu? I need to find Amy. You're behind on the rent? I need to find Amy. Do you not think you're drinking too much? I need to find Amy. Why are you passing blood? I need to find Amy. What do you want for your dinner? I need to find Amy. It's an obsession to beat all obsessions and it never quits, never sleeps and never ends. Not until you find her or it kills you, which brings us on to health.

At the time, I didn't realise what was going on inside my own body, but now I do. It was conspiring to kill me and it had a couple of different strategies. The first was the shortest game. I was drinking far too much; it's not a new story, I self-medicated to the point of excess and I'd been told by doctors already to stop, or I'd die. Audrey was on that journey with me too. How could she not be? My hurt, my pain - was beyond anything I ever thought possible, but Audrey's was worse, ten times as much, if not more. Also, the stress was ripping my body through, shredding my own organs to serrated fibres, wasn't good. Everything I should've been doing – eating and sleeping properly, seeing a therapist- whatever, I was too busy for all that shit, I'll find Amy first. Now, pour another one. The other conspiracy my own body plotted against me was the long game. As we'll see later in this book, that was the master plan that so very nearly worked. I suppose the least important cost - at least to my mind anyway- in relation to Amy's disappearance was the financial one. Your health - mental/ emotional/physical – is your true wealth until – that is – you can't pay for it.

The day before Amy disappeared, we were very comfortable - cash-wise- and 'wealthy' in book terms. We had 9 houses, a bar, a real-estate business - a few cars and a motorbike, and that's just off the top of my head. It was the only reason we were able to give Amy's campaign as much time, traction and profile as we did. Not everyone is so lucky. We knew this. Now we were existing on whatever food was still in-date and could be found under the fridge. My drinking wasn't a problem, we damn surely couldn't afford that either. We had no money left, nothing left to sell or pawn and nothing coming in the door but bills we've never paid - we couldn't. It's that simple. It's the reason why I had to call my father - an old age pensioner, for money. I was beyond shame and humiliation; there were other little luxuries I couldn't afford. Now, compare and contrast that picture against where we were the day before Amy's disappearance. Was it worth it? I'll answer that for you when we eventually get her home. And still, our phones kept ringing (another set of bills way post 'due'), with TV and other media platforms looking for us to give more interviews. For Amy, we never refused but now we were finding it difficult - if not impossible – to get to them. It wasn't due to illness (although, if the truth be told, it probably should've been) rather, it was down to financial geography - we couldn't afford to travel around anymore. It wasn't even something that we could admit to the media because (A) that would become the story and (B) they'd probably offer to cover our costs. Something Audrey and I will never do is accept money for stories. It sickens me when I see other people doing this like this is a business transaction.

All things must end and unfortunately, our Spanish campaign had ground to a halt. We had given it everything. We had and it took it all greedily. We'd nothing to show for all our efforts other than bad health and bankruptcy. My father sent the travel money via Western Union and as soon as I collected it into my grubby little paws, I had to fight some serious temptation not to inject it back into the campaign, that one last 'Hurrah!,' the 'Hail Mary' pass as the clock runs down to zero at the Super Bowl, pride and desperation tugging at you;

"This is it, your last throw of the dice, it'll work! Do it!"

Thank God I didn't because that voice had proved itself to be completely full of shit. Not once did it ever come through on something. Besides, we'd gotten money before from some other good people and did exactly that, but it's only the equivalent of a sticking plaster. Long term, I needed to get back to work, but that wasn't the time for me to do so, both physically and mentally. Booking two – one-way tickets – back to Dublin almost killed me. Telling Audrey that the deed was done was even harder because I just knew what her reaction was going to be;

"No, I'm not going back to Ireland. Forget about it."

I don't know if it was shock, obstinacy, or just fear, but it led to a bit of 'discussion' before common sense prevailed. I wouldn't mind, I actually agree with the reasons why she wanted to stay, but health-wise, we'd both have been dead in a matter of weeks. Again, that's not a dramatic effect, that's honestly how it was. My father - being my father - sent a bit more money than we needed, so with the few bobs we had left over from the plane tickets, we walked across the street to the local supermarket and did something absolutely extravagant, we bought food and petrol. As silly as this may sound, we'll never forget how little that meal cost financially or how much it meant psychologically. It's still one of the nicest meals I've ever eaten. Hunger is a good sauce.

The following day, we met up with all of our friends and broke our sorry news to them face-to-face. They deserved that courtesy after everything they'd done for us. After more than 10 years in Spain, you'd be surprised at how many friends you'd make, I know I was. They were - completely shocked but asked all the correct questions;

"What can we do to keep you here?"

"How long will it be before you come back?"

"Is there anything we can do for you when you go?"

It felt good to see and hear how sincere and lovely they all were to us and it was really quite humbling, as well as a small bit of consolation. It only really hit me when I got home and saw Audrey packing away all of our things, the bits we had left. We were well used to moving at that stage, but it had never felt nearly as sad. It felt like we were packing everything but our souls, they'd wait around just in case Amy showed up. Whatever we couldn't carry, we stuck in a lock-up. Packing complete, we held hands and walked down to the beach. This was where our dreams had started all those years ago, where we talked about bringing the kids over and giving them a better life. A better life for all of us, the world was our oyster. Now, we were taking what felt like our last walk on the beautiful Costa del

Sol. To be honest, I don't remember what we chatted about or if we even chatted because we were in a saddened state of shock. I was processing a new "if only......." with every new wave coming into shore before my buzzing phone intervened;

"Dave?"

"Yeah."

"It's Franco. Franco Rey!"

"Hiya."

"What's all this? I'm hearing about you moving back to Ireland!?"

"Yeah, it's true."

"Why don't we meet up say our goodbyes?"

"Sure. Whatever."

Honestly, I couldn't have given a shite - not just him - anyone; I was downcast and miserable at the world in general. We meet him at a nice little foodie-type bistro. Audrey and I could only afford a burger, chips and a little wine between us, not that Franco would not notice that.

"So, moving back. It's the right thing for you to do."

"Doesn't feel great though."

"Yes, but the search for Amy? It was killing you both."

"Yeah, but we'll never give it up, not so long as we still breathe."

"I see, but you're paying with your lives, Dave, yes?"

"It's what you do when your girl goes missing, Franco."

"So, what are you going to do with your Mercedes?"

"...what?"

"Your car, what will you do with it?"

"Don't know, didn't really think about it."

"No? (Smelling blood)"

"I'll probably leave it parked outside our apartment. It has Amy's posters all over it and everyone in Spain knows my car anyway."

"I have a better idea."

"You do?"

"I'll give you €500.00 for it."

"Franco, it's an old Merc, sure, but we both know it's worth €3,000 if it's worth a penny."

"Maybe, but you go back home tomorrow and you clearly have no money...."

Opportunistic bastard didn't miss a trick, did he? Sharing that burger...........

".... but I do €500.00. Now. Cash. Plus, I'll throw in a life to the airport."

I'm old enough and ugly enough to know a real piece of shit when I see one, and Franco was of the steaming-ice-cream-scoop-twirl variety. I shouldn't have been shocked, but alas, I was. Talk about kicking a man when he's down? It proved everything. I always suspected that about him, lower than the haemorrhoids on a maggot's arsehole. He had us cold, though, so what else could I do? Right at that very moment, €500 felt like a million dollars to us - God knows we needed some travelling money - plus a few bobs when we landed in Dublin. We'd already lost millions in property anyway, so what the hell?

"Fair enough." I'll meet you in the morning with the keys and paperwork."

It kills me to see people exploited - even on TV shows - but truly, how much worse it feels when it lands on your door-step, especially when you know you're being exploited. If it was a total stranger – some scumbag off the street who knew nothing of your troubles - you'd think, "Fair enough, we've all got to eat," but when it's someone you know very well and is intimately aware of the horror you're living through, that's unforgivable. Franco is an extremely wealthy man with connections all the way up the food chain; he was behaving like a total bastard and rubbing our faces in it. C'est la Vie-our friends - our real friends- meet us for a few private drinks on our last Spanish night. It wasn't just hard; it was as difficult as it gets. One of them was deep in conversation with me and noticed that something – apart from all the usual heartache - was eating away at me;

"C'mon Dave, spit it out."

"Ah it's nothing."

"Bollox. Tell me..."

"It's bleedin' Franco."

"That fucking weasel, what'd he do now?!"

(I told him about 'selling' the car to him)

"Dave, I don't like Franco. You know that...."

"That's a bit of an understatement!"

"Exactly! So here (hands me €500) that's for the car..."

"I can't, Franco...."

"Fuck him; listen to me, that's for the car, right? But I'm only renting it off you."

"What?"

"Because when you come back from Spain - and I know you will, - I'll hand it straight back to you - for nothing!"

"That's really generous of you, but I gave my word and..."

"Your word? Fuck all that boy-scout nonsense. This is no 'Man of Honour.' Dave, he's picking the flesh off your bones and Audrey's."

"I don't know," it doesn't feel right... Besides, he's our lift to the airport... No, I ..."

"Yes, you fucking will! How do you know he won't let you down on the lift?"

He had an answer for everything and worse, he was right. Franco is no man of honour- but I am – that was my difficulty, so I couldn't even enjoy "getting one over'' on him.

Franco picked us up the next morning, more stress. I just told him out straight that the deal was off, I'd gone with a ''better offer,'' and if he didn't want to drop us out to the airport, I'd understand. How did he react? Well, my real friend knew

349

I might soften under Franco's wrath, so he prepped me with a silly little joke to deal with the inevitable strop;

"Dave, why did the condom fly across the bedroom?"

"Don't know.''

"Because he was pissed off, get it?! Dave, that's what Franco will be in the morning, a used condom flying off the handle, full of piss!!"

He called that one spot-on, right on the money! Franco went into an almighty strop and had a silent sulk all the way to the airport. Quietest. Car journey. Ever! I had to suppress a fit of the giggles, seeing a bag of 65 yr. Old piss, dropping us off at the airport! God love him if that was the biggest worry in his life. If he'd checked his rear-view-mirror, he would've seen two people with real worries;

We were ill- physically- on arrival at Dublin Airport, our Amy Bubble well and truly burst, our falling bodies screaming in surrender. Audrey was too ill to walk, so once again, she was pushed out of the arrivals lounge in a wheelchair, the perfect psychological metaphor for our inner angst. We clearly wanted to remain under the radar, to be left alone to heal for 5 minutes, but the media had other ideas. Dublin airport has had many media frenzy over the years – Jack's Army coming home from the World Cup - Olympic heroes - Armed forces returning from U.N Duty, etc., but this was our first such experience on home soil! We needed it like a bloody hole in the head, but it's for Amy, so you suck it up and get stuck in. There was one friendly face in the throng- Mick! His booming smile - it even shines out of his eyes! – was an absolute tonic and his hug was a power plant of loving energy. Thanks, Da; you'll never know how much I needed that. Then it was TV interviews, newspaper bombardment and a hasty retreat into Kealys Bar/ restaurant, an old (and favourite) haunt located just beside the airport. We had a spot of lunch and a few drinks with some good friends and then back to Mick's house in Santry, as he had plenty of room. That was the honeymoon period, back living under your daddy's roof after years and years of independence. I'm not being ungrateful for his help - far from it - but if you've ever had to go through something like that, you'll understand.

First thing we did the next morning was head down to the social welfare office. This was a degrading experience as I had never in my life looked for a handout or had to sign on. But we were broke; there was nothing else for it. I left all the talking to Audrey as she'd a little bit of (tiny) experience of this kind from a 'thousand' years ago. We happened upon a very officious female officer, who we didn't want every 'I' dotted and 't' crossed. No, she also wanted blood from us;

"I want letters from the banks in Spain."

"I want evidence to support your 'claim' not to own any more properties."

Fair enough, I can see why such information would be pertinent to such claims, but there's a way of asking too, you know? I tried (really, I did) to explain the differences between the Spanish and Irish banking systems. Over in Spain, if you stop paying your mortgage, you become "dead" to them, and that's no exaggeration. They simply won't deal with you anymore; you are a financial ghost. If you contact them through a solicitor (via séance!), they will push mountains of official paperwork for you to get through, but otherwise, it is all but impossible. We were in a social welfare office looking to sign on the dole, so no way did we have room in our purse for a solicitor, let alone a solicitor with International Banking Experience. So, dear reader, what do you do? We did the only thing we could do and paid a visit to the Spanish Embassy in Dublin. We managed to get a bit of face-to-face with a Spanish Ambassador and explained our case to her. Bless her heart; she was an absolute champion and put together a little package of information backing up everything we said. We handed it over to our friendly neighbourhood social welfare officer;

"Hmmm......."

"Problem?"

"I suppose it will have to suffice."

That was kind of her. It was just as well we didn't get her on a bad day, as I once heard she denied some poor little orphan a bowl of gruel- "More???" So, with the scary lady appeased until the next blood sacrifice on the full-moon cycle, we were officially on the dole. Ouch.

To paraphrase Tom Cruise in "A Few Good Men" (I swear, I'm getting needier the longer the book goes on!) and the hits just keep on coming, why? Audrey's mother got really sick. Ever the dutiful daughter, she split her time between Mick's house in Santry and her parent's house in Artane, another North Dublin Suburb. If you're a G.A.A fan and the name sounds kind of familiar, it's because it's where the 'Artane Boys Band' hails from. Actually, we both ended up spending our time between Santry and Artane because we've always found being apart, as in sleeping apart, to be quite stressful. On the upside, back in Ireland meant that we could reconnect with Dean again. This did so much good for Audrey - seeing him wherever she wanted to - but she no longer had him all to herself; he'd been a busy boy since he got back and was now a dad.

He had a beautiful baby boy and named him Leon. Audrey was a granny! With all the "bussing" between our parent's houses and now with baby Leon on the visit schedule, it made sense to get a car. Again, we worked on a tight budget - being on the dole and broke - so I bought a nice little Rover. It was a lovely, clean little car and did us well. Now, all we needed was to try and find a little roof of our own to sleep under, but this is the Dave and Audrey show, so don't expect smooth seas. Audrey started having to attend the hospital regularly, in and out like a jack-in-the-box, liver cirrhosis. Unfortunately, this wasn't exactly news to us. Back in Spain, Audrey took a leaf out of my book and looked to drinking alcohol as a coping mechanism. Only on a worse scale. She received a fairly hefty prognosis;

"Stop drinking, if you don't receive a new liver, you will die."

The doctors in Ireland were now supporting that diagnosis, too. We had to travel to St. Vincent's hospital to meet the eminent professor, Frank Murray, to whom we had been referred from Beaumont Hospital. He also concurred and put Audrey on a transplant list. As anyone unfortunate enough to be - or know someone - on that list will tell you, it's not like ordering a pizza. It's a long, complicated, convoluted process. People die on that list, it's that serious. I offered to give Audrey my liver or part of my liver (basically whatever they needed), but they turned me down, flat. Why? Because they don't accept living donors in Ireland. I'll give you one guess at what country does and also happens to be the world leader in liver transplants, Yup, Spain. For fuck's sake. Further irony- in case all of that wasn't already enough? - My own psoriasis had cleared up perfectly, so it wouldn't have been a problem.

Next thing to do was to get a place to live in. We'll never be able to thank our parents enough for putting us up, but let's keep it real, nobody wants to overstay their welcome or be a burden and besides, we're two very independent souls. Dublin in 2012 was not an easy place to secure rented accommodation, even when you were the "famous" Dave and Audrey. We'd managed to squirrel away enough of our meagre resources to save up enough for a deposit and we had also managed to qualify for rent allowance. Great news, right? Wrong. Nobody wanted to touch you if you were on rent allowance, so now the task got even harder. Not finding a needle in a haystack, more like finding a specific needle in a needle stack. I tell you, we looked at some properly shit places and even those landlords (although that title is an affront to the trade, wouldn't touch us)

"Rent allowance? Nah, fuck off."

Charming, eh? I was a landlord myself for many years and gave everyone a chance – even some I shouldn't have – and not once was I ever so dismissive of a client or interested client. Now the shoe was on the other foot and all that "good karma" must have gotten lost along the way. Eventually, we came across a nice apartment on Malahide Road - in North Dublin. That was available for rent. It was small   just one bedroom - but it was clean, accessible and affordable. Perfect. We went into the Real estate office in Fairview, just north of the city centre, with rent allowance and deposit safely secured in Audrey's handbag;

"Lovely, lovely, now just show me your references and we'll be done."

"I'm sorry- references?"

"Yeah, you know from your previous landlords and all that?"

"Eh, we don't have any of those."

"No? That's a problem. We need those to proceed."

"Look, we've never had to rent before. We've always been home-owners."

"Oh okay, no problem, I'm sure a work reference will do."

"Ah…"

"Let me guess, another problem?"

"Well… yeah!"

"Talk to me."

"I've always been self-employed, so I've never had a boss before!"

"Hmm… Now, we do have a situation. What about a professional character reference?"

I looked at Audrey and she was flipping through her contacts book and then a smile came across as she underlined a name;

"Reckon, he'll do Dave?"

It was the - then Lord Mayor of Dublin. I called him, but - typical us - he was over in New York for St. Patrick's Day.

"Tell you what, Dave, just head over to my office at the Mansion House and I'll have a reference ready and waiting for you."

The joys of modern technology! The estate agent was impressed by the fact that we had such a person on "speed dial." So, she agreed to wait for us to get it.

Sure enough, when we got to the Mansion House, there it was waiting for us. We got back to Fairview and signed off on the paperwork. Phew! Finally, everything started to click back into gear again and we had a period where- Amy and health issues aside- things were pretty much okay.

Crack! That was kind of the sound my back made every morning since we came back from Spain. But now, it had gotten beyond a joke. My lower back was giving me serious pain and I couldn't ignore it any longer. It was time to see yet another doctor. More money we couldn't afford to spend, but your health is your wealth, really, isn't it? There was a chiropractor in Artane we'd heard good things about, so we went to him. I did a few sessions there, but sadly, no improvement. Audrey then booked me in with her family doctor – Ibrahim - in Donaghmede, an Indian man despite his Arabic-sounding name. We'd had good experiences with him in the past - he helped clear up my skin problem, something the Spanish doctors could never do. I explained what my complaint was - as best as I could – so after a thorough examination, I was sent to Beaumont Hospital for some X-rays. Between Audrey's hospital appointments- here and in Spain - and now me in and out of hospitals where nothing was showing up on the bloody X-rays, my back wasn't the only thing that hurt. I had a pain in my arse with the whole lot of it!!! The pain wasn't going away and for all the medical interventions, it was getting worse - not better. It got to the point where I had to use a walking stick.

Dr. Ibrahim was totally flummoxed, so he next ordered an MRI scan for me. That put my name at the very back of that waiting list, a group so long that Oscar Schindler would've needed a double–take to comprehend. I'd still be on it, maybe halfway down it at this stage. So, I asked about my options. Turns out, you can pay for it privately, so I just said, "Yeah, put me in there." A couple of weeks went by and I received a phone call from Blackrock Clinic, looking to book me in for an M.R.I scan. Happy days…. until I enquired how much it would cost. She told me. I needed to remind myself that it was a price to get an M.R.I scan and not a quote to put her son through university. Holy cow! I told her that I'd get back to her (if I won the lottery!) and looked around for a better deal. Turns out that there was a place in Santry - on our own doorstep! – That was only a third of the price (Result!) and could fit me in the following week (ka-ching!) so it was off to the Santry Sports Clinic for me. It's a fairly routine "procedure," I guess you'd say, but I found it a little bit claustrophobic, something I'm not very good with and as we'll see later, foreshadowed darker times. They sent the results to Dr. Ibrahim, who in turn called me in to see him and discuss where to go next.

"Dave, you need to sit down."

"No kidding! I'm in agony here."

"I've got your M.R.I results and …. It's bad news."

"Great. How bad?"

"You're going to require a total hip replacement."

"Fuck."

"Yes. Fuck. Not what you were expecting, was it?"

Well, no shit, Sherlock! How did a sore back degenerate into a hip replacement? It was time to check my birth certificate – walking stick, new hip- I was only in my 40's, not my 70's! Dr. Ibrahim explained that this "little problem" had Spanish roots.

"Spanish roots? What does that mean?"

"Remember your skin problem?"

"Yeah, you sorted that out for me. They couldn't. So what?"

"Do you remember the steroids they told you to take for it?"

"Of course, I do."

"How long did you take them for?"

"(Thinking) Hmm… six, maybe seven months, why?"

"Did they give you an open-ended prescription, or did you have to renew it?"

"Renewals… every couple of weeks or so."

"Did they ever warn you about any side effects?"

355

"No."

"Didn't think so - you are not supposed to take them for any longer than 4 weeks.''

"Thanks, doc, I think. I can work out the side effects by myself." Shit, I swear to God, if I bought a goldfish, the proxy thing would drown! Ah, well, back to Beaumont for a few more appointments and if that wasn't enough, to satisfy my new-found love of hospitals, their referral of me to the Cappagh hospital in Finglas.

Another hospital, another waiting list. Well, at least it was a consistent process, ain't life just a big 'ol bowl of bleeding Cherries?! What a fun and relaxing year that turned out to be. You can be damn sure I thanked those Spanish doctors every day of it (in my head!) for crumbling my hip bone into chalk with their generous dollop of steroids. In all that time, I was utterly dependent on my walking stick, even for something menial and mundane, such as shuffling across the kitchen to look in the fridge. Actually, that walking stick has a bit of Mahon family provenance as it was first used by my great-grandfather and then by my grandfather. My own dear old dad still had no use for it in his 80's! Ahh, it's the little things that cheer you up, isn't it?! What do you do when you can't walk and your hips dissolve like a fresh lemsip? If you're Dave Mahon, you join a gym. Of course, you do!

Good old Ben Dunne, not content with taking most of my cash on groceries back in the day, now had the audacity to charge me to sweat off all these calories years later! At least he gave us a good deal, so long as three of us joined at the same time. Naturally, I got Dean in on the deal and another guy who I considered to be a friend at the time. More on that later! Anyway, I actually found the gym to be a great source of relief for me as - although there were many exercises my rice paper joints prohibited me from trying – I could swim every day, up to a mile in that lovely, no-impact watery oasis.

So, we had a place to live, a car to drive around in and we were - at least- starting to look into our health situation. Now, we needed to keep our heads above water, save a few quid and inject a bit more pace into Amy's Campaign. It was time to see about a job. Straight away, I had to rule out most of the situations vacant advertisements because I was on a waiting list for a new hip and I could barely walk. I met up with Karl, an old friend of mine who I knew from our taxing days together before I went to Spain. Back in the day, we both had a couple of taxis and as things turned out, he happened to have one for sale. I told him that I was interested, so we agreed on a price and then all I'd have to do was buy a car up in

356

the years, as we say in the trade (3 years old) and renew my P.S.V license, that's what you need to drive a Public Service Vehicle. Because I'd up-sticks and left Ireland around the time of the deregulation fiasco, I'd let my old qualification lapse. Karl couldn't believe it;

"What do you mean you didn't renew it?"

"Jesus, Karl, I was moving to Spain. How was I meant to know Amy would go missing and our whole world would end up falling out of my arse?"

"Jesus, Dave, it won't be easy."

"What do you mean?"

"You've to sit a test and all that now, like – a written test!"

"How hard can it be? I've driven a taxi for years!"

"Yeah, but Dave, you need 80%! That's a pass!"

"Ouch, still, I should be okay…. Shouldn't I?"

"Then you've got to find a company that will insure you."

"Why would that be a problem?"

"(laughing) Sure you're only an 'oul Rubber hips now, aren't you?!!"

"(laughing) Jesus, yeah! I'll have to use your crowd then, won't I?"

"(not quite so jolly) What? What do you mean by that?"

"With your glass eye! They can't be too strict if they'll insure a half-blind taxi driver now. Can they?!!"

I know that might seem a bit cruel, but we were forever slagging each other off about stuff like that. In actual fact, Karl's party piece was to remove his glass eye, drop into a pint and say, "Keep an eye on that drink when I'm gone!" It actually got to a stage -in classic gross out drinking games- where I'd drink his pint and pretend to choke on his eye! I guess it was a bit of an acquired host!! It was for those reasons that I was taken aback by his paranoid response;

"Dave, don't ever say that to anyone. Ever! Okay?"

"Relax, Karl, Jesus, you know me. Why would I ever do that?"

357

In hindsight, his mood swings- giddy to paranoid- should've been a warning shot, but when you "know" someone, you can't always read the signs. We'll come back to this a bit later, too. Anyway, the day of my test arrived and so I went into the centre and sat for the exam. "Piece of cake."

"Mr. Mahon- you've scored 72%. I'm afraid that's short of the pass rate, which is 80%. You've failed."

Huh? Look, I know I didn't study for it or anything, but I know Dublin like the back of my hand, sure - there are one or two new hotels and such springing up here and there, but – me - to fail a test about Dublin?? No way, it must've been a fluke had to be. I did a bit of study and then got right back up on the horse. Time to re-sit the examination, definitely an absolute shoe-in this time around;"

"Mr. Mahon, your score is 76%, which is below the pass rate of 80%. You've failed."

Shit. I sat rooted in my chair, somewhere between disbelief and a sulk, if I'm honest and watched the robotic examiner go from desk to desk, congratulating other people on their success. Then the penny dropped… I wasn't just the only Dubliner at the centre, I was the only Irishman. I waited for the examiner to finish his rounds and then caught his eye;

"Excuse me, can I ask you a few questions?"

"Yes, Mr. Mahon. Ask away."

"How are so many foreign nationals passing the test and I can't?"

"What are you trying to infer?"

"Look, I'm a Dub. I drove a taxi around this city for 12 years!"

"So?"

"So, I know the city like the back of my hand! In fact, pretty much the rest of Ireland, too!"

"And your point?"

"There is no way - zero chance - of any of those others getting near 80% if they lived here for years, and yet somehow, they are?!"

"Ah."

"Ah?"

"Yes. Foreign nationals are only required to reach a passing grade of 60%."

"60%??!"

"Yes"

"Wow! It's no wonder everyone thinks the Irish are stupid, is it?"

Talk about soul-destroying. When you hear your own city - your home- being deliberately prejudiced against its own citizens, it's nonsense. You'd never see that kind of behaviour in Spain or most (if not all) of the cities and countries I'd visited. My heart was no longer in it, but I had to do something and not just for my pocket, but for my sanity. To rub insult into injury, the credit union whom I'd been saving with had refused my loan application to buy a Taxi, even though I'd more than half of the money saved with them. I was then refused car-finance from a different lender. The universe was telling me something, my taxi-driving days were over.

Adding to my good cheer was the proximity of New Year's Day as all of this was going on. Amy was now missing 5 years to the day. It's a nightmare time of the year for Dean, Audrey and myself, whilst the rest of the world sings, dances and celebrates like there's no tomorrow. I don't think we'll ever celebrate another one again. It's an absolute downer for us - anyway, no job, can't get any finance, my hip is screaming in pain whenever I breathe and it's Amy's fifth year on the missing list. What else could possibly go wrong? I decided to get a bit of me time - away from everyone – and drown my sorrows in alcohol. Never underestimate a man's capacity to do something stupid - I drove and deservedly got stopped outside of my father's house in Santry, but no excuses, I was in the wrong. Simple as that. Was I over the limit? Absolutely, like I said, no excuses. I now had a drink-driving charge to add to my woes.

The court date came around and I was presided over by a judge, Ann Watkins. I could go into a lot of detail about her attitude and demeanour etc., but the bottom line is – to use prison parlance – I got "lashed out of it"- a 5-year driving ban and 4 months in prison. And so, it was off to the big house with the oul triangle for my hobbled little self in total shock and Audrey Well, I guess the only way to describe her reaction was discombobulated. My first interactions with the Mountjoy Prison Officers - went something along the lines of;

"What did you do?"

"Drunk driving."

"Did you kill anyone?"

"Nope."

"Have a terrible accident?"

"Nope."

"What's the story then?"

"I sat outside my father's house, but of course, I did drive with a drink on me, yes I'd a few drinks on me."

"That's it? Then they stopped you? Cunts! Who was your judge?"

"Ann Watkins."

"That bleedin' Cow? That's a bleedin' tramp, that thing?"

Audrey, in the meantime, appealed the severity and so, that very night, I got released from Mountjoy. I'd be lying if I were to say exactly "X" amount of money later my appeal was heard - because I honestly don't remember – but it was a few months anyway. Was I hopeful? Sorry, have we even met?!! Me? Hopeful? Not a chance in Hell! Trepidation is a much under used word, but it fits this particular section quite well because I had it by the barrel–full as I walked back into that court. It's a bit like those feelings kids get when they are brought before the headmaster, you know you're getting into trouble, a price will have to be paid (the house always wins and always collects), it's just a question of degrees. My bum had barely warmed the cold, hard bench before that all-too-familiar call;

"Mr. David Mahon, please."

It's your name, you own it and unfortunately, you also own all the baggage it carries and the added weight your load was about to inherit. You look for omens - signs of slim possibility - and nothing jumped out at me. Shit. I had a different judge though. Was that a good - or a bad thing? A man. Were men stricter or harsher than women? I was about to find out;

"Hello, Mr. Mahon, I know who you are....."

(Okay, so – is this good? Is it going to be really bad?)

"……I know that you are the stepfather of missing Amy Fitzpatrick…."

(This is interesting. It's not going to be a sit-on-the fence decision. It's good or awful…)

"……and you are in my prayers."

(Huh! I almost cried - I really wanted to – I wasn't expecting this.)

"Who is here today on behalf of the D.P.P (Director of Public Prosecutions)?"

(Some pencil necked pen pusher stood up and introduced himself.)

"Tell me, what sentence was Mr. Mahon given?"

"He was handed a short custodial sentence, my lord, and a driving ban."

"Well, we can dispense with any talk about custody. How long was the ban for?"

"5 years, my Lord."

"5 years? Hmmm…What is the minimum I can allowably impose?"

"The…eh, minimum, my Lord? (Checks paperwork) This would be 3 years, my Lord."

"3 years (turning to me). Now, Mr. Mahon, as you've heard from my learned friend,

There is a minimum sentence – or 'ban' that I am allowed to impose on you, and that is 3 years. Do you understand that?"

"Yes, Your Honour."

"Very good. I will not be discussing matters in relation to the custody Mr Mahon. That is to say, you will not be returning to prison."

"Thank you, Your Honour."

"However, this court does give you a 3-year ban from driving."

"Yes, Your Honour."

"But… come back to me when 2 years have elapsed and I will give you your license back, okay?"

"Thank you, Your Honour."

"I also will not be giving you any fines."

"Thank you."

"Mr. Mahon, I think that you already have enough on your plate. It is not the interest of this court to add to it."

"Thank you very much, judge.''

"One more thing, Mr. Mahon, the next time it's Amy's anniversary or birthday or matters of that nature…. I'd ask you not to drink and drive. By all means, have a drink, but either get a taxi-home or stay at home."

Talk about a contrast between two judges?! It's easy for me to wax lyrical about how much better one judge was over another, especially when it fell so heavily in my favour, but I do believe it merits at least a comment or two. The law - so we are constantly reminded - is supposed to favour common sense over the black and white ancient, draconian-level text that fills its many books. You'll often read about various senior counsels harping on about an "Affront to common sense to believe…." But we very seldom see it applied. This was one of those rare cases when it was. Yes, I was guilty of drunk-driving, no doubt about it and I'll never deny it. I was caught bang-to-rights and I immediately put my hands up. It's a fair cop guv'nor and all of that. However, even Ray Charles would've seen that there were extenuating circumstances in my case. It was the anniversary of Amy's disappearance and we were thousands of miles away from where she was last seen. You've read my story so far; this doesn't excuse my behaviour, and it is simply the reason why. A good and experienced judge (the second one) could see this and also see past the "punish or perish'' mentality. His final comments to me about getting a taxi home. It was more than a soft touch, an avuncular pat on the back. It was the right thing to say (and a lovely thing to say), but it was also a warning. Had I been caught driving under the influence of alcohol after that, then the D.P.P would (correctly) bring that up and ensure that the book was thrown at me and at me hard. The judge knew that wasn't lost on me, nor was his even-handed decision. He was of the view that I'd learned my lesson. He was right, I have, I'll never again even consider it and that's the perfect scenario. No expense to the state to feed and house me in prison (somewhere north of €70,000, I've been told), and also Audrey and I

362

were free to continue with Amy's Campaign. Unfortunately, these days, we see far too much of the behaviour consistent with my first judge. The law is a guide, not an instruction manual.

Back on planet Dave, my pain wasn't just down to court appearances and bad decisions; my hip was worse than ever and now I couldn't even drive to the shops for tea and biscuits. My own bloody fault, but my lesson didn't just end at the courtroom steps. The 'court of public opinion' was now very much in session and my case was splashed across every newspaper and TV news report. I was suddenly public enemy number one and as embarrassing as this is to admit - it was my first realisation as to how much drunk driving is frowned upon in this country these days. I grew up in a drink-driving culture, a time when everyone knew of at least one driver who drove better drunk than sober. I'm not limiting that to your average punter either - taxi drivers, Garda, ambulances, fire brigades, busses - it was endemic. It was 'just-the-done-thing'. How things have changed, and in that respect -thank God- it has changed for the better. I've tried to explain the drunk-driving culture to younger heads since that fateful day and have been met by nothing but scorn, blank faces and sheer disbelief! It's a practice as alien to our new Irelanders as seeing a teacher smoking in the classroom, another part of my formative years and culture that has also changed for the better.

As much as Audrey and I were learning the new Irish culture and loving the Irish people, our hearts were still in Spain, never more so than when we'd have dealings with our 'wonderful' politicians. Audrey was somehow still able to keep Amy's campaign going despite her regularly increasing hospital visits. Her liver was on its last legs and every doctor she came into contact with reminded her about that fact. What was Audrey's idea of getting her liver issue treated?

"Dave, I've organised for these photos of Amy to be put up on all the bus stops in Dublin, but we're going to focus mostly on the northside, up around the Sword's road and out to the airport...."

It sounds easy, doesn't it? It's not, outdoor advertising is one of the most difficult kinds there is, as you're fighting against the weather, graffiti, and vandalism, but my God, is it worth it. When Audrey and I first saw Amy's face up on the bus shelters, it hit us like a bullet to the heart, just like it did over in Spain. We then took stock for the thousandth time; - we'd advertised her campaign in every format known to mankind and did so relentlessly. Well.... almost. There was one thing we still hadn't tried and that was the time to try it. We were going to write about Amy - for Amy - and the world was going to hear about it. I was soon to discover that was something much easier said than done, but Amy is always worth the pain. Always!

There are two ancient schools of thought about judging books by their covers. The first one – and probably the best known - is that you shouldn't. Simple as that. Case closed. The second one is that we always do. It is a very rare thing when a person enters a bookshop (if they even exist, nowadays!) and doesn't pick up a book where the cover caught their eye. It is for both of these reasons (but especially the latter) that we wanted Amy's face on the front of the book. This, too, was a marketing tool because not only would Amy's beautiful face be instantly recognizable and therefore tick the 'pick-it-up and have-a- look' box, but also when people were finished reading it, they could pass 'her' image on to a friend; leave it beside the post, on a bus - train, plane or in a pub etc. it was keeping her out there, reaching places we usually couldn't. So, we had the cover sorted; now, all we had to do was fill in all of those pesky blank pages in between. It shouldn't be a problem. Lord knows we've enough material, right? Actually yes! For once, the problem wasn't what to put in; rather, it was what to leave out. Audrey went off and wrote down her thoughts, opinions and insights on where we were and I did the same. We made a pact to not read each other's material until we were both finished and then swap them over. It took a long time (longer than you'd think) and it was more than a 'writing job' for us; it was cathartic. It was also a revelation for both of us. We were both amazed by what we had written.

Audrey – in true 'Irish Mammy' fashion - wrote more about her feelings and everything about Amy since she slept in a cradle. You know the usual proud mother stuff - when she was born, how much she weighed, her first tooth, first day at school - all of that, it's unbelievably moving, it makes Amy so much more than a tragic-teen, pouting on 'missing' posters all over Europe and Northern Africa. It makes her real – to you - as she becomes your child too, your friend, your niece, someone you now know. For whoever took her, that stuff becomes a nightmare. They have to worry about who might know it was them, how they might now feel about the 'pay-check' or 'commodity' she once was, now that she's real. Audrey gave the blow-by-blow accounts of how Amy learned to swim, cycle a bike or cook her favourite meal. How she'd eat like a horse and yet look as skinny as a rake and how she'd rub that in when the rest of us had to watch what we ate. I was much more 'blokey' in how I wrote. I put in all the business stuff and was more fact-based than emotional, although that's not to say that my heart wasn't broken as well; it was, but as usual, I felt like I had to stay strong for everyone. When we finished the book, we handed it over to Mick O' Toole, the crime journalist from the Irish Daily Star. He, in turn, handed it to his boss-them director of the Star- Des Gibson, who owns a publishing company.

It was agreed between us that O' Toole would call out to my father's house in Santry (another 'Mick' hence the use of surname) to record our story on his tape recorder. This dragged on and on for weeks and proved to be extremely difficult for Audrey and I, but we trusted the journalist and he did seem to know what question to ask. Around two weeks or so into this process, I noticed that Audrey and I had started getting extremely snarky and snappy at one another- something very much out of character for us- and it was only when we sat back and examined the probable causes why, that it dawned on us. The questions we were being asked were bringing up a raft of difficult feelings we'd been suppressing for years, so writing our book was acting like a conduit to release those emotions like a valve releasing pressure. It's about as close as we'd come to counselling, so it was a worthwhile exercise. Were we happy with the end result? Sadly, no, because we found that an awful lot of the information, we wrote about was removed or "excluded for legal reasons." I still scratch my head about that one, especially when you see outright lies masquerading as facts published every day. Whatever our faults are, Audrey and I aren't liars, so suddenly it's illegal to tell the truth? Whatever, I only hope that this book fares better in that regard.

The book launch was held in the Shelburne Hotel, that famous old dame located off St. Stephen's Green. It was quite the swanky social event with over 80 people in attendance ranging from politicians, lord Mayors, TV and media personalities down to the most important guests, our friends and families. It was a difficult night on so many fronts, but by far, the most painful thing to deal with was the recent loss of Audrey's mother, Mora. She was rushed to Beaumont hospital, never a good thing when you're in 80s, and never recovered, dying there a few weeks later. She was a lovely, lovely woman and Audrey is like her in so many different ways, it's frightening. The irony of my mother's passing just before Amy's disappearance and Audrey's mother passing just before Amy's book launched, wasn't lost on us. It made what was a tough night to begin with that much tougher. All around the room where the book launch was being held were cardboard cut-outs of Amy's face -seven feet high- and hundreds of copies of Amy's book sprinkled generously amongst the guests and tables. A lovely thing to see and behold under other circumstances. It was more than too much for any man or woman to take in, but again, we internally recited our strength mantra: "Do it for Amy – Do it for Amy – Do it for Amy."

There wasn't a shortage of people to step up and say a few encouraging words and again, a joy to see and hear…. under different circumstances. My heart broke time and again that night, wishing that Amy could've been there to see, feel and experience the loss that was there for her. I know that it took real courage -and not of the Dutch kind- to stand up and speak when it was something they'd never normally do and even though their nerves would sometimes show, their words meant the most. As I guess is customary or expected at these events, Audrey and I were pestered in saying a few words, which we did. I can't remember what was said or who said what, but I know we said 'something.' We actually stayed over that night in the famous old hotel, which was a wonderful treat as it's a beautiful place. Something else to do and add to our bucket list when circumstances are different.

Our book was released with the title: "Please find my Amy" with the subtitle "The Amy Fitzpatrick Story" running across the top. The front cover is dominated by Amy's famous pout and those fabulous blue eyes staring out at the world. From a distance, all you can see -are those beams of blue and her name – A M Y- in big red bold-black text, on the bottom-right corner is a lovely little snap of Amy and Audrey- by her mother 'Audrey Fitzpatrick'- the official author, as it should be. It is a striking book cover that could be no mistaking who it's about or what it's about. As the famous brand name would proclaim, "it does exactly what it says on the tin." The bitter-sweet bite for me was (A) seeing the book in most of the shops and (B) seeing the book in most of the shops. I loved that we had managed to get her name-face and story out there, but it shattered my heart to pieces at the same time, seeing her sweet, helpless face on the front of the book that was written about her to find her. I used to feel guilty just turning away and moving on to the next shop, my Irish-guilt (built into our D.N.A) deriding me for 'turning my back' on her face. It really is a confusing thing to live through, let alone try to explain.

The book also helped to re-open some doors that had slammed shut on us. We no longer had any more problems in meeting with various governmental ministers, up to and including the prime minister of the day. Fergus Healy, the Garda Officer in charge of the missing persons unit up at the Phoenix Park, also started to answer our phone calls again. It dropped us back into full-campaigning mode once again and whilst that was great and very important, it came with a high price and our health was running out of credit. Audrey still hadn't allowed herself to grieve properly for her mother and that was a crack you simply can't plaster over, no matter how tough you think you are. Maybe it was how alike they were or maybe it was because Audrey was ''the baby- who knows?'' but they were incredibly close, even by normal mother/daughter standards. It was also a fact that Audrey's father, Joe - wasn't grieving properly either, but that's because he couldn't. He was well into the final stages of that other living nightmare known as Alzheimer's. We couldn't even tell him that his wife was dead because in those rare occasions when he had a semblance of clarity, it would've killed him. Not just once either; every time you'd tell him it would bring with it the same shock, heartache and world-ending-pain as most of us only (thankfully) get to experience once, and that's one time too many. So, if he asked where Mora was – which was often – our answer would have to be some variation of:

"She's up in Beaumont Hospital Joe. Sure, we were all up there with her this morning, do you not remember?"

"Oh…. oh yeah, I remember now."

My heart broke every time, for Joe, for Audrey and for poor Mora, of course. Her family took turns looking after Joe because he couldn't be left at home by himself, a massive indignity for a man who'd spent the whole of his adult life being strong and fiercely independent. The poor man required round-the-clock, 24-hour care and that was on top of regular visits from his professional careers. That was what myself and Audrey would do in our downtime from campaigning Garda and Governments for Amy. We got nowhere fast and to be honest, they probably only met us because of all the media attention that was back on us. I can remember writing to the Irish President, Michael D. Higgins, asking for any help or assistance his office could bring to our campaign. God knows that's hardly a full-time job as it's even more of a figurehead position than the Queen of England, who at least opens the odd supermarket. If anyone should be happy to lend a hand and raise their public profile, Michael D. was surely the man. But he wasn't. He sent a generic, lame response along the following lines;

"I have been in touch with the Garda and they have informed me that they are doing everything in their power…"

In case you have any difficulty in translating political gobbledygook, allow me to translate it for you;

"Dear commoner, fuck off. I couldn't be arsed, now go away." Still, isn't it amazing how one of his predecessors – Mary Robinson – spends more time in Africa than Bono, but when you look for their help about an actual Irish person-in-dire need, the phone is off the hook? Once again, more proof should it ever be needed about how thick the Paddy's' are and we are the butt of golden jokes. I'll tell you how bad we are as a nation; we got more letters and more advice from 10

367

Downing Street and Buckingham Palace than we did from a man and an office known internationally as – "who?" Also, if I had been of a mind to record half of the conversations we had with a Garda Siochana, we'd have made an absolute laughing stock out of them. Heads would've rolled, no tribunals necessary. Nobody that bloody thick could be trusted to order a hamburger, let alone an investigation.

To alleviate the annoyance of such dealings, I'd bought myself one of those electric bikes from a shop on Capel Street. You know, the type - where you have a choice of whether to cycle under your own steam or else switch over and use the throttle. Ideal for old men and younger Dave's still awaiting a new hip. With the driving-ban I'd gotten myself into, it was the closest thing I had to independence and it got me up and back from the gym, my walking stick balancing on the cross-bars, and that was my letting-off-steam sanctuary. It was good to be able to get away from everything and everybody because even though no man is an island, we all need a bit of "me" time every so often. Besides, I had a function to help organize. Where else could I do my thinking and planning?

Yes, you read that correctly, a 'function' or, to be more specific, a 21st Birthday Party for Amy. Our little girl was turning 21, the "key of the door" and all of that, so why not? I know she was still missing -believe me, we knew that better than anyone- but who says we still shouldn't mark the occasion? Not that it stopped a few annoying people from trying to interfere with our business, you know the type;

"That's bleeding, stupid, she's not even here."

Unfortunately, the world is full of them, the type of people who would've sat at the table of the Last Supper and complained about the fact there was no jam. But it wasn't about them, it was about Amy, so they could shove their opinions into the least convenient orifice they could think of.

We invited a small group of family and friends to the champions Bar on the Malahide Road. We dressed the place in balloons and paid professional caterers to do the food and organize a cake. Admittedly, it's still the only 21st I've ever heard of where the guest of honour was 'in absentia,' and for that reason, I'll concede that it felt a little strange, but then again, we'd been living in a world of strange that Dan Sterling would've sold his soul to have written. In the final analysis, it was a good night – enjoyable even - and plenty of people turned up, even some of the naysayers, but in their defence, there's no point in being a hypocrite if you can't prove it. Is there? Not for the first time (and by no means the last), my heart went out to poor Dean. He was there and did his best to be there for both of them, but you don't always need an X-ray to see inner Turmoil. More than any of us, Dean was hurting in ways we'd never fully be able to explore. Amy, wherever you are, your big brother knew early on that your return was never going to happen overnight, but he never gave up on you, even though he gave up on himself at times. He did you proud on the night of your 21st birthday.

No sooner was the ink dry on the bill from the party that I got one of the calls I'd been waiting impatiently for. My new hip was ready and waiting. All I had to do was go under the knife and have it fitted; how hard can that be? It's quite a tough operation, not least of which is where it's located (I can just see you all looking or feeling down to where your hips are – same place as always, right?!) and also how bloody big they are! The procedure takes a few hours and guess what? You have to remain awake during it! You are drowsy though, so it's not all glamour! As for me, I had Bono, Larry, Adam and the Edge to help me through it, although what you want to listen to on your own earphones is entirely up to you! I was given an epidural into the spine; this effectively paralyses you from the waist down, as thousands of mothers already know. When the surgery was over, I felt horrible, every inch of me - all three of them! I could see my feet but couldn't move them for several hours afterwards, a hangover from the medication and your own body, knitting all the neural pathways back together after it had assimilated your new alien body part. Once the medication relief wore off, my body's dying resistance to the alien cells hurt like boiling oil, but there's the breaks.

The doctors turn into drill instructors the next day; you've got to "get out of that bed" and start moving around quickly. You do that for a few days and then you begin your physical therapy and then it's out the door with you. I still had to use the Mahon family walking stick for 6 weeks or so afterwards. I also had an even more impressive "crutch" to lean on the love of a good woman, something and somebody I'll never take for granted. Then, all of a sudden, I didn't need the walking stick or any other physical support. I felt great, invigorated and free. I guess that's how babies feel when they take their first steps, only don't quite have the vocabulary to articulate it! But… but… but… I'm Dave Mahon, so how long was that going to last? Less than a month! Life is all about balance…. My hips knew this. So, my left side decided to give up the ghost. Same process all over again. Doctors/M.R.I/Waiting lists – rinse and repeat. It took another year and a half on the walking stick, but by then, my hip was the least of my worries.

Amy's Dublin Garden

St. Catherine's Primary School, beside Amy's grandmother's house, is one truly unique place. It is not just a school, but a school where Amy loved going to! A far cry from anything Spain had to offer.

It was here that the ever-popular, whip-smart young Amy learned to read, write and talk for Ireland. Sadly, not even her gift-of-the-gab could talk up her math results, but her even Achilles had that whole 'heel deal' didn't he?! When Audrey and I approached her school about an Irish 'Amy's Garden,' we were floored by how well remembered she was, her "smile that lit up the classroom."

Words count, and they are loaded with messages, so we never allowed "Garden of Remembrance" into the lexicon. They're foxes honouring the dead and we're a long way from that. A lot of work went into this garden, but even more love and that's something we'll carry with us forever. The Lord Mayor of Dublin turned up to officially open the Garden.

I know I speak for not just myself and Audrey – but for all our family and friends – when I say that all those little kids who turned up and sang songs – for their Amy, one of their own – and seeing all these little sincere, earnest, innocent little faces, would melt the heart of a sphinx. It was a perfect day and it's the perfect place to visit and to remember our missing daughter. If you're in the area, you can't miss it or the plaque bearing her name outside of it. As perfect as it is, we can't bring ourselves to visit it – still – because it's still too raw, particularly for Audrey, but that's not to say we won't someday. I'd like to take this time to thank all the pupils, teachers and staff at the school for their love and support, like us, we know you'll never give up on her either.

Nostalgia

When your life is in the toilet and dark clouds of gloom follow you, no matter how far or how fast you travel, you need to sit back and re-focus. You'd end up at the bottom of a lake if you didn't have good memories -happy times to look back on- and that's why I've written/indulged in this section of the book. It's just a little section on what we tapped into to get ourselves by, so I guess you could define it as a survival guide.

I'd slump into an empty armchair in the un-lit front room of Amy's house after yet another failed day of searching. I'd be too weary to even bother with the lights; I'd just be worn and broken. That was when I'd look at it, no, it wasn't a magic wand, it was a piece of canvas in a frame, roughly 3 ½ feet by 2 ½ feet. Not huge. Not famous. But it's priceless to me. It was a painting that Audrey bought me on my birthday, one of our first ones together in Spain. Within its dark wooden frame was the image of a naked woman with long hair. Her head is tilted and turned – just so – and its colour scheme consisted of mainly browns and dark oranges. It's really tastefully done, not a hint of smut or pornography. It was a type of art that would complement any family room, as it did ours. Why would such a dark-coloured painting in a twilight-lit room cheer me up? In a word -memories- I can never see it without thinking of Dean and Amy's faces when they first laid eyes on it. They gawked at its boldness- was it rude? Was it acceptable? For ages before the realisation of its simplicity and beauty registered. They loved it. Almost as much as I did. Even when we moved back to Ireland and darkness continued - to reign, that portrait always cheered me up.

Sometimes, "things" matter. Another thing that comes to mind is another painting – and no – we didn't live in an art gallery, but our few humble pieces of art are very special to me. Or rather, in this instance, the memory of how we got it is the happy memory. We (that is Audrey and I) were at an auction for one of the animal charities in Spain, known by the acronym – P.A.D. Anyway, this rather abstract painting came up for auction and the best way my never-at-art college mind could describe it, would be to say that it was 'O.K.' It was a marriage of shapes and styles within a swirl of varieties of bright red shades, it was… bright! Audrey took a fancy to it as it matched the red leather sofa we had at that time. To be honest, she was in two minds about buying it, as it wasn't exactly the Mona Lisa, but it matched our sofa and the money was going to a good cause, so why not? So, the bidding started -nothing noteworthy about that- except who we (we, as in Audrey!) found ourselves bidding against. Do you remember our horrible next-door neighbours, in particular 'the lady' who assaulted Audrey? Yeah! It was her! No way was Audrey coming second in this auction! No matter what the other woman bid, Audrey would wait until the:

"Going once at 'X', going twice at 'X'   going…"

"X plus one!"

Not once, not twice, but as many times as it took! We had deeper pockets back then so Audrey won the bidding war. Brave soul that I am, I waited until we were driving home before I asked;

"Did you even want that picture?"

"What do you mean?"

"Well. It's not great, is it?"

"Ah… it'll match our sofa and it's for a good cause…"

Then she looked at me and the two of us just burst out laughing. We still do!

Not all of our "art collection" came as overpriced as that one. A very good friend of ours – Antonio- was caught a bit short on the day of our engagement. Rather than simply admitting that he'd get us something later on (we couldn't have cared less anyway, not being one of those 'precious' couples who 'expect' presents) he did a quick roll-of-the-eyes;

"Hang on; I'll be back in a minute!"

We thought nothing of it and continued celebrating with our other friends, as you do, until he came back to the bar covered in sweat, carrying something;

"Here you are. Congratulations!"

We thanked him and unwrapped it. It was a beautiful, carved statue of "The Thinking Man," about a foot and a half tall.

"Wow! Nice one, Antonio, it's beautiful. Thanks very much!"

"(Still catching his breath) Ah, no problem, glad you like it."

"So, where'd you get it? I thought all the shops were closed at this time?"

"Eh…"

"Also, you're out of breath and covered in sweat..."

"Um..."

"Did you pay a lot for it?"

"Eh... no... not yet anyway..."

"Huh? 'Not yet'- what does that mean?!"

"I... eh... I borrowed it... I'll pay for it later!"

As it was, we were already having a great night, but the laughs and slagging that went on the rest of the night after that made it truly memorable! As we'd say as kids, he was a "Great Character," and that little statue holds a very dear place in our hearts. We'll never part with it (it's still in Spain with everything else).

Then we went through what I'll call our 'wrought-iron' stage, and two memory filled items in particular. The first was a pair (ironically) of ceiling-light-fittings. Absolutely beautiful, complete with 8 candle-shaped bulbs. Honestly, they wouldn't have looked out of place in a stately home. We had no bloody business putting them up in Amy's house, but we did and they looked fabulous. They were definitely an impulse buy and we were a bit flush at that time. When we made the decision to leave Amy's house, we took them with us and hung them up on the ceiling of our new apartment, where they had even less business being. There is an old Irish custom that has left our shores and caught on around the rest of the world, where a mother will leave a candle burning in the window every night to guide her children home. It's a very serious custom in fishing communities, but, in our situation, those candle-shaped bulbs don't really require further elucidation, do they?

Our other wrought-iron memory concerns our glass-topped dining room table and 6 chairs. We got them at an auction. Another successful bidding war! And we put them out on our balcony. Yes, I'll admit that they did look a little bit out of place there, but they were also - and much more importantly - an "Amy place" where she'd sprawl out and eat her dinners or struggle through some of her rare homework assignments.

We also had the most wonderful shower room built into our bathroom. It was decked out in a lovely mosaic tile pattern with a really cool seat in the shower - very handy when you're a bit worse for wear! With a series of high pressure jets. It had a snazzy blue illumination, which (when coupled with the steam) wouldn't have looked out of place at a Pink Floyd Concert. Oh, and talking about music, it also had a stereo fitted; it was one of my favourite places - ever! It also calls to mind some of my more personal, happy memories, but I'll leave that to your imagination. Let's just say that we'd sometimes go in there to relax and just leave it at that!

A lot of the time, it's the seemingly mundane stuff that recalls smiles from the past. The front door to our home was heavy, distinguished and "Ours" or the little diamond fittings on the kitchen presses that Audrey insisted on, sending me off on three-day camel rides to Malaga time and again until I got them. As usual, she was right. They set off the whole bloody kitchen, lifting it from ordinary to spectacular, unlike yours truly who, passing a curiosity shop on Capel Street, spotted an old deep sea divers' helmet and thought it was the greatest find since the tomb of King Tut. In my defence, it was for our bar in Spain and I had a bit of a 'theme' in mind but fate did too, unfortunately. That coincided with my father's 'heart attack', so it's sentimental for good reason- he survived it.

Sadly, time and unforeseen occurrences have faded and outright eroded all of those -little port keys to more halcyon days, never to be replaced. Even if I had all the money in the world, I wouldn't repurchase them, contradictory, as I'm sure that sounds. I could go on and on forever (as I'm sure you could too, dear reader) about other things we had that meant something very special to us, but that's because I'm a bit of a sentimental old fool at heart, no fool like an old fool, so they say. Also, no matter how hard you try, you can't get toothpaste back into the tube, I should know.

One of those failed experiments concerns a car out of all things. When Amy went missing, I drove a wine-coloured Mercedes in Spain. It became the 'Amy-car,' as I had it covered in Amy's posters for years. When we came back from Spain, I bought a few different types of cars, but soon enough, another wine coloured Mercedes came onto my radar -one difference- it was an automatic, but we still bought it. It took less than 24 hours for us to regret our decision. Boy, did we. Every time we'd look out the window (even when driving), it felt like we should have the kids still in the back with us, driving to Mercadona, a Spanish supermarket the kids loved.

That car picked and prodded our raw, open wounds every time we travelled in it -not the car's fault-ours. One important lesson came out of it, though - it was time to make new memories and stop living in the past. By no means will we ever forget it – no way – because our hearts and souls are still over in Spain, where we feel Amy still is to this day. If we ever did go back, we'd see "her" everywhere we looked – bars we'd been in/ restaurants we had eaten in/ shops -cinemas we'd been to and we'd wither trying to find her, or her absence would kill us. It almost has already, maybe it has and we don't know it yet? Either way, it was time for new memories, but who knew what the future would hold? Who does now?

Dean's Last Night

Dear reader, you've come this far with me and seen me for who I am and for what I am not. Personally, I've read a good few autobiographies and appreciated their honesty but they've been honest "to a point." I've thought long and agonized to the point of absurdity about this next chapter. What you are about to read is completely true, unfiltered and won't put me in a favourable light. That's honesty; call it fool hardy, call it brave, call it what you will, but everything I've written so far has been verifiable both legally/manually and ethically, I can stand over it and will. This next chapter is no exception. So, why this long-winded lead-in? Simply, the 'truth' is written by the victor, this is the only time that someone is in my position. The vanquished antagonist has had the opportunity to set the record straight. This is the truth, the whole truth and nothing but the truth. The narrative, as you "know" it, may very well be about to change.

This, and you've read the book so far, is the hardest thing I've ever had to write. It's impossible to "start" and even harder to "finish," so please, bear with me. My preamble is simple-I'm beyond pissed off and annoyed with the Garda, Guardia Civil, Government officials (home and abroad) and the lecherous slimeballs that constitute tabloid media the world over. Whoever came up with the phrase about lighting never striking twice has never met my family. Dean was and is my family. Yes, I was "only" his stepdad, but any idiot with a positive sperm count can become. As a father, you've got to turn up, be present and work and be as I did; a stepdad, even more so. I love Dean too much to finish his memory, so I'm not going to take the coward's path and speak ill of him. That being said, there was a lot of stuff written about him in the past by the scum-loids that was hurtfully untrue and also hurtfully true. Like the devil, they mix the truth with lies to beef up juicier headlines, so let us set the record straight from who's been in the public domain about him all these years. He wasn't an angelic boy type, but truly, who is? It is true that he developed a drug habit from a very early age, perhaps 10, no older than 11 years of age. Yes, shocking; no child of that age has a clue what they are doing or the consequences and he was no exception. He had a difficult childhood for many different reasons and that resulted in him being committed to Portrane, a mental health institution in North County Dublin, where he was treated for A.D.H.D and self-harm, because Dean was 'a cutter.' A person who cuts themselves to 'relieve' the mental pain and anguish they feel, like most people, when Dean was under the influence of narcotics, he wasn't himself; he would say and do things that a sober Dean would never dream of doing. A recurring theme was to pull the knife, not only on himself but on me a few times too. This is all I'm prepared to go into about his dark half, not least of which is because (a) who am I to judge? And (b) I don't want you, dear reader, to make an early judgement about him, at least not until you get to know the Dean I love.

You see, Dean, for the most part was as happy and loveable a kid as you were ever likely to meet. When he laughed, the whole world laughed with him because 'infectious' was too small a word for it. He had a smile that doesn't require description; I witnessed its effect on the fairer sex too many times over the years to know how beautiful it was. He could have the craic with the lads and maintain gentlemanly decorum around the ladies all at the same time. He was better than great company and was a truly unique young man. I did and continue to think the world about him. I missed him when he moved back to Ireland, so when Audrey and I were compelled into the same action, I did everything I could to build and maintain our relationship.

When we joined Ben Dunne's gym together in Santry, I had high hopes about doing just that. A place to be together, "man time," and to try to keep him healthy and away from that poison he was putting into his system. How wrong I was; my friend John, who also joined the gym with us, helped me with my drunk driving ban by purchasing an electric bike (the same as mine, more or less) to keep me company. It's quite an investment because they're not cheap. It was a pivot point, banter-wise because he was the only one of us working at the time and I had paid all the gym memberships. John was working so he "could've afforded" to, a joke we'd made together over the years, so I guess buying that bike (splurging out) was his way of trying to shut me up! It turned out that the three of us rarely -if ever- trained together. I would do so every day for my stress-free swim, John would train every other day and Dean was more intervals in lifting weights and could turn up in the gym at any time of the day. However, moving on to more germaine matters, as that fateful day. I went to the gym that morning as usual and bumped into Mick, my builder friend also, as usual, we got stuck into each other in some much-rehearsed slagging in the locker room when the door opened and Dean walked through. For one reason or another, we weren't on the best of speaking terms at that moment, typical family tiffs, storm in a teacup type of stuff, so we just gave each other a look of acknowledgement at that exact moment. The reason for our tiff was over a text message conversation. It was something along the lives of:

"I need the nappies."

"How much?"

"€5."

"For nappies?"

"Y (yes)"

"Fuck off."

Context. I knew it was for drugs because this wasn't the first time and also, you can't get nappies for a fiver. Hindsight, the cruel mistress that she is, makes me feel utterly horrible for my choice of reply and the shame I feel even now as I write it is killing me even though I know in my heart that almost every time he'd text me looking for this or that for his child, I'd give it to him, of course I did, but when I realised I was becoming an ATM for his habit, I started drawing the line. Show me a parent or loved one who wouldn't.

So, understandably, there was a bit of tension between us in the locker room. Dean quickly made his way upstairs, no doubt he was lifting a few weights, when Mick asked me, "Who was that man?"

"Oh. That's Dean."

"Dean? Your Dean? Who worked for me over in Spain?"

"Yes."

"But. He didn't even say 'hello' to me?"

"Yeah, I… (I tried thinking up an excuse but failed) I noticed that."

"Dave, I've noticed him looking at my locker before, you know?"

I made my excuses and a hasty exit to see if I could locate Dean. I did a few light weights, hoping he'd walk past or something, but there was no sign, so he must've gone upstairs to where the heavier weights were. You can have all the arguments with your kids and step-kids in the world, but you never stop looking out for them, do you? A couple of minutes into my session, Dean passed me straight to the locker room and left the gym minutes later. This was most unusual and I remember thinking that exact phrase to myself as I saw him leave. It also crossed my mind that he may have been on something, but he was gone. I finished my workout and then proceeded into the steam room and Jacuzzi, as usual, said goodbye to Mick, then showered and left. If that sounds boring, normal or matter of fact, that's because it was, apart from the wee bit of tension, it was a normal morning at the gym. That's important to remember, as you'll discover.

I went over to the spot where I usually parked my bike and as I unlocked it, I couldn't help but think about Dean. Why did he leave so early? Was there something on his mind? Did he need to chat with me about something? But more and more, the nagging thought that he had taken something crossed my mind. He had admitted to me in the past about taking a periodic cocktail of cocaine and steroids, and as anybody who knows anything about drugs can tell you, that is not a good mix for someone with a life-long stance of an anti-drugs nature, this only even strengthened my resolve to speak out against them and to hate them even more than ever, don't get me wrong I have been to parties over in Spain where the cocaine flowed as freely as water. Any amount of it, but it was never for me or for my family. I'll be forever grateful to my parents for that.

As I made my way home, I got the electrics in the bike to do the work. I was tired after the gym session and pre-occupied about Dean. I stopped at a red light at Ballymun Avenue, just before the Swiss Cottage Public House and intuitively reached down for my water bottle for a quick 'slug' before the lights charged. Only it wasn't there, strange? A quick metal recon followed. Did I even bring it? Did I leave it in the gym? Then the penny dropped, Dean! He must've stolen it, it was the sort of thing he'd sometimes do, so I cursed him under my breath for a few seconds, then I just laughed! I remember calling him "a little fucker" under my breath as I completely saw the funny side of it, but I could never let him know that! Then, as I continued on my journey, I thought (for the thousand time) that it "mightn't have been him," so I did a U-turn and headed back to the gym. If it wasn't him, then I'd (mentally) done him an injustice and to be honest, I really wanted to be wrong about him.

When I arrived at the gym, I asked the guys at the front desk if they wouldn't mind checking their C.C.T.V. footage just to put my mind at rest. If it wasn't him, then no harm done and I'd make a mental note to not judge him so quickly next time, but I knew… just knew in my heart of hearts that it was him. Eventually, one of the lads who knew how to operate the C.C.T.V. came to the desk:

"Can I help you?"

"Yeah, look, I know this sounds a bit petty (but then he didn't know that Dean had previously stolen my cars, motorbikes, cameras, phones, etc.), but I think that somebody stole something off my bike."

"Okay, just hang on a second there until I check…"

I watched patiently as he pushed buttons and did his thing, but my mind was in a bit of a quagmire, somewhere between 'Don't let it be Dean 'to' this is the straw to break the camel's back, he's had one last chance too many."

"Okay, yeah, there was definitely someone at your bike alright."

"Can you tell me who it is?"

"No, sorry, you'll have to go to the police and report it to them."

"Right."

"So, can you just confirm that for me?!"

"Look, I'm really sorry, but I can't. You have to go to the police station and report it."

"I'm not going to do that over a bleeding water bottle! If he stole my bike, I still wouldn't do it!"

"Yeah, I hear ya. Look, come back when the manager returns, okay?"

"Sure, will he be long?"

"Well, he's only gone off for lunch, so he won't be too long."

Sounded like as good a plan as any other, so I agreed to do just that. I went outside the gym, scrolled down to Dean's number and pressed 'call,'

"Yeah?"

"Dean, this is Dave."

"Yeah?"

Great, his mono-syllabic attitude was exactly what I didn't need to hear, so I just launched into it and gave him a careful telling off about robbing something off my bike. His response?

"I don't know what you're an about. I didn't go near your bleeding bike ...."

"Don't lie to me! I saw you on C.C.T.V doing it (even though I hadn't)."

Expletives and colourful metaphors were exchanged at high volume before that call ended. That would have to be an end to it… Well, until I saw him next as he was going to get! A piece of my mind. That was the plan, nothing more.

My method for giving out to Dean was born out of my successful Spanish model, which involved a good chastising talk about getting back on the straight and narrow but always in the company of a few good and trusted friends. I wouldn't spring this on my friends; I would've had them well-schooled beforehand so that they could take his side in an avuncular way, something like:

"Dean, why did you rob my car?"

"Ah, leave him alone Dave, sure you used to rob your Da's taxi and collect fares at his age!"

A discussion would then ensue about how things had changed/it's not like it used to be/repercussions are so much more serious these days, etc. So, the result would be Dean learning a lesson at my expense through my mistakes and experiences. It removes the petulant "you don't know what you're talking about" and "you wouldn't understand" arguments, and most importantly, it didn't leave him feeling stupid, as I was the fall guy. Okay, I wasn't his father, but I was his father figure and he knew better than anyone that when the chips were down and he was in a spot of bother, there was no one who would fight harder for him anyway, I was no longer in the mood for seeing the gym manager, so I biked it back to my father's house in Santry.

I was only there when my friend, John McCormack, swung by as he normally would. I told him about my morning up at the gym and he got very pissed off about it. So much so that he insisted that we go back to the gym and speak to the manager. He had his car with him that day, so he drove us down. This time, when we arrived, the manager was there, so I went through the whole C.C.T.V. Rigmarole again. This may sound familiar;

"Yeah. You'll have to go to the police."

"I've been through this already. I'm not doing that."

"Well…?"

"So, then what, can you confirm to me that it was Dean Fitzpatrick?"

"Oh, okay, yes, it was."

"Thank you. I knew anyway, but I needed to confirm it."

"To be honest, we've had our own suspicions about him for some time, tampering with bikes and other items…"

It was all very calm, no shouting or roaring, no threats and no scenes of outrages. It was a mature, reasonable conversation. It was now obvious to me that Dean's card had already been well and truly marked and so, in order to spare him from more trouble and lead him out of temptation, I suggested to the manager that they bar him from the gym. He said that he wouldn't be able to do that unless I went to the police about the incident, so that wasn't ever going to happen. I thanked him for his time, then John and I left the gym and he dropped me home.

I decided to email Ben Dunne's head office to see about barring Dean that way. I already had his email on my contact list as I'd asked him previously about supplying a couple of hundred "Missing Amy" T-shirts, but the old curmudgeon said 'no' now here I was, emailing his office in a futile and desperate attempt to try to save Dean from himself not my proudest ever moment to be fair, almost a week so the day previously, Dean had waited around in the gym reception area for me to give him €50.00 for, well God knows. What I don't forget is that I was on the dole and couldn't work, so that was a significant sum to me. But his son was only an infant and I forced myself to believe the money would've been spent on him. Anyway, I'd spent a king's ransom looking for Amy; Dean was every bit as important, so how couldn't I! Our relationship was as up and down as that was. We were 'up' that week, a week or two prior to that, we were 'down' because of an argument we'd had about Mother's Day. Basically, he didn't get anything for Audrey, so I called him about it and let him have a right ear full. Proper order, too. The call ended with me asking him to our apartment so that I could slip him a few quid on the sly:

"Now, get out there and get your MA some flowers quick!"

"Ah, nice one, great. I'll be back in a minute."

"Don't say anything to Audrey about me giving you the money."

"I won't."

All good, so off he went. "Back in a minute" stretched out to a couple of days. So, God only knows what he did or where he went. I got a bit angry at him at myself, and I couldn't hold it into myself, so I told Audrey the whole sorry role. As angry as I was, we both found ourselves laughing our heads off about it. That was just Dean, what else could you do? Of all the Mother's days Audrey had, that's the one she remembers the most. When he eventually showed up a couple of days later, he had a present of some description for Audrey (I can't remember what it was), but he also had a few lovely T-shirts for me, designer jobs. He knew that I'm too much of a softie to remain angry with him, so we just laughed it off, as you would do. I hope that gives you a bit more insight into the ups and downs of our relationship. There are literally hundreds more stories like that, but through it all, we never stopped loving each other.

On the morning after the bike incident, my friend John phoned me up:

"Fancy a bit of breakfast?"

"Yeah, why not?"

"Audrey free?"

"No, it's her turn to look after her Da today, you know, the Alzheimer?"

Audrey's family were amazing during her father's last days, and they were with that poor man 24/7, a proper family unit. John collected me from our apartment on Burrell Square, just off the Malahide Road, beside the Hilton Hotel on the North side of Dublin. We had the morning to ourselves and I apparently had the day to myself, too, so we weren't in any rush. John drove us out to the Dunes Hotel in Donabate. North County Dublin, although I believe it's called by a different name these days. It's certainly much swankier now than it was then!

As soon as we got there, the salty sea air aroused our taste buds, so we ordered two large fry ups with all the trimmings.

"Sorry, you're too late for breakfast."

Shit. Our stomachs felt like our throats had been cut, it was not a good start to the day. John now had a craving for a fried breakfast, like you wouldn't believe, so we decided to try our luck elsewhere. I didn't mind at all because I'd been looking forward to my fry and besides, it was a lovely drive and we weren't in any real hurry. Like a magnet, we were drawn back to more familiar territory- Kealys bar and restaurant out beside the airport. So, we knew we'd be welcomed there with two breakfasts large enough to have their own postcode. I indulged myself further by washing down all that grease and salt with not one but two deliciously cool bottles of Bulmer's. Now you see why I needed a gym membership! We were having a great oul morning of it, slagging each other off and enjoying the craic and laughs together. Just as I started to get comfortable and before I'd planted roots for the day, John had to bring an end to proceedings because he had a party to go to later that evening and we know each other too well if one of us settled in somewhere, the other was trapped. Out of loyalty, of course! He dropped me off in Santry to my friend Darrin Fagan's house, which is only ten doors away from my father's house.

I suppose it was just as well Darrin was home, wasn't it? He was with Helen, his wife, and the three of us sat in his kitchen for a couple of hours doing what we normally did: talking, laughing and reminiscing about better days.

"Fancy a few beers, Dave?"

"Love a few, but you have a few building quotes to organise, remember?"

"Shit, glass of wine?"

The Pope is Catholic, isn't he? We had a couple of glasses of wine and I could see that Darrin was having a mental tug-of-war between work and having a beer. In my defence, I kept the conversation light and didn't venture into alcohol territory. Darrin had a "Goo" on him for a few pints. I also omitted Dean's situation from our chats because it was totally forgotten about. In the final analysis, I'm only human and Darrin is my best friend, so I succumbed to going out for a few beers:

"C'mon, Dave, we're off. Grab your coat."

"What about your quotes?"

"Ah Dave, that's the beauty about being self-employed, now c'mon!!"

We jumped in a taxi and got out at the Crown Plaza in Santry, so not too far away. This wasn't our first rodeo; we had done this many times and Darrin has been my best friend for over thirty years. We've travelled the world together and know each other inside and out.

We had a nice meal at the Plaza as well as a good few drinks, but this wasn't gluttony, far from it. Darrin and I, in fact, all of our friends would enjoy a few drinks and in so far as is reasonably practicable, we can "handle" our alcohol intake. We've got Black belts in it. Still, it had been a long day and I had definitely consumed more alcohol than food, in other words, had I been driving, then I would've easily been over the limit, but I want to be clear about this, I wasn't drunk, not by a long shot. The way it is with me is always the same. When I've had enough, I disappeared. One minute, I'm there, the next, it's "Where's Dave gone?" The answer is always the same, me making a discreet exit and "Taxi!!" That particular evening was no exception. I ducked out of the Plaza, walked until I hailed a taxi and then it was a taxi home for Dave to Burrell Square. I got in the door, flopped onto the couch and stuck on the T.V. At some point, my phone started ringing and when I answered, it was John McCormack.

"Where are you, Dave?"

"I'm at home, not long in the door."

"Do you mind if I drop around?"

"No, not at all, but are you not out partying with the Missus?!"

"Ah yeah, I'm still out here in clone, but you know yourself!"

I thought that was a bit unusual as it was 10 or 11 PM and clone is a bit of a drive with a good few scoops on you, but c'est la vie, Audrey was staying at her father's house, looking after him, and I didn't need to get up early in the morning or anything, so why not?

When John's call clicked off, I looked at the phone in my hand and thought about calling Dean. I'd invite him up, of course, and do the old Spanish style of bantering with him as John would be there to remind me what a Muppet I was at his age, so once again hope that the message sank in, we'd put it all behind us then have a few laughs and we'd go back to our up and down relationship, just like always. So, my first task was to locate him because Dean, being Dean, could be anywhere! I tried his girlfriend's number first for a couple of reasons. I'd heard it around that they were no longer together and that she'd been with other people already. I'd also heard more than once that she was selling narcotics from home, so there was Dean's son to think about. If all of the above was true, or even some of it, then it might explain some of Dean's recent behaviour. So, I called, she answered and he wasn't with her. I wasn't going into the ins and outs of what was said, but we had an honest exchange of views, let's put it that way. My next call was to Dean's number, and he answered, so I invited him up and he accepted.

Good John would be there and he got on famously with Dean, so in my mind, we'd be able to finish off the night on a good note and Dean would know that we'd still have his back during his difficult break. I decided to call my other friend Karl O' Toole, as he'd be around, driving his taxi and he used to have the critique with

385

Dean as well. I was outnumbering myself slagging wise, but so what? Dean needed a bit of a lift, so why not give it to him? John agreed that it was a good idea too, so I gave Karl a buzz:

"Karl, myself and John are having a few beers at my place. Dean's coming up to join us. Are you interested?"

"Jesus, Dave, I'd love to but I'm working."

"No problem, but if you change your mind, you know where we are."

Karl knew that it sounded like a great-night and I knew from the almost undetectable hesitation in his voice that he might change his mind. Sure enough, Karl's caller ID started flashing up on my phone,

"Fuck you, Dave! I'll come up for a while!"

Karl actually made it to my apartment first, but not by much because as soon as I started pouring his first drink for him, I received a text message from Dean asking me to come down and open the door for him. There were two entrances to the apartment building, one at the front and one at the side. Dean would normally use the side entrance, but that night, he was at the front entrance, where John had also just arrived, all was going as well as I'd hoped so far, and when I went down to let them in, all three of us travelled up together in the lift. All was good, everything was grand. We went into my apartment, where Karl was waiting with his drink.

To give you some idea about the layout of our apartment, it was nothing fancy, a single bedroom with a T.V. room and an open-plan kitchen. John and Karl were primed and ready for me to get the bottle business out of the way so that we could get on with having the craic and a few beers and so on.

"Dean, why did you take my water bottle?"

"I didn't."

That's all it took. All hell started breaking loose, Dean going berserk at me and me shouting at him over nothing.

Like most domestic kitchens, we had one of those knife-blocks with 6 knives housed in it. Dean pulled one out. This is where I'd love to honestly tell you that "I got a fright" or I was "shocked," but I can't tell you that. I can't honestly tell you anything because I don't know how I felt, as it happened too fast. When Dean came at me, it was out of the blue because one moment, the knife was in his hand, and the next, it was in mine. There wasn't even a struggle. The truth is just bizarre sometimes, but that's just the thing; it's the truth. To this day, Audrey still asks me what I said to Dean to make him pull a knife on me. My answer remains the same, I honestly don't know. One minute, we're arguing over a bloody stupid water bottle; the next, I'm disarming him of the knife he came at me with. I don't know if in the moment, he suddenly felt threatened by John and Karl's presence. I can't see that he could've thought that, because he was incredibly fond of John, from all the times he used to come over and visit us in Spain. As for Karl, well he knew Karl. Since he was 12 years old and he knew that both men were just like me, not a violent bone in our bodies, we were all about having a few pints and a bit of a laugh. Wasn't that why we were all there anyway? When I took the knife off Dean, I put it in the back pocket of my jeans, right hand side; why did I do that? I don't exactly know. It was probably insane, who knows? Maybe if I put it back on the kitchen counter, then Dean might've picked it up again? I don't know. I just don't know. I remember turning to John at some point;

"Here, have a word with him (Dean), will you?"

John and Dean walked out to the hallway of our 3rd floor apartment and Karl was still in the T.V. room. I let the lads have a private chat for a minute or two before walking out to see if Dean had calmed down. John was talking to Dean and what it was about and what they were saying, I don't know and truly, I never will. I started giving out to Dean again and then I took the knife out of my back pocket. I held it in my right hand, close to my waist, in about the most non-threatening way you could even hold a knife. There are certain things that will forever be a blur and then there are certain things that are as fresh and raw that it's like they only happened two minutes ago. I can distinctly remember saying certain things to Dean:

"What the fuck are you pulling a knife on your 'oulfello' for?"

With that, Dean ran at me and then made a small noise: -

"Ah."

Not loud, almost an exhalation. Just that one little sound and then he ran off down the stairs. I can remember looking at him running down the stairs and then I said.

"You, gobshite."

Then I looked at the knife I held it out in front of me. It was one of those large kitchen knives, like thousands of others across thousands of homes. Only this one had a small drop of blood on it. Dean's blood, my initial thought was that it must've grazed his side. John was standing to my right beside the lift. Karl was straight in front of me; I really thought that he'd grazed himself. Karl and I went back into my apartment. But John left straight away, pretty much. That was highly unusual, but then, that night was a bizarre of the unusual my way as it only got weirder; for example, think about John's hasty exit. He would've surely met Dean on the way out, did you think? Two entrances, they came in together and left within a proximate time frame. Meanwhile, back in my apartment, Karl insisted on my cleaning the knife. Not just once, either, but over and over again. "Wash the knife Dave, you have to wash the knife. You're not listening to me Dave, wash the bleeding knife..."

"Jesus Karl, relax, will you? You're watching too many movies."

"No, Dave, you have to."

"Relax, Karl, will ya? He's just nicked himself."

Full disclosure. Only I knew the thoughts that were going through my mind, and now you're about to. Right then and there, in that exact moment, I thought that Dean was an absolute gobshite. He'd nicked my stupid water bottle, then lied about it, then pulled yet another knife on me, and then grazed himself on it and I knew, just knew, that he'd be straight around to Audrey the next day to show her his "cut," make an absolute gangster movie about the whole situation and I'd be up to my neck in shit with Audrey for the foreseeable. The only thing I was worried about were the stories he was going to spin to Audrey, and he had the little nick or graze to "prove" what a complete bastard I was. As I write that now, I can see why people assume that I am, but if you read it closely, you'll see the truth. For Dean to "Rat" on me to his mother, he'd have to be alive and fit enough to call around and cause a commotion. At no stage did it ever enter my mind that he wouldn't be, even now forcing myself to re-live those moments, it still feels impossible for my other outcome to have resulted from that night. There was no way that such a tiny graze or incise could develop into anything untoward. I'd spilt more blood slicing onions; I couldn't have been more wrong.

Karl was starting to annoy me with his panicky attitude; he's a windy bastard at the best of times, but this was too much. It was almost as though he was on something. He became really insistent about us getting out of the apartment and heading off somewhere. Anything for a quiet life, so off we went, existing throughout the usual route, which was the side door beside where Karl had parked his taxi. Full disclosure: at no point did we see or hear any signs of Dean being in distress, nothing. We jumped into Karl's taxi and we headed off in a northbound direction. Karl, like most taxi drivers, had a cloth for cleaning off his dashboard, etc. He threw it to me:

"Here, use that to wash the knife."

I threw my eyes up to heaven but did it anyway, and then threw the knife out the window. Karl absolutely lost his reason;

"Dave! What the fuck are you doing?? What did you throw the fucking knife out the window for???"

He was like a man possessed. He drove us out to the Balrothery INN in Balbriggan and we had a drink. Once again, I related my concerns to him about the abuse I was going to get off Audrey; I hadn't a worry in the world about Dean, other than what he was going to say to his mother. We left and on his drive back to Santry, he pulled into Artane Petrol Station to fill up his car and buy his cigarettes. I asked him for his phone, as I was going to stay in my father's house and I wanted to give him a heads up as he's an old man. I tried a few times, but my father wasn't picking up. Anyway, Karl paid for his bits and pieces and then got us back on the road to Santry.

When you drive the route to Santry from Artane, you'd usually go down the old Santry road and there are two lanes. I asked Karl to drop me off there and I'd walk the rest of the way to my father's house. I guess I felt that I needed a breath of fresh air. I suppose, but whatever the reason, Karl agreed and I got out. I took my shortcut route through the two lanes, but when I got to my father's house, Karl had already parked outside; remember what I said earlier about it being a weird night? I couldn't, for the life of me, figure out what Karl was trying to do, but there he was at the front door, larger than life. There was no answer for a while, but Mick eventually opened the door and we both went inside. Boy, did I ever see a different side to Karl once we were inside. As soon as his shoes crossed the threshold, he started yammering away nineteen to the dozen, spewing out word after word about what he believed happened. Once he'd exercised that particular demon, he turned on his heels and left. My father was absolutely flabbergasted and asked me to tell him my version of events. No problem, I told him exactly what had happened.

"Thanks, Dave. Now, can you answer something else for me?"

"Anything."

"Was Karl on something? Do you know if he was taking anything?"

"What do you mean?"

"Is he on drugs?"

"Karl?!! No. Why do you ask?"

"Well, did you not see him, Dave? He was a hundred miles an hour."

To think that Karl would've been anywhere near drugs, let alone be taking them, was a concept too alien for me to even consider... then. My father made his way back up the stairs to bed, but I decided to sit up for a while. I picked up my father's landline phone to call Audrey, but when I first checked the time, I realised it was too late, so I tried Darrin instead; no answer. Probably just as well as I was shattered and tired, so I just went to bed. What a bloody day.

I couldn't have been asleep for more than a few hours before my father came into my room to wake me up. In my waking up/not quite awake yet, I thought he had said the same about 'Dean' and 'Dead:'

"(Groggy) What was that again DA?"

"Dean is dead."

"What? What are you talking about???"

"Son, Dean is dead. It's all over the news."

Bullshit, no way, I had to be dreaming this, it was some sick fucks idea of a bad joke;

"Da, is this some sort of a sick joke or something because it's not true."

"No, Dave. No. Dean is dead."

Fuck. I could hear the words. I understand very well exactly what each and every one of them meant. But it wasn't registering; my brain just could not compute. My father waited for me to get up off the mattress and together we walked down the stairs, into the living room and he turned on the TV.

"Dean Fitzpatrick... Dead..."

Dean. Our Dean. Amy's big brother. Audrey's boy. Dead? I could not believe it. I still can't believe it.

"What are you going to do, Dave?"

"Drop me around to the Police Station in Coolock, please."

And there it was, the sentence that no father wants to hear from his son. As Mick was passing by the flats in (Cromcastle Court in Coolock on the way to the Police Station) I asked him to pull in there and to let me out; that's where John Mc Cormack lives and all I wanted was to let him know. Well, "wanted" isn't exactly the correct word, I 'had' to let him know. John answered the door, good, I didn't know if I could've handled anyone else right then;

"Dean's dead."

"I know. It's on the telly. What are you going to do?"

"I'm on my way to the police station."

"Come on, I'll drop you there."

I went down to Mick and told him that John was going to drop me off at the station.

"Okay, son."

Jesus Christ, the worried look on his poor old face. Fathers want to protect their children and take all the bad away. Sorry, Mick, this was a whole new level of bad that was never going to go away. This deed was done and couldn't ever be undone. Dean is dead. Fuck me. John was talking to me, but I was lost, mentally absent, A.W.O.L devoid of thought. Somehow, I snapped myself back to reality, dark and depressing. As it is;

"What?"

"I was asking you, you know. If you knew last night? What happened?"

"No."

"No?"

"No. I just found out."

"Oh, alright."

"I just thought that Dean.... That Dean.... eh.   I don't know, grazed himself? If I'd have known that he was seriously hurt, I'd have run after him."

"So, what are you going to do?"

A dam burst of thoughts exploded in my mind. Dean's gone?? How the hell?? He was fine, wasn't he? I mean, he ran down the stairs. How can he be dead? How? How did I not realise it sooner? Oh, my God, Audrey Talk about reality starting to kick in? Yet still, I couldn't believe it.

"John, can you give me the number for Coolock Garda Station, please?"

He did and without hesitation, I punched in their number and hit "calls."

"Coolock Garda Station."

"Hello. This is Dave Mahon."

"Yes? How can I help you?"

Make this all go away? Tell me it's a false news story? A different Dean??

"Eh. ... it's been on the news? Dean? Dean Fitzpatrick. Is it true?"

Full disclosure. I've no idea what he said next. I was running on autopilot/ don't remember what I said next;

"It was me. I'm Dean's stepfather; it   it was me."

"Where are you now, Dave? May I send a car around for you?"

"No. I'll.... I'll be there in a few minutes "

That was the moment, right there, the start of the bitter tears I'd cry for Dean for the rest of my life. It wasn't and isn't a pity party, I know that no amount of them will ever bring him back, dear God, if only they could. At some point, I got into John's car and we arrived at the Police Station. How long would it take if we overtook a Sherman tank along the way? I've no idea. When you go into a shock of the black-capped variety, holes start to appear in your mind and in your memory, holes you'll never fill again like the Dean-shaped hock in our lives, I guess. John walked in with me. I thought that was a little odd;

"It's alright John, I've got it from here."

"No, I think I'd better go in as well, Dave."

"Why??"

"They might want to talk to me as well."

Of course, they bloody would. What on earth was I thinking? He was an eyewitness to the whole thing; how did I not realise that? That dear reader, was where my head was at. I was in total shock and didn't realise it. I went up to the desk officer;

"Can I see Eddie Carroll, please?"

"Who are you?"

"Dave Mahon."

"How do you know Eddie Carroll?"

"He was meant to be our liaison office for our missing daughter, Amy."

"What's this about?"

"Dean Fitzpatrick. I'm Dave Mahon, I think I spoke to you on the phone earlier."

"Wait there."

A couple of minutes later (more than enough time to get a taxi to the airport if I'd wanted to, but that little factoid only becomes relevant later), I was ushered into one interview room; John was taken into another. They asked me about everything and I mean everything;

"What happened last night?"

"What happened yesterday?"

"Who were you with?"

"Was it self-defence?"

In case you're wondering, my answer to that last one was "No" it wasn't self-defence. This is why. I've never said it was and never believed it to be. Turns out,

I was right about that and even more right to answer the way I did, but I'm getting too little ahead of myself. There isn't room in this book, to go through all of the questions they fired at me, but I'm sure you can guess what they entailed; I also had my first taste of "Good cop/Bad cop" Garda style and both acting styles were as transparent as glass underwear. I couldn't grasp what was going on. I had phoned them up, told them it was me, handed myself in, told them exactly what happened and it didn't seem to be enough. We read in the news every day about brave Garda and top-notch investigators, but also the financial strain that puts on the economy. There I was, sitting in a cop-shop, telling them every last detail, probably shaving millions off the Garda budget and propaganda campaign, and they didn't believe me??

"Did you kill Dean?"

"No." (Not in that way)

"Was it self-defence?"

"No."

"Sure, sounds like self-defence to me, Dave, huh?"

"No, it wasn't self-defence."

"I think it was Dave anyway. Do you want a solicitor?"

"No."

"No? Fuckin' hard show, huh? Did you even hit Dean?"

"No."

"Were you drunk, Dave, huh? How drunk were you?"

"I... I explained all this already."

"What about Audrey Dave, huh? What about her? Did you even cheat on her?"

"No."

"Are you a religious man, Dave?"

Where did that come from and what was the relevance? I'd discover much later this was a tactic they use to get confessions out of people, something like. "Say a

394

prayer with me, and we will get God's forgiveness for what you did." You'd be amazed at how successful that is. But again, I'd already confessed to my involvement. Into Dean's death, so I was becoming increasingly bewildered by this nonstop questioning, but they were far from finished with me. Next up came something truly tasteless. This pig in a suit motioned right over me and wanted me to stand up and go through a "Re-enactment" of what happened with Dean. The poor boy wasn't even 24 hours dead and they expected me to perform like a circus animal to appease this bad taste and morbid amusements? Well fuck that, no way was I having that. I love the bones of Dean and my heart was torn apart because of what happened. I'd never sully or disrespect his memory for their pleasure (piece of shit), no way. Maybe they were trying to provoke me?

"Do you know Karl O' Toole Dave?" (Interesting, Not John??)

"I do."

"How well do you know him? Would he be a good friend?"

That was a really specific little series of questions. I smelled a rat instantly.

"I know Karl, 20- 30 years or more, but we had a falling out a couple of years ago."

"What about?"

"He accused me years ago of sleeping with his wife."

"Did you?"

"No, I didn't and I wasn't the only person he accused of it either."

(That large rodent smell got a whole lot worse. Karl is one of the most calculating people I've ever known, so there was clearly something they weren't telling me, God only knows what he'd been saying to them).

"You still consider him to be a good friend?"

"Like I said, I've known him most of my life."

Full disclosure - right at that moment, I had the biggest pain in my arse with their bloody questions. Was Karl a good friend? Who gives a fuck, Dean is dead. I desperately needed to see Dean, I still couldn't handle his death. I can't explain it any better than that; it's just so cordately fucked up;

"Can I see Dean, please?

"That wouldn't be advisable."

"I never got to see him, to say 'good-bye' or how sorry I am."

"No."

"How's Audrey? Is she okay?"

"What?"

"Does she know yet? She's over at her father's house in Artane."

-No Answer-

"Does she know?"

"We don't know yet."

"Well, can I see Audrey?"

"No."

"Can I call her?"

"No. Are you hungry, Dave? Want a bit of grub?"

"No."

This was another contender for 'most frequently asked question" that and "self-defence," so they just plopped a cup of tea in front of me. Yeah, right, a cup of tea? Dean was dead, tea wasn't going to bring him back or change what I did, was it? Tea, the answer to all of life's problems, my arse. I had to take in something, though, so I looked up on the tea and chocolate. Sugar gives you a temporary energy boost any way and I knew I still had hours of questioning ahead of me. One of the Guards stuck me in a cell for a few hours; I had no thought of the Shaw shank redemption or escape from there; all I could think about was Dean. Still, even after everything. A part of me didn't believe that he was gone. The amount of times I'd heard that his little sister, Amy, was dead, murdered or worse, you wouldn't believe it. Neither did I, and my answer has always and will always be the same; "show me her body if she's dead, show me. That's part of the reason why I still couldn't believe that Dean was dead." More than anything else, I wanted to see him one last time, hold his hand, toss his hair and tell him I love him. To tell him how sorry I am, that I never meant to ever hurt him, let alone fatally wound him. It's not "closure" because that little word is too small, too cliché and devoid of humanity. It's a psycho-babble word, a shortcut, a cheat, a box ticker. It's a bullshit word... for me, it goes nowhere near the hurt that I feel, the heartache I have to live with every day and will do so until my final breath. "Closure?" Fuck off. I wanted to use every last ounce of energy in my body to scream. All the way up to heaven or to whatever last vest gages of life remained in his body at the sub-atomic level that I was sorry, that I would willingly and happily change places with him. That I could never hurt him, not on purpose and tell him all the things that my heart holds for him still forever private things, shared things, things he'd know were sincere and true. Things he'll never hear. Fuck. Death is so utterly, utterly final. I wanted (and still want) to apologize to Dean and to everyone whose lives he touched and made better in his own unique way. But "apology" is another small cliché to me. It doesn't emote at the level of regret and horror I feel. A better person, a smarter person, would be able to write a computer program on something and hock it up to the same furnishing machine with all these electrodes and stuff protruding from it. You want to know how sorry I am. Hook yourself up to this machine, say the name "Dean Fitzpatrick," and fair warning; be prepared for an emotional onslaught that comes your way. You will not even be suicidal afterwards; you don't get that luxury, you'll know what "Sorry" means for me then, and you'll understand the 'bullshitology' of 'apology' and how it can never fully convey the pain in my heart, or the hearts of all of those who loved him. Until that computer program is written, then to all of you who knew Dean, I'm deeply immeasurably sorry. That is honest and from my heart, but even more so to Dean himself, to Amy and to Audrey.

Meanwhile, back in Coolock Garda station, I was going through the police version of musical chains into a cell, out of a cell, into an interrogation room / out of an interrogation room. They were clearly wasting their time doing head games on me and my head was already wrecked. I just wanted to see and/or talk to Audrey; I desperately wanted to see Dean. The Garda Book of basic psychology was obviously taken down off the top shelf and given its annual dusting down as well:

"You know, Dave (good cop, obviously), the time spent in the cell is every bit as important as the time we spend questioning you."

"Right, yeah."

"You know... (An 'earnest' pause) you might think of something that might help the case."

Help the case? Help the bleedin' case?? Dean is gone. There is no 'helping' of any bloody case. He's gone and nothing's gonna help that. That whole routine, rinse and repeat, rinse and repeat, went on for more than 48 hours. Don't forget, I wasn't under arrest. I volunteered myself into the belly of the beast, but at no time was I told that I could go. My father called in to check how I was doing, they gave him 10 (ten!) minutes, they really broke their hearts. All I can honestly remember was one thing:

"Does... does Audrey know yet?"

"She does, son. She does."

Fuck. Full disclosure. If I had my hands on a gun at that time, I would have shot myself in the head. That is 100% honest. I'm not trying to make light of suicide or sully the memory of the poor souls who have died in such tragic circumstances, but I wanted out. All I wanted, all I needed was to see Dean again and that felt like an obvious method of doing so. I've hated people in my life and have been hated by people in my life, but nobody –NOBODY- has or ever could hate me as much as I hated myself that day. I must've been in quite a state because a doctor was called for me to give me something to calm me down. Then the cops suggested getting a solicitor for me. I didn't know my criminal lawyers in Ireland at the time and it is no doubt obvious. I couldn't have given less of a shit anyway. A solicitor arrived, eventually, from Michael Stains and Company.

"Mr. Mahon have you-..."

"Dave, call me Dave."

"Yes, Mr. Mohan, have you said anything, anything at all?"

"It's Dave, and yes I have."

"Mr. Mahon, I must advise you in the strongest terms not to answer any more questions."

"Why not? I've got nothing to hide."

He was like one of those lawyers you see in science fiction movies, an automation who just coldly, clinically and without the fastest shred of compassion blurts out technical, legal Goddledeegook. I didn't like him. He wasn't for me, if

398

he had known anything about me, he'd have known that shutting me up was utter futility. He left and then the cops started in on me again:

"Did you murder Dean?"

"Was it self-defence?"

On and on and on it went. You cannot hide the facts and I never once tried to. The fact was that Dean Fitzpatrick was dead. The fact was I had the knife in my hand. The fact is that this was going to send Audrey over the edge; she was only just hanging on as it was, and now this??

"The time in the cell is very important Dave..."

Well, he got that right, only not in the way he wanted. I replayed everything in my head over and over; this wasn't a murder and this wasn't self-defence. I'd reinforced those facts into my head, time in the cell well spent, indeed. So, what did I say?

"Maybe Dean ran at the knife to hurt himself..."

Not to the extent that he did, of course, but boy, oh boy, did that ever get blown up out of all proportion.

I still have all of those interview tapes, as I alluded to earlier, and for legal reasons, I had to watch them over several times but I'd rather gore my own eyes out of my head with a spoon than have to view them ever again. There are literally hundreds of questions that they asked over and over and over and unlike the movies, there was no solicitor present. I knew that I was hanging myself out to dry, but I didn't care, remember, I absolutely loathed myself. I was every defence – attorney's nightmare, but I didn't care; I'm not a criminal; I had nothing to hide and I was only telling the truth anyway. I'm not a murderer but I'm also not a Garda with a hard-on for the promotion a murder candied would bring. Was I green? More than an Irish rugby Jersey. Dear reader, learn from my mistakes. By all means, tell the truth, but do so and in the presence of a good solicitor that you can trust.

Next thing I know, I'm getting my fingerprints taken. Then they took every stitch of clothing off me, took all of my mobile phones and they gave me something to wear. In case the word "phones" threw you, I had more than one for several reasons, including different phone numbers we were contactable on, 24x7 for Amy. Then, another team of cops took my runners (training shoes) and other belongings from our apartment. Where does one go from here? This was horrible, all of it, the worst thing in the world because Dean was dead. Gone, gone forever and I still couldn't believe it because the parts of me that started to accept and realize were screaming for a bullet through my fucking brain. I loved him, still love him and one would have to ask themselves? Just how much pain can one heart endure?

Eventually, at some point, I don't know how long exactly, a couple of days anyway, the police said that I could go. The terminology you'll often hear quoted is:

"Released without charge. A file is being prepared for the D.P.P."

The D.P.P. (Director of Public Prosecutions) is Ireland's version of the C.P.S. (Crown Prosecution Service) in the U.K. The "File" that they refer to is a collection of documents, everything from maps to witness statements to photographs, etc. In this sense, and certainly viewed through this particular lens, the police are nothing more than errand boys, putting a bunch of papers together and bringing them to the 'teacher' with a "Please" provision post-it note attached. The 'teacher' in this sense is the D.P.P., which is a collection of legal people. Administrations, devils, solicitors, barristers, etc. Who will, in essence, throw the paperwork against the wall and see what sticks. The 'state' that is the Garda and D.P.P. Make no mistake about that. (Although they always claim that it's you, dear reader, this is a book of honesty really, not a convenient public spin.) They will always look to the headline crimes first to further their career, the murders, rapes and manslaughters. Let's use my case as an example; the "test" for rape must include matters of a sexual nature, so that fails, the D.P.Ps first hurdle. Now, their remit is twofold with murder being the brass ring of career advancement. In this sense, was it Gangland? No. So onto test 2. Was it domestic? Yes. The 'Gold' standard here. Is spousal abuse or uxoricide (husband kills wife), which is always a favourite for the tabloid headlines, a mask of Joe Duffy's and at least one TV documentary? Wrong again, I failed that test. Infanticide is the 'silver' standard in this section (the killing of your children), which I again 'fail' but only on a 'technicality' as I'm "only" a stepfather. Therefore, my conviction, should it come to that, is a "Hi" for career advancement, but is it murder? That's supposed to be a seriously high threshold to reach, so it "could be" or "might also be" manslaughter. That, dear reader, is how the system went. The truth "isn't all it's cracked up to be," as a famous Canady famously said....

Now, let's look at what happened through this lens with Dean, one, we had an argument. That's agreed on all sides. Two, a knife was produced, again. Agreed on all sides. So far, legally speaking, you are looking at three options. Murder,

400

manslaughter or accidental death. Three very different things, carrying very different sentences. As I walked out of Coolock Garda Station that day, I knew (Nor cared) none of that. All I knew was that Dean was dead and I needed to see him one last time. I didn't know if I'd be sent to prison to die there or if I'd even be charged with anything. It was a time for silence, a time for quiet reflection and a time to grieve. Mick was there to drive me home, but he wasn't alone.

As is typical. "If it bleeds, it leads." Every journalist hack, two-bit copywriter, photographer and TV news crew in Hell's creation was waiting for me, too. They weren't there to talk about missing Amy; they were there to get a look at the "broken monster" before calling to fix his hanging. It was a solemn drive back to my father's house in Santry. Not a word was spoken. There was nothing left to say; Dean was dead; what is the use in talking? The answer to that, dear reader, is quite a lot actually, but in my head back then, all was lost. As wise King Solomon once put it, "Everything is futility and a chasing after the wind. Those thoughts filled my head." Whatever journalists couldn't find their way to Coolock Garda Station (I, in fact, thought that they all had, but I was wrong) somehow managed to find my father's house and lay in wait for us there. I hope they never find themselves in a situation similar to what we were experiencing, though that is because only they would they find out how much worse they make everything.

I got in the front door, slumped into a chair and only one thought consumed my mind. Audrey. I had to face Audrey and tell her what happened, to tell her the truth, to tell her everything. I had to see if she was alright "(alright"?? what the fuck would that ever mean to her again??,)" which of course she wouldn't be. She had (and continued to have) every right to finish me off, to erase me off the face of the earth (and who would blame her?), but I didn't care, I had to see her. I picked up my phone (well, my father's phone, mine were still "seized" even though I willingly volunteered them to the police, but as you'll soon realise, words are very important in these matters) and called her right then and there. I was still in a mental fog to end all fogs, so I wasn't even attempting to reconstruct what our little conversation was. I was on absolute auto-pilot, so I can only properly remember the essentials;

"May I call around to the apartment?"

"Yes."

"Okay, I'll be there as soon as I can."

Once again, my father was there for me, for whatever I needed. He drove me back to my apartment, although I thought I was actually somewhere else at first because I didn't recognize the place. There was police parked outside and the media was absolutely everywhere. Clearly, there was nothing else happening in the world that day of a newsworthy nature. But even that didn't faze me that much. What totally discombobulated me, were the flowers. People sweet and well-meaning left a lot of flowers at the lamppost outside of the Hilton hotel. What a beautiful thing for them to do, but it was completely surreal. This was too much of a contrast for me to process, given the nature of everything that had happened.

When I walked into our apartment, a thought hit me like a ton of bricks, Dave, this is the first time you've been in this apartment since Dean's death, every other time, Dean was alive. It was like an emotional bubble. I wouldn't say 'burst' because exploded would be closer to the truth in my very soul. Every molecule in my body felt it. That grim death cloud of reality lowered out of me and transposed itself into my psyche. From that point forward, everything I'd see, smell or touch would be "the first time since Dean's death. Was it early shock on-set or delayed onset of shock? I don't know, but if I live to be one hundred, I hope I never have to experience that abyss of hollow negativity again. I felt as though I was wearing the feet of a drunken giant as I made my way over the molasses thick carpet, such was the effort required not to throw up. All the power just left my body, even breathing was hard. Audrey was there, with her brother, for the life of me, I cannot recall what useless, ineffective nonsense I said to her, probably a combination of shock and the realisation of whatever I said, Dean was dead and it was my fault. I do know that somewhere in my useless wordage were the words:

"I'm sorry "

But you already knew how I felt about that empty expression. I mean, it's fine in situations where you've burned the toast or spilt red wine on the couch, but not for when you've killed the only son of a mother whose losses had already been biblical in scale to begin with. Then, that horrible voice again.

"Dave, this is the first time you've seen Audrey since you killed her son."

There's no getting away from it, and there never will be; at some point, Audrey's brother left us, but I couldn't honestly say when or how or what was said. I was too overwhelmed by grief. It had been days... literally days. Since neither of us had slept, at some point, we both conked out. My last thought before sleep overcame me.

"This is your first proper sleep... since killing Dean."

The next morning and to be fair, the next couple of days are a bit of a blur, well, except for waking up beside Audrey that morning:

"Last time you woke up here, Dave, Dean was alive; can't say that again."

I've come to know that voice a bit too well over the years and to be honest, I can't complain. I'll hear it until I die and it's the least I deserve. My own internal tormentor. That is good enough for me.

For the most part, the police managed to keep the media away from our door, a weird parasitic relationship where money changes hands for access and information and the promise of a public lynching before during and after trial. Still, never underestimate the human appetite for greed because one or two members of the scum-loid fraternity managed to slither their way to our front door.

"Dave! Dave! Have you got anything to say??"

No way was I going to give them a story never in a month of Sundays. But the media succeeded in making us prisoners in our own home, too afraid to venture out because we knew that every photo would be an opinion piece and God forbid, bought a sliced pan:

"Dave on a bread and water diet."

A bottle of wine?

"Killer Mahon hits the booze."

You get the idea. You look sad, it's a story about "crocodile tears," you looked happy (impossible) - "Smirking Killer. Shows no Remorse," or you manage to keep a poker face? "Evil killer shows no emotion." You can't win, so don't even bother; luckily for us, the good friends and reliable family members close to us, called up with edible provisions and heartfelt words of wisdom. I really felt for our friends, having to park underground, a route to avoid the over-present media frenzy. That was pretty much how everything went until the time came to arrange Dean's funeral. Two words together in a sentence that I still can't understand. It disturbs the natural order; it should be Dean and Amy organising our funeral arrangements, not Audrey and I organising Dean's. No matter what way you slice it or from whatever angle you choose to look at it, there's just no avoiding the sheer fucked-up-endless of the whole situation, nice one Dave, now, carry that for the rest of your life. We sat in front of some funeral director and watched his lips moving. I'm sure words were coming out of his mouth, polished to a fine funeral finish, developed over years of such conversations with other poor sods like us, but we didn't hear one of them. When he finished his speech, we just agreed to everything. It wasn't that we weren't bothered or couldn't have cared less, the polar opposite, in fact, but the truth is, once you involve yourself in those discussions, you're letting another little piece of your loved one go, and we weren't even close to ready for that. Then, he was gone just like that. I would love to tell you that Audrey and I got into a blazing row over everything at that point, but that would be a lie. The truth is so much less dramatic and we were spent, all used up, broken people. We may well have been on another planet for all the value we were bringing into this world. Empty shells of the people we once were.

I had no fight left in me; I was a broken and defeated man. I couldn't eat, couldn't sleep and couldn't live with what I'd done. I couldn't live with the sight of Audrey's life disappearing before my eyes. We were zombies, dead, but didn't know it yet. What do you talk about? Where can you go? What can you do? The further you slide into the abyss, the smaller and faster you run the concentric circles of hell. With what was probably my last vestige of hope, I picked up the phone and called our doctor. We'd had him for years and I know he didn't do house calls, but I was going to ask anyway. To Dr. Ibraham's credit, he finished up his clinic in Donaghmede and came straight around once he heard who we were. He gave Audrey an injection and gave me some Xanax. I'm not a medication kind of guy, but when your family doctor insists on it, you should listen. So I did. When he left, you could've sat us both on the runway in Dublin Airport and hit us with a Jumbo jet and we wouldn't have felt a thing. Numb is too small a word; we were transcendental, but the wasp-sting of Dean lying dead at my hand continued seeping its toxins through anyway. There was always plenty of pain waiting for me whenever good king Xanax left my system.

Friends and family of both continued dropping in and out of our apartment like rocket-fuelled yo-yos, a simple gesture of love and support that will never be forgotten or under-valued, trust me on that score. They were the reason why we managed to maintain the microscopic grain of sanity that we had. It was a level of constant pressure that transforms coal into diamonds or humans into apple-crumble. Intense doesn't even make the same sport, let alone the same division. Then, one day, Audrey's brother paid us a visit with yet more misery:

"We have a problem."

"That's a bit of an understatement. What's up?"

It was an understatement, alright. Audrey's other side of the family, basically the other biological half of Dean, didn't want Audrey and me to have anything to do with the funeral arrangements. Me – I can understand totally, I get it but Audrey? His M-O-T-H-E-R??? She is innocent, a victim of this horrendous nightmare, and now she couldn't even bury her own son? Her own flesh, which she carried, birthed, fed-watered and raised with as much love as is humanly possible?? I won't go into too much detail about the ins and outs of what I can only objectively define as vindictiveness, but it got pretty heavy. It went all the way to the High Court. I wanted to go there with Audrey but was advised not to. I can't imagine I would've helped matters, in retrospect, but I didn't want Audrey to be any more alone than she had to be. The crux of the issue is this though, the other side was granted the "Right" (never has that word been used as incorrectly as that) to bury Dean wherever and however they wanted. Audrey was utterly, well… some things don't need to be said, do they? As for me, all I wanted to do was to see Dean one more time, to beg for his forgiveness and say my goodbyes to him. Obviously I wouldn't have been too welcome at his funeral, so I asked about going to the funeral home. The police "strongly advised against it," so that put an end to any chance of that happening. The whole time that this was going on, we were still in the apartment imprisoned.

We took it upon ourselves to just get outside on one of the days, Audrey to meet her friends and family and me to do the same. Sounds easy, doesn't it? Like falling off a bike, right? We walked down to the front door of the complex and there, we were met with a wall of baying media jackals. Audrey and I were more used to the media than your average punter because of all the campaigning work we'd put in for Amy down the years, but it was nothing like that. We'd never seen anything like it. Reporters were actually climbing over each other like starving pigs at the trough. It was absolutely disgusting and as for what they were screaming at us to get a reaction, it's not even fit to repeat. Now, while all of this insanity boils all around us, we can't even jump into a car and drive away from it. We had to wait around for what seemed like an eternity for a taxi. All I could do as we waited was to look down at all the flowers that were left at the spot where Dean must've died. It couldn't have been more than a few yards from the front door. My life was becoming one huge, miserable "If Only," and my internal tormentor was, as always, stoking the coals, reminding me how Dean would still be alive…

We almost had to pull the doors off the taxi to get into it, but we scrummaged past the hungry – snapping – jackals and off we went. Only to be followed by the not too inconspicuous media everywhere we went. That's still the case today too. When the sad morning of Dean's funeral arrived, Audrey dropped another bombshell on me;

"Dave, I'm not going to the funeral."

Shocked wasn't the word for it. I can't even remember how our conversation developed, I was stupefied. At one point, I can remember saying;

"Audrey, don't do this. You'll regret it for the rest of your life..."

But those are just words really, aren't they? They can't change anything. Audrey was adamant that she wasn't going to go and believe me, I knew her well enough to know that when she's adamant about something, then she's not for turning. It was a futile exercise on my part to even try, but I still felt that I had to;

"Dave, how can I watch my son being put in a box and stuck in the ground?" What the hell could I say to that? I – above anyone else – had no right to go there. I was (and continue) to be the author of this tragedy; it was Audrey's call and it was the least I could do to support her. At some point, a knock comes to the door, it was Audrey's brother.

"Don't let him -or anyone else – in."

"Okay."

I answered the door to her brother – Dean's uncle – and told him that Audrey wasn't going to the funeral. I also explained to him that she didn't want to see or talk to anyone and that she was adamant. The poor man was in shock. Who could blame him? He still wanted to come in and I wasn't going to stop him. I just couldn't, who was I to stop him anyway? I killed his nephew, my own stepson, I'm a nobody. It didn't make a difference anyway; Audrey's mind was made up. That's the right of every grieving mother. Respect it.

The day passed. It was a long one, it was tragic and I couldn't re-live it and survive to tell the tale. It's a deeply private experience only we'll ever share with each other. Time dragged on and I started getting one or two more visits from the police. Then, Mick O' Toole, a reporter, came calling. We'd gotten to know. Mick's quite well known over the years as he covered a lot of Amy's disappearance and helped us with our Amy book, so when he said that he wasn't looking for a story, we believed him. Remember this, dear reader, a reporter is always a reporter and nothing is ever really fully "off the record." As fond of him as Audrey and I are, what happened next disgusted us;

"You know that the press is sleeping out in the cemetery?"

"What??"

"Yeah, waiting to get a photo of Dave (me) by Dean's graveside."

"What? Are you serious?"

"I am. So, do you want me to organise a car for you?"

"For what?"

"Well, to bring you to the cemetery…"

Obviously, we refused. Not only did we refuse to be treated like circus monkeys, but it was beyond cheap and disrespectful to Dean's memory. By the way, there is absolutely no doubt in my mind that those media ghouls did, in fact, spend a considerable period of time sleeping in the graveyard, hoping to be "the one" to take that photo. To me, that's just sad and very, very sick. As for you, dear reader, would having a photograph of me visiting Dean's graveside inspire you to purchase that particular "News" paper over all the other ones? If your honest answer is "No," then please read on. If on the other hand, your answer to that was "yes," then maybe this book isn't really for you.

The result of our chat with the reporter was that I couldn't go to the cemetery for a while, while, to be honest, it broke my heart. But we did go up on our own to visit Dean, and as heart-wrenching as I thought it was going to be, well, I wish it had been as "easy" as that. It wasn't 'Jesus.' I did manage to say my few words to Dean, though, from the heart – from the soul and I meant every one of them. Alas, dear reader, they are only ever going to be between myself, Dean and Audrey. I'm sure you'll understand.

Time marched on. Seconds into minutes, into hours. Days – weeks – months, I didn't know exactly how much as the abyss surrounding us just drained everything, but I reached the point of no return as far as our apartment. It's a lovely place – it really is, but it's also a constant reminder of Dean's last night. To some scholars, hell is a fiery Kingdom of tortured souls, rivers and lakes of brilliant orange fire, black–winged demons with sharpened pitch. Folks and all that rubbish, I can tell you for a fact – they're all wrong. Hell is your own private nightmare, the only one you are awake in and live through. That apartment is my hell, "Beware all you who enter here, for all hope is lost." That's not a quote that is a synopsis of the living embodiment of my every working hour within these walls. Audrey's hell wasn't confined to bricks and mortar though; it was killing her that she couldn't even assist with Dean's funeral arrangements. From his funeral all the way down to the choice of his headstone, Audrey – the only mother he ever had and loved more than life – had been erased from existence. Petty vindictiveness should only go so far, or so I formerly thought. She saved up as much money as she could (not a lot as we were broker than broke) and bought a little gravestone. Not the main one, just a small personalised one, with some sentimental words etched into it. She left it on his grave and then left Dean's side for the first time in a long time – feeling like she'd been able to do something for him. For a grieving mother, it's a massive – massive – thing emotionally and psychologically. She went to visit Dean again the next day, looking forward to seeing that little monument of love and connection between them, only it wasn't there. We searched for it high and low before eventually finding it buried under a pile of rubbish in a bin. To whatever piece of dogshit that did this, I hope you feel very proud of yourself for that act of wanton cowardice. You caused Audrey a lot of unnecessary trauma over that, Dean's mother. Don't forget how he would've reacted to that, sure you won't?

Once retrieved, Audrey cleaned it up and brought it home. Today, it resides in a place of special and unique importance to both Dean and Audrey. It'll remain safely there, as only people who truly knew and loved Dean would know where that is, so the cowardly grave – robber will never locate it. It was one trauma too many for Audrey, and in the hellish apartment's final two-fingered salute to us, she overdosed on some sleeping pills. Thank God, she survived that latest brush with death, and when she was able, we up-sticks and left for Blanchard's town. A friend of mine had an apartment there for rent in Ongar, so we took it, as did Fanta and Naranja (Orange), our two cats. We were in a living hell, but at least now our torment was in a nicer apartment. But not for long.

Hammer To Fall

Moving out of the apartment and the Malahide Road was the obvious choice for many and obvious reasons and although the place we moved to in Ongar Village was much better for our mental health, we just could've settled. The biggest problem with it was that it wasn't Spain. That is where our home still was, even though it, too, was riddled with painful memories. I guess you carry your memories with you wherever you go, but at least in Spain, we'd have some chance of breaking life back into Amy's compassion as well as into ourselves.

I told the Irish cops that we were moving back to Spain, but I didn't have to. Could you imagine if I had just upped sticks and left without telling then (something I was within my full legal rights to do)? Their paymasters at Elect-Street would've covered themselves in tons of happy joyshit. "Killer Dave Flee's the Country," "Dave goes on the Run," or some other brand of factious nonsense. As it was, the local plod was less than happy about it, but they knew I was well within my rights, you see, unless you are charged or under arrest, then all they can do is snarl at you."

"We would prefer if you didn't go back."

Tough shit. They had no idea how Audrey and I were feeling or how it felt to live with what we were going through. We were all over the place and Audrey was suicidal. I made a point of leaving my email, mobile phone number and Spanish address with both the cops and my solicitor, as you can never be too careful, can you? I also promised them both that when the D.P.P made a decision either way. That I'd come back to Ireland as soon as possible.

The media attention wasn't too bad over in Spain (well, in comparison to Ireland, living in the Arnotts front window would've been less intrusive), but it did feel like we were living in exile. Maybe we were? It really was just myself and Audrey just waiting and waiting and waiting for the "hammer to fall," as Freddie Mercury would've put it. I couldn't concentrate on making a cup of tea, let alone finding work, but when "Money's too tight to mention" (I promise, no more 80's pop!), you've got to dip your toe into a few bits and pieces, just to make ends meet. It was also a mixed blessing to catch up with some of our friends again, apart from hoping to re-live some painful memories. (Oh, and don't forget that old Mr. Internal Torment travelled over, too. Hey Dave, last time you were here… Dean was alive), memories that were funny and enduring once upon a time were now

409

terrible in emotional intensity. Oh, and then you also have to hear the stupid and unintended hurtful stuff too.

"Hey Dave, if it had been you that died that night, who would have looked after Audrey?"

-Or-

"Ah, sure, Dean was always in trouble anyway."

I guess some people forget to engage their "that would be fucking stupid" gear before opening their mouth and to be as transparently harvest as always. I did snap at some of those well-meaning but grossly insensitive comments. Thank God. I was getting to filter most of them from Audrey because at this stage, she was a complete basket case. Her health was worse than it ever was. I suppose the only thing that was actually going in her favour was that she had been abstaining from alcohol, but unfortunately, that damage had already been done.

It was inevitable and didn't come as too much of a surprise when she had to be rushed to hospital one day. She ended up in the Costa del Sol hospital and it was there that my poor Audrey had to undergo every test in the book. I was a great help sitting beside her, wasting, not knowing what else I could do. If lived waxed lyrical too much about how wonderful doctors and nurses are the world over then I'm sorry, but I'm above to do it again. You don't appreciate their long hours, attention to detail and sheer brilliance until your loved ones are thumping hard on death's door and they somehow manage to stave off the angel of death again and again. Even the grumpy ones with poor bedside manners, lifesavers, every last one of them. They are like gods to me. Soon enough, Audrey's results came back, cirrhosis of the liver.

"If she does not receive a new liver, she will die."

Poor Audrey, another week or so of her life spent in a hospital. The hits came harder and harder and showed no signs of letting up either; it was time for one of my bright ideas, "A cunning plan" in Blackadder Parlance! I say after about four weeks, I then brought Audrey up to an Animal Rescue centre. I think it was called 'P.A.D' but I'm not exactly sure, remember the inside of my head looked like a bowl of porridge, so I can't remember every detail in the preferred cinema scope! In any event, out Baldric, hence, had the intention of looking for a cat or kitten, but on the way, we saw a few gorgeous little pups. They were about as small as pups can be, as they were Jack Russell's and both I and Audrey fell in love with them immediately. A very good friend of ours, Glen, came with us. He is a lovely fella and about as rough as they came, harder than writing code for NASA. Basically, he'd be last on my list of people! Would've expected to be so mushy over a puppy, especially as he already had two dogs, but he too fell for them. We picked one each (that is one for Audrey and I, one for Glen) and then was much quavering on our lips when we were told 'no'!

"No?? Why not??"

"I mean, not yet; they aren't 8 weeks old yet."

Sighs of relief all round! Yes! We were setting a day! I became a 6-year-old again. I couldn't work and neither could Audrey… or Glen! We went up to that animal shelter every day until our 'little girl' was 8 weeks old. We were completely smitten and thank God for that little canine because she was the greatest distraction from the otherwise Orwellian existence we had in our family. Audrey is an animal expert and I'd never had a dog before (well, technically, we did 'have" a dog for a short time, but that's another story), so I was worse than a kid at Christmas. I'm sure I was driving Audrey nuts, but I didn't care. She had a smile on her face and life in her eyes again, to me, that was priceless. Then the big-day arrived, the puppies were 8 weeks old and we couldn't wait to pick her up and bring her home. But first, the paperwork;

Oh my God, there was more paperwork than there was a dog! We even had to get her a passport! Who knew that such things even existed? I know I didn't.

"So, what name shall we put on her passport?"

"(I looked at Audrey) Well?"

"Lili."

Perfect. And so, Lili became the newest member of our family. We brought her back to our little apartment and she spent the first day sniffing all around her new environment and getting cuddled to death by Audrey. Lili lit the spark of life back into Audrey's heart, a tiny pup full of mischief, a loveable pet, never a surrogate for Dean or Amy. Let's be clear about that, but she did bring love and joy back into our hearts, into our lives. I used to take her for a walk every day, well, a "carry" until her legs were long enough. I'll tell you something now, dear reader, that little dog saved our lives, and that's not over stating anything. Think about that, please.

When dog walking started becoming a regular thing, I used to bump into a Spanish woman every morning walking her dog, as you do. However, every time she would come over to me, pick up Lili and say!

"Bonita Gupa Pero."

Which I believe means 'Beautiful dog,' she was right. She loved Lili so much that she would have tears in her eyes when she was hugging her. As my head was still recovering from a breakdown, I was a bit 'sensitive?' I suppose, so her tears would start mine off. Even though it turned into a daily occurrence, tears would start, I'd cry every time. This was the gift that was Lili, crying as much as I was healing without realizing it. Not that I'd ever be truly over Dean, there aren't enough tears in the world for that, but I was being carried through the most difficult period in my life by a tiny dog who's little less ever barely strong enough to carry her own body weight. She was a little miracle, it's as simple as that. It doesn't end there, because after my meaning tears with the Spanish lady, we'd construct forward on our walk to the end of the beach. Here, we would bump into a few of the local fishermen, all Spanish, not a word of English between them. Thankfully, Lili was multi-lingual, so she understood every word and enjoyed her morning playtime with the salty men on the boats. Everyone loved her; I'd take a slightly different route on the way home, which "just happened" to bring us past a little Spanish restaurant. It was hence that I'd order a brandy for Lili and some water for myself, but my Spanish wasn't sneak, so the water would be served in a bowl, "forcing" me to swap over beverages!

Because of Audrey's health issues -physical and mental- she didn't always join us and would stay back to rest, but Lilli's miracle was that Audrey's sporadic appearances with us happened at all. I know that it mightn't sound like such a big deal, but reflect on a moment on everything that Audrey had been through, and you'll see that it was nothing short of heroic. Time did its thing and moved on swiftly and silently, routines of morning walks, crying and playful fishermen continued and I eventually gave up the ghost at our little Spanish restaurant and just ordered the brandy for myself and a bowl of water for Lili in the hope they'd get it wrong but they didn't, one morning there were a bunch of people sitting opposite to us:

"Hello! (English accents)"

"Good Morning! (Me) Woof! (Not me!)"

"Is that Lili?"

"(Surprised) Eh, yeah!"

"Oh, she's beautiful, isn't she?!"

"She is yeah, thanks!?"

That was all good and then, literally minutes later, the same type of questions from another table. To be honest, I was a little confused as to how everyone seemed to know what my dog's name was? Maybe I called her name out at some point and they heard me? Then the owner of the restaurant came out with Lilli's water and my not-so-healthy breakfast. She looked at me like she had something to say,

"Everything okay?"

"Yes, yes. You eh, see the paper this morning?"

"No. I don' bother with them, to be honest."

"Oh..."

"Why do you ask?"

"Eh, is better I show you...."

She was back to my table and returned with a copy of a morning newspaper from page (no less) was a picture (a great photograph to give them their due) of Audrey, myself and you guessed it, Lili, walking along the beach. The headline?

"Dave and Audrey got a new dog."

Clearly, the 68 summit, 60m's exploding in Syria and the Russian annexe of Ukraine weren't 'quite' newsworthy enough that day. Lili took to her new found "stardom" in a totally calm manner; you'd almost believe that she was oblivious to the whole thing…. Oh what, she's a dog, of course, she couldn't have cared less! There you have it folks, proof that a Jack Russell puppy has more sense than a newspaper editor now there's a headline!!

On a more serious note, all that newspaper nonsense burst my little Lili bubble and put me back on tenterhooks about the decision that I was still awaiting from the police and D.P.P back in Ireland; I actually thought that was what I was going to find in the paper. One more unwelcome reminder of the no-man's land. We found ourselves in Amy memories, still mourning over Dean's loss and Audrey's temporary existence being the worst kind of living hell ever imagined. How much

413

more can the heart hope to cope with? Once again, I found myself thanking God for Lili, who was becoming so much more than a distraction. I'd initially brought Audrey to the animal shelter to find a cat. The fact that Audrey still needed a new liver, she was doing well. We'd earned a fair amount of 'Frequent Flyer' miles with the hospital, as people in Audrey's position require a lot of routine check-ups. For all the check-ups and time she was spending around specialists, her eyes were turning a really unhealthy shack of yellow. She was used to waiting, though. Waiting for Amy, waiting for a new liver, waiting for the D.P.P. to release the sword of Damocles over our own heads, for good or ill. We had great memories of friends always on hand, so it wasn't exclusively Dave and Audrey; again, the world type of scenario, but in the dark of night, during those small hours, it was, well, and Lili! Yes, through it all, we still managed to have a lot of laughs. Our hearts are more Spanish than Irish at this stage, so just being around the Med is a 'life' in itself.

But Spain also held darkened emotions for us, nor were the occasions when we'd meet with the Guardia Civil for news and/or updates on the investigation of Amy's disappearance. These were never an easy thing to do, but they were even harder this time around, for a plethora of reasons. First, there was the passage of time, the sheer number of days, weeks, months and years that Amy had been missing, which in turn severed an almost mephistophelian response to the thought of "yet another meeting." We hated everything about their depressive repetition, second I had already had my fill with meetings concerning law enforcement, but affair herding myself into the Garda. Concerning Dean's death, my poisonous choice had well and truly run over. I would've preferred seeking my eyeballs in stinging nettles rather than willingly enter another police station, but it's not about me; it's about Amy, so you just suck it up, last and not "least," by any measure, was Audrey. Take what I just deserved and then multiply that thousands of times, that would put you in the same solar system as where Audrey was, emotionally, but not on the same planet. Then you had to factor in her physical health, such as it was remembered, she couldn't make it through an airport without the assistance of a wheelchair; she was on a waiting list for a new liver (or she'd die) and her skin even her eye-balls had taken on a jaundiced, yellow hue. Oh, and she was also down to about six stone in weight, which by way of context, is essentially your bases and vital organs carried along in a skin bag. Stub bones doesn't register on a weighting scale; I know this to be true as this head strong woman of mine wouldn't even consider (let alone listen) my protests about her attending the meetings. There truly is nothing that Audrey wouldn't do for Amy dying during a three hour meeting with the Guardia Civil included. Thank God it didn't come to that, but dear reader, we had more of chance of that happening than not happening, that is how ill Audrey was.

The Guardia Civil would ask us their usual set of questions and then we'd go through our compendium of thoughts, ideas and unanswered questions.

"Have you interviewed anyone on the lists of suspects yet?"

"Where are you with this?"

"Where are you with that?"

As I've mentioned a couple of times already, sometimes meetings become heard and fractures between us, love and frustration will always fuel that very possibility. Then they asked me about what happened with Dean. I looked at Audrey to see if she was okay with this. Then it would happen, if she wasn't well, they'd be left waiting to know. She gave me a look that I know meant 'Go ahead,' and so I did. I told them everything; it was exactly what I told the Irish Garda; the only difference was that this was said in Audrey's presence , it was never and is never an easy series of events to recount, but by far the hardest and most emotional retelling of events everyone was visibly upset and to be fair, the Spanish police seemed sincere in their sympathy to our situation. Then, a Spanish cop so huge that his clothes were made out of a circus tent plopped his Giant paw on my shoulders and ushered me out of the room, down a corridor and into a larger room. I honestly didn't know what to expect. If there was going to be a "showdown," then they'd selected the wrong guy because if I hit him, then he might feel something, but if he hit me, I'd probably land 15 years from now. It wasn't a showdown (thank God) but yet another 'surreal' encounter to file away like all the rest. A man that big should've had the Granite voice of a small mountain. Instead, his perfect English shows more soft femininity than Mike Tyson and Chris Eubanks love child. It didn't fit, so no wonder he was the sight he was, you had to roughen up to carry a voice like that through your life, it was a room filled with files, lots of files, thousands if not tens of thousands, there was a section filled with 30-40 large lever arch folder, filled to a plump over capacity. He looked at me, then at them, then at me again:

"Dave, don't think that we are doing nothing to help you and Audrey find Amy."

Then he walked me over to the overweight folder collection:

"We are doing all we can."

I looked at the folders. They weren't a prop. They were all about Amy. All of them. Audrey had joined us in the room by now and when we looked up into the face of that man-mountain and saw his carved compassion, we were filled up with tears. Whilst we'll always have our differences. We always tried to leave on amicable terms, mostly with a handshake, sometime with hugs; I'll let you decide how we left the station that day.

We had been back in Spain for quite some time, somewhere between 9 months to a year, when the hammer finally fell. It was like so much bad and unwanted news. A telephone call; it was Detective Sergeant Eddie Carroll.

"The D.P.P. have made a decision, come back to Ireland."

"Okay, no Problem. Can you tell me what the decision was?"

"No."

"No?"

"No, will you come back to Ireland then?"

"Of course, I will. I give you my word."

Some things you just never forget. I remember that it was a Monday, not a manic one, but enough to make me dislike them as much as Bob Geldof. I told Audrey my news the second that the call ended, and then picked the phone straight back up and booked the next available flight back to Ireland, which was the following day, Tuesday. I then made arrangements to get my affairs in order and handed myself in again at Coolock Police station on Thursday.

I made a solo flight back as Audrey wasn't well enough to move and we hadn't enough money as it was. I'd also hoped to be a bit under the radian. As people in the media were used to us marvelling in pairs, but that pipe dream crashed and burned. Dublin Airport was once again filled with the cloven-hoofed bastard scum that is the paparazzi, even down on this day; I never refused any interviews about Amy, even down to the lower detritus of the Hock world, anything to keep her present to a 'relevant' news item because you just never know. Unfortunately, you have to pick and choose once you are in the public eye. There have been some reporters who were nice enough to Audrey and me, even to some of our friends and family, but for the most part, they are nothing but plagiarists and mythmakers. Yeah, I've heard the counter arguments so many times about them "only doing their job" (Shades of Nuremberg?) and other parades of that unsure, but when you're going through hell (as Audrey and I so clearly were); then, it's very difficult to understand or even comprehend the level of balmily invented bullshit they throw up about you.

Judgment without knowledge is the greatest of all crimes, except when that "knowledge" is pure invention; that's probably just a personal reaction to being misjudged so much, but I don't think so. I just wish that the press would drop all the foolishness about saying to order each other with also the most crass and insensitive head live competition. There is no such thing as straight journalism anymore, but a gaping void of where the out rising over live. I was always taught to believe that true journalism would be recognizable by reading a given article and not knowing how the writer felt about the subject under discussion. That some in its place, sits a totem of opinion places subservient to the compensable collective, a defined narrowing assiduously worshipped by per-wielding sycophant. That's enough about that for now, though.

Once again, Mick, my long suffering father, was there to collect me and bring me back to his house in Santry. Most of my family was there waiting for me, with my sister, Dorry, also flying over from England at night to complete the family set and load me up with moral support. I got up on Wednesday morning filled with thoughts of a dark and depressing nature when the phone bounced into life. Bloody hell, who now?? It was Audrey, thank God, the only voice I really wanted to hear, of course, panic set in then and I feared for her health was shot. Why was she calling? Oh God….

"Everything okay?"

"Well, as much as it can be."

"What are you up to?"

"Ah, nothing much, just boarding a plane in Malaga on the way to Dublin. You?"

I was over the moon and furious with her at the same time. She was too ill and too weak to travel by herself, but Audrey is a force of nature, once she sets her mind on something, she does it all the way. My father's home was besieged by swarms of bottom feeder, dishonest hacks, so it was not practical for her to stay in Santry, so we booked ourselves into a hotel for the night in nearby Ballymun. Audrey did pop out to see my family in Santry first anyway, and it was when we were all together that the phase that plastic harbinger of doom kicked off again. It

417

was another reporter, but one of the few we'd managed to develop a good rapport with down the years:

"Dave, can you talk?"

"Sure, go ahead."

"I've got some bad news for you, Dave."

(I swear I'm so sick of that life, it's every other phase, seriously.)

"Yeah, go on."

"Tomorrow morning when you hand yourself in…"

"Yeah."

"You're going to be charged with MURDER…"

I could not believe my ears. Murder? Fucking Murder?? The rest of that call has since faded in the blurry haze of my memory, but I was shocked, to say the least. I think an hour passed, I can't be sure, but about that type of time frame anyway, when I received another phone call. It was (yep, you guessed it) another reporter off our "trusted" short list:

"Dave, a quick 'Heads-up' for you, you'll be charged with MURDER in the morning."

I couldn't keep it to myself any longer, so I shared my latest batch of horrifying news with my shell-shocked family. Every soul in that house was totally shocked and Audrey was struggling to hold it together. We went off to our hotel room to get a bit of time and space together and, if possible, to try to regroup. I called Tony earlier, my solicitor, and shared my terrible news with him.

"Ah, Dave, look, just wait and see. Maybe they got it wrong?"

Dear reader, the Garda and Media are a cosy cartel and lead a shared parasite existence. They weren't getting my thing wrong, the service Garda investigating my case had token another for 'dropsy' of undeclared income from an undeclared expense account (or accounts plural more like), and I knew that in my heart. So did Audrey. Another writer, writing another autobiography, would probably next write something about enjoying a lovely meal and then toddling off to bed. Well, this is me, warts and all, remember? So, I didn't enjoy my meals. I downed a bottle of Jack Daniels and a few Xanax and as far as 'numbing the pain' was concerned, they didn't make a dent, not even a scratch. A blind man could see that it wasn't a murder, so you'll forgive my scepticism at the tired old age of justice being blind' because it's not. Those halcyon days of law, order and an honest cop are dead and gone. There is an analysed echo in a digital age, the new rule of law exists in the realm of newsprint, sound bites and unbalanced media reporting every house, on the hour, sullying the jury pool in the court of public opinion. Murder? Fuck off.

Then the fateful morals came and my father picked us up from the hotel. Dorry came along too and I'll never forget her kindness, as short a journey no sibling ever needs to experience. There wasn't a single poisoned pen or stealing flash bulb in sight at the hotel, so that was good. However, every single one of those misery maggots had camped out at Coolock Garda station. The shadow of the Cadbury's factory loomed overhead and I'm sure that little kids on the road that morning must've thought that the oompa loompas in Dublin weren't at all like the ones in Willy Wonka, all the ones on their doorstep carried a camera and was made of shit, not chocolate.

I trudged through the cesspit of scum-loid Jackals and I was cautiously courteous as I ignored all the …

"Do you reject it, Dave?"

"Do you think you'll get away with it?"

And they were only the polite ones that shouted at me. I remember so well that I wanted to say,

"I know I'm going to be charged with "Murder" you dickheads, because your cop paymasters already leaked the information out."

But it wasn't as difficult as it was to resist it. As I got to the entrance of the Police Station, a familiar face was waiting for me. It was only Eddie Carroll in his best "Look, me, I'm on the 9-0-clock news!' suit." I looked Eddie dead in the eyes and in front of my family, said:

"I already know what the charge is."

"(Straight away) I didn't leak anything to the media."

What an interesting thing for him to say. Look over my comment to him for some more time, please, notice anything? Like, for instance, the absence of the words "media" and "leak" in what I said? Also, please note the absence of accusation in my words. The absence of evidence is evidence of absence. By the same token, hanging yourself with balls of your own shite, a guilty man does make so, sorry Eddie, but your protest fell on unbelieving ears and I don't think you'd blame us either. Anyway, I was brought into an interrogation room:

"Take a seat, Dave."

"Okay."

"Do you want a cup of tea?"

"No."

"Okay. So, Dave Mahon, I formally charge you today with the Murder of Dean Fitzpatrick."

I knew what I was walking into (without any solicitor) and fully expected to hear those…. "Words", but I've got to admit, I was still shocked at hearing them. I was then escorted into a cell in the Garda Station. My family went back to Santry, every bit as shocked as I was. I can't imagine what they were going through; I don't even want to contemplate it. I was held in Coolock just long enough for them to process all the paperwork, but on their Sunday best, pat themselves on the back and prep the media. Then I was brought to the C.C.J (Criminal Courts of Justice), off Parkgate Street beside Phoenix Park). I didn't know what lay ahead of me or what the situation was:

"Do I go straight to prison for the rest of my life?"

Nobody offered answers, there's no guidebook and you don't exactly receive an 'orientation' on arrival. In short, this was all brand new to me. A fish out of water. I made a brief appearance in one of the courts and was then cast off, down into the bowels of the C.C.J; in this neighbourhood of cells, there could be a few hundred prisoners coming and going on a daily basis. Here is where you'll hear the following fun factual exchange:

"Ye' off to da' joy bud?" (Mount joy)

"Nah, bleedin' Wheatfield, kip." (Wheatfield)

"Were, were' ya, de hill?" (Clover till)

"Nah, de Leash" (Portlaoise)

420

"Bleedin' Jockey's der." (Sex-offenders)

"Nah, dec up in Hairy Hill." (Arbor, Hill, Hairy = Hairy APE=Rape)

It was in these cells that I also learned of such wonderful destinations as Cassimere, Cork, Limerick, and what "open" prisons were. I hadn't a clue; there were so many places of detention or classes of prisoners, from sex offenders to lifers to piety criminals. It's pot-luck who you get put in with, unless, of course you get a particularly hopeful turn-key who'll put you in amongst a bunch of strung out psycho junkies, but they must've been all out of them that day or else it was evil turn-keys day off. As I found myself confined amongst a fairly normal group. I hadn't a clue who they were OR what they were "in" for, but they sure as hell knew who 'DAVE MAHON' was and what I was doing there. It's an inverted type of weird 'celebrity,' only the kind you'd never wish to have. I wasn't there too long before getting called up. Remember, I hadn't a clue what was going on or what protocols, if any to follow. So, when the cell door opened and I heard;

"DAVE Mahon."

I didn't know what to say or do. So;

"Yeah?"

"C'mon. (Nod)"

Dear Readers, let me inform you of the Mushroom principle. How does a mushroom grow? It's kept in the dark and fed on shit all dat. The I.P.S and indeed, the entire criminal justice system is built on such lofty concepts as this. So, when I got the verbal and physical response to my affirmative, that is the "C'mon' and the Nod. I should've intuitively cleared that it meant,

"Okay, Dave, your legal team is waiting for you up in court number 'x,' so this way, please."

Anyway, it's Amazing the lack of information you can get by when I got into the courtroom. I was brought directly to the 'dock,' the most visible part of any courtroom barring the 'judges' plinth. You are alone and totally exposed. As close to me as they were allowed to get stood Audrey, Mick (my father), Terry (my brother) and my sister, Dory. I can't describe the look on their faces, but they could probably say the same about me when they saw me, too. I actually waved at them; such was my utter joy at seeing them there. Then the judge arrived. It all gets quite formal when this occurs, like an actor taking to the stage in a play. In fact, when you give the same quick analysis, they are two interrelated beasts. Both stem from English origins; they require wigs and costumes, require a script, an auditorium and bums on seats. Even the Arcane language and formality wouldn't look over of place or the gate. It's probably why courtroom dramas are so popular, as their medium that lends itself so effectively across the various platforms. Anyway, the judge took his seat (more of a throne, actually) and looked down (such is the deliberate geographical layout of courtrooms) on me.

"Good morning, Mr. Mahon."

I can't remember too much else after that, to be honest. Anyway, what was said was said and then I found myself being taken back down into the anal cavity of the C.C.J. I had a different officer escorting me this time, a proper little chatty – Cathy;

"Are you the step-father of Dean Fitzpatrick?

"I am, yes."

"Oh, we had him here a few times!"

The following retort came as far as my lips, but no further;

"Oh, is that right, you smug little smart arse? Go fuck yourself." I sometimes wish that I'd just said it, but on balance, I think my dignified silence spoke louder. It didn't stop his gums from flopping all the way to the cells though, but I think even he got the message.

I was stuck in that foul, piss stenched cell for hours. How many? I've no idea as there are no clocks, but there were plenty of bodies. Ten of us and just the one toilet which of course wouldn't flush and the wash sink had no soap and nothing to wash your hands with, I was sticking out like a sore thumb and not just because of my tabloid notoriety. I was the only guy in there not doing drugs. If you enjoy narcotics and aren't too fussy about personal hygiene or smoking, something that just came out of a "boozer", or a complete stranger just pulled something out of his arse-hole, then hey, this is the life for you! It wasn't for me and never will be. All the other men in the cell spoke in a certain 'shorthand' I suppose you'd call it prison parlance and were knocking our little drug deals nineteen to the dozen as they were getting stoned. It was… educational. Eventually, the cell door-opened and it was my turn to get yet another nod. I got handcuffed and acted like I was the most dangerous man in Ireland, stuck in a prison. Transport Truck, the modern equivalent to the coffin-ships of DD and driven in the horrible junkie piss mobile, off towards Clondalkin. That was when I realised, I wasn't going to Mountjoy, so it was either Wheatfield or Clover-Hill. I looked out of the little reinforced one-way window and saw sights that I'd passed thousands of times back in my taxi-days. We drove down the clover-Hill Road, hitting every bump in the road or least twice and once I saw that we made a sharp left, after the initial right, and then I knew it was Clover-Hill. In hindsight, it's obvious that was where I was only even going to be sent as it's a 'Remand' prison, that is a prison you go to before (but not always) getting sentenced, but I didn't know all of that at the time.

I was fresh out of the jar in terms of prison savvy as I was still expecting to get boiled, as I remembered my solicitors saying something about that very possibility. In the main gates for the first time, a sight I never thought I'd see when I dropped off and collected fares from there. You are then brought in through a small "reception" gate and put into yet another holding cell. There were "only" three of us in that particular cell. If you find yourself in that position, then one of the first questions you'll hear is;

"What are you in for bud?"

As I said, there were three of us in that cell, so;

"Ah, robbed a bleeding car."

"Yeah? I'm in for fraud."

Then they looked at me. Etiquette dictated that I had to "share" I suppose, but before I opened my mouth, the car thief looked of my attire, saw that I was well dressed and made a judgement.

"What about you, bud? Bleeding parking offences?"

"Parking offences? No, I'm in for murder."

"No-Fuckin – way – MAAAAN"

They sat opposite to me, open-mouthed like a couple of petrified cod, and looked at me through different eyes. It was almost like it was a "good" thing to be in the same orbit as a "big one," like it was a badge of honour, murder charges. Apparently were aspirational to some, the stuff of 'legend.' Well, not in my shoes; it wasn't. I couldn't think of anything worse. So, with all of our "jackets" on display, normal cell service (the prison kind, not mobile!) resumed such and such was "a rat," "officer whose face was a kicking bastard", and all kinds of fascinating trivia like that then 'BANG.' The young chap that was in for fraud hit the deck and started having an epileptic fit. I went to the door of the cell and shouted for help. And shouted… and then shouted some more. Eventually, a fat slobby slug of a screw wobbled his key-jangling way down to our cell, lifted up the metal "observation" flap (Think of a hall-door letterbox) and looked in;

"Who?"

"(Pointing) this poor kid just hook an epileptic scene?"

"And?"

"And? He'll probably need a medic or something."

"Fuck him, he'll be great."

I couldn't believe the apathy I was witnessing before my very eyes. I had my own problems and I'm sure that the young kid was no angel and this didn't appear to be his first or even second visit to the Clover-Hill-Hotel, but come on, he was still another human being! Fat boy sounded like he was struggling to find the right key to open the cell door (butter and sausage grease probably weren't helping him), but he eventually managed it, then kicked the door wide open;

"Dave Mahon?"

"Yes (what was this, a telling off for trying to help?)"

"Yeah. Grab your shit, follow me."

Again, I had no idea why I was being moved. It was actually my standard committal interview, everyone gets one. You are walked over to a desk, not unlike the front desk of a police station, and "interviewed." This consists of another prison officer with a pen and a clip-board, so he is clearly a man of immense power and intelligence;

"Rough day, Dave?"

"Absolutely."

"Alright. Name?"

Yeah, I know. He knew me by name and within 3 seconds, he asked what it was. Maybe that was why he carried a clipboard around with him, full of essential reminders;

"Breathe."

"Eat."

"Drink."

"Wash hands after using the toilet."

You know the basics. Anyway, for five mind-numbing minutes, he went through his little prepared sheet of check-boxes. Age, weight, nationality, colour, are you male or female? Are you suicidal? What medication are you on? Then, he gets you to sign it (and take a cursory glance at his spelling mistakes, of which there were quite a few, but I didn't 'go there') before your next indignity: A strip search. Dear reader, I never want to hear those two words again unless they're followed by "Given by some Playboy bunnies" because it's not a lot of fun:

"Turn Around."

"Cough."

"Squat."

"Have you any contraband stuffed up your arse?"

I never knew that my Orpheus held such wild fascination. I definitely have a cunning plan now of how to avoid baggage charges on a Ryan air flight next time I travel! Then you take a very quick shower and dry off with a scratchy sand-paper towel. You go to put on your clothes and realise that they are gone and have been replaced by one-size-fits-nobody prison clothes. Then you see your watch, wallet, etc., on the counter;

"Here, sign these."

Which you do watch them get stuffed into an envelope and spirited away to God-knows-where. You worry about ever seeing them again. If clip-board boy took them, then he'd probably leave them on a bus or try to start his car with your watch. Hey, remember my whole 'hip-thing,' where I was required to walk with the aid of a stick? Well, they took that off me. Here we go:

"I need that to walk."

"What?"

"The walking stick."

"Tough luck."

"If you check my medical file, you'll see that I had a new hip."

"Are you fuckin' deaf? I told you already, tough luck."

Okay, so this was my first problem encounter. How do I handle this? I saw that there was an officer walking past; he looked like a senior guy, so I asked him about getting my stick and honestly, he laughed in my face literally. Okay, so clearly, having a disability was a big joke to these assholes. Fair enough, they were the rules, but rules apply both ways;

"Dave Mahon?"

"Yes."

"C'mon."

"Where?"

"To your cell, where the fuck else?"

"Can't."

"What?"

"I can't."

"Are you refusing an order?"

"No."

"Then, what the fuck are you waiting on? Move Now."

"I CAN'T."

"Stop acting the bollox, fuckin' move!!!"

"I can't."

"Why not?"

"I can't walk without my stick."

"You're not getting your fuckin' stick."

"Then I'm unable to comply with your request.'"

"Well, I'm not going to carry you."

"Just as well, I wouldn't let you."

"What?"

Mahon said nothing – (sorry, dear reader, but in your Face Jack Reacher!!)

"Well?"

Mahon said nothing.

Do you know what the gobshite did next? He stormed over to me like an angry 6 year old and stared into my face Hard. Heck of a poker-player eh? It didn't take 30 seconds to find out which buttons to press on him! His eyes had an insane quality about them, huge control issues going on behind them. I felt pity for his wife, this guy was a model for domestic violence his breath stank of nicotine and alcohol. Odds suddenly turned is his wife's favour, a guy that highly strung and ate cigarettes like skittles, plus couldn't stay off the booze long enough to finish a shift of work, she'd outlive him if she was smart. This little pissing contest lasted long enough for him to realise that I wasn't going to move, so he skulked off and came back with a crutch! He didn't really hand it to me, it was more of a 'foist' in my direction. I honestly thought about refusing to use it, coming out with same insane nonsense about not being qualified to use a crutch and asking if there was a training course or some accreditation required, but didn't I decided to just get on with it... but slowly!

I was brought into the main part of the prison and this was a bit daunting for me. Nothing can ever prepare you for the noises and smells. Then, I was looked into yet another cell. I may as well have been on Mars; this was an Alien world for me. There are many different sections of a prison and the section where I found myself residing was a section known as 23-hour lock-up. Like Ronseal, it does what it says on the tin. Why was I put there? Truth is, I don't know (mushroom treatment), but my gut tells me that it was because they didn't know where else to put me;

"Are you fighting with anyone?"

"Are you mentally unstable?"

"Are you a risk to other prisoners?"

Are you bloody serious?! This was my introduction to prison life. What a lonely, sad and utterly depressing existence it is, so a day is made of 24 hours 23 of which I was locked up for so that left one hour of unlock, where I had what's called "Recreation." What was that, I hear you ask? It was me taken to another cell, with a glass window and a T.V. That is what my recreation was after 3 days of that mental torture I was taken out of my cell, paraded through general population (which after 3 days looking at a wall is actually quite traumatic) and deposited into yet another cell.

It was what is known as a 'shared occupancy' cell in other words, you're not alone; These are basically cells that started off life as a single occupancy cell, then with overcrowding or whatever other politically expedient excuse you care to choose, they started putting in bunk-beds. The cell became double-occupancy or, to use the prison jargon. Two men cells. Then they added another cot and then another etc. Sometimes they just throw a mattress on the floor and add more prisoners that way. They break every rule and controvert human right laws to beat the board, but the right wing press never fully report it, the conditions are simply deplorable. In my case, there were 3 adult men living in space smaller than a box-room. One toilet between us, with a tiny partition wall, no higher than three and a half feet to spare your blushes. No shower, a tiny washbasin/sink and a portable T.V. between us. Oh, and a little Kenwood travel Kettle. Talk about basic, not exactly the 'luxury hotels' that you've been reading about in the press. Are they? But do know something, after three days in solitary confinement (which is what 23-hr lock-up is), it felt great, as solitary is mental torture. You don't know how long you'll be there for (mushrooms again) or what else awaits you. It's tougher than it sounds, it's also how life-sentenced prisoners feel, because how long is "Life"? It's anywhere from 16 years to never, so you can't ever settle; that was one of the possible futures I was facing. I'm not looking for sympathy, I'm just telling my story as it is.

So, what about my family? In prison, you are given two, six-minute, recorded "(For Security purposes)" phone calls per day. That's 12 minutes, not a lot to try and maintain a Family Relationship, is it? 30 seconds for every hour of the clock. Less, If you happen to 'lose' your cell via a bad connection, poor coverage or what-not, in the main prison, you are locked up for 18 ½ hours a day, sometimes more, at least your recreation time resembles some form of actual 'Recreation,' in that you can go out to the yard and walk around in circles for a bit of fresh air, or you can try to grab a game of pool or play a card game called 'Don,' a 4 person game played in every prison.

When I used my "Rec" time to walk the yard, I noticed that everyone either said "Hello" to me by name or else nodded in my direction. After a few laps, two other inmates fell into step with me and started having a chat. They were good fellows and started me on my prison education, giving me the low-down on prison life. I really appreciated it.

"Anything else you need to know, Dave, just ask us."

"Well, there is just this one thing."

"Yeah, man, go ahead."

"How come everyone seems to know my name?"

"(Laughing) Jesus Dave, you haven't been off the news headlined or out of the papers since you got there!"

"Oh!"

I'd have to say that most of the prisoners were okay, but in prison, you have to watch your back -no matter who you are- but especially someone like me -a "high-profile" inmate- splashed across the News! Felt like a bit of a hindrance. To be honest, don't misunderstand me. I'm as social as the next guy, but I wasn't affiliated with any gangs and I didn't have a whole gaggle of friends and family inside either, so, 'alone' in that sense. Apart from phone calls, visits are your lifeline to your family. I thought my first prison visit would never come; I was literally living for it. When the big day arrived (and believe me, it is a big day, you have no idea how much it means to see your family from inside a piss-soaked cage of depression, I was taken out to the 'visits' area), where my father and Audrey were both waiting for me. Some of the lads who'd been showing me the ropes had warned me that my first prison visit would be the hardest and that I might get a little overcome;

"Don't be bleedin' surprised if you have a tear or two, bud." As soon as I locked eyes with my visitors, my loved ones, my rocks, those prophetic words took on a whole new resonance, it was tough. In Clover Hill, all of the visits are behind an impenetrable glass-type screen. These are known as "screen visits," so a lot of thought went into there, eh? So, you can see each other, but you can't touch. No hugs, no hand-holding, no kissing. Nothing. It's like being on Skype or FaceTime, only without privacy. The official reasoning behind this Dickensian cruelty is to prevent the passing over of drugs and/or other contraband, but the reality is that prisons are full-to-capacity with narcotics, so their argument simply doesn't hold

429

water. It was so good to hear Audrey's voice again and to see my father doing his best to make the best out of a bad situation thing.

"What's it like, Dave?"

"Ah, not too bad, you just get on with it."

"What are the other prisoners like? How are they treating you?"

"Ah, the lads are alright, no problems."

"You might get out on bail within a week or so, but it's only a might.'"

"Really? That's good."

It was quite a lot of small talk now that I think back on it, but you see, the truth is, I didn't know if "this" was it. Let me elaborate; I still didn't know if I'd be spending the rest of my natural life in that prison, seeing my family behind a grubby old screen, never again being allowed even to touch Audrey's' hand, let alone hold it. When thoughts like that fill your head, it's difficult to maintain anything close to decent conduct. But you do your best, prisons exist to the beat of a different drum and time moves differently. I don't know how or why exactly, it just does. The screws open your door at "Quarter past when I say so" and close it bang on the appointed time, if not before. Only two things run 'on-time' in a prison "Bang-up" time, officially known as "fall in," like you are in some dog shit, backwards-ass army and visits. Visits hardly ever start when they are supposed to; you'd be forgiven for thinking that the chromes graphical part of their brains were surgically removed en-mosses. That is until your "allocated visiting time" elapses. Then, it's like a whole team of Swiss specialty watchmakers demonically possessed them and BAM!! Just like that, your visitors are handed their visitors Docket (known as the fuck off sheet), and your time is up. You get half an hour. Your visitors do get 30 minutes and not a second, but 30 minutes. Uncanny. When you ask them to do something, you hear, "Yeah, in a minute", and I tell you, I'd love a visit with 30 of those minutes, I'd need an overnight bag! But, it's tough when you spend every waking hour with your partner and you're reduced to half an hour. It's tougher than tough.

Back on my landing and out in the yard, the lads were speculating about what might happen to me in terms of how long I'd do in prison. They knew by my personality that I was no murderer and one of the lads was taking bets on how long I'd get.

"Really? What's the bet's like?!"

"I reckon you'll do 5 years."

"Five? Okay, that's not too bad."

"Yet, the man over there, he said 7."

"7? Right."

"One of the other lads reckons you'll get life 'cos of the papers."

I was glad to be breaking their boredom and bringing a bit of fun into their lives. Not.

"Will you get bail, Dave?"

"Don't really know."

"Ah, you should. How much?"

"How much? Bail."

"Yeah, how much will they set it at?"

"No idea. What do you think?"

"Hmm. A murder charge. Mmm, about fifty grand, plus surety."

"What?? Fuck. What happens if I don't have that much?"

"Do you?"

"No!"

"No?"

"No! Or a surety, whatever that is, what happens then?"

"What, if you can't afford it, you mean?"

"Yeah."

"Simple. You stay in prison."

"Ouch. I put a call in to Tony, my solicitor sharpish;"

"Any news?"

"Yeah, we have a date set for your bail hearing in court." It came quickly. I left Cloverhill prison the exact same way that I came in, only in reverse. The I.P.S., where would it be without all of its rigid procedures? It felt great to slip back into my own clothes again, I felt human, normal. Then it was back into the Paddy wagon and its unique blend of farts, FAG ASH and junkie-urine, permanently. It's tight, ugly little unrolls. The floors and seats look as though they get cleared about as much as Shane McGowan's' teeth. No such thing as seat belts in those death-traps either. You certainly wouldn't leave a tip for the driver!

One badly driven journey later and we were at the C.C.J., A stunning building, scratchy new on the outside. Inside down in the darkened dangerous where the cells are, it's the same, the same old junkies mounting off like a chorus of sloppy mopeds and the smell of ammonia. Stale piss, I took my seat on the converse "bench," hoping that I wasn't sitting on a fleshing Gob or a wet junkie-fart in my clean suit. Every second comment was;

"Ah-nee dooost DER bud, Hav ye?"

"Dooost" = 'Dust,' the colloquialism for Tobacco, because in a pouch, at the cross end, it sort of resembles dust. The cell honestly is like a carcinogenic steam room, thick with smoke. I don't smoke and I already consumed about ten of the horrible cancer sticks by osmosis. Why or how anybody could possibly be 'gummin' for a bleedin' smoke MAAAN is beyond this writer. I couldn't wait to get called up to court to stand before a judge and there's something else I never thought I'd actually write, but it's true!

Meanwhile, up in the clearer courtroom air, my legal team were petitioning the judge for my bail.

"Hmm, I can't see why not. Any objections?"

"Yes, judge."

"And who might you be, sir?

It was Eddie Carroll. What a leach. I couldn't understand why he was objecting. I handed myself in twice to him. He didn't even have to leave his comfortable desk in Coolock Garda station. Thankfully, the judge saw through his nonsense. And granted my Bail Request;

"I'm setting Mr. Mahon's bail at $10,000 and $1000 surety." Great, I was getting out on bail, but Audrey and I were broke, so once again, we had to rely on my father to come to the rescue. There's a part of me that dies inside whenever I have to turn to this loving, reliable, decent human being for help. I'm his son, he's an old man, I should be coming to his rescue, doing things for him, do you know what I mean? I will someday look after him, he won't want me to, but I'm doing it anyway. It's a promise I made to myself and I don't break promises. There were a few other bits and pieces discussed about my case in open court that morning and shame of it all. The only thing I cared about was getting the hell out of there. I can remember the media frenzy, seeing my family there, especially Mick and Audrey. And I can also remember our collective dismay at me not being able to leave there, and then it was back to Cloverhill prison for "processing."

This is yet another layer of bureaucracy and nonsense that our beloved little country simply excels in. Why make something clear and efficient when you can make it messy and slow? Whatever was I thinking? It was the holding cell for me, all 5 plus hours of no air, no water, no television and nothing to do but pace up and down the 14 feet of concert like a caged animal and wonder how long it was all going to take. Boring? You've no idea. Eventually the turn-key jangled his oafish way to my door and asked the million-dollar question;

"Uuuuh… Dave Mahon?"

"Yes."

"Uuuuh, did you get bail?"

(Imagine, dear reader, that I hadn't?! Steve McQueen would've loved an easy escape route like that one! Tunnel? Fuck that. I got bail!)

"Yes."

I'll spare you the rest of that "conversation" because not only is it grossly unfair to stupid people in power all over the world, but you just wouldn't believe it anyway; honestly, I still doubt it and I was there; I was sent back over to the clip-board man.

"Hiya, Dave."

"Alright."

"I see you got bail."

"Yes."

"Okay. Name?"

Oh, sweet Jesus, but, yes, we had to do the whole thing again. He brought out a bag of my stuff and got me to sign it back over to myself. This took more time than you'd think, not because it's difficult, but because they are now. What piece of my property did they "forget" to give me until I had to ask for it? If you said "walking stick", then award yourself a cookie, the most contentious item of all and I had to describe what it looked like. It can't be by accident, can it? I was sent in. One week. The longest of my life.

You know all of these famous movie scenes, where the guy walks out of the prison gates to freedom, brown parcel tied with string under his arm and he looks around and around for a familiar face, a person to bring him home? Well, mine was absolutely nothing like that! I saw a multitude of familiar faces, but only two were friendly. Audrey and Mick, the rest of them had pens, microphones and the ever-clicking cameras. A few other guys were getting out at the same time as me and they also had families waiting for them. Fair play to them, they all offered to form an impenetrable circle around me to protect me from the media, but I politely turned them down. The media were going to follow us around like a love-sick puppy for the duration, but it was a lovely offer. Not as lovely as being able to hold Audrey. My god, I'll never take such things for granted ever again. My father started up the engine;

"Where to, son?"

"Grafton Street, please, let's have a dinner and a few beers." We were followed all the way and even photographed eating, but we didn't let them ruin our enjoyment. We made the best of it while we could. Yes, the sun was shining, but dark clouds were moving in. Soon, there would be court dates. Then would come a trial. My trial for murder.

West Life

So, Dave was back on the streets – great! – The problem, however, was that I couldn't afford to live on them. We were broke. How broke? Well, I owed so much money it was so surreal it bordered on being spiritual. It wasn't looking too hot on the old earning potential either, as both Audrey and I were on disability allowances. Also, every time we went to the shops, we were followed by the slack-jawed human rodents. A mass of never–ending drifters, drifters, alcoholics, whores, scam artists and other forms of media detritus. We so desperately wanted to stay in Dublin close to home base that we even considered renting in areas that were so rough that the Gideon people still wouldn't even deliver Bibles there, but we couldn't even afford them! I guess we had reached a fork in the road of our lives to stay where we were. It was like taking a trip on the denial highway, the only option –a realistic option- for us was to do the 80's pop band thing and go west. Apologies for the pop-culture references, but saying and doing goofy stuff like that with each other is what Audrey and I do, it helps with the otherwise depressing world. We even laugh at certain media photographers trying to hide up in trees or behind the bin to get a "sneaky" picture. Word of advice, guys? A 20-stone man in a red jacket "hiding" on a leafless tree branch (a low one, but hey, 20-stone was your first clue, right?) isn't anyone's idea of "stealth," okay?

Then, of course, they'd "catch" us laughing at them, so the photograph would appear in some rag/mag about what "monsters" we were. I don't know about you, but I can't even recall a monster that laughed. I mean, to me, monsters stalk people and terrorize them, right? They are huge and loud and scary, right? I mean, one could properly compare them to – I don't know – the media?!! As for the type of person who can laugh, show love and generally keep themselves to themselves, well… Isn't that something that most people aspire to? Maybe my worldview is so screwed that I need to be led by more tabloids? Do you want to play a "few" drinking game with some friends? Pick up any red top invariably; there'll be a crime story prominently formed. Ready? Okay, for every mention of the following words: "beast," "monster," "evil," "brute." and "thug," take a three-finger gulp of your favourite sprite. Good luck getting past more than a single page. Those newspaper editors must have a fear of more difficult nouns, or else they're too right to pay for a thesaurus. Then again, they'd probably think that was a dinosaur, a monster!! Okay, rant over. You get my point!

Anyway, we managed to find a lovely house – 3 bedrooms and a large garden – with a rent we could actually afford in the West of Ireland. It was beautiful, even affordable, for a while. We could only manage it for a couple of weeks, and then we tried to heat it. It broke us again. But as always, it bailed down to brass rocks. We lived in our room but had to heat all the rest of the house. Basic economics, but it was another situation that Audrey and I never expected to find ourselves in. We stuck it out for a couple of months but eventually had to cut our losses. We happened upon a 2-bedroomed apartment in the centre of town. I loved it, Audrey loved it and Lily loved it, so finally, we had a roof over our heads and somewhere we could hang our hats. It was a much better "fit" for us than the house had been because not only was it within walking distance of all the local amenities, it was much better for our collective mental health. You see, we were townies in the country, social creatures needing a bit more social interaction than what we were getting "In the sticks."

One of the most surprising discoveries –for me– was to find so many ex-Jacks living there. (Let me explain that little bit of terminology for you – an expat is a countryman in a foreign land, so using that logic, "Jackeen" is not such a wonderful term of "endearment" the other 3 countries of Ireland has fair people from Dublin, ergo – ex-Jacks). Not just general dubs either, but quite a few I know from Swords and Kinsealy. I can't go anywhere, can I?! It seemed like "Jacks" were on my mind a lot, especially concerning Mr. Russell's breed of dog, so we decided to get Lili a little friend of her own. We are big supporters of animal shelters, so it had to be another rescue dog for us. We saw the most beautiful little puppy at the shelter and asked what breed he was;

"Oh, he's a Jack Russell."

"Are you sure?"

"Absolutely."

So, without further ado, we took "Alfi" Mahon home with us. He is a terrific companion for us both and managed to get along fine with Lili once he recognized that she was in charge! Before long, we started to notice some subtle, then more obvious differences between our dogs. The reason? It turns out that "Alfi" is more than the sum of his Jack Russell parts, as in there's a bit of Lurcher in there too! Made no difference to us, though, we loved them both and they were instrumental in getting us out of our apartment every day. Those two little dogs have been our saviours in so many ways it's beyond belief. If ever you feel frightened or alone, try stroking your dog (or pet) for a few minutes. It's the greatest therapy around; please just try it; you'll see for yourself.

It wasn't just animals that we were getting along with either; even people were starting to be nice to us again! We got on famously with our landlord, even though saying that word "landlord" sticks in my craw because once upon a time – that was me! He gave me the occasional job or two whenever they came available, anything from painting, tiling, and carpentry, whatever. I really welcomed the extra modest income when you're living off fumes; fresh air tasted all the sweeter. Besides, it gave me a distraction, something to take my mind off things. My hip was really giving me no end of pain and I was growing impatient with waiting around for replacement. It limited what work I could do, but in so far as was practically possible for me, I wouldn't allow a walking stick to hinder any progress. But nothing can stop or slow down time and on and on she rolled, each day inexorably closer to my murder trial. It still sounds like it was a thing for somebody else, a movie script I was helping somebody to write, a story "real life," not my life anyway. It's an impossible situation; you have delusions to make concrete plans because the ground shifted under your feet all the time. We were keeping Amy's campaign going, but only just because we didn't know if the trial would start "tomorrow" or "next week," so we couldn't give solid commitments to anyone. Unbelievably frustrating and soul-destroying.

It was also a hopeless task to try to stay under the radar because it took less than a week for the local people of the new town, we'd move into to splash us across their front page;

"Dave and Audrey moved to the West of Ireland to avoid media attention."

How bloody "Irish" was that? Nice one, lads. Thanks for respecting our privacy. In order to keep my sanity and maintain my focus, I walked the dogs every day – a couple of times a day – and swam long distances down at the pool. When you're banging out the lengths up and down the pool, you go into a little sub-aquatic zone where it's just you, your breathing and the water; nothing else exists. It's perfect. Then, not entirely out of the blue, I received the first of two calls. I was waiting on.

No, not that one! It was The Cappagh Hospital in Finglas, time for hip number TWO. Another bitter-sweet day. The "sweet" was that, at last, I'd get the bloody thing out of the way, the "bitter" was that I was going to be held up like a helpless man–baby for another 6-8 weeks. Poor Audrey, not exactly eligible to become the poster Girl for Women's Health at the time herself, was now going to be stuck doing everything for me. Again. Shit.

When I left the Cappagh Hospital after my second replacement (you all know the drill by now, no point in making a gangster movie out of every little thing!), my father (who else!) was there to pick me up. He dropped me off at Connolly train station and there was a really unusual experience. Once again, I had been the guy to drop people off at the train station and now I was the person getting dropped off. As a taxi driver, I had experienced hundreds of passengers requiring a porter at the destination, waiting with a wheelchair. Now, that was me, too. I've pushed many wheelchairs around airports (Audrey) and bus stations; it's a very different thing when it's you that in the seat of the wheelchair itself. Mick – as usual – gauged my sober mood and cracked a joke about how he was the old man, yet he was doing the pushing! Sad too, and true. He rolled me all the way up to the ramps and put me into the wheelchair-accessible spot on the train. By the way, the train was totally my idea because Mick and a few of my friends had offered to drive me all the way home, but I'm too independent to put anybody through all of that nonsense.

The train journey was quite fast actually, only about two hours or so, but I'll tell you this, it scared me. No, not the train, not the steady, soothing rhythms of the rail of travel, but the whole wheelchair experience. To be a bit more specific, it was "the look" that other people gave me. When I drove taxis all those years ago and had passengers confined to a wheelchair, I'd always ask them the same question;

"What's the worst thing about being in the chair?"

The answer wasn't always the obvious one you'd expect, rather, it was;

"The sympathetic 'look' that people give you."

That didn't make an ounce of sense to me at that time, but right then, on the train, it sure did. I'm actually ashamed to write this –given my "lifetime" of experience in a wheelchair (a mere two hours) – but by God, do I get it now. Please bear that in mind next time you see somebody in a wheelchair; see the person – not the chair- and for goodness sake, don't do that "look" whatever you do.

Another life experience was done and I was home to rest and recover and wait. That court date loomed ever larger and yet more elusive each day. It was coming through, just like death; it would certainly arrive and its unwelcome odour soured everything and anything until it decided to announce itself. So, what does yours truly do when laid flat on his back for 6-8 weeks? Why, emailing the Department of Foreign Affairs and the Spanish Embassy, of course. What was it that old advert used to say? "Let your fingers do the walking." Well, I had no bloody choice, had

I?! We were still fighting as hard as our health would allow us for Amy, like throwing paper clips at a panzer, to be honest, but we still gave it all we had.

One of the conditions of my bail - most bail cases, actually – was to sign on at the local police station 3 times a week. No big deal, it's certainly better than bloody Clover Hill, but when I got my new hip, it became a problem. I couldn't get down to the police station for obvious reasons so I sent a letter to Garda Eddie Carroll via my solicitor, Tony Collier, stating that I was unable to go to the police station and that when I was back on my feet, I would immediately resume signing on three times a week. All above board, all bases covered – right? Weeks passed, then a month, then a bit more time and I was feeling okay again, I didn't even need a walking stick. Great, all good. I was far more mobile than before, so I emailed Tony again, telling him that I could go back to the police station and start signing back on. All seemed good. Well, not really – the Spanish Embassy and the Irish Government were as useless as ever, but that's not exactly "news" any more. We decided to turn up the heat on these lazy, ineffective assholes once again. What was needed was yet another face-to-face meeting with the Guardia Civil again. Small, tiny problem, though my passport was held with the Garda as part of my bail condition.

This, of course, meant another day in court. I know – right – those poor old legal Professionals, how do they ever get by, eh?! Look, credit where credit is due, the judges had allowed me to leave the jurisdiction before whilst on bail, as I had always handed myself back in and toed – the – line to a ridiculous degree. This particular Judge – Tony Hunt – didn't have any problems with me heading over to Spain again either. In fact, to be fair to him, he was particularly helpful. One of the many boxes to be ticked from the court's perspective was to ask the question in open court;

"Does anyone from the State have an issue with this ruling?"

"Yes, I do judge, yes."

"You do, eh detective?"

"Carroll, judge, Eddie Carroll."

"Okay, Detective Carroll. Please state your objection to the court."

"Yes, judge. Well, judge, he's a flight-risk judge."

"A flight risk?"

"Yes, judge. I must strongly oppose his travel plans, judge."

"Yes, you've said that bit, a 'flight risk', detective?"

"Yes, judge. He is facing a murder trial judge and he once lived in Spain, judge."

"More than once, actually, detective, more than once. Continue."

"Yes, judge, exactly judge, so he knows the lay of the land judge."

"Indeed, he does detective, as he did previously, too. So what?"

"Well, judge, he may not come back this time."

"Or, he 'might' detective, mightn't he?"

"Eh… well, yes, judge, I suppose…"

"So that does not make him a flight-risk detective, wouldn't you agree?"

"Well… eh… eh… no judge."

"No?? Pray tell Detective, why don't you agree?"

"You see judge, he's already broken the terms of his bail agreement…"

"How, detective?"

"…Ah... Sorry judge? Oh, eh, well, he didn't sign on at the station for 2 months."

"So, what you're telling me, detective, is Mr. Mahon didn't sign in?"

"For two-months judge, yes."

"In breach of his court-ordered bail conditions?"

"Yes, judge."

(Oh shit, oh shit, oh shit – where was this going???)

"Well, detective, if Mr. Mahon failed to do so, then he's broken the law…"

"Yes, judge!"

"… and therefore, should be imprisoned…"

"Yes, judge!!"

"Am I right in this, detective?"

"Yes, judge!!!"

(This really wasn't looking good for me, was it?)

"Well then, tell me, detective, why was Mr. Mahon allowed to show such blatant disregard to our very serious bail laws, for so long – months, according to you - and yet you didn't arrest him?"

"Judge?"

"Detective, you have the power of arrest, do you not?"

"I… Yes, Judge…"

"So please – tell the court why didn't you do your job and arrest him?"

(If I was going to go down, I wasn't going alone, it seemed!)

"Well… eh… judge, you see, Mr. Mahon said that he got a new hip…"

"And, Detective? And??"

"Well, judge, he looks fine to me, judge."

"Are you a medical expert detective?"

"No, judge..."

"Are you trying to present medical evidence to this court?"

"Judge?"

As surprised and disgusted as I was with Eddie Carroll for this blatant show of grandstanding for the writers in the peanut gallery, I loved the not-so-gentle deconstruction of his objection from the judge. I was also thankful for having some good legal representation on board. They were next to stand up and address the court. In short, they outlined the fact that my step-daughter went missing over in Spain;

"Yes, I'm very aware of that."

"And our client – Mr. Mahon – has returned to Spain several times to keep the search going and to meet with the Guardia Civil…"

"Go on."

"In fact, my lord, we have numerous emails to that effect…"

"Yes, but what about Mr. Mahon's' failure to sign on for two months?"

"My lord, in relation to that issue – if it may please the court – I have for the court perusal letters from The Cappagh Hospital pertaining to Mr. Mahon's surgery and, indeed my lord, from the surgeon himself, a Doctor Dennis Collins…"

"Yes – yes – yes, so Mr. Mahon did have surgery. But he still has a legal obligation to fulfil the terms of his bail conditions, didn't he?"

"Indeed, he did, your honour, and in fact, up until his operation, he was signing on 3 days a week without fail."

"Yes. But then he stopped for two months!"

"Your honour, that is correct; however, your honour, you may not be fully aware of the volume of correspondence between Mr. Mahon and Detective Carroll via his instructing solicitor, Mr. Tony Collier?"

"Go on…"

A folder – Telephone Directory in thickness – was handed to the judge. All my medical reports and written transcriptions of the communications to Eddie Carroll about my inability to sign on for two months. A paper trial full of conclusive proof that Eddie Carroll was fully aware of and complicit with my temporary break away from signing on. The judge gave Eddie Carroll a withering look that only judges can give and Carroll could only blush loudly and look intently at his shoes. In chess terminology, it was 'check' and 'mate.'

Judge Tony Hunt made sure that my passport was returned and although I didn't see it, I believed he went on to have a side-order of Eddie Carroll's' arse for lunch, but of course, I cannot disclose my sources. When we got to Dublin Airport on the day we were to depart these shores on our way to Spain, it was still dark outside as it was 4 am, because we were booked onto a 6 am flight. It was too early for the media to be waiting for us… only it wasn't.

"Dave, Audrey! Are you off to Spain? Is this about Amy?"

We will never refuse to provide a story about Amy, barring two exceptions.

"The Sunday World and Spain's "Olive Press" – because they represent the dog-shit end of tabloid journalism and can hardly print the date truthfully. This was neither of those rancid rags. However, it was the Irish Independent.

Now, I won't disclose the name of the reporter – for reasons that will soon become obvious;

"How did you know we'd be here at 4 am?"

"We know you have a 6 am flight."

"How?"

"Eddie Carroll told us."

"(blown away) What???"

"Yeah, he called us up and gave us all your flight details."

I couldn't believe what I was hearing. I mean, I could – but I couldn't believe it was being confirmed right in front of me! Dear reader, it is a fact beyond any doubt that the Garda – leak our information to the press all the time – especially about us – and whether or not it was in fact, Detective Eddie Carroll who did it that time is irrelevant. What isn't, however, is that I am 100% positive that the information that day was delivered to the press by the Garda. We thanked the reporter for his candour and then gave them the story about what we hoped to achieve on our trip to Spain. For once, it was reported correctly. Credit when credit is due.

I know I might sound like a broken record here, but it really does feel like "home" whenever we touchdown in Malaga. The sun, the sights, the smells and that Spanish air embracing you in the hugging warmth of an old friend, it's magical. Coming back to Dublin also feels familiar, but more in an "old shoe" kind of way, not quite as romantic, but true! After we got ourselves settled into our accommodation, we took the night off as we were exhausted. Health problems were still an ever-present issue, but you soldiered on. Nobody else was doing a damn thing for Amy, but sure, what else was new? We had arranged to meet the following morning with the Guardia Civil, but for once, we had to get there by bus. It was really weird for me because I had always driven everywhere. When we reached the Municipal Building – Head Office of the Guardia Civil – we had all the usual lads there, waiting to meet and greet us. It felt wonderful. I know how strange that sounds (and you should try writing it, believe me!), but it's the truth. It was great to see some of those familiar faces again, even Ann Marie Perkins, the Scottish woman under whom they've employed as a translator. We gave them hell – as usual – because, at the end of the day, our daughter is still missing. Keep your platitudes; in fact, you can shove them up your arse, just find Amy. Subconsciously, I knew that this might well be the last time I'd see these guys; a trial was pending and if I got a life sentence, then this would be my last hurrah. Perhaps that was why I was even more vocal than usual? I don't honestly know, but what I can say is that at one point, I was pushing so hard that the lizard part of my brain flashed a warning sign across my mind;

"Easy Dave – E –Z – now, this isn't Ireland. These guys can – and do – lock people up over here for up to 4 years without any change. Piss 'em off enough and they might try stitching you up with Amy's disappearance. You've Dean's "Murder" charge hanging over you. It's not out of the question for them."

I've learned to listen to that lizard voice, our reptilian instincts are seldom wrong. I pulled my horses in – not far, but enough – and we left shortly afterwards, still on friendly terms. Admittedly, we did go straight to a little Spanish bar afterwards for a large gin and tonic and a white wine for Audrey. We'd done as much as we could, which was everything. We sat at that bar together and watched silently as the sun set for the last time for us on Spanish soil. Maybe Amy was watching it too, all of us under the same darkening sky for another Spanish sunset. I like to believe we did.

The next day, we arrived back into the comfortable old leather shoe that is Dublin, "home" with a lowercase "h." We met up with the usual friends and family before heading back out West. My murder trial – date still hadn't been set, but it would happen soon. Sooner than I'd want. I dreaded it, even the thought of it, but it had to be faced. I kept running my new mantra around in my head." Not everything that is faced can be charged, but nothing can be charged until it is faced." I'd read it somewhere and it seemed to fit my particular circumstances. The pressure we were under was becoming too intense, and something had to give. I kept thinking about that old science experiment I'd once heard about, the one about the boiling frogs. In case you are unfamiliar with it, it's the one where you place a frog into a pot of cold water, then slowly turn up the heat on the stone. The point of the whole experiment is to demonstrate how the frog will eventually boil to death because it doesn't notice the temperature changes, but if you threw another

444

frog into the already boiled water, then it would jump out (if it could) immediately. My point is that we were – emotionally – at boiling point, finally.

Audrey had started to receive counselling every week, sometimes twice a week; she was totally and understandably out of sorts. She was also on all kind of medication, the very thing her failing liver didn't need. She is still the strongest person I have ever known; how she has survived the protracted, cruel and emotional crucifixion she has endured –for so long – is beyond human. I don't say that lightly. She asked me time and time again to go to counselling sessions, but like a typical man, I refused;

"Please, Dave."

"No."

"Why not?"

"It's not for me, telling all my problems to a stranger? No."

All of that "shrinks" nonsense was for wimps, it was for weaklings and there was no way I was ever going to go. Forget about it. Then, one day, Audrey came into the T.V. room and sat down in front of me. She had her "serious" face on. Great, now what?

"Dave. Will you do me a favour?"

"Of course, name it."

"Will you go to see a counsellor – but – before you answer, will you do it… for me?"

Damn, was she good? Those last two little words, all 5 letters of them, are my kryptonite. She knows that there is nothing I wouldn't do for her and so she played me like an X-box. How could I refuse? Of course, I agreed to see the counsellor;

"Not fair, Audrey! Okay, I'll look into it next week or so…"

"You have an appointment on Wednesday, two days from today."

She played me! So, like the dutiful little brat that I am, I went out that Wednesday to meet the guy. Picture the scene – Dublin Dave with the artificial hips out in the West of Ireland about to walk into the offices of some carrot –

crunching – cliché to tell him my problems? It's like the start of a bad joke. My head was swimming with negativity.

"Not good Dave. Come on, think of a way out of this."

I probably would have, too, except... well, I'd promise Audrey. Shit! Ah well, in I went.

We got off to a good start; the counsellor was from Dublin, so at least there wouldn't be a language barrier!

"Hello, Dave, my name is XXX."

"Hello."

"Now, Dave, tell me why are you here?"

"Because my wife sent me."

Well, he laughed so much at that he almost tripped over his chair! I got lucky. We hit it off straight away, so let the truth be told, that counsellor opened up to me a bit more about his family problems than I did about mine. He explained to me that he had no idea who I was because he didn't have a TV or read newspapers. After our 8 weeks together, he gave me his personal number and to be honest, I did use it once or twice. Did it help? Of course, it did, it always helps to talk to a professional and I'd recommend it highly, so throw all of that "macho" bullshit out the window. When our session had finished, I had a heart-to-heart with Audrey;

"How do you feel, Dave?"

"Okay, given our situation."

"Even though I arranged for you to see the counsellor?"

"Yes, behind my back!"

"Yes, but I arranged for you to meet a Dublin one!"

"Yeah."

"And one that I knew you'd get along with..."

"Right."

"I knew you'd get along together."

"How?"

"I interviewed a few of them before finding you the right one!"

What a woman! Did it solve all my problems? No, because he was a counsellor, not a bloody wizard. People need to remember that. People like him was like writing this book, it helped me to think things through and to see a little clearer. It doesn't stop there either, I find that yoga and exercising also help me to relax and - unpopular as the concept may sound these days - I find that having a few points helps me to cope a little better.

Yet, out of everything, the key to survival for all you slowly boiling frogs out there – as I was – is to talk. Sometimes, the correct answers are the simple ones, why do we feel so compelled to hamstring ourselves with complications? Having said that, sometimes taking the easy road is often the harder journey; that's why it's good to talk to a professional.

I'm told that in America, everyone sees a "shrink," and while I saw that as a weakness, I now say "good luck" and "more power" to them. In Ireland, we have the luxury of going for a pint and talking to good friends, which works for the most part. However, when you straddle with the world-crushing magnitude of what Audrey and I had, I'm sorry, but only a professional will do. Audrey still goes to counselling, but not as often anymore. I think that has something to do with the nervous – breakdown she put her counsellor through! I jest – of course – we owe so much to these mostly unsung heroes.

The Wedding

In this modern world of throw-away consumables, everything appears to have a shelf-life. It wasn't always like this. When I was growing up, a normal family would have the same car for years, fixing it when it broke down and driving it until it literally fell apart or blew up. My point? I'm of a vintage where things were built to last and you learned to fix them if they broke, including relationships, especially marriages. I suppose it's because of that mindset that I committed. From an early age, I wanted to get married when I got older, but only once. Like my parents and their parents before them. Audrey was and is the only woman I was ever going to marry and at this stage in our own story, we had been engaged for about 8 years. Were we afraid of tying the knot? Absolutely not! But, back in 2007, when we got engaged, we had planned on getting married pretty soon afterwards, we had no idea just how much life was conspiring against us, though.

During those halcyon days, little things (as they now appear to be) like running a bar, a real estate business or just the usual ebb? And the flow of family life got in the way. We had always planned on having our wedding even in Spain and even though we had never actually set a date, we were always going to have plenty of family and friends from Ireland over, as well as our large group of Spanish friends. I remember calling my mother when we got engaged and hearing her cries of joy, too excited to believe even her own ears. She insisted on us coming back to Ireland to celebrate with her, which we did, believe me!

When we arrived back at Santry, my mother had already purchased her wedding clothes, giddy as a toddler hiding under a bed "Glamorous Kay," being who she was, insisted on only ever buying the best of clothes and her wedding outfit was no exception with her. Ah, it was not their décor; it was on sale- a bargain!" fabrication already spun out to my curious father. Laurel and Hardy were a funny double act, but sometimes Kay and Mick, how much was that show blew even them away! As you know by now, dear reader, my mother's dream wedding day for me was cruelly taken by cancer and she wore that outfit on her final journey from this world, leaving a hole in my life that no amount of grief will ever fill.

Fast forward then to 2015, and hey-you already know just how much-troubled waters flowed under our bridge in those intervening years. Still, it is high time we made our love "legally official," and so we set the date of May 12th. We chose Kettle's Country Club as our venue, so we booked it and had our civil ceremony, wedding and reception all in one location. I had actually booked the 3 nights prior to the wedding as well because I had a lot of friends and – Ahem! - 'organising to do.' One of my oldest and dearest friend, Tommy Doran, called me up to ask me when I was getting to the Kettle's hotel. I was hoping that was an indication of his being able to make it. Tommy spent a massive part of his time between England and South Africa, the latter being too far a journey for him to reasonably make.

"Sorry, Dave, I'm still in SA (South Africa), but I wanted to make sure that you'd be there when my present arrived."

"Ah, you didn't have to send me a present."

"Shut up, of course I did! How long until you arrive at the hotel?"

"I should be there in a few hours. Why?"

"Just curious, you see, I paid for one of those next-day express things, so it's due today."

"Thanks, Tommy, it won't be the same without you."

"Just one of those things Dave. Anyway, all the best for yourself and Audrey, I promise you, we'll meet again soon, okay?"

It wasn't going to be the same without Tommy, but fair play to him, he not only had the class to call me and tell me himself, he also remembered to send a wedding gift all the way from the other side of the planet. Not too many people would be so thoughtful, would they?

Audrey was staying in a different hotel in Ballymun with Paula - her best friend and bridesmaid. The day before our wedding, they spent a pampering day in Finglas, getting their hair, nails and spray tan done, you know, all of that "girly" stuff! She deserved that little day of pampering, given everything that she's been through, she deserves that every day, but unfortunately, that's beyond my meagre little funds these days! I collected my wedding cake from the Boston Bakery in Santry. My cousin works there and she didn't just bake us a wedding cake, she created a work of art. We needed a wedding cake with no alcohol in it because of Audrey's liver problems (the epithet didn't just go away like they do in the movies, real life sucks like that sometimes!). On top of our cake, my cousin designed a castle with lights built into it. If I could've dreamed of a more perfect metaphor for what that particular castle signified, I couldn't have come close to what my cousin achieved. She didn't stop at that either. Instead of traditional wedding figurines on top of the wedding cake, she created a bald man complete with a kilt and walking stick and a blond bride lifting up the kilt! I was obviously the bald man and yes, I, too, wore a kilt on the big day. Why? I hear you ask.

Well, not only have I not got a single drop of Scottish blood, I've never even stepped foot on their soil and I wouldn't pollute my taste buds with Scotch Whiskey, not when we have the far superior Whiskey over here! Still, I wanted to do something a little different for my wedding day, as I'll only ever do it once. Therefore, I got a kilt shipped over. Hey, if nothing else, it was a great talking point! I was in two minds about staying over in the hotel the night before the wedding. There was a nagging voice in the back of my mind coercing me to just kick back and relax with my father. I was only prevented from doing so by Mick.

"Would you not be better off going up to the hotel, having a few drinks and staying up there?"

"(Un-enthusiastic) Ah. I suppose. Right, see you tomorrow Da- don't be late!"

So, I packed up my car with my wedding cake and our flowers. We decided on La Cala Lilies. I guess the reasons why we decided on them should be obvious by now, right? When I got to the hotel, I was met by the owner and some of his wonderful staff; they really looked after us. In fact, take this as a recommendation. You won't be disappointed when I got out of my car, I walked around it to collect my bags, cake and flowers etc., but I was stopped by the staff.

"Just give us the keys to your car and we will do the rest for you."

"(Confused) Sorry?"

"Let us look after everything for you, please. Go into the bar, have a few drinks and relax!"

I'm not normally a nervous person, but I must admit, on this occasion, I was. Besides, I was never one to refuse a pint when there was an offer on hand for someone else to take over my work! The obedient soul that I am, I handed over the keys and then proceeded into the bar. Just as I was about to order, I heard a very familiar voice.

"Is it yourself or someone else?"

That particular statement was a private joke between me and only one other person, the owner of that voice, my good friend – Tommy Doran! It was up there with the best surprises I've ever had; I was so overcome (in a good way) that it actually brought a tear to my eye. We immediately got stuck into all of our old war stories, the good times, back over in Spain, but I was so grateful for him being there, right there, with me;

"Tommy, your being here is the best present ever. Thank you!"

"That reminds me, I actually do have a present for you."

He brought Audrey and me over a case of Doran's red wine from South Africa. If you thought that Tommy Doran bringing Doran's wine over was a coincidence, a humorous play on words, then you'd be wrong. This was the cream of the crop from his very own vineyard, which made it even more special to us. That night absolutely flew in, but it eventually had to come to an end. I had my big day just over the horizon. I insisted on staying in a regular room that night and to save the honeymoon suite until I was with my new bride. Dear reader, I can't tell you how good it felt to have those words roll off my tongue!

The morning of my wedding had finally arrived, and I was as nervous as a leaving student on exam day who hadn't cracked open a book! My usual "Break glass in case of emergency" remedy for such nervousness was. An infusion of alcoholic beverages and copious amounts thereof, but that just was not going to cut the mustard that day. I went to plan B- A full Irish breakfast, but I couldn't even get that into me when alcohol and fried meat aren't working. I go back to my default position- talking! I phoned everyone and talked their ears off, everyone except Audrey. That is Darren, my best friend and best man, who got me (both barrels) but had the perfect escape. He was picking up Audrey and my father. Mick, even though my father was giving Audrey away in place of her own dad, who was still too ill. She had hoped that one of her brothers would've stood in for her father but sadly, that wasn't to be. Darren used his own pride and joy – an immaculate S-S-Class Mercedes, gold in colour, as our wedding car, the perfect vehicular metaphor for my golden girl!

It was a tough proposition to put my wedding clothes on that morning. Much to Tommy's amusement, who knew that there was so much work into putting on a kilt?! We were also doing a documentary for Amy around then too, so we incorporated some of our wedding footage into it so that also took a bit of time. When all of that was done and dusted, Tommy and I went down the stairs to meet and greet the rest of our guests. It was quite an intimate affair – only about 40 people- but this was by design and not an accident of circumstance. Audrey and I know and love every single person on our exclusive wedding list. Not too many people can say that and mean it. In fact, had I won the lottery that week and had buckets of disposable cash to throw at our wedding, it still wouldn't have made a difference. The guest list, location – nothing would have changed. We were and are blessed to have as many real friends and family as we do, so it was a day for them too. But not as much as it was for us. It was our wedding day; I'm not conceding any ground about that!

Like any other nervous groom on his wedding day (and let's be honest, guys, we all get nervous no matter how cool you think you are!) I was looking to my "mark" for "the signal." This, dear reader, is the nod/wink/thumbs up whatever your 'mark' (be it a friend/relative, etc.) gives you when your bride arrives. I was waiting for one of the Kettle's hotel staff to let me know when Audrey's car was pulling in. This information was to be relayed to Darrin, who was driving her and would call the hotel at a certain point for the "heads-up." I was pacing up and down like a bird on a wire, burning a hole in the carpet with nervous energy. My sister, Olivia, read me like a book and offered some soothing words:

"Dave, you okay?"

"Ah yeah, yeah. yeah eh – a bit nervous."

"Dave."

"Yeah?"

"(Whispers) I don't think Audrey's coming."

Apparently, my jaw bounced off the floor and my face went whiter than an arctic Christmas because first -Olivia- then, well... Everybody else started laughing.

"Ah, I'm only joking with you, Dave!"

I responded with a polite little half–chuckle, but it was the best I could manage because, seriously, it was the most nervous I've ever been in my life. By the way, I've no ill will towards Olivia. I would've done the exact same thing to a nervous eejit like I was, probably even worse. So, it was all good; just a little bit more to wait. Much looking at my watch won't be long now. Another time check... won't be long... won't be long, can't be too much longer, can she? A brandy was put in front of me. It's not usually a good thing for your average brandy; it usually ends badly for the innocent beverage. Then another brandy appeared beside it... then another. I didn't touch any of them. I couldn't stomach them. Any other day and those brandies wouldn't have lasted! Then, one of the lovely Kettle's girls made her way over to me. I thought it was yet another brandy, but she inclined her head towards me conspiratorially.

"(Whispers) Audrey has arrived!"

Yes!! Like a really badly organized military drill, we cropped, fumbled and barged our way into the wedding venue room, took our respective positions like a Marx Brothers sketch and waited for Audrey's arrival. When she entered the room, she was all poise, all sophistication, all grace. Basically, the polar opposite of what had conspired earlier! You know that scene in all the corniest rom-com movies, where the bride walks into the room, all the heads turn and she smiles at the groom? Well, multiply that by ten thousand. Audrey owned that room the second she stepped foot in it. I couldn't have dreamed of a more perfect bride; I had never seen her look so beautiful. She was utter perfection – from the stunning white dress (that she wasn't mad about, but she never looked at it through my eyes) to her gorgeous hair – shaved on one side, long on the other and beautifully blonde as always.

Her beautiful eyes sparkled like precious gemstones, sensationally blue like looking at shining earth in the blackness of space, my very world right there in her eyes. Literally, one of the first things I ever loved about Audrey was her smile and given what life had thrown at us, we didn't have too much cause for smiles, but that day we did. Audrey's smile across the room at me that day was the biggest smile I'd ever seen her wear. Somehow, it made my beautiful bride even more perfect. Wow… just, Wow! She was beyond beauty and she was so completely stunning.

Yeah, I'd started crying; tough guy - right? I didn't care, they were (and I hate a cliché) tears of joy. I'd lived my whole life hearing that hackneyed old expression and thought it was a stupid old phrase you said when, I don't know, Ireland won a match or something. It took my whole life to learn the literal meaning. I was so happy. I was actually joyful, a state of such completeness, your body involuntarily reacts with tears to cope with its overwhelming intensity. Tears of joy. Incredible.

Well, that's just what Audrey does to me, folks! We were blissfully happy in that little moment and hey, I think that we were more than entitled to a great and memorable day in our lives. That was certainly it. Then the ceremony started and we made our vows, meaning each one of them. Then, all of a sudden, seven magical words:

"I now pronounce you husband… and…wife!!!"

Holy shit, after all that time together, we are now Mr. and Mrs. Mahon officially! The deed was sealed with the most important kiss of my life and then Maestro! Cue the music, pour some drinks and get the party started! As Frank Vaile put it – "Oh, what a night!"

What would a wedding be without the speeches, right? Well, a "better one" if Darrin Fagan gives one because his was pure shit! He's my best man, I love him to bits and he's usually the funniest guy in the room, but not that room! I don't know; maybe it was his nerves? Stage fright? Or maybe the distinct lack of Old Dutch courage because he was driving? Whatever the reason, it was the worst wedding speech ever and the most awkward, socially embarrassing moment since Del Boy and Rodney turned up at a funeral dressed up as Batman and Robin. As you may have guessed, I still rib him about it every chance I get, so there was no way it wasn't going to end up in my book now, was there?!! Thank God for Tommy's speech. It was everything. Darrin's wasn't you know, funny, clever, heartfelt... you know? Good!! By the way, in case I forget to mention it, my best man's speech was awful.

My father looked like a million dollars that day. As dapper as a slightly older James Bond with better dance moves! Our Mick busted a few moves on the dance floor that night that hadn't been seen since the heyday of Sammy Davis Jr. Even my sister Olivia and her normally subdued husband caught the old disc fever off him! All of Audrey's good friends were there and not only did they have a great night, they helped make Audrey's one even better, which was really important for her because none of her family members were invited (but her dad) and they wouldn't have turned up anyway.

Audrey and I had a great day, but at the back of our minds was the presence of those absent. It was an occasion tailor-made for my brother, Rory, who would've been the life, soul and entertainment all rolled into one. It was hard not to think about him and miss him. Also absent was my glamorous mother -Kay- who would have been beaming with pride and fawning over Audrey, reminding her every couple of minutes about how spectacular she looked and how happy she was making me. Audrey's parents also missed out on her special day, but for reasons beyond anyone's control, it still didn't make their absence sting any less for her and me because they were such wonderful people. But by far, the greatest void at our wedding was the one created by Dean and Amy. They were the elephants in the room that everybody avoided, except me, during my speech. As much as we enjoyed our fabulous day (well... 3 days!) Dean and Amy were always "there" with us. As Robbie Williams put it, we'd "no regrets" about getting married, save for the fact that we should've done it sooner, when all of our parents and dears were still alive, and before Amy's disappearance. Again, hindsight in all of its 20-20 smugness, I'll let you in on something, though, I still dream of the day when Audrey and I sit down to watch our wedding video with Amy. It will happen.

The first song Audrey and I danced to as a married couple was "Wild Horses" by the Rolling Stones (listen to the lyrics; that's all I need to say), and another song that really stands out was the one sung by Pink. We didn't go off on a honeymoon. To be honest, I still don't know where the money came from to pay for the wedding itself! Thank God for Darrin and my father because their help was invaluable. We were newlywed and nearly dead, such was the incessant toll on our health, especially Audrey, whose heart was still big enough to donate her wedding dress to an Irish Charity for still born babies. Audrey always has been and always will be the love of my life. Audrey and Dave against the world.

Dave and audrey's Wedding

Dave and Audrey having their first dance

Trial by Fire

My solicitor is a lovely guy, not too many former prisoners will ever write, let alone say those words, but they are true. He's a few years younger than me and if you close your eyes and tried to imagine what a solicitor looked like; you'd picture him. To me, anyway, I call him "The Jack Russell" because he's not that much bigger than me, and when he shows his teeth, it's time to worry. Although his bark is actually a lot worse than his bite (which is what a good solicitor should always be), he's every inch a Jack Russell with a low degree. His real name is Mr. Tony Collier and he has been with me from the start of all this, well, pretty much.

I guess ours is a fairly unique solicitor–client relationship in that – from day one, I told him everything and never once held back. At the time, he was just a jobbing solicitor at a big organization, Michael Staines and Company, a company I fell into by fluke. You see when I handed myself into Coolock Garda station and threw myself at their feet, telling them everything about my role in Dean's death. I didn't have a solicitor, so they called one for me. They must've had Staines on speed dial or something because they called his firm and he in turn, sent out one of his juniors. When I met Staines's representative, he was cold and very matter-of-fact about everything. Sorry, it's not good enough; this was Dean. I was not talking about some random stranger who meant nothing to me. A few days after my release from Coolock police station, I went into Staines at his offices in Smithfield, central Dublin.

"Hello, Mr. Mahon."

"Michael, is it?"

"Yes."

"You can call me Dave. Listen, the guy you sent out to me in Coolock?"

"Oh yes, yes…"

"Yeah, I don't want him, he's not for me."

"No problem, Dave – I'll appoint someone else for you."

And so, that's when I met Tony and how we met. For our first consultation, I told him as much as I could (not much) before breaking down. To say that I was still tender and upset would be a massive misrepresentation of how low I was feeling. I was broken, simple as that. He saw how pointless it was to continue (not all solicitors can) and postponed our meeting. In what I can only describe as a human way, I felt like a blubbering fool, but he treated me with kindness and respect. No bullshit. Soon after, began a series of very serious meetings with Tony and I took an instant liking to him. He was very professional, calm and relaxed. At all times except when he needed to rattle my cage or shut me up, that was when I learned how hard he could "bite" when he needed to. Oh yeah, I really liked having him on my side! He was a very different type of lawyer to the ones I used over in Spain for the real-estate stuff and what have you; some of them turned out to become my friends and we also employed a few for Amy's case, but Tony's acid test was coming up fast so I'd get to see how he was under real pressure.

My first time in the C.C.J. with Tony wasn't in a courtroom or before any judges; rather, it was in one of the many consultation rooms housed within that beast. I hate that bloody place; it really puts me on edge and maybe Tony sensed that because he was sussing me out every bit as much as I was him. I'm a total people-watcher and I was really interested in how he interacted with his peers, friends and foes around the court. He mixed in some heavyweight circles, out of his depth back then, but carried a real "fuck you, I belong here, too" attitude, which I liked. We'd gotten to know each other over the courses of several such C.C.J. meetings and I'd grown to trust him, which was why our next scheduled meeting knocked me for six.

Why? Because he wasn't there, instead, Michael Staines himself stood before me with all of my files and paperwork tucked under his arm.

"Hello, David! How are you? (Not a good question)."

"Where's Tony?"

"Tony doesn't work for me anymore."

"Why?"

To be honest, I can't remember the answer he gave me, but then, he is a bloody solicitor!

"I'm your solicitor from now on."

No, I didn't like the turn of events one little bit. His attitude was all wrong, even though he was being nice to me. He never once asked me if I wanted him or someone else to take over my representation like I was some gully off the street without two brain cells to rub together. He stood there all sanctimonious and messianic, "God" himself had stepped down from Mount Zion to care for my interests and boy, I was lucky. He spoke "to" me as if I wasn't there and my bullshit threshold lasted all of a few minutes:

"Have you got Tony's phone number?"

"Huh? Em, no, no – I don't have it, anyway! ..."

"You don't have it?"

"What? Eh, No..."

That was when I knew that something was amiss. That old lizard part of my brain was greatly unsettled, never a good thing. About an hour later, Audrey and I were having a cup of tea right there in the C.C.J. when low and behold, who should we just happen to bump into? Only the bold Tony himself! We had a good little chat, and then I dropped a bombshell;

"I still want you to represent me."

"Dave, you have Michael Staines – himself – Now he's much in demand!"

"So?"

"Dave, he's one of the best-known defence lawyers in Ireland!"

"Tony, I always go with my gut."

Which is always true. After a fairly protested palaver, it turned out that in order to keep Tony, I'd have to fire Michael. So, I let him go and told him that I was sticking with Tony. Okay, so the way it works (or at least worked back then) is to hire a solicitor first. They, and only they hire your Barrister. You can't employ or even talk to a Barrister without a solicitor present. Eventually, in a capital-type trial such as murder especially, you'll end up with a "legal team" along the following lines: (1) Solicitor (Tony Collier), (2) Junior Counsel (known as a B.L), (3) Senior Counsel (known as S.C), (4) Devils (juniors), (5) Legal secretaries. If that all seems a 'top heavy,' it's actually not. If anything, it's not even close to being enough. Why do I think that? You see, under the Irish Constitution, we have an inherent provision known as "Equality of arms." In real terms, this means that if the state (D.P.P) has a solicitor, then you must also be provided with one, so you are both armed "equally." Sadly, this is a fairy tale in every trial situation. Whilst you are provided with a legal team of equal standing, Barrister vs. Barrister, etc., that's where the tampering of the judicial weights and measures begins. Tony Collier – brilliant though he is – is one man. The director (D. P. P) is absolutely legion, a team of prosecutors, heavyweights, the entirety of the Garda's and ownership of state pathologists and a plethora of other governmental agencies with limitless resources, all, "impartial" as a North Korean Election. Let's not even go into the state-sponsored "independent" media at this juncture.

It's now only years after the fact that I know this, but back then, back in the day, it was scratchy new and frustratingly confusing. It took a lot of painstaking meetings with Tony to try and familiarize myself with what was a whole new world for me, and only when I had the most basic grasp of the legal fundamentals did we go through the process of Barrister selection. Tony set up a meeting at the C.C.J. with a senior counsel by the name of Brendan Grehan. I didn't know it at the time, but he is usually the go-to – guy for the D.P.P. and even without that knowledge, he didn't "smell" right. Our meeting with him went okay but only okay. Tony seemed quite excited by it, though, and grabbed me for a quick word afterwards:

"So, Dave, how do you think that meeting went?"

"Yeah, went well, I suppose."

"What do you think of Brendan? He is one of the best in Ireland!"

"I'm not sure, Tony; let me sleep on it, will you?"

"Eh, sure, okay… yeah."

He was a bit put out, I suppose and in retrospect, I don't really blame him. He was fresh out of a big-city firm, I was his fledging but highest-profile client and he'd managed to secure some free time for us with one of the heaviest hitters in the business. It was a major coup for him to even get that far and I could see his strategy. Having his client defended by an Apex Litigator was a statement of his intent going forward. The only stain on his otherwise immaculate tablecloth was… me! Still, I'm a man of my word, so sleep on it I did;

"Morning, Tony."

"Good morning, Dave. Did you sleep on it?"

"I did, sorry Tony, but he's not for me."

"Okay, Dave, thanks for letting me know."

I know what you're probably thinking and to be fair, I'm sure Tony was not too happy about having to let a little air out of Grehan's inflated ego, but you've got to go with your instincts no matter how out of character with the rest of the world they may appear to be.

It took another few weeks, but fair play to Tony. He managed to get another legal Titan into the ring for us to spar with. This time, it was a man by the name of Michael O'Higgins S.C. The meeting went… okay. He was clearly a man with a super-high IQ, and his verbal range was as tough as honeyed Gravel. No doubt, he was a formidable man. He also came from thoroughbred legal bloodstock, so he had that whole 'legacy' thing about him. Once again, Tony grabbed me on the way out:

"I think that went very well for us, Dave."

"Yeah, it was a good meeting."

"So, what did you think about him?"

"Tony, can I sleep on it?"

"Sure."

He must've been fit to strangle me, but you know what I'm like by now. I slept on it, and then Tony gave another early morning phone call;

"Okay, Tony, he's the man for us."

"Why is that?"

"He just is."

"Oh ... Okay."

In fairness to Tony, he didn't push me any further on it. He was probably afraid of whatever other nonsense I'd come out with and decided to leave well enough alone!

I'll say one thing about O'Higgins, he's thorough. We had meeting after meeting after meeting with him. When I say "we," I mean myself, Tony, Audrey and O'Higgins himself. Oh, and when I say "meetings," what I really mean is "consultation," as I was consistently reminded of, but to me, a meeting is a meeting. As we were living way out west, it wasn't always possible for Audrey to attend every meeting, but she was there for more than she missed. That intense level of contact lasted for over a year. This is not to be confused with a complaint. I'm just telling you how it was. Busy-right? That wasn't even half of it. My second hip operation didn't turn out to be a success, so I had to squeeze consultations between visits to both the Cappagh and Beaumont hospitals... on the family walking stick!

So, busy – busy - right? Nope, not nearly enough because somewhere in that time between the minutes, I had to fit in a couple of court appearances. These are basically excuses for a lot of highly paid legal eagles to turn up at court, whip out their diaries and try to agree on a date (or dates) they were free to squash my little case into why this can't be done even the phone or by e-mail is beyond me, unless the cynical side of me is correct, and they do it in open court because they are paid a full hourly rate for each minute they spend in court. Think about it – you can't argue a case today (for example) because you're busy in court to talk about your diary. You are too busy for a trial until at least 3 months. Why? Because most of your court time is taken up by appearances with your diary, to say how busy you are! It's comedy. God, Laurel and Hardy's railway station gag wouldn't have a patch on it. Only it's not a funny story, that's our wonderful court system. I must've looked like a golden goose to them because once they got tired of arguing over whose diary was fuller and agreed on a trial date, I went and threw a spanner in the works on medical grounds because of my hip! Oh, and then we had to wait to receive my 'book of evidence.' This is more properly known as "The Book of Documents." But I don't even think your common or golden variety solicitor would know what a book of documents was anymore. So – whatever you want to call it- What is it? I hear you ask. Like most things in the legal world, it's not very straightforward.

Let's start at the beginning. In every criminal investigation, the first tool out of the police toolbox is a pen, closely followed by a sheet of paper. These are the tools of the trade used for taking statements. The taking of statements constitutes a massive amount of police time, way more than you'd think. Once a statement is signed/countersigned etc., it is sent off for processing. This usually involves typing up a copy of the handwritten version numbered and filed. Eventually, these statements make their merry way to the office of the D.P.P. where they are collated into a massive mess of unorganized ring binders which will someday become your "Discovery documents" and will be dumped on you with reckless and inconsistent abandon to literally, bury you with paperwork whilst you try to work through your book of evidence (let's just call it that). Your book of evidence is the collection of cherry-picked statements highlighting the section of statements (buried in full in your discovery) that best encapsulate your history of Evil-bastardness. It doesn't even have to be real; I actually know of cases where statements about "Ghosts" telling people who killed them have been included in a book of evidence. This, of course, would never see the light of a courtroom jury because the testimony of a ghost wouldn't be "probative." That's yet another fancy legal term, which, in essence, means that you can't call the ghost up on the stand for cross-examination. For obvious reasons, although it would be funny, wouldn't it? Anyway, the D.P.P will sprinkle your B.O.E with non-sense such as that for two reasons: (1)- in the hope that it somehow gets seen by a superstitious juror (in which case a guilty verdict is all but certain) and (2) – to appear "reasonable" when your defence team has to object to it going before a jury. It also works as a misdirection, distracting you from the stuff. This is why you'll never properly have equality of arms, as you'd need.

A small army just to keep pace with the forces of the state. They not only know this; they rely on it and hey – it works.

Your B.O.E will also contain maps, photographs (blurred piss-poor photocopy quality), spreadsheets - you name it, it's in there and none of its good. Now, given all of the many resources available to the state, it would be unthinkable for them to be late in getting your B.O.E to you, wouldn't it? Well, if they gave it to you on time, what would all the media vultures do? So, No- it's always late, that way, those bottom-feeding parasites can take five million unnecessary photos of you coming to and leaving court. This, in turn, continues "the narrative," which is as subtle as it is dangerous. You see, your average punter will read their usual paper every day and after a while, all they'll see is that "Evil Brute" Dave Mahon in court. Again... again... and again. At some basic level, they'd be forgiven for thinking that "that Dave Mahon fella is a bit of serial criminal," sure, he's always in court. Now, if your reaction to that is, "So what?"... well, you've got a point until you consider that the jury pool, your average punter, has now been exposed to and contaminated by "the narrative." Dangerous, isn't it? What's more, nobody ever sees it coming until it's too late. Well, dear reader, not anymore, right?! How long do you think it took for my case to come to trial from day one? If you said a year, you'd be wrong. What about two years, that huge passage of time? Nope, believe it or not, it took 3 years, enough time to begin secondary school - study for and sit a junior certification exam.

Okay, so now I had my court date and we were steamrolling along with me about as prepared as I was ever going to be. The stress that myself and Audrey were going through was intense, but hey-what else was new? Our family and friends were also living on their nerves, especially my long-suffering father. But at no point did we ever lose sight of what all of this was about. Poor Dean. He had a whole other side of his family who were also having to go through hell; his loss was felt on many levels and a lot of families had been destroyed by his death. I've never forgotten that and I hope that someday we can – each of us feel the soothing balm of healing in one form or another. Nobody knows better than me that there are no winners in this case and there never will be.

I can remember my Barrister asking me at one point if I wanted to plead guilty to manslaughter. What a bloody question to be asked ever - but that was what my life had become. Jesus, where to start?

"I don't know what manslaughter is. Is it not the same as murder?"

Turns out it's not. He not only had to explain what manslaughter was but also what murder was, too. They aren't exactly words or terms you'd benefit by looking up in your pocket Oxford or Collin's dictionary either. All you'll glean from them is that manslaughter;

"It is the crime of killing someone without meaning to."

Whereas murder;

"It is the deliberate killing of a person."

Simple, right? Well… No. In Irish case law, the go-to authority frequently cited is a 1970 case- The people (D.P.P) Vs Brophy, where Mr. Justice Pringle directed the jury as follows;

"If you're satisfied, beyond reasonable doubt, that the accused intended to kill or to cause serious injury to Anna Porter (the victim), then you must convict him of murder, if you are not so satisfied, then you convict him of manslaughter."

Doesn't really help either, does it? Somehow, somewhere, some bright spark decided that the process wasn't complicated enough, so now we have "voluntary" and "involuntary" cases of manslaughter and then, resting at a lower level, we now have "corporate" manslaughter and "accidental death." If I got up on my soapbox, I'd fill this and other books with further definitions and arguments for and against each type of category, but that's not the point of my story. So, I'll leave it at that for now. What is actually relevant is that I was charged with murder, which, as anyone can clearly see from the above definitions, is ludicrous. I'll never believe any other reason for this inflated charge other than the fact that I had been in the public eye and spoken out about our lazy, useless authorities and their apathy (at best). About Amy, so vociferously even the best of Irish cops (of which there are many) knew that I wasn't guilty of murder, not in a million years. Once my legal team has explained at some length – what the law has to say about the ins and outs of what constitutes murder charges and the various manslaughter levels. I felt dizzy and was asked once again about offering up a plea of manslaughter. As is my will, I asked for a bit of time to ponder over my options. I had a few weeks to do so anyway, so why not use them?

The truth, as always, is very simple. I'm not a murderer. I wasn't guilty of murder in any way, shape or form. Not morally, not technically, not legally. Was I guilty of manslaughter? Morally and ethically, I'd have to say "No," but legally…? I was struggling to fit square pegs into round holes. Dean was dead. His life ended as a result of something I did. It was not a pre-meditated or intentional act. I held a knife; a fresh occurrence took place and he died tragically. It has all the hallmarks of a stupid accident because some idiot – me- was holding a knife in his hand. If you have to make a choice between the Devil and the deep blue sea, you'd better know how to swim. I do and I also had a team of lifeguards ready to throw me a floatation device if it came to it. Murder- if found guilty – carries but one sentence- life in prison. Manslaughter carries anything from a couple of years all the way up to Life, so a manslaughter plea- although calling – was the only intelligent choice.

Even the cops, when they interviewed me, kept banging on and on about "self–defence" like it was all some sort of game for them. It wasn't and isn't for me; it's the harsh and biting reality I've got to live with, but at no stage did they bandy the word "murder" around. For me, it was, is, and always will be an accidental death, but that wasn't on the table. I bit the bullet and called my legal team to give them the authorization to offer a plea for manslaughter. This was still a few months away from the appointed court date, so I'd be saving everyone a lot of headaches and the trauma of a trial. I knew in my heart that I was screwing myself over, but I also knew that it was for the greater good. All I had to do now was wait for the formality of the D.P.P. to accept and then thrash out. An agreed sentence for me to serve. The call came soon enough and I found my way back into Town to meet with the legal team.

"Dave, the D.P.P. have refused to accept your plea."

It was the only time since I'd met O'Higgins that I found him completely lost for words. Tony Collier was absolutely shocked and stupefied. I was sick to my stomach; this reality didn't look good for me at all. It was a bold and very aggressive move by the state; they were telling us in no uncertain terms that my case was a slam dunk. They never even considered a compromise. Oh. Shit.

Now, I really was facing life in prison. Regardless of the utter shit you are used to reading in the news, "life" in Ireland realistically runs at about 18 years for your average prisoner. For a high-profile case such as mine, you could throw at least another 7 years on top of that. So, all told, I'd be lucky to be out in 25 years. You might as well put 3 bullets into a gun – one for me, one for Audrey (not even her heart could survive that), and with us gone, you may as well shoot Amy, as she'd be forgotten about as she has been only for Audrey and my efforts. Even some of the brightest legal minds were saying off- the record- that my murder change and no-deal attitude was fuelled by my public persona.

Some of the closest people in my life   Audrey, Mick, family and friends   had all said to me at some point that I wanted to go to prison. That my sense of right and wrong was such that I wanted to be punished. I denied their allegations every single time, but when I reflected with honesty on the whole situation, I think they were actually right. Deep down, I needed to pay a price, so I'll have to admit that sometimes my loved ones know me better than I know myself. Still, now I at least knew that I had a murder trial – not manslaughter- to prepare for and I was never so grateful to have such a tight, professional and strong legal team together. Then, just three weeks before my trial, Tony called:

"Dave, I'm sorry, but I have bad news."

"What now?"

"We need to find you another senior counsel."

"What?? Why?"

"Well, you know that whole Anglo–Irish tribunal riots on?"

"Yeah."

"Well, you know the way that's sometimes called the …"

"…O'Higgins case shit."

"Yeah, exactly, he's completely tied up with that."

"Tony, if I'd have known that there was even the slightest possibility of him doing this, I would never have agreed to use him."

This was a real setback because I'd invested a lot of time, energy and trust into this guy. But the reality of the situation was that I was little Dave Mahon from working class nowhere and the Anglo case was full of highfalutin tycoons and paid out millions of Euro in legal fees. When you look at that statue of old lady Justice sitting atop the four courts building, blindfolded with a sword in one hand and scales in the other, try to remember that those scales are for weighing silver (the currency of betrayal since the bible times) and not justice, not any more anyway. Dear reader, I was not a happy bunny, not by a long way. I had poured my heart out – as I told everything to this guy for over a year – about the tragic death of our son Dean. It doesn't get more personal than that, but do you know something - we've always been realists.

In the early days of Amy's disappearance, we had money, more money than we'll ever have again and we knew even then that we were only able to get a lot of stuff done because of that. It's why we always went the extra mile for the families of other missing children, as "there, but for the grace of God go!" The amount of times we'd heard about "good karma" because of that were too many to count, but what we did wasn't about bloody karma; it was simply the right thing to do. Now it appeared that every bank on the planet – even the bank of good karma – was out to screw me ever just as I was fighting for my life of freedom. We were now the "have not's" and there was nobody stepping up to help us out. The lone voice of reason outside of our close-knit unit of friends and family- was Tony Collier. Above and beyond his call of duty, I didn't immediately appreciate that, though;

"Come on, Dave, we're still on track!"

"How?"

"Dave, this is actually a common practice. It happens all the time."

"Well, it shouldn't."

"Don't worry; I'll get you another Barrister!"

"You'll forgive my lack of enthusiasm about that."

"Look, I'll see about getting the court date put back again."

"For fuck's sake, Tony, it's been 3 years already, that's not fair on anybody."

More sleepless nights for Audrey and me. We wouldn't have known what to do with a night's sleep back then if we'd gotten one anyway. Insomnia was the new "normal" for us. "Don't worry!" That's what Tony had said, the one true statement that makes me worry: I don't know about you. Worry? I'd earned a 3rd Dan black belt at it by that stage.

Tony arranged yet another meeting/consultation for me, this time away from the fetid C.C.J and at the law centre building on Church Street in Dublin city centre. At least, that was a positive step. I was about to meet my new counsel – senior and junior- and without any hint of flippancy intended. Tony didn't just pick up the Yellow Pages and pull a couple of legal-sounding names out of it. To his credit, he scoured Dublin, then the rest of Ireland, for the best one or at least a top 3 name that wasn't only available but also somebody that old fussy pants here could work and get along with. I trusted Tony – I still do. So, I knew that whoever it was we'd meet that day, would be good. There was a lot riding on the outcome of that meeting. So, I was glad to have Audrey with me because she's an excellent judge of character. I mean, she married me, didn't she?!! The clock was ticking against us again, so as I pushed open the door into the meeting- I took a deep breath, composed myself and made a mental note to turn on my heels. If I didn't get the right vibe, no more time wasters.

The first sight that I remember was that of a giant. If Tony was the Jack Russell, then Sean Guerin (S.C) was a fearless bear. He stood at least 6' 3." And despite the size difference, there was a certain symmetry between himself and Tony. In that – to me, Tony "looks" like a solicitor and by that same logic, Sean "looks" like a Barrister. I'd like to say that we shook hands like gentlemen, but my tiny paw just got lost in his catcher's mitt of an Appendage! You shouldn't – but we all do judge books by their covers, so I immediately approved of what I saw. As for my new junior - John Fitzsimons (BL) - well, he was the sort of Barrister. I took an instant liking to him, too. His looks, personality and presence dominated even that room. I heard him speak for all of 2 seconds before confirming in my mind that this guy wasn't just smart; he was scalpel sharp. I examined the room – Sean, John, Tony, Audrey - and me. Word of advice: when your life is on the line, always surround yourself with people more intelligent than you are. I was definitely the kid in that room to sit in the corner with the conical dunce's hat on my head, which is good.

"Well, Dave, did you like Sean?"

"He's good."

"How do you feel it went in there?"

"Honestly, as well as it could have."

"Can I take that as a yes or…"

"Let me think about it over the weekend."

"Sure, but know this, it's at the stage now where I'll be seeking another adjournment if I need to find someone else, okay?"

You've heard the expression- "life-changing decision" about as many times as I have, but seldom did it ever hold such resonance for me. It's a horrible position to be in, as you're not alone. I had Audrey, Mick, friends and family- but it's a lonely choice. No one else can make it for you; it comes down to you alone. Just like prison, only you will be doing the time, so you've got to embrace that alien mindset. I had our health to consider, the pain for everyone involved and most importantly, justice for Dean. I called Tony;

"Let's do it, Tony, tell Sean and John."

"Dave, believe me – you've made the right decision."

Guess what happened next- consultation after consultation – and trust me, that went on forever. We had no time and everything to fit into it, so they were intense. I had to relive that fearful night over and over, like a weird Twilight Zone story where a guy was frozen in the same horrific memory, destined to experience it. And experience it forever. Some people think that once the deed is done, then it's done and that there's no justice for the victims. They're wrong. In a case like mine, I'm not only the perpetrator (I despise even hearing that term) I'm also a "victim." Now, I have put queries in there for a reason. Realistically – Dean and only Dean – is the victim because he was the person who lost his life. He is the only victim in the sense of the definite article- "the" victim. Everybody else falls into the category of the indefinite article- "a" victim only, that's not true, in practical terms, because Audrey carried him, birthed him, mothered and raised him. They shared more than D.N.A.; they once existed as one person. So, to my mind, Audrey is the only living person who can properly be described as a victim in the sense of a definite article. I loved Dean (still do), he was my stepson and I miss him more than I ever thought possible, but I'm only 'a' victim in that sense. As bizarre as that sounds, I've suffered because of his death and not "just" because I'm responsible. I'm also the only person who -because of the legal process- had to retell the events of his death and had to see the photographs of his body, his injury and even his autopsy. I'll never articulate this strongly enough, but there are certain things you'd never ever want to see that you can never unsee or forget and in every dark hour for the rest of your life - those horrific images come back and haunt you. If you put those images on a table with a loaded gun beside it, I'd eat the gun every time rather than look again at even one of those photographs. So, when I tell you that my legal meetings were intense, that's what I mean.

Before we knew it, the court date counted down from months to weeks to days, I had to put my 3rd hip operation back a few months; many thanks to Dr. Denis Collins, my orthopaedic surgeon for that. Now, all I needed to do was to find somewhere to lay down my head because making my way up and down from court every day by train wasn't an option. Neither was staying at my father's house, not that I wouldn't have been welcome. Rather it was to spare him medical bombardment that followed me around constantly like shite on the soles of my shoes, their repulsive stink was everywhere. My only real option was to surreptitiously check myself and Audrey into a city centre hotel for the 3 weeks that my trial was expected to last. I must extend every praise to that hotel and its excellent staff for catering to our very specific need for privacy up to and including the use of private rooms for the occasional legal meeting. Given the 24-hour "Sky News – Breaking story" style surveillance I was under, it was a fest of stealth in itself to have remained (somehow) undetected, don't you think?

My Cloverhill experience was still raw, but it did teach me a few things, one of which was how difficult it is to wear a wedding band in prison. They – more often than not – are taken off you, or worse, if I did get convicted and sent to prison and something happened to it, I'd never forgive myself. So, it was something that was on my mind and I came across what I believed to be the perfect solution. I got a wedding ring type tattoo (not the design but the size and shape) on my wedding finger. That was something that they couldn't take off me, or that I could lose... unless I was really careless!! It also gave me something to joke with when Audrey was feeling a bit down, daring her to "show some commitment" too, and other silly stuff like that, anything to lighten the mood, I suppose. The morning when my trial began, for instance.

We got up early that particular morning, dressed casually and went downstairs to the hotel buffet for breakfast. We enjoyed 2 full English fries and copious amounts of tea, I don't know if it was because of nervous energy of whatever, but I wasn't expecting us to eat quite so well, but we did. Sometimes, nothing happens as you imagine it would. When we were all fed and watered, we retired back up to our room, lay on bed and didn't move a muscle. Not even to talk, nothing. Such prolonged silences were very unusual for us, but they signified the importance of what awaited us. So, we just lay there in silence, watching the clock. It was another Twilight Zone experience because time had turned upside down, minutes didn't exist and hours lasted seconds. I had never known time to pass so quickly and to this day, I haven't experienced anything like it again. I showered first, then Audrey and everything was still silent. My phone didn't even ping once, again -strange, again-not to my liking. The hotel kindly agreed to call a taxi for us and at the rate that time was moving for us, it got there far too quickly. Sod's law, the taxi was bizarrely early; still, we didn't want to be late, not for court, not for a murder trial. Not for my murder trial. We climbed into the back of the taxi.

"Well, I don't need to ask where you two are going!"

"What?"

"You're off the C.C.J."

"Yeah, how did you know that?"

"How did I bleedin' know??!"

"Yeah, did the hotel tell you?"

"(Laughing) No-the whole bleedin' country knows!!"

"Oh..."

We were back to our deadly silence again, but the taxi driver was laughing and joking. I knew what he was trying to do. A million years ago, I'd sit where he sat and did what he was doing. It was actually a sign of a good taxi driver, put your passengers at ease and make their journey as pleasant as possible, but nothing and nobody would've succeeded in taking our minds off the horrible, awful situation we were in. Fair play to him for trying, though.

We received our usual red-carpet welcome when we arrived at the C.C.J., a plethora of reporters and photographers who looked like a swarm of angry Cyclops with flashing ray-vision. I asked Audrey – not my first or last dumb question;

"Do you think they're all here for us?"

Fair play to Audrey. With the look, she gave me, an oral bolking wasn't needed! The day continued in its unique and extraordinary way because not one reporter even asked a single question. It was all about getting our photographs; how many more would they need on top of the thousand they already had? We'd only have so many sets of clothes and so many different facial expressions between us, so what's the point? Remember, you dare not smile, or you're a heartless one to the press - "smiling killer" and the rest of the inflated horror lines that permeate the filthy rinse cycle of the news outlets. What a way to earn a living. There's a lot to be said for those guys who jerk off horses at stud farms collecting equine semen, I guess.

Tony Collier met us outside the C.C.J., where we had a brief discussion before walking in together. My father and sister, Dory, were in there already waiting for us, so it was wonderful to have their support. My sister took a few weeks off work and a break from her grown-up children (5 of them!) She was there to support me and she attended every painful day of it. I'm proud and privileged to say that I enjoyed great support over the course of my trial from our network of close friends. Some even made their way over from Spain. There was also a section of good friends who were only there in spirit due to the bloody media again - and who could blame them for that? We certainly didn't. We wouldn't wish the front-page photo of a red top on our enemies, let alone the people we love. By the way, this might be some way to dilute the "narrative" for the next high-profile murder trial you follow, where the accused looks like a weird loner with no friends or support – it's probably not that way at all, just the various arms of the 'judicial' machine pulling together.

Waiting around the C.C.J, for your case to be called, surrounded by solicitors and Barristers milling around like their expensive legal britches were on fire, is a very daunting experience. We didn't know what way was up but felt every eye in the place checking us out judgmentally, the looks of recognition that -yes- that was the Evil Bastard David Mahon back in court. Again, wondering what it was, I was up for this time. Welcome to life in the goldfish bowl; be careful not to drown. We got called; it was show-time, so we walked into the court as a family unit, a united front. The court was packed to the rafters, jammed with noise and chatter- until they noticed us, then the hushed whispers, sneaky pointed fingers, and the not-so-subtle stare of the crowd of attendees, primed by months of Garda propaganda, the code of the sin watching small town that is Ireland. We ignored their puritanical disdain as best we could and sat down together. For less than a minute, Tony had to remind me to sit up in the dock; the perch of every would be jail-bird. Silence. Uncomfortable silence. But at least the relative dimensions of time had folded back into sync; minutes dragged post until the courtroom tip-staff entered the Fray, block capes flowing like a drunken crow;

"All rise! Silence in the court, the honourable judge…"

472

To be honest, with the noise of an entire courtroom jumping to its feet and the rustling of paper – together with my own nervousness – that's all I heard except for the word "presiding" near the end. Then, the judge walked in. My judge. The person whose life had been deemed to rule over the rest of mine. I know her. We had history and none of it was good. Judge Margaret Heneghan. Oh, shit! This was a bad start, I'd entered the judicial lottery and drawn out the booby prize. Our eyes met briefly and it was enough for her to bare her teeth in a rictus of animal hatred. This was the absolute wagon who wouldn't allow me to go back to Spain in my quest to find Amy by refusing me access to my passport. Even her peers had allowed me before because the world and its brother knew that I always came back. Always. She was so unreasonable. We appealed her passport refusal. Who presided over that appeal? She did!! How can that even be legal??! So, she sat back and considered whether to uphold her own decision or to over-rule herself. I lost that appeal. I put on a brave face, but to be honest, my body let me down. My legs went as weak as noodles.

She kicked things off by way of a welcoming speech to the court, then to the jury and then asked both sides for their opening statements. The prosecution -the ones who always bring the actual case - started first, and then the defence team have their say. It's all quite formal, a lot of dotting the I's and crossing the T's, to be honest. Then, the jury (having been whittled down to 12 from a much larger pool of empanelled individuals) is sworn in, which is a very long and protracted process in and of itself. Once again, it's not like it is in the movies; even though you'd be forgiven for thinking you were in a bloody movie, the whole thing is so alien and otherworldly, you know, the type of thing that only happens to other people? We finished early that first day, not too much else of any note happened that I can remember. All those months of anxious build-up for a first day (half day) like that? So, what did I take away from that experience? What did I learn?

A couple of things: first, there is so much pomp and circumstance, you'd be forgiven for Downton Abbey comparisons, I kid you not. Second, my judge – from previous dealings with her was never going to be fair or impartial. We watched each other like hawks over a rabbit hole. Our distrust was mutual. I caught her stealing a few loathsome glances at me, at the crowd and at the jury throughout. At the end of the day, even judges are human, but they are meant to act without fear or favour and certainly shouldn't judge books by their covers, but she did. Random thought entered my mind as I took all this in, alone up there, sitting on the dock. For example, I couldn't think of a case where this is true – you never hear about blind judges, do you? I mean, "Justice is blind" (I'll call bullshit on that), but I've never heard of a blind judge. I personally believe that a blind judge

473

would make a fairer one; no more book covers to prejudice their opinion, only the hearing of evidence.

Audrey and I joined back to our hotel with the pleasurable company of Mick, a few friends and no reporters! When everyone went home for the day, I went down to the bar on my own for a quiet pint of Guinness. Just as I lifted the creamy head of St. Arthur's own nectar to my thirsty lips, the 9 o'clock news came on;

"Good evening, the headlines – Dave Mahon's murder trial..."

Bollox. My name, footage of me walking into and out of court with Audrey. Great. Just marvellous. So much for a quiet pint. You develop a 6th sense; you feel people's eyes on you. At first, you think it's paranoia, but then you soon discover that it isn't. The girl serving behind the bar came over to me;

"Is that you on the television?"

"Yes (any minute now, she's going to call me a scumbag or something)."

"Ah! My boyfriend knows you!"

"(I wasn't expecting that) Does he?"

"Yeah! He spent some time in prison with you before!"

"I'm sorry, but you must be mistaken."

"Why?"

"Well, I've never been in prison before…"

"Yeah, you were, you were taken into Cloverhill and…"

(How did I manage to forget that??)

"…. he told me that you were alright and you'd had a laugh together..."

"I'm sorry, you're absolutely right! What was his name?"

(She said a name that I didn't recognise.)

"No, what was he in for?"

(She told me.)

474

"Ah yeah! I do remember him, he's a funny bloke!"

What a lovely lady she was! It mustn't have been easy for her to approach me and trust me with such personal information, but I was glad she did. It was also a wake-up call as to what was going on around me. Cloverhill had been a very difficult experience for me and yet I'd forgotten about it in the foe of trial stress and publicity. Holy shit – what the hell else was I forgetting? Worrying times.

People can be so loving and so giving, just like the lady working behind the bar. Audrey and I have experienced complete strangers coming up to us on the street and hugging us, wishing us well and giving us good-luck messages, even in the C.C.J. The amount of times I've heard people say that they'd light candles for us was amazing and I remember each and every one of them. They are such an uplifting experience and give us strength when we need it most. Even though I didn't share their optimism, I was so grateful for the "No way will you be going to prison" comments, too, because the mainstream media had worked tirelessly at painting me as Ireland's Jack-the Ripper or some other kind of monstrous entity that it did my heart good to receive positive, face-to-face feedback from real people. As always, the sad and lonely element of trolls - fingers and keyboards sticky with cat semen continued their cowardly basement crusades, but sure, what else can you expect from them? I didn't stay too long at the bar because I didn't want to leave Audrey on her own, but I was too restless to turn in early. I didn't know what to be doing with myself and it was God knows what time when I eventually put my head on the pillow.

Day 2 started off with such similarity to Groundhog Day that you'd be forgiven for thinking we were reliving it down the breakfast, up for a shower and so on. The first real change of the day was that we had a different taxi driver, but he still knew us and didn't need us to tell him where we were going. We had the usual stampede of reporters at the C.C.J, so we scrummaged our way through and I was back up on my perch in the dock before I knew it.

"All rise…"

Judge lonely Heneghan took her place at her own elevated perch, looking as beautiful as never, then squawked;

"Bring the jury down."

The jury of 12 citizens – honest and true, shuffled into place, took their seats and avoided eye-contacts with black and soul-less ocular cavities. I looked at my family for strength and couldn't help but notice Dean's other side of the family taking their seats. When all the people were there in place, the prosecution's counsel – Remy Farrell S.C – stood up and addressed the jury. I saw his mouth open, heard the words that came out of it, but couldn't believe my own ears. In my mind, I was in a movie and he was an actor reading from a poorly written script;

"David Mahon gutted Dean Fitzpatrick like a fish and left him to die."

Please read that again, dear reader, because I can't bear to write it, let alone rewrite it. I was shocked to my core. So was Audrey. So was my father. Come to think of it, a hushed silence descended over the entire courtroom. I gave Tony Collier my best "what the fuck??" glare and didn't process much else of 'oul Remy's' hate-filled bilge. You are told not to look at the jury, but I'm a people watcher and couldn't help myself. Every single one of their faces had 'shock' and 'guilty' etched into it. The verbal barrage continued relentlessly on;

"I ask you, how…"

"So, why is he…?"

"What the…"

"My God, the bastard did…"

On and on and on. Nothing prepares you for that, fuck me, I was in a trial now, I can tell you. Listening to the prosecution's case, I didn't even like myself. Relativity went walk-about again, seconds turned into hours; it felt like three weeks before the 1 o'clock break came. I had a meeting – don't even think of correcting me with "consultation" – word, Tony and my legal team. I wasn't even furious, I was angrier than I had ever been in my life, I didn't (couldn't) hold back.

"How dare you say that?"

"Why didn't you retaliate? You just sat there!!!"

"You didn't open your mouth!"

"Do I have the right legal team? Doesn't bleedin' look like it?"

"Do you know what, I'd be better off representing myself!"

"Even I would've known to stop that straight away…"

I think that it was at about that point when I had to stop to catch my breath, then Sean Guerin spoke;

"Dave, this is actually good news."

"What??? How the hell is THAT good news? Did you not hear what Remy Farrell said???"

"Dave..."

"What? Am I going mad or something?"

"Dave, this is normal practice, the prosecution gets up and puts the worst case forward. Then, after lunch, I get up and state the case for defence, which will be polar opposite of what went on earlier."

"Yeah right – whatever- the damage is already done. Didn't you see the look on everyone's face - everyone's - including my own???"

"Hold on, Dave."

"What?"

"Did you cut Dean like a fish?"

"How fucking dare you?"

"Did you???"

"No! No way. Nothing of the sort."

"That's good."

"How the fuck is that good??"

"Because Remy Farrell came out with a strong, hard-hitting and very dramatic statement. Its sole reason was to elicit that response. Exactly that response, in fact."

"Great, job done. Doesn't help me. Doesn't seem 'good' from my perspective."

"Yes, but David, it's not a statement of fact, is it?"

"No, not at all."

"So, another way of saying that is, it's not true, correct?"

"Yeah, it's a lie."

"So, it's not true and we're going to prove that."

"Okay?"

"Look, he knows he has a weak case, and now, we know - he knows it."

Honeyed words and reasonable counter argument – the stock in trade of any good Barrister – but I was still in the heights of it. Those words – lies though they are - will haunt me forever. We finished our business and headed off for lunch.

There was a bar-restaurant on Parkgate Street beside the C.C.J, so we went there. So did everybody else. The place was jammed full of solicitors and reporters, all there to order lunch, but food wasn't the craving on my pallet. I ordered a large brandy – and trust me on this – it never touched the sides. I couldn't eat; those words and the images they created in my mind, I thought I'd never be able to eat again. I could happily have had several larger brandies, and a little milk of amnesia to dull the pain, but that wasn't the time, the place or anything even close to being a good idea. I composed myself and then headed back into the C.C.J. It was my guy's time to speak, so I prayed that he was even half as good as Tony said he was. I sat up in the dock and waited. The judge was running a little late, no doubt a clever judicial tactic to let Remy Farrell's lies echo off the courtroom walls a little longer and continue contaminating the already Partisan mood.

"All rise…"

Ah, there she was again, looking about as angry and confused as ever.

"Call the jury back down."

They trundled back into position under her wrathful dragon's glare. She gave me a sidelong look of porcine lechery and held it more than long enough to let it burn into the minds of my jury. My senior, Sean Guerin, stood up and said his piece to the jury. This, dear reader, is where I let you down again – memory-wise – because Farrell's lies were all I could think of. I could trawl through my court transcripts and chisel out everything he said, word for word, but I won't because being through a murder trial once is enough for anyone. So, I'll just share a few snippets with you from my memory of the murder trial -in general- as we move on, hopefully, that will be enough. That court day couldn't end quickly enough. I'd never loathed being somewhere so much in life. I actually found it hard to breathe in there, and just wanted to get out of there so badly.

478

Mind you, leaving the C.C.J. that evening was no picnic, either. Every two-bit dime-store hack danced around us like demented dervishes, loving the copy-line we knew they were all going to run with social media erupted into an Inferno of vitriolic hatred and the top story on every news channel-radio and television-was the predictable one. I no longer desire to write. I asked Tony to join us back at the hotel for obvious reasons and we spent considerable time explaining and recriminating. I couldn't see any way out of the hole the prosecution's opening salvo put me in; even my normally reliable and logical lizard brain conceded the point – I was well and truly fucked. How much pain can one heart endure? First blood to Remy Farrell, he won day two by a landslide.

Day 3 started with a kick in Bollox. I turned on the news – Bang - ouch, still the lead story. Then the newspaper review – Bang - every paper crowed in unison and led with that horrific statement.

Two Bangs - one for each ball; it was no wonder neither of us could consume so much as a morsel of breakfast. I think we were still shell-shocked from the previous day. I can remember my thoughts;

"What the fuck is today going to bring?"

"This is only going to get worse."

Those opening statements wouldn't have been good for anyone who ever knew Dean, no matter what side of my nose they were sitting on. We made our usual taxi journey to the C.C.J, met the usual pack of media shit-vultures waiting outside and made our way in. Then we had our little conflate with my legal team;

"How are you? Dave? Audrey?"

"Words can't explain how we feel."

"Did you get any sleep last night?"

"A bit."

"Look, try not to think about yesterday, or the papers, or…."

"Easy for you to say, a bad name sticks like gum in your hair, and you're not the one on trial for your life, are you?"

I wasn't wrong. Neither was he. Weird, because nothing was right either. It was time to sit in the dock again.

"All rise…."

I got up slowly and with no enthusiasm, then watched glumly as the judge practically bounced joyfully out of her chambers, putting all the "ass" into class. She looked happy, but not in a good way. She gave me a strange look- like she'd been fucking someone, only didn't have half-enough yet. Oh yeah, I could count on her impartiality, all right.

"Bring down the jury, please…!"

Please? She was definitely playing to the crowd. I was a mouse; she was a cat, and she was toying with me before the kill. With a pre-existing atmosphere changed with suspense, a courtroom filled with hostile reporters, legal eagles, well-wishers, ill-wishers and many other tribes, it wouldn't be too difficult to see why she wanted to be the shining light in her own theatre. Just my luck to have an evil bitch of a judge who also had delusions of being a Hollywood star. What the hell was happening here?

The first witness called by the prosecution that day was the ambulance driver. The irony of an ambulance chaser of a Barrister calling an actual ambulance driver wasn't lost on me.

Anyway, the value of this witness was to explain what time he received the emergency call and how long it took for him to arrive at the scene. There were also a lot of details provided about what actions he undertook in trying to save Dean's life, things I'd prefer not to go into. There was another witness called from the Dublin Fire Brigade because they, too, attended the scene. Dublin Fire Brigade also being a provider of ambulance services for the city. The purpose of calling this particular witness was to establish certain facts. First is the time factor. As you know, I had already given the police several voluntary statements, telling them exactly what happened. The state would've loved nothing more than to "catch me out" on my timings to prove what a liar I was because if I was a liar, then what else was I? A murderer, perhaps? It also afforded the prosecution every opportunity to feed the Lurid headline snatchers blood, gore and details with which to splash across their sensationalist shit-rags. Anything to fuel the narrative and indoctrinate the masses: Dave-Bad, State-Good. Never underestimate the shock value of such evidence on a jury, either. So, for three days - into my murder trial - all people knew about was Dean being "gutted like a fish" and the blood-soaked crime scene the paramedics arrived into, their brave efforts proving worthless to reverse the brutality of "Evil Dave." No jury in the world was going against the narrative at that point, even if my timings had been proven true, which they were.

The next batches of witnesses concerned what are known as "civilians" that is, not medical or trained professionals. This group mainly concerned the passers-by who witnessed Dean falling down and/or seeing him on the ground bleeding to death. There was a local restaurant nearby and it was mostly patrons from this establishment that provided all this evidence. I have no problem with these people for telling the truth, but I hated how the state kept emphasising the word 'blood' and how 'tragic' it was and how they must've been "scarred" and "repulsed" by what they saw on their way home. Farrell wouldn't give two shits about any of them, he was drip-feeding those words to the jury every chance he got. A sickened juror is a hateful juror, one who'll only ever vote on the side of guilt. He was doing the devil's work well and with a smug look on his face the whole time. Judge Heneghan looked on at him with the sort of adoration you'd expect from a teenage crush. I looked over at Audrey in despair. Her look back at me said it all – "you and me against the world." She was right.

Next up, came the boys in blue, the po-po themselves, our wonderful police force. Have you ever seen a cop on the street? Of course, you have. Now, have you ever seen that same cop on the stand in a court? Chalk and cheese, dear friends, chalk and cheese. I couldn't help but think I was looking at a parade of first communion pupils from Templemore College, as they turned up pretty; polished hairs all in place and in dress uniforms all scratchy new. This, too, is all part of the narrative Cops-Good, Cops-Clean, Dave-Bad. The more cops you can throw in front of a jury, the guiltier you look. Why? Simple, it's because we are hard-wired to think that cops are good. Sure, you'll get the occasional rogue, but not 5 of them… or 10… or 20. Here's the thing, we are right to think that way! Here's the other thing, the majority of cops giving evidence at a murder trial are only there to confirm a chain-of-evidence. Basic stuff, like, "I stood at my post for 6 hours and was relieved by Garda Murphy." Garda Murphy then provided his evidence- "I relieved Garda Byrne, then stood at my post for 6 hours and was then relieved by Garda O'Brien" and on and on this goes. Here's what the jury sees - A clean-cut, polite, well-turned-out Army of public "Hero" protectors making a public stand against me!!

Then there are the other police witnesses, the worst kind when you're sitting in the dock on a murder charge. These are the real heroes, the ones who "caught" me and brought me to justice. You see, the truth gets buried by the narrative drip by drip. I no longer handed myself in, they caught me. Sure, I did walk into Coolock Garda station, but only because I knew they were on to me, I knew it was only a matter of time. Then, they broke me. I thought that I was some kind of a hard man, refusing to answer all of their questions, but they're harder men, so much smarter.

Their tried and tested methods broke me down and I confessed. Not to "murder" of course, because that was a lie too far even for them. But the "confession" to murder was implied. This is all to undermine the case for the defence because any right-minded person would question why there was a need for a trial at all, hadn't I already confessed to it? Why was that Dave Mahon fella' wasting everyone's time?? This is exactly the reason for having a legal team and why cross-examination is so important. It was a very long and tiring day at court. There was a lot of factual information present and a lot of inaccurate innuendo implied and checked in that order. As exhausting as it was, I knew I wouldn't be getting much sleep that night, too much discussion about blood – Dean's blood-for me to deal with. I've seen dozens of television interviews with other authors being asked about their books, and in particular autobiographies;

"So tell me Tom/Dick/Harry, what was it like writing your book?"

"Well, it was very therapeutic…"

Always the same Q&A or variations thereof. To me, that's not only lazy, it's grossly inaccurate. There is absolutely nothing therapeutic to me in having to drag up all of these painful, horrific memories and get them down on paper. It's hell on earth. Spare a thought for Audrey; this is her first-born child we're talking about.

Day four started sometime after day three, but it didn't begin with either myself or Audrey waking up because we hadn't slept. All the legal people can just pack their briefcases, go home to their family, eat dinner, have a regular evening and go to their bed. The same applies to the jury, the cops and most of the spectators. The journalists would file a copy, go to the pub and bribe bent coppers for yet more leaks, then have family time and go to bed. Audrey and I lived - and continue to live - with this all day, every day for the rest of our lives. We couldn't file our emotions into a locked briefcase or file them with a fast, cigar-chewing editor. My trial and Dean's death - on top of Amy's continued disappearance – was our life. No hiding from it or running away, or otherwise avoiding it. When the D.P.P. deliberately bathed their narrative in blood and shocking gore that was Dean's blood, Audrey's blood. So our blood. When the media sensationalised the various gruesome details, they were (and are) our details. Remember, this "bloodied object" was a brother; a father; a son and grandson. He was a friend, a stepson, an employee, a neighbour, a partner. He grew up the same way we all did. Infant → child→ teenager → adult. Think about all of those baby photos - all those memories. Dean Fitzpatrick was a human being. He was loved. He was the apple of Audrey's eye, he was Amy's big brother and he never recovered from her absence. He was hurt in a way very few brothers ever get hurt - thank God for that - and yes, he was a flawed individual, but show me someone who isn't? He dealt with things in his own way, he was his own man. I miss him. I miss him so fucking much it kills me, burns away at me and there's not a day passes when I couldn't beg for the chance to swap places with him. My hell isn't in the C.C.J. or behind any prison wall or any news bulletin. My hell is loving Dean and knowing I'll never see him again, never see him hug his mother again and never be the father he might've been because I held a knife. It's my fault. Until I die, that's my life, every second of every minute forever.

Day four was a no-breakfast day. It was a minimal conversation morning where Audrey jumped into the shower first. I pottered around our empty bedroom, got my clothes and shower, got bits together whilst hating myself all over again. Then I saw it. An empty vodka bottle. Fuck, fuck, fuck, fuck, fuck. Audrey had been off the booze for nigh on three years, her own death sentence butter flying into her life every time she felt a twinge in her liver, now this. This proxy court case had pushed her over the edge. My court case. My fucking fault. I love Audrey all the way, no half measures, if she... look, nothing can happen to her, it's that simple. But what could I say to her? Who the hell was I to say anything to her after what I'd done? It was obvious that she didn't want to tell me, so I'd respect that. If she wanted to tell me, she would. There was a wave of disappointment washing over me - not at Audrey - but because of what my actions were doing to her. If a couple of Vodkas were what she needed to face the unending horror we had to face every day, then so be it. I don't actually know another soul on this little planet of ours who could've handled Audrey's life and not ended it. For the most part, she's as soft as a baby's yawn but teak-tough where you'd least expect it. She needed every last drop of those reserves for what lay ahead.

"All rise…"

Judge Heneghan swooped out her coffin, flapped her black bat wings and settled on her throne of judgement for the fourth consecutive day of our hate-hate relationship.

"Bring the jury down…."

She sounded meaner than ever and wore a face like an explosion in a shirt factory. I think it was at that exact moment, just as the jury looked at her and instinctively reached for crosses and wooden stakes, that the last vestiges of any lingering hope for judicial leniency flew straight out of the courtroom window. I settled into my seat as uncomfortably as a hen in a fox-house, it was going to be another long day.

First up today for the prosecution were the employees from Ben Dunnes Gym up in Santry. This, of course, was the gym I was at on the day my water bottle was taken. The previous day, when the "hero cops" took the stand, they made a massive song and dance about it. That's something that they do, my friends, especially in cases like mine, where they have to juggle a shortage of back-story and a surfeit of plot. According to their testimony (under oath, don't forget), I was

"…........... incensed about the theft of his plastic bottle…."

"…...........He was angry alright, so angry he was roaring, shouting and abusive …………"

"…………. His whole manner became aggressive, threatening even ...."

"…......... even returned with a very large friend of his – over 6 feet tall, with a bald head and a strong, powerful build-to give out some more…"

When I heard all that, I was too shocked to react. Jesus, maybe I was a psychopath? How come I had no memory of any of this? I didn't believe it, but it had to be true, why else would they call the guys from the gym, unless it was to corroborate their evidence?

I recognised their faces, although I didn't know them personally. It was the young chap I spoke to initially at the reception desk and then the manager whom I'd spoken to later that day. To their great credit, they turned up, swore on oath to tell the whole truth, and did exactly that. By the way, the opposite practice - lying under oath - is illegal and known as perjury. It can (and should) carry a custodial sentence, because it is the deliberate falsification of evidence. I don't know if this is an absolute, but from my own (quite significant) observations, no member of the Irish police force has ever done so much as a minute behind bars - or even fined - for that offence. If, through your own research, that does, in fact, turn out to be 100% true, then there is an anomaly for the sitting justice minister to address. Isn't there? Those brave souls from the gym told the truth, but it wasn't made easy for them;

"Who brought it to your attention, about the stolen bottle?"

"Dave did."

"That is, the accused - David Mahon?"

"Yeah, Dave."

"And, tell us, how did he do so?"

"Em… he just told me that something was missing from his bike."

"Did he seem… annoyed?"

"No."

"What about when he raised his voice?"

"He didn't."

"He… didn't?"

"No, not in any way, shape or form…"

"(confused) Oh… okay, will eh…"

"…in fact, he was always courteous with us."

"Right, right. eh… good. Good, so, did he mention anything about C.C.T.V?"

"He did, yeah. He asked if we wouldn't mind checking the C.C.T.V footage."

"Did he say why?"

"Yes, he said he had suspicions about the person tampering with his bike."

"And?"

"He was correct, as were our suspicions about who the person was."

"Who would that be?"

"It was his stepson, Dean Fitzpatrick."

"Did Mr. Mahon then leave and come back later with a much bigger bloke?"

"Yes, but not in the way that's been implied."

"Implied?"

"Yes. We asked Mr. Mahon to come back at a later time because our manager was on a break and that he should feel free to come back when our manager returned from his break."

"And was there a very large man with him on his return? A huge, bald man by the name of John McCormack?"

"Mr. McCormack was there alright, and he was also a member of the gym. Also, speaking as a gym employee, Mr. McCormack wouldn't be among the 'very large' or 'huge' members there, there are much bigger guys."

"Would you agree with the earlier testimony provided about how aggressive Mr. Mahon was when he had Mr. McCormack backing him up?"

"I wouldn't; in fact, we witnessed no animosity at all."

Wow, there you had it, the police were caught on their first lie, the first cast-iron evidence of perjury, but as always, it was swept under the carpet. The D.P.P. were trying hard to turn an otherwise innocent, everyday event into sinister proof of my evil schemes. This was by no means an isolated incident and, to be honest, I'd fill (easily) another volume of further books on their underhanded shenanigans, but the few snippets I'll share in this book are probably enough, after all, I'm not studying for a bloody law degree! Still, if you'll forgive this little indulgence, I'll elucidate further on the above incident.

The implication was that I was bully-boy-Dave and I'd gone off to fetch one of my evil henchmen to apply pressure on the gym employees, secure the proof of Dean's crime and then go off and murder him. I think that's a fairly safe and obvious summation of their strategy. However, it fell apart badly, yet this still minimised the damage. How? The 'who' is actually - John McCormack. You've seen his name throughout my book, we were friends forever. But there's nothing quite like a murder trial to find out who your true friends are. Take it from me, as far as John goes, it's no longer - 'A friend in need is a friend indeed'. It's more a case of "A friend in need can fuck off." Why? It's simple. Did John turn the state's evidence against me? For reasons only he knows. A couple of weeks after Dean's death, John was arrested under Section 4. He left my apartment very soon after Dean and would have had to have either passed him (and not helped) or would've heard some commotion (and still not helped), but in either event/scenario, he would've been the last person to have really known Dean, to see him alive. The D.P.P. sure seemed confident in using him (by name!) as leverage against the gym employees. It would be highly irregular for a barrister to name check another witness at another witness (especially in a high-profile murder trial) and then not call him up to give his own evidence. But that is exactly what happened, worse, in fact, because this - material witness – wasn't just "not called" but was allowed to leave the country (and jurisdiction!) for the remainder of the trial, some friend to me, eh? Fair play to those lads from the gym, I only knew them as a customer, but their truth-telling testimony showed me a greater level of honesty and friendship than John McCormack.

The rest of that day was a blur of hostility and I was tearful, fearful and furious when we got back to our hotel. I was growing ever more despondent about my ability to fight a case where foe was foe and friends didn't know what they were. I expressed my anger -orally- into a bottle of brandy. My head was in a worse mess than Harold Steptoe's junkyard and was filled, spinning in fact, with extraordinary - but nevertheless profoundly conflicting emotions. How – where - could one possibly be able to absorb all of the information, lies and betrayals and make sense of it? The only other person in the universe who could unscramble the car wreck inside my head was Audrey, but she had even more shit to work through than I did.

The Irish media don't miss a trick… unless it's unfavourable to their great golden egg-laying master - the narrative. The papers and news channels all missed out on the big fat lie that the D.P.P. and police had perjured themselves with and instead ran with the more salacious and inaccurate misrepresentations. All the 'brave' cops were still heroes and I was the monster living under the bed, the really scary one that kept you awake at night and your mother could never find. Thank God for the diligent cops, capturing a vile villain like me and keeping me off the streets. If there was any true justice, they'd just hang me already.

"All rise….."

Here we go again. I was determined not to look at the judge, so instead, I looked at my father. He gave me a little wave and I gave him a little smile - he's the greatest. I could feel her eyes burning holes through the back of my head… fuck it, I had to face her. Wow, what a sight - she looked at me like I'd just walked into her chambers and molested a carebear. What was wrong with the bloody wagon?? There was an extra gleam, a malice in her eyes that morning and I didn't understand why until the first witness was called. It was Dean's girlfriend. Both sets of Barristers pinged a barrage of questions at her - about me, about Dean and some background information about the kind of relationship we had. Naturally, there was a lot of focus on the day in question, too.

"How well did you know the accused, Mahon?"

(Why do they feel the need to do that? I'm the only 'accused' person there, so for me, it's a bit like asking, "Did you know the accused, the accused?" or "Mr. Mahon, Mr. Mahon." Just another example of their verbal overkill, I suppose?

"Em… I met him a few times."

"How was he with you?"

"He seemed to like me."

"How was he with you on the day in question?"

"I didn't see him that day, we spoke on the phone."

"Okay, thank you. What was the conversation about?"

"He was looking for Dean, but Dean wasn't answering his phone."

"Why was he looking for Dean?"

"He didn't say, he just asked me to tell Dean to call him back."

"And did you?"

"I told him that Dean had no credit."

"And what did the accused - Mr. Mahon (again!) Have to say about that?"

"He told me to get off my lazy arse and get some credit."

It's true. I did say that. I know I shouldn't have and it would be the easiest thing in the world to call her all the lying bitches under the sun and deny everything, but I think you know me by now and know that isn't how I do things. The fact is, I was pissed off with her that day and I said what I said. The entire courtroom tut-tutted and shook their head in disbelief at my "damning outburst." What she didn't go into at that juncture were the reasons why I was so pissed off at her. But as this is my book- and therefore the best possible platform by which to do so, I will. She and Dean had already parted ways at that stage because she'd cheated on him and was in a relationship with another guy at that time. She used Dean - the father of their child – to get drugs for her. My senior Sean Guerin took to his feet;

"You say you were Dean's girlfriend?"

"Yes."

"At that time?"

"Were you a couple or not?"

"Did you have a child together?"

"Did you take drugs?"

"Were you seeing somebody else?"

"Oh? So, did you cheat on Dean regularly?"

"So, how often did you sell drugs from your house?"

This is an ugly, ugly business and believe me when I tell you, there are no winners. I don't think it comes as a shock to anyone to know that I'm not a fan of Dean's former girlfriend, but I felt that my barrister laid into her a bit too heavily, to be honest. I know that he believed it necessary in order to try to establish Dean's state of mind, but I personally wouldn't have been quite so rough. One of the many reasons why I'm not a senior counsel, I guess! In any trial situation, it is Mr. and Mrs. Joe Public who get battered into thereby the legal prize-fighters and who knows – maybe it is justice? You answer; dear friends are as valid as any others on that score.

I wouldn't be too surprised if Dean's former girlfriend felt as though she was on trial and to be fair, she didn't come across well at all. She was questioned at length about Benzodiazepines and other types of narcotics. Her answers didn't do her any favours. Eventually, the court day came to a close and seeing as it was a Friday, it also brought week one to an end. It was a tough, exhausting week for all concerned. The stress levels on our friends and families – let alone myself and Audrey, were off any known scale measurement. It was becoming more and more habitual for Audrey to disappear from the hotel under the auspices of "a walk" or some other lame form of excuse, but I knew exactly what she was doing. I didn't like it, not one little bit. I always felt that she could tell me anything, trust me with anything and that she didn't need to hide the fact that she was drinking again, especially from me. I pondered hard about this until she returned;

"Audrey, I know that you're back on the soup."

"What??"

"It's alright."

"How do you know?"

"I found a vodka bottle in the hotel room."

"That doesn't mean…"

"Empty."

"Oh."

"I didn't want to tell you."

"Why not?"

"I'm trying to stay strong for you. Audrey, there's no harm in having a few, considering everything we've been through, and now the murder trial? Sure, there would be something wrong with you if you didn't turn to drink for some form of comfort. We are all only human."

"I know, it's just…"

"But please, don't hide it from me – or anyone, you've got nothing to be ashamed of."

I can't recall exactly how the rest of the conversation went, but I do know Audrey and I know that she was a bit more relaxed now that everything was out in the open. Any hopes that we may have had about having a quiet weekend quickly went out the window. It was a wall-to-wall meeting with sleep as an additional extra we could no longer afford. The papers didn't do anyone any favours except the keyboard warriors and the ink manufacturers. Any normal person who may have been sitting on the fence about my case might well have been turned to the dark side by the journalistic orgy of salacious sensationalism that spewed out of their fetid imaginations. It seemed every editorial was ramping up the volatility as the all–powerful narrative went into maximum overdrive. Our phones, in total contrast, didn't stop ringing and pinging all over the weekend with messages of love and support from all quarters. I will never forget the support and seniority of those many well-intentioned well-wishers and like the Good Book says – "…A kind word, at the right time, is oh-so-beautiful and they were."

But I'm a worrier, never in my whole life had I ever been so worried about – me! My worries, up until that time, had always been for others - Kay, Mick, Rory, Graham, Amy, Dean, Audrey, etc. Now, I was the guy with the problems. Now I was the guy looking down the barrel of a 20-year stretch (minimum) and having (but not wanting) to do this, what about Audrey? What would it do to Audrey? My sister – Dorry - stayed over from England and, together with my father, kept our minds and hearts busy when we weren't at court. I remember us all going to a restaurant together on O'Connell Street and believe it or not - we actually managed to eat something and, yes, had a laugh. Dublin, for all of its big city statues, still maintains a judgmental sneer the envy of any small town, and more than a few times did we notice stiff and puritanical glares from some of the other patrons.

As much as we do have gallows - humour (and boy, did that ever come in handy!), we are still only human. We laugh and we cry just like anyone else. My father, however, and uncharacteristically, noticed some of the looks of disapproval we were getting, so he decided to go all-out on his acting-the-maggot just to make us laugh and smile even more. I knew what he was at – the whole 'DADDY' act of getting his children to smile their worries away – but do you know something? It worked! To this day, it always reminds me of something our comedian friend – Dave Young - said to us – "laughter is the best medicine," and he was right, it is. Still, their disapproving looks left a scar, and to this day, I still worry about telling that story in case it's taken out of context, but it is what it is. I'm also strong enough to shrug my shoulders and move on with my life, which still goes on. Then Sunday night came along and did its thing by turning into a Monday morning and then there we were all over again, at the C.C.J. I knew that morning that the courtroom was the last place I'd ever want to be on a Monday morning. What I didn't know was how many more of them I'd be looking at, if any.

Day 6, the first day of week 2, had a preternatural Groundhog Day – Mess about it. For instance – the usual hotel routine; then a taxi to court, paparazzi (the British actress – Dame Helen Mirren, calls them "rat – zis. She's right), then "All - Rise" etc. That was where familiarity almost ended because a very familiar face took the stand, my old friend of many years – Karl O' Toole. That morning was the first time I'd seen him since the 'night of,' almost three years earlier. We bumped into each other in the foyer outside the courtroom earlier. When he approached me, he smelled like a brewery and hey, no better man than me to have a beer, but this was intoxication of a grand scale.

"Yall-Right Dave?"

"Jesus, Karl??"

"C'mon, do you want any tab-lits or Anee-tin, ti re-lax-ye?"

"What??"

To be honest, I was too shocked and too angry to say anything else to him. He - better than most others - knew my stand about drugs, I'd often be the butt-end of anti-drugs jokes, I was so vehemently against drugs, so to offer me drugs in a fucking court complex was a slap in my face. To arrive at my murder trial over Dean's death, pissed up like a street wind, was the height of disrespect.

"Here, Dave, I... I didn't... say any... tin' bout you like... bad, yeah? dat like... Musta' bin Jon Ma- Corr-Mick, right?"

I just walked away from his sorry, drunken ass. The funny thing is, he was as sober (no pun intended) as a judge on that witness stand. It was a polished performance, flawless, in fact. But full of lies. I won't go into all of the ins and outs, but some things really do need to be said. This so-called friend of mine actually said under oath – that:

"Dave told me that he killed Dean."

Which, as you know from earlier, is a total lie. Why would he say that?

Then he said;

"The first time I ever met Dean was on that night."

I couldn't - just could not believe my ears and neither could Audrey. She actually had to get up and walk out of the courtroom, such was her hurt and disbelief. That was "the first time I ever met Dean" Fuck off. Audrey knew as I did that Karl used to drop Dean off to school for us – not once or twice either, but regularly, back when Dean was only a child. Audrey was also there. All the times when Karl came over to visit and stay with us in Spain. How could he sit up on that stand and perjury himself like that? To say that I told him I "killed Dean" when at that stage, I had absolutely no idea as to the extent of Dean's injuries, is beyond belief. He also went on to say (still under oath) that he;

".........wasn't aware of any argument between Dave and Dean......"

When he sat mere feet away in the sitting room, the entire time. I stormed into a meeting with my Barristers as soon as the break came up. I was not apoplectic; I wanted Karl O' Toole torn a new ass-hole up on that stand in full public view. I wanted the world to know what a lying piece of shit he is. Barristers do this whole 'Devil's Advocate' thing, though;

"Dave, he came across very well."

"He's fucking lying, Sean."

"Maybe he didn't witness the argument?"

"Sean, our kitchen and sitting room was an all-in-one space!"

"So then, he must've seen something?"

"Of course, he did, even if he goes down the whole "one eye" routine."

"I'm sorry – one eye?"

"Yeah, he only has one eye."

I thought I'd given Sean more than enough ammunition, but obviously he'd already prepared for the trial using his own tactics. When the incident happened out in the hallway of the apartment complex, Karl O' Toole was standing there and had seen everything. When I made my point to Sean about Karl's' false eye, he seemed a bit shocked;

"Are you sure he only has one eye?"

"Positive. 100%."

"Dave, I've been looking at Mr. O' Toole all morning up on that stand."

"I know."

"Well, he doesn't appear to me to have only one eye."

"He does. I've even had it in my mouth!"

"You.... What?"

"Look, that's not important. It's a very realistic false eye."

"But Dave, it's hard to believe that he could be driving a taxi with only one eye."

"And yet, he is and he does."

I was even more annoyed than ever that my own Barrister was doubting me. That wasn't the worst of it, though. By far the worst part of the day was when Audrey got up and walked out of the court during Karl's' evidence. What made it so horrifically bad wasn't the fact that a person who she knew and trusted lied

493

about knowing her dead son. In a sick kind of way, she was getting used to that, ugly as it sounds. It wasn't even that she was the forgotten victim in all of this and people were cashing in on every drop of Deans spilt blood with shameless abandon. No, what put a hat and a cloak on it was the appallingly bad taste and poor judgement shown by that wig and gowned harpie, Judge Margaret Heneghan. She waited for Audrey to get to her feet, stopped the trial in its tracks and nonchalant flick of her scraggly looking hand, then, in a temper normally found at a crèche and rarely out of the domain of a spoilt 3 year old, stomped her knurled witches feet and screamed at the court guard;

"Get Mrs. Audrey Fitzpatrick back here. Now!!"

Audrey was brought back into the courtroom, summoned like a schoolgirl before the Head-Mistress.

"Will you take the stand?"

"Sure."

"Why did you walk out of the courtroom?"

"As a victim and a civilian, Audrey – I'm sure – had every right to, however."

"Because Karl O' Toole was lying through his teeth."

"Excuse me?"

"He just told the court that he hadn't met Dean before that night. That is a complete lie. He had known Dean for years."

"I don't care."

(Jesus, just think about that.)

"Well, I do care. My son is dead and Karl O' Toole is sitting up here on the stand telling lies."

"I have the power to bar you from the rest of the trial. Do you want that?"

Audrey paused for a moment and the entire courtroom fell into a deafening silence. People subconsciously sat forward in their seats, on absolute tenterhooks. Me? I could only imagine what was about to come out of Audrey's' mouth.

"No."

"Sorry? I can't hear you??"

"No."

"Well, how are you going to behave for the rest of the trial?"

"I will be as quiet as a mouse."

Audrey's' "mouse-voice" was brave, audacious and brilliant! It was a punch on the judge's nose, as there was nothing she could do about it. I know this because if she could've – she would've. What type of a wicked witch beast of a judge did we have on our hands? It was bad enough that she couldn't stand the sight of me – and didn't try to hide that fact – but to hate Audrey? To intentionally and deliberately call her Audrey Fitzpatrick and not Audrey Mahon as she now is legally (and this was a court of law, after all, and they do take those things pretty seriously there) was at best, disrespectful and provocative. Why did she hate Audrey? The only thing she was guilty of was having feelings about yet another piece of shit lying – under oath –about her dead son. What was wrong with that? With that, Audrey stood down, the jury was taken back out of the naughty corner and Karl O' Toole dragged his drugged and drunken ass back into the witness box to spin a few more lies. Ugh, I can't even stomach the thought of what he did and didn't say, but my senior counsel went down in my estimation that day. Not once did he mention a thing about Karl's' eye, the one thing that would've sobered him up into a truth telling style. At some point, the lying -and the trial- ended for yet another day. I headed straight over to Tony and grabbed a quiet corner;

"How much more of this bull shit do I have to take?"

"Not too much longer."

"What – days? Weeks? Months?"

"It's hard to be specific, but…"

"Because I handed myself in, complied with everything, right?"

"You did, and because of that, it'll be a relatively short murder trial."

"As opposed to what?"

"Well, one where we'd have loads of witnesses, etc., to call…"

495

Which brings me conveniently, I suppose, to week two, day 7. A 30-year friendship with somebody should count for something. This was the day that officially ended mine -once and for all- with John McCormack. He was to be called that day to give evidence, but we all know what happened there. On the morning that John was supposed to give evidence – that morning - the guards informed my legal team that he had left the country. We were dumbfounded. Think about it. Think about those weeks and months of intensive trial preparation I'd been through with my legal team. Think about the amount of times that I would've been asked;

"Who was there, with you and Dean?"

"Karl O' Toole and John McCormack."

The two material witnesses - eyewitnesses to what happened, and one of them, a lying, pill-popping snake in the grass had already given "evidence," the whole strategy of what to ask Karl and what to ask John would've been planned in meticulous detail. What to elucidate from each witness, gone -I'm sure that Tony, Sean, etc. had based their cross-examination questions on John and I having had such a long and loyal history together, so his sudden decision to flee from the jurisdiction at the last minute- with the blessing of the state- was a hammer-blow. To this very day, I've yet to hear of any other murder trial where an eye-witness wasn't (A) called to provide evidence or (B) allowed to leave the country. It's unprecedented aid. Let's address the elephant in the room – dodgy as fuck, excuse my French, but it screams of under-handedness and corruption. The massively infuriating element about all of this is that I had put my hands up from the start, handed myself in and admitted what I'd done. There was absolutely no need for all of the cloak and dagger nonsense, but somebody somewhere was hoping to benefit from all the glory that comes from securing a murder conviction that was now obvious. I've scratched my head long and hard about this over the years, and the only strategy I can think of to make any sense is that contained within one of John's statements was the phrase;

"....Dean lunged at Dave......"

A 'lunge' at me would be consistent with self-defence, a road that the cops tried incredibly hard to push me down. The scales have now fallen from my eyes and I see things an awful lot clearer. Had I cracked and lied to keep the cops happy and went along with their self-defence angle, then it was murder. Cut and dried. Black and white game over, the end. Clearly, if John's 'lunge' comment had come out on the stand (and it would've, Tony would have seen to that), then the D.P.P and the cops would've been exposed for what they are. Had the D.P.P wanted him to give evidence, he would've been there with bells on. Remember all of that talk about "Equality of arms" under the Constitution? This is another example of how it doesn't work in the real world. I had a brief consultation with Tony about it;

"Do you want us to get him to appear as a witness?"

"To be honest, I have my doubts about him now."

"Well, Dave, we can put the case on hold until he gets back."

"Really?"

"We can have him return to Ireland and if he refuses, we can have him arrested at Dublin airport when he gets home and summoned to give evidence."

"If he's left the country, do we really want him giving evidence?"

"I think you already know the answer to that one yourself."

"I know. He witnesses a horrific act and then decides to go on his jollies for a few weeks? This justice system is a bloody joke."

Tony said nothing. He didn't need to. I should've bloody known; the signs were right in front of me the whole time, but my loyal friendship blinded me to his treachery. There's no fool like an old fool. He was one of my oldest friends. We grew up together - literally. And I'll never forget how delighted and excited he was being asked to attend my wedding, the way I would've been about the happiest day in the life of one of my friends. I would imagine that would be pretty normal, wouldn't it? I'll also never forget how crushed I was the very next day after I asked him either;

"Dave, I can't come to your wedding."

"What? Why not? What's the matter??"

"I might get my picture taken and it will end up in the papers."

I thought that was a highly unusual thing for him to say, even then.

"I can't guarantee you that it won't happen, but if it does, so what? What difference does it make?"

"I could lose my job."

"What? But you work for Dublin Corporation - how the hell would you lose your job? I didn't get it."

He refused to answer and shook his head like a two-year-old declining food. It was unexpected -to say the least- and also completely out of character for John "The tough guy" who, up until then, was full of;

"You won't be going to prison, Dave."

"How can you be so sure of that?"

"Because of what I have to say to the judge."

"Yeah? Like what?"

"Trust me, Dave. When I'm finished with that judge, the only place you'll be going, is home."

Big talk. Not an isolated incident either, this was a mantra he recited scores of times and not just to me either, but to my father and other close friends too. One of my closest friends smelled a rat long before I did, and as I later discovered, that was out of previous experiences with Big-talking John. Turns out, he had quite the reputation for saying one thing and doing another. I was just too trusting to let any negative press about him to enter my head. Now, however, it's as clear as ice cubes that he was hiding something and I'd be a liar to say that his betrayal didn't sting like crazy, and Judas though he is. I'm not for one second trying to deflect or apportion blame on anyone else about what happened that night but me. Only – ever- me. But something that will forever niggle away at me was how near John's exit was to Dean's from my apartment on that fearful night. I'll never know if John saw him bleeding out and chose to look the other way (or not) because he chose not to give his evidence, deciding on a holiday being more important. Did he step over Dean as he lay there, bleeding to death? What was it that went so far amiss for him that he couldn't attend the wedding of Dean's mother or the trial about Dean's death? Why was John McCormack arrested under a section 4 warrant just weeks after the night of Dean's death, when they took his shoes and clothing for D.N.A. testing? It could all be easily explainable, but John stayed away. He might've been coached by the Garda into what to say and to leave the country during the trial in case he decided to tell the truth and work against the narrative- who knows? Did he come to some arrangements with the cops because he was drunk-driving on that night and didn't want to face another criminal charge? Was that the leverage they were hanging over him? Hard times will always reveal good friendships, unravel the poor ones and cowardice will always show.

Then, day 8 happened. This was the day that the deputy state pathologist – Dr. Curtis- gave his evidence. To look at him, he was quite avuncular and unassuming. An older gentleman with grey hair and salt and pepper stubbly beard. And you'd never imagine the horrors he'd seen and had to give evidence about. To me, he had a clipped, English accent and – as we used to say back in Santry- spoke with marbles in his mouth, or was "ever-so-ever so" as they say in other parts of Ireland. Everything he said was of vital importance, but his delivery was clearly matter-of-fact. He didn't hold back about his autopsy details, the types of illegal drugs in Dean's system, the scarring on his poor body from years of self-harm and all sorts of things too painful and raw to record even to this day. Audrey had been advised not to go to court that day but stubbornly turned up anyway. She left after a couple of minutes of Dr. Curtis' evidence and I, for one, didn't blame her. I only wish I could've left with her. I'll never be able to forget or unhear that evidence ever. And I've tried. Gruesome, horrific, unnatural. I'll spare you and me – the nightmare details. Some of the questions directed at Dr. Curtis included;

"Was Dean murdered?"

"Was he stabbed?"

"Was it intentional?"

"Was it an accident?"

"Was it a self-impalement?"

The good doctor didn't spare the detail in his answers, which weren't always to the D.P.P's benefit;

"Because of the angle of the knife wound…"

"…it is quite possible that it was an accident .."

"…yes, it is possible that he was stabbed, however unlikely…."

My legal team then had their turn with Dr. Curtis:

"Are you still a keen fisherman, doctor?"

"Indeed, I am."

"Would you bait the lines yourself?"

"Of course, yes."

"So between that and your vast experiences, you'd have no problems when it came to, shall we say-killing the fish and preparing them for dinner?"

"No, none whatsoever."

"So, one could say that you'd have an expert knowledge of cutting fish?"

"Somewhat, yes."

"You see doctor, in his opening statement to the jury, counsel for the director - my friend Mr. Farrell here stated that Dean Fitzpatrick had been "gutted like a fish." Now, with your experiences as both a fisherman and pathologist, would you say that my friend was correct?"

"No."

"No?"

"Absolutely not."

"Absolutely not. Correct?"

"Not possible - in fact."

He went on to explain (again, in great detail) what gutting a fish entailed. One could be forgiven for thinking that they'd walked in on an intimate fireside chat about a favoured subject and not a person - a human being. Not Dean. It was beyond surreal, it was Daliesque. I've only skimmed over the facts and indeed, you can look up all the facts if you want to, but that's not something I'm prepared to do. Not now-not ever.

Fair play to Sean Guerin, he was absolutely correct in what he said to me on the day of Remy Farrell's opening statement about how it was a "good" thing that counsel for the D.P.P had made such outrageous comments they had no earthly hope of ever defending. Me, I'm too much of a realist. I'll never agree to the word 'good' in what Remy Farrell said. To me, his words will always resonate with all the class of a pig vomiting. I'm also not sold on calling them 'outrageous comments' either, maybe I'm just too simple and uncomplicated, but a lie is a lie. For Audrey - Dean's mother – to have had to hear about her son being 'gutted like a fish' by her husband is absolutely unforgivable. Remy Farrell, in my opinion, encapsulates all that is wrong with the state prosecution narrative and puts the 'liar' into 'lawyer.' All of this 'little stuff' endlessly seems to fall through the cracks of court reporting and is never heard about or commented on. Why is that? It seems that in Ireland, the only 'victims' with rights are the ones prostituting themselves to low-level tabloids, screaming for the death penalty and yearning for hanging trees to repopulate Phoenix Park, how is that? What about Audrey and other victims like her? What about their rights? Audrey was, is and continues to be an honest citizen, never in a day's trouble her entire life. That makes the machinery of the mighty judiciary her machinery, too, so how did Remy Farrell and his ilk serve her. Nobody next to, near or on the periphery of Dean's death lost as much as Audrey -not even close- but she's not considered worthy of any level of support or sensitivity from the state. Shame. Shame on all of you.

In the courtroom and in what they consider to be "real terms", day 8 was a victory for the defence. It sure didn't feel like one. I could see their point. Remy Farrell was outed for the sensationalist, lying tabloid junkie that he is. Medical evidence had proved that Dean's running at me and into the knife was not only possible but plausible and that angle of the wound etc. completely backed up everything. I'd said from day one. Science has proved the truth of my words and you can't argue against scientific facts, thank God, but do you know what? Dean was still dead, not even science could change that, so there wasn't a whole lot of celebration in the Mahon family. After my legal team had finished showering me with "good news," they asked me what I call a "Columbo" question;

"Dave, just one more thing before you go?"

"Go ahead."

"Do you still intend to offer a plea of manslaughter?"

"Jesus… I... I don't know… eh."

"Well, look, take tonight to think it over."

"Okay."

"But we can't leave it later than tomorrow to let them know."

"Fine, okay."

"Great, good night, Dave."

It wasn't. Then, before I knew it, dawn arrived and it was day 9.

Same hotel, same drill, same entrance.

"All rise."

Same judge. Same expressive face turning milk sour somewhere in the world. She had an extra little sparkle in her eye for me that morning - on a good looking woman, I'd have called it coquettish, but seeing as it was Judge Heneghan, it was probably wind. When she was only a toddler, her father used to call her "pussycat", but it wasn't out of affection because back at the old homestead, she was the only girl around who could catch mice. I knew how they felt. She was purring, so that could only mean that some bad shit was coming down. Bad for me anyway, and I wasn't wrong.

Remy Farrell was back up on his perch and had pages of hate-filled bile scratched out in front of him. From where I sat, it looked like it was written with a Raven's claw. He waited for the courtroom to subdue into a ghoulish silence that cleared his swine-ish sinuses and when he opened his mouth, the hate just gushed on out. He spent 90 hate-filled minutes pontificating his own deluded version of the events of Dean's death. It was the narrative in all of its blood-soaked glory, a new breed of hyperbole that was deliberately exaggerated for obvious effect. It was short on facts but thick and creamy in supposition. I was evil, I was a monster, and I was the spawn of Satan. It was pure catnip for the gutter press, whose behaviour was already bordering on the sleazy fleet- street types in a carry-on movie. But it wasn't just the rat - is playing fast and loose with factual accuracy.

It is the job and responsibility of every trial judge to be the authority and only voice on matters of law. It's a no-brainer. They've every law book and judgement under the sun available at their fingertips. In other words, the best tools of their trade are readily available for their use. Now, I'm no lawyer and I'm certainly not nearly qualified to be a judge. This is also not a law book. Having said that, I've already provided you with the best and most discerns qualification of what murder is deemed to be under law and also a description of how manslaughter is further defined. Well, Judge Heneghan gave a very different description of both at the start of my trial, then took it upon herself to sprinkle vastly different ones over the poor jury at different stages. Here- at the end of Remy's speech- she threw in yet another one. She had been asked several times by the jury Foreman for a clearer clarification of the differences, only to muddy the waters further. It was obvious to everyone that the jury hadn't the first clue about the definition and to be fair, it wasn't their fault. I was the one on trial and I didn't even know. This, dear friends, is yet more of the state's skulduggery. How many times do you have to ask somebody the same question before you feel like an idiot? Or feel like you're bugging the person with nonsense? We all feel that way and the state counts on it. You'd be amazed at how often a person is declared 'guilty' from fear and ignorance, and those dice only ever fall in their favour. Equality of arms? My arse.

At one point, my own legal team had to stand up and interject;

"Your honour, this is the 9th time you've tried to explain…"

She reacted the way one would've expected of any pig. She grunted and snorted in her disapproval and then took a detailed tour through the land of murder manslaughter, something you could only see through the back window of her particular tour bus. If she had printed out a t-shirt with "Find him guilty of murder!" and left it in the jury room, it wouldn't have been as obvious as what she was doing. I had yet another consultation when we broke for lunch.

"Dave, do you want to offer a plea of manslaughter?"

"I don't know, Sean, I really don't. What's your advice?"

"I'm sorry Dave; this has to be down to you."

"Let me talk to my family."

I had a quick, huddled con-flab with Mick and Audrey;

"So, what do you both think I should do?"

"We don't want you to, but it's up to you."

I'd bought a lot of real estate over the years, but I never wanted the location, I found myself in between a rock and a hard place. Literally, my reptilian instincts were steering me down the plea route, and my judge was a total noose-waving lunatic.

"Tony?"

"What's your answer, Dave?"

"Offer them the plea. Again. Please."

This was the second time I'd made that offer and it wasn't any easier, trust me. At this stage of the game, the rest of my life was in the lap of the gods. If they rejected my offer again and I was found guilty of murder, I wouldn't be looking at the "usual" 17-year average sentence for 'life,' because of my high profile nature and my outspokenness about the cops and politicians. I'll be looking at 25 years and above. If they accepted my plea of manslaughter, that loose cannon of a judge might easily give me the maximum sentence available for that, which is also 'life,' so I was not in a good place. You sometimes hear about a judge being lenient or a jury choosing the lesser of two evils when given a choice between murder and manslaughter, but when you're the guy sitting on that precipice, you won't – can't believe any of it. You also ask yourself that question over and over. How the fuck did it ever come to this? It's as bad as it gets. I was quiet, subdued and confused all the way back to the hotel. Audrey squeezed my hand;

"Tough day."

"I'll say."

"What was the worst part?"

"It's hard to say, Remy scared me big time; the judge can't explain the difference between murder and manslaughter and I'm looking at dying in prison."

Day 10 was a Friday and also the end of week 2. I wasn't in any humour for a crunchy, to be honest. This could well be my last weekend with Audrey as a free-man and I would have loved to have planned something special for her, but my head was all over the place. This was also the day for my side -led by Sean Guerin- to stand up and put my case forward to the court. This is the "balance" on the scales of justice you hear so much about- yeah, right.

The first thing he did was apologize to the court - to everyone – on my behalf – for what happened to Dean. This really sickened me because I wanted to do this myself, so I'd like to take this opportunity to do just that. To everyone who was hurt, fevered, and heartbroken and devastated by Dean's tragic and untimely death, I can only offer you – all of you - my deepest and most sincere apologies. I hate the fact that Dean is dead because of my actions and I truly want to make you know that it wasn't pre-meditated, on purpose or done under any cloud of malice. I was at least as shocked as you were to hear of his death and it is an act of shame, regret, sadness and hopelessness I'll carry all the days of my life. I can only hope that you can do something I can't and forgive me.

Sean then moved to re-count his (our) version of events from that tragic, horrible night. He also summarized all of the evidence given over the 2-week duration of the trial. He was able to speak – with conviction -about how the state pathologies version of events complimented and re-enforced what I had said all along. He also spoke about what Dean's state of mind was like and also highlighted to the jury some of the lies that were told under oath. To this day, nobody from my trial has been charged- not even questioned – about their perjury. Make of that, what you will. Sean spoke (or more properly delivered his closing argument) for exactly 1 hour and 41 minutes. I know this because I remember it. I can remember looking at the big Red Digital Clock located just under the judge's platform. I was advised (as I'm sure every defendant is) not to stare at the judge, and you can bet your life I wasn't – I don't hate myself that much – but I did keep an eye on that clock. Call it human nature. At some point, Sean stopped and the judge started, then just before lunch, her parting comment to the jury was;

"Now, go off to your lunch and try to come back with a decision on what you think."

So, no pressure then. I grabbed a quick meeting with my team;

"Will they have a decision today?"

"Hard to say."

"So do you think it might run into next week?"

"On balance…. it will probably be next week."

"Thank God for that."

"Why?"

"My father's dying with the flu, so I sent him home."

Let me rephrase that, I "suggested" he went home, as nobody sends Mick anywhere he doesn't want to go! I told him I'd call him the following day. So he (very) reluctantly agreed to get a taxi home, but only after all of us insisted. The poor man was exhausted and in union with his flu and the never-ending stress surrounding me; the fatigue was written all over his face. He didn't mind quite so much when he noticed that a few of our old neighbours were there to support me, together with some of our friends from Spain and Ireland; with Mick on his way home to his sick bed, we went for some lunch.

Well, certain people ate lunch, I had 2 large brandies, but I might as well have been drinking water for all the good it did me. It was a very fast hour that one. I'll always remember that too. When we landed back at the C.C.J., I had expected a long, drawn out afternoon of waiting around. I was wrong about that. We'd only been there a couple of minutes when word reached us;

"The jury has reached a decision."

There is one universally true in every instance response to those words. You shit your pants, anyone who says otherwise is insane or a liar. My first thoughts concerned my father - poor Mick, who hadn't missed a second of my trial was about to miss its conclusion. He was going to be majorly pissed off when one of the neighbours called him to come back in as the jury had reached a decision.

I sat in the dock again, the loneliest seat on earth. My head was strangely calm, contemplative even. I had thoughts and memories scoot past with laser-guided speed and accuracy. Dean, Amy, Audrey, happy times, unfulfilled dreams, life's long adventure stretching endlessly in front of us in the eternal bliss of Spanish summers. Amy getting married, raising a family, uncle Dean Protective as always, Granny Audrey fussing over little Spanish born babies, life as it could've been. Should've been. Then darkness - Amy – loss, desperation, hopeless hope, finding the unfindable. Dean - death, disbelief, disgust for life as it now was. Audrey - near death experiences, too many to recount, at her own hand and physically failing body. The courtroom walls echoed with the sounds of prosecution speeches, defensive mitigation and endless, tasteless talk about blood, the gutting of fish and stab wounds. At my lowest ebb, my eyes looked up from the floor and met Audrey's. She gives me the tiniest, almost "not-there" nod and what it says can't be contained with these or any amount of pages. What I will say is that it was beyond price. When I someday close my eyes for the very last time, I hope to replay that nod and what it means one more time. I'll force into the unknown then with strength and love and…. so much more, just like I faced another unknown on the dock that day.

My eyes then drifted across to Tony. He was staring at me too, but I had no idea what was in his head. He keeps his cards very close to his chest and isn't a person I'd like to face across a hand of Texas-Hold 'em, that's for sure, then my eyes did a quick dart around the rest of the room and for the life of me, I felt like that mad old polar bear at Dublin zoo with everyone looking at it.

When the judge made her arrival, it was written all over her face that she wanted nothing less than a decision of the black-capped variety, a nostalgic trip down memory lane to the good old days of firing squads and a communal hanging. She wasn't going to get her wish, but she'd settle for the murder verdict, as well as the death sentence, only with less sugar. She had an extra layer of make-up on, knowing that 'this' (whatever it was) was going to be all about her. She was on stage. The cameras were rolling. Lights - camera-

"Have you all agreed on a decision?"

"Yes, Your Honour."

"Mr. Foreman, please hand over your written decision to the registrar."

He did. She handed it to the judge. She read it. No reaction.

"Mr. Foreman, is this the opinion of you all?"

"Yes."

"Very well. You've found the accused - Mr. David Mahon (there it is-again) not guilty on the charge of murder."

"Yes, Your Honour."

Not guilty! Yes, I heard it correctly…. or did I? Shit, this was so confusing. I looked over to Tony, who was clearly reading my mind. He silently mouthed;

"Not guilty."

Nice one. I looked over at Audrey and God love her. She was like a statue, frozen in time. She was in shock, but no matter what the verdict was, she would have been the same. Sure - the trial was over, but her son was still dead. Nothing was sinking in because Dean wasn't coming back. Then the judge cleared her phlegmy gizzard……;

"However…"

She actually said it like that, loving every sweet syllable (not the best word to hear out of the hateful mouth of a power-hungry lunatic with a sharper axe to grind.)

"However, (one word now) the jury do find Mr. David Mahon (now longer accuse)… guilty of manslaughter."

The easiest thing in the world for me right now would be to write about how shocked and devastated I was by that announcement, but the truth is, I wasn't. If I hadn't offered a plea of manslaughter, then I might've walked out of that courtroom and gone home. Then again, that might've left the jury with no option but to find me guilty of murder too, so it wasn't the end of the world. What I'm often asked is, what do I think I should've been convicted of and the truth is I'm guilty of recklessness. I held/produced a knife (phrasing isn't really the point, is it?) that Dean received a life-ending wound from, and of that, I am guilty, but nothing more. When Judge Harpie cackled out her witchy instructions, orders, and pronouncements, I looked over at Audrey. She was 'back in the room', so they say, so I just gave her a little nod before;

"Take him down!"

"All rise…."

…and I was ushered into a little room just outside of the court, not much bigger than a confession box. They must have lined the outer walls with butter. Because somehow, they managed to squeeze me, Tony and the giant that is Sean into that room. The door had to be left slightly ajar as we started to discuss everything we needed to, out of that little crack of light, I could see the judge peering in. Even then, with the trial over and me off to prison, you could still see her primal, animalistic hatred working away at her like a worm in an apple. God only knows the evil thoughts she was brewing up in that all-too-hateful mind of hers ,but for the way the whole "justice" system is set up, I would've loved to have given her a piece of mine.

The crux of the discussion I had with my legal team, concerned the machinery involved in the process of getting me sentenced. In normal language, I wanted to know how long I was going to do in prison, but I wouldn't find out until my next court date, which would be a hearing known as "sentencing". A Ronseal legal team for once. Leaving that stuffy little room meant leaving freedom for the foresee because as soon as my feet crossed the threshold, the guards took over and it was back, once again, to the state-piss stench of the holding cell dungeon of the C.C.J.

Back into a medium sized room -no windows- full of whispering, shuffling people. I didn't know and had no desire to look at the clock on the wall when leaving the courtroom, and then I had no way to tell the time except to know that every second that passed was no longer yours. Reality kicks in. Ouch. It was a view I'd have to get used to, living behind a locked door with power-hungry blue shirts controlling the keys. As a destination, I wouldn't recommend it. The door would open every so often - a name would be called – a person would leave, and then the metal door would slam shut as hard as the nasty screw could bang it. Maybe he wouldn't have been half as up-tight if he went home and tried banging his wife half as hard. As with life, your turn eventually comes up;

"Dave Mahon."

I didn't even answer. I just walked over to him.

"Are you Dave Mahon?"

"Yeah."

"Right, follow me."

I could've been Boris Karloff and just decided to take Dave Mahon's turn, but you didn't exactly get issued with a business card, so to this day, I still can't work out why he asked if I was Dave Mahon and what purpose it served. He had obviously read the rule book on his lunch break because he whipped out a set of hand-cuffs and slapped them to my wrists. Then he realized that I was on a walking stick and had to take them off again. Gobshite. From there, I was put into the little coffee boxes on the paddy wagon/prison transport. Those little cells are called coffin boxes for good reason because they're solid steel, have hardly any ventilation and have no seatbelts. If the driver has a crash, you're getting broken up -badly- there's nothing surer. How they manage to get past the safety inspection is beyond me unless brown envelopes are involved, which seems to be the case more often than not. Remember too, that in most cases, the people being transported are further confined in wrist-breaking figure- 8 handcuffs, so that only exacerbates the danger. Like most of you, I'd seen those vehicles on TV and even pulled up beside them, but I never thought that I'd end up in one of them. I was in one of the bigger ones – 10 cells on each side; the noise and smells were unbearable. You're left in those shit boxes for about an hour until they can locate a screw dumb enough to drive. The selection process for this must be a panic;

"Can you drive?"

"Yeah, tractors, boss, big fuckin' tractors."

"Have you any experience driving in cities?"

"What - like legal?"

"Yes."

"Fuck, no."

"Do you know your way around Dublin?"

"Well, I know how to get from Croke Park to Coppers."

"What about from C.C.J. to say, Mountjoy?"

"Ehh...""

"You'll do!"

There are but two pedals for the driver to use;

Flooring it fast,

Jam-it-dead, brake.

I'm sure there are roller-coasters with fewer whip-lash injuries. I did manage to peep out the little port-hole type window at some stage and see some familiar sights – Hanlons corer, the sign for Anamore drive in Cabra - where my grandparents lived up until they died, together with a thousand other memorable metres along the North Circular road, before Doyle's corner and then the "Big-House" Mountjoy prison itself. I'd driven past this unholy edifice so many times in the past that I didn't even bother acknowledging its existence, but now, here it was in all its Victorian ugliness. Its gates opened up like the jaws of every mythical monster you've ever feared and it swallowed us down its disgusting gullet like the millions of pills its residents have done down the years... then - bang, the screw slammed on the big red pedal with "stop" written on it. In the "coffin box" behind me, I heard an almighty "Thwack" before the inevitable;

"Aww, me bleedin head man.... ye, fuckin Muppet!"

We had arrived at our destination. We were left waiting another hour in that river of fresh piss, puke and stale air. I was beyond bored, so I measured the width of the coffin-box with my walking stick. It was the same width as the stick, so that was a waste of time, a bit like prison itself. In their own good time, the screws eventually decided to let us out of the paddy wagon and marched us into the prison. This was a lot of fun for yours truly because I had to negotiate the steps, stairs and metal - detectors etc., manacled like a Circus bear, only on a walking stick. I took my time about everything too, not only to ease the pressure on my aching hips but also to annoy the screws. They might have had all of the power, but they weren't the only ones who could take their time about things. It was a very similar process

510

to my Cloverhill experience - same uniforms, different numbers on their shoulders, same type of self-important asshole with a clipboard and questionnaire;

"Now, Dave Mahon?"

"Yes."

"Age?"

"Excuse me?"

"Age?"

"Of what?"

"Huh?"

"Age of what?"

"How old are you?"

"Why?"

"What?"

I said nothing.

"Eh, I need it."

"For what?"

"Eh, for my sheet…. records, for our records."

"Oh, right."

"So?"

"What?"

"How old are you?"

"I already told you. (I didn't, but he was in too much of a hurry.)"

"Oh… Ah, yes - here it is; 45. Were you ever in prison before?"

"Yes."

"Where?"

"The same place it says in front of you, on my file."

"What?"

"I can see my file. It's on your clipboard. It's how you know my age."

"Are you reading what's on my I.P.S. folder?"

"It's more of a clipboard, but yes, I'm glad one of us is."

His face contorted into a hilarious mixture of outrage and stupidity. I just won. A smug little grin we both understood to mean, "What's in a hurry, now, mother-fucker, next time don't leave me to sweat too long in the piss mobile!"

"Hmph... Are you fighting with anyone?"

"My wife isn't too happy with me going to prison...."

"Smart-arse? Have you any enemies within the prison population?"

"Not yet, but you've met me – who couldn't love me?!"

I dragged it out like that for ages. Respect is a two-way street and I'd never win that war, but I wasn't about to start my sentence like a Rabbit in the headlights either, even though I was nervous as hell on the inside. Once I was 'processed', I was led out into the belly of the biggest beast there is, and it's terrifying.

Dave and Audrey entering the CCJ for his murder trial

Mick and Audrey leaving the CCJ (Criminal Court of Justice) after a grueling day of Dave's murder trial.

Another grueling day at court

Dave and Audrey leaving the CCJ together for the last time

Audrey and Mick leave the CCJ moments after Dave was sentenced

Dave is escorted by the Garda to the courts

Dave and Audrey walk into the CCJ (Criminal Court of Justice) for his murder trial.

Prisoner # 84976

You don't go to Mountjoy or other prisons really- unless you are sentenced, but there are exceptions to every rule. I wasn't one of those exceptions because I was shuttled back to Cloverhill – a remand prison- until I was given my official sentence. The news crews and social media were in speculation overdrive as to how much time I'd have to do. The most conservative estimates floated around the 3–5- year mark, with life without people and throwing away the key at the other end of the spectrum. The truth - as always – lay between the lives, but I had no idea what end of the graph I was looking at. Not knowing is never easy. Missing Audrey was beyond hard. Knowing how much my father would be hurting was really upsetting as well.

It seemed like everyone had an opinion, but like even the greatest chefs, you couldn't accurately predict how something was going to turn out without all the ingredients. While I waited, I learned a lot about prison life, the ups – the downs, who you can trust and the much larger list of who you couldn't. One of the things you learn fairly quickly in prison is repetition. That little cameo I've just written was pretty much every day of the 7 weeks I spent in Cloverhill, and then it was back to court to see what the future held. I don't mind saying either that by that stage, my hip pain was at an unbearable level and it hurt to think about walking, let alone doing it. My walking stick doubled as a "comfort blanket" of sorts because its familiar sight was my only tactile memory of my former life.

Even though I was no longer a stranger to the court, it looked different this time around, smaller; somehow, maybe that's a prison side-effect? I don't know. In a world of despair and depression, you exist under a blanket of darkness that covers almost everything in its gloom. 'Almost' is the key. Some lights are not so easily extinguished and Audrey -my Audrey- is the bright and shining light in my life. That day was no different. On such a solemn occasion, she had no right to light up that courtroom, but she did. There was a very familiar twinkle behind her eyes and that is never a bad thing. I was stumped as to what that could be, and then she ever so discreetly motioned with her eyes down to her finger. Her wedding ring finger, to be exact. Remember the wedding band tattoo I got? The one I was always teasing Audrey about? Well, she'd only gone and gotten hers done, too! It's all about timing sometimes and on the day of my sentencing, Audrey managed to get a smile out of me! I needed all the smiles and joy I could get as no sooner had the reality of Audrey's lovely gesture sunk in then a dark presence took over the world it was…

"All rise!"

.. Could only be (in my opinion) the epitome of all evil, Judge Heneghan. She rambled on – as she does – in that droning voice of hers, detailing the horrors of my crime with all the sincerity of a whore's orgasm; something wicked was coming this way, that was for sure, still, I must confess, I listened intently to every word she spoke, just like I did at my trial. At one point, she glared down at me with eyes that beamed with bad intentions;

"I would like to sentence you to 10 years…"

[Fuck, 10 years??]

"But…"

[Don't say "LIFE"; don't say "LIFE"]

"…because you showed remorse and cooperated with the Garda and entered an earlier plea of manslaughter, I will, instead, sentence you to 7 years imprisonment…"

There it was, seven years straight. It could've been worse. It should've been better. She also used a word I've grown to hate – "Remorse." It is a non-word, a courtroom word, for me anyway. A rudimentary definition for it would be "having deep regret for your actions" or something similar, but it's not enough. Its alternatives - regret, sorrow, repentance, ruefulness, penitence…. do it for me either. They're hollow, convenient words used by judges and others who don't have the first clue how it feels for me, how much I will always miss Dean and how I felt when I heard that Dean was dead. Seven years is a tough sentence - it's no joke – but it's nothing compared to the sentence I'll share with Audrey until the day we die. I'm not looking for sympathy, pity or anything like it, but if I was to sit on that dock every day of my trial and cried my eyes out continuously, would the judge have said that I was even more remorseful? Less? What is the imperial measurement of remorse anyway? See my point- it's bullshit. So, in the final analysis, what does 7 years mean in real terms? With the exception of a life sentence, every prison term carries an automatic 25% off, which in reality equals to 5 years and 3 months prison time. However, in law, there is now a provision for one-third remission, which would've meant only 4 years and 8 months, but you've more chance of getting mugged by a leprechaun on a unicorn than getting that.

So, my freedom was gone and I've 5 and a bit years before I could go home and do normal stuff again. The man who had made a career out of real estate was

519

on the move again. Goodbye, Cloverhill; never liked you, and I don't miss you. Hello, Mountjoy. I'd been there for processing, knew all the familiar sights along the way and was allocated the first of my many new addresses. - B. Wing. To get there, you've got to walk through the main prison. You see the famous "spiral" staircase, which is actually a helix in shape, but who am I to argue with the rest of the world? You know what. Why not? Henceforth, let it be known as the helix staircase and drive the rest of the world crazy! Also, from the vantage point of the main circle area, you can view hanging on the wall for all to see- the most iconic piece of Irish penology paraphernalia of all time, the 'Auld Triangle' itself. It's a large lump of metal folks in a triangular shape, but it's impossible to look upon it without hearing folk songs going off in your head. That's as good as the sightseeing tour got, and then it was off to my cell on B-wing.

I was there a couple of hours – just long enough to scrub its walls down to 6 inches of Greasy nicotine, puke and snot – before I had my first visitor. He was a 'lifer' and 'listener.' An in-house Samaritan and he was both pleasant and informative. Maybe prison life wasn't going to be so bad, just 5 years, 2 months, 3 weeks and 6 more days to go…

Infamous

Mountjoy is an absolute lie. It's not a mountain. There's not much joy. It's known locally as "The joy." The definitive article of joy; suggesting, by implication, the most joy. Again, not true. Judging a book by its cover and a name must mean something doesn't always ring true and Mountjoy prison is the perfect example. Yes, there's plenty of history in them, their walls -but it's a giant rat-infested dump. I was now its newest member; its Rich history now forever contains some of my D.N.A particles sit alongside. All the rest; the good, the bad and the very ugly.

My first night in prison was a lot different to my first night in "prison" because now I was a convicted criminal with a sentence to serve and a date on my door. You're still locked up, but it definitely feels different. Strange, but true. Anyone's first night in prison is tough – make no mistake about that, but it's worse when you are all over the press and television. Much worse. On the other hand, your brain is still hard-wired to the outside world. So your immediate concern is your family and how hard all of the negative press on them is. Then you have to consider several hundred new neighbours you've suddenly inherited. A large percentage of them will think you're "a bit of walker" just because you were on their T.V. or splashed all over their newspapers. Some will make light of your situation by slagging you about "being famous" or a "celebrity" prisoner;

"Gi's yer bleedin' autograph Dave, will you?!"

But there's also a much nastier element of all things -jealousy – fuels a lot of their hatred;

"You think yer bleedin special, ye Muppet?"

"Think yer great 'cos you're on the telly? Ye pox."

On and on the nonsense goes; when you've got a violent, dangerous criminal with a history of irrational thinking, out of sorts, because people are talking about you and not him, you've got a serious problem. You need to watch your back and I did. For the most part, it slowly fizzles out; my notoriety would be so prominent on the morning papers, making it impossible to escape, but it would mean very little in the afternoons when life and its problems would preoccupy inquisitive minds with their own imprisonment and bullshit. My stint on B-wing didn't last very long, however, because I got the impression that the screws didn't know what to do with me. My hip issues weren't going away. Any time soon and I think they didn't want to keep such 'ailing' prisoner on a main landing because I might have to go to hospital and my cell would lie dormant when other prisoners were having to sleep on a floor. That would cause absolute uproar, understandably. After a few days, I was moved down to the very bottom of the prison - an area known as "The Base." "Was it just me or everything in "the joy" known by definite articles?

The Base is two letters away from being correct because it's basic. It's about as basic as prisons get. It's supposed to be a 23hr lock-up, which means exactly that, you are behind the door, locked in your cell for 23 hours a day, every day. That other is "exercise" for you and also the time to grab a shower and try to make your phone calls. However, like everything else in the I.P.S. the design flow with that system concerns the operations in blue uniforms. Some of the screws know that Mickey Mouse's big arm pointing at the number '12' and the little arm pointing at the number '4' means that it's 4 O'clock. Then, Mickey slowly moves his arms until the little one points at the '5' with the big one still pointing at the number '12' (so there's only one change, let's not make it too complicated), meaning that an hour has passed and it's now 5 O'clock. What all of this means is that most of the time spent in the Base is '24' hour lock up because;

"Ah, I forgot."

"Did you not get your hour's exercise?"

Sometimes, the really diligent ones would let you out... for ten minutes or something as equally futile;

"Fall in."

"It's only been 10 minutes!"

"Fall in, I said, we've got no staff."

I didn't complain. I was only there for a few days or so, anyway and my hip was having a war with my central nervous system because every cough - every sip of tea – anything resulted in excruciating pain emanating from the hip area. I was a happy man the day that my cell door opened and I was told to get my stuff together;

"Why? Where am I going now?"

"The Cappagh hospital."

"Is this for my hip?"

"Don't know."

I was amazed – not about the hospital appointment – but I'd found a "chatty" and "intelligent" screw! I packed up my very few bits and pieces and started my mental preparation for hip number -3 Hip-hip-hip- you know the rest! I dreaded the idea of having to sit in yet another one of those awful paddy wagons, so I was pleasantly surprised at being led out to a car, and off we went.

It was a weird journey. I was only getting used to prison and now I was out already. It was another journey I'd travelled-countless times- in the past, but now I was hand-cuffed and under escort. Your mind goes on a spin cycle of oxymorons a free prisoner- all that kind of things. My little morning of nice surprises continued when we approached the car park at the side of Cappagh Hospital -because waiting there- in their own respective cars - were my father and Owen my brother. It was a wonderful and joyous sight and it shouldn't have felt like a family reunion hosted by Holly Willoughby after 30 years apart, but it did! It was also my first experience of being handcuffed out in public. It felt humiliating. It is humiliating.

As usual, and as I've come to expect, the staff at the Cappagh hospital were amazing, displaying all of the 3 'F's – Fair, Friendly and Fantastic. My hip operation went as perfectly as I couldn't have hoped for and before I knew it, I was in a Recovery room, all to myself. Well…. Not exactly. I was now a really "dangerous" criminal, an actual menace to society, so I had to have 3 highly paid and under-worked prison officers with me at all times, 24 hours a day, 7 days a week. I didn't give a hoot about any of that, though because I was allowed to have visitors, Audrey and my father coming up twice a day. When my best friend – Darrin - came up to see me (twice), I even shed a tear because Darrin is as close to being allergic to hospitals as it gets, yet he put all of that aside to visit me. I could almost see him 'gag' on the smells around him, but like a true friend, he toughed it out. He is a rare man in the very best sense of the word, in that he does what he says;

"I won't come up to see you in prison."

"No brother, I won't blame you."

"I just couldn't bear to see my best friend behind bars."

"Don't worry about it, Darrin."

"But you'll want for nothing."

And for the entirety of my prison sentence, I didn't. We were always going to pick up where we left off when I got out. We've been friends forever and will always be.

One of the most important things you need to do after a hip replacement operation is to get your ass out of that bed – the very next day and walk. In normal circumstances, this is painful but uninhibited. In my circumstances, it was both painful and inhibited, so I had to restrict my walks to the outside of the hospital under the watchful glare of my 3 escorts;

"Don't try making a run-for it, Dave!"

"No chance of that!"

It was kind of funny the first time. Then it wasn't. Then it just got old. Still, at least I was getting in some yards of recovery. It was when I undertook one of those walks that I made an interesting discovery. My brain was changing – not in a bad way - but I started to notice things in ways I hadn't before. Maybe it's down to the sensory deprivation of prison, but I started noticing everything. I've always been a huge lover of the outdoors and it's why being out and capturing photographic images was one of my great hobbies. For the first time in my life, I was loving the scenery around the Cappagh hospital - not exactly a tourist hot spot or a location in any danger of adorning a postcard, yet it was like a Land of Oz to me. It had a beautifully interesting skyline, horses running wild and free, and different birds interacting as they went about their daily business. Sometimes, I need to remind myself to just stop, think, and enjoy this wonderful planet of ours before it's ruined forever. It was when doing just that, when I noticed my father's little Nissan Micra pulling up. Nice one, Mick and Audrey arriving early. I hobbled over to the nearest bench to me, sat down and set my crutches beside me. When the door opened, heaven opened with it- my little dog leapt out and sprinted over to me like the rest of the world was on fire right behind her. Lili, my little white Jack Russell, our rescue pup from Spain, my 4-legged barking, lapping, licking bundle of joy. I was blown away. She was so excited at seeing me that she was crying and pissed herself. So, did I cry, that is, I wouldn't piss myself until a couple of years later- not too shabby at my age! It was a treat I'll never forget, it means more to me now than ever, but we'll get to that. The four of us -Audrey, Mick, Myself and Lili had a really wonderful afternoon, a time to laugh, a time to play, a time to love the world and the horrors that awaited us there were pushed aside for those precious moments.

"Hi, David."

Out of the blue, a familiar voice. It didn't sound angry or aggressive, so I decided it would be safe enough to look away from Lilli's adoring eyes for a couple of seconds. I knew the face, but I couldn't quite place it at first, then clicked into place. It was Paul Reynolds from R.T.E.

"It's okay, Dave, I'm not a tabloid."

I remembered Paul from when Amy went missing over in Spain. He flew down and covered the story in what I've always considered to be a fair and impartial way. For that reason, I considered him to be a great reporter and believe me, over the years, we've learned to recognise the rare good ones from the other buckets of shits.

When the time came for me to leave the hospital and head back to prison, I didn't want to go because Audrey wasn't there to say "good-bye" to me. So I did the same thing you probably would have and blagged my way into staying there as long as I possibly could until she got there. I didn't do too bad a job at it either; I got to stay another night! When Audrey got there, we got to say our 'goodbyes' and when I let her go, I noticed that I'd developed a growth. It was Audrey, holding me tighter than a limpet to a sea-rock and refusing to let me go. (I'd like to say that I've always had that effect on women, but…!!) She wasn't kidding around either, shouting;

"You're not going! You're not going!!"

My heart actually broke for her, knowing how much she'd hate being 'abandoned' yet again. There was nothing we could do though, just keep loving each other, live for the next visit and then it was back to "the joy" again for me. My physical body went back to prison, but my heart remained with Audrey, 24 x 7.

Meanwhile, back at "The Ranch", as they say (see, Mountjoy wasn't the only organization capable of creating definite articles, was it?!!") The management was finding it difficult to find a suitable place for me to live as I was under doctor's orders not to go up or down, any stairs and to exercise as often as I could. So they got all the top brains together from the I.P.S. and put their powerful heads together, a meeting of super minds. You know the scene from Apollo 13, where Tom Hanks and his crew are stranded in space – about to die from the cold or lack of oxygen - and then he utters the famous line;

"Houston…we've got a problem."

The movie shoots back to mission control in N.A.S.A, all the super brains frantically scribbling down numbers-formulate- algorithms on pads of paper, blackboards, whiteboards, orders and instructions are shouted until finally, the leader of the group collates all the information together and summarises it down to two or three fact-filled lines of hope and logic which he relays on to Tom and Co to save the day? Well, this was absolutely nothing like that. I wasn't there to witness it- obviously- but I wouldn't say it is too different from this scenario;

"Jesus, boys, that Jim Gavin is one cute hero."

"Heh?"

"The feckin dubs boys, the feckin dubs! Sure, they're too strong."

"Bollix will be Mayo's year, put your life on it."

"Nah, they'll bottle it..."

"I'm telling ya, it's Mayo's to lose. Mark my words."

"What about yet man - Dave Mahon?"

"Don't know him. What club is he with?"

"He's a prisoner."

"Jesus boy, we're talking Gaelic football here!"

"I know, but look, we need to make a decision first."

"Ah for feck's sake, what's his problem?"

"Hip replacement – doctors don't want him using stairs."

"So feckin - what?"

"They also want him to have regular exercise."

"He should try marking Ciaran Kilkenny for 20 minutes, he's feckin fit him?"

'' (They laugh and pat each other's backs) He can't; he's a dub as well."

"A feckin dub???"

526

"Yeah."

"Simple – so fetch him down to the base."

I was transported back from the hospital as that meeting went on and when I got through the reception, I was stopped by an angry looking man in a uniform and carrying an envelope. He didn't look like Tom Hanks.

"Dave Mahon? (Didn't sound like him either)."

"Yes."

"Follow me. You're going back to the base."

"I can't. I'm not allowed near any stairs."

"Tough."

So, I followed not -Tom- Hanks down each and every faint-inducingly-painful step down to "The Base" and then into another tiny cell for 24- hour lock up. He gave the door an extra-hard slam for dramatic effect, then;

"No feckin stairs in there."

I wasn't angry with him. I felt kind of sorry for him. It must be awful to have such a tiny penis. Ah well, so much for my exercise, I suppose. I sat very slowly, down on my bed/bunk/cot and watched the cockroaches have yet another land war for a while before getting lost in my thoughts. It's just as well I wasn't claustrophobic. That was my only good news.

Incarceration is a funny thing in that it can be a psychological incubator that overheats good news into Euphoria and chills negative news into despondency. I quickly learned to focus on the positives and deal with the negatives when I had to. I strongly believe that those actions got me through my sentence. My new sitting position wasn't quite as impossibly uncomfortable as it first seemed, so I used all the pain-free moments I could get to come up with a plan. Old Mrs Mahon didn't raise no fools, so I put my case forward about the exercise issue at my first opportunity, and it worked!! I was transferred back to a "real" landing (Prison Parlance) and moved into yet another new home, the first cell on the left-hand-side of A-wing.

It wasn't any ordinary cell either, it was wheelchair accessible, so therefore, quite a bit larger than what I was already getting used to. The good news continued to flow upstream, as, when my door opened, it was to bring me down to the visits area. Any time I get to spend with Mick and Audrey is time "out" of prison for me. When we saw each other, I was beaming from ear to ear. Just seeing them again made everything feel so much better;

"So, what's it like in here?"

"It's great, not the animalistic iron-barred enclosure you hear about."

"What are the other in-mates like?"

"Okay, I knew a few of them from Cloverhill, so it was good to know a few faces when I got here."

"What's your cell like?"

So, I answered that and the dozens of other questions every normal person would ask. Before long, our visit ended (they are always too short), and I was taken back to my new landing. When we got to the landing entrance, there was a gang waiting for me, a not-so-welcoming committee, so the officer took me on a detour;

"It's not safe for you on that landing Dave. I'll have to move you."

And he did. Back into the bloody base again. I was beginning to feel like a boomerang. All of that bloody nonsense in the papers and on the T.V had clearly shaken awake the drug-addicts brain cell in some junkie's heads;

"Who does he think he is?"

… And now I was being transferred over it again. I still had a new hip; therefore, I still needed exercise, ergo, my argument about being in. The base still held true. I used it again, this time using really small syllables and using my grown-up voice. Something worked because I was brought up to stay in the medical unit -sorry, it was Mountjoy- so it was; "The Medical Unit!"

This was another learning curve in my whistle-stop tour of Mountjoy because this was the first cell I'd walked into that was reasonably clean. It was smaller than the wheelchair on A-wing, but it was clean, convenient and my newest, new home, so I made the best of it. It was a much smaller landing than I was used to (even thinking that so fresh into my sentence was strange!) As there were only about 10 other inmates, most of whom were trying to come off drugs. They were a bit wary of me at first (well, I was the dangerous, vicious psycho-killer from the papers, after all), but after a week or so, they got used to seeing me and saw the passive wood from the tabloid trees. As for the screws, well, that's an entirely different story. They came in 3 different groups, the largest of which being the aggressive, alcoholic types. The next largest was the "buddy" type who'd talk to you and sentiments sounded admirable, but all they were really doing was softening you up for stories to sell to the media. The third and smallest group was the one or two genuine guys who had a job of work to do, showed you some courtesy and left you alone if you weren't causing trouble.

I was on that little landing to try to rehabilitate my hip, so my exercise regime consisted of walking 30 steps, turning around, walking 30 steps- rinse and repeat. It was quite a confined little place, but so what, it did the trick. I stuck to that workout for about a month or so until I started tackling the stairs. Then, whenever I was allowed, I'd go up the stairs and lift a few weights in the gym. I felt like I'd settled in nicely to the medical unit, so, wanting to stay there a bit longer, I put in a half sheet (this is a written request to the Governor) to the Governor. It was 5-months until Christmas, so my hope was that I'd see in the New Year (not celebrate it) on the medical unit then transfer to another 'normal' landing in January. I heard nothing back until I was on a visit with Audrey one day and the Governor came over to us to introduce himself. I must say that he came across as very fair, affable and quite forward-thinking. He was quite sympathetic to my predicament and assured us that -as per my half sheet- I'd be left alone until at least January.

"At which point we'll assess the situation, so get yourself settled in."

This was more great news as it meant that Audrey could visit me twice a week. She could get the train straight into Connolly station in Dublin Amiens street and walk the short journey to "the joy." Happy days, everyone a winner and to quote the great Derek Trotter, "Kushdi Rodders, you know it makes sense!" It didn't take long, just minutes after I hung up my crutches for the last time, my cell door flew open.

"Pack up your stuff, you're getting transferred."

It hadn't even been 3 weeks since the Governor spoke to me on the visit. I was starting to learn a lot about prison life and its poisonous policies.

"Where am I going?"

"Transfer."

"Yeah, what landing?"

"Landing?"

"Yeah."

"No - transferred out. You're going to Wheatfield."

Another Paddy wagon stuffed to the gills with noise, piss, and the not-so-sweet aroma of skunk weed. Wheatfield prison is another misnamed oxymoron because I didn't see any wheat (except in my breakfast cereal) and if there have been fields behind those high walls once, they were long since gone when I got there.

There must be a special shop out there somewhere that sells giant metal doors, as I went through yet another one to get into Wheatfield. Then I saw my first major difference between there and 'The Joy'- Wheatfield was tiny by comparison. It was like a tiny little body letting on prison, yet it regularly houses in excess of 500 inmates. It was a bit confusing. The coffin-box opened and I was taken out of the Paddy wagon with my usual bling handcuffs and a walking stick. I'm sure there's a joke in there somewhere? You're led into a tiny, cramped little corridor, which no exaggeration- stinks of a weird marriage between cabbage and rotten eggs, then led up some stairs into the main reception area. This consists of 3 little changing areas (so you can strip off all of your clothes and wrap an orange, scratchy towel around what's left of your dignity. You then sit on what is known as "The Boss" chair (what is it about prisons are their fascination with definite articles anyway?), which reliably informed, detects if you have a mobile phone or a weapon hidden up your "Brenda Fricker" (more prison parlance – Brenda Fricker- Gicker-bum-hole). I guess it beeps if you do? You then walk through a metal detector because – as we say in Ireland- "To be sure, to be sure."

This was a complete pain for me because of all the metal in my body (hips, for example). I would – of course – light up the bloody thing like a Christmas tree.

"Hang on their horse; are you carrying anything metal on you?"

"Yes, my hips and some pins in my…"

"Huh? Your… what?"

"I've a new hip and… look, it's all in my file there."

The usual back and forth then occurred with me having to explain what a new hip entails, why I'd require metal pins in my leg and that everything was in my life, if they'd only open it up and read it. Eventually, they patted me down, let me get dressed again (after a shower) and put me into the world's smallest holding cell to wait for a few minutes. Literally. Then, I was given the usual directions;

"Grab your kit and follow me."

I was brought straight over to a landing known as 7F. Now, in case you were thinking that "F" was really far away, like a logically minded person, as in - A,B,C,D,E,F – then you'd be wrong like I was. 'F' section is the first floor section and 'G' section is for the ground floor locations. On each floor, there are 10 landings, so my new home was the 7th landing on the first floor. Welcome to the 'organised' mess that is Wheatfield. On the way to my landing, I was amazed by the length of the corridors- basically the entire length of the prison. I was badly lit and very institutional, a lot like school actually, only with gates every 100 feet or so.

My new home was a new experience in lots of ways, not the least of which was my living arrangements. I had a room-man, or to use the correct prison terminology. A cellmate. I didn't know him from Adam, but it was clear that housekeeping wasn't high on his list of priorities. The cell had ambitions to one day be clean enough to be called a filthy kip. It was still a long way from achieving that particular milestone. Now, I'm an extremely clean person, like most decent folk. My mother instilled in us a habit of cleanliness being next to Godliness, so for me, say that the place was beyond cleaning. You can take that to the bank. The place also reeked to high heaven; it's best described as having a stench that was both earthy and enormous. I physically shuddered at the thought of what could possibly be giving off such an odour. Then my cellmate walked in and answered that question. I really want to be fair to him and not run him down too much, so I've chosen my words with kindness and humanity. He stank like a 3-day old shite that just got fucked in a puddle of vomit. I had wanted to blend- in, get lost in the mainstream of prison life and was willing to do whatever it took to do that. It was only standing in that public health hazard that I added one main caveat - not at the expense of my own personal hygiene.

I spent my first night in the "new" cell with my clothes close to my pillow- anything but the other numerous, odious and interesting smells that surrounded me. It worked because I did manage to get a wee bit of shut-eye. My new cell-mate woke up just after I did;

"Morning, bud."

531

He had half a smile on his face an attempt at being friendly I guess- but all I saw was a set of delph that would've given Shane Mc' Gowan nightmares. What little teeth he still had were so yellow and greasy you could've actually buttered toast with them.

"Good morning."

I didn't smile. I wasn't being unfriendly, I just didn't want to open my mouth more than I needed to, for fear one of the many tiny flies buzzing around him decided to escape into it. When the screw opened the door for breakfast, a gust of stale, piss-laden prison air rushed in. It smelled like a field of roses to me.

When we opened up proper, at half-nine or so, I shot out like a bat out of hell and grabbed as many cleaning products and a large bin as quickly as I could. I filled the bin, but the totality of my efforts had been for naught, the place looked and stank as bad as ever. Most of the other lads on 7F were alright with me, but not all - because of all the media nonsense. They viewed me with suspicion and were as cautious as serpents around me. When you are the F.N.G (fucking new guy) in a new prison, you see the prison governor on the next available morning. That is the governor and/or one of their deputies. You don't ask for this, it's just a fair-accompli, so I was given a 2-Bar Chief.

"David Mahon?"

"Yes."

"I'm Chief 'X', how are you settling in?"

"Great."

"You won't be on this wing for long. You'll go over to East-wing next week."

"East wing?"

"Yeah. The I.M will see you about a job later."

"The I.M?"

"Yeah. Next!"

Not for the first time or last time in prison did I feel like I'd fallen down the rabbit hole and arrived in a different land. I asked one of the lads on the landing what an I.M was;

"Industrial Manager."

"A what?"

"He's a two-bar chief; he gives you a job in a workshop."

"Alright. What's east-wing?"

"It's a separate wing, built for jockeys (sex offenders), but now it's full of bleedin' rats. It's a rats landing. Why?"

"The chief said I'd be going there, but I won't if it's full of snitches."

"Yeah, true dat bro, snitches -get- stitches, what?!"

"Too right."

"They'll probably send you over anyway, bro -not calling you a rat- but you're kinda famous, a 'profile' prisoner, know what I mean?"

I did. Great. Now, thanks to the media, I was going to be grouped together with a bunch of informers. That's not putting a target on my back at all, is it? Then the I.M met with me;

"Hiya, David, settling in alright?"

"Yes, thanks."

"I'm the I.M. My name is Mr. "X" and it's my job to find you one!"

"Okay."

"So, how do you feel about woodwork?"

"Great, no problem."

"Are you handy at all?"

"Yeah, not too bad."

"Okay, come with me so I'll bring you to the joinery shop."

And he did. I actually loved it down there; it was a great way to spend my time and kept me busy. There were only two problems, though. The first was that you could only work a few hours a day and it was, therefore, a little stop-start. The second is that the screw-in-charge down there is a total and utter prick. In the land of the shit-head, this guy would be king. Anyway, I got on great with my fellow "lads" and we worked hard but had great craic along the way. After two weeks had passed, I asked to see the chief who'd told me about going to East wing. Don't get me wrong. I still wasn't a snitch, but a few of the lads I worked with lived over there and they weren't either;

"Chief, you told me two weeks ago that I'd be over to East wing in under a week and …."

"…No, I didn't. I never said that."

"Do you not remember? It was my first morning on 7F, you asked how I was getting on, then we'll get you over to East wing next week?"

"No, I would never have said that. Normally, you have to do 8 weeks in here and be a good boy (No.P19's or disciplinarians) before we'd ever consider …moving you."

Another prison. Another chief. Same old lies. I ended up changing cells on 7F later that same week because 14 days and 14 nights of cleaning and scrubbing, that cell had achieved the square root of nothing. I'd grown to be paranoid about its smell following me around like that kid with the blanket in the Charley Brown cartoons. Such was my paranoia; I'd almost scrubbed off a layer of skin in the shower, but thankfully, it hadn't.

My new cell and cellmate were a much cleaner experience altogether - not too hard! He was only a young fellow actually, a kid, really. He was very clean and very quiet and was imprisoned for the monstrous crime of Stealing a push bike. It was as clear as the nose on your face that he has psychological issues and it has always been my opinion that he did not belong in prison. I'll give you a quick example as to why, every week, you are allowed to order something from the Tuck-shop, I used to buy him a bag of sweets and he'd be overjoyed like a child. He would also laugh out loud or cry his eyes out for no apparent reason. In a hate-filled environment like Wheatfield, even the other lads looked out for him, highly irregular. I didn't spend too long with him because I was soon moved into another cell -another 2 man cell- but this time I was on my own. It was great. You don't appreciate your own company until you haven't had it for a while. Of course, nothing lasts forever and a couple of weeks later, I was given a new cellmate in, on top of me. He was a smoker and a bully.

If you let him, he was what I would call a passive–aggressive bully because he'd insinuate rather than outright challenge and would do little, stupid things to "prove" his dominance. I'm quite easy going, but it was starting to grate on me. Then, one day, I caught him snooping around in my stuff – a major no-no in a prison environment. Was this a once off? Hardly.

"Were you going through my stuff?"

"N…No."

"If I ever see you touching anything belonging to me, I'll chop your bleedin' hands off!!!"

This big, tough bully put in a transfer the following morning. When news of his transfer hit the landing, one of the lads approached me;

"I see your mate ran away!"

"He was no mate of mine."

"Here – is it true you told him that you'd chop his hand off?"

"I did. Yeah."

"Did ye?!!"

"Yeah, but not literally!"

"(laughing) Well, he took it bleedin' literally!!"

I found out after that, that he'd once bullied the young kid I'd been doubled up with, so I was delighted my tongue-in-cheek comment put the fear of God in him. It just proves true the old adage that all bullies are cowards, doesn't it?

Life ticked along with the same routine, day-in, day-out, more or less. I was still working in a joinery shop and really enjoyed making a few bits and pieces for myself, especially the flower boxes. As always, I was eager to learn new things and in particular, a wooden bench caught my eye. I had noticed it on my very first day working there and I had promised myself I'd give it a shot once I'd polished up my skills. As I did in Mountjoy, I went to the gym as often as I was allowed in Wheatfield, too, which was around 3 times a week on average. I pushed myself as hard as my hips would allow and I started giving myself endurance targets to meet-achieve, then raising them incrementally. One such goal was on the exercise bike

- a low impact but high cardio exercise – that didn't tax my hips like, say - a treadmill would. I remember being up in the gym one particular day and breaking one of my endurance goals and headed off to my shower-exhausted – but feeling pretty good about myself.

As I walked into my shower, there was a really weasel looking character standing at the next cubicle. I didn't pay him too much heed, but my lizard brain went on high alert. That's normally a good barometer for trouble, but I decided to concentrate on showering without falling first, then I'd log in with my resident lizard.

I left my cubicle, walked over to the changing area and then everything went dark. What had happened was that two cowardly rats jumped me and knocked me unconscious before I could get any retaliation in. When I came to, I shook my head clear of the myopic fog and got to my feet screaming revenge and meaning every word of it. I must've gotten up too quickly, as no sooner had I started making a move toward those two yellow pieces of shit that my legs went wobbly and I had to plank my backside on a bench until the blood started flowing back into them. Before that could happen, the gym officer heard the commotion and came in to see what had happened. I withdrew to the toilet to see what damage was done and clean away the blood before the screw saw it. It looked pretty bad and as soon as the screw saw me, he was all over me, peppering me with questions I wouldn't answer. They may have been scumbags, but I was never a snitch and wasn't about to start over them. As the screw walked away, he almost walked into the sneaky little weasel who'd been lying in wait at the showers. He'd been there the whole time to see if I'd said anything.

I was brought back to my cell feeling disoriented and humiliated. I'm not a hard man and I'm not a stranger to a row, but I'd always at least lose honourably and not like the victim I was being made to feel like. Suddenly, prison seemed alien and antagonistic, and despite the numerous;

"Are you alright, Dave?"

"Great."

My dishevelled and bruised appearance suggested otherwise. I licked my wounds in the cell for a while and then I was brought down to the medics.

"You've got a lot of bruising, Dave."

"I know."

"We'll send you out for an X-ray."

"No need, it's a couple of black eyes. I'll be great."

I was right. So that, dear reader, is exactly how and what happened in full. Fast forward a couple of days;

"Dave Mahon attacked in showers - beaten to a pulp!"

"Battered Dave's jaw broken!"

And on and on. I never once said who it was that attacked me and you don't live on this planet as long as I have without making a few enemies. Of course, the flip side to that coin is that you make some friends along the way, so I decided to make a few phone calls. I had to be careful, though, because prison creates a field atmosphere in which small infections can grow into large sores. My pride was hurt; let's call a spade a spade, so my psychological and emotional equilibrium was completely out of sync. There was a balance I needed to address between waiting to avoid confrontation and not falling prey to the bitterness, aggression and violence that were always bubbling away not too far below the prison surface.

Within a couple of days, I was approached by a younger inmate whose uncles were known to me. He had heard that I was making a few phone calls;

"If you drop it, the lads will drop it as well."

"Give me 24 hours. I'll think about it."

Ego can be a terrible thing if you let it control you. It wasn't an easy decision because those cowards shouldn't be allowed to get away with what they did. But, a truce, an end to hostilities would be better all around, so I agreed to it. I still made a point of going back to the gym, just once, to show face and to let it be known that I wasn't going to turn into one of those vulnerable prisoners who needed protection. It was also a full-stop I needed to do.

I eventually got moved over to the "promised land" of East 1, at that time, the best place to be in Wheatfield. It was a drug-free landing. Yeah, right, you could've counted all the non-drug users on one hand, out of the hundred or so inmates that were over there. The big advantages were that you had your own single and larger cell, with your own shower. I'd say in total, there were 50 prisoners on each of its three landings; it also had its own gym, library and yard for its "enhanced" prisoners. It was at that point that I was offered a job out on the grounds. It's the best job in the place, so I accepted. Grounds workers are trustees and only about 10 inmates are chosen, so it's a good job. When I started, which was in January 2017, the prison was still doing its rescue dog project, so on my very first day, a new dog was brought in. A Jack Russell!! I couldn't believe my luck, as I love dogs and had 2 Jack Russells of my own. He was a gorgeous little thing - brown and white, about 2 kilograms in weight, filthy dirty and tried to bite everyone he came in contact with. He'd obviously been abused in the past, the poor thing. I claimed him straight away and it was up to me to look after him. I felt like I'd won the lottery. Better even.

I walked that little dog every day, 7 days a week come rain or shine. He would still snip at people, but I'd managed to bond with him and he allowed me to wash him. It took 3 or 4 good scrubs before I got him properly clean and it was worth the effort. I noticed as I washed him, that his side was especially tender and incredibly sore for him, so in my opinion, he must've been kicked around by the brainless thugs who abandoned him. Well, those days were over for him now. Being his 'handler', I was next given the job of naming him. For me, his name had to sum him up to be an extension of his personality. He was a feisty little thing. So, when the officer asked me what I'd 'christened' him, there was only one name on the shortest short-list in history;

"Feisty!"

"I can see why! Good name."

It was, and so the name stuck, Feisty by name and nature. Within a matter of weeks, he was my best pal. He grew to love all the other lads out in the grounds but hated the officers. Maybe it's a uniform thing with dogs-postmen and all that. But I think it was different with my Feisty. One of the officers asked me if I was training him to be that way, but honestly – I wasn't! I think that Feisty's screw-hatred was born out of some of them hitting his cage at night time and as he'd only see the uniform and hear the jangling keys, that -to me anyway- makes the most sense. Apart from looking after Feisty, I had other duties (like the rest of the lads out there), such as cleaning up all the rubbish and doing gardening duties. During the spring/summer months, we also had to plant approximately 60,000 plug plants into pots, sow them and then put them together- somewhere in the region of - 1,800 flower baskets. These would be sold around most of the other prisons, in the I.P.S. as well as to the prison staff. I really enjoyed this kind of work and anyway, it beat sitting in a cell. Didn't it?

My little broma with Feisty came to an abrupt end just 4 months into it;

"Great news, Dave!"

"What's that?"

"We found a new home for Feisty!"

I was delighted for my little pal because prison is no place for a dog and he deserved a home where he'd be loved and treated as he should've been all along. On a personal level, I was absolutely gutted; I was really going to miss him. I stayed with him all that day until it was time for him to go and I said my goodbyes to him. Not all officers are dick-heads, and one in particular had a heart and more. He saw how much Feisty meant to me, so he very kindly gave me a photo of him and his collar. Feisty's, that is! That mightn't sound like much, but it truly was. Three weeks passed;

"Great news, Dave!"

"What was this, déjà-vu?"

"What?"

"Feisty's back!"

That started a cascade of gags;

"He's back off T.R! (Temporary release)"

"He got done for A.B.H! (Actually badly harm)"

"Poor Feisty, talk about Ruff Justice!"

Well, you get the idea! Apparently, he had been sent back because he'd bitten the owner, but I didn't care. I had my little Feisty back and we enjoyed the work and the fresh air together. I got on very well with the lads out in the grounds and I also had a few friends I'd meet up with every night in the library, from 5:30 p.m. to 7 p.m., more or less. We'd talk about anything and everything; it was like meeting up with a couple of friends after work in the pub. Only with books. And no alcohol. But you get the idea! I was doing pretty well in prison, apart from my grief, memories and unfathomable pain about Amy, Audrey and Dean. It was with those concerns foremost in my mind that I went back to my cell one Friday evening and was locked up as usual. Then, literally, 2 minutes later, my door flew open and 4 burley officers stormed in. It's not in the least bit pleasant and is what the screws like to do during a search or whatever in order to remind you that in prison, "might is right," "Grab some of your stuff, Dave."

"Why? What's wrong here?"

"You're being moved up to West 2."

"What did I do wrong?"

"There's a hit on your life."

And it was up to 24 hours of protective custody for me, but you know about that already from the prologue. Now that you know a bit more about me, it probably won't surprise you to know that I missed my little Feisty so much. I actually started dreaming about him! Luckily for me, my good friend from the grounds was allowed in to see me. (I still don't know how he managed to pull that one off!!) And he promised to look after Feisty for me until I got back. He had his own dog to look after anyway, so I didn't get too jealous!

When in solitary, there's not a huge amount to do. So I filled my days reading voraciously and growing the germ of the idea that you now hold in your hands. I was still able to have my 2-6 minute phone calls to Audrey and thank God for them and Audrey. I am in no doubt that those 12 precious minutes each day and the photos of her that my friend was able to get for me got me through my time in solitary. I memorised every millimetre of those photographs, two of our wedding and one of Audrey sitting with her feet in a fish pool over in Spain. When I finally got to meet with a chief and a Governor who were willing to talk to me, we had an interesting discussion,"

"Well, Dave, how are you?"

"Why am I here?"

"Well… there's a phone call from Mountjoy and money was offered to have you sliced up… or worse."

"And?"

"The… eh, prisoner who was contacted to carry this out…"

"What about him?"

"You see, it's weird. It doesn't fit his profile."

"Why?"

"Well, he's over on East and…"

He realised that he'd said too much, so he just shut up. What did I extract from all of that? Well, clearly, there was a price on my head, so whether that came from some of Dean's so-called friends or from the Wilsons was anybody's guess. Certainly, what didn't help was the likes of the irresponsible Sunday World and their crusade to publish only the nastiest articles filled with vitriol and such viciousness that they could only know exactly what they were doing. They weren't alone.

My sixth day on protection started off like all the other ones - up out of bed, a cup of tea, and watched Ireland a.m., the morning show of choice for every prisoner. How's that? Anyway, along came the newspaper review and the headlines on the star that morning made for grim reading;

"Dave in lock-up as a known criminal wants him dead."

That wasn't going to help matters. I wanted to try and get my hands on a copy of that rag (it being the paper of choice for drug dealers and purse snatchers - a demographic that Wheatfield covered in Spades) as I might've been able to get more information out of that than in prison. As it happened, I had a visit booked that day with my father and Audrey, so I had hoped that they would've read the article and given me whatever information it contained. I also called Tony, and he was trying to book in for a visit with me, but the prison kept putting him off. I then saw another one of Wheatfield's many governors on the landing and made a point of talking to him;

"How long do I have to stay here for?"

"Em…What did the other governor say?"

Either they were completely stupid or else decided to keep their cards very close to their chest. I could be mistaken, but I'm fairly sure that I was their only high-profile prisoner with a death threat on him who was splashed all over the paper that day. Do you seriously believe that wouldn't have been discussed that morning? No? Me either. Welcome to the prison system.

As I was being brought down to my visit, I bumped into a few of my friends and they seemed genuinely shocked to see me. They tried to talk to me, to ask me a few questions, but I was ushered along by my escort. In the visit box, both Mick and Audrey looked terrible. My father was unusually pale and shaken, and Audrey had a few drinks on her, not knowing what else to do because neither of us was in charge anymore. It was up to the governors; God help us. Audrey and I had a little bit of a snap at each other during an otherwise lovely visit (given the circumstances), but that's to be expected every so often. We're not the bloody Brady bunch!

The following day, I met yet another governor, a full week into solitary;

"How long are you going to keep me here?"

"Em…What did the other..."

"Look, can you make a decision on me? Today??"

"Well, the guy who is meant to carry this out, he's still over on East…"

"What?"

"Yeah, he's still over there…"

"So, you never even approached him?"

"No."

"He's meant to kill me; you know who he is. You know he's on the super-duper good boy landing, and you leave him there?"

"Eh… yes."

"And put me - who's a trustee and hasn't threatened anybody, enter a punishment landing for my own protection?"

"Yes!"

Well, you get the idea of how parsimonious governors can be, so I won't labour the point. I did eventually get back onto the East Wing, where an even more dangerous set of tests awaited me, but we'll get to that. In general, my normal prison day reverted back to the grounds, then the library in the evenings. I took a few classes up at the school, hacked all the boxes I needed to tick, and collected plenty of certificates along the way. By far, my favourite class was Spanish, not just because I love the country so much, but because the guy teaching it was the only real teacher in the place. He knew his stuff and learning it was fun.

I'm often asked if I was lonely in prison. My answer is that solitude and loneliness are two completely different experiences. Why? Because not for one moment during all my time in solitary (or in prison) did I ever feel lonely. When I was out on the grounds, the grimy architecture of the prison was softened by my little Feisty bouncing along after me, and the nasal-moped-monotone of junkies shouting through windows was dissolved by the sounds of bird-song. Planting flowers and trees kept me in touch with nature and life, whilst within the landing walls lay only tales of vengeance and death. Wasn't it Oscar Wilde who noted that we were all in the gutter, yet some of us look up and see the stars? I know where my focus was, but sadly, that didn't go for everyone.

Remember that bench I wanted to make? I actually did it! It now adorns my father's award-winning garden, but I also asked to have two more made to be donated to the Cappagh Hospital as a thank you for everything they did for me. I was refused. I'm not a charity case, so of course, I offered to pay for all the materials and preparation costs, the whole nine yards. Again, I was refused because there was "a waiting list for items going to charity." I persisted for a full year, even providing documentation from the hospital, but they never allowed me to do it. Rehabilitation? Paying a debt to Society? Coming out as a better person? With better management, what hope does the average prisoner have of that?

Cancer - Dave

Let me just get this out of the way. I'm not looking for sympathy. I'm no angel, but nobody, and I do mean nobody, either wants or deserves cancer. Yes, I was in prison and Dean's death begins and ends with me. I accept that, I never hid from it and I have to try and live with that each and every day. What follows is a brief synopsis of my cancer story, not only because it forms a massive part of who I am today but also because it might just help somebody – if they find themselves in a similar situation.

I'm not a moaner or complainer by nature, but due to the experiences of my poor mother and dear father, I'd learned to take my health extremely seriously. That's not to say that. I run to the hospital at the first sign of a runny nose, far from it, but mysterious lump and bumps appearing at random. I don't ignore those. In June of 2017, I felt a bit of a lump in the left-hand side of my neck. Typical male that I am, I actually thought about leaving it, but that's only vanity, my parents didn't get an early warning sign, I might get lucky. It might be nothing. Either way, I put my name down to see the prison doctor.

There is a world of difference between a doctor and a prison doctor. You don't get second opinions and usually, you don't receive anything, even pretending to be dressed up as an "examination." Usually, you sit on the horns of the following dilemma - option (A) – A course of antibiotics or option (B) - A paracetamol; I received option (A). It didn't work. So, after a week of trying, I went back to the doctor. When he finished his examination (I got lucky, it was a proper medical exam), he uttered the word I feared most in the world out loud for the first time - "It might be a cyst, or it could be cancer." There it was, old Mr. Cancer had been stalking me in the shadows since my mother's epic battle, and now here he was, sinking his sabre-sharp poisonous claws into my - literal- throat. I hate cancer almost as much as I fear it. Back then, it was the beginning of the sum of all fears for me. It 'might' be a cyst, but if it wasn't, I'd have a fight on my hands. A fight for my life.

How do you fight cancer, though? For me, you couldn't. What does it look like? How do you hope to stop it? Those thoughts are negative and useless, you'll die for sure. So here's what I did, I personalized it. My cancer became my 'Shark.' Why? Both are terrifying, man-eating death machines. They consume flesh, blood, bone and organs with impurity and when they're not doing that, they propagate their family line. Sharks make baby sharks who, in turn, carry on down the line

544

cancer cells… you get the point, I don't need to labour it any further. But here's the thing: sharks can die; they can be eaten. So can cancer. Ironically, it was pointed out to me (much later) that sharks can't get cancer! Anyway, the point is if you have a big-scary monster trying to kill you, then you need to kill it first.

Back in June 2017, I was swimming in a pool that may or may not have had a shark in it. We didn't know, so the doctor arranged for me to go the Eye and Ear Hospital on Adelaide road, or to give its full and grandiose moniker - The Royal Victoria Eye and Ear Hospital, Dublin. Going from prison to, well, anywhere really is a lovely experience once you get past "The procedure." It is mind-numbingly predictable and never… ever changes. For my first trip to the hospital, it was no big deal, but what I didn't know then was that I'd be such a constant on the prison escort service. Bear in mind this happened every single time:

You are assigned three randomly selected officers to escort you.

You are taken from your cell to the reception area.

At this stage, you undress fully in their presence, then searched… fully.

You are then made to sit on the "Boss" chair, which electronically searches out your most private areas for contraband.

You are then taken through the metal detector, like you would at an airport.

Due to my hip replacements, I set this off every single time. This meant I had to explain it. Every. Single. Time.

You then get to suit up, get manicured into two sets of hand-cuffs and off you go. When you return to prison, it's the exact same process, but in reverse. Now, I'm not saying that the entire process was deliberately designed to be so degrading and dehumanising, but…

Anyway, back to the actual journey and it was a wonderful experience. Why? Well, for reasons that all non-prisoners (including myself back in my pre-prison days) take completely for granted. Dublin, for me, as a former taxi driver in this fair city, holds a story on memory on every corner. It literally brought joy to my heart to see places such as the motorbike shop on Nass road, then on to the Mercedes Garage and as we got closer to the city centre, the bars that I used to frequent! The Headline Bar, The Bleeding Horse, The Harcourt and then Conrad hotel – all filled with great times and a world away from prison life! I had read something before about the 'past being a different country' and that our memories are the closest thing we have to a Time Machine. I had never appreciated those statements until that moment where I was safe and happy in my little time machine capsule and blissfully unaware of what lay ahead. My little time capsule also helped insulate me from the mind-numbing drivel that the screws were spouting on about. For the journey there and the journey back, it was non-stop whining about money, overtime time and a half etc. They knew the price of everything but the value of nothing.

When we arrived at the hospital, the first thing I heard was the clunk-click of the cuffs going back on, and then I was let out of the van like a dog on a lead. One of the few "perks" of being a guest of the state's pleasure is that you don't do a lot in the way of queuing up. The reasons are quite obvious when you think about it because who wants to wait around in line standing behind a guy chained up like a stand in for Hannibal Lecter? It's a sight that must be extremely disconcerting for the young, elderly and the vulnerable. Unfortunately, it's a practice very necessary for only a handful of Irish prisoners but not all, not by a long way. It is humiliating beyond belief to be the cause of fear for sweet little old ladies and little children who physically stop and stare in horror at the 'Monster' in the Cannibal costume. It's just one in a long list of Draconian systems still in practice by the I.P.S and the best way I found to deal with it was to pretend to myself that I was in a movie and it was just a role I was playing, that's how surreal the whole thing is.

It didn't take long before I was seen by a young doctor (a sure sign you're getting along in years is when doctors look like school-children!) started examining me. It was basic stuff:

"Is the lump sore?"

"No."

"Has it gotten bigger?"

"No."

"Have you lost weight?"

"No."

He seemed like a nice enough chap but nervous. I soon found out why. As "terrifying" as I might've looked in all my chairs, I didn't hold a candle to what walked in next. It was his boss. A strong, strident, independent Irish lady, knocking on the door of sixty and oozing power and professionalism from every pose. This lady was ruler-straight and needle-sharp. She issued orders to her team with the assured expectation that they would be followed – to the letter - without question. She was a straight talker, too. I liked her. My officer-escorts clearly weren't paying attention or respect to her presence and efforts to consult with me. That would be typical of the arrogance and ignorance of that particular crew. It was also a big mistake. She shot them a look – singular one! And they shut up like slapped children. A couple of minutes later, they started yapping again. That was a bigger mistake! It only took a few sharp, cutting words of surgical precision to rip apart their boisterous façade and leave them needing stitches. Now I really liked her! Once the ignorant screws were sitting silently on the naughty step, she turned her attention back to my pre-pubescent doctor, who was instructed to put a camera up my nose and down my throat.

God love him. He didn't do it right and got a right old scolding for his trouble. She put it right and then sat down beside me and asked if she could discuss my case in front of "them." Nodding her head in the direction of the naughty step, I gave my consent but insisted that I had a word with them first. She seemed genuinely taken back to be spoken to in this way! I asked the officers not to discuss my case with anyone in the prison or to go to the papers. They agreed. The opinion of this incredible doctor a professor no less – inspired me with hope!

"Nothing sinister. It's a cyst; it will require an operation to have it removed. We'll have you in within the next six weeks."

Wow! Great news, it's not cancer. The relief was almost overpowering. I hadn't had the best of luck up 'till then and certainly, my family had been cursed – if anything, by the Big-C, so I was overjoyed. Who could blame me? I went back to the prison doctor a few days later and told him the good news. In fairness, he seemed genuinely delighted as he was typing everything down and updating my medical file. I asked him if he shouldn't wait to get the files from the hospital first so that he'd at least have all of the correct medical terminology that a layman like me couldn't hope to understand, but he assured me that it wasn't a problem. On the surface, all appeared well, but below the surface, old Mister Shark was developing an appetite…

Time, as it does, moved on and so just a few weeks later – in July – I got called back in for an appointment at the Eye and Ear hospital. The Queen of Mean must've been off that day as I was seen by a different doctor. Something you need to get used to as a prisoner-patient is the repetition of questioning. This was no exception. In point of fact, I was asked all of the exact same questions in the exact same order, it kind of makes you think that they worked off standard pro-forma or something. I am a patient man by nature, but I had to draw the line when they once again wanted to perform the old camera-down- the neck trick. This wasn't exactly inspiring confidence, so I asked them to go and find my other doctor, Professor Terror herself. After checking their notes for a few minutes, they looked at me with blank expressions;

"What was the name of this doctor?"

I hadn't a clue! The last thing I expected to be asked about that day was the name of a doctor, so I couldn't help them... or me. Having drawn a blank, they told me that they'd have to do a biopsy and a scan "before we can see what." Little warning alarms started to beep inside my head. "It's normally benign..." Hang on... benign? I'd heard that word before, deep in the trenches of my nightmares... that was a cancer word, wasn't it? I managed to keep my emotions in check and put on my poker face for the journey back to Wheatfield. I'd have to wait about six weeks for my next appointment, which in real terms meant that my shark was feeding freely for about two months before having to worry about getting caught. Sharks can consume an awful lot of flesh in that time.

Just as I was starting to come to grips with a cancer possibility coming back onto the table, I got called – completely out of the blue - for another hospital appointment. It had been four days since my last. Not good. Something else unexpected happened when we arrived at St. James's Hospital. This was getting weirder and more worry-some by the second. We waited in the accident and emergency department (in full-Hannibal costume) for ages, causing no end of worried, scared and judgmental looks from all corners of the busy hospital until I was eventually called to the doctor's office. Here, I was met by a very professional and extremely polite Northern Irish doctor who – surprise, surprise- started asking me all the same questions all over again.

"Have you lost weight?"

"No."

"Is it sore?"

"No, look, I think I'm here for a scan and biopsy..."

"Huh??"

This was clearly news to her, so I went through the story so far with her. And it was obvious that the more I explained, the more perplexed she got. She was a smart cookie, though, so she grabbed the bull by the horns and called the Eye and Ear right in front of me.

"I'm very sorry, Mr Mahon, but the Eye and Ear just confirmed that they are dealing with you, so there is no need for you to be here."

"So why am I here? Who made the mistake?

"I don't know… maybe the doctor in the prison?"

Now, wouldn't you agree that this was a very strange series of events? Anyway, the doctor wished me luck and she went back off on her rounds. I was escorted off to the hospital waiting area, rattling in chains like an old ghost with the three prison officers, when one of either Larry, curly or Moe called the driver of the "Paddy Wagon"- prison slang/parlance for the prison transport vehicle. Now, during the consultation I was having with the doctor, these three ignorant clowns were busy on their mobile phones like distracted teenagers. No respect. As we waited (and then waited for some more) they started making a big kerfuffle about how long everything was taking and how we'd be better off going outside to meet the van. Well, lo-and-behold, wouldn't you know it, there just so happened to be some press photographers hanging around outside waiting for us. I mean, what a complete coincidence that was. I'm not a betting man, but I'd love to hear what kind of odds Paddy Power would've given for that freak occurrence to happen on a day and at a place when I wasn't even meant to be. Even more unlucky was the fact that the van couldn't get any parking and had to drive around the block again. Two days later, I was splashed all over the Sunday world again. What another stroke of good luck for the Sunday world to have had their photographer at St. James that day. Somebody somewhere made a nice few quid for themselves out of that and even though I was still no closer to knowing if I had the Big-C, there was a little bit of an upside.

The problem with being chained up to a goon is that when your photograph is published, the goon makes it into shot. When three goons are with you, they all run the risk of being caught on camera. When some higher-up at the I.P.S. looked through their Sunday papers. They took a right old shot at seeing their prized prison officers out of official uniform and being equally as casual with their safety. A directive "from the top" was issued and questions were asked. Further, there was to be no more relaxing of the escort rules. All prison officers were to wear full uniform, complete with stab vests, etc., the whole nine yards across all prisons for all escorts, with no exceptions. This caused absolute uproar across the prison estates, not by the prisoners, but the officers. Apparently, the poor little bunnies were "sweating like paedophiles in bravery suits" during the warm weather, and there was much concern about "chaffing" and "dizzy spells." As a result, good enough for them. Unfortunately, this practice was soon abandoned anyway due to the weak and toothless management the I.P.S prides itself on. Believe it or not, this is a very real problem and yet nobody is blowing any whistles about it. What we have is a classic case of a free-for-all discipline light system, with no checks and balances where bully-boys roam free to run the school. But I had bigger problems; I had found another lump at the side of my neck. That wasn't good. I couldn't be bothered telling the prison doctor about it either. Soon, he might've sent me to bloody spec-savers or something!

The day of my next hospital appointment eventually arrived. So it was another early start, down to reception and through "the procedure" once again. The only difference this time was that the officers were wearing all of their full uniforms - stab proof- finery. Not only that, but as I was waiting in the holding cell, I overheard one of the senior officers on their two-way radios say,

"This is a very high-profile prisoner, boys. By the book, all the way."

It was food for thought. How could such a "high-profile" (their terminology, not mine) prisoner such as little-old me be taken out of prison to a place he wasn't meant to be, with not so much as a basic paperwork scan or a simple phone call to confirm an appointment? Yet, that had happened and now it was "by the book" day? What if, instead of St. James Hospital, they took me to a secluded area somewhere, with a few dangerous junkies lying in wait with knives instead of a tabloid reporter? That's how easy it would've been to have me killed and what 'spin' would've been put on that?

As I walked to the van with my chained escorts, I couldn't resist.

"Full uniforms today, lads?"

"Oh yeah. We got into trouble the last time..."

They actually admitted the whole casual/uniform debate. The idiots. Naturally, they had to at least try and save face, as – lest we forget- they are bullies, and this is their playground.

"Ah, Jesus, Dave, you're very photogenic."

"Jaysus, the papers won't leave you alone, will they?"

I blanked out all their taunts and just drifted off to my time capsule, only that day, I moved to a future day, where I'd visit all of my old haunts once again, with Audrey holding my hand.

When we get to the Eye and Ear, I have to move out of my mental time capsule and back into my "movie space" as I traipse through the hospital in my Cannibal regalia. We get to the nurses' station and guess what happens next? We are a week early! The bumbling idiots had gotten their dates mixed up. I kid you not. You couldn't make this stuff up, "by the book" day, alright! I couldn't help but laugh and when the stooges glared at me from the nurses' station, I said (to the nurses).

"Ah well, this is progress. The last time, we went to the wrong hospital!!"

It was a much quieter journey back to the prison!

A week later, the same drill, journey and uniforms, only this time, we were meant to be where we should've been at the right time – the right place. Third time works a charm. I was put through the scan first and then I was given my biopsy. This is not a nice experience as they puncture your neck – three times- with a big bloody needle, and then they scan you again. When you're done, you're done. As a prisoner, I couldn't be told when I could expect to receive my results, whereas a citizen would at least be provided with a date. Turned out, mine would arrive the following week, September 22nd, and for reasons I won't go into. I knew the date in advance anyway. Hey, there are always ways around every problem!

The days turned into weeks, then the weeks turned into months and before I knew it, December had arrived. During all of this time, the lumps got bigger, the shark grew stronger and I existed in a physical and emotional no-man's-land, not knowing if I did or didn't have cancer. There was also the not unimportant matter of where my treatment would continue – from home or from prison? My appeal was already heard and I received something known as a "reserved judgment." In plain, ordinary language, this is a process where the C.C.A (court of Criminal Appeal) squeezes every last drop of hope out of the "Appellant" (that would be me) and makes you wait on your nerves to see if you were successful or not. It is a truly interesting phenomenon in this country as it almost always gets used in high-profile/media-friendly cases, such as mine. They are an absolute God-send for the media, as the process lends itself to multiple, easy headlines. For example, the day the appeal is heard, the following morning's headlines bleed all the details on their front pages in their usual alliterative finery, such as "Mad Mahon", or "Deadly Dave", or "Convicted criminal", etc. How the red-tops love their alliteration! Then, just as that settles down, the day of the actual judgement comes along "hence reserved" and they get to lazily regurgitate the bile all over again. As you can imagine, on the seventh of December 2017, the furthest thing from my mind was cancer and I entered the courts with a little bit of hope. Well, that was short-lived, I lost. In prison parlance, this is known as a "carry-on", as in you just carry on doing the sentence you were doing and, therefore, has no bearing at all on the classic Barbara Windsor and Sid James comedies.

The newspaper headlines the following morning were a journalistic orgy of salacious sensationalism of the Red Top variety. It was the usual crowd-pleasing snake oil trading hacks, emptily indulging in their misapprehending and cruel re-telling of the facts, crudely re-imagining the ghostly tableau of what they thought my miserable existence should be. Something that they all failed to report was that my legal team actually won that appeal hands-down, a first-round knockout, it wasn't even a contest, so the C.C.A only succeeded in highlighting the morass of institutional incompetence (see, I can do alliteration too!!) that possess for "justice" in this country. Those three deciding judges: Michael Perth, Alan Mahon (no relation) and George "Justice" T- Beauford of Dukes of Hazard fame Birmingham, should be ashamed of themselves and they know it. Anyway, thank God for my friends back at Wheatfield, as they got me through it. It's funny, but in prison, you develop what is known as "gallows humour" – you have to, as they are horribly depressing places of torment and flooding rivers of bad news. When I got back to my cell, my friends were waiting for me with a pack of "celebratory" cigars! It was a good-natured celebration soaked with slagging and sarcasm in equal measure, and it eased my concerns about the following day's hospital appointment.

Yes, you read that correctly. I had just lost my appeal and I was unexpectedly called back to the hospital the following day. I should have noticed the dark, menacing dorsal fin in the water. At that point, I had only had my M.R.I the previous week, but nothing even fully prepares you for a death sentence. When I arrived at the hospital, it was full-on. Dr. Lecter time, as not only was I splashed across every paper in the land, but I was also blessed to have the three worst sadist this side of Hell's creation as my escorts. Any chance they got or hh manufactured to pull on my chains like I was a rabid dog or opportunity to call attention to me as a "celebrity prisoner" (an oxymoronic title if ever one existed), they seized upon with great gusto. It was an exercise in state-sponsored humiliation of the gravest kind and they were enjoying it way too much. I guess it's true what they say about tiny minds loving petty torments. It was because of this continuous barrage of cruel and unusual punishment (to coin the phrase any good student of the Geneva Conventions would slap on them) that I thought had made my doctor so jittery and uncomfortable, but alas, I was wrong about that.

Hindsight is indeed twenty-twenty, but everything just felt "off" that day. Even casting aside the media coverage, the Hitler-youth escort and the fact that I wasn't expecting to be there, the whole scenario just felt out of place and wrong. As a dog biscuit on a communion plate. Where was the professor and her steely glare today? What I wouldn't have given to see her tear a few strips off the Black-and-Tan wannabes, I was still chained to. Maybe she was too busy for the likes of me now that I was merely tabloid fodder once again? Why did this new doctor look so worried?

"Mr. Mahon?"

(Not "Dave." He was getting more uneasy by the second. Not good.)

"We... eh... we have your results."

(Don't say cancer please, don't say cancer.)

"Em... Well, look, we need to book you in for next Tuesday..."

"Doctor, is it cancer?"

The answer I wanted to hear - what everyone wants to hear in that situation – is a loud, solid and resounding "No!" What I got was a very sad, sympathetic look and then he put his hand on my left shoulder, looked me in the eyes and

"Dave (not Mr. Mahon), how old are you?"

Oh, dear God, why was he answering my question with a question? Why did he want to know my age? Hang on; was I going to be fresh out of birthdays now?

"I'm... eh... (actually I couldn't remember, it took me a minute)... eh, forty six I think... look, is it cancer?"

"Well Dave, If I was a betting man... I'd say... yes... yes... you do."

Nope. It hadn't been the press coverage or the pack of dogs I was chained to, after all. It was just plain old bad news. He'd obviously drawn the short straw in the canteen that morning and it was "on" him to tell me something nobody wants to hear ever. Old man Cancer is stalking me through the shadows of time and space. Since sucking the life out of my dear mother had finally announced himself by sinking his sharp claws into my literal throat. It was the moment in jaws when Chief Brody and the shark came face to face and he says "We're gonna need a bigger boat"- yes, I was shocked, depressed, terrified and so much more, but I'd also looked at my enemy in the eye, and even though he was bigger, stronger, scarier than life itself, I didn't blink or back down.

I must use this opportunity to commend that young doctor on his bravery, compassion and professionalism. Yes, it was news I didn't want, but it must've been awful for him, too. To his eternal credit - and to the armies of healthcare professionals just like him across the world - he was outstanding under more pressure than normal, as he had to not only deal with me but had to conduct his business under the arrogant, watchful glare of three sadistic idiots who were everything he'd never be, who laughed and joked about utter nonsense as he delivered his news. As their churlish banter continued increasing in its vulgarity and poor taste, he continued my next line of treatment;

"Here's what happens next. The lump (remember when it was only a cyst?) on the left side of your neck has grown extremely large. What we need to do is take a piece of it out and see if we can find out what type of cancer it is. We can discuss the best course of treatments at that stage, okay?"

"Okay, thanks doc."

"No problem Dave, see you on Tuesday. Take care…."

I can't exactly remember the rest, but I do remember thinking that he was sitting on the fence a bit until he was sure of what he was dealing with. The journey back to prison was as cruel, degrading and miserable as the rest of the day had been. For example, I'd just been told to my face that I had throat cancer and yet all one of the officers could think about was bringing me to McDonalds because you've missed your lunch. That's good, Dave, isn't it?! Mac. Don. Alds!!" like I was a bloody kid. I declined the kind offer of a clown-based junk meal, but that didn't stop them going there anyway. "Are you sure, Dave?" We're all entitled to one as we've all missed our lunch hour because of you. It's great, it won't even cost us anything as we can claim the money back on expenses!!"

Well, whoopee -bloody- doo for them. As banal as it already sounds, it got even more surreal well let's call him "Percy" (in honour of that nasty, petty, horrible screw out of "The green mile" who danced joyfully on a mouse as he killed it and fried another inmate on "old sparky," because, well, it suits him) proceeded to give a running commentary about all the things the poor McDonalds worker was doing wrong as she served their "food, nd I should know, I used to be a manager at McDonalds." I'm sure old Ronald McDonald cried his eyes out of the day "Percy" tendered his notice to join the I.P.S. The only thing I asked for was "a cup of tea", and they "forgot" to get it for me.

I managed to hold my thoughts and tears together when I travelled back and when I walked through the prison, as you can't show any signs of weakness in prison – Ever. Not so much around my friend, but the vast majority of the rest were nothing more than a pack of sneering, opportunistic jackals. Back in my cell, I composed myself, made a cup of tea (you can keep your McDonalds freebie, Percy) and rehearsed that phone call I was about to make, as I wasn't "allowed" to do so from the hospital or on the journey back, Good "oul Percy" a manager at McDonalds? He couldn't manage his own ass on the toilet, but I had to put my focus back on important matters.

Being locked up takes away many freedoms, but it gives you an abundance of time, and time is never wasted if you use it wisely. I did, I'd composed myself and had a rough idea of how I was going to handle things. That took about an hour. The next thing I knew, the little hatch on my cell door lifted up and thank God, it was a familiar and friendly face. It was my good friend Sean and he could tell just by looking at me that something was seriously amiss. When my door was unlocked, he just marched right in and gave me a big hug. Now, hugging another man is neither "cool" nor "macho" in the way male perceptions are judged (between heterosexual men) in most walks of life, but especially so in prison. I'll go even further than that. If the wrong people happen to see it, that can become downright dangerous, but to Sean's everlasting credit, he couldn't have given a hoot; that's just the type of caring, decent man that he is. Up to that very moment, I had been in prison for almost two years and never cried, never even contemplated doing so. That changed in an instant-all that horrible news shattered dreams and nightmarish memories of Mick and Kay's experiences. The tears just wouldn't stop. Fair play to Sean. He stayed with me until I finally managed to scramble my "persona - Dave" back to life and crack a few jokes. It put me in mind of a famous quote I'd read from Nelson Mandela, who said that "prison is an incubator of friendship", and I can testify to the truth of those words. I checked the time on the TV; I had fifteen minutes until my father was due to visit and the phone call would have to wait.

In most prisons in Ireland, there is an officer in charge of each landing known as a "Class – Officer." This is the guy who is in charge of a "class" or "landing", as it's also known. Sean went to the class officer in charge that day and explained that I had received some very bad news (as could be evidenced by my still-red eyes anyway) without going into the details of what it was. He put me in touch with a chief officer (Identified as such by the two gold stripes called "Bars" on their shoulders) who was very sympathetic. She didn't even blink before promising me a Box-visit (a visit in a private room, away from all those cruel eyes studying you) and, two extra calls every day and whatever else I'd need. She left me with the cleanest of impressions that my request was reasonable and very straightforward and it was for situations exactly like mine that such procedure existed for compassionate grounds. It was a much needed soothing balm for my heavy and broken heart, so I went out to see my father with renewed optimism.

It never happened. Experience is a tough teacher and it gives you the exam before the lesson, as I soon discovered. I met with the assistant chief officer (or A.C.O) of the visits as soon as I got out there, fully expecting him to be aware of my situation from the chief. Bear in mind, an A.C.O is basically an assistant manager in any other profession and the gap between his one stripe and her two is vast. It's a no-brainer. My first dialogue with this particularly aloof potentate was crushing. I was polite, I was courteous, and I remembered my lowly station and humbly put my request forward. It was inconceivable that he hadn't already been aware of my news, both from the chief and from other officers, who, as a rule, gossip more than a sewing circle at a back-biters convention. It was surely a done deal, a foregone conclusion. Every prison character posted throughout their estate boasted of meeting inmates with "humanity," "respect" and "compassion." Revelling in their self-appointed image of responsible custodians. He towered over me, standing too close and blocked me like a bad metaphor;

"No."

"(Stunned) Please, is there anything you can do? I've received terrible news."

"So what?"

It was pointless, just another school yard bully flexing his muscles. I was well-shocked as I walked into the main visiting area to see my father, who was expecting to hear all about my appeal, not expecting what was about to come. I didn't have the mental or emotional strength left to stick to the plan formulated in my cell over a cup of tea. I only had the words out of my mouth - hadn't even hugged him yet. Before the tears came, and when I saw the realization in his face of the word "cancer", I lost it completely. I've never been what could be called a crying man, but boy, when I do, there is no such thing as half measures. There, I was a fully grown man, father, husband (and I'm sure many other things besides!), but at that moment, I was a child again, crying to my daddy, hoping that he'd somehow make it all go away. I'd been through a year's worth of emotions in one day and yet Mick, somehow, managed to make me laugh. I don't know how he manages to do it. The rest of the visit went as well as could be expected and typically, he felt that it mightn't be as bad as I'd feared. I hoped he was right. I also couldn't help but wonder if he had similar conversations with my mother back when they faced their individual battles with this evil plague. To this day, I don't know where he gets his strength from, as cancer conversations must be among the most horrific to have with any family member, let alone multiple members. There are few better to have them with than Mick, but other difficult conversations lay ahead.

I got back to my cell with a head full of implacably depressing thoughts, random as tombstones in their overwhelming complexity. Your focus determines your reality, so I had to focus on what little I could do. Everything else, no matter how big or seemingly important before today, had to wait. So far, I knew - Mick and Sean knew and probably every screw in Ireland too, so I made it my mission to let my friends who didn't know, hear it from me directly. God forbid they might hear it from a screw… or worse. Yet, for all of those worthy names listed, there was one missing, the most important one of all. Audrey - my beautiful, sweet, loving wife. She'd already helped me through my mother's death; then we had the trauma from Amy, then Dean, then prison and now this… Death sentence. How much pain could one heart endure? I hoped this wasn't the final push over the edge for her, she deserves so much better. But there was no way I could hide this from her; I wouldn't even try to, our marriage is built on the foundation of trust that means warts n'all. That's why we had managed to survive hell, because we knew that no matter what, we had each other's backs ready to take bullets for each other. All I'd ever wanted to do was to protect her and make her feel happy and safe, just like any other husband. Happiness is contingent on making the right choices; there could be no happiness here, but she had to know that wasn't a choice.

It was one of the hardest calls I ever had to make. Audrey deserved so much more than to be given news of this magnitude over the phone, but the cat was well and truly out of the bag and I'd be damned if she didn't hear it from me first. My poor Audrey's heart shattered like glass as I knew it would, and her voice -as soft as falling snow- was filled with sadness. But the strength of her love still burst through. All I wanted in the world right then was to hold her, feel her crying in her arms and feed off each other's strength, getting through all of this the best we could. I thought of Mick's words – from our visit that day - coming back to me, so I tried using them to Audrey in a vain effort to keep hope alive;

"It mightn't be as bad as we think."

"What do you mean?"

"Well… we might get lucky."

"Ah, c'mon Dave, when were we ever lucky?!!"

She was right. For some reason, I found myself apologising before a sound – as beautiful as it was unexpected and welcome - Audrey was laughing! Broke my concentration;

"What on earth are you apologising for?"

"I…. eh… I don't know."

I kind of did know, though. I felt like I had let her down… again. I was supposed to be the strong one, and even from prison, I was trying to be her rock, but in that moment of apology, who knew what lay ahead? What use could I be to her – to Amy- if I became too weak to do anything? Telling my friends the unwelcome news after Audrey's call was an easier experience but tougher than expected.

You don't really expect men convicted of the most serious and brutal crimes - to show love, sympathy, and even empathy in some cases so freely, but they did. This gallery of modern rogues infused me with strength and hope I could scarcely have imagined. There is a great lesson in all of this, we need to see the person in front of us and look into their hearts, not their headlines. It's not an exaggeration to say that some of the warmest, kindest people I've ever met, I met in prison. I went back to my cell laughing, which was a blessing, especially at lock-up time and this was down to my friends too. In particular, it was my friend who gave me the celebratory cigars;

"Oh yeah, thanks again for the cigar!"

"What do you mean?"

"Well, you gave me a cigar yesterday, and now today I've got cancer!"

Let's just say that my tongue-in-cheek comment started so close to the bone bonder that only a bunch of guys living in the vacuum of joy that prison is, would properly understand, but we all laughed long and hard at each other. Behind closed doors, in the dark witching hours of a day that had already been a festival of the unlikely, I tried to occupy my mind with the most banal of thoughts just to try and ground myself. Should I go out to my job in the morning? Should I tell the senior officers out there that I report to? Routine was my happy place, my comfort zone and I needed some of that. There would be no quick fix out of this, no point in training for sprints when I would have to run a marathon. As that long and difficult day finally pulled the curtain of sleep over me, I was restless, fidgety as a mouse on Red Bull and frankly, terrified. Old Mr. Cancer had dug his roots in good and deep and there was blood in the water.

The manic events of December 8th discombobulated me so much that the events of the following days are lost to me... forever. December 11th, however, still exists (partially) in my mind only because I still have a copy of the letter that I wrote to the surgeon that day. It speaks for itself. It's a basic history of my treatment up until that point and is unapologetically honest and to the point. It wouldn't take a handwriting expert to gauge my state of mind or levels of anxiety at that time, and this is actually a deadly combination. I would soon find out that worry leads to added stress, leads to loss of sleep, promotes fatigue and low levels of energy, and leads to poor decision making. It is paving the pathway to Hell and self-destruction.

11/12/17
David Mahon
Wheatfield Prison
Prison number: 84976

To whom it may concern (surgeon).

I, David Mahon, have attended the Eye & Ear Hospital this August 2017.

I have been back 7 or 8 times since, on my first appointment, I was introduced to a female doctor (Professor). She put a camera up on my nose and down my neck. Her verdict was it is a cyst, nothing sinister. She stated that within six weeks, I will have an operation.

This did not happen.

On another appointment, I had a biopsy. The results were inclusive. I was told by another doctor that maybe went into early; people panic when they see a lump, and we have to do another biopsy maybe in January 2018.

I had a 2nd biopsy and M.R.I. Now, a different doctor has told me, "If he is a betting man, I have cancer", and will be operated next Tuesday (12/12/17) to find out which type of cancer it is."

You can imagine my concerns. Before my operation, can I have someone explain to me my prognosis and discuss my case with my wife, 0874491085

Regards,

Don't succumb to it. Destruction, don't succumb to it ever. Back in my metaphorical swimming pool, I was "chumming' the water and ringing the dinner bell for Mr. Shark. See what I mean about poor decision making? When the facts speak, it is a wise man who listens.

To a lot of people -my vintage and beyond- December 12th will forever be associated with the birthday celebrations of ol' Blue eyes. As far as these brown eyes are concerned, it will forever be the day my cancer treatment began in earnest. Incidentally, the chairman-of -the-board had his own battles with the Big-C around his throat, so if I was looking for omens, this wasn't the best place to start, but I'd do it... my way! There it goes again, my gallus humour, but you have to stay positive. Don't just take my word for it, who better than John Wayne, perhaps the most famous casualty of this killer disease, who said shortly before his passing- "Never underestimate a man's potential to just want to play." The "Duke" was right, do what you can to keep your spirits up.

I was actually at the hospital that day for a (in my humble opinion) biopsy. I remember trying to make light of the situation with the doctor, "I'm only here for a small operation." His reply was dark and serious, "This is not a small operation." Wow. Short and to the point. Not good. All I was expecting to happen was a small incision to be cut into my neck and then they'd take out a little piece of flesh, job done. I'd also hoped to get answers to my letter, which I'd handed to my consultant, Prof. Con Timon - and asked him to read it before my operation. He didn't pass any comment about it. You soon find out that cancer doesn't like plans, don't ever forget, it's a flesh-eating machine, so my "procedure" morphed into a lot more than expected.

The first change was that the surgeon went in through my mouth, not my neck. As he removed a piece of the infected flesh, he noticed that my tonsils were now too showing signs of a malignant growth, the left side in particular. They needed to come out and they duly did. Right then, no messing. When cancer announces itself (and at this juncture, the information being fed to me was that cancer was still only an "80-90%" possibility), who did they think they were fooling? It appears at what looks to be a slow, gradual crawl, but once it takes hold, it gallops. It was eating through my throat and vocal cords, turning screams into growls, leaving a trail of flesh-eating open sores in its wake. There was no doubting the fact that the shark had noticed me and taken a liking to my flesh. Chomp - a small tissue removal, chomp-chomp, no more tonsils and everybody knows a tiny set of tonsils won't satisfy the appetite of a hungry shark. Okay - reflection time – the shark had taken a couple of bites out of me and drawn blood, but I'd taken out some of its poisonous offspring in the process. Round one was a draw on the judges' scorecard.

There was some good news that day too; I had to stay overnight at that hospital! I was spoiled rotten - visits wise, too. Not only did my father come in to see me - twice! But he also dropped my brother, Owen, in to see me and my best friend, Darren. Family are always welcome and you can never see them enough, but I was on cloud nine to see Darren. I'd missed him so much!! He'd told me before my trial that if things went south - he wouldn't, couldn't come to see me in prison. He was upfront and honest with that. That doesn't mean that he forgot about me, though, and – thanks to him! I wanted nothing in prison, be it runners, clothing, money, etc. If you ever want to know who your real friends are, you find out when you go to prison. My poor Da just continued to take everything in his stride, but he also looked exhausted. He never faltered, though, not ever. I guess, you know by now, he's an absolutely incredible man and I can never thank him enough.

At some point, the surgeon dropped in to see how I was post–operation and used the light off his mobile phone to look down my mouth/throat. I didn't find it very clinical or hygienic, if I'm honest, but these guys are rock stars, in my opinion, and exist in worlds of pressure most mortals will never comprehend, so I wasn't going to make an issue out of it! There was no conversation out of him, though, so again, it was not a good omen. Later that night, a Chinese doctor came into my room and asked if I had any questions for him. I asked him more questions than a naughty four-year-old at bedtime. "Do I have cancer?"

"Statistically, you have an 80-90 percent chance."

"When will you know more?"

"We will have to wait until we get your results back."

"When will that be?"

"Early January."

Oh my God, Amy will be missing for ten years in "Early January," the hits just kept on coming... hard. No matter what they were, I'd have to be strong for Audrey. I had asked a ton of other questions, too - such as "Will I lose my voice?" etc. But what I really wanted to know was if I was going to die and how long I had left.

The next morning, a whole team of doctors -including my Chinese friend- came around to see me on their calls. He must've been a glutton for punishment, as yet again he asked me if I'd any questions!

"Do I have cancer, and if so, how bad is it?"

"It's not that easy. We can't just look into your mouth and see if it's cancer..."

"I understand that. So why did you remove my tonsils?"

"Because the left one looked bad."

562

"As in, "cancerous" looking?"

He couldn't and didn't answer that, so once more, I was left in no-man's land. I'd later find out the exact date of my biopsy results would be January 12th 2018, but not without a massive struggle. I asked my wife to call the hospital to find out, only for poor Audrey to be told that no information about me was to be given out "orders from the prison." My father called the hospital and explained who he was, then turned up at the hospital passport in hand - to identify himself, but always the same answer: "No orders from the prison." I won't say how I eventually found out, but it was important that I did as I needed to have a clearer head than ever to process a potential death sentence. Plenty would happen in the meantime.

I returned back to Wheatfield prison -minus my tonsils- the following day, December 13th, had a family room booked for my visit with Audrey and my dad. It was to be the first time I'd see Audrey since I'd received my news and boy, did we ever need that precious contact. It was beyond words to see her and hold her again. We've walked through actual nightmares together, yet with her by my side. Defeat is only momentary and nothing looks quite so dark. She took a keen interest (evidenced by the ever tightening grip on my hand!) in the conversation I had with the Chinese doctor. His vague and non-committal answers didn't help ease any of our tensions. That was a major factor resulting in her phone calls to the hospital trying to find out when my results would be ready. Audrey -as my wife- has every legal right to ask those questions and to expect honest answers. Therefore, by implication, the I.P.S had no right in denying her the information. Yet again, "might – is – right" in the continuing morass of institutional incompetence. Don't misunderstand me, I would absolutely agree -and understand- this refusal if some reporter called them, chancing his arm, and got refused, proper order, none of their business. But therein lies the rub, somehow, they always seem to find out anyway and it wouldn't require detection levels at the standard of Sherlock Holmes to find out why.

Something else that isn't immediately obvious to people is Audrey's struggle in all of this. We had a fantastically open and honest conversation on our visit, most of it about painful and depressing topics and the more we chatted, the clearer it became to me that she was drinking heavily again. This, by itself, is not a situation she needed to find herself in and who could blame her? But there were deeper issues. She clearly wasn't taking everything on board and I feared that she was on the verge of a nervous breakdown. I wasn't too far off the mark and she admitted to giving serious consideration to booking herself into Rehab. She had even located a residential centre in Co. Donegal where you could go and get treatment for four weeks. I thought that was a good move.

I didn't discuss my failed appeal with Mick and Audrey -they had enough on their plates- but it was still on my mind. I don't like injustice in any of its forms and I really can't stress strongly enough how obvious it was that we won it, yet "Appeal refused." It was a travesty, we were almost home and dry, but 'almost' doesn't make the bread rise. My Senior Counsel, Sean Guerin, was snarling and apoplectic when he received the judgement and that is even rarer than a papal visit. He was adamant that I appeal it again, only straight to the Supreme Court and I turned him down on the basis that my family and I were already under enough stress, we didn't need any more. But still… it gnawed away at me relentlessly. Tony, my solicitor, came up to see me later that night, as I'd given the bad news to him on the phone the previous day. He was still reeling from the shock of my cancer fears but still put a strong case forward for my appeal. "You've nothing to lose, Dave." I told him that I'd sleep on it.

Sleep on it I did and I didn't realise until much later how difficult sleep was going to be, and what a luxury when it happens. It is said that certain kind of sharks doesn't sleep…. let me tell you, "Cancer shark" is one of them. He feeds relentlessly. The next time I spoke to Tony was just before Christmas, on December 23rd. I asked him to get in touch with Professor Timon at the Eye and Ear to see if he could find out about my results. Unfortunately, he wasn't able to shake anything out of the tree for me, but deep down, I knew what it was. I spent the Christmas of 2017 eating as much as I possibly could. I'm not exactly a glutton by nature, and it wasn't as though I was stuffing myself with rubbish - biscuits, chocolates, etc., just because I was suddenly unable to resist all of its glorious sugary exuberance. In some ways, it was comfort eating, but for the most part, I was trying desperately to put on a few pounds, but it didn't happen. I was packing in hundreds of calories daily and still losing weight. Was it Cancer? Was it Stress? We know now, and let me tell you, trying to gain weight wasn't my extra battle, I had the odious task of chasing Governors, Chiefs and Medics in order to get my medication and for them to provide me with the diet the Eye and Ear insisted on. This is a recurring motif of prison life. It was all just adding layers upon layers of additional stress and anger that I didn't need.

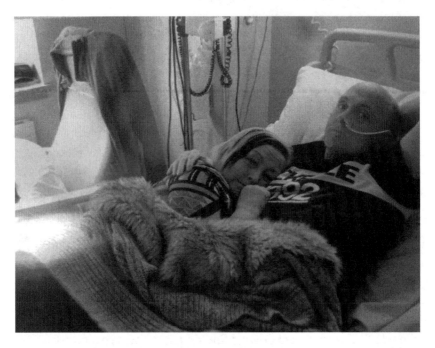

Dave in the early stages of his treatment for Cancer in St Luke's, supported by his wife Audrey.

January 2018 finally arrived. Amy was now missing for a decade – depressed beyond belief and the thoughts assaulting my mind on the morning of my hospital visit were a miasma of negativity. I was convinced that I'd be given six months left to live and I'd die, never knowing the truth about Amy. We listen to our dark narrations all the time because the Devil's voice is so sweet, but if you're going to throw down with the BIG-C, you've got to cough that straight out of you. Be strong, stay positive and remember never ain't hence yet. Easier said than done? I've said it; I've done it. So can you. Pessimism is corrosive; don't let it in. Back on the cold January morning, however, my mind was all about time limits - will I have a long or short prognosis? Will I be able to refuse treatment so that I can be given permission to go home and die? Will I be allowed to die in comfort, surrounded by my Father and Audrey? I had discussed these possibilities with Audrey and she had accepted where I was coming from. It was impossible for me to divorce myself from my mother's predicament. She had been given only five months to live, and that was with treatment. It would've been better for her not to have had any treatment given the decaying quality of life she endured toward the end. As I write this now, I'm reminded of Mark Twain's famous quote – "I have had a great many troubles, but most of them never happened"- And how I could've used it back then, especially as I entered the hospital. I was escorted -in chains naturally- and all I could think was – "This is it. This is it…" I had let Audrey and my Father know the time and date of my appointment through a special code we had created for our (Always) monitored phone calls. A mixture of Spanish and "Mahon-ish", so I knew they'd be inside waiting for me.

It would be next to impossible for me to impress upon you the finality of my thoughts and fears as I trudged through the hospital waiting area. There was no doubt in my mind that I was going to be handed a death sentence at any moment. I've been a fighter all my life, fighting for business, fighting for Amy, fighting for other people and soon I'd be told that all my fighting would come to an end. There would be nothing I could do about it. Now, I'm more than aware of the fact that when it comes to memory (especially in autobiographies), we all stack the deck, but that's not what this book is about. I promised you honesty, so honesty will continue to be. These were the thoughts and emotions of what I was living in that moment. I was tired, I was (And felt) utterly defeated and I was convinced I was going to die. Be very wary of those betraying thoughts because we all fool ourselves so much that we could do it for a living. My only little corner of comfort existed in my hope that maybe I'd get lucky and see my mother, Rory and Dean once again. If Amy was dead, then I could be with her again and finally discover the truth of this terrible nightmare. I couldn't even "enjoy" these miserable thoughts in peace, thanks to my three escort/companions gossiping endlessly about utter banalities as they shuffled me along, chains clanging and keys jingling to my despicable fate, like a cow down a slaughterhouse chute.

Part of my honesty in this story must always include instances of giving credit when credit is due, and to be fair to one of my officer escorts that day, he saw my father before I did (he recognized his face from our many prison visits) and made sure we had a bit of time together. He didn't have to do that; it went above and beyond his job description, but things were looking up. This particular officer – who turned out to be a lovely person and didn't look unlike a small Spaniard-had managed to put my father a bit more at ease and that, in turn, gave me the strength to put on my Dave 'personal-face,' but I was still dying inside, it distracted me enough to not see Audrey spring mysteriously out of seemingly – nowhere which is always the most welcome of sights. Things were now really starting to look up. I was still nervous but also happy, proving another old saying about how the sun even shines on a dog's ass some days! That nice officer managed to find a private little corner – which he managed to get screened off – where myself, Audrey, Mick and the officers could sit together, away from prying eyes.

Our little conversation was utterly dominated by my tales of doom and gloom, how I was "sure to die" and how the doctor would only be able to give me "X" amount of time and when I get that news, I'd forego my treatment. I'd managed to persuade Audrey into my no-treatment crusade but- not for the first time – I hadn't reckoned on Mick. He was dead – against my views on treatment and told me - correctly- that I was "jumping the gun." The Lesson? When you've got someone around like him, with a vast reservoir of knowledge and experience from which to draw, be humble (and wise) enough to listen.

Given the gravity of the situation, we managed to talk about a lot of important and necessary stuff, which was driven by my desire to get through everything quickly, as I was still a prisoner and could've been whipped off at any time. The nice officer removed my handcuffs, which was really something and just as I was settling into my un-chained novelty, I got called to the doctor's office. The short distance to see Professor Timon in his office felt like it was a thousand acres, each filled with death, misery and pandemonium. Here we go. It's show time.

"Morning Doc, do you have any good news for me?"

"I'm afraid I don't."

I know Professor Timon; he's a great guy, professionalism personified, and I'm sure he delivered my news with great care and sensitivity, but to me, it had all the grace and finesse of an axe murderer.

"You have cancer."

"Fuck."

I know, not my finest hour, nor was it a shining example of a beautifully constructed and well thought out response, but I'm being totally honest. I have bad language as a rule, but that's how it was, and be honest, what would you think and/or say? I could've sugar-coated my response and lied to you, but no, you deserve the truth. I know I've explained all about how sure I was that I was going to receive a death – sentence because it's true, but it's also true that camping quietly on the precipice of my subconscious was a niggling Rebel called "Hope." He was there to remind me that it wasn't so long ago that another Professor had told me that it was only "a cyst" in her best God voice and that another doctor had thought me foolish for coming in a "bit early" and for "panicking" because I saw a lump. That little Rebel started crumbling under the weight of his own absurdity. It was cancer. I knew it was and it was folly to have tried to "hope" it away. I had even gone so far as to compile a list of written questions – in my very pocket at that moment – prepared for that exact eventuality, but I couldn't summon the strength to take them out.

"How long do I have?"

"Dave, we hope to treat this cancer."

(I had nothing, completely dumbstruck.)

"It's going to be a difficult ride, but let's try."

"So you're not saying I've only 6 months or a year to live?"

"Let's treat it and see what happens."

"Okay, so... what are the percentages of me living to old age?"

"Dave, because you don't smoke and are otherwise healthy, I'm giving you a 70-80 percent chance of survival."

That was great news. I'd grow to take 70-80% percent on face value as being close to certain as that. After all, it was more than the percentage I was given for it being cancer and that worked out. I looked at my father and Audrey; they looked happy too. I know it's surreal, isn't it? I've got cancer and we're happy, but that had everything to do with my chances of survival.

Before I continue that little consultation with the Professor, I need to provide a little more in terms of context. I am in no way a deeply religious man, but I've come to think that sometimes love conveys its own psychic powers. On the eighth of January, just before my hospital visit, I had a very strange and vivid dream. It was about my mother. I could see her face as clear as day and not in that tacky, 'night-fog' way you see in the movies. I could actually feel her hand (and every son recognizes his mother's distinctive touch) touching the left-hand side of my neck, and then she spoke to me. I can still hear her; "You are going to be alright," I can remember seeing her reassuring smile and then something that didn't make immediate sense but does now, she said, "Seven… two a week." I've racked my brains about this ever since to see if I could remember her saying anything so cryptic to me when she was alive, and in the spirit of honesty and full disclosure, I can't. I since come to realise that dreams mostly tell the truth.

I was completely flummoxed at the time, I mean, what did "Seven… two a week" mean to anybody? I even quoted this to my prison pals. Shay, Sean and Ozzy about it. Nothing. I told Audrey and Mick. Nothing there either. It was bothering me so much that I even wrote it down in my little pad. Okay, back to Professor Timon:

"You have Squamous cell carcinoma of the head and neck. It is not a very common type of cancer. Only about Four Hundred People are diagnosed in Ireland each year."

Well. Lucky. Bloody. Me. A one-in-four-hundred chance and yours truly gets it. He went on to explain how it starts in the lining of your mouth, nose, throat, tongue or ear. It is more common in men than in women. I had a list of questions to ask how I could've got it – was it the inordinate amount of stress I'd been under since Amy's disappearance? Was it a result of my two hip operations, or was it as a result of the attack I suffered in Wheatfield? I have a bit of a confession to make now; I wasn't entirely forth-coming to my medical team about my former drinking habits. It's not that I was a 'lush' or anything, but I enjoy a drink, like the next man, but I did hit it harder than I would've liked when the extra-ordinary pressures Audrey and I endured, Hey, I'm only human and ask yourself – what would you have done to cope? My therapist was Mr. John Daniels and he got me through some dark, dark times. The net result was that I consumed more than ten-units per week. Just saying. Okay, back to Professor Timon again:

"Your cancer is, specifically, in two places, the lymph nodes and the neck."

Could that be something to do with the "two" in my dream? I wondered.

"You will be receiving seven weeks of treatment..."

Yep, there it was, a "seven"... coincidence? I know what you're thinking! But there it was, I was to get seven weeks of treatment with two different methods of attacking the cancer, namely chemotherapy and Radiotherapy. Remember what my mother said? "Seven... two a week." I looked from Professor Timon to Mick and Audrey; I didn't have to say a word. They got it, too.

Looking back, I'm surprised how we all just 'accepted' this news in our stride. Not that we'd any choice in the matter, but we'd no histrionics and use (somehow) managed to remain as dignified as a rolled-up umbrella and Bowler - Hat. Then again, getting bad news was becoming a bit of a forte for us. Ah well, another day, another battle on our hands. In fairness to the medical staff at the Hospital, they were fantastic that day. They answered my questions that day as quickly as I could ask them, and believe me, being starved of so much information in prison, I asked a lot! Most of my questions were answered by "Diet" or "Exercise", but I would've been lost like a babe-in-the-woods if it wasn't for all the wonderful publications on cancer that they provided me with. These are too many to mention here, so I've included them at the back of this book in the Appendices. In this case, the Bibliography in Appendix "B" live also included the question I so carefully prepared - but left it in my pocket! But never asked Professor Timon in Appendix "C." I had also prepared two other lists of questions prior to my Hospital visit - the first (Appendix "D" was for the chief and their open and innocent nature highlighted my worried shore of mind at the time. As for Appendix "E" - questions for the (Prison) Doctor, well, that's a different case entirely.

On Wednesday, January 3rd, I had asked to see the prison doctor. I stressed the urgency to the medics, as my lumps were much worse and I was very worried. This was at about seven p.m. up at the Nurse's dispensary. Thursday arrived, nothing. On Friday the 5th, I stayed back, waiting for the doctor, only to be told to "Go to work and get off the landing." When I tried explaining to the official about how important it was for me to see the doctor, our ACO, all I got was, "See the chief, go on now, see the chief." Nothing happened on that day or over the weekend. On Monday the 8th, I asked the medic for my tablets, but she wouldn't give them to me, that's prison. The next day, the 9th, I asked that same medic for my medication and she once again refused me. I then asked her two very clear questions – why can't I have my medication and could she please put my name down on the doctor's list. Her response was to stare at me with a face like a hard-boiled-balloc and mutter nasty and acerbic comments under her breath. The next day – the 10th my tablets were A.W.O.L once again and shock-horror. My name wasn't added to the doctor's list. It was absolutely imperative on what they consider 'urgent.' By the time the 11th rolled around, it was 'T-minus' one day until my hospital appointment and I was reaching the end of my tether. I noticed an A.C.O. on the landing, so I asked him if I could see the doctor. This was the fourth time. I reminded him about the fact that the doctor said I could "see him any day of the week." He asked the nurses/medics to get me over to the doctor. They told him – "No." He didn't put up much of a fight. Therein lies yet another staring example of the I.P.S roil wagging the I.P.S dog. I, again, tried explaining the seriousness of my condition, but it was like teaching Hindu to a Beagle.

Meanwhile, back on the ranch that was my hospital appointments, the nice "Spanish" officer saw to it that I got to spend a couple of precious hours with my family. Eventually, the driver arrived back to take me away, but first, I had to be fed, one of the officers – a non-Spanish one, let's just leave it at that – went to get me a roll for my lunch. This isn't done out of the Goodness of their hearts, by the way, as it is a legal requirement to get you some food if you are out over your lunch. I'm usually a pretty easy-going type of guy about such things, just get me a regular roll; I don't need or respect the government treatment. The officer was gone for an unfeasibly long time, so I thought that he'd gone to Gordon Ramsay's house, gotten him out of bed and stood over him every step of the way through the Roll-making process and then had it gift-wrapped at Arnott's! It would've been quicker, if anything. We all thought it a very strange thing to do anyway, considering there was already a café in the hospital. Ah well, maybe he just liked lunch rolls or something? When he eventually made it back, I offered to share it with Mick and Audrey – Mick declined – so it was just myself and Audrey, having a 'Lady and the Tramp' moment over a bread roll! It was great just to be able to do the simple thing again. Whether hunger is good sauce or if Chef Ramsay made it, either way, it was delicious, so I asked the officer where he got it from.

"Ah, just around the corner."

I didn't believe him, he had been gone far too long, but I didn't pursue it. I had more important things to discuss. I also didn't want to scuff the sheen off the priceless support I'd received that day from Audrey and Mick. Our short time together came to an end - as all good things do – and I found it really hard to leave Audrey. We had gone into a precious little happy – bubble, sharing lunch, holding hands and doing what we do best – talking, but bubbles are a fragile beast and can't last forever. We walked out to the Hospital steps together, where I was once again cuffed up to the nines. Mick and Audrey started to walk just in front of me and to my not so surprised face, I heard a sudden… click. Right there in front of us was yet another photographer. You'd think we'd have been used to all this by now, but it's always a sickening shock. How did they as they always hunt in packs – know that we were going to be at that exact spot, at that exact time? A cynical person might think that they were tipped off by somebody, but, well, I'll leave that up to you.

It was back to prison after that, again we work through the 'Procedure' and on the way back to the landing, I bumped into a chief officer. I had to fight back the tears as I was telling him that I had cancer, I really confided in him. He could see the anguish in my face and told me that if I needed anything, I'd only have to ask. I asked for extra phone calls and he told me that he'd give me two extra a week and box visits etc… it was just like the last time. Chapter and verse. Just like the last time I heard such promises, they never materialised. In my experience, senior officers are just like politicians. They tell you what you want to hear; they are all style, but no substance. When I got back to my cell, my good friend Sean dropped by, I gave him the latest news. He noticed that I didn't seem nearly as upset as the last time I'd come back, even though I now officially had cancer. I was right and the difference this time around could be encapsulated in just one word – Audrey. The fact that the doctors seemed confident about treating and that Mick was his calming, Zen-like influence too, didn't hurt. His reaction to our getting "pepped" is better in his own words.

"The only way they could've known you were there was from the officers selling information to the papers again."

Again, I'll let you make your own decisions about that, dear reader bottom line, however, was that we were splashed all over the front pages the following morning, but there was a chink of sunshine poking through the clouds-they still didn't know about the cancer, so that bought Mick enough time to ring around and provide my friends and family with the now confirmed updates. I finally managed to get an appointment with the lesser-spotted prison doctor too, Dr. Suto and he was genuinely sympathetic. He always struck me as being a compassionate doctor/man. A copy of the diet I was to be put on "immediately," It was a high protein, plenty of carb diet plus multi-vitamins and full-fat milk to build me up. I was due back to the hospital on the 15th at 11 a.m.

The days leading up to that, namely the 13th and the 14th, resulted in, yes, you've guessed it. No special diet provided, I felt it encumber of me to state that this lack of nutritional adherence was in no way the fault of DR. Suto. The problem was with Wheatfield, and I know it was not a personality clash, as plenty of other inmates received the same lack of treatment. At any given time, there are between three to five governors of varying grades, none of which seem capable of communicating with one another or even like one another. No one wants to make a "decision", so therefore – despite all the organisational charts pointing to the contrary – there is not one person in sole charge of the prison. They are all about as trustworthy as a lawyer's smile. The chiefs – three bar and two bar – do the actual day–to–day running of the chaos they call "Good order," and that is mostly by way of delegation down to the assistant chief officers, most of whom are despotic wannabes with less backbone than a jellyfish. Case in point? Let's see what happened on my next hospital appointment on the 15th.

My appointment was for 11 a.m. at St. James Hospital. We didn't leave the prison until ten minutes to twelve. I still had to go through the "Procedure" – the only thing that seems to happen consistently and boy-oh-boy, was I ever hand-picked with the three worst screws in escort duty history. A more insincere, sermonising bunch of simpering shit-heads you couldn't imagine. Whatever class they'd ever hope to attain would only ever be of the low variety. I was given the whole "by-the-book" speech again, you know, the one that worked so well last time out. Never under-estimate the ability of the I.P.S to come upon a logical solution to something and just flush it down the toilet in favour of something with no chance of success. When we eventually arrived – Really, Really late – At the hospital, they conspired on how they could produce the dumbest course of action. So, they parked – outside and then there was a flurry of messages over their radio, with "Dave Mahon" being the two morose words. Well, they are little words, after all.

Eventually, one of the officers got out of the van and made some calls on his mobile. He then proceeded to walk around the van in big, soft cartoon steps – like Elmer Fudd – and then continued his very unsubtle and non-ninja stalk around the hospital entrance and the car park opposite the entrance in what had to be-surely-an attempt to draw attention to us? He finally managed to make it back to the van (probably needed SAT-VAN), opened the sliding door and then quite abruptly stared.

"Dave, if a member of your family is in here, then I'm not bringing you in. This is not a visit. Also, I hope that there is no press here." He kept his most threatening stare and tone for the next bit:

"You are not to speak to anyone."

I took a few seconds, a little moment – no more – in stunned wonderment as to the exact whereabouts of the Dumb Tree he'd fallen out of. If I wasn't older, I was certainly wiser than him, so I just said "okay," and we went inside… And not before time.

The pantomime continued. We entered the building and they started looking around the waiting area like meerkats. They made an absolute show of themselves and didn't seem to have the ability to know how to stop. For once, I wasn't ashamed to be seen in chains, I was embarrassed to be seen with these imbeciles, it was excruciating. The best part was that I was in the "care" of these nitwits!! I was getting desperate,

"Can you take the cuffs off, please?"

"No."

I was told this with a snarl and a trail of spittle for my obvious impertinent. To compose myself, I took a really deep breath;

"Look, if there is a member of my family inside, then nobody is going to stop me talking to them…"

I stared hard and deep into all of their vacant eyes, and yes, I did raise my voice before continuing;

"Plus… you should know that if the press are here…

… then you'd know about it, as you are the ones selling the stories, not me."

Their response – when I came, was more muted and straight out of the textbook:

"Dave, we have been given orders…"

"I appreciate that, but you have brought unnecessary attention to yourselves and to me."

I tried to keep my comments short, punchy and to the point, using the smallest words possible… I know what I was having to deal with. We shuffled over to Dr.

Nasmy's office, skipping the queue as usual (which the dumb bullies took a sick pleasure in doing) and in the presence – at last- of a mature, responsible adult, I again asked for my cuffs to be removed.

"No."

It was more sulky than aggressive this time, but it still meant that I couldn't shake my hand when he introduced himself. Through no fault of my own, I'd insulted him. Great start. We sat down, then he looked me directly in my eyes and stared, peeling the poisoned fruitage of my cancer right then and there. At some point – I'm not exactly sure when; we were interrupted by the uncoordinated fumbling of the screw I was still chained to, as he tried to unshackle me, he eventually succeeded in taking my cuffs off. Obviously, the seriousness of my situation – this "not a visit" situation – had dawned on him. I know this because I saw the moment of clarity as it happened – in went the enormity of cancer treatment and then, out – exited all those stupid thoughts, emerging for and fresh from his brain all-too-large stupid zone it took a while, but he got there.

My treatment was to be of the Monday to Friday kind for seven weeks, consisting of hours of Chemotherapy and Radiotherapy. I wasn't 100% sure about what each of these treatments would entail, so I asked. Below are the responses I received. If you are about to go through cancer treatments, then this may be of help; if you are not, it's interesting stuff anyway. So then, what is 'chemo'?

"Chemotherapy is a systematic treatment. Systematic means that it can affect all the cells in your body. The treatment itself consists of the use of drugs to cure or control cancer cells. It can be given before, during or after radiotherapy and surgery. When given together with radiotherapy, it is known as a process we call chemoradiation."

"Fair enough. How is that different to radiotherapy?"

"Radiotherapy is, as the name suggests – the use of high-energy X-rays to kill or shrink the cancer cells. If given after your surgery, it can destroy any cancer cells we left behind."

"How do you think these treatments will affect me?"

"It's actually impossible to predict how each patient will react to any treatment, too many variables …"

"What about weight loss? I feel like I'm losing weight…"

"You might need special build-up supplements to stop that, especially during your treatment."

"So I'm going to need a special diet then?"

"Oh, God, yes, most definitely."

"Okay, but I'm in prison and it's not really…"

"That doesn't matter. We'll be writing to the prison about this."

"You are under our care, they'll have to comply."

"Alright, I get that, but I'm already supposed to be on one…"

"Well, they can't ignore this. It's too serious."

"What about side effects?"

"We'll get to those if or when we need to. You will have to get your teeth checked though, that's very important. Due to the intensity of your treatments, you might have problems with some of your teeth, especially after the radiotherapy.

"Is there anything else I should be doing?"

"Well… (Sighs) it's an awful pity you smoke…"

Between the ins and outs of our conversation, he made three references to my 'smoking':

"So, doctor, what would my chances be if I didn't smoke?"

"Oh! Much better!"

"Well, that's great because I've never smoked in my life."

"You… eh (checked his notes) you've never… (Re-checks notes) you say you've 'never' smoked?"

"Correct."

"Oh… well then, I guess somebody made a mistake somewhere…"

"I guess so. What do you think my chances of survival are, now that I don't smoke?"

"Much better, of course… hmm… definitely up there in the seventy to eighty percent…"

This was deeply encouraging, not to mention wholly consistent with the doctors at the eye and ear.

"I have to warn you though, the treatment is as tough as it gets."

And so it was that we headed back to Wheatfield. There wasn't much in the way of conversation on this journey, as my travelling cohort sat as stiff as Puritans with bold, perpetual scowls across their sulky faces. This was a situation borne out of the fact that I'd dared to challenge them. If I'd known that their tiny minds had been more impressionable than wet-cement before the journey, I'd have barked at them back in the prison hold area! Dimwits. As for me? Well, seeing their stupid expressions was deeply gratifying, so I rubbed it in further by looking as happy as a child humming in his cot, all the way back. I received the silent treatment all through 'The Procedure' and back to my cell. When I was about to enter through my cell door, the sulky/Bully screw actually apologised to me about how he handled the whole situation. He tried explaining his actions, but I just cut him off. Explanations, after all, are such cheap poetry. It's our actions that define us.

A few days later, I was back at St. James Hospital again. In that short time between visits, my shark had been busy. His incessant biting into my flesh was no longer 'just' meddlesome, it was downright painful. Did you ever cut-say-your finger, then get salt, or alcohol, etc., into the still raw wound? Then, sods-law being what it is, bang it off something accidentally, then somehow manage to burn it pouring a cup of tea for yourself and so on? The point being that a tiny wound, superficial and innocuous, over time becomes ever-large until you finally have to do something about it. That, is a very loose – but accurate portrayal of how cancer sets to work, gnawing away at you until it kills you.

When we arrived at the hospital this time, we didn't have any more attempts by the keystone cops to practice their "Blending in" techniques rather, they pulled up to the side of the building where two of the hospital's security guards were waiting for us. Their involvement had already increased the I.Q. levels of this particular adventure, thank goodness, but to be honest, I thought it was all a bit much. I mean, seriously, I needed cancer treatment to save my life and I'm not exactly Mark 'Chopper' Read, so why all the additional security? Anyway, it is what it is, no point in complaining. I was escorted – very safely! – To the chemotherapy doctor. Are you ready for a bit of déjà-vu? Here goes!

"Are you a heavy smoker?"

"No. I don't smoke."

"Do you drink?"

"No. I haven't drank in… oh… two years now!"

"Where you a heavy drinker?"

"No, just the average, I suppose."

Okay, confession time, dear reader. We both know that this is a bit of a white lie now, don't we?! The truth is, all of these doctors – as brilliant as they are, no doubt have a list of questions they need to ask before assessing you for treatment. Also, I was surrounded by prison officers who, let's be fair, have been known to, well, "let things slip" from time to time. If I had gone into the details of why I drank heavily after Amy's disappearance and so forth… well, some headlines just write themselves, don't they?

After she'd gone through her list of questions – and I don't mean that in a flippant way – cancer is serious business, she provided me with some more of my treatment plan and what it would entail:

"You were scheduled to receive chemotherapy once a week for seven weeks but because you are young and healthy (I'm not making that bit up, honestly!) I'm prescribing you with the higher dosage of chemotherapy for your body size."

"Okay."

"You'll also be getting it three times."

"Okay."

"Most likely, you'll be very sick."

"Okay."

"We need to start your treatment very soon."

"Then it was back to prison all over again. Now, just in case you're thinking that's "okay" as a response to pretty much everything the doctor told me was a bit lame, then you need to appreciate the gravity of the situation. Everything, every stage of the process, is surreal. You feel like an observer – not a participant, in your own life. You are seeing through your own eyes, but your life is up on the big screen. Your words, your actions, the very steps that you take, feel like they are being played by an actor at the direction and whim of a scriptwriter. In a very real sense, you are tip-toeing through a vivid sleep-walking dream. Only you're not. It's all real, too real and if you don't learn to wake up out of it, you'll die. It was only when I was back in my prison cell that it dawned on me… When was my treatment starting? Had I missed that bit? I wake up out of my stupor just in time for my dental appointment. It was the 18th of January.

I don't know about you, but I'm of a generation and an opinion that your teeth are important. We have them for a reason, they are necessary and are far more than a fashion statement, in short, they matter... A lot. I have always been proud of my 'choppers' and I've gone to great pains - all my life to keep them in as close to perfect working order as I possibly could. Ever have a toothache? Hurts more than taxes, doesn't it?! Dentists, in my well-versed aunty experience opinion - are great professionals. I had never in my life met a dentist who thought an extraction was a first and only option until that day in January of 18. The first thing I noticed about him was how young he was. This is not always a bad omen; sometimes, these young whizz-kids are the cats-meow and are farm-fresh of wonderful innovations. This guy... wasn't. I'll lay out the facts for you and in the end, you can decide on his level of competence. For me though, he was about as much use as an ice-cream candle.

Introduction wasn't one of his strong suits. He sat open-mouthed, gawping at me until I seized the initiative and told him who I was and why I was there sitting in front of him. It was in relation to getting prepared for my cancer treatment, so it was serious business.

"Oh yeah… I know about your cancer."

It wasn't kind and reassuring, but at least – thought he'd done his homework. I never met a straw I wouldn't grasp, but this wasn't encouraging. Something about him just felt… wrong.

"I need to do a few X-rays."

It wasn't a request and it didn't sound like one; opening my mouth – even to speak – was a painful ordeal (not that it stopped me!), but having to open it wide, wider than wider again, for this guy, brought me to the limit of my pain threshold. The left side of my throat gums felt like a thousand angry wasps got trapped in there and had to stink their way out. It was awful.

"Your teeth look well."

To be fair, they were all whiter than dry-cleaned 106 coats, every previous dental professional I'd seen had told me so and yes, they were a matter of pride for me, I won't lie.

"Shame."

"What?"

"I've got some bad news for you."

- (Oh my God, now what? I'm sick and bored of 'bad news,' how bad?) –

"Oh yeah? What's that?"

"I have to take ten of your teeth out."

Right. Context. That equates to just less than half of all your teeth. They will never grow back. Ten teeth. My teeth. Teeth, every dentist – ever – gushed over and complemented - ten vitally important mouth utensils that helped me to eat, feeding my body fights the cancer, keeps me strong. Gut reaction? This guy is deliciously deluded if he thinks I'm going to 'just agree' to this insanity.

"No."

"No?"

"No."

"No what?"

"No. You're not."

"I have to. This is a must!"

"Then I want a second opinion."

"You can't have one."

"Why not?"

"Because you are in prison."

"Then my teeth are staying in my head."

To this day, I still can't believe what next come out of his mouth:

"Why don't you want your teeth pulled out?"

I kid you not, they are his exact words. Don't forget this is a dentist, not some character out of a Roald Dahl novel, trying to scare children into brushing their teeth. This… head-banger had decided to dedicate his life to a career in dentistry. He could be looking into the mouth of a child – maybe even your child – tomorrow morning and here he was – A bloody dentist (!!!) asking me that???

"Eh, because they are my teeth, that's why."

"But…"

"Drop me back to my cell, please. Now."

I was absolutely seething. Hard as it may be to believe, I honestly took this news harder than my cancer diagnosis. I mean, I knew something was very wrong with my neck and throat, but my teeth? They were perfect. Also, sometimes you've got to choose your battles and say "Enough" to all of the prison nonsense and utter stupidity. This was one of those times. I got back to my cell and just sat on my bed, stewing in my righteous rage.

Just over an hour passed and a screw came to my door. I'd been summoned back to the dentist. Oh joy.

"Ah, Dave…"

(Like we were mates and I'd just popped around to see him)

"… I managed to get a second opinion for you."

(Yeah, right)

"Oh. From where?"

"I eh… emailed them to someone."

Weird. Right? So, jokingly, I asked:

"From where? Lincoln place?!"

- This is at the facility where dentists go to train, behind Trinity College –

"Yes."

So there it was the truth. He was a trainee, not a real dentist yet.

"So what's the verdict?"

"I have to remove three teeth."

"Big difference"

He proceeded to take out one of my teeth, which took almost one hour. The pain was unbelievable, but my temper overruled it. The officer that was in the room must stay there however, he even left. The dentist started to proceed to my next tooth; I stopped him and said you will not be doing any more work on me. I want a different dentist. The following day, I received a different dentist and he pulled out the other two teeth in half an hour with no pain.

A sore jaw, which meant I couldn't eat. As I sat in the darkness of my cell, wondering when my cancer treatment would start, the tall-dark-dorsal fin of cancer-shark snapped and thrust around me, turning the pool water into boiling foam. He still had a mouthful of sharp, jagged teeth and they loved to just bite, and bite, and bite. Oh, just in case you were wondering, I did ask for pain relief and I got handed a leaflet! An apt letter to describe how dreadfully painful the experience was! Remember the trouble I had with the medics, trying to get over to see the doctor? I may have mentioned that I was in pain (!!), so immediately after leaving the dentist, I made a bee-line for the medics. It was four P.M

"Oh. I won't have any painkillers until tonight."

In jail parlance, 'tonight' means a quarter to seven. So I go up, I actually get some.

"They will last for the next few hours!"

"What will I do when they wear off?"

"Ring the night, Nurse."

"In real terms, this means pressing the "call" button on the cell wall, where – in theory, the officer comes to your cell and opens the 'flap' on your door to see what you want. You explain the 'night nurse' conversation, he goes and gets you the medic working the night shift and hey-presto, Robert is your mother's brother, sort to speak. In practice... yeah, it doesn't run so smooth, and so at a quarters-to-ten exactly, I press the "call" button. I had been in prison for over two years and never once had to do that. Even after a hip replacement, that will give you some idea of the pain I was in. One hour and forty minutes later, that is six thousand excruciatingly painful seconds later, little Miss Sunshine finally condescends to see me.

No, 'how are you feeling?' etc., just a steady torrent of bile and abuse (for pressing the "bell)" before tossing some pills at me, then telling me in a voice with the nasal squeal of an un-oiled tool, "do not take them until one a.m., that's what it says here (pointing) on the directions, every six hours." I was drained, running on fumes if not already empty, so I just shared my leaflet here, like a pathetic orphan in a Dickens tale. She didn't want to know. This came neither as a shock nor a surprise.

Another week at whacky – Wheatfield passed and then I had another visit. This time, the destination was St. Luke's Hospital in Rathgar. I was told nothing before or during the journey to St. Luke's, so I didn't know if this was going to be the start of my treatment. Or Not. Whatever it was going to be, the prison doctors and staff were keeping me in the dark about it by accident or design, I don't know. St. Luke's – as the name suggests – is named after the Bible writer of the longest Gospel and the book of Acts. He was known as the "physician," hence his obvious link to the world of modern-day medicine. However, it was historical information of a different kind that occupied my thoughts as we pulled up outside the entrance. As a Dublin taxi driver, many years before, I had dropped plenty of fares off at the exact spot I was now sitting at. They were always memorable journeys – each and every one of them – as they were tinged with sadness without exception. One of the most important but underappreciated aides to memory is your sense of smell. I mention this only because I remember that particular – and unique – scent as soon as we arrived. Even outside. Maybe it's just the way my brain is wired, but to me, that has always been and will forever be the smell of death.

Memories, as they sometimes do, came flooding back. Here I was, a man in my mind – forties, recalling with crystal clarity, a comment I made to myself back in my early twenties – "If I ever end up in here, shoot me." I wonder what the 'Dave' I was then would've made out of the 'Dave' I was now, been shackled into the very mouth of death, chained to these prison officers. It was a surreal experience. The first guy I spoke to in the hospital did nothing to arrange the little festival of the surreal my day was developing into:

"Hi Dave, you're here for your mask?"

You could understand if I thought. 'A mask? Now? Why are the medics here? It's a bit late for a mask' – but that was one of the many thoughts bouncing around inside my head. Think about it, how many conversations do you have with people – outside of Halloween – where you'll hear the word – "mask?" Anyway, I didn't let it show. I reacted (outwardly) like it was the most normal thing in the world like I'd been fitted for a mask thousands of times – who hasn't?!

"Yeah… yeah, that's right, the… eh… mask."

"Exactly. Now, you'll need to stay completely still."

"Oh?"

"Well, yes, this mask has to set, so that it fits your face exactly."

"Okay."

"You might get a bit nervous, but it's alright. Most people do."

I was actually grand, though. They placed well – whatever the substance is called – over my face and it was a nice sensation, like the host-towels you get on an airplane. Then the mask guy rubbed his fingers over my face, head and neck in order to create an exact impression of my features. It only takes about fifteen minutes all-told, but you have to keep your mouth and eyes closed for the duration and breathe only through your nose. Once that little procedure was complete, it was 'thanks very much' and back to prison. My first contact with the world of the 'cancer hospital' and its stench of death was short and sweet. It was a positive start.

Back at the prison, I enquired from the staff as to when my treatment would begin in earnest I was told "in two weeks," so I called Audrey and asked her to try asking the hospital to see if they'd confirm that. They couldn't have been nicer to her, full of concern, understanding and the very height of professionalism. They answered each and every question she had with patience and full attention to even the slightest niggling detail, it didn't exactly put her mind at ease (I had cancer, so nothing could), but at least this time, she knew exactly where she stood. Meanwhile, back in the Wally world, that is Wheatfield, professionalism was A.W.O.L.

Incredibly, the medics had gone from bad to worse and so much so, I started keeping a journey of mishaps. They became so frequent that I eventually just plotted down bullet points as otherwise, I'd have been writing full-time. I won't bore you with every single detail – I'm sure you can already join the dots from my previous travails, but I will mention a few.

Remember the Diet I received from the Hospital, the one that was essential to my treatment? On February 6^{th,} I asked a screw at the Food server area for my special diet meal.

"No."

"Okay, well, can I have an extra slice of cheese, please?"

"What??! Extra cheese?? Who do you think you are?"

Abrupt eh? I had to see the doctor that same day due to shooting pains I was getting from my neck into my shoulder. I've done enough training over the years to recognize a bone or muscle pain when I had one, and this definitely wasn't either. The doctor examined me by looking in my ears and placing a stethoscope on my chest and back. He proceeded by asking me to breathe in and out and then told me that I might have a problem with my lungs. I don't know about you, but when I hear the words "cancer" and "lungs" in the same sentence, I get worried. This went on for about twenty minutes or so and then on the way out of the surgery, I asked what the issue was.

"It's probably a trapped nerve."

Now, if I hadn't asked that question, I would've left that surgery thinking all sorts of doomsday scenarios. He scribbled on a pad.

"I'll prescribe you some painkillers."

That was ironic. Only a few weeks previously, I had tried and tried to see the doctor but couldn't do it. Then I had a psychopathic chipmunk chisel away at my teeth until he satisfied himself with the fact that it was impossible to extract any more pain from a human being, and I couldn't get a pain – killer for love nor money. Now here I was, in front of a doctor, offering me pain-killers and … I didn't want them. Had I taken them; I would've been on over twenty painkillers a day, that is not healthy. Funny thing is, given the appalling nature of the prison medics, I wouldn't have gotten them anyway.

As is always the case, the 6th followed by the 7th and that, in turn was replaced by the 8th. February 8th 2018. The day my Cancer treatment began.

It was a Thursday. It's funny the little things you remember, isn't it? In my prison life, Thursdays were important to me because they were usually my visit days, together with Mondays. St. Lukes is a formidable place too, as not only did it put me in mind of death, but its strange voodoo seemed to rub off on the prison officers too, as – much to my surprise - they took all of the cuffs off as we got to the hospital reception. This made a huge difference. For me, because I could be 'Dave' once again, Hannibal was on holiday. I'd like to say that it made me feel 'normal', but there's nothing normal about cancer, so I'll say that I felt 'Almost' normal well, at least – that was – until we were asked to sit in the waiting area, where about ten other people sat and stared at me – to the three fully uniformed officers - with me etc. It was like watching spectators at the devil's own tennis match. Yet another occasion we can chalk down to the surreal. Actually, this raises an important point. Why don't the I.P. S just swallow their pride and allow their officers to wear their "civvies" (normal attire, out of uniform) when on hospital detail to places such as St. Lukes? I'm not saying this for the benefit of the inmates, but for the ease and comfort of the patients, staff and families of everyone else. It's just a complete unnecessary and unwelcome distraction, just saying.

I was last in but first to be called again because of the unfair way the deck is stacked in favour of prisoners in and out and out of harm's way as quickly as possible. No matter what way you cut it, it's skipping the queue and I was always mortified to be a part (unwilling one) of it. Even to this day, writing about it sickens me still. I was led down a sterile smelling corridor and into a room dominated by a Giant machine. This was clearly where I was going to receive my radiotherapy – no flies on me eh?! It was a terrifying room and not just because of what just promised for me in terms of treatment. There was a cold, humourless metal bar hanging close to the ceiling.

Running along the length of it, it looked like human heads. Well, I say "heads," what they actually were - after close scrutiny. Once my heart fell back into my chest after dropping out of my mouth – were masks in the shape of human heads. Adding to this bony décor was a jar floating with false teeth. It was a macabre sight, the sort of room you'd expect to have been furnished by Dr. Frankenstein, or my old friend Dr. Lever. It wasn't just me being a drama – queen either. The look of controlled terror in the faces of all three prison officers attested to that. It honestly looked like the kind of room where vampires came to die. Eventually, one of the nurses came into our little chamber of horrors and told me to take my top off and lie down on the machine. Being a fully paid member of the red-blooded Irish male society, these were a series of words strung together to form a sentence I'd longed to hear since I first hit puberty, but not today, not in the crypt. I had to check for wooden stakes before settling down on the machine!

"Now, are you okay there?"

"Yes, thank you."

"This should only take about ten minutes."

"No problem."

"Good. Oh, it's also going to be quite loud."

Hah, piece of cake. Ten minutes and a bit of noise? No bother, sure, that sounds like a quiet night in Wheatfield! I just lay back and closed my eyes while the nurses re-aligned the machine for me.

"Dave?"

"Yes?"

"We're just going to put the mask over your face, okay?"

"Yeah, no problem."

"Then we'll have to leave the room until your treatment is finished."

"Okay, Great."

"If there are any problems, just raise your hand."

"No problem."

I didn't know what all the fuss was about. It's only ten minutes of lying down with a mask on in a strange room. I know plenty of people who'd pay top-dollar for that kind of experience! What could possibly go wrong? Anyway, on goes the mask-which was skin tight, believe me – encasing my forehead, cheek-bones, nose, mouth and chin. It's not a pleasant sensation. To put it another way, I'd go so far as to say that it awakens our primal fears of drowning and suffocation. It's incredibly unsettling. I focused my mind as best I could and concentrated like a chess master on happy thoughts. Then, a surprising thing happened.

It was a panic attack. My hand shot up and I tried calling out for help, but nothing could come out, my face and mouth sealed up tighter than a tomb. Thank God for the great nurses, they got in and removed my mask quicker than a hiccup. I let out a long, strangled breath, it was such a release, but my God, was I ever embarrassed. I felt like such an idiot. Like most men, I like to think that I'm mentally strong and all of that bravado nonsense, but no, that episode completely knocked me for six. The nurses were full of reassurances about how this happens

587

a lot and such, but I was shocked. How did that happen? After a few minutes of calm, we went again. This would be different. I know what to expect. Happy thoughts first, then they'd put the mask on and all would be fine. It's only ten minutes. So, on went the mask…

It was still uncomfortable and well "weird", but I was breathing through my nose and holding it together. The nurses then clipped me to the bench – a series of five separate clips – that pin your shoulders and head in place, tighter than a fish's ass, and that's water-tight. This is important because your head really shouldn't move; the radiation has to hit the exact spot, focusing all its terrible power on my killer tumour. It's a precision procedure, pin-point in the truest form of the expression. Okay, so once more, onto the breach…

Bang. Another panic attack. This was so unlike me. I was told – correctly, I'm sure – that it took a mere thirty seconds for the nurses to come back in and, well, 'rescue' me, but it felt like an eternity. As soon as the clips came off, I bolted upright and started sucking in big, lung-busting breaths. My mind was a maze of lost hope, I was never going to be able to do this simple treatment, and therefore I'm as good as dead already. Didn't even put up a fight. One of the nurses came over to me. I couldn't even look at her. I was so ashamed.

"Dave?"

"Yeah."

"Do you mind if I make a suggestion?"

Of course I didn't, something had to change.

"Take one of these."

"What is it?"

"It's a relaxant. It's called Xanax."

"Okay."

"Now, there's only one thing."

"What's that?"

"It'll delay your treatment. It takes about forty minutes before it takes effect."

Music to my ears, a break from the chamber of horrors and that awful death mask. I'm not one for medication at the best of times, but that Xanax didn't even touch the sides on the way down, it just bought me forty minutes. All nurses are quick studies and fast - learners. The staff at St. Luke's are no exception, the officers and I were brought to a small private room to wait for the relaxant to take effect. No fuss, no problem and no preying eyes. A clear demonstration of thinking on your feet, putting patient first and knowing – intuitively – the right thing to do, every time. As the chemical changes brought about by my little pill started to take effect, a nurse called out one of the officers, wanting to speak to him privately. A few minutes later, he came back in, so I asked what that was all about. He told me that the nurse said we could use that private room for our appointments over the next seven weeks and asked if it were possible for them not to wear their prison uniforms, as it might make the other patients nervous and uncomfortable. See? What did I tell you?!!

As promised, I was re-called to the house of horrors exactly thirty-nine minutes and fifty-nine seconds after taking my tablet, so it was off with my shirt, onto the 'slab' (in keeping with the rest of the creepy décor, it kinda fits!) and back on with the mask. Even though I had a happy little Xanax sauntering through my system dropping rose-petals and preaching 'peace and love man,' my heart was still going like the clappers and I was as nervous as a mouse in a lion's cage. I closed my eyes, breathed slowly through my nose and listened to the five clips snapping into place. I remember hearing the door closing as the nurses vacated the room and then the clunk-hum as the machine powered up. Panic. My heart was jumping out of my chest, so I tried opening my eyes to 'see' how silly I was being, that would surely calm me down a little. The thing is, I couldn't open my eyes, even a fraction because the mask was too tight. This wasn't at all helpful, now my natural curiosity couldn't be satisfied, so I'd nothing to do with the emotions born out of that frustration other than channel them into my already over-fed panic. I'd be damned if I was going to raise my hand up in defeat for a third time, I'd felt bad enough as it was, a common reaction or not. It was a long ten minutes, a period of torture where every second of it is dragged with the super-slow-motion of a bubble in a honey jar. Finally, mercifully, all the noises stopped and my treatment was over. The nurses were their reliable, speedy sieves and had me unstrapped and unmasked faster than a formula - one pit crew, thank God. The relief was so palpable but short-lived, as it suddenly dawned on me that this was my life now; I'd one session done. One.

As strange as it may seem, that not very strenuous activity had left me exhausted, so I said 'Goodbye' to the nurses and readied myself for a trip back to prison and my bed that was now screaming out to me. However, nothing in my life ever goes smoothly and wouldn't you just know it, with the exit doors in sight, I was approached by a young doctor.

"Dave, where are you going?"

"Why?"

"Because you're coming with me – Now!"

"Okay…"

(Yeah, okay, I'll admit it, I almost said, "What's up doc?" before I realised just how bloody stupid that would've been!)

"Yes, you're getting your first treatment of your chemotherapy today."

Well, that was a shock completely out of the blue. Why hadn't I been told before now? A 'little' bit of time to prepare or compose myself wouldn't have hurt, surely? Anyway, shock aside, I wasn't going to complain, no way. Old Mr. Shark had been taking lumps out of me with reckless abandon long enough, and it was long overdue retaliation now. Let's see how he likes that. We hurried along to the chemotherapy section of St. Luke's with a renewed, energetic vigour in my step, which only seconds before had one foot in my bed. This was a good thing.

I was brought into a small room and put lying down in a hospital bed. It was too small a space for the few doctors, nurses and prison officers to crowd around me and discuss my treatment plan, so I asked the officers to leave and in fairness, they did. It's not a spectator sport, after all. Anyone who's ever gone through 'chemo' will agree with me – it takes a long time. It was a good two hours attached to a saline drip as the short-killing ingredients entered my body. Then, another fifteen minutes of intravenous painkillers followed by another two hours of cisplatin, the 'harpoon' for my treatment - while once done - you get yet another half an hour of drip-fed saline and drugs. This was protracted but great. I was finally in the game, not just lying down and taking it… which was a bit ironic, considering I was lying down in a bed… And taking medication, but you know what I mean! So, what do you do when all this is happening? For me, I was more and more concerned about my father and Audrey. I had been in hospital for over twelve hours and not a single phone call to them all day. I knew that they would've been worried sick. You've read my story so far – ask yourself? Do I strike you as the sort of person that you think, "Ah, sure it's Dave, I'm sure he is good, he never comes to harm?" Exactly and my dad and Audrey knew me even better, so they would've been climbing the walls! Worse than that, they had both wanted to come to the hospital and be with me that day but after the last time at the Eye and Ear, I thought it more prudent for them to stay at home.

I'll get back on my soap box now – you know that I'm writing this book with warts 'n' all honesty, whether it be good or bad. I've given you insights into some of the meaner prison staff and also the good. All of it is honest. What happened next is another example of a good guy being a human being. One of the officers saw a look of distress on my face, checked his watch and then:

"Are you alright, Dave?"

"Yeah."

"Long day for you."

"That's for sure."

"Want to call home?"

"Yeah, but sure (I nodded at the drip and shrugged my shoulders)."

"Here, use my phone."

Wow, this was a gift! I know it seems like a small thing, but trust me, this was a very big deal. I called Audrey, gave her a run-down on my day and told her not to worry, that I was fine, which was the truth. When all my treatments were completed, it was back to prison, weirdly. I couldn't wait to get back. I never in my life expected to look forward to going to prison, but I honestly was. It had been an unexpectedly long, hard day and I was out on my feet. Lots of new faces, new expressions and straight into a series of alien treatments I'd need to know intimately along that hard old road to recovery. A little bit of solitude was exactly what I wanted. My doctor – Dr. Nassem - handed me a letter and a prescription to give to the medical staff at Wheatfield. He told me that he'd put me on a plethora of medications, from anti-sickness drugs to God knows - what. In turn, I explained my concerns about the lack of treatment from the prison medics and how unlikely it was that they'd adhere to his written instructions. I had already prepared a little something for him in writing because I knew that moment would arrive at some point. He told me he'd look into it and after reading what I wrote, promised me that he'd discuss it with Dr. Suto. He then wrote out a note that I was to hand to Dr. Suto in person.

Back at Wheatfield, I gave the prescription stuff to the chief in charge of the Medics. A medic then handed me some tablets to get me through that night and or if I felt sick. I was also given some tablets to be taken at seven a.m. the following morning. Just then, the chief medic noticed a letter in my hand addressed to the doctor from Dr. Nassem.

"Give me that."

"No."

"Now!"

"I was told to hand-deliver this too..."

"No… you just have to trust me."

"Well, trust works both ways..."

"Give me the letter now."

"Okay (no choice), can I get some mouthwash?"

"No."

"It's part of my prescription."

"I'll get you some later."

"Okay, I'll trust you to do that."

"What's that in your other hand?"

"My medication for tonight and for 7 a.m."

"I'll take them too."

"If you check your screen (in front of her) you'll see that I don't like taking tablets and …"

"Back to your cell."

So, back to my cell, it was. The last thing I wanted was for her to notice the thermometer I'd been given in St. Luke, as that would've been confiscated too. I'd also managed to keep the little jar of mouthwash hidden from her, which I shouldn't have had to do, but that's what you are dealing with. My parting shot to her was that she was "adding to my stress," to which she wouldn't and couldn't reply. My "medication" that night consisted of a cup of tea and an entire packet of Bourbon creams; it had been a long day! I had a lovely hot shower and then a shave using some E45 cream and jumped into my bed at 21:21 exactly. I closed my eyes and sleep came quickly. I was feeling good, but my body and mind were battered, it had been a good day, but I had a long seven weeks ahead of me.

Day two, February 9th, started badly. One of the filthiest, dirtiest habit – in my opinion – is spitting. It looks, sounds and is disgusting. Yet, that is what I found myself having to do constantly all morning. My throat was quite sore, so I didn't even try to eat, but I was filling tissue after tissue with long strings of throaty mucus. It was a new experience and proof – positive of the powerful side effects of my treatment. As with most difficult experiences in my life, I tried metalizing the situation to my benefit, so the tissue filling ceased to be known (internally) as 'spitting' and was re-branded as cancer-removal. It's not exactly in the same league as Marathon to Snickers, but it worked for me. Another area of concern to the bad start of that day was the screws assigned to my escort. They weren't the worst bunch I'd ever had, but they were organised only in terms of chaos – running around late, blaming this, that and the other on everyone but themselves. Be that as it may, we made it to the hospital and they had enough Guile to take the cuffs off me, so I'll credit them that. Life, however, is all about balance – yin and yang/ night and day/ decent screws. Bad hospital staff. I'm sorry to say that I managed to be dealt a dud card in the otherwise always excellent hospital pack. It wasn't even something truly bad, but rude, imperfections and flat-out snobbish. She was an English (by accent anyway) school-mam type administrator who looked much taller than she actually was due to the height of the saddle on her high horse. Such a shame. She located us a couple of feet below the end of her nose and in a voice so prim and proper.

She made the Queen of England sound like Imelda May:

"You there."

(directed at the prison officers.)

"Yes, you wait with him over there."

(pointing the way to a small room.)

Yesterday, all the staff called me Dave or David, I was a patient – no more/ no less – afforded the absolute zenith of professional healthcare. Today, I'm 'him,' a piece of dirt. In fairness, the screws were too, as the room would've been too small to pass building regulations as a toilet. Our waiting time was approximately one hour, but I couldn't – and wouldn't – take any more than two minutes of us trying to fit the equivalent of a key into a kettle.

"Sorry, lads, I'll wait in the waiting room, just like everyone else."

The screws were delighted with my decision, so that's what we did. As I waited, I thought about the previous day and what I'd have to face that day and then suddenly, a huge wave of relief washed over me. I'd started on a Thursday, today was Friday – I'd have the weekend off, thank God for that! Happy thoughts don't last in such situations, so before I knew it, I was back to the radiotherapy room and its Addams – family- décor.

Everything went pretty much the same as the first day, bar the panic attacks, courtesy of Xanax. The tight-fitting mask was still a terrifying challenge I'd have to try to overcome. As I was receiving treatment scary nurse approached one of the officers and told him that:

"In the future, you'll have to stay in the small waiting room."

I know this because – even though the walls and noisy machine – she spoke softly at the decibel rate of a medieval town-crier…. but posher! Like an Idiot, he agreed. Please don't get me wrong, I realise better than most that a lot of the members of the public would be frightened at the thought of having to sit next to a "chained maniac" shackled to three brave prison officers. If my own mother had still been alive, she would've been one of the frightened masses, but only until she spoke to them and realised how normal most prisoners are- myself included- and when it comes to a place like St. Luke's, public or prisoner, cancer doesn't discriminate, we are all as scared and nervous as each other. I suggested to the officers that they get permission from the governor to wear their civvies for such occasions and that I would also do what I could by way of a written request. I also informed them about a nurse - the day before - who asked the other officers the same thing. It was one of those rare occasions where everyone screws/prisoners/public/hospital staff – all agreed on the same logical, obvious solution. It was doomed to failure at I.P.S level, as to them – "logic" witchcraft and punishable by death on a fiery stroke. This will become clearer as my story develops. Anyway, back to my treatment.

Day two of radiotherapy was much, much harder in terms of recovery. I was starving, but I couldn't eat, thirsty but unable to swallow. It was beyond frustrating.

My mood wasn't helped by having to wait around for about five hours in the tiny "family room" (a family of Smurfs may be able to fit in) for the transport back to prison to arrive. A normal 'not scary' nurse gave me a cup of tea and toast at one point. But they stuck in my throat and I had to spit them out, like everything else. My doctor then came over to me and asked if I received my medication from the previous night and that morning. I told him exactly what happened and his amazement was surpassed only by his fury. He stormed off and made several heated calls to the Wallyworld medics. When he came back to me, he provided me with assurances that everything would be sorted out. He wrote out another prescription and handed it to me. I decided to make a note of all my medications; exact names and exact dosages, including the mouthwash. As I knew with all the certainty of gravity that everything would be taken back off me when I got back to prison.

When we got back to Wheatfield… everything was taken off me (bare my notes). Who saw that coming?!! I managed to keep a hold of all the cancer booklets I'd been given in St. Lukes as I felt it was high time, I educated myself on the type of cancer I had and the medications treating it. They were essential reading and, in my opinion, compulsory if you're going through it. I explained to the arrogant-not listening chief medic that I hadn't received the medication and mouthwash, etc. that she told me to trust her with.

"You'll get them, in time."

"I'm meant to be on a high protein and carb diet. It was given to you by the Eye and Ear Hospital. Further Dr. Suto issued strict instructions to the chiefs and governors that this be facilitated."

"And?"

"Well, it hasn't happened. My treatment has now started and all you've given me is a multi-vitamin. I'm still not receiving my tablets."

"There are certain tablets we can't give you in prison."

"The doctors told me that I'll end up on morphine."

"No."

"No?"

"No. We don't issue that in here. I'll see about giving you a morphine patch… when the time comes."

"All I want is what the doctors prescribe for me, nothing more."

"We're done here. Go back to your cell."

I knew there was going to be a problem as soon as I saw her not – so friendly face. I could only hope that the doctor from St. Luke's had spoken to her earlier, chewed her up and spat her out. It would go some way to explain her catty attitude. It was bad enough having to go into battle with a shock every day, but what made it worse was also having to do battle with his little shock minions, dressed in I.P.S. medical tunics. Welcome to prison healthcare.

With one or two exceptions, all of the prison staff were adding to my stress levels. Stress is a word in Cancer's hand, and he doesn't hold back from using it. It had been a long day, a stressful meeting with the chief medic and lots of additional pressures closing in on me from all sides of the prison system machinery. Added to this demonic cocktail were the after–effects of my chemotherapy, leading to a long night of vomit and fatigue. Even writing about it, all this time later, I can still remember that horrible metallic taste in my stomach. It was the end of day two and I was sick and unable to eat. If I didn't get my medication issue resolved, I'd be dead by the end of the month.

It was a long night, full of thoughts running through my head about death, pain and general gloom. It struck me at stupid- o'clock in the morning that I had been doing nothing but listen to screws telling me their cancer horror stories:

"My gamy had it, Jesus, she'd an awful hard death."

"Officer "X" I used to work with... when he died, he looked like a skeleton."

"My brother's wife died of cancer."

"My sister had it; she's not out of the woods yet."

"Jesus, I'd hate to have cancer."

"Do you think you'll live through this?"

"Is it right that you'll have to be fed through a tube now?"

On and on they went. At first, I was interested, my mother's story was never far from my heart and ultimately, we're all human, aren't we? Empathy is a wonderful thing, but there was only so much negativity I could listen to. It was making a tough time even worse. At some point, I'd have to address all of that. Saturday morning starts with my door getting unlocked.

"Breakfast?"

"No."

Bang. Metal on metal, wallop, a child would have more sense. An hour or so later, the landing gets unlocked again, and this time, the class officer - the snide, sneaky one - pokes his weasel face in through the door.

"You're alive anyway."

Some comments are unworthy of reply, even contempt.

"What did they say to you at the hospital?"

I had to be careful what I said to this guy. He has the Sunday World on speed dial. Also, it's none of his business, but you have to be civil.

"They said I'd a hard road ahead."

"Yeah?"

"Yeah."

"What else?"

"I'd die if my medication and diet aren't sorted out."

"Oh…."

It was a little bit of a white lie, but it was a true statement; they just hadn't said it yet. It was also a little dig at him and his inept cronies and couldn't be reported back to his tabloid buddies. It shows a light on their negligence. He got stuck on what to say next, stuck on "oh" with the same stupid look on his face as a toddler who filled his pants half a second after realizing it was a bit more than a fart, then shuffled off to bother someone else. Good. I was glad.

One of the medics eventually made her way to my cell, she didn't look to be happy in her work, so business as usual, she gave me a hard stare, a silence that said "How dare you have cancer? The cheek of you, being sick I suppose you want me to help or something? Ah sure why not, I've nothing better to be doing."

"Morning, nurse."

"Hmph…"

"Is my medication sorted our yet?"

"Have an anti-sickness tablet for you."

"Thank you, I've been feeling very sick…"

"(Sigh) Right."

"I'm not able to eat anything and I find that I'm constantly having to cough up (didn't want to even use the word 'spit') a thick, filmy type of mucus."

"Here, you can take this pain-killer as well."

She slammed the two little tablets on my food counter with all the sermonizing contempt of a puritan minister and stormed off before I could waste any more of her valuable gossip-time. I didn't get a chance to ask about my special diet or to tell her about the painful ringing in my ears. Nor that there would've been any point; sure she didn't even condescend to answer my question about my medication.

As unhelpful as her whole attitude and demeanour had been, it turned out that the 'help' she'd given in the form of the pills she'd left - had been worse. The pain-killer she left, was something no cancer patient should ever have been given. Remember the thermometer I'd managed to sneak back in from the hospital? Well, that wasn't me trying to be the king of Contraband; that was a potential game-changer. Why? The answer is best left to the express; the following is a direct quote from the literature I'd been given in St. Luke's:

"If you develop a temperature at any time during your treatment, it is considered a medical emergency. An infection during cancer treatment can be life-threatening."

Four words literally jump off the page for me "medical emergency… life threatening and that's not scare tactics, that's from the people who know their craft. The pain-killer I'd been given was well known for disguising a temperature, something for me even at that stage of my treatment that could've been fatal. I need to add some additional context to all of this; I know and completely understand that the medics in the prison system are not oncology Doctors or nurses, not should they be expected to be, yet they only needed to follow the clear and reasonable instructions supplied to them, from the relevant experts. There was no excuse for their culturally comatose and self-absorbed attitude, it wasn't just rude, it was now dangerous. One thing all prison medics are all too aware of, is that other little word hiding in the middle of the St. Luke's quotation "infection."

Putting it yet another way, prisons are choc-full of all types of germs and infections-Hepatitis, colds, flu, H.I.V., scabies, S.T.I.'s, etc. it's a who's - who of guests you'd never invite to the cancer party, yet here they are. I kept thinking about that quote from 'The Shaw shank Redemption' – "Get busy livin; or get busy dyin" so I decided to extend my life as much as possible. Not being able to eat, I put the knife and fork away and replaced them with pen and paper. A flurry of letters came out of this decision – Charlie Flanagan (the justice minister of the day), The Irish prison service, the governor of Wheatfield and to my doctors at St. Luke's. In these letters I stated quite-clearly my untenable situation and my wish to be hospitalized for all of my treatment. My requests were supported by the prison doctor - Dr. Suto, who, to his external credit, was brave enough to stick his head above the trenches and not toe the company line. There lies the difference of a doctor who swore an oath and lived up to it. He knew exactly what was going on, he was strangled by their petty-polities just as much as I was and wasn't oblivious to the fact that I wouldn't get anything near "proper" treatment at Wheatfield. If the status-quo remained, you wouldn't be reading these words, I'd have died in prison, another annoying 'Anomaly' in the annual report from the inspector of prisons.

My letters were a damning synopsis of a different kind of institutional abuse and trust me when I tell you I didn't sugar-coat any of it. I'd love to include all of their replies in this book but… they never replied…. Not one of them. When Monday rolled around, it was back to the hospital for more treatment and I still hadn't eaten. In fact, I wouldn't eat again until February 17th when I managed to consume two eggs and a spice burger. Back at the hospital, I asked to see Doctor Nazmy and I handed him a copy of my letter. He took it very seriously and promised to get a social worker onto the prison. True to his word, he did, a Ms. Bernadette Donnelly, who was a senior medical social worker and managed to put a 'few' manners on the bratty medics. However, at those early treatment stages, there was no need for my hospitalization, according to Doctor Nazmy, and thanks to the efforts of Ms. Donnelly, he was right.

The rest of that week passed as advertised daily trips to the hospital for my treatments: all of my medications were suddenly made available, including the mouthwash, which is so important when you have extreme pain in the mouth and gums. As mentioned, I couldn't eat and the ringing in my ears was increasing with the intensity of a built in Parisian hunchback inside my skull, yet mentally, I was feeling strong. Really strong. Now that I was also receiving the correct – non-fatal painkillers, I was starting to cope a lot better. My shark, however, was gorging himself on my excess weight, and I wasn't yet aware of it.

In prison, you lose all concept of time; repeat, repeat and repeat again. My second week went the same as the first, except that I could eat normally, felt great and had plenty of energy. But I started noticing side effects, namely I couldn't taste my food properly, not a hundred percent. This was exactly as the reading materials described (on radiotherapy)

"The short-term side effects tend to develop towards the end of the second week…. Xerostomia (dry mouth) taste changes, sticky mucus, sore throat/ mouth, difficulty eating and drinking…."

Again, if you are unfortunate enough to be going through this, then read all the materials and trust your medical team completely. I cannot over-emphasise just how accurate they are about everything.

Furthering this point, the next few weeks followed the guidebook like a Swiss watch. The side effects continued, and then fatigue kicked in. The rinse-repeat nature of prison and the reception 'procedure' were wearing me out. The long walks to and from the transport and having to get dressed/undressed/ dressed again like a busy prostitute are not conducive to cancer treatment. Fatigue is as much a part of cancer as sickness and chemotherapy. I'll come back to that again, though, because there were one or two little highlights of the following weeks I wanted to address first.

Let's start with the good old prison medics. One, in particular, happened to be pregnant and had a real issue with me. What issue, I hear you ask? Why, dear reader, I was receiving radiotherapy and that made me "Radio-Active." Yep, yours truly was now a Marvel superhero. I had become 'Radio-Active-man'!! Not content with displaying just any old display of ignorance, she compounded it further by insisting I be sent up to the punishment wing – west-two, that god for sake Kip I was in at the start of this book. Why on earth would she want to do that, you probably wonder? Well, that's simple. Radioactive people cannot be around pregnant ladies. Did I mention that she was a 'medic'? Be assured, dear reader, this 'health-care professional' wanted to ship a patient who was undergoing intensive cancer treatment up to a punishment cell, cold and uncomfortable, with less than one hour of out-of-cell time, surrounded by diseased, lunatic junkies screaming and banging on doors all-night, because he had become "Radio-active." I was furious, but I bit my tongue and tried to reason logically with her. I handed her one of my cancer information booklets and directed her to the section that read, and I quote:

"The Radiotherapy does not make you radioactive."

It is perfectly safe for you to mix freely with family and friends."

"her reaction?"

"Get away from me! You're RADIOACTIVE!!"

She went straight to management; I went to the phone and called my solicitor. I was moved out of my cell, alright. Only to a bigger 'medical' cell with wheel-chair access and a few more comforts, good one to Tony, came through for me once again!

The problem with a scorpion, though, is that once you've neutralized his pincers, he stings you with his tail. My 'sting' for being a Radio-Active pest in a swanky new cell (Mahon-Estates on Tour, as my friends were quick to deride me about!) was administered when my sister, Dory, visited me. She flew over from England, where she lives, to see her baby brother because he had cancer, just like any normal, decent person would. Her reward for all the expense and time away from her children? One, ten-minute visit, they couldn't have been any more petty or vindictive if they tried. You see, they always have to win and then rub your nose in the mess of your defeat.

As February bled into March, I found the going getting tougher in terms of the strain on my energy levels. I eventually had to request a chair in the reception area, and that's not something my personality would usually allow. Some of the escort officers would just give me a general pat-down, as it was now beyond obvious that I wasn't a well man. As usual, most didn't and made sure I went through every step of the 'Procedure,' this had medical consequences. To be specific, there were several 'near-misses' for me in terms of getting sick in the van or getting caught short for the toilet. Bear in mind that I was handcuffed at all times, so there wouldn't have been any 'winners' in that situation. The closer of calls happened on one of the weeks of my treatment when I had just sat down in the van, the engine started and "Sorry lads, but I have to use the toilet - now." It was a lucky thing that we hadn't even left the car park, as I wouldn't have made it in time otherwise. It was a humiliating time for me, a grown man barely in control of his bowel movements, having to rely on other adults to get me to the toilet like a child. That's cancer for you and I was lucky, lots of poor souls have it much worse, believe me.

I made a point of keeping my doctors fully in the loop of my 'new life' and changing circumstances:

"How are you feeling today, Dave?"

"Tired. Really, really tired."

"That's normal, Dave. Remember, when you're going through radio and chemotherapies, your body takes a hammering."

"When will I get some energy back?"

"That, unfortunately, doesn't have a specific answer."

"What do you mean?"

"Well, your energy levels should improve six months to a year after treatment."

"That long!"

"I'm afraid so, in fact, some people still feel tired two years after their cancer treatment has ended."

As usual, they were spot-on. As far as predictions went, mystic Meg was only in the ha'penny place!

"Are you eating okay?"

I wasn't. I was only able to take a few small morsels on board before feeling sore and bloated.

"I'm trying to."

"You've lost weight, Dave. Keep an eye on that."

I had so many things to "keep an eye on" now a spider would've struggled to not run out of them! Between my food, medication, energy and temperature and well, everything in between it was like everything became exhausting. As if life wasn't already hard enough, one of my hospital appointments had to be cancelled on Friday, March 2nd, because of… snow! That's me in a nutshell, that is, wait for the worst snow storms in nearly forty years before starting cancer treatment!

On the next Wednesday, March 7th, I noticed for the first time just how much weight I had lost. My clothes tight fitting and snug only weeks earlier, now felt like they'd been borrowed from a giant. I'm not a huge man by any means, but when I caught my reflection in the mirror getting dressed, I looked no bigger than a mouse. I didn't recognize myself when I got to the hospital Dr. Nazmy was called to see me straight away. That was unsettling and it worried me. Hey, it's cancer, you always assume the worst; of course you do. He examined me and he wasn't happy, not a bit. He sent a nurse over to me to go through a few more tests. Now, with one noticeable exception (Riding a high horse will always make you stand out), the nursing staff, in fact, all the staff at St. Luke's are lovely, lovely people. This particular nurse was the nicest of them all, a great professional with the funniest personality you'd ever meet. We got on like a house on fire and she had a way of breaking bad news like it was the very thing you wanted to hear:

"(Whispering) You're not going back to prison today!"

"(Smiling!!) Yeah? Great! How come?!"

"Remember you were 84kg?"

"Yeah!"

"Well, now you're 73kg, that's over 10 percent!"

I was waiting for the punch-live, as this nurse was forever cracking little jokes, but she just tipped me a conspiratorial wink and headed off. Minutes later, the doctor came back and told me that I'd have to be hospitalized straight away.

I stole a glance at the nurse, who just popped up behind him and mouthed a silent "Told you so!!" with that little 'All is well with the world' smile of hers!

This news actually pleased me, believe it or not! From my perspective, I was in the only place where I had a fighting chance of survival. Back at Wheatfield, It was Russian roulette as to getting/not getting the proper medication. I was out of luck most of the time and not only was I unable to eat, but there was no sign of my special diet appearing over the horizon. The doctor was in a 'serious -mood' with me:

"You've lost over ten percent of your body weight…"

Again, I side a glance at my nurse. She mimed a perfect 'struck by lightning bolt'

Expression before silently mouthing a perfectly slap-stick "Duh! I told you that!!"

"…. And if you were to lose any more weight, we'll have to feed you through a peg…."

Another glance at my nurse who mimed perfectly synchronized "A bleedin' 'PEG'?!" with its silent movie panache of an inform Charlie Chaplin. This is serious stuff, literal life and death conversations, as bleak and depressing as you'd ever want to hear, yet there I was, trying not to laugh! Cancer, we know only too well, is an affliction of soul-sapping, joy-murdering consequence where bad news is piled atop worse news every minute of the day; as a patient, I needed light relief like this and I will never have a word said against it.

"…. A peg, by the way, is what we call the tuber we feed you through into your stomach."

It was horrible news, gross in the truest sense, but I was smiling. I wasn't happy about the thought of a tube going into my gut, but the sting was drown out of the prognosis. Unfortunately, I was still unable to eat anything later that evening and believe me, I tried, really tried, as I didn't want that peg under any circumstances. They decided to give me the Nasogastric tube instead of the PEG; I was in the danger zone, though, so like it or not, out came the tube. First, it is inserted up your noise, then down your neck and into your stomach. I can't get worse luck! Instead, it took them three very un-heroic (on my part!) Attempts at this procedure before it was done. Also trust me on this, it's a mighty sore experience and feels every bit as horrible as you'd think. I mean you even feel it hitting your stomach from the inside…. yuk.

The best thing you can do when trying to swallow a two-feet-tube through your nose is to think about something, anything else, just get your mind the hell out of there. I tried to focus on "why?" why can I not eat? Why didn't/they do something else? Why didn't I try harder? I settled upon a few reasonable conclusions to those and so many other questions. I was under-medicated, totally the fault of the prison. In particular, my little inhaler had run out about three days ago, had led to my nose and throat becoming totally congested and made it nigh-on-impossible to swallow.

I had also started getting snappy at my friends back on the landing and had started to not want Audrey and my father to come to Wheatfield when I was going through treatment. It was horribly selfish stuff, but it is also text-book behaviour for cancer sufferers. I had underestimated the effects of fatigue. I wouldn't mind, I had been warned:

"What other side effects doctors?"

"Fatigue really, you need to be cognizant of that….."

"You mean 'tiredness."

"No Dave, fatigue."

"What's the difference?"

"You'll have no energy for friends or family…."

"Well that wouldn't be me," I thought… wrongly.

"….so be careful you don't adversely affect those relationships with what will come across as 'impatience' with them."

Suddenly I wasn't so sure. Was I showing impatience? Was I pushing them away?

"You'll find it hard, maybe impossible to complete even the smallest of chores…"

Yep, you could tick that box

"….. even have trouble thinking or making decisions……"

Tick.

"In short, you'll feel as though you could spend whole days in bed and still have no energy……"

Tick, tick, and tick again. All the boxes were full. The Irish cancer society even quotes the following in their literature.

"It can be hard for anyone to understand how much fatigue can affect your life unless they have experienced it themselves."

If you take nothing else from my cancer story, take that take it to the bank. You'll never read a more accurate statement; every word of it is true. This was why my slapstick nurse was so important; I enjoyed our little chats together. She gets cancer. She gets cancer patients with fatigue; you're encouraged to "find time to do something you enjoy each day." I also enjoyed time with my friends, my father and of course, Audrey. I had almost started to push them all away. I got lucky my dad had been through this, and Audrey…. my life was a picnic compared to what she'd been through, so I was flanked on all sides by the most loving, patient and understandable people on earth. Not everybody can say that. Thank god I can.

Breathing with a tube squatting in one of your nostrils and taking up residence down your throat into your tummy is not easy and feels anything but natural. I was coming to terms with this further alien inconvenience when my bed started on a journey down to the X-ray room.

"What's wrong?"

"Ah, don't worry, Dave, we just have to give you a quick X-ray to make sure the tube is in the right place."

"Will I get used to this tube?"

I was told that I would, but I didn't. You don't. You can't! At least the X-ray tuned out fine. Also, it could've been much worse; I might've needed that dreaded Peg.

In prison, you live in a cell. Mine had a spectacular view of…. A wall, you've got a little plastic and a useless chair and your sink, shower and toilet are all, essentially, connected together. Therefore, sick as I was, I was loving my hospital bedroom. A nice bed, pleaser surroundings and no jangling keys or the subliminal stench of tobacco and urine; it was an average room in every respect, but the view was a different matter. I was truly blessed as I had an amazing view of the beautifully maintained, pristine gardens. My eyes were drawn to that lovely little view more times than I cared to count. It was a special little breath of freedom, the real world, without walls or razor wire. I couldn't quite believe the joy I'd experience by just looking at birds feeding outside, wild and free. I felt little jolts of excitement at seeing the many grey squirrels going about their bust days. For the entire world, I could've passed as a kind old pensioner staring out a window…… except I had three prison officers camped outside my door twenty-four-seven.

At the beginning of my stay at St. Luke's, a few of the more 'conscientious' officers thought it prudent and in the best interests of the safety of the state to stay at my bedside all day, every day. They would even sleep in a chair beside me. I had the usual mixture of the good, the bad and outrageously ugly officer selection, but as usual, there was one, well, special one. He was a gigantic boondoggle of a human being, the sort of person who, when he sits in a chair (any chair) it disappears until he sits on thin air, like a long lost zeppelin. Unfortunately, he was as meddlesome as he was huge. For example, on one of our cosy little sleepovers, he proceeded to drag the chair along the floor - metal legs screaming in migraine inducing stereo until he got it 'just so' at the door, then slumped into it. He could've easily picked the chair up, wedged the meat from his super-sited-dinner out of the gaps between his teeth with it, and then gently placed it back down again so as not to wake up the entire hospital full of sick and dying cancer patients.

Alas, no. He had a charming little habit of snorting every last drop of snot and phlegm up into the back of his very roomy nose, then adding a very protracted "Haaaaackkkk" guttural noise at the back of his throat before gulping it all down in an Adam's-apple wobbling swallow. Invariably, a loud rancid belch would follow after jamming the door to my room closed with the chair, and then securing the room further by filling the narrow doorway with his substantial bulk (if I really wanted to escape, there was still a big window!!) he settled himself in for the night by turning off the light and the TV that I was in the middle of watching. I was going to kick up, but I decided to wait... this individual required my special attention.

It didn't take too long. He forced and spluttered himself into a deep sleep, a sight I can only compare to a fat old tabby snoozing on a mouse hole. I turned the TV on, nice and loud too.

"Huwhuuwhuh."

"Excuse me?"

"I was asleep."

"I wasn't."

"Do you mind??"

"What?"

"The telly, I can't sleep with it on."

"I can't sleep with the noise of your snoring."

He mumbled something crude and vulgar before making a big deal of bashing his too big frame off the door a few times and then closed his eyes, forcing sleep. As most people with a mind of their own already know, hospitals don't close, they operate all day, all night, always. The staff work on shifts just like the prison officers, so it shouldn't have come as a shock to my bulky companion that as a patient, the nursing staff would require full and free access to my room to check on me. It was inevitable....

(Outside) "Dave? Dave? Are you okay? Are you on the floor?"

"No, I'm great."

"Are you sure? I can't seem to open the door?"

"No, I'm in my bed…"

"Have you something blocking the door?"

"Eh… sort…. of!"

"You have? What? Why?"

"Well, eh, it's a prison officer!"

(Officer) "What's the problem?"

"Who's that?"

"I'm a member of the Irish prison service. I'm doing my duty. I'm detailed to ensure…"

(interrupting) "I don't care who you are, this is a hospital, Dave is a patient, I'm his nurse and you're in the way, now… MOVE!!"

What an absolute plonker! I remember sharing this story months later with some of the lads back in Wheatfield and it cracked them up! One guy in particular was a massive fan of the show 'Game of Thrones,' a show I've never seen, and compared that screw to one of its characters called 'Hodor.' Apparently, he was also a "Giant Dope" of a man who got his name by crying "Hold the door! Hold the door!" over and over. I must admit, it did share a certain resonance.

Over time, the majority of the officers realized that I wasn't a troublemaker and decided to give me (and themselves) a bit of privacy and stayed outside my room for the remainder of my stay. The nursing staff clocked up a lot of frequent flyer miles, bustling in and out of my room all of the time, no doubt a result of my fragile condition coupled with the curiosity factor, wondering what type of criminal still required three burly prison officers whilst stuck in a hospital bed.

Hospitals, like prisons, give you plenty of downtime, space to muse and reflect on your life and your thoughts. I had a serious niggle. I was finding it really difficult to take myself seriously. To be blunt, I considered myself a bit of a fraud; you see, I'd heard people saying stuff over the years such as "I beat cancer", or "I survived cancer" and "cancer is not going to kill me", and so forth. Yet for all of that, there I was in a hospital bed, yes, I was feeling sick and feeling tired, but I was nothing like what I'd seen in the movies. I was nothing like the way I remembered my poor mother. The nurses fussed around me all day, carrying out all manner of tests, taking blood every day and being generally world class at their jobs. I was still able to walk around the grounds of the hospital, albeit slowly. Also, it must be said that the garden in St. Luke's is an absolute credit to whoever looks after it.

I used to walk around that garden three times a day and when Audrey and my dad visited. They'd join in with me. It felt, well, 'normal'; it was wonderful. The only concerns I was having were for them, I felt good, I was grand. Every day, I'd get called for radiotherapy, but because I was now an inpatient, the times would vary. For all my positive thoughts and feelings though, radiotherapy is a crafty beast. It gets into where the dirt can't and bores away at you like a worm into an apple. Before I knew it and without any hint, clue or warning… Bang! Fatigue. It was like taking the plug out of a bathtub. You don't see an immediate emptying of the water, but before you know it, it's gone.

The fun continued; my neck had suddenly become sore to the touch and had developed a vast and angry redness to it. The left side of my jaw felt like it had horses kicking it and now, all of a sudden, I was in serious trouble, it hurt to even think about opening my mouth, let alone actually doing it, so eating and drinking... Forget about it. Everything had to go down the nasogastric tube. My weight was of deep concern. This is where the shark went into over-drive. I rapidly plummeted from 84kg to 70kg and then to rock-bottom-near-death, 68kg. I wouldn't mind, but I love my grub and the food looked delicious. St. Luke's even boasts an actual menu, a long way from prison food, believe me, but it was impossible.

Thank god for my visits, especially then. My son, Graham, came up to see me every week and the hours we spent together were priceless. We'd discuss his job, his next holiday to the Canary Islands, his new house and his home and family life. Darrin, my best friend, came up to see me a few times as well, like Graham, I hadn't seen Darrin for two years, and boy, did we make up for that! We covered everything, the great and the good topics ranging from clothes, the good times, the bad times, the next times. Everything except the rags-on-a-stick I was transforming into before their very eyes. Only for them, though, I wouldn't have made it. No way, always count your blessings and I am blessed with an amazingly supportive family. My brothers and sisters came up as often as they could and this was my 'food.' I was gorging on their love and support, savouring every last drop of their care and compassion.

In prison, you rarely, if ever, hear a positive report about solicitors fully justified in a lot of cases, to be fair, but not all. I was that rarest of endangered species, and I praised mine to the rooftops. Tony, my solicitor, was another welcome visitor. He knows me inside out and I'd honestly place him amongst my dear friend. We can and did talk about any subject, what I'd do when I got out, work wise and what I'd do in terms of travel etc. It was always positive and gave me great hope.

Speaking of prison, one of the chaplains, a lady named Jean, came up to see me a good few times. That came as a bit of a welcome surprise to me, as I'm not exactly a religious man. I'm often asked if I believe in a higher power. My answer? I have a tattoo on my back of Jesus on the cross. Coming down from his hands are the scales of justice, with two names under that: Rory, my brother and Kay, my mother. I don't believe in the justice of this world, but I do believe in a god. I pray that there is a god; this was amongst the many topics of conversation I had with Jean, together with other aspects of life. She also kindly brought me a get-well-card signed by a few of my friends back in prison; It meant the world to me to know that they wished me well. Unlike my other visitors, they couldn't get in to see me, but I was in their thoughts. They were pulling for me too, more positivity, more food.

Not all officers Moonlight as over-stuffed door-stops, and occasionally, the better ones would pop their head in for chats, and good ones too. A lot of good banter can be had with the oul Scooby-Doo's (screws, a prison thing!) from time to time, so little things like recycling my mother's old joke about me 'Going-Bald' from the chemo' and the negative effects it was having on my self-confidence. Even obvious tongue-in-cheek comments like that could only be said (always in jest) to certain screws, as too many of them would take it seriously and you'd end up either seeing a psychologist, having a 'Depressed Dave' story leaks to the tabloids, or both. Seemingly innocuous things, too, like getting thrush in my mouth, a side effect from chemotherapy, could be twisted and turned into any number of malicious ways by the media, so you become adept at keeping your cards close and your mouth shut.

When I wasn't chatting to people (Always been one of my favourite pastimes!) I found other ways to pass the time. T.V. isn't great at the best of times, although I do love my soaps! And I wasn't in much of a mood for movies, so reading became a new and exciting mistress for me. Being a Dub and former taxi driver, I'd always been curious about James Joyce. A world famous, critically renowned author from right here on our very doorstep. I picked up 'Dubliners' and loved it, then 'a portrait of the Artist as a young man,' excellent stuff. Then, I tried Ulysses. Twice, not for me, in fact, I didn't know what was worse, that or cancer! Meeting 'normal' people, seeing local wildlife, cars, trucks etc. then hearing everyday noises really put me into a 'Freedom' state of mind. I didn't realize it then, but all those thoughts and 'freeing' my mind with great books were adding layers of hope into my subconscious. Instead of thinking about pain and death, I was thinking about walking around the streets of Dublin, name checking all the little touchstones from Joyce's books. Instead of obsessing about grave diggers being the only profession to build houses that last until doomsday, I was dreaming about buying a Toyota Landcruiser (commercial) and doing a bit of painting to make ends meet. I'd reached for the stars long enough and their radiation almost killed me. No, it was a normal, simple life for me, peace quiet, family and love. That's all I want.

I ended up staying in St. Luke's for five weeks straight. Do you want to know how all of your hard-earned tax money was spent during this time? Of course, you do! So here it is, every day of it, I had six prison officers by my side, three at any given time due to their twelve-hour shifts. The officers came from anywhere and everywhere; Wheatfield, Mountjoy, Arbour Hill, Shelton Abbey and Cloverhill, so all you have to do is find out their average hourly rate, multiply that by the number of screws by the number of hours and then add say 12%? For expenses and you'll be in the right ballpark. I have been and will continue to be of the opinion that this was complete overkill and nothing more than a 'jolly.' A handy day out for the officers, but you, dear reader, are the taxpayer, so it's over to you! I did my part; I put it in writing to the relevant authorities before I was hospitalized. Their reply must be lost in the post…. Then again, maybe they'd no money left for stamps!

Back on the treatment table, however, I was getting pushed to my limits. They say that the actual radiotherapy isn't a painful process but more of a discomfort for the area receiving treatment. All I knew was that I was in terrible pain, especially in my targeted area. I had dreaded chemotherapy more, even its name stuck fear in my heart, yet there are people out there who go through it with little or no side effects, please god, that will include you should you ever go through it; which of course I hope you don't. For the rest of us mere mortals (and radioactive superheroes like me!) the side-effects come aplenty but can for the most part, be eased with medication. I ticked all the following boxes: sore mouth, taste changes, loss of appetite, nausea, vomiting, diarrhoea, infection, fatigue, hair loss (my beautiful thorn-like golden looks, forever lost!) and numbness or tingling sensations in my feet and hands.

What you don't expect is the 'chronic sunburn' wounds running down your throat on the inside or to be hooked up to a drip six hours a day for chemotherapy. You'll feel alright on the day and the next, but on day three, you'll be flattened. By the mid-point of my treatment, I was a poster boy for the effects of fatigue on the human body. It was difficult to walk, to talk, to read, in short, everything. No more walks in the garden. No more banter with my usual visitors or energy to have the craic with my unexpected visitors, such as the couple of inner-city ladies who popped in, off-the-cuff and just started yapping to me like we grew up in some house or something! They came from a family line of flower-sellers on Moore Street and Grafton Street and sold all kinds of seasonal extras such as wrapping paper and that sort of thin. As is common with me, we drank in some of the same pubs over the years, so we'd great stories to tell and exchange. Those ladies had faced cancer down and beat it senseless; they were also a much-needed positivity tonic. One of my last visits, before I fell into the quagmire of fatigue, was from one of those ladies. She popped in and handed me a gift that I treasure to this day, a 'good luck' Guardia Angel crying. It only cost me a hug, which I was only too happy to provide and I'll admit it brought a tear to my eye. My kind of people and I'll tell you something else too… when I was in the depths of chronic fatigue. That little Guardia Angel above my bed became my focal point, instilling a mantra from deep within- "the people who brought this, beat cancer, c'mon Dave, beat it too…"

I had been at a point in my treatment where I felt like a fraud, and it was too easy; there was no fight, no battle. Well, I was in the fight now. "Death, where is the sting? The good book questioned; I had the answer. Boy, did I ever, for the first time in my life, I was in a battle I had no hope of winning alone. I was way out of my depth, in the realm of that biting, snapping super-predator who had me eat all ends up. I was done. Finished, I'd nothing left, no energy, no more fight…. This is it, the end, Dave Mahon, R.I.P. I closed my eyes and fell into a deep sleep I was never coming out of.

Chomp, searing, unbearable, supernaturally wicked pain jolted me out of death and forced my face into the sick bucket. Violent vomiting, another little side-effect hidden in the small print. Was I dead? Was this hell? My neck was certainly on fire, so I knew it wasn't heaven. Every bone in my body groaned and ached and the whole world left a bitter, metallic taste. My head flopped back onto my pillow and I looked up at my angel and then looked at the cards and well-wishes on my bedside locker fight. Fight, I owed it to my dad, I owed it to Audrey, I owed it to all my family and friends pulling for me. The Moral support I'd received and continued to receive was going to get me through, I'd 'died' because I wasn't thinking, I'd 'lived' because they believed in me and willed me back from the abyss. Audrey was travelling up all the long- way from Carrick-on-Shannon to see me several times a week. My father, an octogenarian, for goodness's sake, was driving an eighteen-year-old Nissan Micra up to see me every day. Why? To see me. To give me moral support because they love me. No way was I going to let them down again. I owe my life to these two people; no overgrown fish was going to change that. Game on cancer, let's go.

I fought back every day after that, slowly at first as I'm not really a Marvel superhero, despite the prison medic's insistence. Sometimes, just looking at the medical team I had around me was enough to harpoon away the shark for short baits of time anyway. The brilliant Dr. Nazmy would make a point of coming to see me at least twice a week and tell me in plain English (unlike most doctors) exactly what was happening and what to expect next. He was a man first and a doctor second, so I felt more than comfortable discussing my concerns with him and knowing I'd be assured of his understanding. It is true to say that without the excellence permeating through every pore of my incredible medical team, I wouldn't be here today. It's for those very reasons that I'll never be one of these people to say "I" beat cancer; you don't. You can't. It takes a team to beat a plague and to refuse to acknowledge that is insulting to the love, patience and support of your family and the people who dedicate their lives to facing this global killer every day. But back at that time, I still had a lot of woods to make my way out of.

For all the love, joy and support that my visitors brought me, I had reached fatigue saturation level and it was all I could do to just lie there and listen to them. I simply hadn't the strength to try and engage with them. I felt terrible about that, but like I said before, I am blessed with the best. You can never hope to pay back that kink of debt in understanding.

Now, I'm an anti-drugs kind of guy. Always have been to say that I actually thanked God during my struggles for morphine and anti-sickness medication tells its own tale and requires no further elucidation. I was on that stuff for breakfast, dinner and tea, but it wasn't a "fix," oh no, for me, it was a weapon. I utilized these deadly weapons to build up the strength to get up out of bed, to strip off for my shower, to look in the mirror and see…. A skinny-wrinkled-old-man with no muscles and big, insectivore eyes blinking back at me. As you might have noticed, I'm not a vulgar man, not the type to just fall into a colourful metaphor for convenience's sake, but I'm also honest. So, forgive me, but my honest reaction to what stared out of the mirror at me was encapsulated in one, all-encompassing exhalation.

"Fuck."

I felt the fight draining out of me all over again. I looked pathetic and hopeless; I just couldn't see any way back for me anymore. I considered checking out to save everybody a whole lot of trouble for something that clearly wasn't working. What stopped me? I thought about Audrey and my father; how would they cope with my death? Hadn't they already been through enough? They had invested so much of themselves, their hearts and souls into keeping me going. What kind of a selfish idiot was I to even consider such a thing? But I did; I was in such a bad way physically, emotionally, and mentally that death seemed like a cosy blanket of warmth and relief. I stood under the jets of water in the shower and had all kinds of difficult thoughts. I did my little metalizing exercise, where I was in the shark pool and I was treading water the colour of blood, my blood. I took a deep breath and dived under to where the blood wasn't floating and looked the shark right in the eye. My, had he grown. His cruel, intelligent eyes acknowledged my thoughts, so he bowed his head, welcoming my decision, then opened his massive jaws to their world swallowing limit and waited. I moved my head slowly into their maw, accepting my hopeless fare…. Then I stopped. He opened his eyes; I saw surprise in them, uncertainty. I paddled back away from him only a fraction, then kicked him straight into his monster sized balls:

"Fuck You Cancer."

I might be dying, but I'm still my mother's son and like her, I'm a fighter. Game back on cancer. Let's do this.

The shower was a turning point. It not only washed away the fleshly dirt, it cleansed my negative thoughts away, too. Like the old song goes, I was clean, the cleanest I'd been, an end to the tears and the in between years and the troubles I'd seen…. now I was clean. "A different kind of context perhaps, but the message was true. Stage one was to not look at my reflection as I got out of the shower.

614

After all, it wasn't magic leading me out of bloody Narnia. Reality check, Dave! Good, the old me was coming back.

Always remember these doctors are smart people. Exceedingly so if you notice that you've turned into the physical manifestation of an extra from Schindler's list.... Count on it, they do too. A day or two after my life Affirming shower, my doctors had a little conference with me:

"Dave, your weight is low.... Dangerously low."

"Yeah.... I eh..."

"We've had a discussion about your treatment...."

--- Oh, oh ---
"..... And we're a little undecided about allowing you to go through your last chemotherapy treatment....
"I'm doing it."
".... As you mightn't....
I'm sorry, what did you say?"
"I'm up for it. I'll do it."
"Are you sure?"
"Of course, I'm sure. That's what I'm here to do, just give me whatever you have to, anything, just do it, I'm ready."

It might read like heroic or macho nonsense, but it honestly wasn't. I was fully committed to my fight, even if it killed me. Even today, I wonder what would have happened if I turned it down. I'd certainly be dead, but how long would I have lasted? How would my family have taken my failure to do all I could to have saved myself?

I was skeletal and fatigued beyond all common sense after that particular treatment. Then, my radiotherapy bombed me onto another planet. I was completely dependent on morphine and anti-sickness pills, such was the pain it put me through, Mr. Shark's blood was also in the water now as well. I was going down with a fight, after all. I wasn't able for visitors though and that was breaking my heart as I know how much effort it took for them to get here, only to get a few grunts and growls out of me, and that was only if I was strong enough to stay awake. In prison, visits are everything, but phone calls are a close second. In the hospital, my visits were even better, and because of how ill I'd become, a phone had been fitted in my room. It could 'only' receive calls, but it was an absolute lifeline for me, especially as Audrey couldn't travel every day. Hospitals are great like that; they consider the wider picture, how cancer hurts the families as well and how a friendly voice on the end of the phone in the small hours can make all the difference. If I needed to call Audrey, I could press "I" and give the number out to the operator, but she almost always called me instead. In prison on the enhanced regime - you can make two six-minute phone calls a day. The system in place for me at the hospital was just as secure because (A) I still had three screws present morning, noon and night (B) all incoming calls were recorded and (c) all outgoing calls were recorded via the operator. It was a flawless and fool proof system that worked like a Swiss clock for three weeks until an officer complained about it.

It was a Sunday night. I was feeling good about myself as I'd managed to force a small drink of juice or cordial or something into me, and then my under-used plumbing sparked back into action, forcing me over to my little toilet room to call nature. It was an almighty struggle even to shuffle over those few yards, but it was worth it. Another little victory on my road to recovery. I could hear a bit of a commotion down the corridor and noticed that it was getting closer. This was the sort of guy you'd always hear first.

He burst in through my door, strutting about like jack-off-jack, the pool room snake with a face twitching in a cat's cradle of rage and hate. Sweat ran down the face of this credulous idiot in sharply aromatic rivulets. As far as I'm concerned, his will always be a face crying out for a fist in it. If our speech can often be a reflection of who we are inside and how we view others, then his was overwhelmingly loud, obnoxious, below contempt and downright disgusting. I wouldn't have expected this from even the lowest form of scumbag, but this wasn't a prison, wasn't an escaped lunatic, wasn't even a common garden variety screw with an itch in his crotch. This was prison management itself. A chief from Wheatfield, his vocabulary was steeped in the language of a vulgar variety and he was in such an infant's rage that he never stopped to consider that he was in the presence of a female nurse, unless of course, this was all an elaborate attempt at showing off to her, flexing his manhood like a peacock discovering Viagra for the first time.

I didn't even get the time to button up my fly fully, a fact that champions for ignorance jumped upon:

"What were you doing, Dave… having a piss?"

Volcanoes erupted with less noise.

"Yes."

I was exposed, exhausted and totally vulnerable, so I kept it short. He just stood there, piping loud and purple with blood, struggling to think of a funny or inappropriate retort. Rule or ruin is the policy of every human dictator, this guy wanted both and I knew that the next noise to spew forth from his sewer of a mouth would be some other reflection of his anxious narcissism, so I just flopped back down on my bed. As expected, he launched forward with a homemade list of rules – arbitrary, of course - designed to retain, constrain and imprison. Some people just have a challenging personality.

"Blah- Blah-Blah, you are not to be using THAT phone."

His face had now morphed into the shape of a melted wellington and he couldn't help but continue to make an unedifying spectacle of himself. I just lay there, looking at him, completely uninterested in his circus act."

"We have to take that phone away…."

-His arms were gesticulating as though he was singing arias-

"….. So, you'll use the phone up at the nurse's station…."

-A journey as far as China to me then-

"…. Where you can make two…"

-He actually held up the appropriate number of fingers, you know, in case I didn't know how many Two was or maybe he was still showing off? —

"…. calls a day for five…."

--Yep, you guessed it! —

"…. minutes a day."

"Five."

"Oh, and I'm taking that phone away."

"Do what you like with it."

"Give it to me."

"I can't. But it's plugged into the wall if you want to get it.." He desperately wanted me to get it so that he wouldn't have to, but feeble mindedness of his inept and ignorant thoughts flashed across his eyes. What was the I.P.S. thinking about when they moved this guy into management? Anyone could see that when you promoted an ape-like this, it was like giving a hammer to a child. Pretty soon, everything would start to look like a nail. The big hand on his internal stupid clock finally reached 'Decision-o-clock', so he leaned over me, reeking like a small distillery and grabbed the phone, ripping it out of the wall. He wrapped the cord around it and stuffed it into his jacket, all over the situation like a tramp on a bag of chips. As he stormed back out of the room, he paused at the door, looked back at me and growled. A grunt would've suited him better. I lay on my bed and gazed at the ceiling, wondering what the hell just happened, then turned over on my side to turn off my lamp. The book I was reading was open on the lamp stand. I'd delved into Shakespeare just to give it a go. It was from Macbeth, act five, scene five and it read.'

"It is a tale told by an idiot, full of sound and fury, signifying nothing"… wise words, so let us waste no more about him.

I had to use the phone the following morning, to let Audrey know about the new communications arrangement, and I was glad I did, as she would have thought the worst if she had kept calling and I didn't answer. I loved hearing Audrey's voice again, but unfortunately, hers wasn't the only one I was listening to in the collective wisdom of the I.P.S management. I was planted in the middle of a busy nurse's station. They still had jobs to do important jobs and they couldn't just stop all of that just to give me a few minutes peace and quiet. Nor would I ever have expected them to. To make matters even more difficult, I had to endure three looming shadows in blue uniforms standing behind me for every call, either through accident or design. I felt like the world's greatest burden to everybody, so I never spent too long on those calls. Probably just as well, given my lack of energy, be warned Dear reader, cancer treatment can be more enfeebling than the disease. I'm not writing this for shock value either, rather, I'm trying to present you with a braining lucid portrait of the daily realities of life with what is, for many, a terminal illness.

If you happen to have the misfortune of being in prison whilst dealing with the "BIG C," then just stay strong and positive and try to use my story as your own shock-repellent H-Bomb. Unfortunately, I haven't yet discovered an I.P.S. irritation antidote and as you'll continue to see, we need one of those too.

Part of my call to Audrey at the busy nurse's hub concerned news on a documentary we'd made about Amy. Even dying of CANCER is not a reason to stop looking for her. There is no excuse for anyone close to her to ever stop. Not then. Not EVER. I had received a letter from David Cumming at Waddle Media, based in Hollywood, Co Down. He had written a lovely letter wishing me well and letting us know when we were to expect a screening on R.T.E. television of our documentary. He was a fellow survivor and a hell of a Nice Guy. With the offences eavesdropping on my every word to Audrey, we were rightly worried about yet more leaks to the press. It's not a way to fight cancer, is it?

You take the good with the bad, though. Living in your head, a head fraught with fears, Regress and tumultuous Ruminations, the last thing you need is another Percy at Shaw Shank, but wouldn't you just know it. Let's call this guy 'Saville' because he looks and acted like a sexual predator. I don't use those terms loosely, so I'll provide context by way of a few examples.

Remember my dad-Mick- the Retired, cancer surviving, eight-year widower? Of course, you do; everyone does, including prison officers. Not Saville though, oh no. He'd make a big display out of standing in my father's way every time he was on duty and giving him the third degree. Without his uniform, he is a nobody. With it, he was the kind of lickspittle and leech that could only have been handpicked by the 'Brave-with-drink on him' chief. He was exactly the type of obsequious sycophant who'd worship the Emperor's new clothes and doff his prison issue cap whilst laughing raucously but misguidedly in deference to a man who bullies those he can get away with it to satisfy his own narcissism. As you read this, ask yourself – do I have any identification documents on me? I would say that the answer, for the most part, would be – "NO," and why would you? You're a private citizen, after all. This would be a typical example of salute badgering.

"Who are you?"

"Ah hello there, I'm Dave's father. How is he?"

"Dave? Dave who?"

"I'm sorry, what?"

"Are you deaf?"

Dave.

Fucking. Who?"

"Dave, David Mahon. He's my son. He's just in th…"

"His father?"

"… there… What? Yes, yes, I'm his father…"

"Prove it."

"Excuse me?"

"Can you prove it?"

"I can."

"Yeah?

"How?"

"Here's my passport (handing it to him)."

"(snatching it out of his head) Michael Mahon. That's you?"

"It is."

"Well, aren't you the lucky one?"

"How do you mean?"

"The way you "just" happened to have your passport on you."

"(laughing) Sure, I always carry that!"

"Oh yeah? Why's that?"

"Ah, you never know when you might need it!"

There were even occasions when Saville's colleagues recognized my da in a friendly way – "Howya' Mick, on your own today?" - type of thing and just wave him in, but Saville would have to hop up like a villainous sprite and puff his budgie chest out before beginning his questioning, sometimes the other officers would tell Mick to just ignore him and go in, but he wouldn't stand aside until he felt the fabric of my fathers' travel-documents. Luckily, Mick is a master gardener and has yet to meet a weed he couldn't handle, but it bothers me. As weak as I was, I could've wrung his scrawny neck and, especially when it came to Audrey. He'd go through the same vulgar questioning, only you could see he was getting off on it. The more he got in her face, the more aroused he became. Even from my dad, I could see a little bulge in his pants, the same approximate shape of a penis, only smaller. Most of the other officers would wait outside the room and give us a bit of space - not that we could do anything anyway. I was on so much pain medicine it took all of my strength to raise a smile! – But not Saville. He waits at the door and stare in… with a stupid little smile on his maggot's face. My family had been the wellspring of my formidable resilience to Mr. Shark, but that Saville pervert, he was making me burn up energy – anger energy – that I couldn't replace and that might've been fatal. It is by such small margins that disaster has struck before. I was lucky. Whenever Audrey would be getting ready to go home, he'd open the door, bounce up and down on his toes like a child waiting to go in to see Santa at a department store and smirk-blatantly- at us, dying to let us in on the world's creepiest thoughts running around in his head. He was the reason why dogs mysteriously howled at night and you got chills all over your body but couldn't wait to jump into the shower anyway because you felt "dirty".

Was he capable of leaking stories to the newspapers? I honestly believe he is capable of much, much worse, but he did have a "Gotchya!" grain on his face one morning. "I remember watching Ireland A.M that day, as I usually did anyway- even in prison- and they started reading out the newspaper headlines. One of the Read-Tops had something 'tasteful' like "Dave Mahon has cancer" or something equally as information and it honestly felt like they were talking about somebody else. It's yet another entry for my long list of the surreal things I've experienced. It wasn't the first time a story had been shamelessly bundled out of Wheatfield sexual deviant licking his lips in front of me when they Read it. Most of those stories, incidentally, are a patchwork Quilt of outrageous lies; normal lies, little lies, A few flies and the odd sprinkle of truth. They always maintain a negative spin, though, no matter how bad and rudimentary the 'story' actually is. A quick example – I buy a bar of chocolate from the prison tuck shop. Big deal, who cares? That would be spun into "Mad Mahon munches Mars bars with Murdering Mates." Paints a picture, doesn't it? A "Twix" just doesn't have the same loud alliteration and as for Milky Bars?

All of this nonsense was happening around the time of Dean's birthday. He was born in 1990, so he would've turned 28 that day. Twenty Eight. That's' no age at all. I felt horrible and I was heartbroken thinking of how things could've-should've been different. I really missed him; I miss him still. I can't even write his name without thoughts of the horrible, tragic night coming back to me. The pain of those thoughts cut even deeper, more painfully than cancer and I'm not exaggerating the point. I can't even imagine the suffering Audrey must have – and continues to – endure on those landmark days. For all you Right-wings 'throw away the key' thinkers out there, trust me, the familiar torpor of prison life is like staying in a country, my Real sentence, not prison.

I distinctly remember closing my eyes that day and thinking that if I died, I'd get to see Dean again. On his birthday. Honestly, I welcomed that concept. Audrey came up to see me later that day. Yes, there was a massive elephant in the room that we both knew was there, but neither of us had the strength to discuss it. Audrey took out her phone to show me a video she had on it. She pressed 'play', and onto the little screen popped up an image of Andrea Bocelli singing with his sons. I fell to pieces and cried my heart out, and it was all too much.

Another landmark day came hot on the heels of that one-Mother's Day. Oh, dear God. I was still in St. Luke's and even though it was a Sunday, Audrey didn't come up to see me. It doesn't have to be said, but I'll say it anyway, no way – No way could she have ever made that trip. 'Mother's' Day can be such a cruel concept. Try (if you can) to imagine that you lose your first child to a miscarriage. Your second child, a beautiful, amazing son now lay dead in his grave and your third, your baby girl, was somewhere… missing. You want to turn to your husband for support, a hug, a cuddle, anything – but you can't because he's lying up in the hospital, fighting for his life against cancer. He's also guarded by three prison officers because he also happens to be the reason why your baby boy lies cold in his grave. I think a bottle of vodka and a box or ten of Kleenex were on the cards for her that day, and who'd begrudge it to her. I was lucky, I had morphine on tap.

Completing the set of landmark hospital days was my own birthday on April 13th, but to be honest, that is just another day. The important thing for me was that my hospital treatments had finished at long last. I thought incorrectly that I'd be turned out of St. Luke's and back to prison as soon as they could do it, but they kept me for another couple of weeks. I actually felt as though I was ready for a return to Wheatfield and I said it to the doctor. He thought it was hilarious, as he'd never had a patient ask to go back to prison before! Then it dawned on me, I was still hooked up to feeding tubes and drips and so forth. It's amazing how quickly your body adapts, isn't it?

"I'll tell you what, Dave, once we take out that feeding tube and you can drink Fresubin (ensures), then we'll dismiss you, okay?"

That sounded like a good deal to me, so later that day, I asked a nurse to remove my tube, and she did. I then started taking my energy drinks in the normal - non-tubular – way. It was a great feeling just to be able to do that simple little thing. Wisely, though, they kept me a bit longer as I still wasn't healthy enough for prison, but I was getting there. Before I knew it, my time had come. I'll never forget it; it was a Wednesday afternoon and Doctor Nasmy came around to see me.

"How are you feeling, Dave?"

"Great… under the circumstances."

"Before I release you…"

-Yes!!! –

"—I need to hear a few answers from you, okay?"

"Yeah, Great!"

"So, exercise. What can you do?"

"Not much, but I'll walk when I can."

"What about rest?"

"Sleep when I can."

"Good. Remember, you're going back to prison, so don't forget how important it is to stay positive and keep your spirits up, okay?"

"Absolutely, I'm very lucky in there two, always have had support from some fellow inmates."

"I know. I've seen your friends and family. They're important."

"Several times I thought I was done; it was so easy to take the just give up' option, but I didn't."

"Why?"

"Lots of reasons, Audrey, Mick..."

"Outside of your family, anything?"

"Books, Reading ..." especially Lance Armstrong,"

"And outside of that?"

He was clearly testing me and wearing me out. I wasn't used to so many questions coming at me and coming at me in the relentless way he was peppering them at me.

"Well... Lance Armstrong."

"The… eh, cyclist?"

"Yeah!"

"Go on......."

"Another cancer sufferer, I found him inspirational."

"He did?"

"Yeah! (I picked up his book and went to a part I had marked). His motto was, pain is temporary and to get your ass back on the saddle, so I will!"

"(Laughing) Laughter is great medicine too. Your humour helps!" And it does, don't forget that. He then shined a few of his observation skills at me. Everything from going to mass twice a week, walking around the grounds three times a day when I could - and then grilled me on my medications.

"Dave, you're going to need to stay on top of this."

"I know, I'll try. It's not easy in Wheatfield."

"That's why you'll have to make sure you have all the proper medication."

"Will you give those written directions?"

"Absolutely."

One of the most important medications I'd need, incredibly, was the little Ensure drinks. In some cases, it can take up to nine months to recover from radiotherapy to the mouth. The advice is to sip cool drinks - plain water being the best. You are also supposed to have four - to - six-mouth dental check-ups when the treatment finishes. You are prison-savvy by now, dear readers; do I even have to go there? Didn't think so! I suppose I should also mention that your hair is meant to grow back two to three months after finishing your treatment, but sadly, mine never did! One thing I definitely worried about was the swallowing difficulties I'd had during and after my treatment. Even something as harmless as a soggy terabit felt like trying to swallow a mouthful of boiling thumb tacks, it just couldn't happen. Sipping Ensure drinks was the closest I'd get to solid food for months. Just as well they are loaded with calories (400), so that's almost a meal.

"Well, I guess I'm ready, doc."

"You are. All the best, Dave, you are officially released!"

I can't tell you how long I'd wanted to hear those words. I was finally getting out of the hospital! Then, as I slowly shuffled back to the prison, not really the "Released" was a subjective term. I was still going back to prison. Really, the release I'd wanted, but hey, my shark was still swimming around mosses with a pain in his balls, so I wasn't the only one suffering and that was great!

Back to Wheatfield, back into the procedure, then the stop/start hike down the endless corridors until finally, back - breathless – to my East 1 landing. The first person I saw was my good friend - S.G. and he wore a big smile and gave me a massive hug. To be honest, it was the same with all my other friends, too, an honest-to-God uplifting experience, in a weird way, it was good to be back in prison again. In the realm of 'Wow, I never thought I'd ever write that! Moments, here's another entry getting back into my cell, with all my personal belongings, felt like a sort of homecoming. Well... almost. It didn't help them during my absence; my room/cell had been well and truly turned over by the search team and their delicate touch was evidenced by the fact that my clothes were all over the place and the shelves that I'd put up on the wall to keep my toiletries, had been smashed off the well. Searches happen in prison every couple of months, so I wouldn't have expected anything less. How can I compose to somebody who'd never been to prison? It's like coming home from the world's worst holiday to find that your house has been vandalised by a gang of street junkies. A little "Welcome back, Dave!" courtesy of the I.P.S Still not even that could detract from the warmth of support from my friends, especially S.W. and S.G. Even some of the nicer officers had been asking after me, important that, as some of them are, in fact, human, good people. I found it so strange to think about prison as 'home', though. I guess it had something to do with the 'Groundhog Day' Routine that you just Autopilot back into.

Prisons will be famed for their dynamic ability to change. Top of the class in that regard would be the prison medics, Satan's own sisters of sarcasm. The treatment I received on my first two weeks back in Wallyworld would border on the cruel and harder kind. On my first night back-knackered, just getting my thrashed cell back together, with chronic pain and fatigue - I crashed asleep at early-o-clock. At eleven — o'clock, my door crashes open with a fanfare of noise and hostility. Two officers rushed into my room and shook me awake. The shock could - and almost- killed me. I didn't know who I was, where I was or what on earth was going on. Then I looked at the shadow figure standing in the doorway. Nurse ratchet. Wherever she spoke, wolves howled, babies cried and somewhere in the world, a puppy died. It was one of those voices. Leaving her broomstick at the door, she floored a foul blackish-green mist. In her scaly, old lady paw, at least fifteen different tablets.

"Here. You have to take these. Now!"

It takes a couple of seconds to decode her shrick-laden-rasp of a voice. Then it dawned on me, she's insane. No way could she possibly be serious. I had never had to take so many tablets All at once in my whole life... ever.

"Sorry, but can you tell me exactly what they are?"

I've seen rattle snakes with a better bedside manner. She hissed:

"Painkillers... Morphine… Tablets... These make you, SHIT."

"I'm, I'm sorry, they what?"

"Shite... These ones? Are, Sick... Ness. These? Anti. De. Press. Ants."

"Hang on, Anti-depressors?"

"Did I stutter?"

"No."

"Then you heard me."

"Who prescribed them?"

"The doc did."

"I've never been on anti-depressants in my life. Why did he do that?"

"How would I fuckin' know? Do you want them or not?"

"No thanks."

"Then you can't have ANY of the medication."

"Fine. I want to see the doctor tomorrow."

BANG. That was the door almost coming off the hinges. The cell does a fine trade in echo, by the way, wonderful noise in full and surround sound for a few minutes. It developed into a rough night. I was extremely sick all the way through it and into the following morning.

Naturally, I had to fight my way over to the doctors' surgery the following day because nothing is ever done properly in Prison. It wasn't the regular Doctor, so that wasn't a great start.

"Good morning, doctor."

"Prison number?" (I gave it to him).

"David Mahon? Yes?"

"Yes. Now look, did you prescribe anti-depressant tablets for me?"

"No."

"No??"

"It must have been the other doctor."

Right away, I know this wasn't true. Not a chance, but I didn't pass a comment.

"The other doctor, so it wasn't you?"

"No, not me."

"Okay, so why would you think the doctor prescribed anti-depressants for me?"

"Because you have cancer and you might be depressed."

Only thing worse than a liar is a liar lying about being a liar.

"Do you think he was right? Would you prescribe medication for me without an examination or consultation?"

"No, I wouldn't."

The guilty look all over his face confirmed my earlier suspicions. It was him, but he was trying to bluff his way out of it. I didn't have the strength or energy to pursue it further. You can't win anyway.

627

"Anyway, I didn't get any of my medication since I got back from the hospital. Can you help me?"

"Of course. What do you need?"

"You should have a note of everything from the hospital. I know it came in with me yesterday. My oncologist was very clear about that."

He moved a few papers around his desk in a show of looking for it, but no surprise:

"No, I don't seem to have it... here... eh..."

"What about on the computer system?"

He rapped away blindly on the keyboard; it was just like that sketch out of Little Britain. The computer says no to every question:

"No, I checked, nothing on your file..."

"Nothing on my file?? So, the prison is unaware of my cancer?!"

"Oh no, we know about that... eh... eh... do you know what tablets you need?"

Have you ever heard about Hanlon's Razor? It's a philosophy tailor-made for this exact situation. It states: "One should never attribute to malice that which is adequately explained by neglect." The medical team were guilty or something; you choose yourself between malice or neglect, and either one is a disgrace.

"Actually, doctor, I do. Should I list them?"

"(Disbelief all over his expressive puss) Yes, please do!"

"Dexamethasone, that's a steroid..."

"Hmm steroids... 'Might' be a problem. Continue."

"Maxolon, I get those three times a day."

"Go on."

"BMX, that's a mouthwash, again, three times a day."

"Hmm, I'll need to check that. Next?"

"Solpadol 500/36's, four times a day."

"That's a big problem. Keep going."

"Myostatin, five times a day.

"Ensure drinks because I can't eat…"

"They're problematic, keep going."

"I'm also on morphine…"

He didn't even dignify that with another "problem," just sucked in a deep breath through his teeth, then shook his head in a "no chance" way on the exhale. I'd almost become a chemist overnight in order to memorize all that stuff, but he couldn't have cared less. Yet, for all of that, he tickled my ears with "I'll sort this all out" platitudes before I left the surgery, thus, I held out a sliver of hope on my way back to my cell. It didn't last.

I couldn't eat, no matter how hungry I got. Hunger pain isn't a patch on the throat cancer pain, so it wasn't an option. In such a situation, you are completely dependent on the ensuring/Fresubin supplements. I was presented roughly half a dozen different concoctions of this stuff, totalling 2,200 calories a day. That equates to the average calorie consumption for a man my size/Age/Shape, etc. I didn't receive a single one for over four days. I complained until I was Blue-in-the -Face, but you'd have better odds trying to nail a trifle to the wall. It got to the point that I was too weak to complain. Think about that. Not enough energy to even have a moan! My good friend S.G. called into my cell – to see how I was – And almost died of fright. Not a good confidence booster, believe me! He had to literally lean into my face to hear what I was saying. That's how weak I'd become. He shot off to the medics and fair play to him. An hour later, some drinks arrived. This was to be a regular occurrence, let you go to your weakest point, then parachute in some last-minute supplies. I'd become wise to their neglect, though, so I made sure to keep a little supply of bottles hidden in my cell. I remembered my chats with Dr. Nasmy about positivity, so I found a lot of solace in my books. A quote that stood me in great stead came from 'The Ballad of Sir Andrew Barton.' It went: "I am hurt, but I am not slain, so I'll lay me down and bleed awhile, then I will rise and fight again."

My friends provided a mighty arsenal in that fight. Yes, I was bruised and battered, starved and ignored, but I'd got great support from my real friends, so much so that it reached a point where you couldn't distinguish between my blood and the shark's. The pool was a deep shade of red and his attacks were less frequent.

The great thing about having friends around you is that they 'know' you and sometimes they know better than you do, when to give you a good kick-up the back-side. They'd hassle me all the time about getting back out to work on the grounds. It was getting into the busy season, all the flowers had to be planted, hanging baskets put together, gardening and general duties, so there was a bit of a buzz about the place. Unfortunately, I was barely able to walk; I was struggling and panting to go a few feet up the landing and back. After what must have been a good six weeks, S.W. finally broke me down. His kindness and logic were top class – "C'mon Dave, excuses are like arse–holes, we've all got them, now come on, you're not staying back today, and so it was then I made my first tentative steps back out to work.

It was great, what a feeling – the sun was shining, the air was fresh and the heat was slowly starting to build into what was to become one of the Hottest summonses in our history. It was even good to see a few of the officers out there again. I'd also met a few of the new faces out there and most of them were okay. I lasted half an hour before I started to fade, so S.W. brought me back in. In fact, he would be the one to bring me in and out whenever I needed, a true friend, a real rock. He'd been there for me all the way through this – whatever I'd need; laundry, shopping, even offered to help with some personal chores if it came to it – the sort of thing only a professional carer would do on the outside – but thankfully it didn't come to that. His greatest gift to me, though, was his friendship and the chat's we'd have every evening – without fail – he'd appear at my cell door as it opened at five thirty. Both of us could chat for Ireland, so even when I was too tired to talk, he'd take up the slack and just bring the craic! After a couple of weeks, I felt my strength started coming back.

Annoyingly, frustratingly, for all of that progress, fatigue was proving to be a sticking point. I was still having to sleep a lot more than I usually did, but I continued to push myself as hard as I could. As Ian Mc Ewan so eloquently put it, "A person is, among all else, a material thing, easily torn and not easily mended." The way I found to repair myself was as simple as it was effective; I walked!

My muscles had been inactive for the longest period in my life and re-awakening them was tough. Fatigue, of course, makes everything a trudge, but like the little-engine-that-could, I pumped out step after step after step until those muscles screamed themselves awake. Remember, 'muscle memory' isn't just a slogan on a T-shirt; it's a real thing, remind your body that it was strong once and will be strong again. Falling down is not the mark of failure; staying down is. I wasn't going to stay down anymore, no matter how gnarled and tortuous my journey got. I gave it even more, then more again. Besides, Walking was always my 'thing,' I love walking and always have. It has always been a bit of a safe place for me to be alone in my thoughts and de-stress myself, decompress all of life's many frustrations. In Wheatfield, walking around the grounds was my 'escape' – maybe not the best of words to use in a prison context! – but in my mind's eye. I could see my two dogs, Lili and Alfi, walking with me. I'd get lost in those little thoughts and believe it or not, I caught myself calling after them from time to time! Whatever gets you through, eh?! But it does prove the old adage that anything in life, every problem can become an opportunity. I was now an artist of my imagination, and the best part of that was that my dogs had jumped into the pond with me and had developed a craving for fresh shark!

Old Mr. Shark hadn't come near me since the arrival of my 'dogs', but the lumps he'd chomped out of me hadn't gone away. I was still back and forth to hospitals quite a lot, spreading myself between the St James and St. Luke's. The consensus was that I was improving, but I needed to get back to eating and fast. I got a stark reminder at the Radiotherapy Torture chamber at St. Luke's when I was shown my panic-inducing mask. It will always envelop me in instant claustrophobia because of how tight it was to my face and how difficult it was to breathe through. I could open my eyes, mouth, everything in it now; that's how much I'd lost, and that was only on my face. Again, I had to remind myself of the positives, everything else was going great and I was doing great. I wouldn't be getting any indication of exactly where I stood with regard to cured/not cured – and wouldn't for at least four months – but five years was the most important period of time to me and every cancer warrior worldwide. That's how long an all-clear takes if you're lucky to even have that hope. I had also learned to live in 'the now,' so I pushed all long-term targets to the back of my mind and cut right to the chase:

"What will I do if it's not gone?"

"If it's still there in your lymph nodes (neck), we should be able to operate."

"What if it's in my throat?"

"That's a different matter. That would be very serious."

That was the end of the conversation for me. His considered and honest response told me all I needed to know, so I didn't – couldn't press him on it. My logic was based on a recent tragedy back in Wheatfield, where I wasn't the only inmate with cancer... for a while.

His name was Samuel Jennings and he was doing a life sentence. I neither know nor care what he was convicted of; it isn't the point of his short entry into my story. He used to send me over already made-up and mounted jigsaw puzzles; a lot of inmates would hang these on their cell walls as you would a poster. For Samuel, it was one cancer warrior being supportive of another. He was seventy-two years old and had fought cancer for a number of years. He lost that fight. A day or two before he died, he was made to walk all the way up the stairs to the nurse's station to collect his medication. I now knew more about chronic fatigue than I did then, so I am more than aware of how difficult that must've been for him and sadly, how utterly unnecessary. His medication or hospice bed, but they weren't. Instead, he was forced to expend energy he didn't have and then, to add insult to injury – had to face what would become his final humiliation. He soiled himself front and back. It wasn't his fault, he had nothing left, he'd no energy, but yet the simple-minded junkie-scum Neanderthals frequenting this place mocked and jeered him all the way back to his cell, looking at his lonely journey reminded me of the sad image I saw many years ago on a wildlife documentary. It concerned an old African elephant slowly limping his long way to a so-called Elephant's graveyard. It was said that they don't die of old age, rather, they wear their teeth out over a lifetime and then starve to death because they can no longer eat. It is not unlike cancer, is it? But this was a human-being, not an animal, and he didn't have David Attenborough's dulcet tones accompanied by sombre mood-music to extenuate his sad demise. His was the mocking of an idiot's gallery and the shame of how helpless he'd become. It took another inmate-another 'lifer' as it happened – to go into his cell and help clean him up. It's as well he did, as otherwise, he would've left this world choking in the smell and stickiness of his own putrid filth. The only hint of 'humanity' came from the month of an African medic, she told me that "he should be in a hospital, but I don't recall her rushing to his aid.

The official 'company-tone or I.P.S.' I'm led to believe is that Samuel died in hospital. This is not true, why? Well, prisoners "don't die in prison" because then the state is financially culpable for the autopsy, funeral and associated expenses. If they die in a hospital or the back of an ambulance, then the costs revert back to the family or somewhere else. The facts about Samuel are that he died in his cell sometime between 7:15 pm – 9:02 pm. I know this because not only did I take contemporaneous notes to that effect, I was also in a cell directly across from his, so I could hear – EVERYTHING. Using my notes, I can tell you that at 22:14, there was still no sign of ambulance for him. It might well have been outside the jail by then, as it takes hours – sometimes – to get clearance. Everything was ghostly quiet until I eventually fell asleep at quarter to eleven that night.

At un-lock the following morning, 8:15am, we heard confirmation that Samuel had died the previous night at the hospital. This is a disgusting practice – surely the families/friends deserve to know the exact time – date – and location of the time their Father/Brother/Son/Friend died? I felt his passing more than most – not that we were especially close (we weren't), but because that was a potential prophecy for me, how my life would end. No way. I bided my time on the landing until the usual procession of suits and management deigned to honour us with their Ivory-towered-presence to visit Samuel's cell "out of respect" – Read "Ass coverage" and assure us all that everything is awesome and we're so lucky to be in such a healthy, caring environment.

Vulture-in-chief suited Governor O'Neill, Wheatfield's numero UNO, I headed over to him and introduced myself. I explained to him that I had been dealing with a female Governor up until then, Governor McGuiness.

"She's gone to another prison."

"So, can I deal with you then?"

"Oh, absolutely."

"You're sure?"

"Of course, I'm the Head Governor around here."

I gave him a detailed summary (if that's not too much of an oxymoron, but you've got to get your best case across-and fast-in person) of where exactly I was with my treatment, what my fears were, and so forth.

"Don't worry; I'm dealing with it now."

"Do I have your word on that Governor?"

"You do."

"Can we shake hands on that?"

This is a highly unusual occurrence on a landing in any jail anywhere. You just don't doorstep a governor and then often shake his hand, but I did. He took it, and we shook hands on the deal.

"Thanks, Governor."

"No problem."

"So, when can I expect to hear from you?"

"I'll get back to you – personally within a working day or two" tip service. I'm still waiting to hear from him! I find it absolutely cross for the death of any man to be used by selfish individuals to perpetuate their own egotistical legacy, but that's what we continue to find ourselves faced with.

Back on my own battleground, I faced another hospital appointment at St. James' on July 10th 2018. As usual, I had a three-officer escort, only this time, I had two male officers and one female. I was still chained up to the hilt, but I was more curious than before, as I had not only lost all that weight but the presence of a female chained to me drew a few strange looks. The decibel volume of her potty-mouthed running commentary on the "Fuckin' state of this… that (dat) and the other…"

"Fuckin' state of this… that (dat) and the other…" Really wasn't helping anyone much. We did our usual business of scaring half the people there – 'dangerous criminal in chains' – and then proceeded to annoy the other half by that bloody queue-jumping rule. Once again, if you- dear reader – were one of those inconvenienced on that day, I humbly apologise. Not that it was much of a help, to be fair, as I ended up having to wait over two and a half hours to see the doctor anyway. I was glad of that as I wasn't going anywhere because I still had a good bit of prison to do, but my 'entourage' got into a real sulk… I love it when that happens! While I was waiting for the doctor, I had my blood taken and sat around people watching, just as happy as a clam. It was a day for the ladies as the doctor that attended me that day was also of the fairer sex and I didn't think that she was assigned to me at first because I'd never seen her before. Inevitably. A clipboard was produced and the questions began.

"How are you feeling?"

"Great."

"Have you given up smoking yet?"

"No."

"Why?"

"Because I've never smoked in my life."

Unless I see cast-iron evidence to the contrary, I will always be of the opinion that every oncologist has the 'smoking' question stamped across their clipboards in large, bold-type font. The examination began just as the questions ended. It seemed very unscientific compared to what I was used to. She checked my neck using only her hands and looked down my throat using the naked eye and not a camera. I guess people of my vintage would call that "old school" nowadays!

"You look great, Dave!"

"Yeah, I know... thanks!"

We had a good laugh about that, even though we had all three officers in the examination room with us, there is no such thing as privacy. The consultation ended with the doctor telling me that I'd be back on July 27th 2018, to get a C.T. Scan (A.K.A. A 'CAT' SCAN), which would involve me having to consume a dye first, which allows the scanning machine to find whatever it's looking for. The thought of knocking back some dye didn't exactly appeal to me... then again, if it came out of a Jack Daniel's bottle, I'd take as much as I could! Everything is relative, isn't it? She also told me that I'd get my results from the C.T. a few weeks after it, which would've been around August. I didn't get an exact date because the doctor - to be fair - didn't have one, but – and I don't mean to seem disingenuous – waiting is tortuous with cancer as you'll always fear the worst. As the doctor walked away, I noticed the officers whispering in a huddle. Strange.

"Do you want some lunch, Dave?"

"I'd love some, but I still can't really eat much."

"Are you sure?"

You know what they say about months and gift horses, right?

"Well, I wouldn't mind a bowl of soup and I have a few ensures in my carrier bag..."

"Right then, let's go..."

Confession time, I was no more in the mood for food than the man on the moon, but sitting around in the real-world people–watching beats the hell out of sitting in a cell staring at the four walls, don't you think? It's funny how things change. I'd dropped off many a fare at St. James' back in the day but never knew it had a restaurant upstairs. The place was packed out with people, so I was relieved to be sans-cuffs for the duration. I people-watched like a tourist, as I struggled through my soup, ensures and a bottle of coke. It was a long way from doing the people-watching-thing sitting outside Bruxelles off Grafton Street with a creamy pint of Guinness in front of me, but beggars can't be too choosey when you're doing time! It was a good time though, as simple as it was, then it was time to go. Back on with the shackles and then paraded through the heaving throng of hospital traffic, which meant my mind was elsewhere, in 'Dave-the-movie' world of my subconscious. Before I knew it, we were back at Wally world and walking through the 'Procedure' once again.

I called Audrey when I got back, just to let her know that I was back safely, went through some of the tests and bits I'd been through and all was good. Life progressed in prison normally until that Sunday when I made my usual call to Audrey. Straight away, I sensed a problem, so I asked what was up!

"Ah… the papers have been on to me again."

"Who?"

"The Star."

"Why?"

"There's a story in the Sunday world about you and they wanted to see if I'd give them my side of it."

Naturally, she didn't, as if you do, you fan the flames of a non-story into a red-top inferno. I managed to get my hands on a copy of The Sunday World later on that day. Never a problem in prison as that's their target demographic anyway; junkies, scumbags and wife bashers masquerading as wannabe gangsters (but not all of them). My stomach lurched and constricted with what I read.

They had filled two pages with an article framed with their normal, banal nonsense, so I'll spare you the perils of their poor writing, but they printed what can only ever be generously termed – outrageous lies. Their malicious gossip rag proclaimed that my cancer had spread to my stomach and groin area. Note to the crayon–wielding "writers" at that paper, the spread of cancer from one part of your body to other tissues and organs is called METASTASIS. That's – 'ME. TAS. TAS. IS'. Sunday World, the "Article" continued with its lying through-line, stating that I had received this bad news on my last visit to St. James Hospital on the 10th of July 2018. When you write for this worthless rag and the editor tells you to fill two pages, don't panic about running out of wax for your crayon and just slap an oversized photo across both pages. This was duly adhered to, with another "lucky-your-photographer-just-happened-to-be-there-and-wasn't-tipped-off-by-the-screws" photo of me and two of the screws in question on that fateful day. Oh, they also added that I was "dying of cancer." The problem with dirt media like the Sunday World is that we all know that the only thing they ever get right is the date, but still when you have cancer and find yourself awaiting results. You can't help but wonder, "What if?" That article added no end of stress and worry to my family – and – to me, which, lest we forget, could've actually killed me, thus fulfilling their otherwise colour sheer of lies and prediction.

I called Audrey the next day as she was very shaken and upset. Her day went from bad to worse after talking to me the previous day. Her phone – and my father hadn't stopped for a rest all day, always concerning that horrible rag. It was nice - in a weird way- that so many people took the trouble to call and offer their support. That is always a welcome, loving thing, but seriously, the "No smoke without fire" doomsayers needed to remember who it was they were calling – An eighty-years-old-widower-with-a-heart-condition and Audrey, you know – missing – Amy's mum? If you know of two more people less deserving of yet more stress in their lives, you'd be doing well. This is what Jango-journalism never considers, the collateral damage. Slag me off all you want. Just don't hurt my family. Please.

Anyway, the article was so untruthful and offensive I called Tony, my solicitor, about it, but that takes us off the cancer track, so we'll come back to that. I think you'll agree though, irresponsible at best, isn't it?

Back in the real, non-Sunday world, time ticked slowly on until, at last, August 14th arrived. I still had concerns at the back of my mind about 'what-if' they knew something I didn't about my own diagnosis, so I was ravenous for answers. I was at St. James to get a PET scan. This is another radiation treatment. This time, you are injected with radiation and then left to sit in a vacuum of isolation where you are not even allowed to read a book, which I thought was a bit strange, so I asked the doctor about it;

"When you read, you use both sides of your brain."

"Okay?"

"No. You have to be completely relaxed."

Fair enough. They are most definitely experts in their field. When they tell you something- Listen? You want to get better? Okay. You could not be in better hands; they don't talk just to hear themselves. That's been my experience, anyway. As ever, my three officers are with me, but this time, they have to wait outside. As usual, they do nothing the easy way. As I previously mentioned, the room itself was a type of non-sensory room. A place to be at peace and in quiet with your thoughts so that you decompress both sides of your brain. In the little world of the obscure. One of the screws and their baby brain thought that it would be quite acceptable to leave her mobile phone plugged into a socket, charging away. Given that I was still a prisoner and I'd have been alone in a room with one of the taboos' pieces of contraband known under the sun... she left the door open. Even security conscious, aren't they? Well, so am I, at least that is when it comes to the security of my health, so I waited for one of my oncology team to pass by and called him into my room.

"Hi Dave, you okay?"

"Not really, no."

"Oh? What's up?

"I'm feeling really stressed."

"Oh, Dave, that's really not good. You're supposed to be avoiding stressful situations. I thought that we were very clear about that?"

"You were, but it's not my fault."

"Okay, so what's the problem?"

"You see that phone charging down there (pointing)."

"Yes."

"Well, it's not supposed to be in here, is it?"

"No, it's not. Nothing is. I thought you knew that?"

"It's not mine and what's worse is, the person who owns it won't close the door while I'm in here with it."

"Is that right...?"

He tore her to ribbons. He didn't exactly throw her phone back at her, but he didn't place it gently back into her soup-bowl-paws either. His lecture was first class, a dressing-down of epic proportions, a child's scolding on how it was a hospital, not a carphone warehouse, how a depleted battery does not have the same crushing impact as a lost life and how they – the hospital - carried around the PhD's and would therefore trust their own well-informed, highly educated opinions on what doors would be left open – or not – in their own buildings. The peanut gallery remained quiet. Smartest thing they'd ever said. The doctor came back in to see me and noticed that I looked anxious and full of nervous energy.

"Don't worry about them, Dave."

"I'm not."

"Really? You see a bit shaken."

"It's not them…. It's the scanners."

"Are you claustrophobic?"

"I wasn't before, but since I had to wear that mask in radiotherapy…."

To be brutally honest, that mask had done serious – possibly irreparable – psychological damage to me. Every scanner machine was caked in coffin-block icing for me now and I needed a relaxant. When the doctors offered one up for me, I almost bit it out of hand, I was that scared. As soon as I swallowed the pill, I knew I'd be under the scanner in less than thirty minutes…. And I was.

The scan itself took only twenty-five minutes, but you have to lie perfectly still with your arms straight up behind your head. They also strap you into the machine around the waist - but I was unaware of that until I tried getting up! I'm putting that down on the table as I was half – asleep, but that's fine. It's a lot better than being a nervous wreck. Tired as I was, I was still cheeky enough to ask the nurses about getting my results before going. Not a chance, of course, but if you don't ask, you don't get it I suppose/ Ah well, God loves a trier!

"Are you still under Dr. Nasmy?"

"I am."

"He should have your results by tomorrow and he'll get in touch with you in due course, okay?"

That was a lot more than "okay", even though I would've wanted the news right there and then, but Dr. Nasmy is better than a rock star as far as I'm concerned. He's a rock star with a lot of time for Audrey; he'd take her call if it came to it. Scan complete? It's time to eat!

I was brought back upstairs to the restaurant in St. James and even though I still wasn't able to eat properly, I enjoyed a banana and my bottle of coke. The officers didn't bother cuffing me, but they insisted on keeping me on a chain…. Like a dog… it's degrading but scary for Mr. and Mrs. Jo Public.

People, understandably enough, are really uncomfortable about having to shell out their hard-earned cash only to have to sit beside some potentially dangerous convict, shackled with chains by three prison officers. I'll level with you; I still wouldn't like to do it and I'd rather have a meal elsewhere if I had a child or elderly person with me. The I.P.S. should simply address this issue by providing a pre-packed sandwich and having a private place where you can eat it, but I digress. My main concern – apart from my results, obviously – was if those pesky photographers would be waiting outside again. I'm used to all of that nonsense by now, but what you never get used to are the harmful lies they continually perpetuate in their salacious gossip-rags. I found myself just waiting to get back to my then-home in prison. As much as the walls press you in, they also act as protection from the outside too.

I called Audrey when I got back and told her that Dr. Nazmy would have my results the next day. We knew that our calls were always scrutinised and Analyzed, so what Audrey knew to take from my single line of dialogue was to call Dr. Nazmy, find out as much as she could and let me know about it on a visit. That's why I continued:

"It will probably be two or three weeks before I get the news, good or bad."

We both knew that if she got the bad news of Nazmy, then that's when the news would be leaked from the prison. It also gave her a "free-run" if she looked upset on our next visit, as the screws still wouldn't know what she did. It's terrible the lengths you have to go through. Audrey called Dr. Nazmy and got to talk to him over the next couple of days. Through the good doctors – and his team – Audrey was provided with a much fuller picture of where we were at.

As an 'enhanced' prisoner, I was allowed two phone calls per day and more often than not, I used these on Audrey, given the fact that I'd called her so often. You'd be forgiven for thinking that one would be the same as the next. On August

17th 2018, you'd have been wrong for thinking that. All wrong - our usual phone - etiquette of carefulness went out the window.

"Dave, I've good news for you!"

"You do? Okay, what's the good news?"

"The cancer is gone!!"

"What?!"

"You heard me; your cancer is gone!"

"Really?"

"Really!!"

"How do you know?!"

She had been on to St. Luke's and one of the staff members explained that they couldn't just hand out personal information like that. Rightly so. However, Audrey got lucky in that she happened across a staff member she had gotten to know very well, somebody who appreciated all the stress that we were going through and knew Audrey could be trusted.

"Let's just say that you have nothing to worry about!"

This was the best news EVER! When I got back to my room, I let out a scream of joyous relief and let loose a few first pumps! I don't know where they came from, but that wouldn't be my normal thing, not that me getting good news could ever be a 'normal' thing! As if to prove that point, life had to give us another kick in the guts. Lily, my poor little Jack Russell, had to go to the vet with pancreatic problems.

Back in my cell, my head was spinning and whirling like a dervish. This was yet another quantum leap in my fortunes and now, I could dare to dream again. We would have a second chance to look for Amy, to go back to work on her appeal with a vengeance. Or would I be forced to give up and retire – would Audrey be okay – when I got out? Too many questions and too much going through the processors in my head at one time to make the right decisions; I needed this to all sink in. Better things would lie ahead. That was more than enough for now. But I couldn't relax everything. I tried to just sit down and chill out, I'd spring back up out of the chair and think of something else;

"When do I tell the screws?"

"Will I even bother?"

"When should I tell the inmates?"

"The papers, they'll find out, but do they already? Could that call with Audrey already be on the printing presses?"

In the end, common sense prevailed and I decided to share my news with only my good friends, those who had been with me all the way through, the ones who had proved trustworthy. Of that small group, only two remained that particular day, S.W and J.R, one of which gave me a big hug-much needed and again very much out of character for a prison situation. I found myself getting very emotional and as I was telling J.R. the news, I had to stop myself a couple of times to get some composure back, I was welling up. These tears of joy were a dam burst of dreams morphing into reality. My death sentence had been revoked I had the same two visitors to my cell later that evening, it was truly glorious news that we wanted to shout about, but it had to remain under-wraps as long as possible. One of the lads hung back a bit longer at the end, he had something to say and wanted to do so in private;

"Dave, I'd love to bring you out and buy you a celebratory Brandy or Jack Daniels, but we're stuck in here, 'so I wait.' Hence, this is the best I can do, enjoy!"

It was a little bit of Cadbury's drinking chocolate, a very rare commodity to have in Wheatfield prison. That night, when we were all banged up in our cells, I poured some milk into a plastic bag and then struck it into a kettle of water to boil. You see, this was prison. You had to immense milk in this way in order to boil it. It was worth it though, a tasty treat that came out of the blue, always appreciated. Yet, it was such a long way from what I'd grown accustomed to on the outside – in the Real world – and all I really wanted was to be out there with my Audrey and my father. The two people who'd helped me through every painful and deathly step, held my hand, laughed with me, cried with me and probably would've died with me. I raised my little cup of chocolate and toasted them in my empty cell. I think it was Helen Keller who said, "The most beautiful things in the world cannot be seen or touched; they must be felt in the heart." Mick and Audrey will never fully know how much love I felt for them in that moment. There are no words to articulate it, but those feelings are etched forever in the depths of my heart. Eternal. Immovable. Indescribable.

Waking up over the next few mornings was an absolute joy. Why? Because it wasn't a dream! I became a vastly different Dave until the doors were unlocked and I'd have to put on the 'just-Dave' persona, but 'bouncy-bouncy-happy-bunny-Dave' would hide under my bed until it was safe to be him again. I loved this little subterfuge as keeping secrets in prison is like catching lightning in a jam jar, it just can't be done, but there I was, doing it! It was my week to pull off the impossible. Let the good times roll!

That was a close approximation to how prison life went on until August 29th, 2018. I woke up in my bouncy-bunny-jolliness and that lasted until my door opened a little earlier than usual that morning. Usually, that's not a good omen; it's a glitch in the Matrix, so your primal sense of survival takes over. In short, you're on edge.

"Alright, Dave?"

"Yeah."

"You're going to hospital today, okay?"

"Yeah, great. Just give me a while to get ready."

So, it was off with my work clothes and on with my good clothes. The outside, normal person clothes. They say "clothes make the man" and that's very true because I felt 'normal' and 'free' in that particular ensemble. All dressed and ready, I caught my reflection in the mirror again. I looked a bit like that fella' from the papers, that Dave Mahon bloke, only thinner! It was a healthier looking me than that skeleton who stared back at me only a couple of months ago. Then reality came slamming down on top of me – I was going back to St. Luke's… What if Audrey heard the message wrong? Maybe she picked it up wrong? Maybe the nurse read off the wrong chart? Maybe, maybe, maybe, what if? I was back on edge, doubting myself, doubting everything.

I saw my two friends passing by my cell on their way to work, the only other people who knew, and they gave me discreet thumbs-ups and wished me well. The lads shuffled on to work. I went through reception and 'the procedure' and met with my usual cadre of a three-screw-escort. I knew all three of them, two were quiet and one was so full of beans that he reminded me of a pent-up house dog who finally saw the lease come out of the drawer. They're pretty much par for the course, but whatever floats your boat.

As much as I'd always loved the journey to St. Luke's, my little nostalgia tour, looking out the window at all those memories, was tinged with a sense of foreboding. I closed my eyes and transported myself back to the shark pool. It was blood-stained with blackened walls but was otherwise empty. Strange. No sign of me or the shark. What could that mean? At the back of the pool, there was an exit door. I walked up to it and gave it a push. It opened. Outside was what looked for all the world like an old graveyard, complete with a low over-hanging mist of rain and ancient headstones poking out of too-green grass. At the edge of this cemetery stood a pile of freshly dug earth and a small crowd huddled in black mourning cloths under Raven-Black umbrellas blocking out their features. Clearly, this is a funeral, but for who? Was this a premonition? What did it all mean?

"C'mon, Dave, are you right?"

"Huh?"

"We're here, come on, let's go."

We walked into St. Luke's and as we entered the foyer, the screws took my cuffs off. Fair play to them. I had only once before not received that courtesy, so that was an excellent result as prison escorts go. All of the nurses that I'd come to know and appreciate greatly, came straight over to see me and say 'hello,' what beautiful people they are.

"Ah, Jesus, you look great!"

"Dave, what are you doing back here?!"

"Did you miss us, Dave?!"

Great, great people, talk about a warm welcome! I pray that you never get cancer, but if you do. You'll understand for yourself just what it is that I'm trying to say here. To put it another way, if the government stopped urinating money up against the wall by stopping just a few of the I.P.S. practices I've highlighted in this book and poured these savings into the staff of the various hospitals I've attended, it still wouldn't be enough. Politicians and other vacuous parasites are sucking the money out of our society, stick em' on a nurse wage and see what happens. Put the nurses on a politician's wage. At least they earn it, and then some? These - and other thoughts rattled around in my all-too-nervous mind as the eternity I had to wait to get called (it was only 15-20 minutes, but they dragged like hard butter on soft bread). Then, just like that, Dr. Nazmy beckoned me over. Hence, it comes, the moment of truth.

In the consultation room, I was greeted by Dr. Nazmy and three other medical professionals – doctors, nurses and dieticians. I stopped at the door and locked at the three officers shadowing me;

"Excuse me, lads, do you mind? I'd like some privacy, please" They looked at me, then beyond me at the panel of PhD's and numerous other academic accolades and decided on discretion being the better course of valour for once. I went into the consultation room and sat down, still clutching my new book (it was a Martha Long book called "Ma, Now I'm Goin Up in the World) for dear life. I didn't read a single page that day, I was far too nervous. I kept my eyes fixed on Dr. Nazmy.

"I've good news for you Dave, the cancer is gone!"

OH.MY.GOD. There it was, in full Technicolor and no ambiguity. Black and white. Cut and dried. This. Is. It. My cancer was gone! I was on cloud nine. It was true, it was all true! It took me a minute or two to get back down to earth and then I was back to myself, laughing, joking and having the craic with the doctors. The only thing missing was a round of drinks! It had been a very long time since I'd been able to do that. Back in prison, I'd kept myself subdued, but it felt great to just be me again.

"Anything else on your mind, Dave? Now's the time…"

There was. I brought up that disgusting web of lies published in the fifth-ridden Sunday world. The reaction in a room full of highly educated professionals who save lives on a daily basis and are accountable for the decisions they make was as I expected. Shock, speechless and horror. They could not believe that anybody could be so blatantly callous and unashamedly faced with such malicious lies. Dr. Nazmy fleeted his fingers and started typing furiously on his computer keyboard.

"Dave, come over here and have a look at this."

It was a detailed analysis of my results. I was checked from head to toe, every cell and molecule in my body - and yes, Sunday world, that did include my neck, pelvis, groin, stomach, etc. – and all the results said the same thing cancer free. I was elated; I've had a lot of meetings in my life that one still ranks up there with the best of them.

We eventually broke for a bit of lunch in the hospital and again, I couldn't eat very much. What I lacked in calorie consumption I ingested in great conversation and even better company. All the doctors and nursing staff were over, wishing me well and congratulating me. There were a lot of lovely moments during that lunch, but one really special one stands out. My old co-conspirator nurse worked her way over, suppressing her world-famous grin.

"You bleeding knew already!"

"What?"

"You bleeding knew! Look at the big guilty head on ya!"

"You what? What are you talking about?!"

"(Then the smile came out!) Your results! You knew weeks ago!"

"What? How… sure, how could I?!"

"Cos I'm the one who told your wife, you Muppet!!"

We both just burst out laughing. The game was up, she had me bang to rights and I walked into it! The only thing missing was being free to pop out to the shops and shower them with flowers and chocolates in a small way of my utmost thanks. But I wasn't going to be locked up forever and when I got released. I did just that.

I said nothing to the officers about my news on the way back, but I'm sure they could've guessed just by looking at me. Also, they weren't deaf and seemed a little too interested in the high-jinx and frivolity of my earlier lunch. We got back to Wally world at about two O'clock, which gave me about two minutes to change out of my jacket, but I left the rest of my good clothes on. I was out to the grounds to walk in the fresh air and clear my mind. On the way out there, one of the officers – at the top of his voice – said,

"I believe you got great news today, Dave!"

This was blurted out in front of about twenty people, inmates and officers alike in a normal environment, I know what I would've said about him and his big bloody mouth, but it wasn't a normal environment; it was bite-your-tongue and don't take bait prison, so I just nodded at him. Ah well, the cat was well and truly out of the bag, wasn't it? Just to accentuate that point, I bumped into a masked medic at the entrance to the grounds.

"Great news, I believe?!"

Was it? This was the guy who refused to drop my medication down to my cell when I first came back and couldn't move an eyelid. This was the animal that refused to give me water to help me ease down the tablets he handed me. Knowing the pain, I was in and the impossibility of swallowing rocks through hot sandpaper, now he was full of smiles and false platitudes, basking in my good news like he had anything to do with it.

Sleep came easily to me that night. I lay my head down and when I closed my eyes, I was transported back to the funeral scene I'd been at earlier. As I drew ever closer to the freshly dug grave, I was struck by the size of it. It was huge, easily the largest I'd ever seen. I looked at the faces of the mourners surrounding it. There was Dr. Nazmy and his oncology team. They looked at me, smiled politely and then walked away. Every face I looked at, I recognized and was thankful for knowing. But they'd just nod at me with a knowing smile, then peel away into the mist. Eventually, only two remained, the grave digger and a beautiful woman dressed in Black, glamorous and somehow familiar. She was looking down into the grave until she sensed my approach towards her. She turned toward me, lifted her head and veil away from her face and gave me a smile that melted me on the spot.

"Hello again, son."

"Ma?!"

"You did it, you beat it!"

"Ma, I... Is it really you?!"

"You beat cancer son, I couldn't be more proud!"

"I... I miss you ma…. So much…"

She raised her index finger to her lips, softly shushing me, then directed my gaze into the grave.

"We had some job getting him in there! His fin was so big!"

"Is that…"

"Yes, Dave, there's your shark! Big one, wasn't he?"

"Wow. I never realised…"

"You look after yourself, Dave, do you hear me? If he comes back, he might be stronger than before, don't let him."

"Ma, I… I…"

"You need to make changes Dave. Express yourself through art, writing, anything, but promise me, you'll be careful?'

"Ma, I… I promise."

"Thanks, son. I love you."

I went over to her, to give her a hug, but she wouldn't let me.

"No, son. Not yet. Not for a long time."

"Ma?"

"It's not your time!"

"But ma, I…, don't go, don't leave me."

She smiled, her famous glamorous 'Kay-smile' and threw a black rose onto the shark-coffin. It landed with an unexpected thud.

"I never did, son. I was always with you."

Then she was gone. I stared out into the mist, trying desperately to see just one glimpse of her… then I heard a massive 'thud' behind me. It was the grave digger, starting to fill in the hole... and he was laughing.

"Are we going for a drink?!"

"Sorry?"

"A drink! But I want to go somewhere where they'll let me sing!"

"Rory!"

"He was big Dave, wasn't he?"

"The shark? Yeah."

"Hey, Dave?"

"Yeah?"

"Fuck him!"

"Rory! Language…."

But then he was gone too. Just the echo of his happy little laugh hung in the air. I took a last look at the headstone.

"Cancer Shark. Died For Good – 29/8/2018."

Amen to that.

Epilogue

And so, finally, I made it! My seven-year sentence came to an end in Wheatfield, on the even more super – deluxe good-boy landing of 5G, A 'progressive' landing/Loughlan House, an open-prison much nearer to home that was not afforded to Audrey and me. Great time together; looking back on it all, it wasn't too bad apart from death threats, getting beaten up, getting cancer, appallingly horrific treatment from the so-called "medical" staff and everything in between.

As Dickens famously wrote in 'A Tale of Two Cities,' "It was the best of times. It was the worst of times." The better times large consisted of forging some solid friendships with other inmates. Not everything the courts do or the papers say is correct - never lose sight of that – and I'm proud to count certain prisoners as friends. It's an experience that is often compared to soldiers who once served together – The suffering, the pain, the losses, the hope and the despair. You experience feelings that leave a lasting impression on your mind – love, joy, grief and companionship, and it makes us all better people to share it. On balance, it is also fair to say that there are some terrific prison officers as well, folks that would only ever try to do you a good turn and view their job for what it is - a pay cheque at the end of the week and not a license to behave like a total asshole. I think you know, at this point, that the vile, key gangling Percy – wannabes far outweigh the decent ones and if you happen to be reading this as a prison officer and don't know which of those camps you belong to, then you're more than likely too/much of an asshole to work it out!

I had butterflies in my stomach on the day of my release, swarms of them. That hip-hop song from the 1980's kept running around my head – "Back to Life Back to Reality." Waiting for me outside, as always, were my father and Audrey. It was the most wonderful feeling in the world. But I'd dreamed of this day for several years and I had made myself a little promise;

"Da, can you drive me to the C.C.J?"

"What??!"

"The C.C.J., please!"

"Why on earth would you ever want to go back to that place?"

650

"It's just a thing I need to do and have wanted to from day one."

"What's that?"

"Well, I walked into the C.C.J. on a Friday. The 3 of us did. But only 2 of you walked back out. I was brought off to a place I didn't want to go to. It's high time I redressed that balance. I was going to walk in there, take a breath of fresh air and walk back out again. I need to exorcise all those demons and lay them to rest; I don't want their stink on me anymore. It's a chapter that needs to end, so I'm putting a cap on it."

So, I did just that. Unless you've been through what I've been through, then that may appear a little crazy, but to me, it makes perfect sense. I can't even pretend that it's a 'prison thing' because, as far as I know, I'm the only one to have done it. It's just something I felt I needed to do. When I walked back out of those now – famous doors, my thoughts weren't banal or – self-congratulatory like – "Yay! I did it," they were entirely on Dean. It was a little moment – fleeting in the great scheme of things of extreme regret and sorrow. A wave of loss and heartache, tiny in duration but unfathomably deep in pain, washed near me. I never missed him more than I did at that moment.

It gave me a new mission. A trip to the cemetery to have a heart-to-heart with him, which is all I'm willing to say about it because the last thing I'd want that to be is a story or a photo-op. I also made a personal vow to visit my mother and Rory's plot as well. Sooner rather than later, I had other goals that I'd set for myself in my cell that I would make good on. Nothing Earth-shattering, basic – simple stuff – like walking around Howth with my father, letting the sea air build up an appetite and feeding it with fish and chips and icecream for dessert. A '99,' a happy memory meal from my childhood, revitalising the classics! I'd also spent many a long evening thinking about having a few pints of the Black Stuff with the lads and enjoying a tale or two. I even pondered the possibility of there not being any more pubs with a decent atmosphere left, given how dull and beige the world was turning.

More than anything else though, I just wanted to be with my wife again. The immeasurable joy of being able to sit in our house together and spend the entire night without someone telling us that "times up" or being anyone else. That is a priceless gift. I used to listen to the lyrics over and over from a song by the script;

"Sitting up all night/drinking a bottle of jack and cheap wine/

Talk about things we haven't done for a while."

Then, doing things we hadn't done for a while, I wasn't the only person to have these thoughts either. I am not exactly known for standing on ceremony, Audrey's exact words to me were;

"You only thought you were locked up; I'm going to lock you up in this house for a good while!"

Sounds great! And so, it was off to the west of Ireland for Mr. And Mrs. Mahon, but I did feel a bit sorry for Mr. Mahon senior, as I'd been looking forward to spending a night or two over at Mick's house, but Audrey is the Boss now so I promised to call my father and arrange to pop up to him for a few days... once I was let!

If only that last life was the happy ending to my story, but nobody ever truly rides off into the sunset and lives happily ever after, do they? Audrey and I continue to keep the campaign for our Amy alive, but not at the frenetic pace we once had. We can't. We've nowhere near the requisite levels of health and fitness needed for what we did in the past and to be honest, it would kill us off once and for all. When I look back at it, I don't know how we did what we did. This book that you're reading is a part of our campaign because by just reading it, you're keeping hope and Amy alive. You are part of a small club, the last of the decent folk we deal with because with every new generation comes a new batch of reporters, cops and politicians, but readers - such as you - are timeless, so thank you.

When I was asked what kind of book I was writing, I thought long and hard about how to answer, the 'easy' answer would be to call it an 'autobiography', but that wouldn't be true. It would be dishonest. Admittedly, there are a lot of autobiographical elements, but to me my answer is this – It's a collection of love letters. My love – letters to Audrey, to my father, to Rory, to my mother, to Dean, to Graham and to Amy. To all of the above – Alive and no longer with us – I owe an unplayable debt of gratitude to. I'm not smart enough or strong enough to still be around today, if I hadn't stood on the shoulders of such giants, it's that simple. I hope that every time this book is read, that a small part of Rory, Kay or Dean can be given enough oxygen to breathe again and live – even for a short time – in your or someone else's thoughts. That, for me, is the magic of books.

We turned to the Guardia Civil.

We turned to a Garda Siochana.

We turned to the underworld.

We turned to the Irish and Spanish Governments.

We turned to the media.

We turned to Heads of States.

We turned to Psychics.

We turned to God.

We turned until there was nowhere left to turn, but we'll always think of something. Now that I'm out of prison, people ask what I'm going to do for work, what will I do? I just tell them that I've "Retired" because it's easier than having to explain everything to them, but dear reader, now that you know me so much better than them, let me leave you with one last question: Do you think that I've finally retired?

Printed and bound by CPI Group (UK) Ltd, Croydon, CR0 4YY
08/12/2023
03616087-0001